# ADVENTURES in SOCIAL RESEARCH

Tenth Edition

*To our students:*
*Past, present, and future—*
*We challenge each other and profit from it.*

Sara Miller McCune founded SAGE Publishing in 1965 to support the dissemination of usable knowledge and educate a global community. SAGE publishes more than 1000 journals and over 800 new books each year, spanning a wide range of subject areas. Our growing selection of library products includes archives, data, case studies and video. SAGE remains majority owned by our founder and after her lifetime will become owned by a charitable trust that secures the company's continued independence.

Los Angeles | London | New Delhi | Singapore | Washington DC | Melbourne

# ADVENTURES in SOCIAL RESEARCH

## Data Analysis Using IBM® SPSS® Statistics

### Tenth Edition

**Earl Babbie**
*Chapman University*

**William E. Wagner III**
*California State University, Channel Islands*

**Jeanne Zaino**
*Iona College*

Los Angeles | London | New Delhi
Singapore | Washington DC | Melbourne

FOR INFORMATION:

SAGE Publications, Inc.
2455 Teller Road
Thousand Oaks, California 91320
E-mail: order@sagepub.com

SAGE Publications Ltd.
1 Oliver's Yard
55 City Road
London EC1Y 1SP
United Kingdom

SAGE Publications India Pvt. Ltd.
B 1/I 1 Mohan Cooperative Industrial Area
Mathura Road, New Delhi 110 044
India

SAGE Publications Asia-Pacific Pte. Ltd.
3 Church Street
#10-04 Samsung Hub
Singapore 049483

Acquisitions Editor:  Jeff Lasser
Content Development Editor:  Sarah Dillard
Editorial Assistant:  Adeline Wilson
Production Editor:  Jane Haenel
Copy Editor:  Jared Leighton
Typesetter:  C&M Digitals (P) Ltd.
Proofreader:  Tricia Currie-Knight
Cover Designer:  Dally Verghese
Marketing Manager:  Kara Kindstrom

*Library of Congress Cataloging-in-Publication Data*

Names: Babbie, Earl R., author. | Wagner, William E. (William Edward), author. | Zaino, Jeanne, author.

Title: Adventures in social research : data analysis using IBM SPSS statistics / Earl Babbie, Chapman University, William E. Wagner III, California State University, Channel Islands, Jeanne Zaino, Iona College.

Description: 10th edition. | Los Angeles : SAGE, [2019] | Includes index.

Identifiers: LCCN 2018014647 | ISBN 9781506362779 (pbk.)

Subjects: LCSH: Social sciences—Statistical methods—Computer programs. | SPSS for Windows.

Classification: LCC HA32 .B286 2019 | DDC 300.285/555—dc23

LC record available at https://lccn.loc.gov/2018014647

18 19 20 21 22 10 9 8 7 6 5 4 3 2 1

# BRIEF CONTENTS

# DETAILED CONTENTS

## PART II • UNIVARIATE ANALYSIS         29

### Chapter 4 • Using SPSS Statistics: Some Basics      31

### Chapter 5 • Describing Your Data: Religiosity      49

# PREFACE

This workbook is offered to you with a number of aims in mind. To begin, we want to provide students with a practical and hands-on introduction to the logic of social science research, particularly survey research. Moreover, we want to give students an accessible book that guides them, step by step, through the process of data analysis using current General Social Survey (GSS) data and the latest versions of IBM® SPSS® Statistics* for either Windows or Macintosh computers. Most importantly, we want to involve students directly in the practice of social research, allow them to experience the excitement and wonder of this enterprise, and inspire them to pursue their own adventures in social research.

As we pursue these goals, however, there are a number of agendas in the background of this book. For example, students who complete the book will have learned a very useful, employable skill. Increasingly, job applicants are asked about their facility with various computer programs: word processing, spreadsheets, and data analysis. As of this writing, SPSS Statistics is still clearly the most popular professional program available for social science data analysis—hence, our choice of it as a vehicle for teaching social research.

## A FOCUS ON DEVELOPING PROFESSIONAL AND INTELLECTUAL SKILLS

What sets this book apart from others that teach SPSS Statistics or similar programs is that we present this particular skill within the context of social research as a logical enterprise.

Thus, in addition to learning to use SPSS Statistics, students are learning the intellectual "skills" of conceptualization, measurement, and association. Even though those who know only SPSS Statistics can assist in data analysis, our intention is that students will also be able to think for themselves, mapping out analytic paths into the understanding of social data. As they polish these intellectual skills, they should be able to progress to higher levels of research and to the administration of research enterprises.

More generally, we aim to train students who *will use* computers rather than *be used by* them. In our experience, when students first confront computers in school, they tend to fall into two groups: those who recognize computers as powerful instruments for pursuing their goals in life, or at least as the grandest of toys, and those who are intimidated by computers and seek the earliest possible refuge from them. Our intention is to reveal the former possibility to students and to coax them into a productive relationship with computers.

Educators are being challenged increasingly to demonstrate the practical value of instruction, no less in the social sciences than in other fields. Too often, an overreaction to this demand results in superficial vocational courses that offer no intellectual meaning or courses hastily contrived as a home for current buzzwords, whose popularity is often short-lived. We are excited to be able to offer an educational experience that is genuinely practical for students and that also represents an intellectual adventure.

Those who have taught methods or statistics courses typically find themselves with a daunting task: to ignite their often involuntary students with the fire of enthusiasm they feel for the detective work of social research at its best. In this book, we seek to engage students' curiosity by setting them about the task of understanding issues that are already points of interest for them: topics such as abortion, religion, politics, poverty, gender roles, sexual attitudes, mass media, gun control, child-rearing, racial prejudice, and others. For many of our readers, we imagine that *mathematical analysis*

---

*SPSS is a registered trademark of International Business Machines Corporation.

still smacks of trains leaving Point A and Point B at different speeds and so on. Now, they are going to learn that some facility with the logic and mathematics of social research can let them focus the light of understanding on the dark turbulence of opinion and hysteria.

We do not tell students about opinions on abortion as much as we show them how to find out for themselves. We think that will get students to Point C ahead of either of the trains.

## A FOCUS ON ACTIVE AND COLLABORATIVE LEARNING

As we are teaching students to learn for themselves, this book offers a good example of what educators have taken to calling *active learning*. We have set up all of our demonstrations so that students should be executing the same SPSS Statistics operations we are discussing at any given point. Although we may give them the "answers" to assure them that they are on the right track, we leave them on their own often enough to require that they do the work rather than simply read about it.

Finally, the culture of personal computers has been one of *collaborative learning* from its very beginning. More than people in any other field of activity, perhaps, computer users have always delighted in sharing what they know with others. There is probably no better context within which to ask for help: Those who know the answer are quick to respond, and those who do not often turn their attention to finding an answer, delighting in the challenge.

Because this book is self-contained, even introductory students can walk through the chapters and exercises on their own, without outside assistance. We imagine, however, that students will want to work together as they progress through this book. That has been our experience in student testing and in earlier courses we have taught involving computers. We suggest that you encourage cooperation among students; we are certain that they will learn more that way and will enjoy the course more. In fact, those who are initially intimidated by computers should especially be encouraged to find buddies with whom to work.

## INTENDED FOR STUDENTS IN VARIOUS SOCIAL SCIENCE DISCIPLINES

This book is intended for use in any social science course that either introduces or focuses exclusively on social research methods, social statistics, data analysis, or survey research. It can be easily combined with or used as a supplement to most standard social science textbooks, including but not limited to those in fields as varied as communication science, criminal justice, health studies, political science, public policy, social work, and sociology.

As far as possible, we have designed this book to be "self-writing" and "open-ended" to ensure it is relevant to students with varying interests across numerous disciplines. Throughout the text, we encourage students to focus on issues and questions relevant to their particular areas of interest. After walking through the demonstrations that introduce the fundamentals of the data analysis process, students are given a chance to apply what they have learned. In many of the lab exercises, students are encouraged to design their own hypotheses, choose their own variables, and interpret the results. Moreover, we encourage instructors to apply the principles, techniques, and methods discussed to other data sets relevant to their fields.

## INTENDED FOR BOTH BEGINNING AND MORE ADVANCED STUDENTS

We have designed and structured this book to support students at a variety of levels. This includes both those students who are taking their first course in social research and more advanced students (including graduate students) who either want to hone their social research, statistical, and data analysis skills or merely want to become acquainted or reacquainted with the latest versions of SPSS Statistics for Windows or Macintosh. More advanced students who come at this book full speed may choose either to work through the text from beginning to end or to skip around and focus on particular chapters and sections.

It is important to note, however, that because this book is "self-contained" and guides the student analyst step by step through the demonstrations and exercises, no previous experience with social research, statistics, computers, Windows, Macintosh, or SPSS Statistics is required. Those who have never taken a research methods, statistics, or computer-based course will find that they can easily progress through this book.

## THE BOOK AND THE FREE COMPANION WEBSITE: WHAT IS INCLUDED?

The book and *Adventures in Social Research* companion website provide the instructions and data needed to introduce students to social science data analysis. Most college and university computing services make SPSS Statistics software available to students. A student version of IBM SPSS Statistics may be purchased bundled with this textbook through SAGE. The companion website includes the data sets that are used throughout the book: DEMO.SAV and EXER.SAV, which can be analyzed by most versions of SPSS Statistics on Windows or Macintosh computers. As you will see, although we have provided for analysis in some depth in a few instances, the variables cover a fairly broad terrain. In addition to working their way through the demonstrations and exercises presented in the book, students will be able to find original lines of inquiry that grow out of their own interests and insights.

This book will illustrate the use of SPSS Statistics, using version 24.0 for Windows and Macintosh. While the text focuses specifically on the current version of SPSS Statistics, it can also be easily used with most of the earlier versions. Regardless of the version you are using, throughout the text, we will refer to the program simply as "SPSS Statistics," which is identical to PASW Statistics. (Versions 17 and 18 were known as PASW as part of a branding shift, before SPSS was acquired by IBM in 2009 and the name reverted to SPSS.) SPSS Statistics comes with extensive help screens. They are almost like having a coach built into your computer! Begin with the menu farthest to the right.

You can click **Help** to see the options available to you. "Topics" will usually be your most useful choice. This will give you three options: "Contents," "Index," and "Search." "Contents" and "Index" present you with two ways of zeroing in on the topic of interest to you. "Search" will search for the specific terms or keywords you indicate. You should experiment with these options to discover what works best for you.

## ORGANIZATION AND CONTENT

The chapters are arranged in an order that roughly parallels the organization of most introductory social science research methods texts. Part I (Chapters 1–3) includes an overview of the essentials of social research and description of the 2016 GSS from which come the data files you will be working (DEMO.SAV and EXER.SAV). Parts II, III, and IV (Chapters 4–20) introduce readers to SPSS Statistics and data analysis, beginning with univariate analysis, then bivariate analysis, and finally multivariate analysis, respectively. Part V (Chapters 21–22) focuses on primary research and additional avenues for secondary research.

Part I includes three chapters that help prepare students for social research using the General Social Survey. Our goal in these chapters is to give students an introduction to some of the fundamental elements of social scientific research, particularly those they will encounter later in the text.

Chapter 1 discusses the main purposes of the text and introduces students to some of the historical background that lies behind computerized social research, data analysis, and statistical software packages. It also introduces readers to the process of social research. Chapter 2 continues this focus by examining the logic of important aspects of social research, including theory, research, and measurement. Chapter 3 is designed to introduce readers to the GSS and the data sets included with this book.

Part II is designed to help students get started using SPSS Statistics and to give them practice with the basics of univariate analysis. Chapter 4 introduces students to SPSS Statistics by guiding them through the steps involved in launching the program, opening their data sets, and exploring the variables contained on the disk that accompanies this book.

The rest of this section (Chapters 5–9) is devoted to data analysis. In Chapter 5, we introduce frequency distributions, descriptive statistics, and saving and printing data. Chapter 6 focuses on the graphic presentation of univariate data by covering the commands for creating bar and pie charts, line graphs, and histograms. In Chapters 7 and 8, students are given a chance to practice recoding and creating composite variables. The final chapter in this section (Chapter 9) allows students to strike out on their own and apply the methods and techniques they have learned in this section to other topics.

Part III focuses primarily on bivariate analyses. In Chapters 10 through 12, we limit our discussion to the analysis of percentage tables. In Chapters 13, 14, and 15, we introduce other methods for examining the extent to which two variables are related to each other.

Chapter 13 focuses on some common measures of association for nominal and ordinal variables, including lambda and gamma. Chapter 14 focuses on correlation and regression analysis, by exploring Pearson's $r$, $r^2$, and OLS (ordinary least squares) regression. Chapter 15 introduces tests of statistical significance, such as chi-square, $t$ tests, and ANOVA. In Chapter 16, students are once again given a chance to apply the bivariate techniques and methods discussed in Part III to other topics and issues.

Our discussion of data analysis concludes in Part IV with a discussion of multivariate analyses. Chapter 17 focuses primarily on multiple causation. Chapter 18 picks up on some of the loose threads of our bivariate analyses and pursues them further, while Chapter 19 guides students through the steps involved in creating composite measures to predict opinions. Finally, in Chapter 20, students are given a chance to apply the methods and techniques discussed in Part IV to other topics and issues.

The final section comprises two chapters that explore some further opportunities for social research. Because students often express an interest in collecting their own data, Chapter 21 focuses on primary research. We introduce students to the steps involved in designing and administering a survey, defining and entering data in SPSS Statistics, and writing a research report. This chapter is supplemented by several articles on the *Adventures in Social Research* companion website that are intended to give students additional information regarding preparing a research proposal, designing and administering a survey, constructing a sample questionnaire, and writing a research report. Chapter 22 suggests other avenues for pursuing secondary social research by focusing on the unabridged GSS, additional data sources, and other statistical software packages that students may find useful.

The text contains a codebook (Appendix A) that describes all of the variables in the data files used in this book. The full GSS Codebook is included on the companion website, along with the full GSS file for 2016. A sample questionnaire designed for student use (with instructions in Chapter 21) is provided in Appendix B. We have also updated and expanded the references, index, and glossary.

The *Adventures in Social Research* companion website contains not only our data sets (DEMO. SAV, EXER.SAV, and GSS2016.SAV) but also articles relevant to the discussion of primary research in Chapter 21, a comprehensive list of all of the SPSS Statistics Commands introduced in the text, and recommended readings that relate to topics and issues covered in the text.

## STRUCTURE OF EACH CHAPTER

Chapters include explanations of basic research principles and techniques; specific instructions regarding how to use SPSS Statistics; and demonstrations, writing boxes, a brief conclusion, a list of main points, key terms, SPSS Statistics commands introduced in the chapter, review questions, and SPSS Statistics lab exercises. Students are expected to follow along with the demonstrations in the body of each chapter. They are aided in this process by both the text, which walks them, step by step, through the process of data analysis, and screen captures, which help them understand what they should be seeing on their own monitor.

In an effort to stress the importance of describing research findings in prose, most chapters include writing boxes, which give readers an example of how a professional social scientist might describe the findings being discussed. The review questions at the end of each chapter are designed to test the students' knowledge of the material presented in the text. Because they do not require SPSS Statistics, these questions can be assigned as either class work or homework assignments.

In the SPSS Statistics lab exercises, students are given a chance to apply what they learned in the explanatory sections and demonstrations. These exercises generally follow a fill-in-the-blank format for presenting, analyzing, and summarizing results. Instructors may wish to assign these exercises as lab assignments to be completed either in the lab or as homework, provided students have access to SPSS Statistics, either the full or the student version, on Windows or Macintosh.

Although the book is designed to guide students through the process of computerized data analysis from beginning to end, we encourage instructors—and particularly more advanced students—to skip around and focus on chapters and sections that are of interest to them. We designed the book with the understanding that students at various levels may find different demonstrations, techniques, discussions, and methods of varying interest. Consequently, all of the chapters are self-contained, and both students and instructors should feel comfortable picking and choosing among topics, issues, and material of particular interest to them.

Instructors and students who choose to take this approach may want to refer to the table of contents, introductions to each part, chapter conclusions, and summaries of main points to get a better sense of which sections and chapters they want to focus on.

## SOFTWARE SUPPORT AND SERVICE

If you or your students should run into any problems using this package, there are several sources of support that should serve your needs. Frequently, college and university computing centers have student assistants who are very helpful to new computer users. In fact, most academic computing centers employ a user services coordinator who can help faculty plan student use of the school's computers and provide aid when problems arise.

One source of SPSS Statistics assistance available via the Internet is the product's Customer Resource page at https://www.ibm.com/analytics/us/en/technology/spss. (SPSS has been an IBM company since 2009.) In addition to providing answers to frequently asked questions, it offers a variety of tips and white papers on important issues in data analysis. Registered users may submit specific questions to consultants via an online form at the Business Analytics Client Center. SPSS Statistics requests that a legitimate license or serial number be submitted with questions in order to receive a response. Be forewarned that SPSS cannot give assistance with pedagogical or substantive problems. It has been our experience that the best help comes from local resources.

## ACKNOWLEDGMENTS

In conclusion, we would like to acknowledge a number of people who have been instrumental in making this book a reality. First on the list is Jerry Westby of SAGE/Pine Forge Press. Our thanks also go to former Pine Forge Press editor Steve Rutter and the many others at SAGE/Pine Forge Press who aided us along the way, particularly Claudia Hoffman, Kristin Snow, and Vonessa Vondera for their work on the fifth edition and Denise Santoyo, Cheryl Rivard, and Kim Suarez for their work on the sixth edition. Special thanks go also to Megan Granger and Nichole O'Grady for their work on the seventh edition, and again to Megan Granger for her work on the eighth edition. Paula Fleming was our copyeditor for the ninth edition, and Jared Leighton for the tenth edition.

We would also like to thank the many reviewers who helped us along the way: Monika Ardelt, University of Florida; Karen August, Humboldt State University; Dhruba J. Bora, Wheeling Jesuit University; Tom Buchanan, The University of Tennessee at Chattanooga; Gregg Lee Carter, Bryant University; James Cassell, Indiana State University; Christina DeJong, Michigan State University; Xiaogang Deng, University of Massachusetts, Boston; Stephen J. Farnsworth, Mary

Washington College; Ellen Granberg, Clemson University; Jessica Greene, University of Oregon; John R. Hagen, Health Strategies Inc.; Jade Hsuan Huang, Hawaii Pacific University; Steven L. Jones, University of Virginia; Quentin Kidd, Christopher Newport University; Wanda Kosinski, Ramapo College of New Jersey; Mary Jane Kuffner Hirt, Indiana University of Pennsylvania; Peter Allen Lee, San Jose State University; Kim Lloyd, Washington State University; William H. Lockhart, University of Virginia; Karyn D. McKinney, Penn State University, Altoona College; Maureen McLeod, The Sage Colleges; Josh Meisel, Humboldt State University; Philip Meyer, University of North Carolina; Amanda Miller, University of Indianapolis; David B. Miller, Case Western Reserve University; Ojmarrh Mitchell, University of Nevada–Las Vegas; Melanie Moore, University of Northern Colorado; Thomas O'Rourke, University of Illinois at Urbana-Champaign; Graham Ousey, University of Delaware; Linda Owens, University of Illinois; Boyka Stefanova, University of Texas, San Antonio; Sue Strickler, Eastern New Mexico University; Mangala Subramaniam, Purdue University; Jennifer L. S. Teller, Kent State University; Lanny Thomson, University of Puerto Rico; John Tinker, California State University–Fresno; Madine VanderPlaat, Saint Mary's University; Roland Wagner, San Jose State University; Joshua J. Weikert, West Chester University; Assata Zerai, Syracuse University; and Thomas G. Zullo, University of Pittsburgh.

We reserve our final acknowledgment for our students, to whom this book is dedicated. We recognize that we have often asked them to think and do things that they sometimes felt were beyond their abilities. We have admired their courage for trying anyway, and we have shared in their growth.

# ABOUT THE AUTHORS

**Earl Babbie** was born in Detroit, Michigan, in 1938, but his family chose to return to Vermont 3 months later, and he grew up there and in New Hampshire. In 1956, he set off for Harvard Yard, where he spent the next 4 years learning more than he initially planned. After 3 years with the U.S. Marine Corps, mostly in Asia, he began graduate studies at the University of California, Berkeley. He received his PhD from Berkeley in 1969. He taught sociology at the University of Hawaii from 1968 through 1979, took time off from teaching and research to write full-time for 8 years, and then joined the faculty at Chapman University in Southern California in 1987. Although he is the author of several research articles and monographs, he is best known for the many textbooks he has written, which have been widely adopted in colleges throughout the United States and the world. He also has been active in the American Sociological Association (ASA) for 25 years and currently serves on the ASA's executive committee. He is also past president of both the Pacific Sociological Association and the California Sociological Association.

**William E. Wagner III,** professor of health science and sociology at California State University, Channel Islands, served as a member of the faculty and director of the Institute for Social and Community Research at California State University, Bakersfield, prior to coming to Cal State, Channel Islands. His MA and PhD degrees in sociology are from the University of Illinois, Chicago. In addition, Dr. Wagner earned a master's of public health (MPH) degree from California State University, Northridge. He holds two separate bachelor's degrees, one in mathematics and the other in sociology/anthropology, both from Saint Mary's College of Maryland. His work on topics such as urban sociology, sports, homophobia, academic status, and sexual behavior has been published in national and regional scholarly journals. He was elected as a vice president of the California Sociological Association for 2 years and served for 7 years as the chair of the Pacific Sociological Association's Committee on the Status of GLBT Persons. Dr. Wagner has also authored *Using IBM SPSS Statistics for Research Methods and Social Science Statistics,* 6th edition (SAGE, 2016), as well as two co-authored books: *The Practice of Survey Research* (2016), with Erin Ruel and Brian Gillespie, and *Using and Interpreting Statistics in the Social, Behavioral, and Health Sciences,* with Brian Gillespie (forthcoming). His faculty website can be found at http://faculty.csuci.edu/william.wagner.

**Jeanne Zaino**, professor of political science, Iona College, earned a bachelor's degree in political science and a master's degree in survey research at the University of Connecticut, Storrs. During that time, she worked as a research assistant at the Roper Center for Public Opinion Research. She went on to earn a master's degree and PhD in political science from the University of Massachusetts, Amherst. She is currently chair of the Political Science Department at Iona College in New Rochelle, New York, where she teaches courses in American government, institutions, research methods, social statistics, public opinion, scope, and methods. She and her husband, Jeff, are the proud parents of two sons, Maxim and Logan.

# PREPARING FOR DATA ANALYSIS

In the opening chapters, we introduce you to computerized data analysis, the logic of social science research, and the data you will be using throughout this text.

In Chapter 1, we begin by looking at how and why social scientists use computers and computer programs. Then, we introduce you to the two main pillars of social research: logic and observation. We will demonstrate how theory—the *logic* component—informs our investigations, makes sense out of our *observations*, and sometimes offers predictions about what we will find. We will also touch on another important aspect of research: the collection and analysis of data, such as those collected in a survey.

In Chapter 2, we delve more deeply into one central component of scientific inquiry: measurement. We look at some of the criteria for measurement quality and start examining the kinds of measurements represented by the data at hand.

In Chapter 3, we introduce you to the data you will be using throughout the text. The data come from the 2016 General Social Survey (GSS). The GSS reflects the attitudes of a representative sample of American adults on a variety of issues from religion, politics, abortion, and child-rearing to the mass media, sex, law enforcement, and immigration.

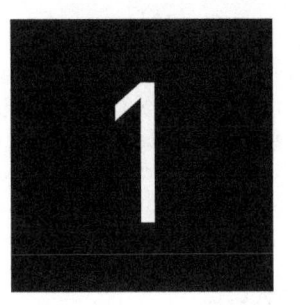

# INTRODUCTION

## The Theory and Practice of Social Research

Social research is the detective work involved in answering big questions. Whereas a conventional detective tries to find out who committed a specific crime, a social researcher looks for the causes of crime in general. The logic of social scientific investigation extends beyond crime to include all aspects of social life, such as careers, marriage and family, voting, health, prejudice, environment, and poverty. In fact, anything that is likely to concern you as an individual is the subject of social science research.

## OVERVIEW

The purpose of this book is to lead you through a series of investigative adventures in social research. We can't predict exactly where these adventures will lead because you are going to be the detective. Our purpose is to show you some simple tools (and some truly amazing ones) that you can use in social investigations.

We'll also provide you with a body of data, collected in a national survey, that is so rich you will have the opportunity to undertake investigations that no one else has ever pursued.

If you have access to a computer that uses a recent Microsoft Windows or Mac OS configuration and IBM SPSS Statistics (or the even the older temporarily branded PASW, Predictive Analytics Software), this book and the website associated with it (https://study.sagepub.com/babbie10e) contain everything you need for a wide range of social investigations.[1] The website is designed specifically for exploring data by way of a fascinating computer game. Instead of fighting off alien attacks or escaping from dank dungeons, you'll be pitting your abilities and imagination against real life, but you'll be looking at a side of life that you may not now be aware of.

This tool is also well designed to aid in the creation of college term papers, and throughout this book, we suggest ways to present the data you discover in the context of a typical term paper in the social sciences. Whereas most students are limited in their term papers to reporting what other investigators have learned about society, you will be able to offer your own insights and discoveries.

Finally, the data set included on the website is being analyzed by professional social scientists today. Moreover, the analytical tools that we've provided for you are as powerful as those used by many professional researchers. Frankly, there's no reason you can't use these materials for original

---

1. Earlier versions of SPSS Statistics for Windows or Macintosh may be used, but some of the instructions, procedures, and screens may be somewhat different from those in this book. SPSS 15.0 and higher require Windows 7 or 8. PASW Statistics 18 requires Windows 7 or Mac OS X Leopard (10.5) or Snow Leopard (10.6), while SPSS 22 requires the Mac OS to be at least 10.6 (Snow Leopard), 10.7 (Lion), or higher. This book uses IBM SPSS Statistics 24 for Mac, requiring OS X 10.10 (Yosemite). The identical version (24) for Windows requires Windows 7 or higher. For more detail, visit the IBM SPSS website: https://www.ibm .com/analytics/us/en/technology/spss.

research worthy of publication in a research journal. All it takes is curiosity, imagination, practice, and a healthy obsession with knowing the answers to things. In our experience, what sets professional researchers apart from others is that they have much greater curiosity about the world around them and, in fact, are passionately driven to understand it; they bring a powerful imagination to bear on this task; and they are willing to put in the time necessary for effective investigation.

## WHY USE A DATABASE?

As do physical scientists, social scientists use observations of the empirical world to develop and evaluate theories. Much of the social scientist's work involves ascertaining whether logically derived relationships expressed in social theories correspond to empirically observed relationships among social data. For instance, a theory may suggest that Catholics are more opposed to abortion than are non-Catholics, but we don't have scientific evidence until we poll Catholics and non-Catholics and evaluate their differences on abortion. To have confidence in our findings, we must poll a large number of people for their positions on abortion and their religious preferences. And for sure, we probably would feel that any explanation of difference was incomplete until other factors, such as each respondent's gender, age, social class, and so forth, were included. We don't have to stretch our imagination very far to realize that even simple research can soon generate a large mass of data, given the number of cases and variables that we need to provide credible evidence for or against a theory.

Given the sheer number of observations commonly made by social scientists, researchers need to use a database to take into account all relevant data in their research. The full 2016 General Social Survey (GSS) data file we have included with this book, for example, contains more than 790 variables for more than 2,800 individuals. Initial analysis of data requires that they be sorted, categorized, and recategorized before statistics may be computed for them. With more than 1.5 million data points available for use, we clearly need to use a database to complete a meaningful analysis this semester!

## SPSS STATISTICS

Today, the two statistical packages most widely used by social scientists are **SPSS Statistics** (originally known as the Statistical Package for the Social Sciences, temporarily branded as **PASW Statistics** for version 18; since 2009, IBM SPSS Statistics), and **SAS (Statistical Analysis System)**.[2] We have selected SPSS Statistics for use with this textbook for three reasons. First, early versions of SPSS date back to 1968. The package is well known, and hardly any social scientists who have earned a graduate degree in the past 50 years have not had some contact with SPSS. Second, SPSS takes you through all of the basic issues of using a statistical package. This knowledge will give you a head start if you learn some other package later. Finally, recent versions of SPSS Statistics are suitable for computers running Microsoft Windows Me, 7, 8, or higher. SPSS Statistics version 24 for Windows does require Microsoft Windows 7, 8, or higher. There are also versions available for Apple Macintosh computers running Mac OS X. SPSS Statistics version 24 for Mac does require OS X 10.10 (Snow Yosemite) or later.

The SPSS Statistics Base is sold as the basic package. Then, if the buyer wishes, it can be upgraded with powerful statistical accessories, all of which are beyond the scope of this book. You can think of it like a car: The base price includes basic features, and then, you can add options like a great sound system and high-performance tires. Other upgraded software packages include SPSS Professional and the ultimate model, SPSS Premium.

SPSS also offers two packages specifically designed for students: SPSS Statistics Student Version (last offered for version 18 of PASW Statistics and discontinued until release 22.0) and SPSS Statistics

---

2. While SPSS originally stood for and is still most commonly referred to as Statistical Package for the Social Sciences, SPSS Inc. recently said it had "updated the meaning of the letters to more accurately reflect the company and its products. Today, SPSS stands for 'Statistical Product and Service Solutions.'" The PASW acronym stands for Predictive Analytics Software, and after SPSS Inc. became part of IBM in 2009, it was determined that the brand would become IBM SPSS Statistics, referred to as SPSS Statistics for short.

Graduate Pack. Although both versions are available for use with Windows or Mac, they differ in terms of their capabilities. Unlike the SPSS Statistics Base system or the SPSS Statistics Graduate Pack, the **SPSS Statistics Student Version** is limited to 50 variables and 1,500 cases and cannot be upgraded. IBM had not authorized the student version since version 18, before reintroducing it for version 22. Version 24 of the Student Version is available to accompany this book. The student version has fewer statistical procedures but has most of the procedures that will ever be needed by an undergraduate social science major or a master's-level graduate student, so it is sufficient to use in tandem with this book.

The SPSS Statistics Graduate Pack contains the SPSS Statistics Base system plus two advanced statistical modules. The graduate pack is commonly available at college and university bookstores. You can learn more about IBM SPSS Statistics and the various versions that are available by visiting the company's online store at https://www.ibm.com/analytics/us/en/technology/spss.[3] IBM may change the configurations or offerings of these packages or modules in the future, so be sure to check the website for the latest details.

While having a copy of SPSS Statistics on your personal computer is convenient, you may not need to purchase the software to complete the exercises in this book. Most colleges and universities offer SPSS Statistics to their students through the school's network. More recently, client/server desktop application technology has been adopted at some colleges and universities. With this technology, your school can provide you with client software (e.g., Citrix) and settings to put on your personal Windows or Macintosh computer. You will then be able to run the university's version of SPSS Statistics from its server through your computer desktop application as though the software were directly installed on your computer. Of course, you will need to remain connected to the Internet, and a high-speed connection is required for this software to be useful. Check with your school's IT (information technology) office to see if this capability is available. Other universities may offer temporary student licenses for enrolled students, where students are granted a temporary license to install a copy of the base software on their personal computer.

## SOCIAL RESEARCH: A PRIMER

This book addresses the techniques of social science data analysis. Thus, we're going to be spending most of our time using SPSS Statistics to analyze data and reach conclusions about the people who answered questions in the GSS, as described in more detail in Chapter 3.

Data analysis, however, doesn't occur in a vacuum. Scientific inquiry is a matter of both observing and reasoning. Consequently, before focusing on SPSS Statistics, let's take a few minutes to consider some of the central components of social science research. We will begin here by looking at the role of theory in conjunction with the social research process. In the following chapter, we will turn our attention to another fundamental aspect of scientific inquiry: measurement. The goal is not to make you an expert in the social research process but to give you the background necessary to master the techniques of data analysis presented in the remainder of this book.[4]

## CONCEPTS AND THEORIES: DEPRIVATION THEORY

Given the variety of topics examined in social science research, no single, established set of procedures is always followed in social scientific inquiry. Nevertheless, data analysis almost always has a

---

3. Throughout this book, we suggest various websites you may find useful. Keep in mind, however, that the World Wide Web is constantly changing. For this reason, some websites and online content referred to may no longer be available. If particular websites are no longer available, try using a search engine to find the information you need.

4. If you are thinking about designing a research study or just want to learn more about the process and practice of scientific inquiry, you may find the discussion in this book's last two chapters and accompanying appendices a useful starting point. You may also want to browse through the Reference section on the student study website at https://study.sagepub.com/babbie10e for citations of texts that focus on the nature of social scientific inquiry, designing a research project, and other important aspects of the research process.

bigger purpose than the simple manipulation of numbers. Our larger aim is to learn something of general value about human social behavior. This commitment lies in the realm of theory. A primary goal of social scientific research is to examine the various concepts that constitute our knowledge of the social world and then develop them into theories that help us explain, understand, and make sense of the social world.

*Concepts* are general ideas or understandings that form the basis of social scientific research. Some of the social scientific concepts with which you are familiar might include social class, deviance, political orientations, prejudice, and alienation. The most useful concepts describe variations among people or groups. When thinking about social class, for example, we might distinguish upper class, middle class, and working class, while the concept of prejudice leads us to consider those who are more prejudiced and those who are less prejudiced.

A *theory* is a statement or set of statements describing the relationships among concepts. Theories provide explanations about the patterns we find in human social life. Developing social theories is a matter of discovering causal relationships between concepts, and we start to develop a theory by asking questions that help us begin to investigate those causal relationships. Examples of such questions include, "Does education reduce prejudice?" "Does gender affect how much people are paid?" "Are minority group members more liberal than majority group members?" and, "Are women more religious than men?" As for the last question, American social research has consistently shown that women are more religious than men, and the key concepts in that observed pattern are religiosity and gender. Because one of the subjects we are going to examine in this textbook is religiosity, we will begin with an example of a theory deriving from the sociology of religion.

The sociologists Glock, Ringer, and Babbie[5] developed what they called the deprivation theory of church involvement. Having asked why some church members participated more in their churches than did others, the researchers' analyses led them to conclude that those who were deprived of gratification (e.g., money, prestige, power, opportunities, and freedom) in secular society would be more likely to be active in church life than would those who enjoyed the rewards of secular society. In this case, the concepts under examination are deprivation, gratification, and church involvement. Some people are more deprived of gratification than others, and some people are more religiously involved than others. The research question is to find out if the degree to which people are deprived of secular gratification is somehow related to their degree of religious involvement.

Deprivation theory offers a plausible explanation of how the concepts of deprivation and religious involvement are related. It gives us a possible explanation—a theory—to help us make sense of why some people are more religious or more active in church than others. In this form, however, the concepts are too general for us to be able to test the theory empirically. Before we can test a theory, we must take the additional step of creating hypotheses. Unlike theories, well-developed hypotheses posit relationships between variables that are specific enough to permit testing.

In short, while theory is an important starting point in social science research, the empirical relationships predicted by the theory must be tested. To do that, we shift our focus from relationships between concepts to relationships between variables and, therefore, from theories to hypotheses.

## VARIABLES AND HYPOTHESES: RELIGIOSITY

*Variables* are empirical indicators of the concepts we are researching. Variables, as their name implies, have the ability to take on two or more values. For instance, people can be classified in terms of their gender (male or female) or religious involvement (involved or not involved). When we identify empirical indicators for our concepts, they become variables.

A *hypothesis* is a statement of expectation derived from a theory that proposes a relationship between two or more variables. Specifically, a hypothesis is a tentative statement that proposes that variation in one variable "causes" or leads to variation in the other variable. We put *cause* in quotes here because more than a simple association is needed to attribute cause. To be a cause, a related

---

5. Glock, C. Y., Ringer, B. B., & Babbie, E. R. (1967). *To comfort and to challenge: A dilemma of the contemporary church*. Berkeley: University of California Press.

variable must (among other requirements) precede the dependent variable in time and not be related to some other variable that is also related to the dependent variable. A ***dependent variable*** is the variable you are trying to explain (e.g., church involvement/religiosity), while an ***independent variable*** is the variable hypothesized to "cause," lead to, or explain variation in another variable (e.g., gender). We'll explore this further in Chapter 17.

Table 1.1 illustrates the differences between theories and hypotheses. Theories specify relationships between concepts in the world of ideas, while hypotheses specify expected relationships between variables in the world of empirical experiences.

| TABLE 1.1 ■ Concepts, Theories, Variables, and Hypotheses | |
|---|---|
| **World of Ideas** | **Concepts** |
| | 1. Secular deprivation |
| | 2. Religious involvement |
| | Theory: The more people experience secular deprivation, the more likely they will be religiously involved. |
| | Variables representing dimensions of secular deprivation |
| | a. Age |
| | b. Gender |
| | c. Socioeconomic status |
| **World of Experiences** | **Hypotheses** |
| | a. As people get older, their religious participation increases. |
| | Independent variable: Age |
| | Dependent variable: Religiosity |
| | b. Women will have greater religious participation than will men. |
| | Independent variable: Gender/sex |
| | Dependent variable: Religiosity |
| | c. The lower your income, the more likely you will be to participate in religious activities. |
| | Independent variable: Income |
| | Dependent variable: Religiosity |

Also, please note that relationships such as the one predicted in the hypotheses in Table 1.1 are ***probabilistic***, meaning that people displaying certain characteristics will have a higher probability of exhibiting certain behaviors but are not guaranteed to exhibit those behaviors. For example, Hypothesis B says that women, as a group, will have a higher average level of religious participation than will men, as a group. This does not mean that all women are more involved in religion than any men. It does mean, however, that if we asked men and women whether they attend church every week, a higher percentage of women than of men would say yes, even though some men would say yes, and some women would say no. That is the nature of probabilistic relationships.

As Table 1.2 demonstrates, each variable contains two or more ***categories***, which are defined as the specific attributes that make up a variable. For instance, the categories of the variable *gender* are *male* and *female*, while the categories of the variable *social class* may be *upper class*, *middle class*, and *working class*.

| TABLE 1.2 ■ Variables and Categories | |
|---|---|
| **Variables** | **Categories** |
| Gender | Female |
| | Male |
| Religious involvement | Involved |
| | Not involved |
| Party identification | Democrat |
| | Independent |
| | Republican |
| Social class | Upper class |
| | Middle class |
| | Working class |

The categories of each variable must meet two requirements: They should be both exhaustive and mutually exclusive. By *exhaustive*, we mean comprehensive enough that it is possible to categorize every observation using those categories. Imagine, for instance, that you are conducting a survey, and one of your variables is religious affiliation. In order to measure respondents' religion, you devise a question that asks respondents simply, "What is your religion?" Let's say you give respondents only three choices: Protestant, Catholic, and Jewish. While most Americans would identify with one of these religious traditions, the categories certainly are not exhaustive. Muslims and Hindus, among others, would not find any of these categories to be descriptive of their traditions. To correct this problem, we would have to add more traditions, an "other" category, or both so that all respondents could fit themselves into at least one category. Moreover, we'd want a "none" category for those with no religious affiliation.

*Mutually exclusive* means every observation must fit into only one category. For instance, if we asked people for their religious affiliation and gave them the choices of Christian, Protestant, Catholic, and Jewish, then the categories would not be mutually exclusive since Protestants and Catholics would see themselves as being in the Christian category as well.

# SOCIAL RESEARCH STRATEGIES: INDUCTIVE AND DEDUCTIVE

After developing a hypothesis, a researcher may decide to design and conduct a scientific study to test whether there is a relationship such as the one proposed between gender and church involvement. Social scientists generally approach research in one of two ways: inductively or deductively.

In the previously mentioned study by Glock, Ringer, and Babbie, the researchers employed an *inductive research* strategy. First, they collected data regarding people's religious involvement and gender. After they completed their observations, they examined the data and constructed a theory to explain the relationships found among the variables.

An alternative and somewhat more common approach is *deductive research*. Unlike inductive research, which begins with data collection, deductive research begins with social theory. A specific hypothesis is then deduced from the theory and tested to discover whether there is evidence to support it. To continue our example, the deprivation theory suggests that people who lack secular gratification will be more involved in religious activities. From that, we could derive the hypothesis that persons of lower socioeconomic status will attend church more often than will those of higher socioeconomic status. We could then collect data about people's socioeconomic status and church attendance and examine the data to see whether lower-status people really do attend church more than higher-status people. This would be considered deductive research because we began with the theory and tested a hypothesis with data.

Perhaps the simplest way to distinguish between inductive and deductive research approaches is by where they begin and end. While inductive research begins with data analysis and then moves to theory, deductive research begins with theory and then proceeds to data analysis and back to theory again. More simply, deduction can be seen as reasoning from general understandings to specific expectations, whereas induction can be seen as reasoning from specific observations to general explanations.

You can see, then, that whether an inductive or a deductive approach is used, the social research process involved many steps or stages.

*Inductive Research*

1. Collect data.

2. Analyze data.

3. *Induce* a theory to account for data.

*Deductive Research*

1. Find or formulate a theory.

2. *Deduce* hypotheses to test theory.

3. Collect data.

4. Analyze data.

5. Evaluate hypotheses.

While in practice, the process of social research is not nearly as linear as these steps suggest, you can see that whether a researcher employs a deductive or an inductive strategy, the goal is always the same: to develop theories that help us explain, make sense of, and understand human social behavior.

The possible topics for exploration are, as you can imagine, endless. Whereas some social researchers are interested in understanding religiosity, others are interested in issues such as spousal abuse, child abuse, violence in schools, unemployment, political party identification, poverty, alcoholism, drug addiction, health care, crime, malnutrition, overpopulation, governmental corruption, and so on. The problems and issues of concern to social scientists are as manifold and complicated as human beings themselves. Despite the diversity of these questions and concerns, what connects social scientists is the belief that if used properly, the techniques and process of social science research can help us examine and begin to understand these complicated issues. Only when we understand what causes these problems, how they come about, and why they persist will we be able to solve them.

While the primary focus of this book is on one stage of the social research process—data analysis—we hope this book will inspire you to take some time to reflect on which of the many problems in contemporary life interest you. What issues or questions are you passionate about? What social problems or issues would you like to examine, understand, and potentially address?

# THEORY AND RESEARCH IN PRACTICE

Now that we have focused a little on the relationship between theory and the social research process, let's examine some of the theoretical work that informs two of the many subjects we are going to analyze together in this book: political orientations and attitudes toward abortion.

## Example 1: Political Orientations

One of the more familiar variables in social science is political orientation, which typically ranges from liberal to conservative. Political orientation lies at the heart of much voting behavior, and it also relates to a number of nonpolitical variables that you are going to discover for yourself shortly.

Each concept or variable we deal with in social research may have different aspects, which we call **dimensions**. Three commonly examined dimensions of political orientation are (1) social attitudes, (2) economic attitudes, and (3) foreign policy attitudes. Let's examine each dimension briefly.

Some specific social attitudes and related behaviors might include abortion, same-sex marriage, and capital punishment. Let's see where liberals and conservatives generally stand on these issues:

| Issue | Liberals | Conservatives |
|---|---|---|
| Abortion | Permissive | Restrictive |
| Same-sex marriage | Permissive | Restrictive |
| Capital punishment | Opposed | In favor of |

In terms of economic issues, liberals are generally more supportive than conservatives of government programs such as unemployment insurance, welfare, and Medicare and of government economic regulation such as progressive taxation (the rich being taxed at higher rates), minimum-wage laws, and regulation of industry. By the same token, liberals are likely to be more supportive of labor unions than are conservatives.

## Example 2: Attitudes Toward Abortion

Abortion is a social issue that has figured importantly in religious and political debates for years. The GSS contains several variables dealing with attitudes toward abortion. Each asks whether a woman should be allowed to get an abortion for a variety of reasons. The following list shows these reasons, along with the **abbreviated variable names** you'll be using for them in your analyses later on.

| Abbreviated Variable Name | |
|---|---|
| ABDEFECT | Because there is a strong chance of a serious defect |
| ABNOMORE | Because a family wants no more children |
| ABHLTH | Because the woman's health would be seriously endangered |
| ABPOOR | Because a family is too poor to afford more children |
| ABRAPE | Because the pregnancy resulted from rape |
| ABSINGLE | Because the woman is unmarried |
| ABANY | Because the woman wants it, for any reason |

Before we begin examining answers to the abortion attitude questions, it is worth taking a moment to reflect on their logical implications. Which of these items do you suppose would receive the least support? That is, which will have the smallest percentage of respondents agreeing with it? Think about that before continuing.

Logically, we should expect the smallest percentage to support ABANY because it contains all the others. For example, those who would support abortion in the case of rape might not support it for other reasons, such as the family's poverty. Those who support ABANY, however, would have to agree with both of those more specific items, plus all the rest.

Three of the items tap into reasons that would seem to excuse the pregnant woman from responsibility:

| Abbreviated Variable Name | |
|---|---|
| ABDEFECT | Because there is a strong chance of a serious defect |
| ABHLTH | Because the woman's health would be seriously endangered |
| ABRAPE | Because the pregnancy resulted from rape |

We might expect the highest percentages to agree with these items. We'll come back to this issue later to find out whether our expectations are correct.

When we analyze this topic using data, we will discover useful ways of measuring overall attitudes toward abortion. Once we've done that, we'll be in a position to find out why some people are generally supportive of abortion rights and why others are generally opposed.

# CONCLUSION

This book has two educational aims. First, we want to share with you the excitement of social scientific research. You are going to learn that a table of numerical data, which may seem pretty boring on the face of it, can hold within it the answers to many questions about why people think and act the way they do. Finding those answers requires that you learn some skills of logical inquiry. Second, we will show you how to use a computer program that is popular among social scientists: SPSS Statistics. It's the tool you will use to unlock the mysteries of society, just as a biologist might use a microscope or an astronomer might use a telescope.

Before getting started using SPSS Statistics, however, it is important that you have at least an initial appreciation for social research. In this chapter, we have focused in particular on the relationship between theory and the social research process. This examination will continue throughout the book. While most of our attention will focus on the skills involved in analyzing data, we will always want to make logical sense out of what we learn from our manipulations of the numbers. Measurement is a fundamental topic that bridges theory and research, so we turn our attention to that topic next.

## Main Points

- The main purpose of this text is to introduce you to the logic and practice of social scientific research by showing you some simple tools you can use to analyze real-life data.

- Social and behavioral scientists' use of computer programs has evolved over many years because of the need to analyze large amounts of data.

- SPSS Statistics is a widely used, state-of-the-art statistical software program that will take you through all of the basics of using any sophisticated statistical package.

- A theory is a general statement or set of statements that describes and explains how different concepts are related to one another.

- A hypothesis is a tentative statement of expectation derived from a theory.

- A hypothesis proposes a relationship between two or more variables (independent and dependent variables) that can be tested by researchers employing scientific methods.

- The categories of variables must be both exhaustive and mutually exclusive.

- When a social scientist proceeds from theory to hypothesis development, data collection, and data analysis, the process is called deductive research.

- When a social scientist moves from data collection to data analysis and then induces a general theory based on those observations, the process is called inductive research.

- Theoretical work informs all of the subjects we are going to analyze in this book and, indeed, all of questions and issues of relevance to social scientists.

# Key Terms

Abbreviated variable names  10
Categories  7
Concepts  6
Deductive research  8
Dependent variable  7
Dimensions  10

Exhaustive  8
Hypothesis  6
Independent variable  7
Inductive research  8
Mutually exclusive  8
PASW Statistics  4

Probabilistic  7
SAS (Statistical Analysis System)  4
SPSS Statistics  4
SPSS Statistics Student Version  5
Theory  6
Variable  6

# Review Questions

1. What are the two statistical packages most widely used by social scientists today?

2. Which of the versions of SPSS Statistics described is the least powerful in terms of the number of cases and variables it can handle? (Hint: It was discontinued by IBM after SPSS/PASW version 18, prior to its renaissance with version 22 continuing to the present with version 24.)

3. Which version of SPSS Statistics is the most powerful in this regard?

4. What version (or versions) of SPSS Statistics are you using?

5. Name two tasks for which one could use a statistical package, such as SPSS Statistics.

6. What is the primary goal of social scientific research?

7. Name two social scientific concepts.

8. What is the relationship between theories and hypotheses?

9. Complete the following statement: Theories are to concepts as hypotheses are to _____
_____ .

10. Does a hypothesis propose a relationship between dimensions or variables?

11. The categories of each variable should meet what two requirements?

12. What, if anything, is the problem with the following categories of the variable *political views*: liberal and moderate? If there is a problem, how might you correct it?

13. What, if anything, is the problem with the following categories of the variable *political perspective*: liberal, Democrat, Republican, and conservative? If there is a problem, how might you correct it?

14. Construct a hypothesis based on the deprivation theory of church involvement, using level of education as your independent variable.

15. List the categories of the variables you used to construct your hypothesis in response to Question 14.

16. Construct potential hypotheses to relate the following concepts, and identify the independent and dependent variable in each hypothesis. In addition, list the categories of each variable.

    a. Age and health

    b. Race and attitude toward affirmative action

    c. Gender and income

17. Which of the following is not a dependent variable: grade point average, church attendance, age, or number of children?

18. Which of the following is not a variable: occupation, amount of television viewing, female, or education level?

19. Consider the following hypothesis: People who earn more than $50,000 a year are more likely to vote Republican than people who earn less than $50,000 a year. Does this mean that all people who earn more than $50,000 a year vote Republican? Why, or why not?

20. Is the following statement true or false? A researcher who begins by collecting data and then develops a theory to explain his or her findings is engaged in deductive research.

21. A researcher formulates a hypothesis based on the "magic bullet theory" and then selects independent and dependent variables to test this hypothesis. What process is the researcher engaged in?

22. A researcher collects data on the spread of AIDS in the United States and then, based on his or her findings, develops a theory to explain why the rate of exposure and infection to the disease is higher among certain racial and ethnic groups than among others. In what process is the researcher engaged?

# THE LOGIC OF MEASUREMENT

Measurement is one of the most fundamental elements of science. In the case of social research, the task of measurement is typically one of characterizing individuals in terms of the issues under study. Thus, a study of voting will characterize respondents in terms of the candidate for whom they plan to vote, and a study of abortion will describe people in terms of their attitudes on that topic.

## VALIDITY PROBLEMS

*Validity* is a term used casually in everyday language, but it has a precise meaning in social research. It describes an indicator of a concept. Most simply, an indicator is said to be valid if it really measures the concept it is intended to measure; it is invalid if it doesn't.

As a simple example, let's consider political orientation, ranging from very liberal to very conservative. For an example of a clearly valid measure of this concept, here's the way the General Social Survey (GSS) asked about it.

POLVIEWS: We hear a lot of talk these days about liberals and conservatives. I'm going to show you a seven-point scale on which political views that people might hold are arranged from extremely liberal to extremely conservative. Where would you place yourself on this scale?

1. Extremely liberal

2. Liberal

3. Slightly liberal

4. Moderate, middle-of-the-road

5. Slightly conservative

6. Conservative

7. Extremely conservative

At the opposite extreme, a simple question about respondent gender would not be a valid measure of political orientation because political orientation and gender are different concepts. But now, let's consider another questionnaire item that does not come from the GSS. This item lies somewhere in between these two extremes of validity with regard to measuring political orientation.

Question: Which of the two major political parties do you most identify with?

1. Democratic Party

2. Republican Party

3. Neither

This second item is another reasonable measure of political orientation. Moreover, it is related to the first because Democrats are, on the whole, more liberal than Republicans. On the other hand, there are conservative Democrats and liberal Republicans. If our purpose is to tap into the liberal–conservative dimension, the initial item that asks directly about political orientation is obviously a more valid indicator of the concept than is the item about political party.

This particular example offers us a clear choice as to the most valid indicator of the concept at hand, but matters are not always so clear-cut. If we were measuring levels of prejudice, for example, we could not simply ask, "How prejudiced are you?" both because no one is likely to admit to being prejudiced and because it's possible for someone to be prejudiced without knowing it. As we search for workable indicators of a concept such as prejudice, the matter of validity becomes something to which we must pay careful attention.

Validity is a concern not only when you collect and analyze your own data—a process known as *primary research*—but also when you reanalyze data previously collected by someone else, as we do in this book. The process of reanalyzing someone else's data is referred to as *secondary analysis*. Even if you can think of a survey question that would have captured your concept perfectly, the original researchers might not have asked it. Hence, you often need to use ingenuity in constructing measures that capture the quality in which you are interested. In the case of political orientation, for example, you might combine the responses to several questions—asking for attitudes about civil liberties, past voting behavior, political party identification, and so forth. We'll return to the use of multiple indicators shortly.

In large part, the question of validity is settled on *prima facie* grounds: We judge an indicator to be relatively valid or invalid on the face of it. It was on this basis that you had no trouble seeing that asking directly about political orientation was a valid indicator of that concept, whereas asking about a person's gender was definitely not a valid measure of political orientation. Later in this book, we'll explore some simple methodological techniques that are also used to test the validity of measures.

## RELIABILITY PROBLEMS

Reliability is a different but equally important quality of measurement. **Reliability** refers to the quality of a measuring instrument that would cause it to report the same value in successive observations of a given case (provided the phenomenon being measured has not changed). For instance, if you step on a bathroom scale five times in a row and each time it gives you a different weight, the scale has a reliability problem. Conversely, if you step on a bathroom scale five times in a row and the scale gives you the same weight each time (even if the weight is wrong), the scale is reliable.

Similarly, if your statistics instructor administered the same test to you three times and each time you got a different score, even though your knowledge of statistics had not changed in the interim, the test would have a reliability problem. Conversely, if your instructor administered the same test three times and your score was the same each time, the test would be reliable.

In the context of survey research, reliability also concerns whether we can trust the answers that people give us even when their misstatements are honest ones. For instance, in medical research, some patients report in one survey that they have had a particular organ removed, only to indicate in subsequent surveys that they still have that organ.[1] Similarly, students of voting behavior regularly encounter individuals who claim on one survey that they did vote in the past presidential election and then claim in subsequent surveys that they either did not vote or do not remember whether they voted. As noted previously, these statements are often honest ones because it is difficult enough for most of us to recall what we did a few months ago, let alone several years ago.

Conceptually, the test of reliability is whether respondents would give the same answers repeatedly if the measurement could be made in such a way that (a) their situations had not changed (e.g., they hadn't had additional surgery to remove organs) and (b) they couldn't remember the answer they gave before.

As we suggested, empirically testing the reliability of an item requires multiple measures (e.g., your instructor must administer the statistics test at least two times in order to determine its reliability). However, we can sometimes assess the reliability of a single item based on its practicality.

---

1. The authors are grateful to Professor Randall MacIntosh, California State University–Sacramento, for this suggestion.

For example, years ago, one of us was asked to help administer a survey to teenage drivers in California. Over researcher objections, the client insisted on asking the question, "How many miles have you driven?" and providing a space for the teenager to write in his or her response. Perhaps you can recognize the problem in this question by attempting to answer it yourself. Unless you have never driven an automobile, we doubt that you can report how many miles you have driven with any accuracy. In the survey mentioned, some teenagers reported driving hundreds of thousands of miles—highly questionable results for people who had only been driving for a few years. Unless they have been keeping a driving log their whole life, most people cannot report with any accuracy how many total miles they have driven.

In this situation, it would be better to provide respondents with a set of categories realistically reflecting the number of miles they are likely to have driven: fewer than 1,000 miles; 1,000 to 4,999 miles; 5,000 to 9,999 miles; and so on. Such a set of categories gives respondents a framework within which to place their own situations. Even though they still may not know exactly how much they have driven, there is a fair likelihood that the categories they choose will contain their correct answers. The success of this technique depends on our having a good idea in advance of what constitutes reasonable categories, perhaps as determined by previous research. As an alternative, we might ask respondents to volunteer the number of miles they have driven but limit the time period to something they are likely to remember. Thus, we might ask how many miles they drove during the preceding week or month.

# DISTINGUISHING BETWEEN VALIDITY AND RELIABILITY

Perhaps the difference between validity and reliability can be seen most clearly in our previous example of weighing oneself on a bathroom scale. If you step on the scale repeatedly and it gives you a different weight each time, then the scale has a reliability problem. On the other hand, if the scale tells you that you weigh 125 pounds every time you step on it, then it's pretty reliable. However, if you actually weigh 225 pounds, then the scale, though reliable, has a problem in the validity department; it doesn't indicate your weight accurately.

Both validity and reliability are important in the analysis of data. If you are interested in learning why some people have deeply held religious beliefs and others do not, then asking people how often they attend church will be problematic. This question doesn't really provide a valid measure of the concept that interests you (religious belief) because anything you learn from asking the question will explain the causes of church attendance, not religious belief. Plus, if you asked people how many times they had attended church in the past year, any answers you received would probably not be reliable since, as with the driver survey mentioned previously, most people can't remember that far back. (It would be better, once again, to give them categories from which to choose.) Therefore, anything you might think you had learned about the causes of church attendance might be only a function of the errors people made in answering the question. You would have no assurance that another study would yield the same result, so your study would not be reliable.

# MULTIPLE INDICATORS

Often, the solution to the problems just discussed lies in the creation of ***composite measures***, measurements of variables that combine two or more indicators of the variable, and the use of ***multiple indicators***, or several questions about the same concept. As a simple example, to measure the degree to which a sample group of church members holds Christian beliefs, you might ask the members of that group questions about several issues, each dealing with a particular belief:

- Belief in God

- Belief that Jesus was divine

- Belief in the existence of the Devil

- Belief in an afterlife: heaven and hell
- Belief in the literal truth of the Bible

The various answers respondents give to these questions could be used to create an overall measure of their Christian religious belief or lack thereof. In the simplest procedure, you could give respondents 1 point for each belief with which they agreed, allowing you to score them from 0 to 5 on the index. Notice that this is the same logic by which you may earn 1 point for each correct answer on an exam, with the total score being taken as an indication of how well you know the material.

Some social science concepts are implicitly multidimensional. Consider the concept of *social class*, for example. Typically, this term is used in reference to a combination of education, income, and occupation and, sometimes, dimensions such as social class identification and prestige. For the purpose of data analysis, this concept would therefore be measured through the use of multiple indicators. When it becomes appropriate in the analyses we are going to undertake together, we'll show you how to create and use some simple composite measures.

# LEVELS OF MEASUREMENT

As we convert the concepts in our minds into empirical measurements in the form of variables, we sometimes have options as to those variables' level of statistical sophistication. Specifically, there are a number of different possibilities regarding the relationships among the categories constituting a variable. Therefore, in social research, we commonly speak of four **levels of measurement**: nominal, ordinal, ratio, and interval.

## Nominal Variables

Some variables simply distinguish different kinds of people. Gender is a good example of such a variable in the General Social Survey; the two categories of the variable, male and female, distinguish between men and women. Of course, such a treatment of this variable may not suit all research purposes, as transgender and intersex individuals are achieving more visibility, and there is more scholarly interest in them. The way we conceptualize and study gender will, no doubt, evolve in the coming years. Similarly, political party distinguishes Democrats from Republicans and from members of other parties; religious affiliation distinguishes Protestants from Catholics, Jews, and so forth. We refer to these variables as "nominal" because the categories constituting the variables are based on names.

*Nominal variables* simply name the different attributes constituting them. The attributes constituting a nominal variable (e.g., religious affiliation composed of Protestant, Catholic, Jewish, etc.) are simply different on their face. Republicans and Democrats are different from each other, as are Protestants and Catholics. In other cases, however, we can say more about the attributes making up variables.

## Ordinal Variables

Many social scientific variables go a step beyond simply naming the different attributes constituting a variable. *Ordinal variables* arrange those attributes in some order: from low to high, from more to less, and so on. Whereas the nominal variable *religious affiliation* classifies people into different religious groups, *religiosity* might order them into groups such as very religious, somewhat religious, and not-at-all religious. And whereas the nominal variable *political party identification* simply distinguishes different groups (e.g., Democrats and Republicans), an ordinal measure of political philosophy might rank-order the very liberal, the somewhat liberal, the middle-of-the-road, the somewhat conservative, and the very conservative. Ordinal variables share the nominal variable's quality of distinguishing differences among people, but they add the quality of *rank ordering* those differences.

At the same time, it is not meaningful to talk about the distances separating the attributes that make up an ordinal variable. For example, we have no basis for talking about the amount of liberalism separating the very liberal from the somewhat liberal or the somewhat liberal from the middle-of-the-road. We can say that the first group in each comparison is more liberal than the second, but we can't say by how much.

## Ratio Variables

Some variables allow us to speak more precisely about the distances between the attributes constituting them. Consider age for a moment. The distance between 10 years old and 20 years old is exactly the same as that between 60 years old and 70 years old. Thus, it makes sense to talk about the distance between two ages (e.g., they are 10 years apart). Moreover, variables such as age have the quality of containing a genuine zero point—in this case, 0 years old. This quality is what allows us to examine ratios among the categories constituting such variables. Thus, we can say that a 20-year-old is twice as old as a 10-year-old. By comparison, we would have no grounds for saying one person is twice as religious as another, so religion can only be measured as a nominal or ordinal variable.

*Ratio variables*, then, share all of the qualities associated with nominal and ordinal variables, but they also have a zero point, and their categories can be separated by fixed units of distance and can thus be compared as ratios. Other examples of ratio measures include income, years of schooling, and hours worked per week.

## Interval Variables

Rarer in social research are ***interval variables***, which have the quality of standard intervals of measurement but lack a genuine zero point. One example is intelligence quotient, or IQ. Although IQ is calculated in such a way as to allow for a score of zero, such a score would not indicate a complete lack of intelligence because the person would at least have been able to take the test.

Moving outside the social sciences, consider temperature. The Celsius and Fahrenheit temperature scales both have 0° marks, but neither represents a total lack of heat, given that temperatures below zero are possible. The Kelvin scale, by contrast, is based on an absolute zero, which does represent a total lack of heat (measured in terms of molecular motion).

For most statistics used by social scientists, interval and ratio scales may be considered the same. When we start using SPSS Statistics, we'll see that its creators have lumped interval and ratio variables into a single category called ***scale***. Although these variables may be combined for practical purposes, the distinction between them helps us understand why a negative income might be interpreted as debt and why a negative age is impossible!

# MEASUREMENT AND INFORMATION

Knowing a variable's level of measurement is important for selecting an appropriate statistic. Variables of different levels of measurement contain different amounts of information. The only information we have about nominal variables is the number of cases that share a common attribute. With ordinal variables, in addition to knowing how many cases fall into a given category, we know a greater than/less than relationship between the cases. Variables measured at the interval level have points that are equidistant from one another, so we know how much greater or less each case is than the others. Finally, with ratio variables, we have all of the characteristics of nominal, ordinal, and interval variables, plus the knowledge that zero is not arbitrary but means an absence of the phenomenon.

The statistics that SPSS Statistics has been programmed to compute are designed to make maximum use of the information preserved in a level of measurement. Using the mode on a sample of grade point averages ignores information used by the mean. Conversely, using the mean for a sample of religious preferences assumes information (equidistant points) not contained in a nominal measure. Responsible use of statistics requires selecting a statistic that matches the data's level of measurement. We'll talk about this more later. Right now, we want you to know that being able to identify a variable's level of measurement is essential for selecting the right statistical tool. We don't want to see you using a screwdriver when you need a hammer.

Table 2.1 displays the three primary levels of measurement that we discuss in this book: nominal, ordinal, and interval/ratio (scale). We purposefully designed the table as a series of steps to remind you that there is a hierarchy implied in the levels of measurement idea. Variables at the nominal level (the bottom step) contain the least amount of information, variables at the ordinal level (the middle step) contain more information, and variables at the interval/ratio level (the highest step) contain the most information. You should also note that as you move from the nominal to the ordinal and finally to the interval/ratio level, each level has the qualities of the level(s) below it, plus a new trait.

| TABLE 2.1  ■  Levels of Measurement | | |
|---|---|---|
| | | INTERVAL/RATIO Distance between categories is meaningful. Examples: income (measured in thousands of dollars); age (measured in years) |
| | ORDINAL Categories can be rank ordered. Examples: social class (lower, working, middle, upper); attitudes toward gun control (strongly oppose, oppose, favor, strongly favor) | |
| NOMINAL Categories differ in name. Examples: gender (male, female); party identification (Democrat, Republican) | | |

## MEASUREMENT OPTIONS

Sometimes, you will have options regarding the levels of measurement to be created in variables. For instance, although age can qualify as a ratio variable, it can be measured as ordinal (e.g., young, middle-aged, and old) or even as nominal (baby boomer or not baby boomer).

The significance of these levels of measurement will become more apparent when we begin to analyze the variables in our data set. As you'll discover, some analytic techniques are appropriate to nominal variables, some to ordinal variables, and some to ratio variables. On the one hand, you will need to know a variable's level of measurement to determine which analytic techniques are appropriate. On the other hand, where you have options for measurement, your choice of measurement level may be determined by the techniques you want to employ.

## CLASSIFYING VARIABLES AS DISCRETE OR CONTINUOUS

In addition to distinguishing variables by their level of measurement, researchers sometimes classify variables as discrete or continuous. Just as distinguishing between levels of measurement helps us choose appropriate statistics, so too does knowing whether variables are discrete or continuous.

***Discrete variables*** are variables whose values are completely separate from one another. In the GSS data, these include variables such as NUMBER OF SIBLINGS and SEX. These are variables with a limited number of distinct (i.e., discrete) values or categories that cannot be reduced or subdivided into smaller units or numbers. Discrete variables can be nominal (sex), ordinal (class rank), or interval/ratio (number of siblings). All of these variables are discrete because their values cannot be subdivided or reduced. A respondent may, for instance, have 1 dog, but he or she cannot have 0.5 or 0.25 dogs. Dogs, like people, come in discrete units of 1; they simply cannot be subdivided into smaller units.

(Note that it is possible to have an average number of dogs per family in a town that is not a whole number, say 1.5 dogs. This is an average; it does not and cannot indicate that any single family has a fractional physical dog—dogs, like people, are whole creatures only, like Mina in the photo to the right posing with a previous edition of *Adventures in Social Research*!)

***Continuous variables***, on the other hand, are variables whose values can be infinitely subdivided, such as AGE or EDUC (education measured in years). These variables are continuous both because they have a time dimension and because time can be infinitely subdivided (i.e., years, months, weeks, days, hours, minutes, seconds, etc.). The level of measurement for continuous variables can be either interval/ratio (age measured in years) or ordinal (age measured as infant, toddler, adolescent, preteen, teenager, etc.).

Unlike levels of measurement, which tell us the amount of information provided by a measure, the discrete versus continuous distinction gives us information about the underlying characteristics of a variable. In particular, it refers to the phenomenon's divisibility, or whether the values of a variable can be subdivided into ever-smaller units, as described in Table 2.2.

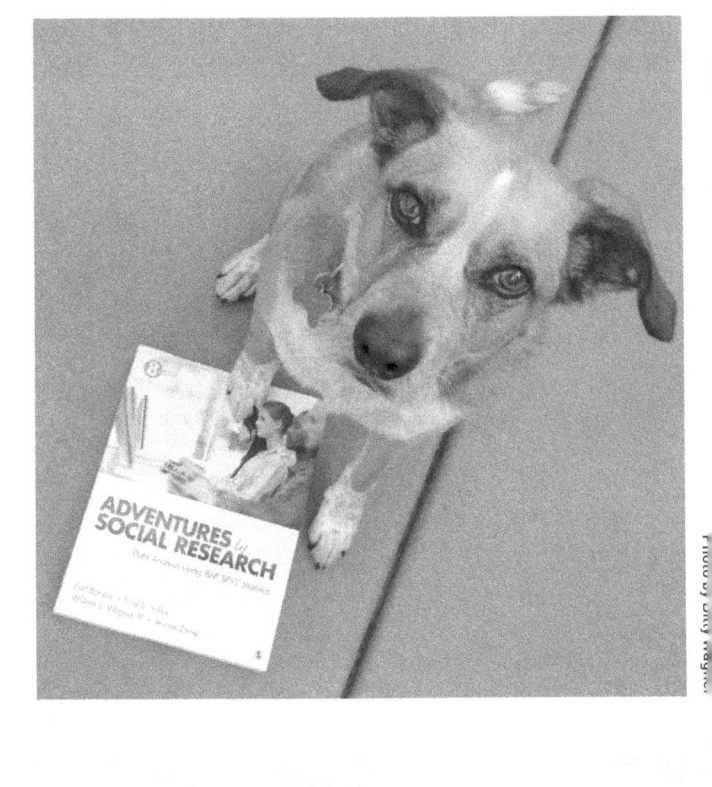

| TABLE 2.2 ■ Tips for Distinguishing Between Discrete and Continuous Variables | |
|---|---|
| **Discrete Variable** | **Example: Number of Siblings** |
| | • Units CANNOT be reduced to ever-smaller units. |
| | • There is NOT an infinite number of other possible categories between any two categories of this variable (i.e., 1 and 2 siblings, or 2 and 3 siblings, etc.). |
| | • Variables can be nominal, ordinal, or interval/ratio (scale). |
| **Continuous Variable** | **Example: Age Measured in Years** |
| | • Units CAN be further reduced to smaller units (i.e., months, weeks, days, hours, minutes, seconds, etc.). |
| | • There ARE an infinite number of other possible categories between any two categories of this variable (i.e., 19 and 20 years old, 20 and 21 years old, etc.). |
| | • Variables can be interval or ratio (scale). |

# CONCLUSION

Measurement is a fundamental aspect of social science research. It may be seen as the transition from concepts to variables—from sometimes ambiguous mental images to precise, empirical measures. Whereas we often speak casually about such concepts as prejudice, social class, and liberalism in everyday conversation, social scientists must be more precise in their use of these terms.

Chapters 1 and 2 have given you a brief overview of two important issues in social scientific inquiry that are directly relevant to our primary focus—computerized statistical analysis. The chapters that follow build on this discussion of theory and measurement and show you the concrete techniques you need to engage in data analysis.

## Main Points

- Measurement is a vital component of social scientific research.

- In designing and evaluating measurements, social scientists must pay particular attention to the problems of validity and reliability.

- A common remedy for problems of validity and reliability is the construction of composite measures using multiple indicators.

- Level of measurement signifies the different amounts and types of information obtained about a variable, and consideration of level of measurement is essential for selecting appropriate statistical tools.

- The four levels of measurement are nominal, ordinal, ratio, and interval.

- Variables of different levels of measurement contain different amounts of information.

- There is an implied hierarchy of the various levels of measurement, with the nominal level being at the bottom (meaning it can provide the least information), the ordinal level in the middle, and the interval and ratio levels being at the top (meaning they can provide the most information).

- In addition to classifying variables by their level of measurement, researchers distinguish between discrete and continuous variables.

- Discrete variables cannot be infinitely subdivided into ever-smaller units, whereas continuous variables can.

## Key Terms

Composite measures 15

Continuous variables 19

Discrete variables 18

Interval variables 17

Levels of measurement 16

Multiple indicators 15

Nominal variables 16

Ordinal variables 16

Primary research 14

Ratio variables 17

Reliability 14

Scale 17

Secondary analysis 14

Validity 13

## Review Questions

1. A researcher sets out to measure drug use on U.S. college campuses by asking a representative sample of undergraduates whether they are currently receiving federal grants or loans. What is the problem with this measure?

2. A researcher asks a representative sample of baby boomers how much alcohol they consumed during their college years and includes on the survey form a space for them to write in the actual number of drinks they consumed. One month later, the researcher administers the same questionnaire to the same respondents, and more than half the respondents report consuming much less alcohol during their college years than they reported just a month earlier. What is the problem with this measure?

3. Multiple indicators are useful in dealing with what types of problems?

4. Name one reason why it is important to know or be able to identify a variable's level of measurement.

5. Ordinal variables have all the qualities of variables at which other level of measurement?

6. Ratio variables have all the qualities of variables at which other levels of measurement?

7. The creators of SPSS Statistics have combined ratio and interval variables into one category that they refer to as _____.

8. A variable whose values can be infinitely subdivided is called a _____ variable.

*Identify the level of measurement of each of the following variables, and classify the variables as either discrete or continuous (Questions 9–11).*

9. A researcher measures respondents' attitudes toward premarital sex by asking the following question: "If a man and woman have sexual relations before marriage, do you think it is always wrong, almost always wrong, wrong only sometimes, or not wrong at all?"

10. A researcher measures the amount of television viewing by asking the following question: "On the average day, how many hours do you personally watch television?" The researcher then asks respondents to fill in the actual number of hours in a space provided.

11. A researcher measures marital status by asking respondents whether they are currently married, widowed, divorced, separated, or never married.

*Indicate whether the following statements (Questions 12–17) are true or false.*

12. Certain variables can be measured at both the nominal and ordinal levels.

13. You are invited to watch a screening of a new movie and then rate it as excellent, good, fair, or poor. The level of measurement is nominal because the ratings differ in name.

14. A researcher asks respondents to indicate the last four digits of their Social Security numbers. The level of measurement for this variable is interval/ratio because the distance between categories is meaningful.

15. A researcher asks respondents how many siblings they have. This variable can be categorized as continuous.

16. A researcher asks respondents how long they have lived at their current residence. This variable can be categorized as continuous.

17. Discrete variables can be either nominal or ordinal but not interval/ratio.

*Complete the activities below (Questions 18–20).*

18. Construct measures of *annual income* at two levels of measurement.

19. Classify the variables you constructed in response to Question 18 as either discrete or continuous.

20. Construct measures of *individual age* at two levels of measurement.

# DESCRIPTION OF DATA SETS

## The General Social Survey

The data we provide for your use here are real. They come from the responses of 2,867 adult Americans selected as a representative sample of the United States in 2016. These data are a major resource for professional social scientists and are the basis of many published books and articles.

The **General Social Survey (GSS)** is conducted regularly by the **National Opinion Research Center (NORC)** in Chicago, with financial support from the National Science Foundation and private sources. The purpose of the GSS program is to provide the nation's social scientists with accurate data for analysis.

This survey was the brainchild of Jim Davis, considered one of the most visionary social scientists of our lifetime. The GSS, which began in 1972, was conducted annually until 1994, when it became biennial.[1] Over the past 38 years, the GSS has asked more than 48,500 respondents more than 4,500 questions on topics ranging from attitudes toward abortion to star signs in the zodiac. In recent years, the GSS asked questions on issues such as Internet use, religious transformations, spirituality, genetic testing, heredity, stress, violence in the workplace, immigration, altruism, alcohol consumption, sexual behavior, social networks, and group membership.

While this chapter provides you with a brief overview of some of the central components of the GSS, you can access further information about the GSS and other data by visiting one of the following websites:

- NORC is a nonprofit corporation, affiliated with the University of Chicago, that conducts the GSS. Visit the NORC home page at http://www.norc.org. Once there, click on *Projects* and filter on *General Social Survey* or go directly to http://gss.norc.org. The GSS Data Explorer website is particularly useful for examining and obtaining GSS data: https://gssdataexplorer.norc.org.

- The Inter-University Consortium for Political and Social Research (ICPSR) is associated with the University of Michigan. Part of its mission is to maintain and provide access to a vast archive of social science data for research and instruction. ICPSR's home page can be found at http://www.icpsr.umich.edu.

- The Roper Center for Public Opinion Research is an archive of public opinion research, affiliated with the Cornell University (formerly affiliated with the University of Connecticut), that provides access to the GSS. The Roper Center home page is at https://ropercenter.cornell.edu. Click on *Search Datasets* and enter "General Social Survey," or visit https://ropercenter.cornell.edu/general-social-survey.

- You can also access this information online by using your favorite search engine. Simply search using one of the following terms: *General Social Survey (GSS), GSS 2016, National Opinion Research Center (NORC), Inter-University Consortium for Political and Social Research (ICPSR)*, or *Roper Center for Public Opinion Research*. If you do such a search, you

---

1. Funding shortages precluded GSS studies in 1979, 1981, and 1992.

will find that Canada also has a GSS sponsored by Statistics Canada, the equivalent of the United States Census Bureau.

## SAMPLING

The data provided by the GSS are a representative sample of American adults. This means that anything we learn about the 2,867 people sampled can be taken as an accurate reflection of what all (noninstitutionalized, English-speaking) American adults (18 years of age or older) would have said if we could have interviewed them all.

Creating a truly representative sample requires developing a selection technique that ensures every person in the population has an equal probability of being included. Since the previous GSS, the U.S. Postal Service and the U.S. Census Bureau have made available lists of household units representing 72% of the U.S. population. With the aid of computers, random samples of households are drawn from the lists for inclusion in the GSS sample. For the 28% of the population not on household lists, Census tracts and enumeration districts are selected, and then, housing units are randomly drawn for inclusion.

This complex and sophisticated sampling process makes it possible for the responses of 2,876 individuals to provide an accurate reflection of the feelings of all adult Americans. The U.S. Census Bureau uses similar techniques for the purpose of government planning, as do polling firms that predict voting behavior with relative accuracy.

For a detailed description of the sample design the GSS uses, see "Appendix A: Sampling Design and Weighting" in the *General Social Surveys 1972–2016 Cumulative Codebook.*[2]

The *Adventures in Social Research* student study site (https://study.sagepub.com/babbie10e) includes three data files. One, named ***GSS2016.SAV***, includes all 2,867 cases across 960 variables from the GSS. We have also created subset data files, ***DEMO.SAV*** and ***EXER.SAV***, by reducing the size of the GSS sample to 1,500 cases (through random subselection) so that those who are using the student version of SPSS (for both Windows and Macintosh) can access the GSS 2012 data. As we noted in Chapter 1, whereas the professional and graduate versions of SPSS Statistics for Windows and Macintosh are, for all practical purposes, limited only by the size of the computer on which they are installed, the student version for both operating systems is limited to 1,500 cases and 50 variables.

We have selected 43 of the variables from the GSS to include in the DEMO.SAV data file. Likewise, we have chosen 46 variables from the GSS for inclusion in the EXER.SAV data file. The DEMO.SAV data file contains the data that are used in the examples in each of the chapters, demonstrating the techniques and analysis. The EXER.SAV data file contains the data needed to answer the Laboratory Assignment questions at the end of each chapter, starting with Chapter 4.

The data you have at hand, then, can be taken as an accurate reflection of the characteristics, attitudes, and behaviors of noninstitutionalized Americans 18 years of age and older in 2016. This statement does need to be qualified slightly, however. When you analyze the data and learn that 46.2% (variable: ABANY, GSS, 2016) of the sample said that they supported a woman's unrestricted right to have an abortion for any reason, you are safe in assuming that about 46% of the entire U.S. adult population feels that way. Because the data are based on a sample rather than on asking everyone, however, we need to anticipate some degree of sampling error. You can think of ***sampling error*** as the extent to which the responses of those sampled differ from the responses of the larger population (English-speaking persons 18 years of age and older living in noninstitutionalized arrangements within the United States in 2016). As a general rule, the greater the sampling error, the less representative the sample. It would not be strange, based on the example given, to discover that 44% to 48% of the total adult population (rather than exactly 46%) support a woman's unrestricted right to have an abortion for any reason. It is inconceivable, however, that as few as 10% or as many as 90% hold the opinion in question.

---

2. Available at http://gss.norc.org/documents/codebook/GSS_Codebook.pdf.

As a rough guideline, you can assume that the sampling error in this data set is plus or minus only a few percentage points. Later in the book, we'll talk about how to calculate sampling error for specific pieces of data.

Even granting the possibility of sampling error, however, our best estimate of what's true among the total U.S. population is what we have learned from probability samples. Thus, if you had to bet on the percentage of the total U.S. population who support a woman's unrestricted right to an abortion, you should put your money on 46%. You would be better off, however, betting on the range of 44% to 48%.

# DATA COLLECTION

The GSS data were collected in face-to-face household interviews. Once the sample households were selected, professional interviewers were dispatched to call on each one. The interviewers asked each of the questions and wrote down the respondents' answers. Each interview took about 90 minutes.

To maximize the amount of information that can be collected in this massive interviewing project, the GSS uses a split-ballot design, such that NORC asked some questions of a random subsample of the households and other questions of the other households. Still other questions were asked of all respondents. When we begin analyzing the GSS data, you will notice that some data items have a substantial number of respondents marked *missing data*. For the most part, this term refers to respondents who were not asked that particular question.

Although some of the questions were posed to only a subsample of households, you can still take the responses as representative of the U.S. adult population, except that the degree of sampling error, mentioned previously, is larger.

For more information about how the GSS data were collected, see "Appendix B: Field Work and Interviewer Specifications" and "Appendix C: General Coding Instructions" in the *General Social Surveys 1972–2016 Cumulative Codebook*.

# THE CODEBOOK: APPENDIX A

The questionnaire items included in the files you will be using throughout this text (DEMO.SAV and EXER.SAV) are listed in Appendix A of this book. We attempted to choose variables that are not only interesting but also relevant to students from a variety of social science disciplines, including communications, criminal justice, education, health studies, political science, public administration, social work, and sociology.

Before proceeding to the next chapter, you may want to take a few minutes to review the variables in Appendix A. Before long, you'll be getting much more familiar with them. As you analyze survey data, it is important to know exactly how questions were asked if you are to understand the meaning of the answers given in response. Appendix A includes the following information for each of the variables contained in your DEMO.SAV and EXER.SAV files.

- Abbreviated variable names—used by SPSS Statistics to access variables

- Question wording—how the interviewer asked the question

- *Values*—sometimes called *numeric values* or *numeric codes*, used to code responses

- *Value labels*—used to identify categories represented by values. Please note that in Appendix A, we have excluded the following value labels: *NA (no answer)*, *DK (don't know)*, and *IAP (inapplicable)*. These labels refer to cases when the respondent offered "no answer," the respondent said he or she "did not know," or the question was not asked and, thus, is "inapplicable."

- Level of measurement for each variable

### Data Set 1: DEMO.SAV

*DEMO.SAV* will be used and referred to in the demonstrations in the body of the chapters that follow this one. You can follow along with these examples on your own computer. This file contains a randomly selected subsample of 1,500 cases and 43 variables drawn from the 2016 GSS. The items are arranged according to the following subject categories: demographics, abortion, family, religion, social-political opinions, and sexual attitudes and behavior.

### Data Set 2: EXER.SAV

*EXER.SAV* is made available for completion of the Lab Exercises, which start with Chapter 4. Like DEMO.SAV, this file contains a randomly selected subsample of 1,500 cases and 46 variables drawn from the 2016 GSS. The items are arranged according to the following subject categories: demographics, sex roles, law enforcement, health, mass media, national government spending priorities, teen sex, affirmative action, hiring practices in education, sexual behavior, and voting.

### Data Set 3: GSS2016.SAV

*GSS2016.SAV* is the full 2016 GSS file. It includes all 2,867 cases, as well as all 960 original variables. The *GSS Cumulative Codebook*, also provided on the *Adventures in Social Research* website, provides details for each of the variables in this data set.

## CONCLUSION

After reading this chapter and Appendix A, you should be familiar with the General Social Survey and the variables with which you will be working. The data you will be using are real and can be taken as an accurate reflection of the attitudes, opinions, beliefs, characteristics, and behaviors of adult Americans in 2016.

In the next chapter, we are going to get started using SPSS Statistics. Once you have learned how to launch an SPSS Statistics session and access the files on the *Adventures in Social Research* website (https://study.sagepub.com/babbie10e), you will be ready to begin exploring your data. With the help of SPSS Statistics and some simple tools, we think you will find that the possibilities for discovery are both rich and rewarding.

## Main Points

- The General Social Survey (GSS) is a national survey of adult Americans that has been conducted annually or every other year since 1972.

- The 2016 data are based on a sample of 2,867 adult Americans and can be taken as an accurate reflection of noninstitutionalized, English-speaking adult Americans in 2016.

- The data were collected in face-to-face household interviews averaging about 90 minutes each.

- The website associated with this book (https://study.sagepub.com/babbie10e) contains three data files: DEMO.SAV, EXER.SAV, and GSS2016.SAV.

- DEMO.SAV is the file you will be using as you work your way through the chapters. You will use EXER.SAV to complete the exercises at the end of each chapter.

- The DEMO.SAV data file contains data from 1,500 respondents and 43 variables from the full GSS 2016 data set, while the EXER.SAV data file contains data from 1,500 respondents and a different selection of 46 variables.

## Key Terms

DEMO.SAV 24

DK (don't know) 25

EXER.SAV 24

General Social Survey (GSS) 23

GSS2016.SAV 24

IAP (inapplicable) 25

Missing data 25

NA (no answer) 25

National Opinion Research
Center (NORC) 23

Sampling error 24

Value labels 25

Values 25

## Review Questions

1. What is the General Social Survey (GSS)?

2. When were the data discussed in this chapter collected?

3. If the data show that 60% of respondents favor capital punishment (60.4% favor capital punishment; GSS, 2016), what will be your best estimate of the percentage(s) of adult Americans who feel this way?

4. Is it possible, based on this example, that as little as 5% to 10% of adult Americans favor capital punishment? Why, or why not?

5. When social scientists refer to *sampling error*, to what are they referring?

6. Would you agree that as a general rule, the smaller the sampling error, the less likely the data are representative of the population?

*Indicate whether the following statements (Questions 7–11) are true or false.*

7. Respondents to the 2016 GSS were interviewed over the telephone.

8. Each interview takes approximately 1.5 hours.

9. When an interviewer forgets to ask a respondent a particular question, the nonresponse is called *missing data.*

10. The label *DK* is used when a respondent refuses to answer a question.

11. The label *IAP* is used when a respondent is not asked a particular question.

*In order to answer Questions 12 through 14, consult Appendix A.*

12. List three items from the DEMO.SAV file that deal with sexual behavior or attitudes.

13. List three items from the EXER.SAV file that deal with opinions about who should be able to teach.

14. The DEMO.SAV file and the EXER.SAV file contain several variables addressing a variety of issues. Once you have looked through the codebook in Appendix A, answer the following questions: Which of the issues most interest you? What would you like to learn about these issues? Why?

# UNIVARIATE ANALYSIS

Chapter 4 provides you with some initial familiarization with the version of SPSS Statistics you will be using throughout the text. This and each of the following chapters contain a series of demonstrations you can follow along with on your computer. When the images on your computer screen match ours in the book, you will know that you successfully used SPSS Statistics commands. In Chapter 4, for instance, we begin with Demonstration 4.1, "Starting an SPSS Statistics Session," and end with Demonstration 4.7, "Ending Your SPSS Statistics Session." By the time you work your way through these demonstrations, you should be fairly comfortable accessing SPSS Statistics, moving through the Data Editor, opening a data file, and ending your SPSS Statistics session. You can further check your abilities by completing the lab exercise at the end of the chapter.

In the body of each of the following chapters, we are going to pay special attention to three concepts: religiosity, political orientations, and attitudes toward abortion. In the exercises at the ends of these chapters, you will have a chance to explore other issues, such as sex roles, law enforcement, health, mass media, national government spending priorities, teen sex, affirmative action, and terrorism preparedness. We've chosen these topics on the basis of general interest and the possibilities they hold for analysis.

Chapter 5 begins our discussion of univariate analysis, the analysis of one variable at a time. In this chapter, we will examine several different ways we might measure the religiosity of the respondents to the General Social Survey (GSS), distinguishing the religious from the nonreligious and noting variations in between. In so doing, we are going to learn how to instruct SPSS to create frequency distributions, produce descriptive statistics, and save and print our output.

In Chapter 6, we continue our focus on univariate analysis by looking at differences in political orientations. We will show you how to present your data in graphic form by reviewing commands for creating bar charts, pie charts, line graphs, and histograms.

Chapters 7 and 8 provide you with two additional skills that many social researchers find useful: recoding and creating composite measures. In Chapter 7, we teach you how to combine the categories from one variable to create a new variable. This process, known as recoding, is most useful when you are working with variables with a large number of categories. In addition to recoding, social researchers often combine several responses into more sophisticated measures of the concepts under study. In Chapter 8, you'll learn a few basic techniques for doing this.

Finally, Chapter 9 suggests a number of other topics you might be interested in exploring: desired family size, child-rearing attitudes, sexual behavior, and prejudice. We'll give you some guidance in applying the techniques we've focused on in the previous chapters to examine these topics. The major goals of this chapter are not only to review the SPSS techniques discussed in the previous chapters but also to give you the opportunity to strike out on your own and experience some of the open-endedness of social research. The exercises at the end of this chapter are designed to assist you with writing up your research results.

# USING SPSS STATISTICS

## Some Basics

Like most data analysis programs, SPSS Statistics is capable of computing many different statistical procedures with different kinds of data. This makes SPSS Statistics a very powerful and useful tool, but because of its generalization, we need to specify what we want it to do for us.

In many ways, SPSS Statistics is a vehicle for discovering differences and relationships in data, the same way a car is a vehicle for discovering places we have not yet visited. The car does not know where we want to go or what we wish to see. We, rather than the car, plan the trip and set the direction. Similarly, when we use SPSS Statistics, we choose the data we wish to explore and select the statistical procedures we wish to use. Sitting at our computer keyboards, we are in SPSS's driver's seat.

## DEMONSTRATION 4.1: STARTING AN SPSS STATISTICS SESSION

Starting an SPSS Statistics session is simple. Once you have started Windows (7, 8, or later) or the Macintosh OS X (Yosemite, or later), you will see a "desktop" that may contain several small graphics (called icons) representing programs. The desktop also contains access to pull-down menus and can have a dock, on which program or file icons are displayed. At this point, you have several options, and two of the most basic are summarized in SPSS Statistics Command 4.1.

---

**SPSS Statistics Command 4.1:
Starting an SPSS Statistics Session**

Once you are in Windows (or Mac OS), you have two major options:

*Option 1*

Double-click **SPSS Statistics icon**

*Option 2*

Click **Start → Programs** OR **All Programs → SPSS Statistics**

For Macintosh OS users, find the SPSS Statistics icon in the Applications folder or on the dock. (If it's not there already, you may wish to place it on the dock.)

---

Whenever we introduce a new command, we will provide you with a summary of the command in a box such as the one above (SPSS Statistics Command 4.1). The box contains a brief description of the command, as well as a summary of how to accomplish the procedure. You will also find a list of new SPSS Statistics commands at the end of the chapter. In addition, the *Adventures in Social Research* student study website (https://study.sagepub.com/babbie10e) contains more resources related to the SPSS Statistics commands introduced in the text.

If neither of these alternatives works, you can panic if you like. Better yet, verify that SPSS Statistics has been installed on your computer, or ask your instructor for assistance.

After launching SPSS Statistics, you may see an SPSS Statistics ***dialog box*** asking, "What would you like to do?"[1] For now, click on the **Cancel** button or the **X** (Close button) in the upper right-hand corner, and this box will disappear. SPSS Statistics will finish loading, and you should see something like what is shown in the following screen.

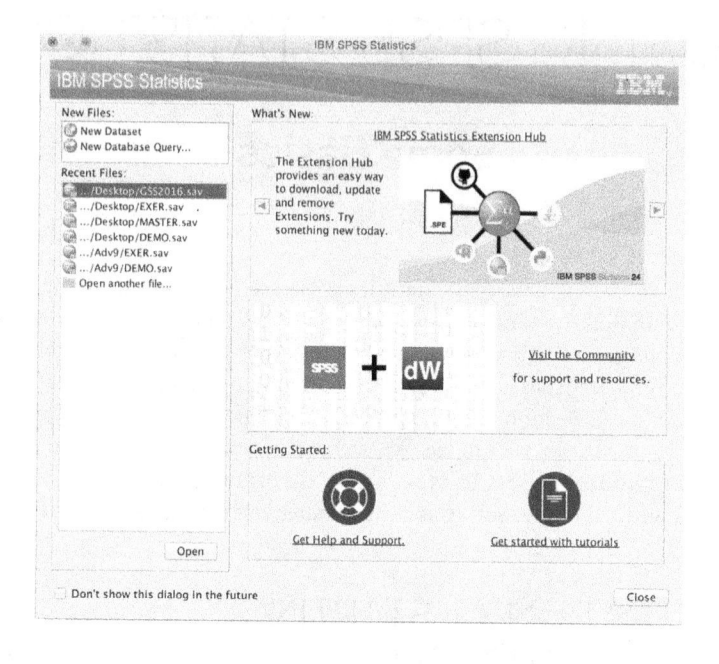

Once SPSS Statistics opens, you will notice that most of the screen is taken up by the SPSS Statistics ***Data Editor***. You can find that name in the ***title bar*** on the top left-hand side of your screen. In the example, note that it is labeled "IBM SPSS Statistics Data Editor."

---

1. If you do not see this dialog box, don't worry. It just means that someone using SPSS Statistics before you requested that this box not be displayed every time the program is opened.

The Data Editor displays the contents of the active file. Because we haven't loaded any data yet, the screen is currently empty (thus, the name "Untitled1").

If you look to the bottom left-hand corner of the screen, you will notice two tabs representing the two primary components of the Data Editor: **Data View** and **Variable View**. Both screens contain important information about the data with which you are working. The Data View screen, the one you are looking at now, is designed to hold raw data for analysis. The Variable View screen contains information about that data.

We are going to examine each aspect of the Data Editor in turn, beginning with the Data View screen.

# DEMONSTRATION 4.2: EXPLORING THE DATA VIEW PORTION OF THE DATA EDITOR

## Menu Bar

The Data View screen is designed to hold data for analysis. If you wished, you could enter data directly into the screen now and analyze it. Instead, however, we are going to load a portion of the General Social Survey (GSS) data set into the screen in a moment. Directly beneath the title bar is a set of menus called a **menu bar**, running from "File" on the left to "Help" on the right. You are going to become very familiar with these menus because they are the control system or the primary means through which you will operate SPSS Statistics.

As a preview, click **File** on the menu bar, and a drop-down menu will appear. Notice that some commands in the drop-down menu appear black, whereas others are faint gray. Whenever you see a list such as this, you can execute the black commands (by clicking on them), but the gray ones are not currently available to you. Right now, for example, you can **Open** a data set, but you can't click **Save** because there's nothing to be saved at this time.

You will also notice that some of the options in the drop-down menu (i.e., New, Open, Open Database, Display Data File Information, Repository, Recently Used Data, and Recently Used Files) are followed by a right-pointing arrow. The arrow signifies that several additional commands will appear on a submenu when the category is picked. If you hold your cursor over **Open** for a moment, you will notice that a submenu of options appears on the screen. Now click on **File** again, and the list disappears. Do that now to get rid of the File menu, and we'll come back to it shortly.

## Getting Help

At the far right-hand side of the menu bar, you will see the SPSS Statistics Help menu, something that you may want to take note of in case you need to use it later. As you are now aware, SPSS Statistics is a powerful state-of-the-art statistical package that allows users to accomplish numerous tasks and procedures. While this textbook introduces you to a variety of SPSS Statistics commands, options, and procedures, we cannot hope to cover all of the program's capabilities. If you find that you want to use SPSS Statistics to perform a procedure not covered in the text or if you have a question or problem that hasn't been addressed in the book, you may want to consult the Help feature. All you have to do is click on **Help**, and a drop-down menu containing several options will appear.

The first option available in the Help menu is "Topics." Click on **Topics**, and you will see that this box gives you several options for getting assistance. The Index tab, for instance, is organized in alphabetical order and provides a searchable index that makes it easy to find specific topics; the Search tab allows you to type in a word or phrase to be found. To close this box, simply click on the **X** (Close button) in the upper right-hand corner.

Another Help feature you may find useful is the online tutorial that gives a comprehensive overview of SPSS Statistics basics. You can access the tutorial by clicking **Help** and then selecting **Tutorial** from the drop-down menu. You will have an opportunity to explore the tutorial in the exercises at the end of this chapter.

---

### SPSS Statistics Command 4.2:
### Accessing the Help Menu

Click **Help** → Select Help option you wish to access (i.e., **Topics, Tutorial**, etc.)

---

These are just some of the Help features available. In addition to the Help menu, assistance is also available in other ways. We will mention some of these as we go on.

## Toolbar

In addition to the menu bar, a second common way to communicate with SPSS Statistics is through the use of the *toolbar*. The toolbar is the line of buttons, or tools, running from left to right directly below the menu bar. Although you can use the menu bar and drop-down menus to perform most tasks, sometimes it's easier just to click a button on the toolbar.

You can find out what tasks each button on the toolbar performs by hovering your cursor over the button and waiting a moment until a brief description of the tool pops up onscreen. For instance, if you place your cursor on the button toward the left end of the toolbar that contains a picture of a disk, you will soon see the words "Save File" pop up on the screen. This, of course, lets us know that we can use this tool to save a file.

If you want to take a moment to explore what other tools are available on the toolbar, you can do that now. Otherwise, we will move ahead to the dialog boxes.

## Dialog Boxes

Often when you click on one of the toolbars or choose an option from the menu bar, SPSS Statistics responds by opening a dialog box. If, for instance, you click on the **Open Data** tool on the far left-hand side of your toolbar (the tool depicting a partially opened file), SPSS Statistics responds by displaying the Open Data dialog box.

Dialog boxes are important because they tell you what else SPSS Statistics needs to know in order to fulfill your command. In short, they serve as a collection of prompts or hints indicating what other information is necessary in order for SPSS Statistics to do what you've asked it to do. Recall when we said earlier that there are other ways to get assistance beyond using the Help option on the menu bar. One of the primary ways to access assistance on SPSS Statistics is through dialog boxes. There are two methods of getting help once you have opened a dialog box.

The first option is to right-click on any control in the dialog box to display a description of the option and directions for its use. The second option is to click on the **Help** button. Most dialog boxes contain a Help button that takes you directly to the Help Topic for that particular dialog box. This Help Topic will provide you with general information and links to related issues.

---

### SPSS Statistics Command 4.3: Getting Help in a Dialog Box

*Option 1*

Right-click any control/command

*Option 2*

Click **Help** button

---

## Scroll Bars: Moving Through the Data Editor

Before we move on, we want to mention one last set of bars that will make it easier for you to move through the Data Editor: the *scroll bars*.

The horizontal scroll bar, situated across the bottom right side of your screen, allows you to move from left to right, while the vertical scroll bar, located on the far right side of your screen, allows you to move up and down.

In addition to the scroll bars, you can also use your cursor or the arrow keys on the keyboard to move through the data screen. If you take a moment to experiment with these options, you may notice that you can move the *active cell* (the cell in the screen outlined with thick black lines). Once a cell has been designated as the active cell, you can enter data in it (or modify existing data), something we will focus on in the next demonstration.

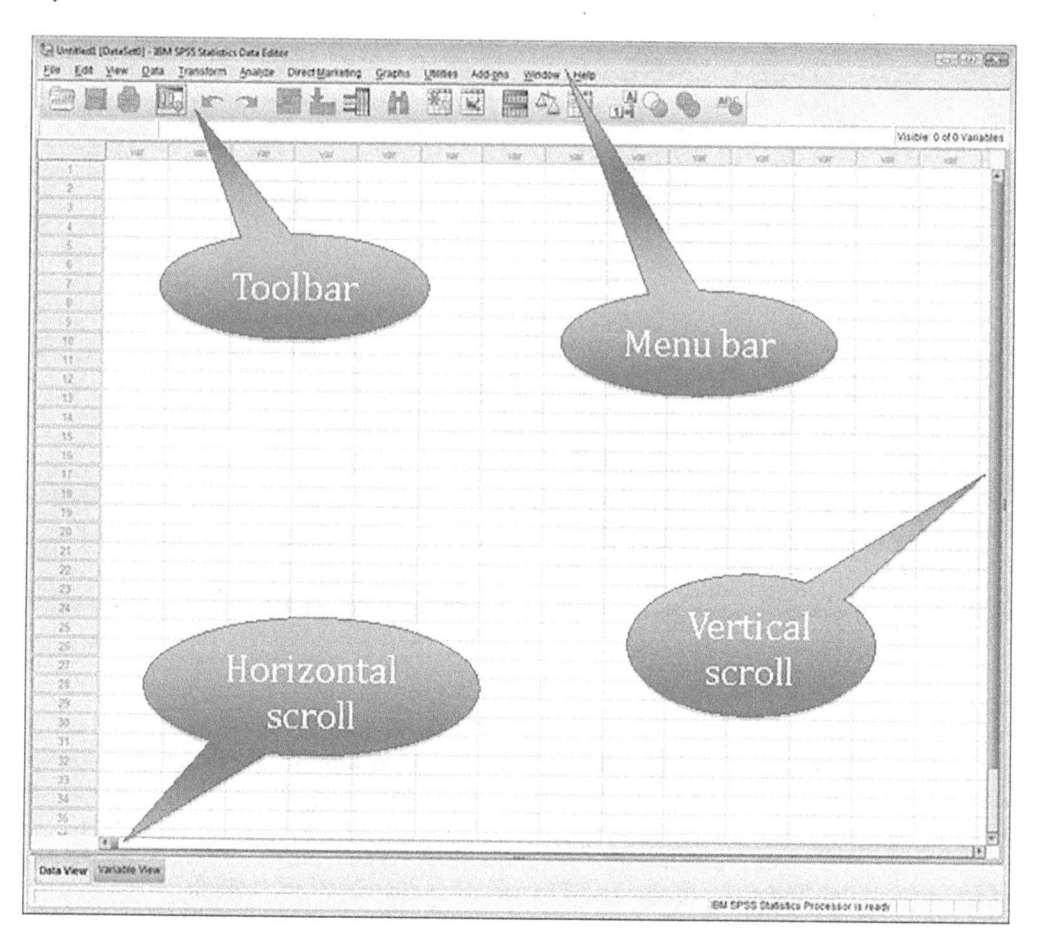

---

**SPSS Statistics Command 4.4:
Moving Through the Data Screen**

*Option 1*

Use horizontal and/or vertical scroll bars

*Option 2*

Use cursor → Click

*Option 3*

Use arrow keys on keyboard

---

# DEMONSTRATION 4.3: ENTERING DATA—A PREVIEW

Take a moment now to designate the cell in the upper left-hand corner as the active cell. Once you have done that, you are ready to begin entering data for analysis. In fact, if you decide to conduct your own survey later on, this is how you will enter those data. As a quick preview of this feature, type a **1**, and press the **Enter** key on your keyboard.

You have now created the world's smallest data set, with one piece of information about one person. The **1** on the left of the screen represents Person 1. If you enter another number as you just did, you will bring Person 2 into existence with one piece of information. Why don't you do that now—enter a **2** for Person 2.

The "VAR00001" at the head of the column in the screen represents the specific information we are storing about each person. It might represent gender, for example. Moreover, a value of 1.00 might mean male, and a value of 2.00 might mean female. In that case, we would have indicated that Person 1 is a man and Person 2 a woman.

This is the basic structure of the data sets analyzed by SPSS Statistics. The good news for you is that we've already prepared large data sets for your use, so you won't have to keep entering data like this. However, if you are interested in using SPSS Statistics to create your own data file, you may want to consult Chapter 21, which takes you through this process step by step.

Before loading our GSS data, we want to close the small data set we just created. To do that, click **File → Close**. At this point, SPSS Statistics will ask you if you want to "save the contents of data editor to Untitled?" which is just a fancy way of asking if you want to save the "world's smallest data set" that we just created. Because we are not interested in saving this data set, click **No**. If we wanted to save the data, we would click **Yes** and follow the instructions in the dialog box.

# DEMONSTRATION 4.4: LOADING A DATA SET

At this point, you should once again be looking at an empty screen—but not for long because we are finally ready to load one of the GSS data sets provided with this book.

Once you have downloaded the DEMO.SAV file from the *Adventures in Social Research* website, you have two options. If you wish to use the menu bar, simply click **File**, and from the drop-down menu, choose **Open** and then **Data**. If you want to use the toolbar, all you have to do is click on the **Open Data** tool. Either way, SPSS Statistics will respond by displaying the Open Data dialog box, similar to the one shown on the next page. This box will assist us in selecting the data set we want.

File → Open → Data

Now your computer needs to be directed to the DEMO.SAV file. As noted in Chapter 3, the file is maintained on the *Adventures in Social Research* student study site (https://study.sagepub.com/babbie10e). You may want to save the SPSS Statistics data files you use to a jump/thumb/flash drive, a network drive, Dropbox, a cloud server, or another easily accessible location. By doing that, you can retrieve versions of the data files you have altered and saved and not be limited to just the unaltered data files found on the website. For example, if you use data manipulation techniques, such as recoding variables, you'll add new variables to the file. (This will be addressed in Chapter 7.)

Once you download the DEMO.SAV file from the study site, return to SPSS Statistics and click on **File → Open Data**. In the dialog box that appears, go to the location on your hard drive or other storage device to which you downloaded the DEMO.SAV file. Then, make sure SPSS Statistics–format (or PASW Statistics–format) data files (.sav extension) are displayed in the "Files of type:" drop-down list. If not, simply click on the down arrow and select the suffix for SPSS Statistics data files, **SPSS Statistics (\*.sav)**. Now, you should see the file you just downloaded. To select **DEMO.SAV**, highlight it and double-click or click the **Open** button in the lower right-hand corner of the dialog box. In a few seconds, SPSS Statistics will display the GSS data in the Data View portion of the Data Editor.

---

### SPSS Statistics Command 4.5: Opening a Data File

*Option 1: Menu bar*

Click **File → Open Data**

*Option 2: Toolbar*

Click **Open Data tool**

*Once the Open Data dialog box is displayed:*

Click **Look in field**: → Select drive that contains your file → Navigate to folder where you have saved your file → Click down arrow to choose **SPSS Statistics (\*.sav)** from "Files of type": drop-down list → Highlight name of data file and double-click OR click **Open**

---

## DEMONSTRATION 4.5: RAW DATA IN DATA VIEW

Now, you should be looking at the data in the DEMO.SAV file. This is the subsample of GSS 2016 data we will be using for the demonstrations in the body of each of the following chapters. The information in the Data View portion of the Data Editor consists of variables and respondents or cases.

Each row (horizontal) represents a person or ***respondent*** to the survey (what is sometimes referred to as a *case*). Based on our discussion in Chapter 3, we already know the DEMO.SAV file has 1,500 rows representing each of the 1,500 respondents or cases in this subsample. (Remember that there are 2,867 in the full file, but so that our DEMO file will run on all packages of SPSS, we've taken a random subsample of 1,500 cases.) You may want to take a few minutes to scroll from the first case or respondent (Row 1) to the last respondent (Row 1,500).

Each column (vertical) represents a variable, indicated by the abbreviated variable name in the column heading. This data set contains 43 variables, or columns. If you scroll from left to right across the screen, you can see that this file contains variables ranging from ABANY to XMOVIE. You can get a brief description of each abbreviated variable name by hovering your cursor over the name at the top of each column and waiting for a moment until the description pops up on the screen. For instance, if you place your cursor over the variable name ATTEND, a brief description of the variable that reads, "How often R [respondent] attends religious services," will magically appear on your screen.

# FINDING VARIABLE
# INFORMATION: VALUES AND LABELS

Now, turn your attention to respondent Record Number 1 and the variable MARITAL. Be careful not to confuse the ***record numbers***, which run down the far left side of the screen, with the ID numbers (an actual variable usually listed in the first column). They have no "ID" variable in the DEMO.SAV or EXER.SAV files, though it is a simple matter to create one. Initially, the variable would be identical to the record number, since ID numbers are assigned consecutively, beginning with the number 1. In many types of files, however, they are not the same. Also, when data are sorted, sampled, or split into subsamples, the ID numbers will no longer correspond to the record numbers.

You will notice that respondent Record Number 1 has a 5 in the MARITAL column. This variable reflects respondents' marital statuses. (If you forgot that, place your cursor over the variable name at the head of the column, and a brief description of the variable will appear on your screen.) As you may recall from the list of variables in Appendix A, a 3 (the ***numeric value*** or code) on MARITAL means the respondent was "never married" (the ***value label***). If you didn't recall this, don't worry. There are several ways you can use SPSS Statistics to access the information.

## Option 1: Variables Dialog Box

One option is to click on the **Utilities** menu and select **Variables**. Alternatively, you can click on the **Variables icon** on the toolbar (the one with the question mark on it). Either way, SPSS Statistics will respond by opening the Variables dialog box, as shown below.

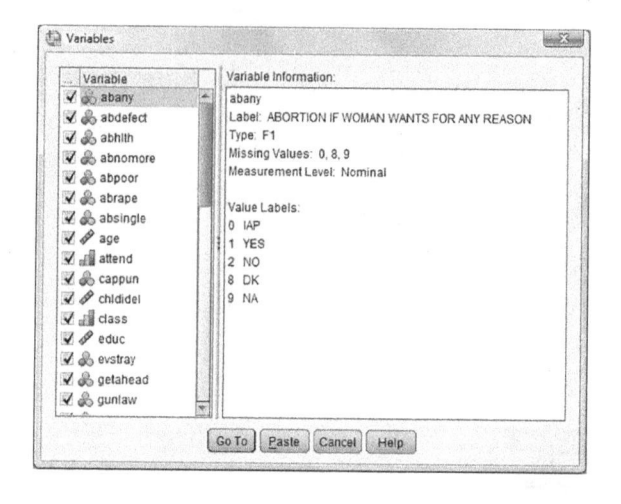

As you can see, the Variables dialog box has two main parts. On the left is a list of the variables contained in our data set. On the right is some information about the highlighted variable ID.

If you don't already see it, click on the variable **ABANY** (abortion if woman wants for any reason) in the list on the left side of the box. This is the second variable listed. Notice how information about the highlighted variable ABANY is displayed on the right side of the dialog box, including the information we are looking for: numeric values and value labels. This box tells us that for the variable ABANY, a 1 (value) means "yes" (label), a 2 (value) means "no" (label), and so on.

Consequently, if you didn't recall what a value of 3 on MARITAL means, you can easily access the information by scrolling down through the list of variables until you see MARITAL.[2] Now, click on **MARITAL**, and this is what you should see.

```
Variables

Variable                    Variable Information:
√ educ                      marital
√ evstray                   Label: MARITAL STATUS
√ getahead                  Type: F1
√ gunlaw                    Missing Values: 9
√ helpoth                   Measurement Level: Nominal
√ hispanic
√ homosex                   Value Labels:
√ income                    1 MARRIED
√ maeduc                    2 WIDOWED
√ marblk                    3 DIVORCED
√ marital                   4 SEPARATED
√ obey                      5 NEVER MARRIED
√ paeduc                    9 NA
√ partners
√ partyid
√ pikupsex

        Go To   Paste   Cancel   Help
```

---

2. In addition to scrolling, there are several other ways to move through the list of variables on the left side. You can, for instance, click on the up and down arrows on the right-hand side of the variable list. You can also use the arrow keys on your keyboard or type the first letter of the variable's name; the highlight will then move to the first variable in your data set that begins with that letter.

The box on the right side tells us that anyone with a code of 1 is married, anyone with a 2 is widowed, and so forth. You might want to take a minute to explore some of the other variables in the data set because familiarity with them will be useful later.

When you get bored with the Variables dialog box, there are a couple of ways to leave it. You can click either the **Close** button or the **X**. Either action will produce the same result.

## Option 2: Toggling Between Numeric Values and Value Labels

Another way to find out what a numeric value (such as a 5 on MARITAL) means is to click on **View** in the menu bar. Then click on **Value Labels** in the drop-down menu. This command tells SPSS Statistics to change the numeric values in the data screen into descriptive value labels. You will see, for instance, that the numeric value 5 under MARITAL for Respondent 1 has been replaced by a descriptive value label indicating that the respondent was never married.

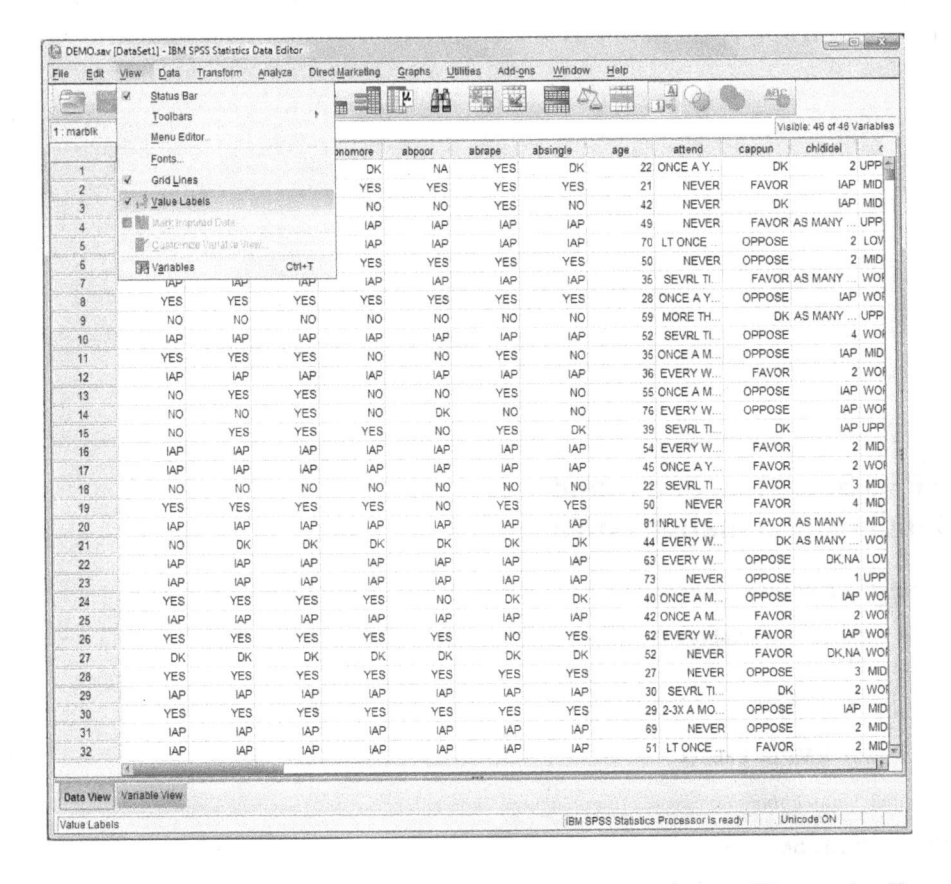

To display numeric values in the data screen once again, just click on **View** again. You will now see a check mark next to Value Labels in the drop-down menu. Click on **Value Labels** and the check mark will disappear. You should now see the numeric values in the data screen once again. This process of switching back and forth between numeric values and value labels is known as *toggling*.

## Option 3: Value Labels Tool

A third way to discover what a numeric value refers to is to click on the button in the toolbar that shows arrows pointing to both an A and a 1, the **Value Labels** tool (second from the right side of the toolbar). You will notice that the numeric values in the data screen have now magically changed into value labels. To change the value labels back into numeric values, all you have to do is click on the **Value Labels** tool once again.

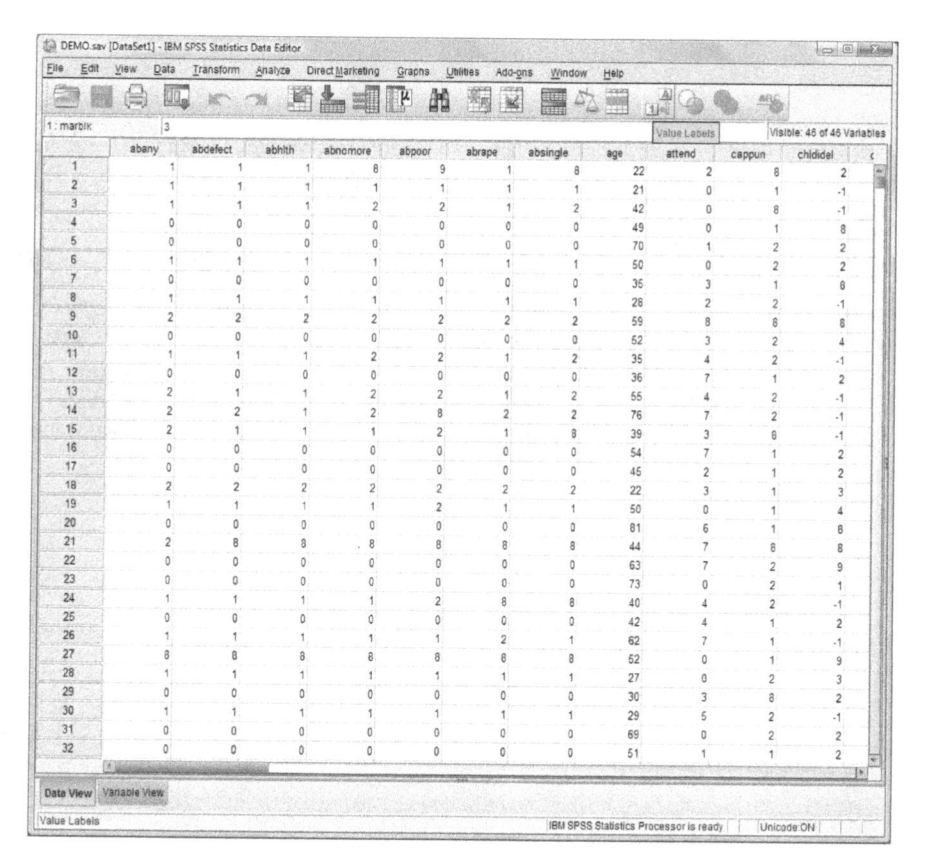

---

## SPSS Statistics Command 4.6: Finding Information on Variables

*Option 1: Variables dialog box*

Click **Utilities → Variables** OR Click **Variables** icon on toolbar and highlight variable name in list on left side

*Option 2: Toggling*

Click **View → Value Labels**

*Option 3: Value Labels tool*

Click **Value Labels tool**

---

# DEMONSTRATION 4.6: VARIABLE VIEW TAB

A fourth way to determine value labels is through the Variable View portion of the Data Editor. So far, we have focused primarily on the Data View screen, which contains the raw data for analysis; however, the Variable View tab also contains important information about the data in your file. In particular, Variable View contains descriptions of the attributes of each variable in your data file.

Click on the **Variable View** tab at the bottom left side of the screen. You will notice that in Variable View, rows represent variables. Take a moment and scroll from the first variable, ABANY (Row 1), to the last, XMOVIE (Row 46).

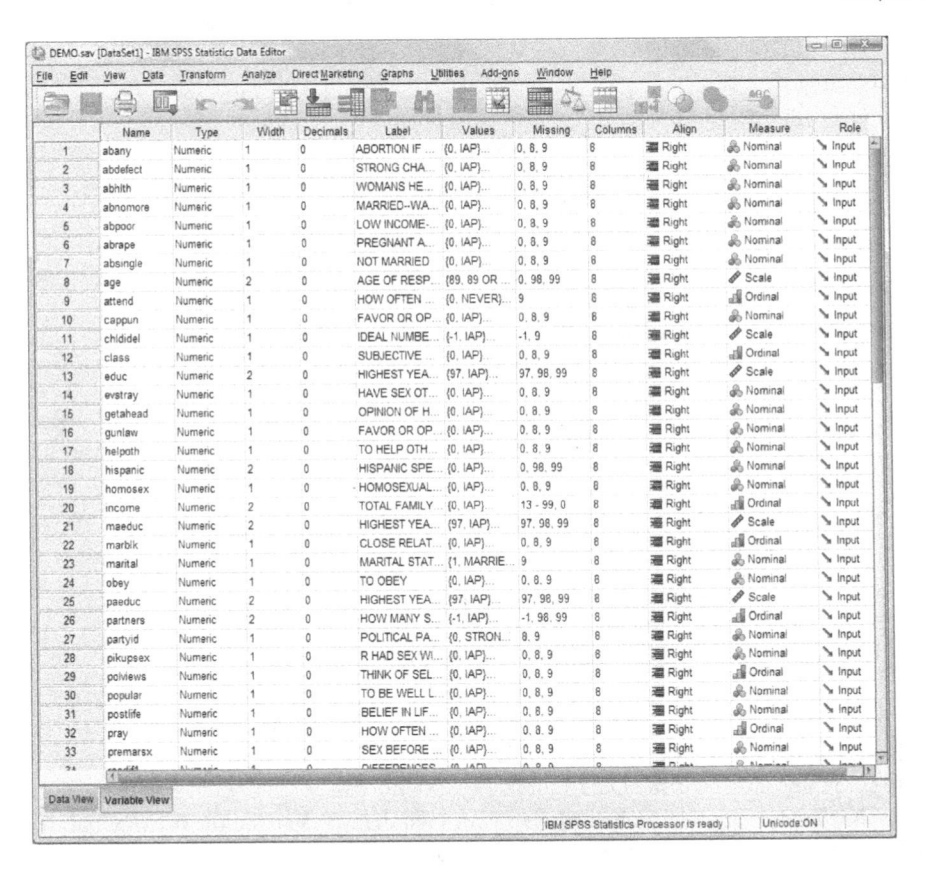

Unlike in Data View, here, each column is an attribute associated with the variables. The 11 columns, or attributes, are listed below, followed by a brief description of their contents:

Name  Abbreviated variable name (e.g., ABANY, ABDEFECT)

Type  Data type (e.g., numeric or string)

Width  Number of digits or characters

Decimals  Number of decimal places

Label  Variable labels or description of variable (i.e., respondent ID number; abortion if woman wants for any reason; strong chance of serious defect)

Values  Values and labels (e.g., ABANY: 0 = IAP, 1 = Yes, 2 = No, 8 = DK, 9 = NA)

Missing  Missing values (values designated as "missing")

Columns  Column width (width of column in Data View)

Align  Alignment (alignment of data in Data View, either to right, left, or center)

Measure  Level of measurement (i.e., nominal, ordinal, or scale)

Role  The origin of the data: whether they were input (by you or whoever created the file), recoded or calculated from another variable (a target variable), etc.

When in the Variable View, you can add or delete variables and modify the attributes of each variable. We will focus more specifically on how to modify attributes in Variable View later in the text.

For now, it is enough that you are aware that the Values column in the Variable View window is another way to find information about values and labels. Earlier, for instance, we were focusing on the variable MARITAL. In Variable View, identify the cell corresponding to the variable MARITAL (row) and the Values column. Now, double-click in the far right side of that cell (intersection between MARITAL and Values), and the Value Labels dialog box will open. Note that rather than double-clicking, you can click once and then click the button with three dots (ellipsis). Once the dialog box opens, you can see that the values and labels for the variable MARITAL are listed. To close the box, click **Close** or the **X** in the upper right-hand corner.

---

### SPSS Statistics Command 4.7: Finding Information on Variables in Variable View

*Option 4: Variable View*

In Variable View portion of Data Editor . . .

Click on cell corresponding with the variable in question (row) and the Values column

---

## DEMONSTRATION 4.7: ENDING YOUR SPSS STATISTICS SESSION

When you've finished this session, you have a few options. First, you can use the **X** in the upper right-hand corner to close the program.[3] If you click the **X** now, SPSS Statistics will ask if you want to save the contents of the Data Editor. Because the data set is already saved, you can safely click the **No** button now. If you had entered your own data or changed the existing data set, you would definitely want to save the data, in which case the computer would ask you to name the new data set.

You can also end your session by clicking **File** and then **Exit**. Before terminating your session, SPSS Statistics will ask if you want to save the file. Once again, you can click **No** because you have not altered the data file.

---

### SPSS Statistics Command 4.8: Ending Your SPSS Statistics Session

*Option 1: Close button*

Click on **X** (Close button)

*Option 2: File menu*

Click **File** → **Exit**

Mac OS users, click **File** → **Quit SPSS Statistics**

---

## CONCLUSION

In this first encounter, you've learned how to launch SPSS Statistics, load a data set, and explore it. In the next chapter, we'll revisit some of the variables in the data set and see how SPSS Statistics lets us explore more deeply than we've done in this first incursion.

---

3. Don't forget that the Minimize and Maximize buttons to the left of the close button are particularly useful if you are working with SPSS Statistics and other files simultaneously.

## Main Points

- Because SPSS Statistics is generalized, we use SPSS Statistics commands to tell it specifically what to do.

- The SPSS Statistics Data Editor is a screen designed to receive, display, and hold data for analysis.

- The two major components of the Data Editor are Data View and Variable View screens.

- The Data View screen contains the raw data in your file.

- Variable View contains descriptions of the attributes of each of the variables in your data file.

- You can use SPSS Statistics either to enter data or to load an existing data set, such as the data provided on this book's website (https://study.sagepub.com/babbie10e).

- In Data View, rows represent respondents or cases, and columns represent variables.

- In Variable View, each row is a variable, and each column is an attribute associated with the variables.

## Key Terms

Active cell 35
Data Editor 32
Data View 33
Dialog box 32
Menu bar 33

Numeric value 39
Record numbers 39
Respondent 39
Scroll bars 35
Title bar 32

Toggling 41
Toolbar 34
Value label 39
Variable View 33

## SPSS Statistics Commands Introduced in This Chapter

4.1.  Starting an SPSS Statistics Session

4.2.  Accessing the Help Menu

4.3.  Getting Help in a Dialog Box

4.4.  Moving Through the Data Screen

4.5.  Opening a Data File

4.6.  Finding Information on Variables

4.7.  Finding Information on Variables in Variable View

4.8.  Ending Your SPSS Statistics Session

## Review Questions

1. What are the two main sections (tabs) in the SPSS Statistics Data Editor?

2. What type of information does the Data View screen contain?

3. What type of information does the Variable View screen contain?

4. In Data View, rows represent _____, and columns represent _____.

5. In Variable View, rows represent _____, and columns represent _____.

6. If a researcher has conducted a survey and wants to enter the raw data into SPSS Statistics, would he or she enter it into the Data View, Variable View, or Utilities View portion of the Data Editor?

7. If you have a question or problem, what is one of the features SPSS Statistics provides to offer you assistance?

8. If you don't recall what a value of a particular variable in your data set means, what three SPSS Statistics commands can you use to find this information?

9. What does the term *toggling* mean?

(Continued)

(Continued)

10. If you are using several documents at once, which Windows (or Mac OS) features might you want to take advantage of?

11. If you use SPSS Statistics to enter your own data or change an existing data set, what one thing should you do before ending your SPSS Statistics session?

# SPSS Statistics Lab Exercise 4.1

NAME: _____

CLASS: _____

INSTRUCTOR: _____

DATE: _____

*To complete the following exercises, load the data file EXER.SAV (found on the* Adventures in Social Research *website:* https://study.sagepub.com/babbie10e).

1. What does the variable COLCOM measure? (Hint: In Data View, place your cursor over the column heading to determine the descriptive variable label, OR in Variable View, double-click on the cell corresponding to COLCOM and the Label column.)

2. Using the variable COLCOM, note the numeric value for each of the following respondents (listed by record number, the column on the far left side of the screen). Then, open the Variables dialog box to determine the value label.

|  | **Numeric Value** | **Value Label** |
|---|---|---|
| Record No. 89 | _____ | _____ |
| Record No. 837 | _____ | _____ |
| Record No. 1240 | _____ | _____ |

3. What does the variable COLRAC measure?

4. Using the variable COLRAC, note the numeric value for each of the following respondents (listed by record number). Then, use the toggle command to determine the appropriate value label.

|  | **Numeric Value** | **Value Label** |
|---|---|---|
| Record No. 3 | _____ | _____ |
| Record No. 505 | _____ | _____ |
| Record No. 1460 | _____ | _____ |

5. What does the variable COLHOMO measure?

6. Using the variable COLHOMO, note the numeric value for each of the following respondents (listed by record number). Then, use the Value Labels tool to determine the appropriate value label.

|  | **Numeric Value** | **Value Label** |
|---|---|---|
| Record No. 14 | _____ | _____ |
| Record No. 233 | _____ | _____ |
| Record No. 1475 | _____ | _____ |

*(Continued)*

(Continued)

7. What does the variable COLATH measure?

8. Using the variable COLATH, note the numeric value for each of the following respondents (listed by record number). Then, access the Variable View tab, identify the cell that corresponds to COLATH and the Values column, and double-click to access the Value Labels dialog box. Use the Value Labels box to determine the appropriate value label.

Record No. 7 _____    _____

Record No. 158 _____    _____

Record No. 1235 _____    _____

9. Select any variable that interests you from the EXER.SAV file (other than those we have worked with previously in this exercise). Then, use SPSS Statistics to find the following variable information:

   a. What is the abbreviated variable name? _____

   b. What does the variable measure (i.e., variable label)? _____

   c. List the numeric values and value labels for the variable.

   **Numeric Value**                              **Value Label**

   _____            _____

   _____            _____

   _____            _____

   _____            _____

   _____            _____

   _____            _____

   d. Choose three respondents, and list how they responded to the variable/question item you chose (list case number, numeric value, and value label).

   **Case Number**                **Numeric Value**                **Value Label**

   Case No. _____    _____    _____

   Case No. _____    _____    _____

   Case No. _____    _____    _____

10. Access the SPSS Statistics Help feature Tutorial. (*Hint:* Click **Help → Tutorial.**) Once you have opened the Table of Contents, work your way through the following aspects of the tutorial: Introduction, Using the Help System, and Reading Data. To exit or close the Tutorial, click on the **X** (Close button).

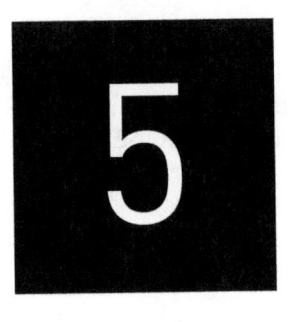

# DESCRIBING YOUR DATA

## Religiosity

In this chapter, we are going to analyze data. Before we begin, we want to give you a few shortcuts for opening frequently used data files. We also want to show you how to set display options for SPSS Statistics and define values as missing. This will help ensure that what you see on your screen matches the screens in the text.

In order to begin, you'll need to launch SPSS Statistics, as described in the previous chapter. If you have trouble recalling how to open the program, simply refer to the discussion in those pages.

## DEMONSTRATION 5.1: OPENING FREQUENTLY USED DATA FILES

If the SPSS Statistics (or PASW Statistics, for some older versions) "What would you like to do?" dialog box is displayed when you open SPSS Statistics, you can access a recently used data file by clicking the button labeled "Open an existing data source" next to the SPSS Statistics icon (the first option displayed).[1] If the DEMO.SAV file is listed, highlight it, and click **OK**. This feature is available in prior versions of SPSS software, going back to at least version 18.

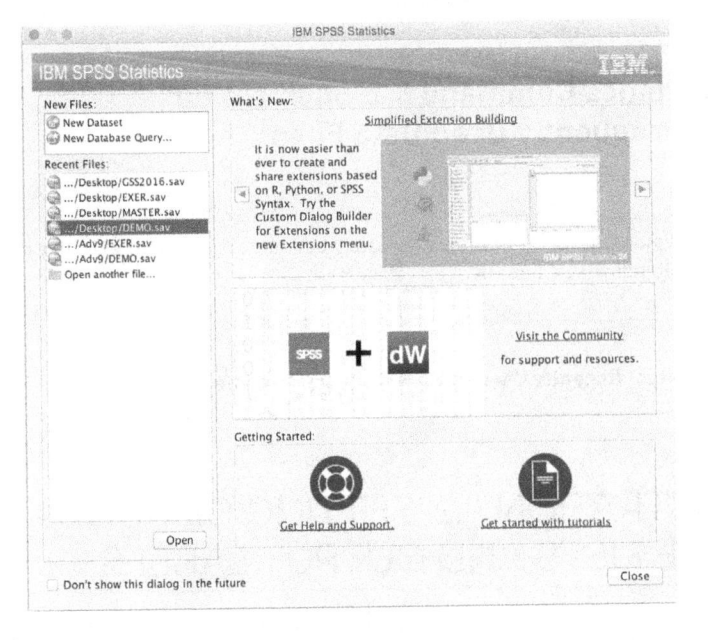

---

1. If you don't see this box, it is probably because someone using SPSS Statistics before you requested that it not be displayed every time the program is opened. If you prefer this dialog box not be displayed when you open SPSS Statistics, click the "Don't show this dialog in the future" option in the bottom left corner.

Another shortcut for opening a frequently used file is to select **File** on the menu bar and then click **Recently Used Data** in the drop-down menu. Since SPSS Statistics keeps track of files that have been used recently, you may see the DEMO.SAV file listed in the box. To access the file, click **DEMO.SAV**.

If the DEMO.SAV file is not listed, don't panic—everything is still OK. You can also open the file by following the instructions given in Chapter 4 for opening a data file.

---

## SPSS Statistics Command 5.1: Shortcut for Opening Frequently Used Data Files

*Option 1*

In the "What would you like to do now?" dialog box, select **Open an existing data source** → Highlight the file name → Click **OK**

*Option 2*

Click **File** → **Select Recently Used Data** → Click on file name

---

# DEMONSTRATION 5.2: SETTING OPTIONS—VARIABLE LISTS AND OUTPUT LABELS

Before we begin analyzing data, we want to make a few changes in the way SPSS Statistics displays information. This will make it easier for us to tell SPSS Statistics what we want it to do when we start running frequencies.

To set options, begin by clicking on **Edit** (located on the menu bar). Now choose **Options**, and the Options window will open. You will see a series of tabs along the top of the box. Select **General** (if it is not already visible).

Toward the top of the dialog box, you will now see the Variable Lists options. In that area, choose **Display names** and **Alphabetical**. Now, click **OK** at the bottom of the dialog. You may get a warning telling you that "Changing any option in the Variable List group will reset all dialog box settings to their defaults, and all open dialogs will be closed." If so, click **OK** once again.

**Edit → Options**

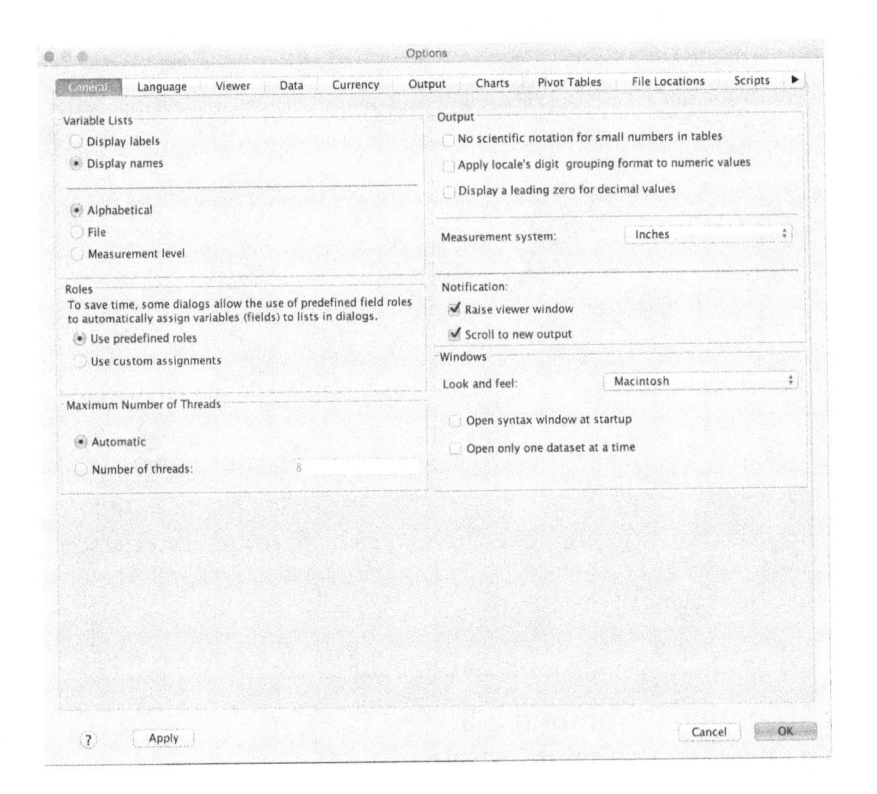

What we have just done is tell SPSS Statistics to display abbreviated variable names alphabetically whenever it is listing variables. This will make it easier for us to find variables when we need them.

---

**SPSS Statistics Command 5.2: Setting Options—Displaying Abbreviated Variable Names Alphabetically**

Click **Edit → Options → General tab → Display names → Alphabetical → OK → OK**

---

A second change we want to make deals with the way SPSS Statistics displays output (such as frequency distribution tables, charts, graphs, etc.). By following the commands listed subsequently, you can ensure that SPSS Statistics will display both the value and label for each variable you select for analysis, as well as abbreviated variable names and variable labels.

Simply choose **Edit** and **Options** once again. This time, click on the **Output** tab located at the top of the Options window.

At the bottom left-hand corner of this tab, under the heading "Pivot Table Labeling," you will see two drop-down menus labeled "Variables in labels shown as:" and "Variable values in labels shown as:". Click on the down arrow on the first drop-down ("Variables in labels shown as:"), and choose the third option, **Names and Labels**. Now click on the down arrow on the second drop-down ("Variable values in labels shown as:"), and select **Values and Labels**; then, click **OK.**

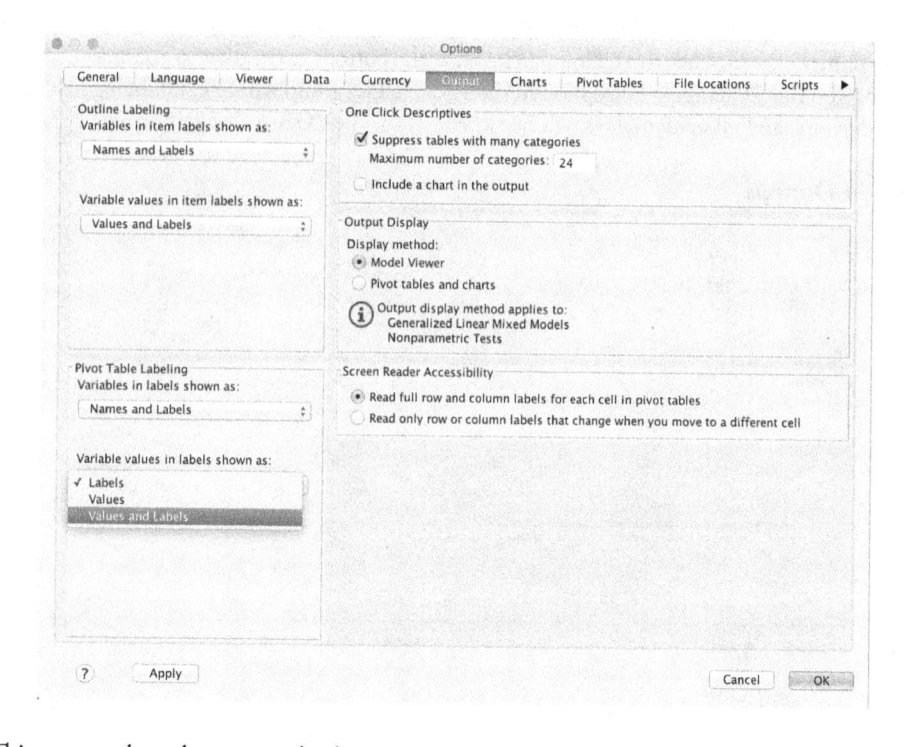

This ensures that when we are displaying output, we see both variable names and labels and value names and labels. When we begin producing frequency distributions, you will see why access to all of this information is helpful.

---

### SPSS Statistics Command 5.3:
### Setting Options—Output Labels

Click **Edit → Options → Output Labels tab →** Click down arrow on "Variables in labels shown as:" → **Names and Labels**

Click down arrow on "Variable values in labels shown as:" → **Values and Labels → OK**

---

One last thing we want to do before running frequencies is to show you how to set values and labels as "missing." This simple process will help ensure that what you see on your screen matches what you see in this book. It is also important because when you begin analyzing data, you will want to be able to define values as missing.

Defining values and labels as missing is not difficult. Since we will be working with our four religious variables frequently throughout this chapter, we will demonstrate this procedure using these variables: RELIG, respondent's religious preference; ATTEND, how often the respondent attends religious services; POSTLIFE, respondent's belief in life after death; and PRAY, how often the respondent prays. Click on the **Variable View** tab. Scroll down until you can see the values and labels for our first variable, RELIG, by clicking on the right side of the cell that corresponds to RELIG and the Values column. As you can see, this variable has several categories and labels ranging from 0 = "IAP" (inapplicable), 1 = "Protestant," and 2 = "Catholic" all the way to 13 = "Inter-nondenominational," 98 = DK (don't know), and 99 = NA (no answer). When we are running frequencies and conducting other analyses, we may want to exclude those respondents who were not asked the question (IAP), said they didn't know (DK), or had no answer (NA).

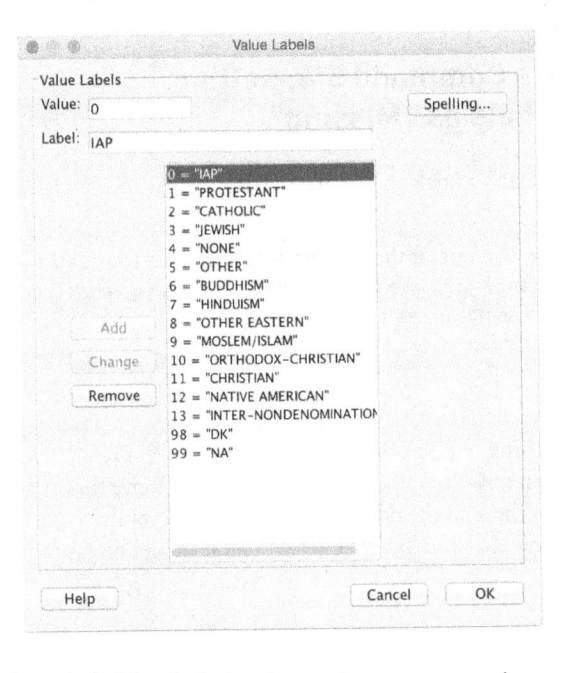

Cases may be easily excluded by declaring categories we want to ignore as "missing." In the Variable View tab, click on **Cancel** to close the Value Labels dialog box. Now, click on the right side of the cell that corresponds to the variable RELIG and Missing. On opening that box, you can see that you have several options:

- If you do not want any values/labels defined as missing, you can choose the "No missing values" option and click **OK**.

- If you want one to three values/labels set as missing, click on the option labeled "Discrete missing values," type the values in the box, and click **OK**.

- If you want a range plus one value defined as missing, you can choose the last option ("Range plus one optional discrete missing value"), type in the range and discrete value, and click **OK**.[2]

In the case of RELIG, you may already see that the values 0, 98, and 99 have been labeled as missing. If that's the case, then you needn't do the following. If, however, you see only the values 0 and 99, we want to verify that 98 is classified as missing so that we also exclude those people who said they don't know their religion. To do this, simply make sure the option labeled "Discrete missing values" is selected, type **98** in the remaining box, if applicable, and click **OK.**

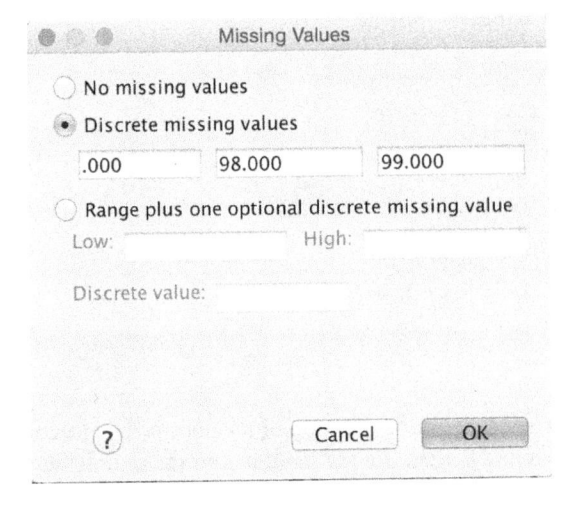

---

2. We include a demonstration involving this option in Chapter 9, Demonstration 9.3.

---

### SPSS Statistics Command 5.4: Setting Values and Labels as "Missing"

Access **Variable View tab** → Click on cell that corresponds to column Missing and row containing appropriate variable

In Missing Values box, use one of the options available to set variables as missing ("Discrete missing values" or "Range plus one optional discrete missing value"), or ensure there are no missing values ("No missing values")

---

To make sure you are comfortable setting values as missing, go ahead and set the values for the following variables as missing: ATTEND, 9; POSTLIFE, 0, 8, 9; PRAY, 0, 8, 9. These should already be set in your data file, but it is very important to check. As we move through the text, if you find that your screens don't match those in the book, it may be because you have not set values as a particular value or as "missing." Now that you know how to do so, it should be easy to rectify the problem!

# DEMONSTRATION 5.3: FREQUENCY DISTRIBUTIONS

Now that we have loaded the DEMO.SAV file, set options for SPSS Statistics, and defined selected values as "missing," we are ready to begin looking at some aspects of religious behavior. We will do this by first asking SPSS Statistics to construct a *frequency distribution*. A frequency distribution is a numeric display of the number of times (frequency) and the relative percentage of times each value of a variable occurs in a given sample.

We instruct SPSS Statistics to run a frequency distribution by selecting **Analyze** from the menu bar and then choosing **Descriptive Statistics**, then **Frequencies** in the drop-down menus.

Once you've completed these steps, you should be looking at the following screen:

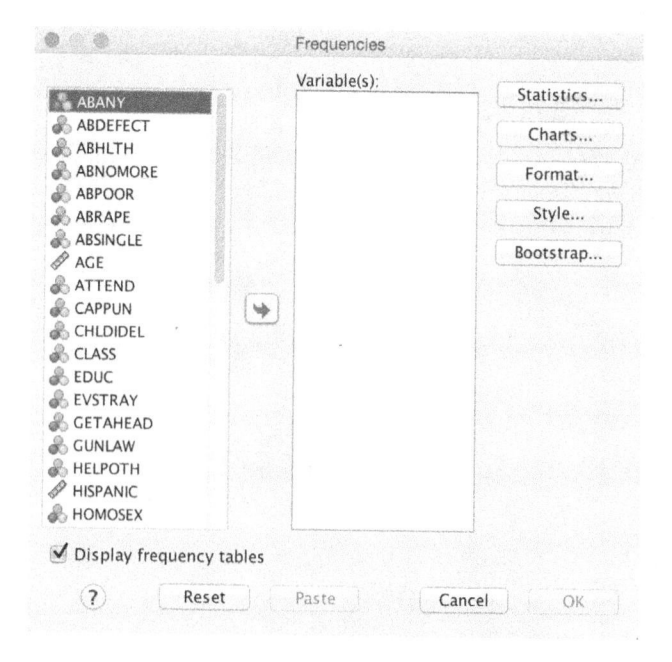

Let's start by looking first at the distribution of religious preferences among the sample. This is easily accomplished as follows: First, use the scroll bar on the right-hand side of the list of variable names to move down until RELIG is visible.

You may notice that it is fairly easy to find RELIG because the abbreviated variable names are displayed in alphabetical order (as opposed to the variable labels, which can be cumbersome to sift through). This is a result of our first task in this chapter, setting the options so SPSS Statistics shows abbreviated variable names alphabetically. If you notice that your variables are not formatted properly, you can revisit that discussion earlier in this chapter—or you can right-click (or if you have a one-button Macintosh mouse, press the **<control>** key while you click)—and options will appear for sorting and displaying variable information.

Once you locate RELIG, highlight it, and click on the arrow to the right of the list. This will transfer the variable name to the "Variable(s):" field. Alternatively, you can also transfer a variable to the "Variable(s):" field by double-clicking it.

If you transfer the wrong variable, don't worry. You can move the variable from the "Variable(s):" field back to the variable list by highlighting it and clicking on the left-pointing arrow or simply double-clicking the abbreviated variable name.

Once RELIG has been successfully transferred to the "Variable(s):" field, you can display its values and labels by highlighting it and then right-clicking (or with a one-button Macintosh mouse, by holding down the **<control>** key while clicking). From the drop-down menu, select **Variable Information** (see figure at the top of page 56).

You will now see a box with the name, label, measurement, and value labels for the variable RELIG. Click on the down arrow on the "Value labels:" drop-down to access a complete list of values and labels.

Once you have moved RELIG to the "Variable(s):" field, click **OK**. This will set SPSS Statistics going on its assigned task. Depending on the kind of computer you are using, this operation may take a few seconds to complete. Eventually, a new window called the ***SPSS Statistics Viewer*** will be brought to the front of the screen, and you should see the figure at the bottom of page 56.

If you don't see the entire table as shown, don't worry. It's probably because of resolution/size differences between computer screens. To see all of the information, simply use the vertical scroll bar.

---

## SPSS Statistics Command 5.5:
## Running Frequency Distributions

Click **Analyze → Descriptive Statistics → Frequencies**

→ Highlight abbreviated variable name → Click on arrow (pointing toward "Variable(s):" field) OR double-click variable name → **OK**

### The SPSS Statistics Viewer: Output

You should now be looking at the SPSS Statistics Viewer. After you run a procedure such as a table, graph, or chart, the results are displayed in the Viewer. This window is divided into two main parts or panes: the *Outline pane* (on the left) and the *Contents pane* (on the right). As its name suggests, the Outline pane contains an outline of all of the information stored in the Viewer. This outline gives us a complete list of everything we have instructed SPSS Statistics to do in this session. If you use SPSS Statistics for several hours to run a large amount of analysis, this useful feature will let you navigate through your output. If, for instance, you want to find a specific table, all you have to do is select the name of the table in the Outline and wait a moment. The table will then appear in the Contents pane, that part of the Viewer where charts, tables, and other text output are displayed.

There are several ways to navigate through the SPSS Statistics Viewer. You can use your vertical and horizontal scroll bars, or you can use the arrow keys or "page up" and "page down" keys on your keyboard. For easier navigation, simply click on an item in the Outline pane, and your results will be displayed in the Contents pane.

---

### SPSS Statistics Command 5.6: Navigating Through the SPSS Statistics Viewer

*Option 1*

Use vertical or horizontal scroll bars

*Option 2*

Use the arrow or "page up" and "page down" keys on your keyboard

*Option 3*

Click on an item in Outline pane

---

You can also change the width of the Outline pane by clicking and dragging the border to the right of the pane (the border that separates the Outline and Contents panes). You may want to take a few moments to experiment with each of these options before we move ahead.

---

### SPSS Statistics Command 5.7: Changing the Width of the Outline Pane

Click and drag border to right of Outline pane

---

### Hiding and Displaying Results in the Viewer

There are several ways to hide a particular table or chart. You can simply double-click on its **book icon** in the Outline pane. Alternatively, you can highlight the item in the Outline pane, and then, from the menu bar, choose **View** and **Hide**. To display it again, highlight the item in the Outline pane, and select **View** and then **Show** from the drop-down menu. Easier yet, you can highlight the item in the Outline pane and then click on the **Hide** icon (closed book) on the Outlining toolbar. To display it again, just highlight the item and then click on the **Show** icon (open book) on the Outlining toolbar.

---

### SPSS Statistics Command 5.8: Hiding and Displaying Results in the Viewer

*Option 1*

Double-click **book icon** in Outline pane

To display again, double-click **book icon** again

*Option 2*

Highlight item in Outline pane → Click **View** → **Hide**

To display it again, highlight item in Outline pane → Click **View** → **Show**

*Option 3*

Highlight item → Click **Hide** icon (closed book)

To display it again, highlight item in Outline pane → Click **Show** icon (open book)

---

In addition, you can hide all of the results from a procedure by clicking on the box with a minus (–) sign to the left of the procedure name in the Outline pane. Once you do this, you will notice that the minus sign turns into a plus (+) sign. This not only hides the results in your Contents pane but also compresses the Outline itself. To display the results again, simply click on the plus (+) sign; it will turn into a minus (–) sign, and your results will display.

---

### SPSS Statistics Command 5.9: Hiding and Displaying All Results From a Procedure

Click on box with minus (–) sign to left of procedure name in Outline pane

To display results again, click on box with plus (+) sign

---

Don't forget, you can also hide the SPSS Statistics Viewer itself by using the minimizing and reducing options. There are several more advanced ways of working with SPSS Statistics output and using the SPSS Statistics Viewer. You can, for instance, change the order in which output is displayed, delete results, change the formatting of text within a table, and so on.

We are going to mention some of these more advanced options as we go along. In addition, the lab exercises at the end of this chapter give you an opportunity to work through a part of the SPSS Statistics Tutorial that provides an overview of some of these more advanced options.

### Reading Frequency Distributions

Now that we are more familiar with the SPSS Statistics Viewer, let's take a few minutes to analyze the output for the variable RELIG, which is located in the Contents pane.

The small box titled "Statistics" tells us that of the 1,500 respondents in our subsample of the 2016 General Social Survey (GSS), 1,492 gave valid answers to this question, whereas 8 respondents have been labeled as "missing."[3] The larger box below, marked "RELIG R's religious preference," contains the data for which we are really looking.

---

3. *Reminder:* If your frequency table looks different from the one shown in the book, it may be a result of the "missing" values for the variable RELIG. We ran this frequency distribution with the values 0, 98, and 99 missing. The procedures for defining missing values are outlined earlier in this chapter.

Let's go through this table piece by piece. As we requested when we changed the options earlier, the first line identifies the variable, presenting both its abbreviated variable name and label. Variable names are the key to identifying variables in SPSS Statistics commands. Earlier versions of SPSS software limited variable names to eight characters, a convention that has been continued by the GSS data analysts. Sometimes, it is possible to express the name of a variable clearly in eight or fewer characters (e.g., SEX, RACE), and sometimes the task requires some ingenuity (e.g., CHLDIDEL, for the respondent's ideal number of children).[4]

The leftmost column in the table lists the numeric values and value labels (recall that we asked SPSS Statistics to display both when we changed the options) of the several categories constituting the variable RELIG. These include (1) Protestant, (2) Catholic, (3) Jewish, (4) None, (5) Other, and so on. As we discussed, the numeric values (sometimes called *numeric codes* or simply *values*) are the actual numbers used to code the data when they were entered. The value labels (or just labels) are short descriptions of the response categories; they remind us of the meaning of the numeric values or codes. As you'll see later on, you can change both kinds of labels if you choose.

The *frequency column* tells how many of the 1,500 respondents said they identified with the various religious groups. We see, for example, that the majority (690) said they were Protestant, 339 said they were Catholic, and so forth. Note that in this context, "None" means that some respondents said they had no religious identification; it does not mean that they didn't answer. Near the bottom of the table, we see that only 6 people failed to answer the question by selecting one of these substantive choices. (They may have answered by saying "I don't know" or "idk," but those instances would be classified as missing cases.)

The next column tells us what percentage of the whole sample each of the religious groups represents. Thus, for example, 46% are Protestant, calculated by dividing the 690 Protestants by the total sample of 1,500. Usually, you will want to work with the *valid percentage*, presented in the next column. As you can see, this percentage is based on the elimination of those who gave no answer, so the first number here means that 46.2% of those giving an answer said they were Protestant.

The final column presents the *cumulative percentage*, adding the individual percentages of the previous column as you move down the list. Sometimes, this will be useful to you. In this case, for example, you might note that 68.9% of those giving an answer were in traditional Christian denominations, or either some type of Protestant or Catholic.

# DEMONSTRATION 5.4: FREQUENCY DISTRIBUTIONS—RUNNING TWO OR MORE VARIABLES AT ONE TIME

Now that we've examined the method and logic of this procedure, let's use it more extensively. As you may have already figured out, SPSS Statistics doesn't limit us to one variable at a time. (If you tried that on your own before we said you could, you get two points for being adventurous. Hey, this is supposed to be fun as well as useful!)

So return to the Frequencies window with the following actions:

**Analyze → Descriptive Statistics → Frequencies**

If you are doing this all in one session, you may find that RELIG is still in the "Variable(s):" field. If so, you have a few options. You can double-click on **RELIG** to move it back to the variable list. Alternatively, you can highlight it. Once you do that, you will notice that the arrow between the two fields changes direction. By clicking on the arrow (which should now be pointing left), you can return RELIG to its original location. A third option is to simply click the **Reset** button. Choose whichever option appeals to you to move the RELIG variable back to its original position.

---

4. For a brief overview of the rules regarding abbreviated variable names, access the Help feature of SPSS Statistics. Select **Topics** and **Index,** and then search for **Variable Names → Rules**.

Now, let's get some other variables relating to religion. One at a time, highlight and transfer **ATTEND**, **POSTLIFE**, and **PRAY**.[5] When all three are in the "Variables(s):" field, click **OK**.

After a few seconds of cogitation, SPSS Statistics will present you with the Viewer window again. You should now be looking at the results of our latest analysis. Bear in mind that if you are doing this all in one session, the results of the latest procedure we ran (a frequency distribution for RELIG) may still be listed in the Outline and displayed in the Contents pane directly above the current procedure. If so, just scroll down until your screen looks like this:

---

5. *Reminder:* For the variable ATTEND, the value 9 should be labeled as "missing." For the variables POSTLIFE and PRAY, values 0, 8, and 9 should be labeled as "missing." The procedures for defining values as missing are outlined earlier in this chapter.

## SPSS Statistics Command 5.10: Running Frequency Distributions With Two or More Variables

Click **Analyze** → **Descriptive Statistics** → **Frequencies** → Double-click on variable name OR highlight variable name → Click right-pointing arrow

Repeat this step until all variables have been transferred to the "Variable(s):" field → **OK**

Take a few minutes to study the new table. The structure of the table is the same as the one we saw earlier for religious preference. This one presents the distribution of answers to the question concerning the frequency of attendance at religious services. Notice that the respondents were given several categories to choose from, ranging from "Never" to "More than once a week." The final category combines those who answered "Don't know" (DK) with those who gave "No answer" (NA).

Notice that religious service attendance is an ordinal variable. The different frequencies of religious service attendance can be arranged in order, but the distances between categories vary. Had the questionnaire asked, "How many times did you attend religious services last year?" the resulting data would have constituted a ratio variable. The problem with that measurement strategy, however, is one of reliability: We couldn't bank on all the respondents recalling exactly how many times they had attended religious services.

The most common response in the distribution is "Never." About one quarter, or 24.7%, of respondents (valid cases) gave that answer. The most common answer is referred to as the **mode**. This percentage is followed by 16.9% of the respondents, who reported that they attend religious services "Every week."

If we combine the respondents who report attending religious services weekly with the category immediately below them, more than once a week, we might say that roughly 23.4% of our sample report attending religious services at least once a week. If we add those who report attending nearly every week, we see that 28.6% attend religious services about weekly. Combining adjacent values of a variable in this fashion is called **collapsing categories**. It is commonly done when the number of categories is large and/or some of the values have relatively few cases. In this instance, we might collapse categories further, for example:

| | |
|---|---|
| About weekly | 29% |
| 1 to 3 times a month | 16% |
| Seldom | 30% |
| Never | 25% |

*Note:* Percentages add to 100% in this case, but don't be alarmed if in another instance they add up to 101% or only 99% due to rounding of percentages within categories.

Compare this abbreviated table with the original, and be sure you understand how this one was created. Notice that we have rounded off the percentages here, dropping the decimal points. As is the case in this instance, combined percentages can add to slightly more *or* slightly less than 100% due to rounding of the individual categories. Typically, data such as these do not warrant the precision implied by the use of decimal points because the answers given are themselves approximations for many of the respondents. Later, we'll show you how to tell SPSS Statistics to combine categories in this fashion. That will be especially important when we want to use variables in more complex analyses.

Now, let's look at the other two religious variables, beginning with POSTLIFE (see figure on next page).

As you can see, significantly fewer categories make up this variable: just "Yes" and "No." Missing value categories are listed only when there are missing cases to report. One hundred and forty-eight respondents indicated that they don't know (DK) if there is an afterlife, while five respondents gave

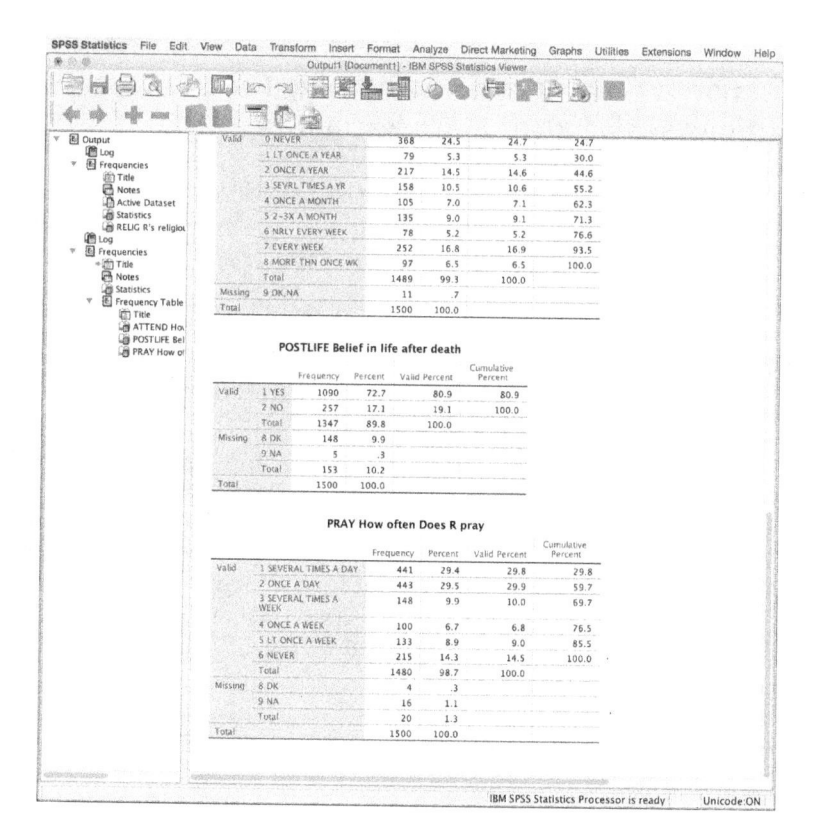

| | | Frequency | Percent | Valid Percent | Cumulative Percent |
|---|---|---|---|---|---|
| Valid | 0 NEVER | 368 | 24.5 | 24.7 | 24.7 |
| | 1 LT ONCE A YEAR | 79 | 5.3 | 5.3 | 30.0 |
| | 2 ONCE A YEAR | 217 | 14.5 | 14.6 | 44.6 |
| | 3 SEVRL TIMES A YR | 158 | 10.5 | 10.6 | 55.2 |
| | 4 ONCE A MONTH | 105 | 7.0 | 7.1 | 62.3 |
| | 5 2-3X A MONTH | 135 | 9.0 | 9.1 | 71.3 |
| | 6 NRLY EVERY WEEK | 78 | 5.2 | 5.2 | 76.6 |
| | 7 EVERY WEEK | 252 | 16.8 | 16.9 | 93.5 |
| | 8 MORE THN ONCE WK | 97 | 6.5 | 6.5 | 100.0 |
| | Total | 1489 | 99.3 | 100.0 | |
| Missing | 9 DK, NA | 11 | .7 | | |
| Total | | 1500 | 100.0 | | |

**POSTLIFE Belief in life after death**

| | | Frequency | Percent | Valid Percent | Cumulative Percent |
|---|---|---|---|---|---|
| Valid | 1 YES | 1090 | 72.7 | 80.9 | 80.9 |
| | 2 NO | 257 | 17.1 | 19.1 | 100.0 |
| | Total | 1347 | 89.8 | 100.0 | |
| Missing | 8 DK | 148 | 9.9 | | |
| | 9 NA | 5 | .3 | | |
| | Total | 153 | 10.2 | | |
| Total | | 1500 | 100.0 | | |

**PRAY How often Does R pray**

| | | Frequency | Percent | Valid Percent | Cumulative Percent |
|---|---|---|---|---|---|
| Valid | 1 SEVERAL TIMES A DAY | 441 | 29.4 | 29.8 | 29.8 |
| | 2 ONCE A DAY | 443 | 29.5 | 29.9 | 59.7 |
| | 3 SEVERAL TIMES A WEEK | 148 | 9.9 | 10.0 | 69.7 |
| | 4 ONCE A WEEK | 100 | 6.7 | 6.8 | 76.5 |
| | 5 LT ONCE A WEEK | 133 | 8.9 | 9.0 | 85.5 |
| | 6 NEVER | 215 | 14.3 | 14.5 | 100.0 |
| | Total | 1480 | 98.7 | 100.0 | |
| Missing | 8 DK | 4 | .3 | | |
| | 9 NA | 16 | 1.1 | | |
| | Total | 20 | 1.3 | | |
| Total | | 1500 | 100.0 | | |

no answer (NA). The "IAP" missing category, Inapplicable, is not shown, indicating that there were no respondents who were not asked this particular question. Thus, all 1,500 in the sample were asked this question. A number of questions, like this one, are asked of everyone or almost everyone; however, due to the split-ballot nature of the GSS data design, many questions are not asked of all respondents. To collect data on a large number of topics, the GSS asks only subsets of the sample some of the questions. Thus, if you were a GSS survey participant, you might be asked whether you believe in an afterlife but not asked your opinions on abortion. Someone else might be asked about abortion but not about the afterlife. Still other respondents will be asked about both. We will explore the data for some questions put only to some respondents later.

Notice that more than four out of five American adults who have an opinion on the subject believe in an afterlife, according to the Valid Percent column. Is that higher or lower than you would have predicted? Part of the fun of analyses such as these is discovering aspects of our society that you might not have known about. We'll have numerous opportunities for that sort of discovery throughout the remainder of the book.

Now, let's look at the final religious variable, PRAY. One quick observation you can make from the distribution is that more than three fourths of Americans pray at least once a week. Is this higher or lower than you were expecting?

# WRITING BOX 5.1

Once you've made an interesting discovery, you will undoubtedly want to share it with others. Often, the people who read our research have difficulty interpreting tables, so it becomes necessary for us to present our findings in prose. A rule of thumb for writing research is to write so your ideas can be understood by reading either the tables or the prose alone. To aid you in this process, throughout the text we have incorporated "Writing Boxes" using a style appropriate for professional reports or journal articles. In this box, for instance, we present in prose findings from the variables we just examined.

Almost half the respondents in our study (49%) identify themselves as Protestants, while a little less than a quarter (23.3%) are Roman Catholics. Jews make up only 1.7%

of the sample, and 1 in 5 (19.9%) say they have no religious identification. The rest, as you can see, are spread thinly across a wide variety of other religious persuasions.

Religious identification is not the same as religious practice. For example, while 80% claimed a religious affiliation, only a little more than a quarter (28.6%) attend religious services about weekly. Another 16.2% reported attending one, two, or three times a month. About 30% reported attending services several times a year or less, leaving about a quarter (24.7%) who never attend religious services.

Religious belief is another dimension of religiosity. In the study, respondents were asked whether they believed in a life after death. The vast majority of those who held an opinion—4 out of 5 (80.9%)—said they did.

Finally, respondents were asked how often they prayed, if at all. Responses to this question bear a striking contrast to earlier answers. Recall that 20% said they had no religious affiliation, but about 86% of the respondents said they pray *at least* now and then. Clearly, some respondents separate their spirituality from membership in formal religious organizations. More than half of all respondents (59.7%) said they pray at least once every day.

This just about completes our introduction to frequency distributions. Now that you understand the logic of variables and the values that constitute them and know how to examine them with SPSS Statistics, you may want to spend some time looking at other variables in the data set. You can see them by using the steps we've just gone through.

If you create a frequency distribution for AGE (with values 0, 98, and 99 set as missing), you may notice the following: 0.1% of the sample is 18 years of age, 1.1% is 19, 1% is 20, and so forth (by looking in the Valid Percent column). You may also notice that the table is *not* very useful for analysis. It is not only long (more than 70 values) and cumbersome but also difficult to interpret as well. This is due primarily to the fact that AGE is presented here as a continuous, interval/ratio variable.

The Frequencies procedure we just reviewed is generally preferred when you are dealing with discrete variables. If you want to describe the distribution of a continuous variable, such as AGE, you will probably want to do one of two things. One option is to use the Descriptives procedure to display some basic summary statistics, such as common measures of central tendency and dispersion. (We also use descriptive statistics when working with discrete variables.) Alternatively, you might consider combining adjacent values of the variable (as we did with ATTEND previously) to decrease the number of categories, making the variable more manageable and conducive to a frequency distribution. When we collapse categories on SPSS Statistics, this is called recoding. We will consider the first option (running basic measures of central tendency and dispersion) in this chapter and save the second option (recoding) for Chapter 7.

# DESCRIPTIVE STATISTICS: BASIC MEASURES OF CENTRAL TENDENCY AND DISPERSION

While it is fairly easy to learn how to request basic statistics through SPSS Statistics, it is more difficult to learn which statistics are appropriate for variables of different types and at different levels of measurement. At your command, SPSS Statistics will calculate statistics for variables even when the measure is inappropriate. If, for instance, you ask SPSS Statistics to calculate the mean of the variable SEX, it will dutifully comply and give you an answer of 1.55. Of course, in this instance, the answer is meaningless because it would make no sense to report the average gender for the 2016 GSS and thus the average gender in the United States during 2016 as 1.55. What, after all, does that mean?

When it comes to a discrete, nominal variable, such as SEX, the mode, not the mean, is the appropriate measure of central tendency. Since the GSS measures SEX as a dichotomy (having exactly two categories), the mean does tell us that there are more females than males. (Since males are coded "1" and females are coded "2," the value is closer to 2.) It also tells us the proportion of one category to the other. However, for all other nominal variables that are not dichotomous, the value provides no useful immediate information.

Consequently, before running measures of central tendency and dispersion, we want to provide a brief overview of which measures are appropriate for variables of different types (Table 5.1) and at different levels of measurement (Table 5.2).[6] An *X* indicates that the measure is generally considered both appropriate and useful, whereas a long dash [—] indicates that the measure is permissible but not generally considered very useful. For example, Table 5.2 shows that the mode is appropriate for variables at the nominal level, whereas the median, range, and perhaps the mode are appropriate for variables at the ordinal level, and every measure listed is generally appropriate for ratio- and interval-level data. Note the exception that for interval/ratio variables that have skewed distributions, the median is generally a better central tendency measure than the mean.

You are probably already familiar with the three ***measures of central tendency*** listed earlier. As we noted in the previous section, the mode refers to the most common value (answer or response) in a given distribution. The ***median*** is the middle category in a distribution, and the ***mean*** (sometimes imprecisely called the *average*) is the sum of the values of all the cases divided by the total number of cases.

| TABLE 5.1  ■  Basic Descriptive Statistics Appropriate for Different Types of Variables | | | | | | |
|---|---|---|---|---|---|---|
| | Measures of Central Tendency | | | Measures of Dispersion | | |
| Type of Variables | Mode | Median | Mean | Range | Interquartile Range | Variance and Standard Deviation |
| Discrete | X | X | — | — | — | — |
| Continuous | — | X | X | X | X | X |

| TABLE 5.2  ■  Basic Descriptive Statistics Appropriate for Different Levels of Measurement | | | | | | |
|---|---|---|---|---|---|---|
| | Measures of Central Tendency | | | Measures of Dispersion | | |
| | Mode | Median | Mean | Median | Interquartile Range | Variance and Standard Deviation |
| Nominal | X | — | — | — | — | — |
| Ordinal | — | X | — | X | X | — |
| Interval/ratio | — | — | X | X | X | X |

You may already be familiar with some of the ***measures of dispersion*** as well. In this section, we will focus on three: range, interquartile range, and standard deviation. While ***variance*** is also listed in the tables, we'll save it for later in the text. The ***range*** indicates the distance separating the lowest and highest values in a distribution, whereas the ***interquartile range (IQR)*** is the difference between the upper quartile (Q3, 75th percentile) and lower quartile (Q1, 25th percentile), or the range of the middle 50% of the distribution. The ***standard deviation*** indicates the extent to which the values are clustered around the mean or spread away from it.

---

6. In addition to the variables' type and level of measurement, other issues may enter into the choice of particular statistics. Additional considerations beyond the scope of this text include (but are not limited to) your research objective and the shape of the distribution (i.e., symmetrical or skewed).

## Demonstration 5.5: The Frequencies Procedure

Several of the procedures in SPSS Statistics produce descriptive statistics. To start, we are going to examine descriptive statistics options in the Frequencies procedure.

Open the Frequencies dialog box by choosing **Analyze → Descriptive Statistics → Frequencies**. Then, select **Statistics** in the upper right portion of the dialog box. The Statistics box that appears allows us to instruct SPSS Statistics to calculate all of the measures of central tendency and dispersion listed in Tables 5.1 and 5.2.[7] The Frequencies procedure is generally preferred for discrete variables because, in addition to calculating most basic statistics, it presents you with a frequency distribution table (something not particularly useful for continuous variables), though you do have the option to suppress the frequency table.

If there are any variables listed in the "Variable(s):" window now, click **Reset** to clear them. We will use a simple example to show you the commands, and then, you can practice on your own with other variables. Enter the variable **SEX,** and then click **Statistics** to the right of the window.

**Analyze → Descriptive Statistics → Frequencies**

When the Statistics window opens, you will see the measures of central tendency listed in the area in the upper right-hand corner and the measures of dispersion listed in the area in the lower left-hand corner. To select an option, simply click in the check box next to the appropriate measure. For our simple example, all we have to do is click the box next to **Mode** (in the Central Tendency area). After you have made your selection(s), click **Continue**. You will now be back in the Frequencies box, and you can select **OK** (see figure at the top of the next page).

You should now see your output displayed in the Viewer (see bottom figure on the next page). Remember, the output should include both the mode and frequencies for the variable SEX. By just looking at the frequencies, you should be able to say quite easily what the mode (the most frequent response or value given) is for this variable. You can check to make sure you are right by comparing your answer with the one calculated by SPSS Statistics.

---

7. To determine the interquartile range, simply select **Quartiles**; then, use your output to subtract Q1 from Q3 (Q3 – Q1, or Quartile 3 – Quartile 1).

By glancing through our output, we find that the mode in this instance is 2 because there are more females (numeric value 2) than males (numeric value 1) in our data set. There are 819 females (54.6%) and 681 males (45.4%).

---

**SPSS Statistics Command 5.11: The Frequencies Procedure—Descriptive Statistics (Discrete Variables)**

Click **Analyze** → **Descriptive Statistics** → **Frequencies**

Highlight the variable name and click on the right-pointing arrow OR double-click on the variable name → Select **Statistics** → Choose statistics by clicking in the boxes next to the appropriate measures

Click **Continue** → **OK**

---

You may want to practice this command by choosing another discrete variable from the DEMO .SAV file, determining the appropriate measure(s) for the variable, and following the procedure listed previously.

# DEMONSTRATION 5.6: THE DESCRIPTIVES PROCEDURE—CALCULATING DESCRIPTIVE STATISTICS FOR CONTINUOUS VARIABLES

We can also instruct SPSS Statistics to calculate basic statistics using the Descriptives procedure. This option is generally preferred when you are working with continuous, interval/ratio variables or when you do not want to produce a frequency table. Bear in mind, the Descriptives procedure allows you to run all of the measures outlined in Tables 5.1 and 5.2 except mode, median, and interquartile range.

If you want to use SPSS Statistics to determine descriptive statistics for AGE, you can do that by clicking **Analyze** in the menu bar. Next, select **Descriptive Statistics** and then **Descriptives** from the drop-down menus. You should now be looking at the Descriptives dialog box, shown below.

If any variables are displayed in the "Variable(s):" box, go ahead and click **Reset**. Then, move **AGE** from the variable list on the left side to the "Variable(s):" box, either by double-clicking it or by highlighting it and clicking on the arrow between the two fields. Once you have done that, AGE will appear in the "Variable(s):" field. Now select **Options** at the top right of the window. This opens the Options window, which lets you specify what statistics you want SPSS Statistics to calculate.

The **Mean**, **Standard deviation**, **Minimum**, and **Maximum** options may already be selected. If not, select those options by clicking in the boxes next to them. You can also request **Range**, although in this case, it is not necessary because calculating the measure by hand is just as easy. Now that you have specified which statistics you want SPSS Statistics to run, click **Continue** and then **OK** in the Descriptives box.

| Descriptive Statistics | | | | | |
|---|---|---|---|---|---|
| | N | Minimum | Maximum | Mean | Std. Deviation |
| AGE Age of respondent | 1,495 | 18 | 89 | 49.16 | 17.476 |
| Valid N (listwise) | 1,495 | | | | |

We can see that the mean age of respondents in this study is 49.16. As we already know, this was calculated by adding the individual ages and dividing that total by 1,495, the number of people who gave their ages. Also, note that the Valid N is 1,495, five short of our total subsample of 1,500. So where did those other five other people go? Did we lose them? No, they opted out of the question by giving no answer (NA). Theoretically, one or more of them could have responded that they didn't know their own age (DK), but that was not the case here. (You can always confirm this by looking at the full frequency distribution.)

We can also see that the minimum age reported was 18 and the maximum 89. The distance between these two values is the range, in this case, 71 years (89 − 18).[8] The standard deviation tells

---

8. *Reminder:* For the variable AGE, the values 0 and 99 should be labeled as "missing." The procedure for defining values as missing is outlined earlier in this chapter.

us the extent to which the individual ages are clustered around the mean or spread out from it. It also tells us how far we would need to go above and below the mean to include about two thirds of all the cases. In this instance, about two thirds of the 1,495 respondents have ages between 31.684 and 66.636 (49.16 ± 17.476). Later, we'll discover other uses for the standard deviation.

---

**SPSS Statistics Command 5.12: The Descriptives Procedure—Descriptive Statistics (Continuous Variables)**

Click Analyze → Descriptive Statistics → Descriptives

Highlight variable name and double-click OR click on the right-pointing arrow

Click **Options** → Choose statistic(s) by clicking the check box next to the appropriate measure(s)

Click **Continue** → **OK**

---

You may want to practice using the Descriptives command by choosing other continuous variables and running appropriate statistics. If you run into any problems, simply review the steps outlined before.

# DEMONSTRATION 5.7: PRINTING YOUR OUTPUT (VIEWER)

If you would like to print your output, you have several options. First, make sure that the SPSS Statistics Viewer is the *active window* (i.e., it is the window displayed on your screen). From the menu, choose **File** and then **Print**. You can control the items that are printed by selecting either **All visible output** (allows you to print only the items currently displayed in the Contents pane, as opposed to hidden items, for instance) or **Selection** (prints only items currently selected in the Outline or Contents panes). Then, click **OK**.

If, for instance, you want to print only a selected item (such as the frequency distribution for the variable ATTEND), you click directly on the table or the name of the table in the Outline. Once you have done this, you can access the Print Preview option to preview what will be printed on each page. Conversely, you can select output you don't want to print and remove it by pressing the **Delete** key.

To access Print Preview, select **File** and then **Print Preview** from the drop-down menu. When you are ready to return to the SPSS Statistics Viewer, select **Close**.

You can then click **File → Print → Selection → OK** to print your output.

---

**SPSS Statistics Command 5.13: Printing Your Output (Viewer)**

Make sure SPSS Viewer is active window

Highlight item in Contents or Outline pane

*To select only certain items to print:*

Click **File → Print → Selection → OK**

*To print all visible output:*

Click **File → Print → All visible output → OK**

---

---

**SPSS Statistics Command 5.14: Print Preview**

Click **File** → **Print** → **Preview**

---

## DEMONSTRATION 5.8: ADDING HEADERS/ FOOTERS AND TITLES/TEXT

Headers and footers are the information printed at the top and bottom of the page. When you are in the SPSS Statistics Viewer and ready to print output, you may want to enter text as headers and footers. This is particularly useful for those of you working in a classroom or laboratory setting and using shared printers so you can readily identify which printed output is yours.

You can add headers and footers by selecting **File** and then **Page Setup** from the drop-down menu. Now, click on **Options**, and add any information you want in the Header and/or Footer fields (such as your name, the date, title for the table, etc.). Then click **OK** and **OK** once again to return to the SPSS Statistics Viewer.

You may want to use the Print Preview option discussed earlier to see how your headers and/or footers will look on the printed page.

---

**SPSS Statistics Command 5.15:
Adding Headers and Footers**

Click **File** → **Page Setup** → **Options**

Add information in Header and/or Footer fields

Click **OK** → **OK**

---

In addition to adding headers and footers, you can also add text and titles to your output by clicking on the place in either the Outline or Contents pane where you wish to add the title/text. Now, simply click on the **Insert Title** or **Insert Text** tool on the toolbar or click **Insert** → **New Title** or **New Text** in the menu bar. SPSS Statistics will then display an area for you to add your title or text.

After inserting your text or title, you may want to use the Print Preview option to see how your text/title will appear on the printed page.

---

**SPSS Statistics Command 5.16: Adding Titles/Text**

Click on area in Contents or Outline pane where you wish to add title or text → Click on **Insert Title** OR **Insert Text** tool on the toolbar

Add text or titles OR click **Insert** on the menu bar

Click **New Title** OR **New Text**

Add text or title

---

## DEMONSTRATION 5.9: SAVING YOUR OUTPUT (VIEWER)

That's enough work for now. But before we stop, let's save the work we've done in this session so we won't have to repeat it all when we start up again.

Any changes you have made to the file (such as defining values as missing) and any output you have created are being held only in the computer's volatile memory. That means if you leave SPSS Statistics right now, the changes and output will disappear. To avoid this, simply follow the instructions here. This section walks you briefly through steps involved in saving output. The next section gives you instructions for saving changes to your data file.

If you are writing a term paper that will use the frequencies and other tables created during this session, you can probably copy portions of the output and paste it into your word processor document. To save the Output window, first make sure it is the window front-most on your screen. Then, select **Save As** under the **File** menu or choose the **Save File** tool on the toolbar. Either way, SPSS Statistics will present you with the following window:

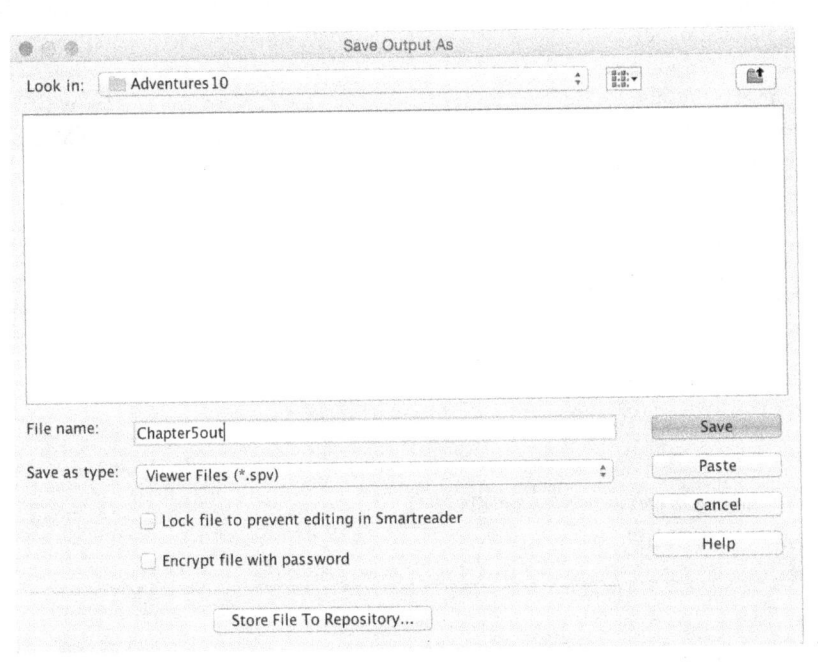

In this example, we've decided to save our output to the Documents folder on our computer's hard drive under the name "Chapter5out" (which SPSS Statistics thoughtfully provided as a default name). If you are using a public or shared computer, you may want to save the file to a portable drive or accessible Internet location (e.g., thumb/jump/flash drive, USB drive, or network drive).

As an alternative, you might like to use a name such as "Out1022" to indicate that it was the output saved on October 22, or some similar naming convention. Either way, insert your drive if necessary, change the file name if you wish, choose the appropriate location in the "Look in:" field, and then click **Save**.

---

### SPSS Statistics Command 5.17: Saving Your Output (Viewer)

Make sure the SPSS Viewer/Output is the active window.

Click **File Save As** OR click on **Save File** tool → Choose appropriate drive → Name your file → Click **Save**

---

# DEMONSTRATION 5.10: SAVING CHANGES TO YOUR DATA SET

If you have made no changes to labels, missing values, and so on, then there is no need to resave the data file; the one you already accessed today is up-to-date. If you did make changes, we will want to maintain the labels we set for our variables as missing, so let's go ahead and save the data file. If you are sharing a computer with other users, you should save DEMO.SAV on a removable or network drive for safekeeping. If you are using your own personal computer, you can save your work on your computer's hard drive.

Keep in mind that whenever you save a file in SPSS Statistics (whether you are saving output or your data set), you are saving only what is visible in the active window. To save your data set, you need to make sure the Data Editor is the active window. You can do that by either clicking on **DEMO.SAV** in the taskbar or choosing **Window** in the menu bar and then selecting **DEMO.SAV** from the drop-down menu. Then, go to the **File** menu and select **Save As**. From the "Save in:" drop-down menu at the top of the Save As window, select a location for your data to be saved—either a USB drive, a network drive, a cloud server, your Dropbox folder, or the computer's hard drive.

Type the name for your file in the "File Name:" window. Although you can choose any name you wish, in this case, we will use "DEMOPLUS" to refer to the file that contains our basic DEMO file with any changes you might have made today. Then, click **Save**. Now, you can leave SPSS Statistics with the **File → Exit** command. If you open this file the next time you start an SPSS Statistics session, it will have all of the new, added labels.

---

### SPSS Statistics Command 5.18: Saving Changes Made to an Existing Data Set

Make sure the Data Editor is the active window

Click **File → Save As**

Select appropriate drive → Name your file

Click **Save**

---

# CONCLUSION

You've now completed your first interaction with data. Even though this is barely the tip of the iceberg, you should have begun to get some sense of the possibilities that exist in a data set such as this. Many of the concepts with which social scientists deal are the subjects of opinion in everyday conversations.

A data set such as the one you are using in this book is powerfully different from opinion. From time to time, you probably hear people make statements such as these:

Almost no one goes to church anymore.

Americans are pretty conservative, by and large.

Most people are opposed to abortion.

Sometimes, opinions such as these are an accurate reflection of the state of affairs; sometimes, they are far from the truth. In ordinary conversation, the apparent validity of such assertions typically hinges on the force with which they are expressed and/or the purported wisdom of the speaker. Already in this book, you have discovered a better way to evaluate such assertions. In this chapter, you've learned some facts about people and religion in the United States today. The next few chapters take you into the realms of politics and attitudes toward abortion.

## Main Points

- In this chapter, we began our discussion of univariate analysis by focusing on two basic ways of examining the religiosity of individuals in our subsample of 1,500 randomly selected respondents to the 2016 General Social Survey (GSS): running frequency distributions and producing basic descriptive statistics.

- Before embarking on our analysis, we reviewed a shortcut for opening a frequently used data file and learned to change the way SPSS Statistics displays information and output, as well as how to define certain values as "missing."

- The Frequencies command can be used to produce frequencies for one or more variables at a time.

- When we request tables, charts, or graphs on SPSS Statistics, the results appear in the SPSS Statistics Viewer.

- There are two main parts, or panes, in the Viewer: Outline (on the left) and Contents (on the right).

- The Outline pane lists the results of our output for the entire session.

- The Contents pane presents the results of our analyses.

- Frequency distributions are more appropriate for discrete, rather than continuous, variables.

- When working with continuous variables, a better option for describing your distribution is either to produce descriptive statistics or to reduce the number of categories by recoding.

- Certain measures of central tendency and dispersion are appropriate for variables of different types and at different levels of measurement.

- There are several ways to run measures of central tendency and dispersion on SPSS Statistics. We reviewed two: the Frequencies procedure and the Descriptives procedure.

- When you are ready to end your SPSS Statistics session, you may want to save and/or print your output so you can use it later.

- Before exiting SPSS Statistics, don't forget to save any changes you made to the existing data set.

## Key Terms

Active window 69
Collapsing categories 61
Contents pane 57
Cumulative percentage 59
Frequency column 59
Frequency distribution 54

Interquartile range (IQR) 64
Mean 64
Measures of central tendency 64
Measures of dispersion 64
Median 64
Mode 61

Outline pane 57
Range 64
SPSS Statistics Viewer 55
Standard deviation 64
Valid percentage 59
Variance 64

## SPSS Statistics Commands Introduced in This Chapter

5.1. Shortcut for Opening Frequently Used Data Files

5.2. Setting Options—Displaying Abbreviated Variable Names Alphabetically

5.3. Setting Options—Output Labels

5.4. Setting Values and Labels as "Missing"

5.5. Running Frequency Distributions

5.6. Navigating Through the SPSS Statistics Viewer

5.7. Changing the Width of the Outline Pane

5.8. Hiding and Displaying Results in the Viewer

5.9. Hiding and Displaying All Results From a Procedure

5.10. Running Frequency Distributions With Two or More Variables

5.11. The Frequencies Procedure—Descriptive Statistics (Discrete Variables)

5.12. The Descriptives Procedure—Descriptive Statistics (Continuous Variables)

*(Continued)*

(Continued)

5.13.   Printing Your Output (Viewer)

5.14.   Print Preview

5.15.   Adding Headers and Footers

5.16.   Adding Titles/Text

5.17.   Saving Your Output (Viewer)

5.18.   Saving Changes Made to an Existing Data Set

# Review Questions

1.   Analysis of one variable at a time is often referred to as what type of analysis?

2.   What are the two parts of the SPSS Statistics Viewer called?

3.   What is a frequency distribution?

4.   In a frequency distribution, what information does the column labeled "Frequency" contain?

5.   In a frequency distribution, what information does the column labeled "Valid Percent" contain?

6.   Is a frequency distribution generally preferred for continuous or discrete variables? Why?

7.   List the measures of central tendency and dispersion appropriate for variables at each of the following levels of measurement:

a.   Ordinal

b.   Nominal

c.   Interval/ratio

8.   List the measures of central tendency and dispersion appropriate for each of the following types of variables:

a.   Discrete

b.   Continuous

9.   Calculate the mode, median, mean, and range for the following distribution: 7, 5, 2, 4, 4, 0, 1, 9, 6.

10.   If Q1 (Quartile 1) = 25 and Q3 (Quartile 3) = 40, what is the interquartile range for the distribution?

11.   Is the standard deviation a measure of central tendency or dispersion?

12.   In general terms, what information does the standard deviation tell us?

13.   Explain why, for certain GSS variables, a large number of the responses may be labeled "missing," coded as IAP.

14.   In order to save or print output, which SPSS Statistics window should be the "active window"?

15.   In order to save your data file, which SPSS Statistics window should be the "active window"?

## SPSS Statistics Lab Exercise 5.1

NAME: _____

CLASS: _____

INSTRUCTOR: _____

DATE: _____

*To complete the following exercises, you need to open the EXER.SAV file.*

Produce and analyze frequency distributions and appropriate measures of central tendency for the variables RACE, HEALTH, and TEENSEX. Then, use your output to answer Questions 1 through 6.

Before you begin, make sure to define values for the following variables as "missing":

RACE: 0

HEALTH: 0, 8, 9

TEENSEX: 0, 8, 9

1. (RACE) The largest racial grouping of respondents to the 2016 GSS was _white_____, with _71.0_____%. The second-largest grouping was _____, with _____%.

2. Which measure of central tendency is most appropriate to summarize the distribution of RACE, and why? The value of that measure is __mode_____. _because the nominal_

3. (HEALTH) _____% of respondents to the 2016 GSS reported that they are in good health. This was followed by _____% of respondents who reported being in excellent health, whereas about _____% of respondents reported being in either fair or poor health.

4. Which measure of central tendency is most appropriate to summarize the distribution of HEALTH, and why? The value of that measure is __Median_____. _because it ordinal_

5. (TEENSEX) Nearly _____% of respondents to the 2016 GSS believe that sex before marriage, particularly for teens 14 to 16 years of age, is either always wrong or almost always wrong. Only _____% think it is not wrong at all, whereas _____% think it is sometimes wrong.

6. Which measure of central tendency is most appropriate to summarize the distribution of TEENSEX, and why? The value of that measure is __mode belive_____.

Use the Descriptives procedure to examine the variables EDUC and TVHOURS. Then, use your output to answer Questions 7 and 8.

Before you begin, make sure to define values for the following variables as "missing":

EDUC: 97, 98, 99

TVHOURS: −1, 98, 99

7. (EDUC) The mean number of years of education of respondents to the 2016 GSS is _13.51_____, and two thirds of respondents report having between _____ and _____ years of education.

*(Continued)*

(Continued)

8. (TVHOURS) Respondents to the 2016 GSS report watching an "average" of _____ hours of television a day, with two thirds of them watching between _____ and _____ hours of television per day.

9. Are respondents to the 2016 GSS generally satisfied that the government is doing enough to halt the rising crime rate (NATCRIME) and deal with drug addiction (NATDRUG)? (Hint: Consider the type and level of measurement for each variable before using either the Frequencies or Descriptives command to produce frequency tables and/or descriptive statistics. For the variables NATCRIME and NATDRUG, values 0, 8, and 9 should be set as "missing.")

Choose three variables you are interested in from the EXER.SAV file. Then, based on each variable's type and level of measurement, use either the Descriptives or Frequencies command to produce a frequency table and/or appropriate descriptive statistics for that variable.

List the variable name and the values you set as "missing" below. Then, describe your findings in the space provided (Questions 10–12).

10. Abbreviated variable name: _____

    Values labeled "missing": _____

    Written analysis:

11. Abbreviated variable name: _____

    Values labeled "missing": _____

    Written analysis:

12. Abbreviated variable name: _____

    Values labeled "missing": _____

    Written analysis:

13. Access the SPSS Statistics Help feature Tutorial.

    Hint: Click **Help** → **Tutorial** → and then work your way through the following sections: "Using the Data Editor" and "Working With Output."

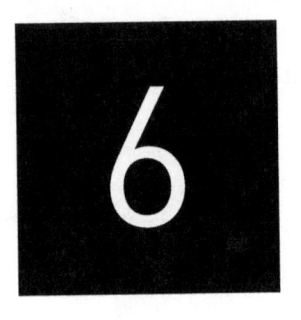

# PRESENTING YOUR DATA IN GRAPHIC FORM

## Political Orientations

Now, let's turn our attention from religion to politics. Some people feel so strongly about politics that they joke about it being a religion. The General Social Survey (GSS) data set has several items that reflect political issues. Two are key political items: POLVIEWS and PARTYID. These items will be the primary focus in this chapter. In the process of examining these variables, we are going to learn not only more about the political orientations of respondents to the 2016 GSS but also how to use SPSS Statistics to produce and interpret data in graphic form.

You will recall that in the previous chapter, we focused on a variety of ways of displaying univariate distributions (frequency tables) and summarizing them (measures of central tendency and dispersion). In this chapter, we are going to build on that discussion by focusing on several ways of presenting your data graphically.

We will begin by focusing on two charts that are useful for variables at the nominal and ordinal levels: bar charts and pie charts. We will then consider two graphs appropriate for interval/ratio variables: histograms and line charts.

## GRAPHING DATA WITH DIRECT "LEGACY" DIALOGS

SPSS Statistics gives us a variety of ways to present data graphically. Clicking the Graphs option on the menu bar will give you three options for building charts: Chart Builder, Interactive, and Legacy Dialogs. These take you to two chart-building methods developed by SPSS over the past 25 years. Chart Builder is the more recent.

We have chosen to introduce you to graphing data with the Legacy Dialogs because the dialogs guide new users through the creation of a graph a step at a time. The newer methods require a user to be fairly familiar with graphics issues and nomenclature. While the Chart Builder makes greater use of the Microsoft Windows and Apple Macintosh graphic interfaces, we think you will appreciate starting with this established method. After you develop a sense of graph making's issues and options, we encourage you to try out the Chart Builder and Interactive methods. Once you understand the procedure using Legacy dialogs, the Chart Builder becomes easy to understand.

## DEMONSTRATION 6.1: FREQUENCY TABLE—POLVIEWS

We'll start our examination of political orientations with POLVIEWS. Before we get started, make sure to define the values 0, 8, and 9 as "missing." Then, use the Frequencies command to find out what this variable measures.

**Analyze → Descriptive Statistics → Frequencies**

Take a few minutes to examine this table. As you can see, POLVIEWS taps into basic political philosophy, ranging from "extremely liberal" to "extremely conservative." As you might expect, most people are clustered near the center, with fewer numbers on either extreme.

### POLVIEWS Think of Self as Liberal or Conservative

| | | Frequency | Percent | Valid Percent | Cumulative Percent |
|---|---|---|---|---|---|
| Valid | 1 EXTREMELY LIBERAL | 72 | 4.8 | 5.0 | 5.0 |
| | 2 LIBERAL | 188 | 12.5 | 13.1 | 18.1 |
| | 3 SLIGHTLY LIBERAL | 156 | 10.4 | 10.8 | 28.9 |
| | 4 MODERATE | 519 | 34.6 | 36.1 | 65.0 |
| | 5 SLGHTLY CONSERVATIVE | 210 | 14.0 | 14.6 | 79.6 |
| | 6 CONSERVATIVE | 227 | 15.1 | 15.8 | 95.4 |
| | 7 EXTRMLY CONSERVATIVE | 66 | 4.4 | 4.6 | 100.0 |
| | Total | 1438 | 95.9 | 100.0 | |
| Missing | 8 DK | 43 | 2.9 | | |
| | 9 NA | 19 | 1.3 | | |
| | Total | 62 | 4.1 | | |
| Total | | 1500 | 100.0 | | |

## Bar Chart: POLVIEWS

Sometimes, the information in a univariate analysis can be grasped more quickly if it is presented in graphic form rather than in a table of numbers. Without looking back at the table you just created, take a moment to think about the distribution of political orientations for respondents to the 2016 GSS. You may recall that most respondents were clustered near the center, but do you remember the relative sizes of the different groups? Was the "moderate" group a little bigger than the others or a lot bigger? Sometimes, a graphic presentation of such data sticks in your mind more than a table of numbers.

In this section, we are going to focus on one basic procedure to construct a simple *bar chart* for POLVIEWS. Bar charts display the same type of information as frequency tables do (the number or percentage of cases in a category). The difference is that bar charts display this information graphically rather than in a table.

SPSS Statistics offers an easy method for producing a simple bar chart. Under the **Graphs** menu, select **Legacy Dialogs**, then **Bar**, and the Bar Charts dialog box will open. This box will give you an opportunity to select the kind of graph you would like: simple, clustered, or stacked. Because we have only one variable, we want to choose the **Simple** type.

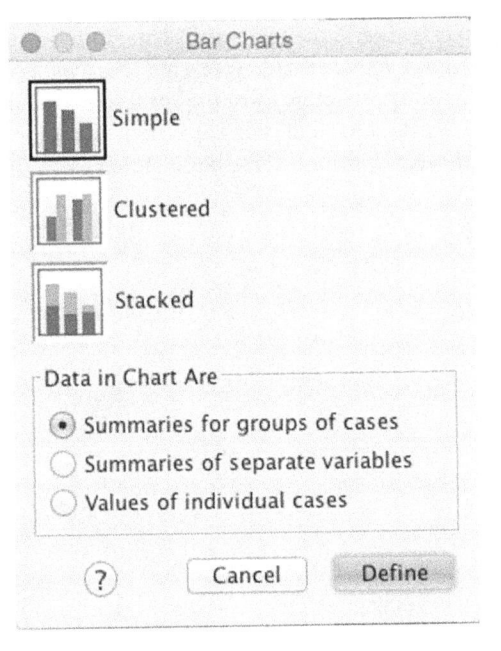

Probably that's the one already selected, but you can click it again to be sure. Then, click the **Define** button.

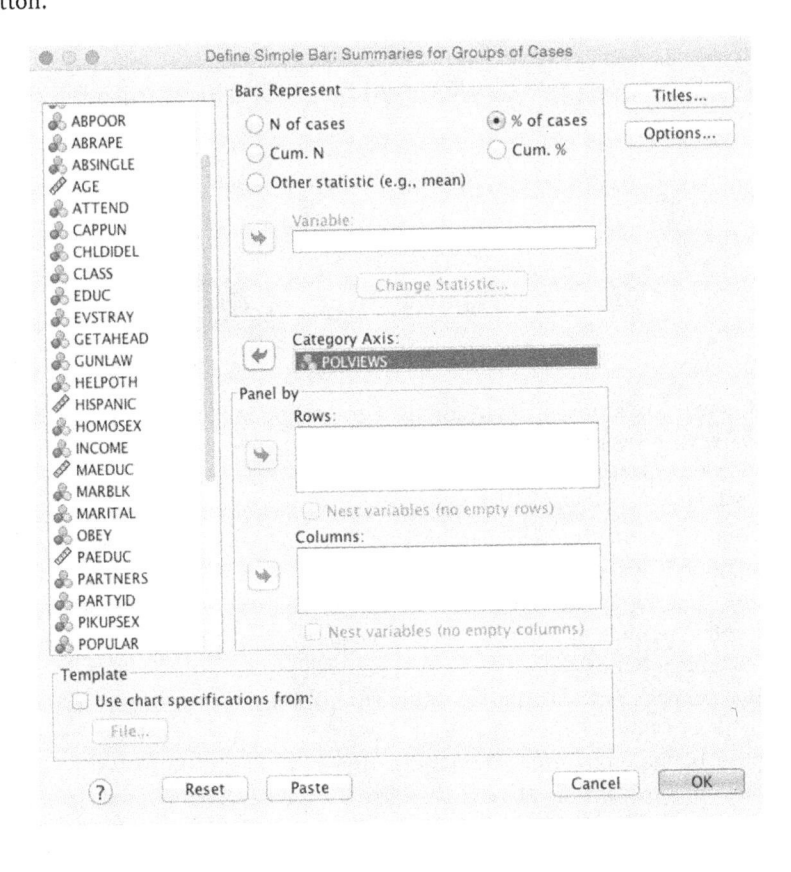

The next window allows you to specify further the kind of bar chart you would like, including which variable(s) will be graphed. As a start, let's find POLVIEWS in the variable list and highlight it. Now click the right-pointing arrow next to the "Category Axis:" box. This lets SPSS Statistics know that you want to construct the bar chart with the categories of POLVIEWS (extremely liberal, liberal, slightly liberal, etc.) on the *horizontal* (x) *axis*.

The "Bars Represent" box at the top of the window allows you to specify a format for the *vertical* (y) *axis* of the bar chart. In other words, you can choose to display "N of cases" (frequencies), "% of cases" (percentages), "Cum. N" (cumulative frequencies), or "Cum. %" (cumulative percentages). For now, let's click on **% of cases.**

Next, click on the **Options** button in the upper right-hand corner. After you do this, you will be presented with a screen that allows you to select how missing values will be treated. Because we are not interested in cases coded as "missing," make sure that the box next to the line that says "Display groups defined by missing values" is *not* checked. If the box has a check in it, simply click on the box to make the mark disappear, and then select **Continue**. If the box is already blank, just click **Continue**.

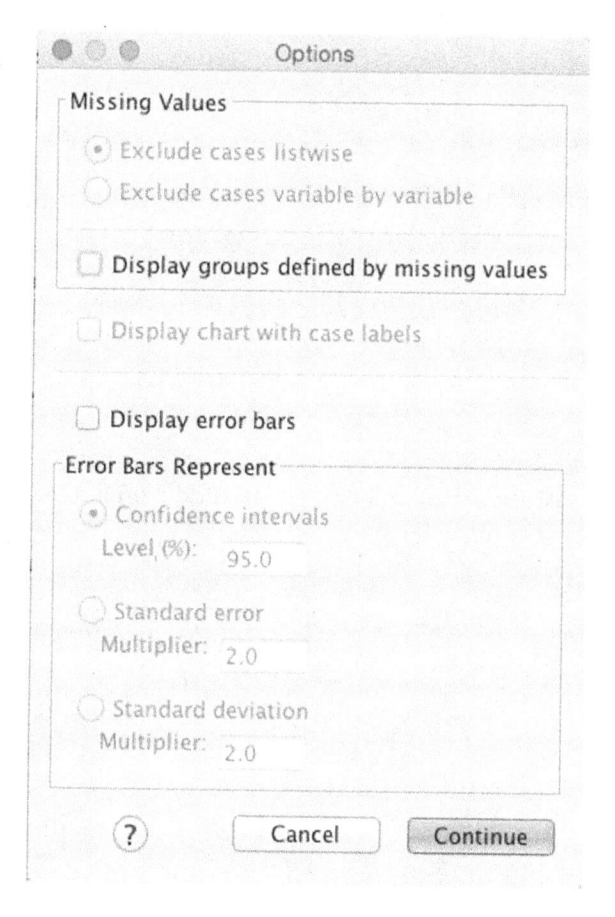

You should now be back in the Define Simple Bar dialog box. Before we tell SPSS Statistics to produce the chart, we want to draw your attention to one option you may find useful. The **Titles** button, located in the upper right-hand corner, opens a dialog box that allows you to specify titles, subtitles, and/or footnotes to define your chart further. While we are not going to do that now, you may want to keep this option in mind, particularly if you are planning to prepare charts for a presentation or inclusion in a paper, report, or publication.

Now that you are ready to instruct SPSS Statistics to produce the chart, click **OK**. It may take SPSS Statistics a few seconds to construct the bar graph to your specifications, depending on the speed of your computer, but in a short time, your chart will appear in the SPSS Statistics Viewer.

If you take a moment now to compare your bar chart with the frequency table you ran for POLVIEWS, it should become clear why graphic presentations are sometimes preferred to tables and why they can be more powerful. Viewing the data in graphic form makes it easy to see that most people are "middle-of-the road" and very few people are extreme in their political views.

Graphic presentations are useful because they often do a better job of communicating the relative sizes of the different groups than does a table of numbers. Chances are, for instance, that after analyzing this chart, you will have a more vivid memory of the distribution of political views in the United States.

Moreover, it should also be clear that bar charts are essentially just the graphic or visual equivalent of a frequency distribution—equivalent in the sense that they convey essentially the same information in a different format. Each category of the variable is represented by a bar whose height is proportional to the percentage of the category.

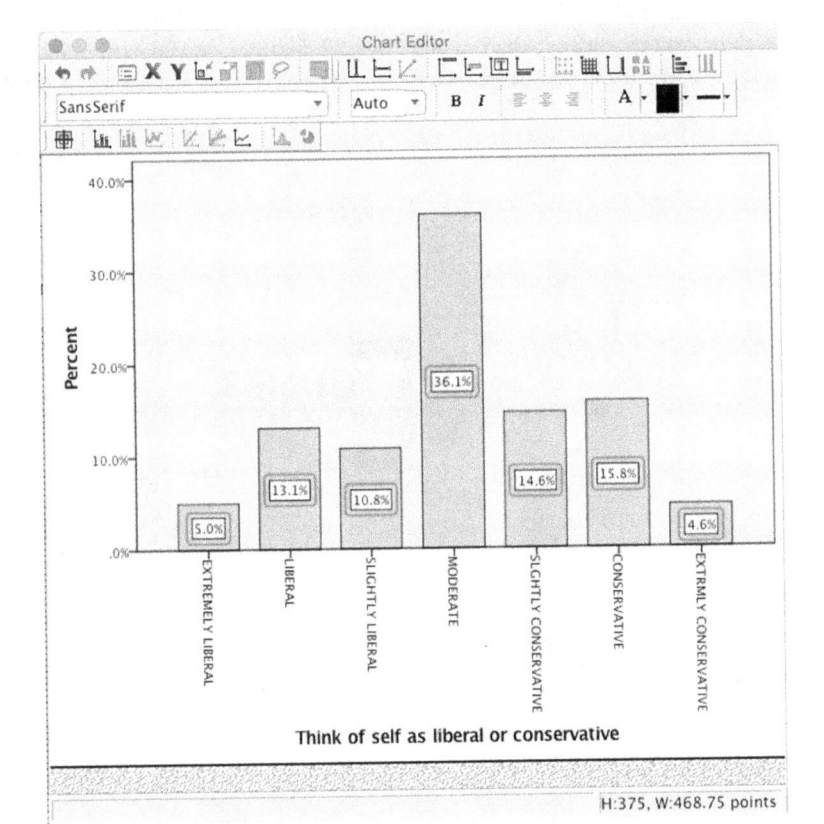

---

### SPSS Statistics Command 6.1: Simple Bar Chart

Click **Graphs** → **Legacy Dialogs** → **Bar** → **Simple** → **Define**

Highlight the variable name → Click arrow pointing to the "Category Axis:" box → Select option for vertical (y) axis in "Bars Represent" box

Click **Options** → Make sure there is NOT a check mark next to the "Display groups defined by missing values" option

Click **Continue** → **OK**

---

# DEMONSTRATION 6.2: SPSS STATISTICS CHART EDITOR

After studying your chart, you may decide you would like to change the appearance (i.e., color, style, etc.) of this graphic. The good news is that SPSS Statistics allows you to do this quite easily in the Chart Editor. To start the Chart Editor, place your cursor on your bar chart and double-click. You should now see the Chart Editor, which provides you with a variety of options.

The Chart Editor can be very useful, particularly if you are planning to present, publish, or otherwise share your analysis. While we can't cover nearly all of the possibilities available, we will introduce you to a few fun and useful options. Remember, once you are familiar with how to access the Chart Editor, you can experiment on your own.

Once the Chart Editor is open, you can change the color of your chart. Single-click on any bar in the chart to select all of the bars. Then, select the **Show Properties** window on the Chart Editor toolbar (the third from the left). Alternatively, you can also click on **Edit → Properties**.

Once the Properties dialog box opens, click on the **Fill & Border** tab. To change either the color or borders of the bars, select **Fill** OR **Border** → the color of your choice → **Apply**. You can see that this dialog box also allows you to edit your chart in other ways. If, for instance, you want to insert a pattern, you can click on the down arrow next to **Pattern** → select the pattern of your choice → **Apply**.

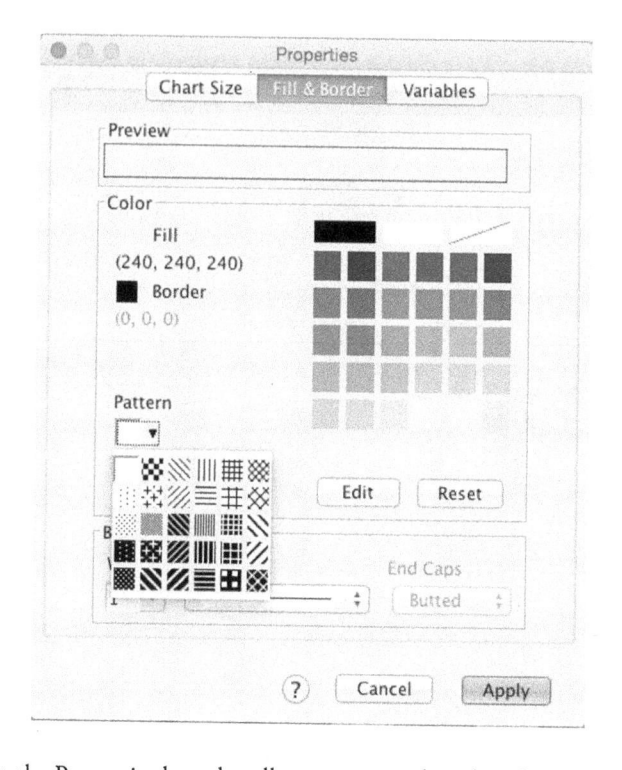

You can see that the Properties box also allows you to make other changes to your chart. If you want to change the style of your bar, for instance, you can click on the tab labeled **Depth and Angle**. On the upper left side, you will see that you have the option of choosing either "Flat," "Shadow," or "3-D Effect." Go ahead and select **3-D Effect**, then click **Apply**, and you will see how it changes the appearance of your chart.

The Properties box enables you to edit your chart in other ways as well. Take a few minutes to examine each of the tabs at the top (click the left or right arrows to move back and forth between all of the tabs), and then, once you are done, click **Close** or **X**. The Chart Editor has many other useful aspects yet to explore. The last option we will mention for now also happens to be one of the most useful. You can add percentages to each bar on your chart by clicking on the **Show Data Labels** icon (the one that looks like a bar chart, second from the left, in the row immediately above the chart). Alternatively, you can select **Elements → Show Data Labels**. As you can see, both methods display the percentages for each bar.

The Data Value Labels tab of the Properties dialog box allows you to customize this display. Take a few moments to experiment with some of those options, such as customizing the label position. When you are done, click on **Close** or the **X**. Remember, if at a later date you want to remove the percentages, choose **Elements → Hide Data Labels** or click on the **Hide Data Labels** icon (second from the left, immediately above the chart).

These are only a few of the Chart Editor's capabilities. You should experiment with the Chart Editor features on your own. Remember, once you are done, you can exit the Chart Editor by selecting **X** or **File → Close** from the drop-down menu.

Familiarity with the Chart Editor makes it easy to modify SPSS's charts for use in black-and-white publications, color overhead transparencies, and computer presentations. We will try to do our part by mentioning some other options as we go along. In addition, in the last step of Lab Exercise 7.1, you will be given an opportunity to work with an aspect of the SPSS Tutorial that focuses on creating and editing charts.

---

### SPSS Statistics Command 6.2:
### SPSS Statistics Chart Editor

Double-click on chart

Click on appropriate icon in SPSS Chart Editor to make necessary changes

---

Before we turn to another basic chart useful for nominal and ordinal variables, let's take a few minutes to practice creating a simple bar chart. We will use the POLVIEWS variable again, but this time, construct your chart so the bars represent the number of cases, as opposed to the percentage of cases. (Hint: Select **N of cases** in the "Bars Represent" area.) By following the instructions listed in SPSS Statistics Command 6.1, you should get the following chart.

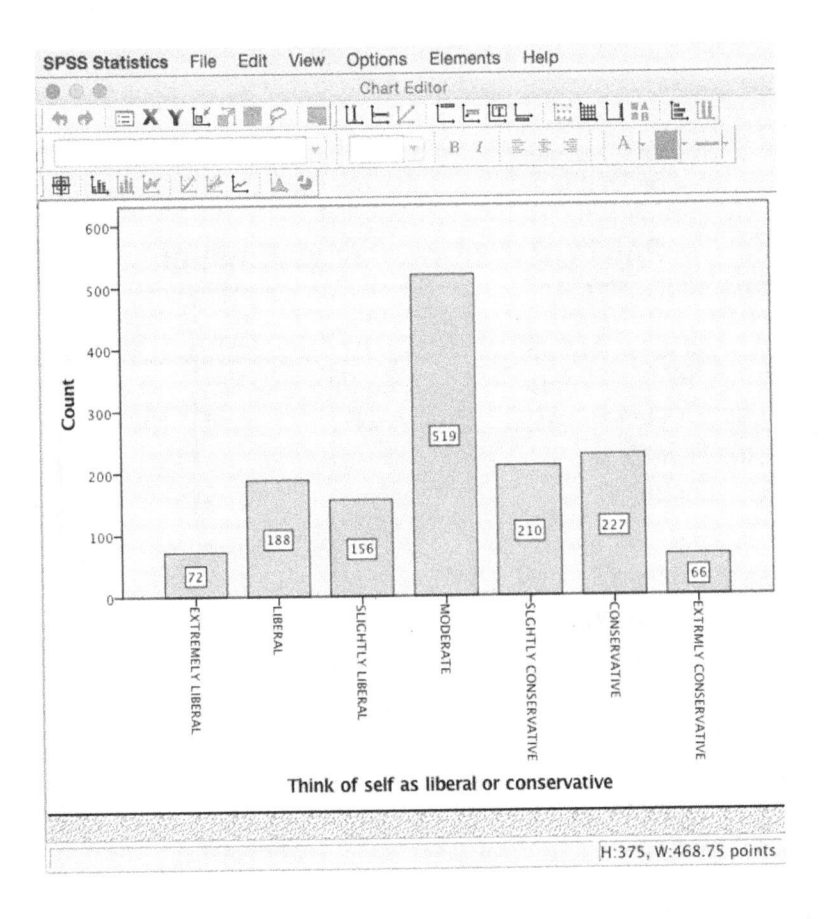

## DEMONSTRATION 6.3:
## FREQUENCY TABLE—PARTYID

Another basic indicator of a person's political orientation is found in the party with which she or he tends to identify. Let's turn now to the variable PARTYID, referring to political party identification.

Before we get the Frequencies for this variable, make sure to define the values 8 and 9 as "missing." Once you have done that, go ahead and run Frequencies for PARTYID.

You should get the following results:

## PARTYID Political Party Affiliation

| | | Frequency | Percent | Valid Percent | Cumulative Percent |
|---|---|---|---|---|---|
| Valid | 0 STRONG DEMOCRAT | 239 | 15.9 | 16.2 | 16.2 |
| | 1 NOT STR DEMOCRAT | 247 | 16.5 | 16.7 | 32.9 |
| | 2 IND,NEAR DEM | 210 | 14.0 | 14.2 | 47.1 |
| | 3 INDEPENDENT | 250 | 16.7 | 16.9 | 64.0 |
| | 4 IND,NEAR REP | 147 | 9.8 | 9.9 | 74.0 |
| | 5 NOT STR REPUBLICAN | 199 | 13.3 | 13.5 | 87.4 |
| | 6 STRONG REPUBLICAN | 152 | 10.1 | 10.3 | 97.7 |
| | 7 OTHER PARTY | 34 | 2.3 | 2.3 | 100.0 |
| | Total | 1478 | 98.5 | 100.0 | |
| Missing | 9 NA | 22 | 1.5 | | |
| Total | | 1500 | 100.0 | | |

## Pie Chart: PARTYID

Pie charts are another common way of presenting nominal and ordinal data graphically. Like bar charts, *pie charts* depict graphically the same type of information found in a frequency table—the differences in frequencies or percentages among categories of a nominal or ordinal variable. However, in this case, the information is not displayed on the x- and y-axes but as segments of a circle or, as the name suggests, slices of a pie. The segments add up to 100%.

To create a pie chart, simply select **Graphs**, **Legacy Dialogs**, and then **Pie** from the drop-down menu. Once the Pie Charts dialog box opens, you will see that by default, SPSS Statistics has selected the option that is appropriate for our purposes: "Summaries for groups of cases." To accept this and open the Define Pie dialog box, click **Define**.

The Define Pie dialog box may look somewhat familiar to you because it's similar to the Define Simple Bar dialog box we used previously. In this case, the main difference is that after highlighting the variable **PARTYID** on the left, you need to click on the arrow pointing to the "Define Slices by:" box.

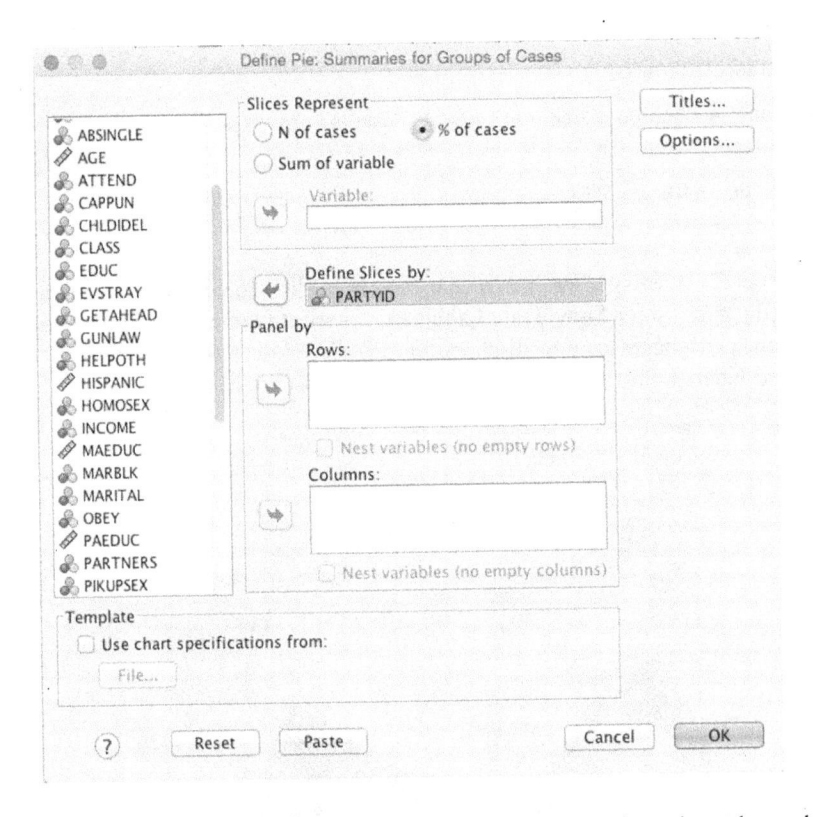

The rest of the steps are probably so familiar that you will not need much guidance, but just in case, follow the subsequent steps.

In the "Slices Represent" area at the top, select **% of cases**. Choose **Options** at the top right, and turn off the "Display groups defined by missing values" option by clicking in the box to the left and removing the check mark. Click **Continue** to return to the Define Pie box. Notice that similar to the Define Bar box, you can use the **Titles** option to insert titles, subtitles, and/or text. When you are ready to run your pie chart, click **OK.**

You will see that SPSS Statistics does not, by default, display the percentages for each slice. Nevertheless, it appears that the largest slices are "Strong Democrat," "Not Strong Democrat," "Independent," and "Not Strong Republican."

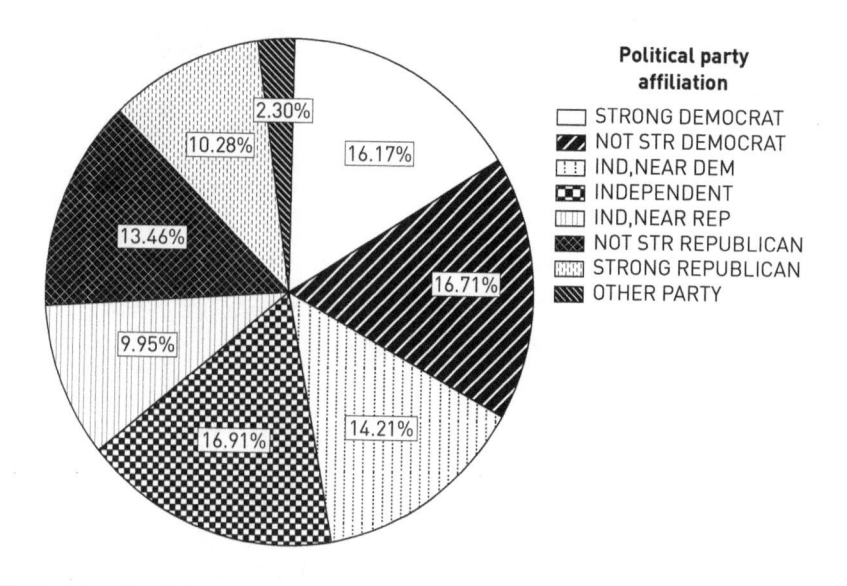

---

## SPSS Statistics Command 6.3: Pie Chart

Click **Graphs** → **Legacy Dialogs** → **Pie** → **Define**

Highlight variable name → Click arrow pointing to "Define Slices by:" → Select desired option in "Slices Represent" area

Click **Options** → Click on check mark next to "Display groups defined by missing values" to remove it

Click **Continue** → **OK**

---

We can request percentages for each slice by accessing the SPSS Statistics Chart Editor. To do that, once again, click on the **Show Data Labels** icon or select **Elements** → **Show Data Labels**. As you can see, the percentages are now displayed in each slice of the pie chart.

To close the Chart Editor, select **File** and then **Close** OR click **X**.

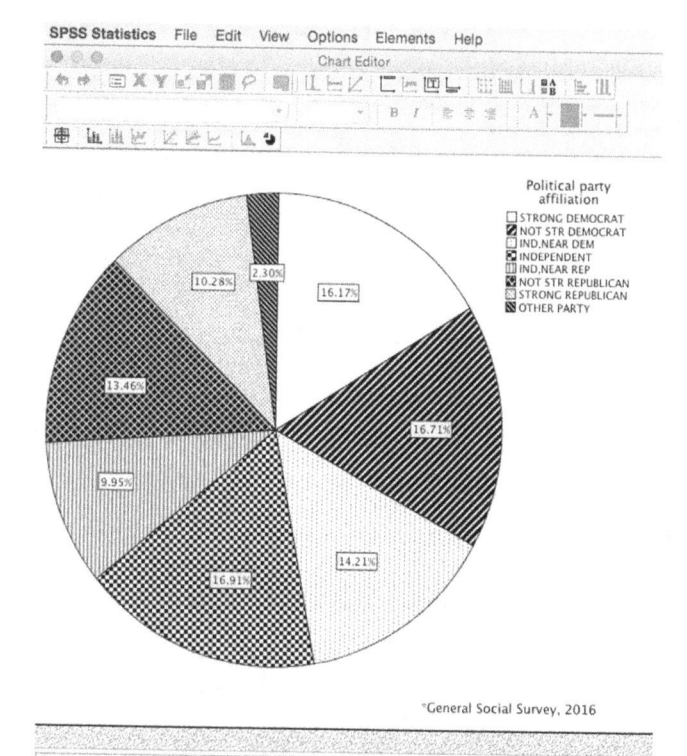

---

**SPSS Statistics Command 6.4:
Accessing Pie Options (SPSS Statistics Chart Editor)**

Double-click on pie chart in SPSS Statistics Viewer

**Select Data Labels** icon OR **Elements** → **Show Data Labels**

---

Remember that in addition to adding (or deleting) percentages and values for your pie chart, you can also change the color and text, "explode" a slice for emphasis, and so on. The ability to vary fill patterns, for example, is especially useful when preparing charts for reproduction in black and white. To experiment with this, access the SPSS Statistics Chart Editor once again.

Open the Properties dialog box by selecting the **Show Properties Window** icon or **Edit →
Properties**. Now select the **Fill & Border** tab. This tab should look familiar because we used it to change the color of the bar chart. You can also use this option to edit the colors of a pie chart or use the "Pattern" option to experiment with fill patterns. Once you are done experimenting, close the Chart Editor.

Before we work with other variables, let's take a few minutes to practice creating a pie chart. We will use the PARTYID variable again, but this time, construct your chart so the slices represent the number of cases, as opposed to the percentage of cases. (Hint: Select **N of cases** in the "Slices Represent" box.) By following the instructions listed in SPSS Statistics Command 6.3, you should get the following chart.

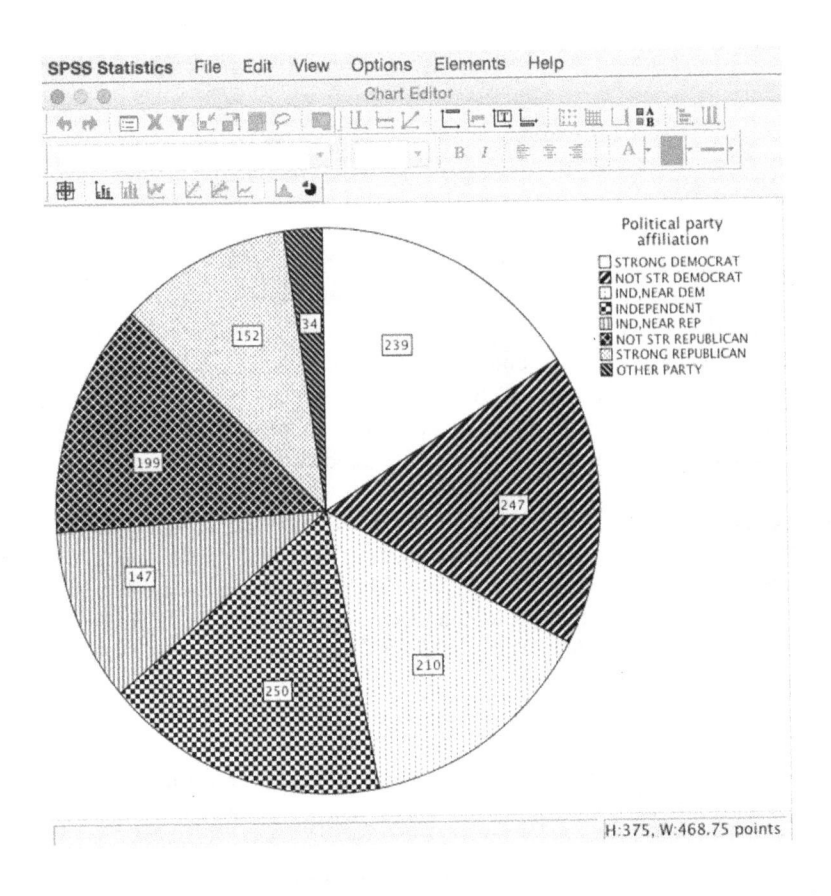

Note that you can also change the type of labels directly in the SPSS Statistics Chart Editor. In the Properties window, as seen below, click the **Data Value Labels** tab, and options will be presented for what kinds of labels are "Displayed" and "Not Displayed." You can move a label type (e.g., Percent) from the "Displayed" box to the "Not Displayed" box to remove it from the graph or vice versa.

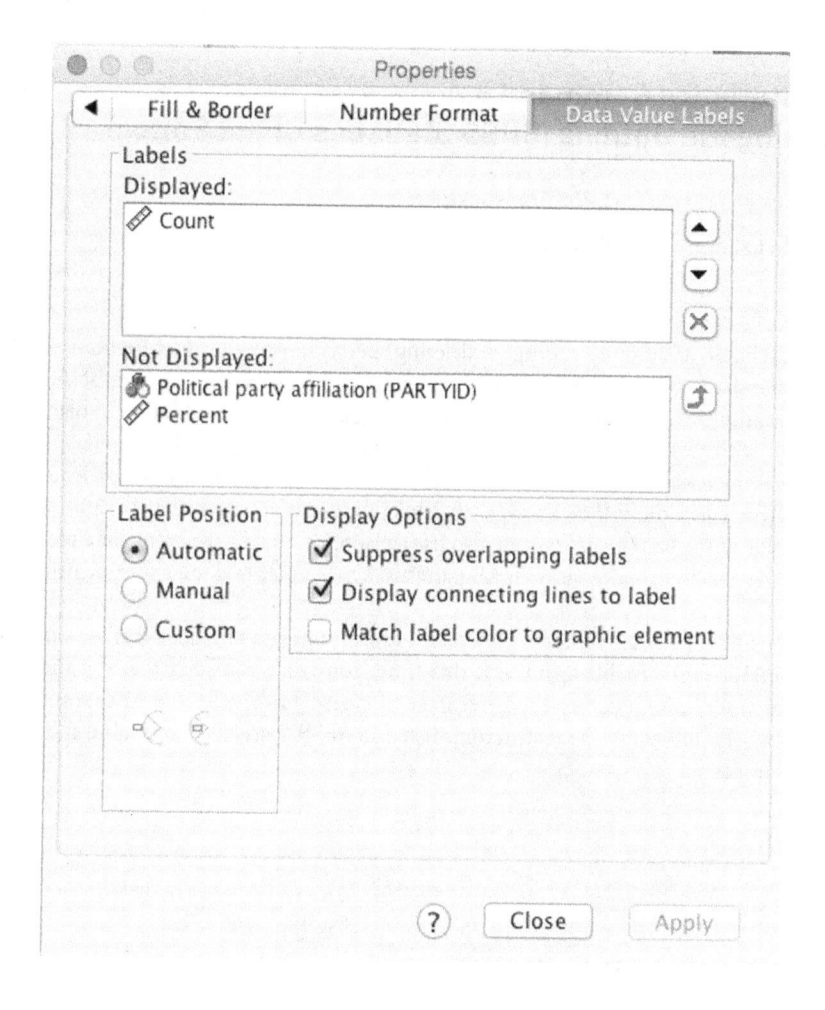

# DEMONSTRATION 6.4: POLITICAL ATTITUDES

The GSS data set contains other variables that tap into people's political orientations. For instance, GUNLAW measures how people feel about the registration of firearms. This has been a controversial issue in the United States for a number of years, involving, on one hand, Second Amendment guarantees of the right to bear arms and, on the other hand, high rates of violent crime, often involving firearms. In addition, CAPPUN measures whether respondents favor or oppose capital punishment, another topic associated with political attitudes.

As you can see, there is no lack of ways to explore people's political outlooks in the data set. We're going to focus on some of these items in later sections of the book, but you should take some time now to explore some of them on your own. Take capital punishment, for example. How do you think the American people feel about this issue? Do you think most are in favor of it or most are opposed? This is your chance to find out for yourself. If you have any interest in political matters, you should enjoy this exercise.

You may have your own personal opinion about premarital sex or homosexuality or whether it's OK to watch an X-rated movie, but do you have any idea how the general population feels about such things? How about the death penalty and permits to purchase firearms? Or how many people do you think have viewed an X-rated movie in the last year? Take a moment to think about how the general public feels about these issues.

Be sure to set appropriate values for each variable as "missing" before you proceed. We defined 0, 8, and 9 as "missing" for all five of these variables: HOMOSEX, PREMARSX, XMOVIE, CAPPUN, and GUNLAW.

You can check to see if you were correct by running charts and graphs for each variable. Once you have done that, compare your findings with those in Writing Box 6.1.

# WRITING BOX 6.1

Here's where the sample stood on a number of controversial issues. There is overwhelming support (71%) for requiring people to obtain police permits in order to buy a gun. About three-fifths (61%) support the death penalty for persons convicted of murder.

Three questions had to do with sexual matters, and levels of support differed widely among the three items. Asked whether premarital sex was always wrong, almost always wrong, sometimes wrong, or not wrong at all, 60% chose the last of these, saying it is always alright. Interestingly, 21%—the next most popular response—said it was always wrong, pointing to a polarization of opinions on this topic.

The same question was asked with regard to homosexuality: "sexual relations between two adults of the same sex." Again, opinions were polarized. About 39% said it was always wrong, while about 52% said it was not wrong at all. Note that this is in contrast to prior General Social Surveys. In 2012, for example, 46% disapproved, while 45% believed it was not wrong at all. The GSS can also help us to examine a changing social environment over time.

Finally, respondents were asked whether they had seen an X-rated movie during the past year. More than one quarter (27%) said they had.

## DEMONSTRATION 6.5: HISTOGRAM—AGE

In the next few sections, we will examine two other types of graphs appropriate for interval/ratio variables: histograms and line charts.

Like bar charts, **histograms** have two axes, the vertical ($y$) axis and the horizontal ($x$) axis. The categories of the variable are displayed along the horizontal axis, while frequencies or percentages are displayed along the vertical axis. Unlike bar charts, the categories of a histogram are displayed as contiguous bars (bars that touch each other). Both the height and width of each bar are proportional to the frequency or percentage of cases in each category. On a histogram, the sum of the areas covered by all of the contiguous bars is 1, or 100%, if proportions or percentages are graphed. If frequencies are graphed, the sum of the areas is the number of cases.

Here's how SPSS Statistics can be instructed to produce a histogram for an interval/ratio variable. Because the political items we have been focusing on in this chapter are nominal and/or ordinal, we need to turn our attention to another issue. For now, let's focus on AGE (respondents' ages at the time of the interview), a measure that you may suspect is at least peripherally related to political orientation and party identification.

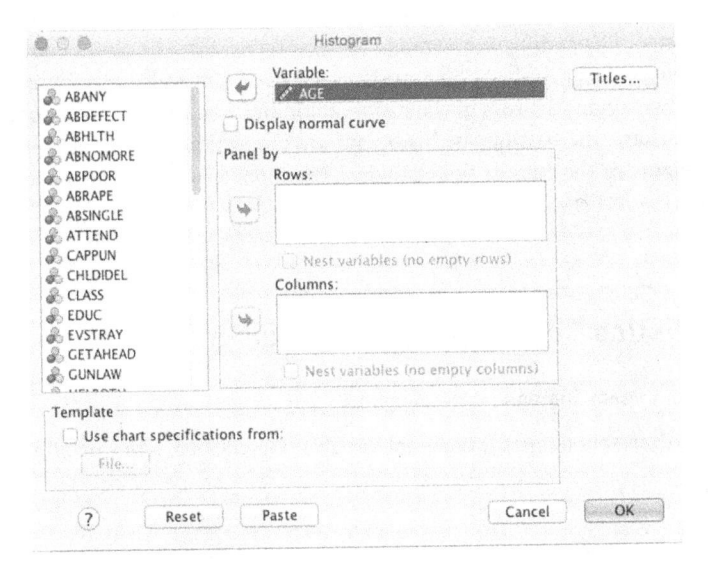

Before we instruct SPSS Statistics to create a histogram, make sure the values 98 and 99 are defined as "missing" for the variable AGE. Now select **Graphs**, **Legacy Dialogs**, and then **Histogram** from the drop-down menu. Highlight the variable **AGE** and then either double-click or click the arrow pointing toward the "Variable:" field. For this chart, we don't have to worry about missing values because SPSS Statistics automatically removes them from display.

You will notice that, once again, you have the option of adding titles, subtitles, and/or footnotes (by clicking the **Titles** button) or displaying a line graph of the normal distribution across your histogram. But we won't do those things now; instead, we will go ahead and run the histogram by clicking **OK**.

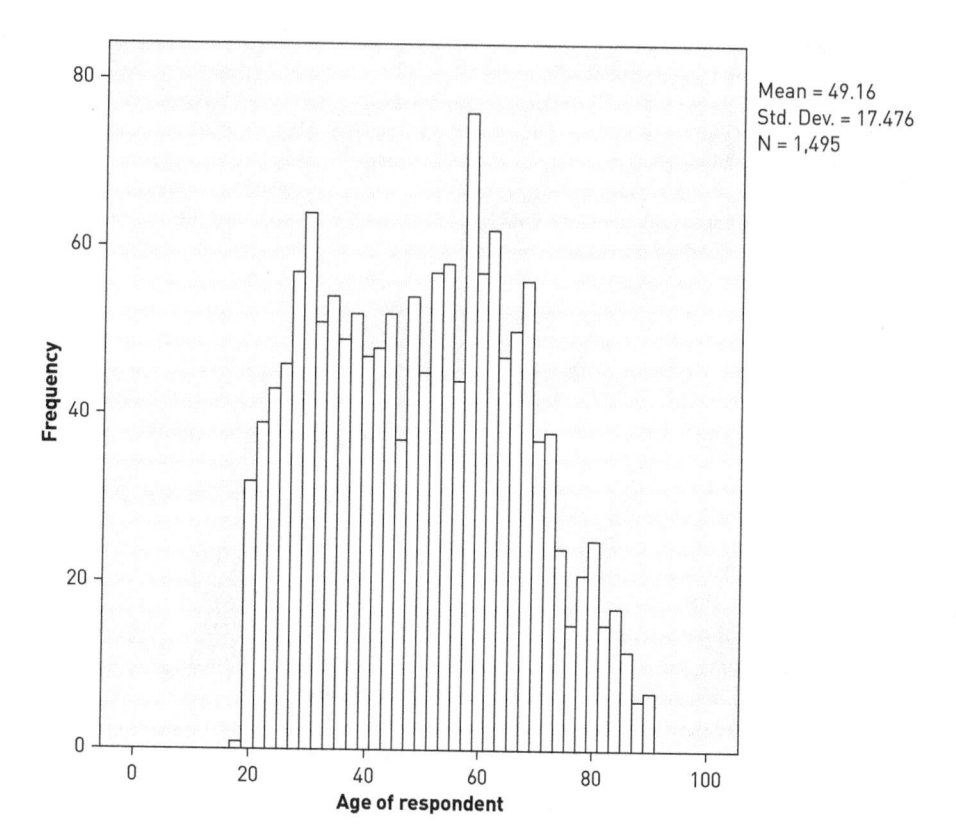

As with bar charts, the horizontal (*x*) axis shows categories of AGE that SPSS Statistics has automatically created. Depending on the range of the variable, SPSS Statistics computes an interval width for each category. For AGE, SPSS Statistics created 37 intervals, each with a width of about 2 years. The numbers under the bars of the histogram indicate the ages of the respondents. As with the bars on a bar chart, the bars on the histogram are proportional to the number of cases in the intervals. The heights of the bars in the histogram correspond to the frequency of respondents in that age category.

---

### SPSS Statistics Command 6.5: Histogram

Click **Graphs** → **Legacy Dialogs** → **Histogram**

Double-click on variable name OR highlight variable and click on arrow pointing toward variable field

Click **OK**

---

The Chart Editor can be used to customize your histogram. Take a few moments to experiment with this option and see if you can improve on the way SPSS Statistics made your chart.

# DEMONSTRATION 6.6: LINE CHART—INCOME

Total family income (INCOME) is another interval/ratio variable somewhat related to political orientations and party identification. While it is possible to represent this distribution using a histogram, we are going to consider another type of graph you are probably already familiar with, a ***line chart*** (sometimes also called a *frequency polygon*).

A line chart is similar to a histogram and bar chart in that the categories for the variable are displayed on the horizontal (*x*) axis, and the frequency or percentage is situated on the vertical (*y*) axis. Unlike the bar chart or histogram, however, the line chart has a single line running from the far left to the far right of the graph that connects points representing the frequency or percentage of cases for each category of the variable.

Line charts are particularly useful in showing the overall shape or distribution of variables with a large number of values or categories. Consequently, while bar and pie charts are generally used to display discrete variables, histograms and line charts are most often used to display the distribution of continuous, interval/ratio variables.

Before we produce our line chart, make sure the values 13, 98, and 99 for INCOME are defined as "missing." To begin, click **Graphs → Legacy Dialogs** once again. This time, however, select **Line**, and the Line Charts dialog box will open, as shown below.

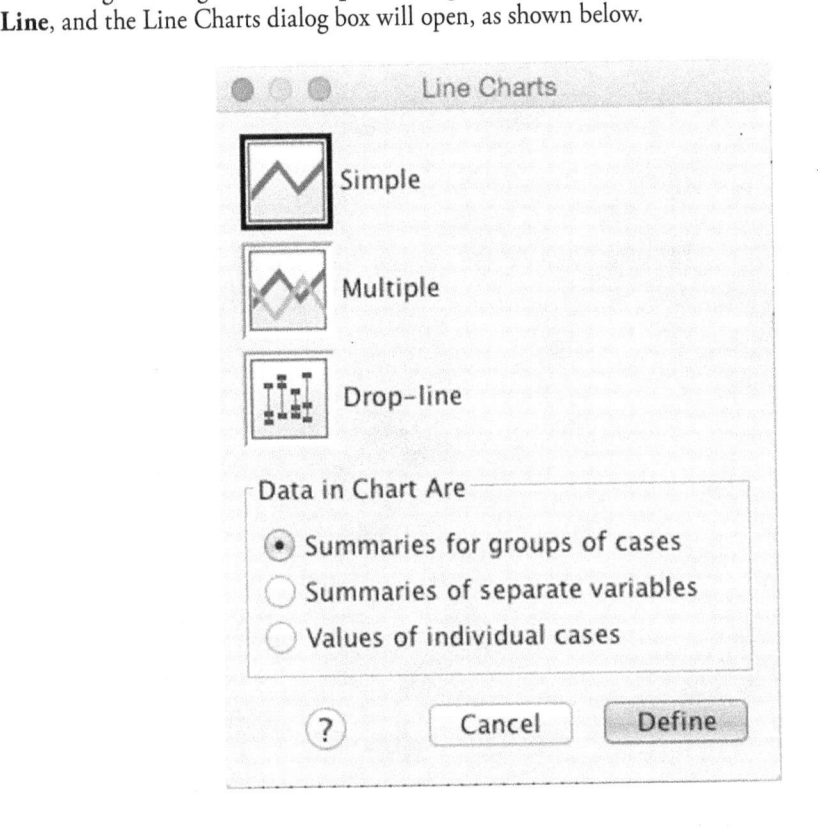

You see three types of graphs listed: simple, multiple, and drop-line. Because we are charting only one variable, we want to choose **Simple**, which is probably already highlighted, but you can click on it once again just to be sure. Now click the **Define** button, and the Define Simple Line dialog box will open (see figure at the top of the next page).

On the left side of the box, you can see the list of variables. Scroll down the list until you find **INCOME**, and highlight it. Now click on the arrow next to the "Category Axis:" box to transfer the variable name. This time, under "Line Represents," choose **N of cases** as opposed to **% of cases**. (It may already be selected.) Then, click the **Options** button to make sure there is no check mark next to the "Display groups defined by missing values" option. After you have done that, click **Continue**, and you will be back in the Define Simple Line dialog box. As in the previous chart dialog boxes, the **Titles** option can be used to add titles, subtitles, and/or footnotes to the chart. You can explore that option now or just click on **OK** if you are ready to produce your line chart. Once you do that, you should see the line chart on the next page displayed in your Viewer.

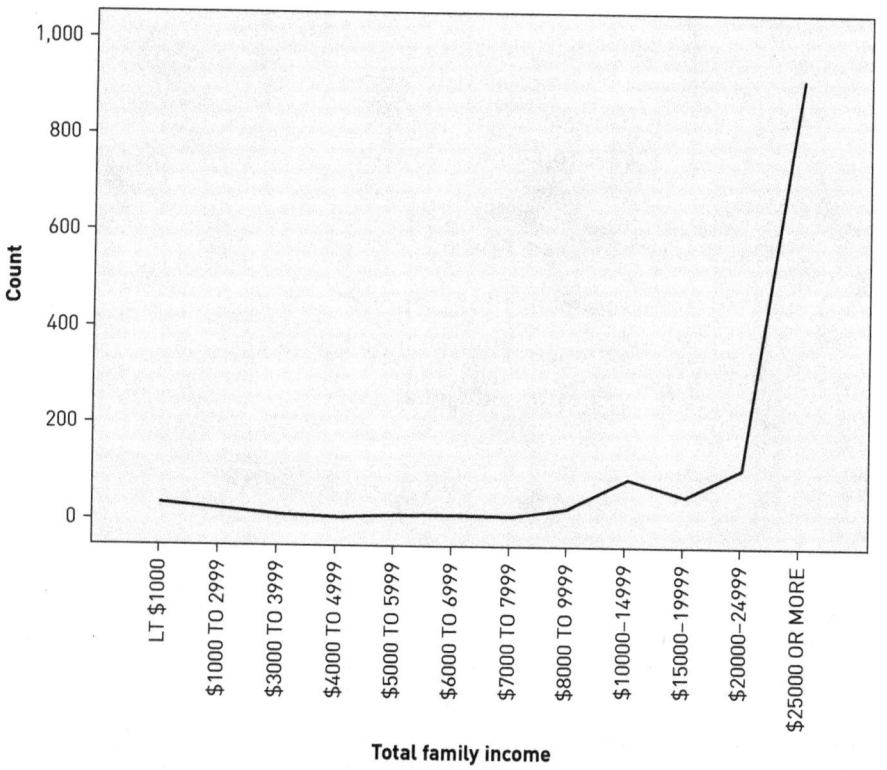

Take some time to review your line chart. You can see how respondents' reported annual income ranged from those who received less than $1,000 to those who received more than $25,000 in 2016. You may want to take note of the shape of the distribution and whether the sample is concentrated in a specific area or fairly evenly spread out. (Hint: Part of the explanation lies in the distribution of income in the United States. The other part lies in the coding of this variable: The last category includes all respondents making $25,000 or more per year.)

---

## SPSS Statistics Command 6.6: Simple Line Chart

Click **Graphs** → **Legacy Dialogs** → **Line** → **Simple** → **Define**

Highlight the variable name → Click arrow pointing toward the "Category Axis:" box

Click **Options** → Click on the box next to the "Display groups defined by missing values" option to make sure it is NOT checked

Click **Continue** → **OK**

---

As before, you can use the Chart Editor to change the appearance of your line graph. You can, for instance, change the style or color of your new chart, as well as experiment with several other options available through the Chart Editor.

## Some Guidelines for Choosing a Chart or Graph

In this chapter, we have focused on four common and useful charts. The following tables present a summary of the discussion regarding which charts are appropriate for variables of different types (Table 6.1) and at different levels of measurement (Table 6.2). Bear in mind that you can also use SPSS Statistics to produce a number of additional types of charts and graphs. To get a sense of the options available, click **Graphs** on the toolbar. You can see that, in addition to the four options discussed in this chapter, you have the opportunity to work with many other types of charts.

**TABLE 6.1 ■ Charts Appropriate for Variables of Different Types**

|  | Type of Variable | |
|---|---|---|
|  | Discrete | Continuous |
| Bar chart | X | — |
| Pie chart | X | — |
| Histogram | — | X |
| Line chart | — | X |

**TABLE 6.2 ■ Charts Appropriate for Variables at Different Levels of Measurement**

|  | Level of Measurement | | |
|---|---|---|---|
|  | Nominal | Ordinal | Interval/Ratio |
| Bar chart | X | X | — |
| Pie chart | X | X | — |
| Histogram | — | — | X |
| Line chart | — | — | X |

While it is fairly easy to learn how to produce charts on SPSS Statistics or any other statistical package, it is more difficult to learn which types of graphs are appropriate for variables of different types and at different levels of measurement. Remember, at your command, SPSS Statistics will produce any chart or graph you request, regardless of whether it is meaningful or appropriate.

## SAVING AND PRINTING YOUR CHARTS

That's enough work for now. If you are interested in saving or printing any of your charts or if you want to save the changes we made to the DEMO.SAV (or DEMOPLUS.SAV) file (e.g., defining certain values as missing), you can do so by following the commands for saving and printing output discussed at the end of the previous chapter.

## CONCLUSION

Politics is a favorite topic for many Americans, often marked by the expression of unsubstantiated opinions. Now, you can begin examining the facts of political views. In later chapters, we'll move beyond describing political orientations and start examining why people have the political views they have.

## Main Points

- In this chapter, we focused on two key political items: POLVIEWS and PARTYID.

- POLVIEWS taps into basic political philosophy, whereas PARTYID measures political party affiliation.

- A graph or chart can sometimes communicate the relative sizes of different groups or the shape of the distribution of a variable more powerfully than can a table of numbers.

- You can use SPSS Statistics to produce two charts appropriate for discrete, nominal, or ordinal variables: simple bar charts and pie charts.

- Bar and pie charts are the graphic equivalent of frequency tables, best used for variables with a limited number of categories.

- You can also use SPSS Statistics to produce two charts appropriate for continuous, interval/ratio variables: histograms and line charts.

- Line charts and histograms are most useful for variables with numerous response categories.

## Key Terms

Bar chart 79
Histogram 89

Horizontal (x) axis 80
Line chart 91

Pie chart 84
Vertical (y) axis 80

## SPSS Statistics Commands Introduced in This Chapter

6.1.   Simple Bar Chart

6.2.   SPSS Statistics Chart Editor

6.3.   Pie Chart

6.4.   Accessing Pie Options (SPSS Statistics Chart Editor)

6.5.   Histogram

6.6.   Simple Line Chart

## Review Questions

1. What does the variable POLVIEWS measure?

2. What does the variable PARTYID measure?

3. If you wanted to produce a chart for a discrete variable, which type of chart would be your best option: bar chart, line chart, or histogram?

4. If you wanted to produce a chart for a variable with many categories or values, which type of chart would be your best option: bar chart, pie chart, or line graph?

5. Why are graphic presentations of data useful?

6. Name one reason why you might make a pie chart, as opposed to a line chart, for the variable PARTYID.

7. Name two measures of political attitudes (other than POLVIEWS and PARTYID) contained on DEMO.SAV.

8. List the types of chart(s) or graph(s) generally recommended for variables at the following levels of measurement:

   a. Nominal

   b. Ordinal

   c. Interval/ratio

9. List the types of chart(s) or graph(s) generally recommended for variables of the following types:

   a. Discrete

   b. Continuous

10. A researcher creates a problematic, overcategorized bar chart for the variable AGE (measured in years). Which of the following would *not* be a solution to this problem?

    a. Combine categories of the variable AGE (recode) and produce a bar chart for the recoded variable.

    b. Produce a pie chart for the variable AGE.

    c. Produce a line chart for the variable AGE.

## SPSS Statistics Lab Exercise 6.1

NAME: _____

CLASS: _____

INSTRUCTOR: _____

DATE: _____

*To complete the following exercises, access the EXER.SAV file.*

1.  (NEWS) 0, 8, and 9 should be defined as "missing."

    a. What does the variable NEWS measure (hint: variable label)?

    b. What is the variable's level of measurement? _____

    c. List one type of chart appropriate for this variable: _____

    d. Produce the chart listed in response to Question 1(c) above, and then, based on your output, fill in the blanks below.

    About _____% of respondents read the newspaper once a week or more, whereas about _____% read the newspaper less than once a week. Only _____% of the sample said they never read the newspaper.

2.  (TVHOURS) –1, 98, and 99 should be defined as "missing."

    a. What does the variable TVHOURS measure?

    b. Would you describe the variable as discrete or continuous? _____

    c. List two charts appropriate for this variable: _____ and _____

    d. Produce one of the charts listed in response to Question 2(c) above that will allow you to answer the question that follows. (Hint: When you run a histogram, SPSS Statistics automatically calculates two statistics that are useful for answering this question—mean and standard deviation.)

    Using the standard deviation, we would expect two thirds of respondents to watch between _____ hour(s) and _____ hours of television per day.

Questions 3 and 4: After you have produced and analyzed the charts for CONPRESS and CONTV, briefly describe the distribution of values for these variables in the spaces provided. You may want to note the largest and smallest categories for the items, as well as any other interesting or pertinent information.

3.  (CONPRESS) 0, 8, and 9 should be defined as "missing."

    a. List one type of chart appropriate for this variable: _____

    b. Description of chart:

4.  (CONTV) 0, 8, and 9 should be defined as "missing."

    a. List one type of chart appropriate for this variable: _____

    b. Description of chart:

*(Continued)*

(Continued)

5.  (EDUC) 97, 98, and 99 should be defined as "missing."

    a. List one type of chart appropriate for this variable: _____

    b. Produce the chart listed in response to Question 5(a), and then, describe the distribution below:

6.  How do American adults feel about sex education in public schools? Produce and analyze a chart for the variable SEXEDUC (0, 8, and 9 should be defined as "missing"). Then, describe your findings below:

7.  Do Americans tend to think sex before marriage for teens 14 to 16 is appropriate or inappropriate? Produce and analyze a chart for the variable TEENSEX (0, 8, and 9 should be defined as "missing"); then, describe your findings below:

8.  Choose three variables in your EXER.SAV file related to personal sexual behavior. Then, list the abbreviated variable names and variable labels below:

|  | **Abbreviated Variable Name** | **Variable Label** |
|---|---|---|
| Variable 1: | _____ | _____ |
| Variable 2: | _____ | _____ |
| Variable 3: | _____ | _____ |

9.  Produce and analyze charts for the three sexual behavior variables listed in response to Question 8. Based on your findings, how would you describe the sexual behavior of Americans?

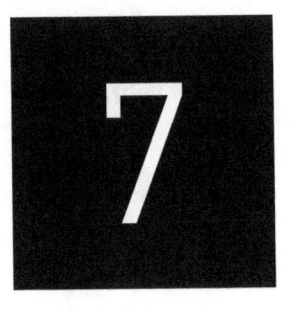

# RECODING YOUR DATA

## Religiosity and Political Orientations

At the end of our discussion of frequency distributions, we mentioned that frequency tables are not particularly useful when you are working with continuous variables or any variables with a larger number of response categories. As an alternative, we suggested you may want to use basic measures of central tendency and dispersion to describe a distribution. That's what we did with AGE in Chapter 5.

But often, instead of using statistics to describe a variable, we want to use a set of meaningful groupings that suit our research. Even when we know our respondents' exact ages, it may be more useful to group them in categories such as young, middle, and older. The groups are formed by collapsing categories of the variable and recoding them. Those of you who have worked with frequency distributions may recognize that what we are doing is similar to the creation of a grouped frequency distribution. Only, in this case, it is much easier because we have SPSS Statistics to assist in the process.

SPSS Statistics can be instructed to combine adjacent categories using the Recode command. **Recoding** is a technique that allows us to combine or group two or more categories of a variable together in order to simplify the process of analysis. When we recode, we can take a variable such as ATTEND with nine valid categories and combine them to create, say, four categories. Recoding is a useful technique to master for several reasons. In addition to helping us create easier-to-read tables and identify patterns in responses, it also enables us to group continuous data into categories so we don't present our readers with an excessively long table. If you don't believe this could be a problem, try imagining the size of a table relating our DEMO.SAV file variables EDUC and AGE!

Recoding takes several steps. While it may take a little time to get used to the process of recoding, if you follow along with the demonstrations that follow and practice them using the lab exercises, you should get the hang of it quickly. If you have trouble recalling the steps at first, don't worry: You will have plenty of opportunities to practice recoding in later chapters and exercises.

## DEMONSTRATION 7.1: MODIFYING VARIABLES WITH RECODE—ATTEND → CHATT

Throughout this chapter, we will use a number of variables from the DEMO.SAV file that you have worked with in previous chapters, beginning with ATTEND. You may recall that ATTEND measures how often the respondent attends religious services. To help refresh your memory, go ahead and run a frequency distribution for this variable. You should get a table that matches the one below.

## ATTEND How Often R Attends Religious Services

| | | Frequency | Percent | Valid Percent | Cumulative Percent |
|---|---|---|---|---|---|
| Valid | 0 NEVER | 368 | 24.5 | 24.7 | 24.7 |
| | 1 LT ONCE A YEAR | 79 | 5.3 | 5.3 | 30.0 |
| | 2 ONCE A YEAR | 217 | 14.5 | 14.6 | 44.6 |
| | 3 SEVRL TIMES A YR | 158 | 10.5 | 10.6 | 55.2 |
| | 4 ONCE A MONTH | 105 | 7.0 | 7.1 | 62.3 |
| | 5 2-3X A MONTH | 135 | 9.0 | 9.1 | 71.3 |
| | 6 NRLY EVERY WEEK | 78 | 5.2 | 5.2 | 76.6 |
| | 7 EVERY WEEK | 252 | 16.8 | 16.9 | 93.5 |
| | 8 MORE THN ONCE WK | 97 | 6.5 | 6.5 | 100.0 |
| | Total | 1489 | 99.3 | 100.0 | |
| Missing | 9 DK,NA | 11 | .7 | | |
| Total | | 1500 | 100.0 | | |

The recoding process will allow us to make this variable more manageable by combining adjacent categories. The result will be a new variable with four, as opposed to nine, response categories. When we are done, you will be able to compare the frequency for the new variable with the frequency table you just ran and see the difference firsthand.

To begin this process, select **Transform** and then choose **Recode** from the drop-down menu. SPSS Statistics now asks if you want to replace the existing values of the variables with the new, recoded ones. Select **Into Different Variables** because we are going to assign a new name to the new, recoded values.[1] SPSS Statistics now presents you with the following screen, in which you can describe the recoding you want.

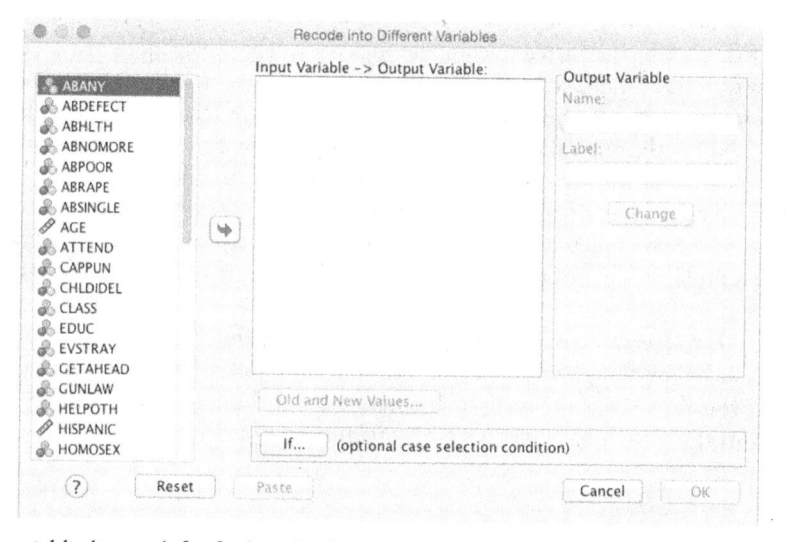

In the variable list at left, find and select **ATTEND**. To transfer ATTEND to the "Input Variable → Output Variable:" field, either double-click on **ATTEND** or click on the arrow to the right of the variable list.

Notice that you need to tell SPSS Statistics what you would like to name the new, recoded variable. You can accomplish this easily in the area of the window called "Output Variable." Let's name

---

1. Because the student version of SPSS Statistics limits the number of variables that can be used to 50, if you are using a student version, you might want to save the recode under the same name as the original variable. It's OK to do this if you save the modified data set later under a different name (e.g., DEMO01.SAV). That way, you can reopen the modified data set or you can retrieve the original data in its unrecoded form. Note that the DEMO.SAV and EXER.SAV files do not use all 50 allowed variable slots, so there is room to add a few recoded variables and save to a usable data file for both of those data files.

the recoded variable "CHATT" (for CHurch ATTendance). Type **CHATT** into the space provided for the output variable name, and then label the variable (perhaps "Recoded Church Attendance"). When you are done, click the **Change** button. As you can see in the middle field, SPSS Statistics will now modify the entry to read "ATTEND → CHATT."

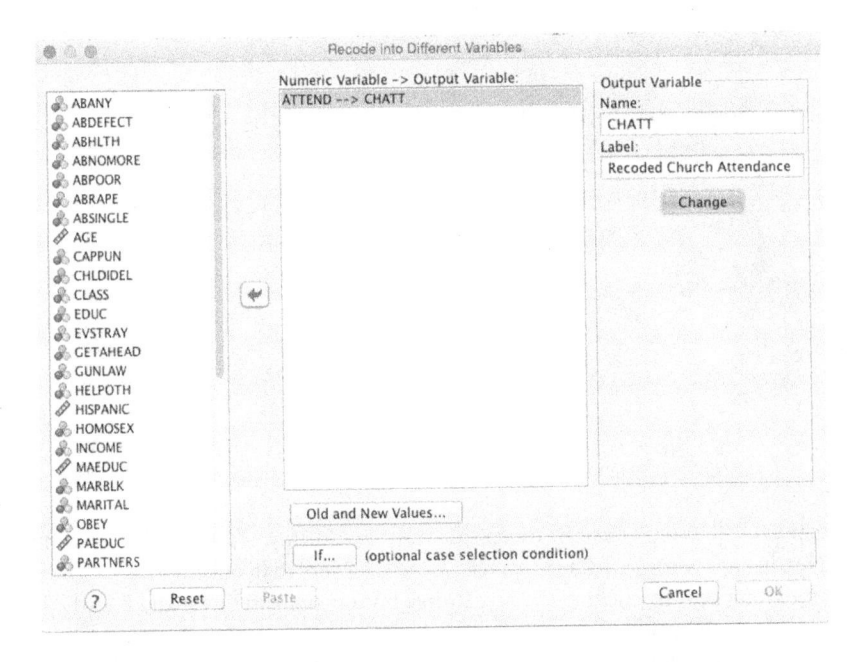

If, instead, you see "ATTEND → ?," then you still need to click the **Change** button.

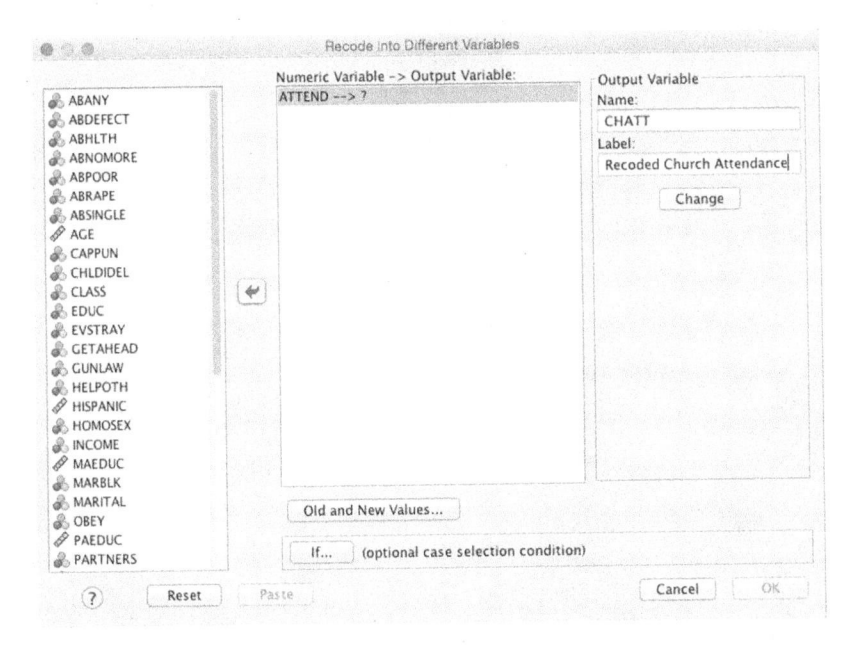

Thus far, we have created a new variable, but we haven't entered any data into it. We initiate this final step by clicking the **Old and New Values** button. Now, SPSS Statistics presents you with the window shown at the top of page 102.

The left side of this window provides us with several options for specifying the old values we want to recode. The first, which SPSS Statistics has selected as a default, lets us specify a single value on the original variable, such as 8 ("More than once a week"). A more efficient option for our present purposes is found farther down the list, letting us specify a range of values. (Remember, to find the numerical codes assigned to ATTEND, you can use one of the several options discussed in Chapter 4.)

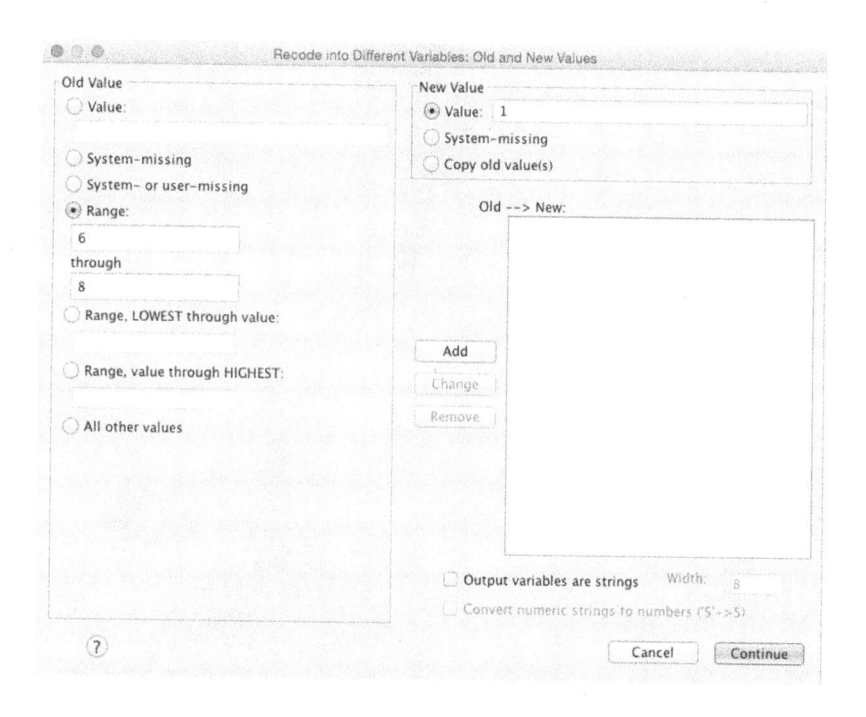

In our manual collapsing of categories on this variable earlier, you'll recall that we combined the values 6 ("Nearly every week"), 7 ("Every week"), and 8 ("More than once a week"). We can accomplish the same thing now by clicking the first **Range** button and entering 6 and 8 in the two boxes.

At the top of the right side of the window, notice that there is a space for you to enter the new value for this combination of responses. Let's recode it 1. Enter that number in the field provided, as shown below.

Once you've added the recode value, notice that the **Add** button in the middle of the dialog box, which was grayed out, is now illuminated and available for use. Click it.

This action causes the expression "6 thru 8 → 1" to appear in the field (see figure at the top of the next page). We've given SPSS Statistics one recoding instruction. Now, let's continue.

Click **Range** again, and now, let's combine values 4 ("Once a month") and 5 ("Two to three times a month"). Give this new combined category the value of 2. Click **Add** to add it to the list of recodes. Now combine categories 1 ("Less than once a year"), 2 ("Once a year"), and 3 ("Several

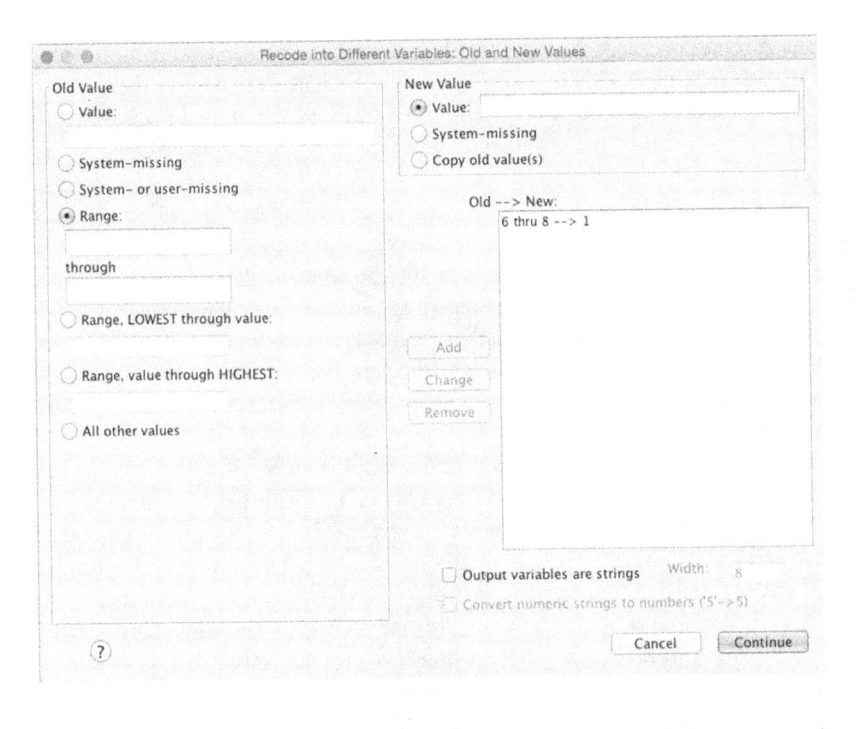

times a year"). Recode the new category as 3, and **Add** it to the list. Finally, let's recode 0 ("Never") as 4. On the left side of the window, use the **Value** button to accomplish this. Enter 0 there, and enter 4 as the new value. Click on **Add**.

To tidy up our recoding, we could have SPSS Statistics maintain the missing data values of the original variable. We would accomplish this by clicking **System- or user-missing** as an old value (on the left side) and **System-missing** as the new value (on the right side) and then clicking **Add**. Although it is good practice to consciously recode every category, in this case, it is not necessary. Any cases not covered by the range of the old values will be undefined and treated as missing values.

Your Recode window should now look like this:

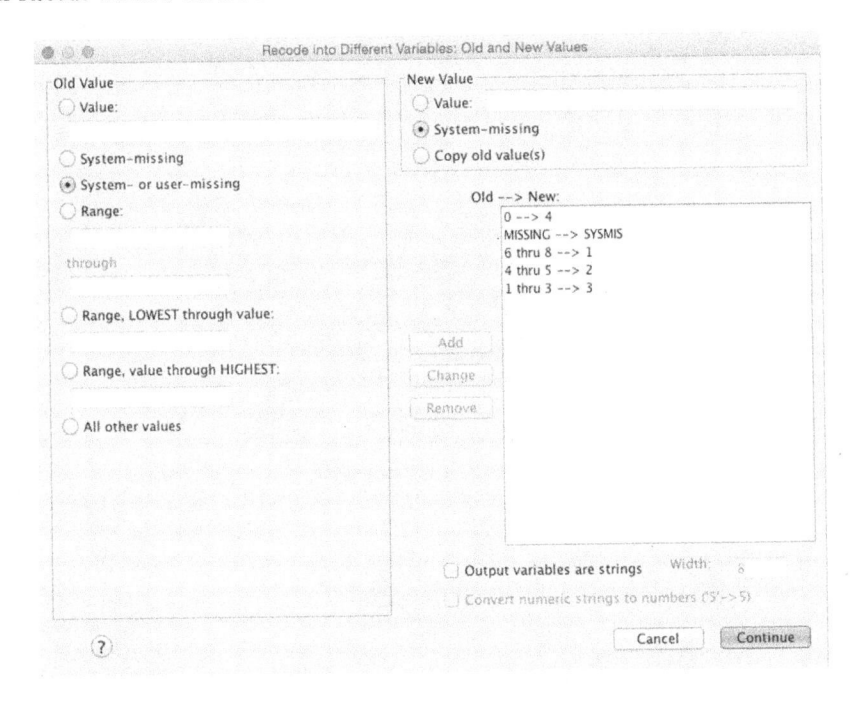

As we wrap up, we should repeat that there are no hard-and-fast rules for choosing which categories to combine in a recoding process such as this. There are, however, two rules of thumb to guide you: one logical, the other empirical.

First, there is sometimes a logical basis for choosing cutting points at which to divide the resulting categories. In recoding AGE, for example, it is often smart to make one break at 21 years (the traditional definition of adulthood) and another at 65 (the traditional age of retirement). In the case of church attendance (attendance at religious services), our first combined category observes the Christian norm of weekly church attendance.

The second guideline is based on the advantage of having sufficient numbers of cases in each of the combined categories because a very small category will hamper subsequent analyses. Ideally, each of the combined categories should have roughly the same number of cases.

How do you suppose we'd continue the recoding process? Click **Continue**, you say? Hey, you may be a natural at this. Do that. This takes you back to the Recode into Different Variables window. Now that you've completed your specification of the recoding of this variable, all that remains is to click **OK** at the bottom of the window. SPSS Statistics may take a few seconds now to accomplish the recoding you've specified.

Go to the Data View portion of the Data Editor window now. To see your new variable, scroll across the columns of the window until you discover CHATT in the last column used thus far.[2] Notice the values listed in the column. Notice that Case No. 1 (denoting Respondent 1) has a 3 recorded for CHATT. That's correct because everyone with a 1, 2, or 3 in the original variable (ATTEND) was recoded as a 3 in the new variable, CHATT. Similarly, notice that Case No. 2 has a 0 in ATTEND. That, too, is correct because everyone with a 0 in the original variable was recoded as a 4 in CHATT. You can check a few more people if you want to verify that the coding was accomplished as we instructed. This is a good idea, by the way, to ensure that you haven't made a mistake. (Presumably, SPSS Statistics doesn't make computational mistakes.)

The next step in recoding is to define your new, recoded variable CHATT. We can do this by accessing the Variable View tab. Once you are in Variable View, scroll to the bottom of your screen until you see CHATT listed in the last row, as shown below.

---

2. If you used the same variable name, look at ATTEND.

Remember that the Variable View tab stores important information about each of our variables. Since we just created the variable CHATT, we need to specify its characteristics.

Let's begin with the column labeled "Decimals." Simply point and click on the cell that corresponds to the Decimals column and the variable CHATT. Notice that up and down arrows appear on the right side of the cell. Because decimal points are of no use to us in this situation, let's get rid of them by using the down arrow to change the number of decimal places to 0. Now move to the column labeled "Width" directly to the left. To do that, click on the cell that corresponds to the Width column and the CHATT row. Because our recoded variable contains codes that range from 1 to 4, the width need only be set at 1—though leaving it set at 8 will not make any discernible difference for the analysis in this book. Again, if you wish, use the down arrow to change the width to 1.

Recall that when we began the process of recoding, we not only named our new variable CHATT but also labeled it "Recoded Church Attendance" (in the Recode into Different Variables dialog box). Consequently, you do not have to change any of the information in the Label column for the variable CHATT. However, if you want to view the entire label or if you want to change the label, simply double-click on the cell that corresponds with the Label column and the CHATT row. You will notice that the width of the cell increases so you can better view the entire label and, if you desire, modify the variable label.

The next column, labeled "Values," is important because it allows us to store labels for the values of our new variable. To do this, click on the right side of the cell that corresponds to the Variables column and the CHATT variable. The Value Labels box will appear on the screen, as shown below.

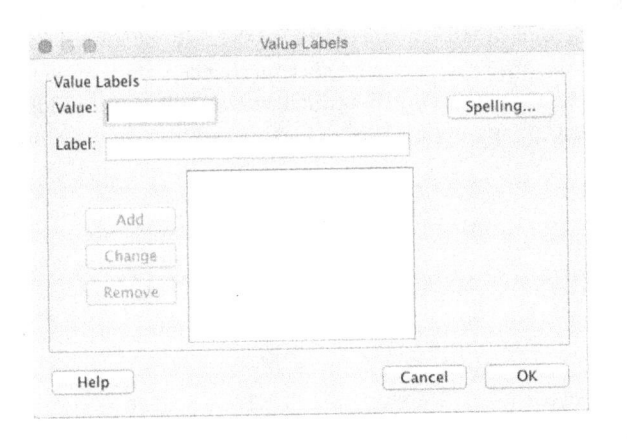

To add the values and labels for our new variable, simply type "1" in the "Value:" field. Recall that this value represents people who originally scored 6 ("Nearly every week"), 7 ("Every week"), and 8 ("More than once a week"). Let's call this new, combined category "About weekly." Type that description in the "Label:" field, and click **Add**. You can see that the information now appears in the field below, telling us that 1 = "About weekly." Now, enter the remaining value labels as indicated below. Once you have entered all of the value and label information (and your screen looks like ours below), click **OK**.

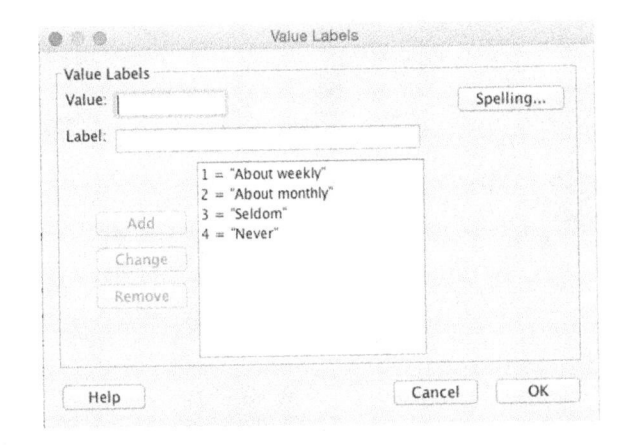

If you accidentally add the wrong information, don't worry. You can delete the information by highlighting it and clicking **Remove**. Alternatively, as shown below, you can correct the value or label and then click the **Change** button, which will become usable once you begin typing something different into the "Value:" or "Label:" field.

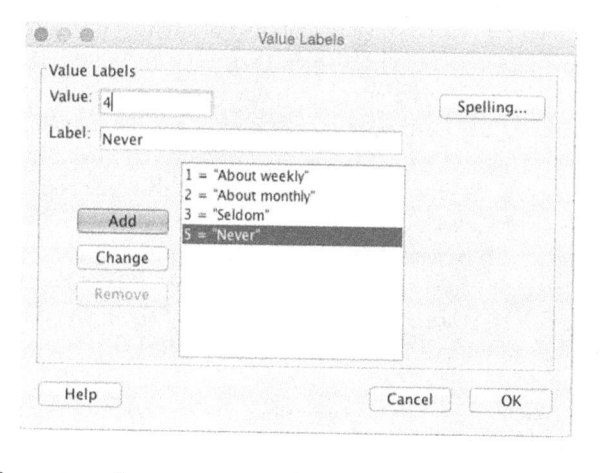

The last bit of information of concern to us at this point is the variable's level of measurement. We can easily select the appropriate level of measurement by clicking on the cell that corresponds to the Measure column (the second-to-last column on the far right side of your Variable View tab) and the CHATT row. Notice that once you point and click on that cell, three options appear, representing each of the levels of measurement: nominal, ordinal, and scale (interval/ratio). Use the down arrow and your mouse to select the appropriate level of measurement (in this case, ordinal).

Now that we have used the Variable View tab to define our variable, let's review the results of our recoding process. We can do this most easily through the use of the now familiar Frequencies command. Once you have accessed the Frequencies dialog box, scroll down the variable list. You'll see that CHATT is now included in the list (which is in alphabetical order).

Once you have found CHATT, go ahead and run a frequency distribution for the variable CHATT. Your table should be similar to the one shown in the screen below.

## CHATT Recoded Church Attendance

|  |  | Frequency | Percent | Valid Percent | Cumulative Percent |
|---|---|---|---|---|---|
| Valid | 1 About weekly | 427 | 28.5 | 28.7 | 28.7 |
|  | 2 About monthly | 240 | 16.0 | 16.1 | 44.8 |
|  | 3 Seldom | 454 | 30.3 | 30.5 | 75.3 |
|  | 4 Never | 368 | 24.5 | 24.7 | 100.0 |
|  | Total | 1489 | 99.3 | 100.0 |  |
| Missing | System | 11 | .7 |  |  |
| Total |  | 1500 | 100.0 |  |  |

Notice how much more manageable the recoded variable is. Now, we can use the recoded variable in our later analyses.

## Summary of Steps Involved in Recoding

### Step 1: Preparing to Recode a Variable

- Identify which variable you want to recode (e.g., ATTEND).

- Run a frequency distribution for the variable you want to recode to see its current coding (as we did with ATTEND).

- Figure out which values you want to combine to create the new variable (as we did with ATTEND). Keep in mind the loose guidelines for recoding discussed earlier. You should also consider the level of measurement for your new recoded variable because it will impact the type of statistical analyses you can perform.

- Many of us find it helpful to make a list of the old values and new values with their labels before we start the recoding process. Here's what we did for ATTEND.

- Decide on a name and label for your new (recoded) variable (i.e., CHATT for CHurch ATTendance, "Recoded Church Attendance").

| Old Variable ATTEND | | | New Variable CHATT | |
|---|---|---|---|---|
| Values | Labels | | Values | Labels |
| 0 | Never | → | 4 | Never |
| 1 | Less than once a year | → | 3 | Seldom |
| 2 | Once a year | → | 3 | |
| 3 | Several times a year | → | 3 | |
| 4 | Once a month | → | 2 | About monthly |
| 5 | Two to three times a month | → | 2 | |

*(Continued)*

(Continued)

| Old Variable ATTEND | | | New Variable CHATT | |
|---|---|---|---|---|
| Values | Labels | | Values | Labels |
| 6 | Nearly every week | → | 1 | About weekly |
| 7 | Every week | → | 1 | |
| 8 | More than once a week | → | 1 | |

### Step 2: Recoding

Use the SPSS Statistics Recode command to create your new variable (i.e., **Transform Recode → Into Different Variables**).

### Step 3: Checking Your Recode in the Data Editor

Check your new variable in the Data View portion of the Data Editor to make sure your recoding was correct.

### Step 4: Defining Your Variable

Define your new variable using the Variable View tab (i.e., decimals, width, label, values, and measure).

### Step 5: Running a Frequency Distribution

Run a frequency distribution for your new variable to ensure the recoding was done correctly.

# DEMONSTRATION 7.2: RECODING AGE → AGECAT

The value of recoding is especially evident in the case of continuous interval/ratio variables, such as age and education. Because these types of variables have so many categories, they are totally unmanageable in some forms of analysis. Fortunately, we can recode scale variables as easily as we just recoded ATTEND.

Why don't we go ahead and recode the variable AGE because, in addition to giving us more practice with recoding, it will allow us to take advantage of an additional feature in the recoding process.

If you follow the steps listed previously, you will note that in accordance with Step 1, we have already identified the variable we want to recode (AGE). Now, take a moment to run a frequency distribution for AGE so you can see the categories we want to combine. Feel free to look back at the instructions given earlier in the chapter if you have any problem recalling how to run a frequency distribution.

In this case, we want to collapse this multitude of categories into four more manageable categories as follows:

| Old Variable AGE: Values | | New Variable AGECAT: Values | Labels |
|---|---|---|---|
| 18 to 20 | → | 1 | Under 21 |
| 21 to 39 | → | 2 | 21 to 39 |
| 40 to 64 | → | 3 | 40 to 64 |
| 65 to 89 | → | 4 | 65 and older |

Note in this instance that the oldest respondent to the 2016 General Social Survey (GSS) was 89 years old. A value of 99 in this case refers to "NA," or people who did not answer the question, rather than the actual age of a respondent. In this case, the value of 99 for the variable AGE should be labeled as "missing." Go ahead and do that, or verify that it has already been done, before continuing with the recode. If you have any problems setting values as "missing," see the discussion in the previous chapter.

We will call our new, recoded variable AGECAT (to represent AGE CATegories) and label the variable "Recoded AGE." Now we are ready to use the Recode command to create our new variable. To do that, simply select **Transform → Recode → Into Different Variables** again. Notice that the Recode into Different Variables window still shows our recoding of ATTEND. Clear the boards by clicking **Reset** at the bottom of the window.

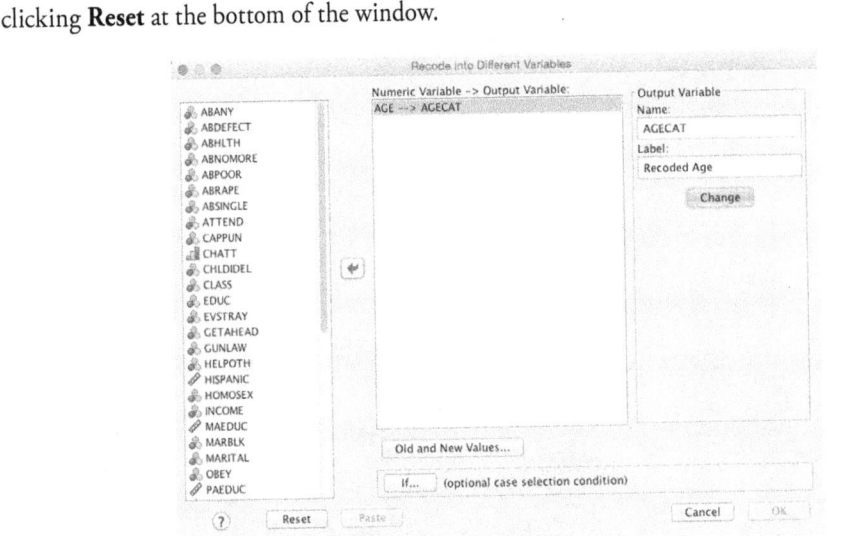

Then, select **AGE** and move it to the "Numeric Variable → Output Variable:" window. Name the new variable "AGECAT," add the variable label, and click **Change**. Now you can select **Old and New Values** to tell SPSS Statistics how to recode.

In recoding AGE, we want to make use of the range option again, but for our first recode, check the **Range, LOWEST through value:** option. This will ensure that our youngest category will include the youngest respondents. Enter 20 in the box, specify the new value as 1, and click **Add**.

You may also want to take advantage of the other range option, **Range, value through HIGHEST**. When you do this, however, beware! Although the lowest and highest range specifications are handy, they must be used with care. If we hadn't run a frequency distribution for AGE and checked on our missing values, we could easily specify "65 through highest" as the range and not notice that in this case, 99 refers to "NA." As a result, we may run the risk of including 10 people who didn't specify their ages as 65 years and older.

Now, do what you have to do to create the remaining recode instructions indicated below.

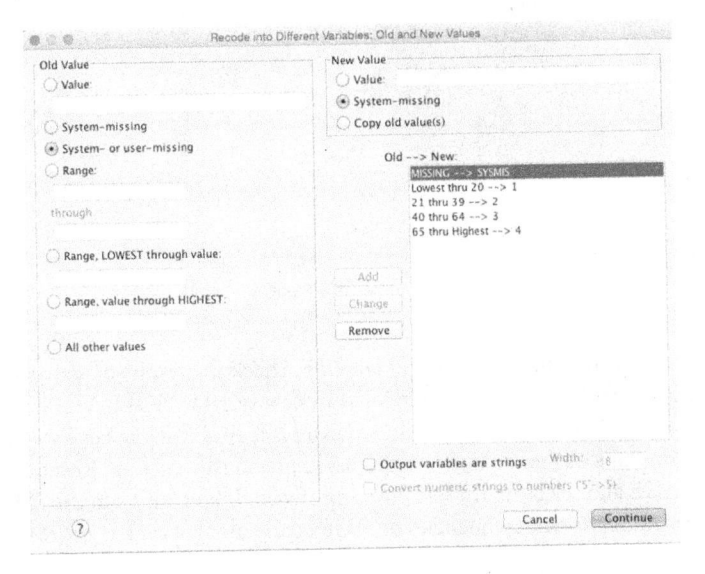

Click **Continue** to return to the main Recode window and then **OK** to make the recoding changes.

Now go to the Data View portion of the Data Editor, and you should see your new, recoded variable, AGECAT, in the rightmost column. Check it out.

To complete the recode process, follow Steps 3 and 4. Check your new variable, AGECAT, against the old variable, AGE, in Data View; then, define AGECAT in Variable View. When defining your variable, remember to set your decimals to 0 and your width to 1. Then, list the values and labels for AGECAT, and select the appropriate level of measurement (in this case, ordinal), as shown below.

Once you've completed the recoding and labeling, check the results of your labors by following Step 5 and running a frequency distribution for your new variable, AGECAT. Notice that AGE may still be in the list of variables to be analyzed. You can place AGE back in the list of abbreviated variable names by using one of the methods we discussed previously (clicking **Reset**, or double-clicking or highlighting **AGE** and selecting the left-pointing arrow). If you fail to do this, SPSS Statistics will simply calculate and report the frequencies on AGE again, along with any other variables selected.

**AGECAT Recoded Age**

| | | Frequency | Percent | Valid Percent | Cumulative Percent |
|---|---|---|---|---|---|
| Valid | 1 Under 21 | 33 | 2.2 | 2.2 | 2.2 |
| | 2 21-39 years old | 479 | 31.9 | 32.0 | 34.2 |
| | 3 40-64 years old | 660 | 44.0 | 44.1 | 78.4 |
| | 4 65 and older | 323 | 21.5 | 21.6 | 100.0 |
| | Total | 1495 | 99.7 | 100.0 | |
| Missing | System | 5 | .3 | | |
| Total | | 1500 | 100.0 | | |

# WRITING BOX 7.1

The largest percentage of respondents to the 2016 GSS is between the ages of 40 and 64 (44%). This is followed by 32% of respondents who are 21 to 39. Only 22% of respondents are retirement age (65 and older), while about 2% are under 21 years of age.

---

## SPSS Statistics Command 7.1: Recoding a Variable

Click **Transform → Compute → Into Different Variables**

Highlight name of variable to be recoded → Click right-pointing arrow OR double-click variable name → In "Output Variable" field, type name and label of new variable

Click **Change → Old and New Values**

Choose option for specifying old values you want to recode (i.e., Range, etc.) → Enter old value codes → Enter new value recodes → Click Add → (Repeat this step until all old values are recoded)

Click **Continue → OK**

*To Define New, Recoded Variable*

Select **Variable View tab** → Identify new, recoded variable in last row → Click on cells corresponding with new, recoded variable and the following columns to change Width, Decimals, Values, and Measure

---

# DEMONSTRATION 7.3: RECODING POLVIEWS → POLREC

Now that we have recoded ATTEND and AGE, let's turn to two of the political variables we examined in the previous chapter. You may recall that in Chapter 6 we examined the respondent's basic political philosophy using the variable POLVIEWS. We also looked at the respondent's party identification using the variable PARTYID. You may also recall that both of these variables had seven or more valid categories. In the following two demonstrations, we will use the Recode command to reduce the number of categories for these variables to a more manageable size.

We will begin with the variable POLVIEWS. Go ahead and run a frequency table for this variable. Your results should be the same as those below.

## POLVIEWS Think of Self as Liberal or Conservative

| | | Frequency | Percent | Valid Percent | Cumulative Percent |
|---|---|---|---|---|---|
| Valid | 1 EXTREMELY LIBERAL | 72 | 4.8 | 5.0 | 5.0 |
| | 2 LIBERAL | 188 | 12.5 | 13.1 | 18.1 |
| | 3 SLIGHTLY LIBERAL | 156 | 10.4 | 10.8 | 28.9 |
| | 4 MODERATE | 519 | 34.6 | 36.1 | 65.0 |
| | 5 SLGHTLY CONSERVATIVE | 210 | 14.0 | 14.6 | 79.6 |
| | 6 CONSERVATIVE | 227 | 15.1 | 15.8 | 95.4 |
| | 7 EXTRMLY CONSERVATIVE | 66 | 4.4 | 4.6 | 100.0 |
| | Total | 1438 | 95.9 | 100.0 | |
| Missing | 8 DK | 43 | 2.9 | | |
| | 9 NA | 19 | 1.3 | | |
| | Total | 62 | 4.1 | | |
| Total | | 1500 | 100.0 | | |

As you can see, POLVIEWS has seven valid categories ranging from "Extremely liberal" to "Extremely conservative." If you simply wanted a measure of liberals versus conservatives, you might decide to recode the variable into just three categories: Liberal, Moderate, and Conservative.

Let's go ahead and do that. We will create a new variable called "POLREC" by recoding POLVIEWS as follows:

1 through 3 → 1     *Liberal*

4 → 2     *Moderate*

5 through 7 → 3     *Conservative*

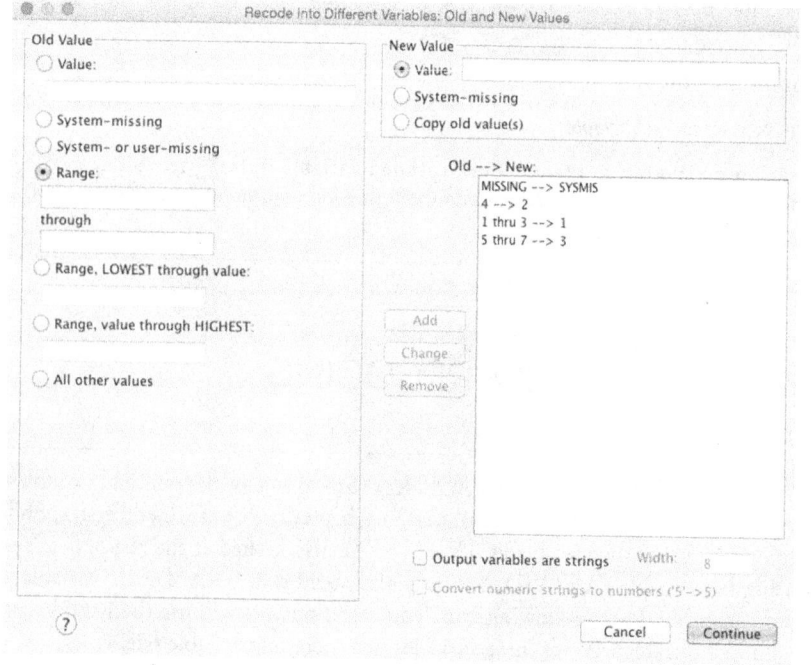

Once you have successfully recoded POLVIEWS, remember to access the Variable View tab and set the decimals, width, values, and appropriate level of measurement for your new, recoded variable POLREC. In this case, assign new labels to the values of POLREC as follows:

1 = "Liberal"

2 = "Moderate"

3 = "Conservative"

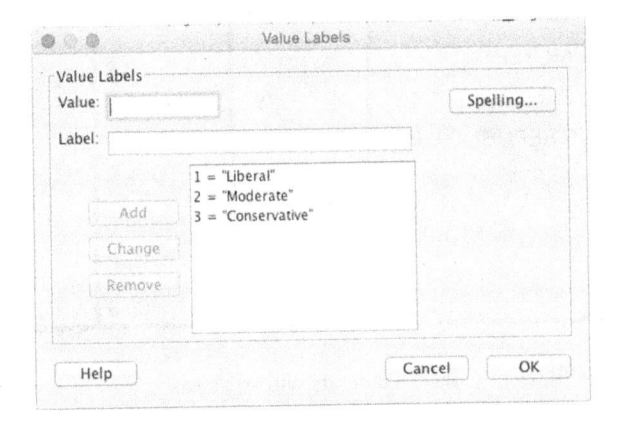

To see the results of our recoding, we repeat the Frequencies command with the new variable POLREC.

### POLREC Recoded POLVIEWS

| | | Frequency | Percent | Valid Percent | Cumulative Percent |
|---|---|---|---|---|---|
| Valid | 1 Liberal | 416 | 27.7 | 28.9 | 28.9 |
| | 2 Moderate | 519 | 34.6 | 36.1 | 65.0 |
| | 3 Conservative | 503 | 33.5 | 35.0 | 100.0 |
| | Total | 1438 | 95.9 | 100.0 | |
| Missing | System | 62 | 4.1 | | |
| Total | | 1500 | 100.0 | | |

If your screen looks like the one shown above, congratulations! You have mastered the art of recoding and are ready to move ahead. If not, don't worry, you may just need to go back and review the steps outlined earlier.

# DEMONSTRATION 7.4:
# RECODING PARTYID → PARTY

As a final demonstration, let's go ahead and recode the variable PARTYID. You may recall that **PARTYID** contains eight categories ranging from "Strong Democrat" to "Other party." If you want to refresh your memory, go ahead and run a frequency table for this variable, as shown on the next page.

As the frequency table shows, this variable probably has more answer categories than we will be able to manage easily. Consequently, we should recode PARTYID to create a new, less cumbersome measure of party identification called "PARTY."

It makes sense to combine the first two categories: the "strong" and "not strong" Democrats (0 and 1). Similarly, we will combine the corresponding Republican categories (5 and 6). Two of the categories, however, need a little more discussion: the two Independent groups who said, when pressed by interviewers, that they were "near" one of the two parties.

## PARTYID Political Party Affiliation

| | | Frequency | Percent | Valid Percent | Cumulative Percent |
|---|---|---|---|---|---|
| Valid | 0 STRONG DEMOCRAT | 239 | 15.9 | 16.2 | 16.2 |
| | 1 NOT STR DEMOCRAT | 247 | 16.5 | 16.7 | 32.9 |
| | 2 IND,NEAR DEM | 210 | 14.0 | 14.2 | 47.1 |
| | 3 INDEPENDENT | 250 | 16.7 | 16.9 | 64.0 |
| | 4 IND,NEAR REP | 147 | 9.8 | 9.9 | 74.0 |
| | 5 NOT STR REPUBLICAN | 199 | 13.3 | 13.5 | 87.4 |
| | 6 STRONG REPUBLICAN | 152 | 10.1 | 10.3 | 97.7 |
| | 7 OTHER PARTY | 34 | 2.3 | 2.3 | 100.0 |
| | Total | 1478 | 98.5 | 100.0 | |
| Missing | 9 NA | 22 | 1.5 | | |
| Total | | 1500 | 100.0 | | |

Should we combine those near the Democrats with that party, for example, or should we combine them with the other Independents? There are a number of methods for resolving this question. For now, however, we are going to choose the simplest method. As we continue our analyses, it will be useful if we have ample numbers of respondents in each category, so we will recode with an eye to creating roughly equal-sized groups. In this instance, that means combining the three Independent categories (2, 3, and 4) into one group. So let's recode as follows:

0 through 1 → 1        *Democrat*

2 through 4 → 2        *Independent*

5 through 6 → 3        *Republican*

7 → 4                  *Other*

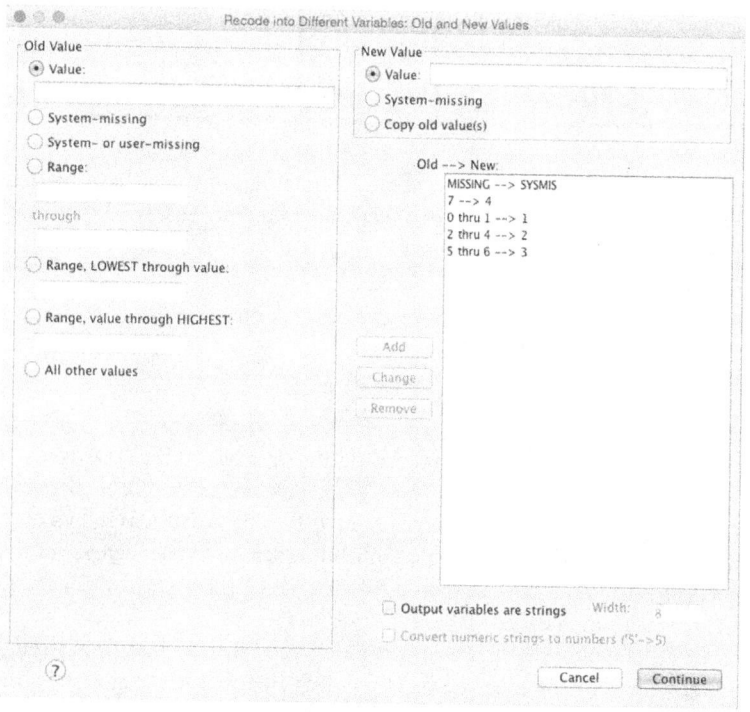

Then, label PARTY as follows: 1 = "Democrat," 2 = "Independent," 3 = "Republican," 4 = "Other."

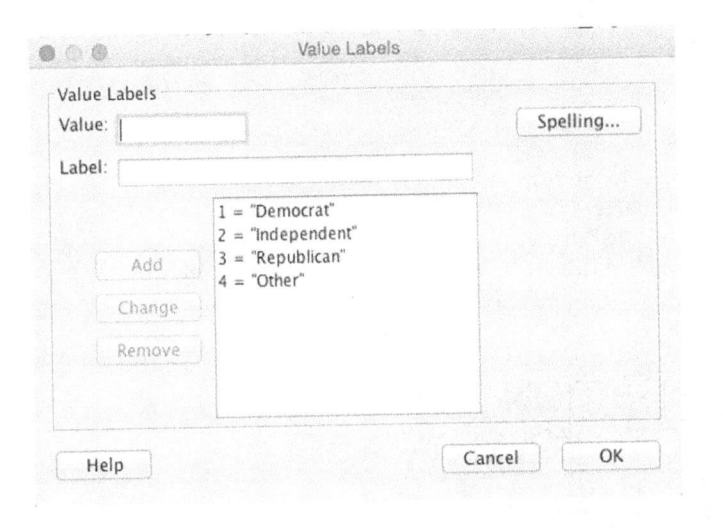

Enter and execute these commands now. Once you've done so, we'll be ready to create a frequency table and either a pie or bar chart for the new variable, as shown below. (Tip: You can use the Charts button in the Frequencies dialog box, rather than performing a second request for the pie chart.)

## PARTY Political Party

|  |  | Frequency | Percent | Valid Percent | Cumulative Percent |
|---|---|---|---|---|---|
| Valid | 1 Democrat | 486 | 32.4 | 32.9 | 32.9 |
|  | 2 Independent | 607 | 40.5 | 41.1 | 74.0 |
|  | 3 Republican | 351 | 23.4 | 23.7 | 97.7 |
|  | 4 Other | 34 | 2.3 | 2.3 | 100.0 |
|  | Total | 1478 | 98.5 | 100.0 |  |
| Missing | System | 22 | 1.5 |  |  |
| Total |  | 1500 | 100.0 |  |  |

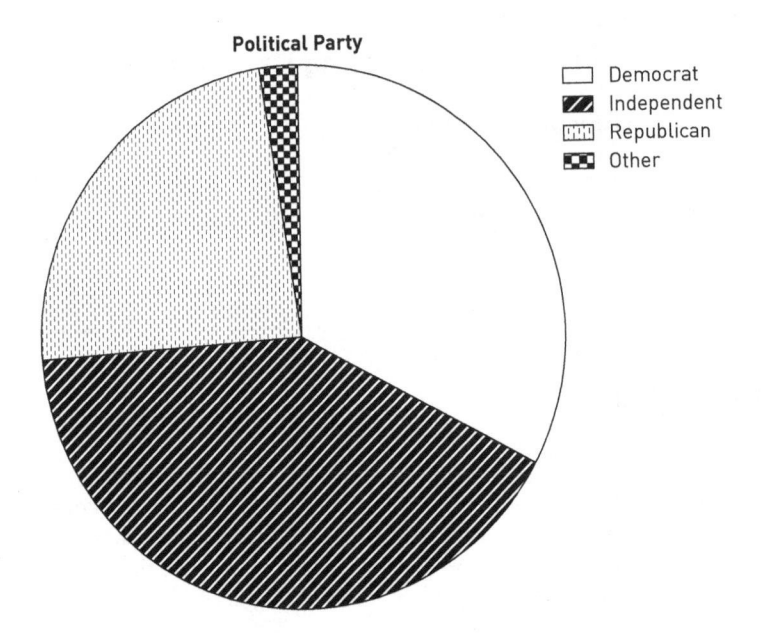

Political Party

☐ Democrat
▨ Independent
▦ Republican
▨ Other

# WRITING BOX 7.2

Whereas about one third of respondents (33%) to the 2016 GSS are Democrats, only a bit more than a quarter (29%) describe themselves as "liberal." On the other hand, 24% of respondents identify with the Republican Party, but 35% describe themselves as "conservative." More than one-third of the respondents say they are moderate (36%), and a higher number describe themselves as Independents (41%).

## DEMONSTRATION 7.5: SAVING CHANGES TO YOUR DATA SET

That's enough work for now. But before we stop, let's save the work we've done in this session so we won't have to repeat it all when we start up again. The recoding you've done so far is being held only in the computer's volatile memory. That means if you leave SPSS Statistics right now, all the recoding changes will disappear. Because we will want to use the recoded variables CHATT, AGECAT, POLREC, and PARTY later, a simple procedure will save us time at our next session.

If you are sharing a computer with other users, you should save DEMO.SAV as "DEMOPLUS. SAV" for safekeeping. Keep in mind that whenever you save a file in SPSS Statistics (whether you are saving output or your data set), you are saving only what is visible in the active window.

To save your data set, you need to make sure the Data Editor is the active window. You can do that by either clicking on **DEMO.SAV** in the taskbar or choosing **Window** in the menu bar and then selecting **DEMO.SAV** from the drop-down menu. Then, go to the **File** menu, and select **Save As**. From the "Save in:" drop-down menu at the top of the Save As window, select a location for your data to be saved—either a USB drive, a network drive, a cloud server, or the computer's hard drive.

Type the name for your file in the "File Name" field. Although you can choose any name you wish, in this case, we will use "DEMOPLUS.SAV" to refer to the file that contains our basic DEMO.SAV file with the changes we made today using the instructions in Chapter 7 (i.e., four newly recoded variables). Then, click **Save**. Now, you can leave SPSS Statistics with the **File → Exit** command (or **FILE → Quit SPSS** on a Macintosh computer.) If you open this file the next time you start an SPSS Statistics session, it will have all of the new, recoded variables.

---

### SPSS Statistics Command 7.2:
### Saving Changes Made to an Existing Data Set

Make sure the Data Editor is the active window

Click **File → Save As**

Select appropriate drive → Name your file (DEMOPLUS.SAV, DEMOPLUSCHAP7.SAV, or something else)

Click **Save**

---

## CONCLUSION

Social scientists have a variety of options when it comes to working with data. While in the previous two chapters we examined variables relating to religious and political attitudes, we were somewhat restricted. In this chapter, we learned that although the researchers who collected the GSS data opted to distinguish between people who go to church two to three times a month and people who go to church nearly every week, using SPSS Statistics we can combine adjacent categories and create a new, more manageable variable. Similarly, while some researchers may want to know the exact age of respondents, others may want to combine categories of this variable to create age range categories.

Thankfully, the software we are using allows us to do this fairly easily. By recoding into new variables, we have the luxury of examining the variables in their original format and combining categories to create a wholly new, more accessible version as well.

## Main Points

- When working with continuous variables, one option often used to describe your distribution is to reduce the number of categories by recoding.

- Modifying variables in SPSS Statistics by combining adjacent categories is called collapsing categories.

- Recoding is particularly useful when you are dealing with continuous variables or variables with many response categories.

- There are no rules for deciding which categories to combine when you are recoding. There are, however, two guidelines—one logical and the other empirical.

- Before exiting SPSS Statistics, don't forget to save any changes you made to the existing data set.

## Key Term

Recoding  99

## SPSS Statistics Commands Introduced in This Chapter

7.1.  Recoding a Variable

7.2.  Saving Changes Made to an Existing Data Set

## Review Questions

1. What are the two general guidelines you should keep in mind when deciding how to combine adjacent categories for recoding?

2. It makes most sense to consider recoding if a variable has which of the following characteristics?

    a.  It is a nominal variable.

    b.  It is a discrete variable.

    c.  It is a continuous variable.

    d.  None of the above

3. It makes most sense to consider recoding if a variable has which of the following characteristics?

    a.  It has a small number of response categories.

    b.  It has a larger number of response categories.

    c.  It has a large number of missing data.

    d.  None of the above

4. If you were going to recode the variable CHLDIDEL, which measures the respondent's ideal number of children, how might you collapse (or combine) the following categories?

    a.  None

    b.  One

    c.  Two

    d.  Three

    e.  Four

    f.  Five

    g.  Six

    h.  Seven or more

    i.  As many as you want

(Continued)

(Continued)

5.  If you were going to recode the variable PRAY, which measures how often the respondent prays, how might you collapse (or combine) the following categories?

    a.  Several times a day

    b.  Once a day

    c.  Several times a week

    d.  Once a week

    e.  Less than once a week

    f.  Never

6.  After recoding a variable and going back to the Data Editor window, we recommend that you access the Variable View tab because it allows you to accomplish what specific task(s)?

7.  After recoding, which SPSS Statistics procedure gives you the best way to check your new, recoded variable?

8.  In order to save your data file, which SPSS Statistics window should be the active window?

# SPSS Statistics Lab Exercise 7.1

NAME: _____

CLASS: _____

INSTRUCTOR: _____

DATE: _____

*To complete the following exercises, you should open your EXER.SAV or EXERPLUS.SAV file.*

1.  What does the variable FEHIRE measure? (Hint: Check the variable label.)

2.  Produce a frequency distribution for the variable FEHIRE, and use your findings to fill in the blanks below. Before you begin, make sure you define the values 0, 8, and 9 as "missing."

### Valid Percentage

1.  Strongly agree _____

2.  Agree _____

3.  Neither agree nor disagree _____

4.  Disagree _____

5.  Strongly disagree _____

3.  Now, follow these steps to recode the variable FEHIRE to create a new variable, RECFHIRE.

| Old Variable FEHIRE | | New Variable RECFHIRE | |
| Values | Labels | Values | Labels |
|---|---|---|---|
| 1 | Strongly agree | 1 | Agree |
| 2 | Agree | 1 | |
| 3 | Neither agree nor disagree | 2 | Neither |
| 4 | Disagree | 3 | Disagree |
| 5 | Strongly disagree | 3 | |

*(recoded FEHIRE), as follows:*

a.  Use the Recode command to create your new, recoded variable: RECFHIRE

b.  Define your new variable.

c.  Run a frequency distribution for the variable RECFHIRE; then, list the valid percentages for each category below.

### Valid Percentage

1.  Agree _____

2.  Neither agree nor disagree _____

3.  Strongly disagree _____

d.  Print out your frequency table, attach it to this sheet, and then write a brief analysis of your table below.

*(Continued)*

(Continued)

4. Produce a frequency distribution for the variable NEWS, and use your findings to fill in the blanks below. Before you begin, make sure you define the values 0, 8, and 9 as "missing."

**Valid Percentage**

1. Every day _____

2. Few times a week _____

3. Once a week _____

4. Less than once a week _____

| Old Variable NEWS | | New Variable RECNEWS | |
| --- | --- | --- | --- |
| Values | Labels | Values | Labels |
| 1 | Every day | 1 | Few times a week or more |
| 2 | Few times a week | 1 | |
| 3 | Once a week | 2 | Once a week or less46 |
| 4 | Less than once a week | 2 | |
| 5 | Never | 3 | Never |

5. Never _____

5. Now, follow these steps to recode the variable NEWS to create a new variable, RECNEWS (recoded NEWS), as follows:

a. Use the Recode command to create your new, recoded variable RECNEWS.

b. Define your new variable.

c. Run a frequency distribution for the variable RECNEWS, and then, list the valid percentages for each category below.

**Valid Percentage**

1. Few times a week or more _____

2. Once a week or less _____

3. Never _____

d. Print out your frequency table, attach it to this sheet, and then write a brief analysis of your table below.

6. What does the variable EDUC measure? (Hint: Check the variable label.)

7. Produce a frequency distribution for the variable EDUC. Print out your frequency distribution, and attach it to this sheet. Before you begin, make sure you define the values 97, 98, and 99 as "missing."

8. Now, follow these steps to recode the variable EDUC to create a new variable, EDCAT (recoded EDUC), as follows:

| Old Variable EDUC Values (years) | New Variable EDCAT | |
|---|---|---|
| | Values | Labels |
| 0 to 11 | 1 | Less than high school education |
| 12 | 2 | High school graduate |
| 13 to 15 | 3 | Some college |
| 16 | 4 | College graduate |
| 17 to 20 | 5 | Graduate studies and beyond |

a. Use the Recode command to create your new, recoded variable EDCAT.

b. Define your new variable.

c. Run a frequency distribution for the variable EDCAT, and then, list the labels and valid percentages for each category below.

**Labels**                                              **Valid Percentage**

1 _____      _____

2 _____      _____

3 _____      _____

4 _____      _____

5 _____      _____

d. Print out your frequency table, attach it to this sheet, and then write a brief analysis of your table below.

9. Choose one variable from the EXER.SAV file that you want to recode. Then, fill in the information requested below.

a. Name of the variable being recoded: _____

b. Run a frequency table for this variable, attach a copy to this sheet, and describe the frequency table below.

c. List the categories of the variable, and indicate how you will collapse them below.

*(Continued)*

(Continued)

    d. Name of the new variable you are creating: _____

    e. Complete the steps for recoding the variable.

    f. Run a frequency distribution for your new variable, attach it to this sheet, and describe the table below.

10. Save your recoded variables so we can refer to them later. Save the changes using the file name "EXERPLUS.SAV."

11. Access the SPSS Statistics Help feature Tutorial, and work your way through the section titled "Modifying Data Values."

# CREATING COMPOSITE MEASURES

## Exploring Attitudes Toward Abortion in More Depth

Now that you've had a chance to become familiar with univariate analysis, we are going to add a little more sophistication to the process.

You may recall that in Chapter 1, we discussed abortion. The 2016 General Social Survey (GSS) contains several measures of American attitudes toward this issue. We are going to explore these attitudes in more depth in this chapter. We will begin by identifying the relevant variables and running frequencies. Then, we will learn how to combine the multiple measures of abortion into a single variable, which, as noted in Chapter 2, is called a composite measure.

## DEMONSTRATION 8.1: IDENTIFYING THE SEVEN ABORTION VARIABLES—FILE INFO

To start the process, we will instruct SPSS Statistics to produce frequency tables for the abortion attitude variables contained in the file DEMOPLUS.SAV (and DEMO.SAV). If you do not recall the names of the seven variables used to measure abortion attitudes, you can review the list of variables in the codebook (Appendix A). Alternatively, you may view the variables with SPSS Statistics by selecting **Utilities** and clicking on **Variables**. In a moment, information about the variables on your DEMO.SAV file should appear.

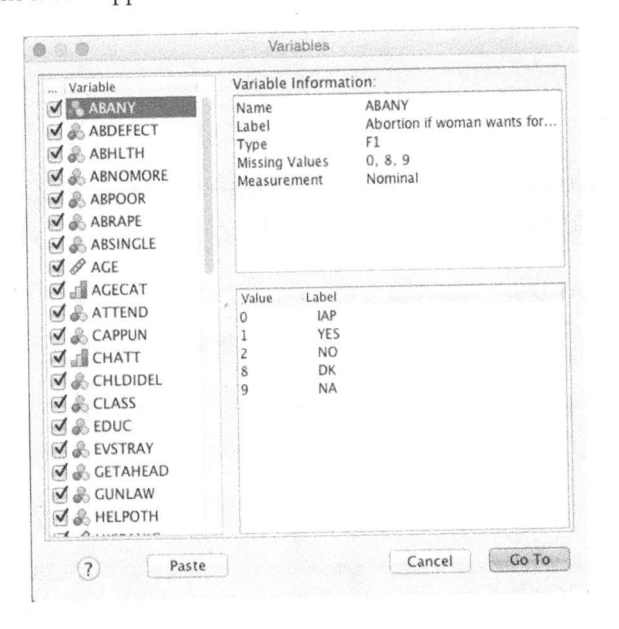

With the file arranged alphabetically, you can see the seven abortion variables contained in the DEMO.SAV file at the beginning of the list: ABANY, ABDEFECT, ABHLTH, ABNOMORE, ABPOOR, ABRAPE, and ABSINGLE.

---

**SPSS Statistics Command 8.1:**
**Identifying Variables—File Info**

Click **Utilities → Variables**

---

## DEMONSTRATION 8.2: RUNNING FREQUENCIES FOR SEVERAL VARIABLES AT ONCE

Once you have identified the names of the abortion attitude variables, you can easily instruct SPSS Statistics to run frequencies for all the items at once.[1] If the variables are clustered together (as the abortion opinion items in our DEMO.SAV file are), you can select the entire cluster by clicking on the first and last variables while holding down the **Shift** key and then clicking the right-pointing arrow to transfer them to the "Variable(s):" field.

If the variables are not clustered together, you can transfer them all at once by holding down the **Ctrl (Control)** key (or **Apple** key for Macintosh computers) on your keyboard as you click the name of each item. After all of the items have been highlighted, click on the right-pointing arrow to transfer them to the "Variable(s):" field.

You may want to experiment with both of these options. One way or another, you ultimately want to transfer all seven abortion items to the "Variable(s):" field, as shown below.

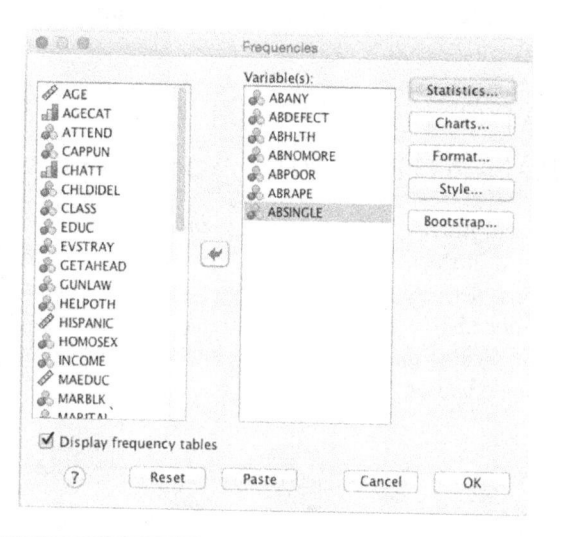

---

**SPSS Statistics Command 8.2: Running Frequencies for Several Variables (Not Clustered)[2]**

Click **Analyze → Descriptive Statistics → Frequencies**

Press and hold Ctrl (Control) key, or Apple key for Macintosh computers, on the keyboard as you click on the names of the variables

Click right-pointing arrow to transfer selected variables to "Variable(s):" field

Click **OK**

---

1. For each of the seven abortion variables, the values 0, 8, and 9 should be defined as "missing."
2. To run frequencies for several variables at once when the variables are clustered, see the discussion in Chapter 5, "SPSS Statistics Command 5.10: Running Frequency Distributions With Two or More Variables."

Once you have given SPSS Statistics the command that will generate frequency distributions for the various abortion items, you should get the results in your Output window. The tables discussed next indicate the different levels of support for abortion under various circumstances.

## Items With the Highest Levels of Support

It would seem at first glance that very high percentages of the general public support a woman's right to an abortion if the woman's health is at risk, if the pregnancy is a result of rape, and if there is a strong chance of serious birth defects. As the tables show, the large majority of respondents (75%–88%) to the 2016 GSS said they would support abortion in each of these cases.[3]

### ABHLTH Woman's Health Seriously Endangered

|         |         | Frequency | Percent | Valid Percent | Cumulative Percent |
|---------|---------|-----------|---------|---------------|--------------------|
| Valid   | 1 YES   | 834       | 55.6    | 88.3          | 88.3               |
|         | 2 NO    | 110       | 7.3     | 11.7          | 100.0              |
|         | Total   | 944       | 62.9    | 100.0         |                    |
| Missing | 0 IAP   | 516       | 34.4    |               |                    |
|         | 8 DK    | 27        | 1.8     |               |                    |
|         | 9 NA    | 13        | .9      |               |                    |
|         | Total   | 556       | 37.1    |               |                    |
| Total   |         | 1500      | 100.0   |               |                    |

### ABRAPE Pregnant as Result of Rape

|         |         | Frequency | Percent | Valid Percent | Cumulative Percent |
|---------|---------|-----------|---------|---------------|--------------------|
| Valid   | 1 YES   | 737       | 49.1    | 77.4          | 77.4               |
|         | 2 NO    | 215       | 14.3    | 22.6          | 100.0              |
|         | Total   | 952       | 63.5    | 100.0         |                    |
| Missing | 0 IAP   | 516       | 34.4    |               |                    |
|         | 8 DK    | 17        | 1.1     |               |                    |
|         | 9 NA    | 15        | 1.0     |               |                    |
|         | Total   | 548       | 36.5    |               |                    |
| Total   |         | 1500      | 100.0   |               |                    |

### ABDEFECT Strong Chance of Serious Defect

|         |         | Frequency | Percent | Valid Percent | Cumulative Percent |
|---------|---------|-----------|---------|---------------|--------------------|
| Valid   | 1 YES   | 710       | 47.3    | 75.1          | 75.1               |
|         | 2 NO    | 236       | 15.7    | 24.9          | 100.0              |
|         | Total   | 946       | 63.1    | 100.0         |                    |
| Missing | 0 IAP   | 516       | 34.4    |               |                    |
|         | 8 DK    | 23        | 1.5     |               |                    |
|         | 9 NA    | 15        | 1.0     |               |                    |
|         | Total   | 554       | 36.9    |               |                    |
| Total   |         | 1500      | 100.0   |               |                    |

3. In each instance, the percentages have been rounded.

### Items With Less Support

When you examine the other three items, however, you will find a significant decrease in levels of support for women getting an abortion. As the tables that follow show, support for a woman getting an abortion if she is not married, has low income and cannot afford any more children, or doesn't want any more children range from 44% to 48%.[4]

## ABSINGLE Not Married

|  |  | Frequency | Percent | Valid Percent | Cumulative Percent |
|---|---|---|---|---|---|
| Valid | 1 YES | 421 | 28.1 | 43.9 | 43.9 |
|  | 2 NO | 538 | 35.9 | 56.1 | 100.0 |
|  | Total | 959 | 63.9 | 100.0 |  |
| Missing | 0 IAP | 516 | 34.4 |  |  |
|  | 8 DK | 11 | .7 |  |  |
|  | 9 NA | 14 | .9 |  |  |
|  | Total | 541 | 36.1 |  |  |
| Total |  | 1500 | 100.0 |  |  |

## ABPOOR Low Income—Can't Afford More Children

|  |  | Frequency | Percent | Valid Percent | Cumulative Percent |
|---|---|---|---|---|---|
| Valid | 1 YES | 428 | 28.5 | 45.1 | 45.1 |
|  | 2 NO | 521 | 34.7 | 54.9 | 100.0 |
|  | Total | 949 | 63.3 | 100.0 |  |
| Missing | 0 IAP | 516 | 34.4 |  |  |
|  | 8 DK | 24 | 1.6 |  |  |
|  | 9 NA | 11 | .7 |  |  |
|  | Total | 551 | 36.7 |  |  |
| Total |  | 1500 | 100.0 |  |  |

## ABNOMORE Married—Wants No More Children

|  |  | Frequency | Percent | Valid Percent | Cumulative Percent |
|---|---|---|---|---|---|
| Valid | 1 YES | 459 | 30.6 | 48.2 | 48.2 |
|  | 2 NO | 493 | 32.9 | 51.8 | 100.0 |
|  | Total | 952 | 63.5 | 100.0 |  |
| Missing | 0 IAP | 516 | 34.4 |  |  |
|  | 8 DK | 21 | 1.4 |  |  |
|  | 9 NA | 11 | .7 |  |  |
|  | Total | 548 | 36.5 |  |  |
| Total |  | 1500 | 100.0 |  |  |

---

4. In each instance, the percentages have been rounded.

## Unconditional Support for Abortion

Finally, let's see what proportion of the population would support a woman having unrestricted freedom to choose an abortion for any reason.

### ABANY Abortion If Woman Wants for Any Reason

| | | Frequency | Percent | Valid Percent | Cumulative Percent |
|---|---|---|---|---|---|
| Valid | 1 YES | 441 | 29.4 | 46.8 | 46.8 |
| | 2 NO | 502 | 33.5 | 53.2 | 100.0 |
| | Total | 943 | 62.9 | 100.0 | |
| Missing | 0 IAP | 516 | 34.4 | | |
| | 8 DK | 25 | 1.7 | | |
| | 9 NA | 16 | 1.1 | | |
| | Total | 557 | 37.1 | | |
| Total | | 1500 | 100.0 | | |

Notice that about the same proportion (47%) supports a woman's unrestricted freedom to choose abortion as support abortion in the specific situations described in ABNOMORE (48%), ABPOOR (45%), and ABSINGLE (44%). Yes, that's right: A slightly smaller percentage of respondents support the choice of abortion for women who are not married than do those respondents who would support unrestricted freedom to choose abortion. Can you think of any reasons why the results are such?

## Support for Abortion: An Overview

It is often useful to bring related tables together in an abbreviated table, so let's construct a table that summarizes those tables we've just examined. See Table 8.1 for a summary of abortion support across all variables.

The tables suggest that attitudes toward abortion fall into three basic groups. There is a small minority of no more than 12% who are opposed to abortion under absolutely any circumstances whatsoever. We conclude this because 88% would support abortion if the woman's life were seriously endangered—the highest level of support in the scenarios given.

Another group, about 47% of the population, would support a woman's free choice of abortion for any reason. The remainder of the population would support abortion in only a few circumstances involving medical danger and/or rape.

While the separate abortion items are helpful, they make it difficult for us to get a clear picture of how Americans feel about abortion overall. Consequently, to explore attitudes toward abortion further, it may be useful to have a single variable, a composite measure, that captures the complexities of attitudes toward abortion overall—in other words, a single variable that takes into account the complexity of attitudes by capturing the three major positions on this issue.

Now that we have raised the issue, you will probably not be surprised to learn that SPSS Statistics allows us to create such a variable, or a composite measure made up of multiple indicators of a single concept. By employing the **Count command**, we can use the scores on two or more variables to compute a new variable that summarizes attitudes toward a complicated issue or ambiguous concept, such as abortion, sexual permissiveness, religiosity, prejudice, and so on. We will begin this chapter with a fairly simple two-item index indicating anti-abortion attitudes and then move to a somewhat more sophisticated measure indicating pro-abortion attitudes.

| TABLE 8.1 ■ Variations in Levels of Support for Abortion | |
| --- | --- |
| **Percentage Who Support a Woman's Right to Choose Abortion Because ...** | |
| the woman's health would be seriously endangered | 88% |
| the pregnancy resulted from rape | 77% |
| there is a strong sense of a serious defect | 75% |
| a married woman wants no more children | 48% |
| the woman is unmarried | 44% |
| the woman is too poor to afford any more children | 45% |
| the woman wants it for any reason | 47% |

# INDEX: A FORM OF COMPOSITE MEASURE

An *index* is a form of composite measure; that is, an index is composed of more than one indicator of the variable under study. The score on a multiple-choice quiz is an example of a very simple index. Each question is an "item" that indicates some of the student's knowledge of the subject matter. Together, all of the items form an index of the student's knowledge. Just as we would not think that a single-question quiz would give us a very accurate assessment of a student's knowledge, so it is when we measure attitudes. We do a better job measuring respondents' attitudes with multiple items.

In addition, using an index has two other advantages. First, indices include multiple dimensions of the subject under study. In this case, an index composed of ABDEFECT and ABSINGLE will combine two aspects of the debate over abortion rather than being limited to only one (e.g., just the impact of birth defects). Second, composite measures, including indices, tap into a greater range of variation between the extremes of a variable. If we were simply to use one of the abortion items, we would distinguish two groups of respondents: the pros and the antis. Combining two items will allow us to distinguish three groups. A later example will extend this range of variation even further.

## ABORT Index

As we noted, the Count command allows us to create a new summary variable based on information from existing variables. The new variable can then be saved in your data set and used like any other variable.[5]

The Count command scans a list of variables for each respondent and counts the number of variables containing a particular code. For instance, the abortion variables have been consistently coded 1 to indicate approval of abortion and 2 to indicate disapproval of abortion. When the time comes, we will instruct Count to count either the number of 1s or the 2s, depending on whether we want our index to reflect overall approval or disapproval of abortion.

Our first index will be based on the two variables mentioned previously: ABDEFECT and ABSINGLE. As you probably recall, ABDEFECT measures respondents' support for abortion if there is a chance of serious defect in the baby, whereas ABSINGLE measures respondents' support for abortion if the woman is not married and does not want to marry the "man." You may want to refer to the codebook (Appendix A) to find the exact wording of each question. If you do that, you will notice that both items are coded as follows:

*Value/Code—Value Label*

0—IAP (missing value)

1—Yes

---

5. If you follow the demonstrations and exercises in this chapter, you will be asked to compute a handful of new variables. If you are using the student version of SPSS Statistics, remember that it is limited to a maximum of 50 variables in a data file.

2—No

8—DK (missing value)

9—NA (missing value)

## ABORT Index Scores

We are going to treat ABDEFECT and ABSINGLE as if they were items on a quiz designed to find out how much our respondents disapprove of abortion. On this quiz, we will count only the "right" answers, those who answered "No." Consequently, a respondent who answered "No" to both questions will get 2 points. Someone answering "No" to only one question and "Yes" to the other will get 1 point, and a respondent answering "Yes" to both will get a score of 0. On this quiz, then, the higher the score, the more respondents disapprove of abortion.

We will use the Count command to instruct SPSS Statistics to create a new variable (ABORT) based on respondents' scores on ABDEFECT and ABSINGLE. Again, our index (ABORT) will be made up of three possible scores; the steps for creating these scores are subsequently demonstrated.

0—Respondent approves of abortion in both cases (if there is a chance of a serious birth defect and if the woman is single).

1—Respondent approves of abortion in one circumstance (primarily birth defects) but not the other.

2—Respondent disapproves of abortion in both cases (if there is a chance of a serious birth defect and if the woman is single).

When we are done, if a respondent has a 1 ("Yes") on both ABDEFECT and ABSINGLE, his or her score will be a 0 on our new index. If a respondent has a 1 ("Yes") on ABDEFECT and a 2 ("No") on ABSINGLE (or vice versa), his or her score will be a 1 on our new index. And if a respondent has a 2 ("No") for both component variables, his or her score will be 2 on our index.

# DEMONSTRATION 8.3: ABORT INDEX

Before we get started, you should check to make sure the values 0, 8, and 9 are defined as "missing" for both ABDEFECT and ABSINGLE.

Once you have done that, go ahead and click **Transform** in the menu bar and then select **Count Values within Cases** in the drop-down menu. This will open the Count Occurrences of Values within Cases dialog box, as shown below.

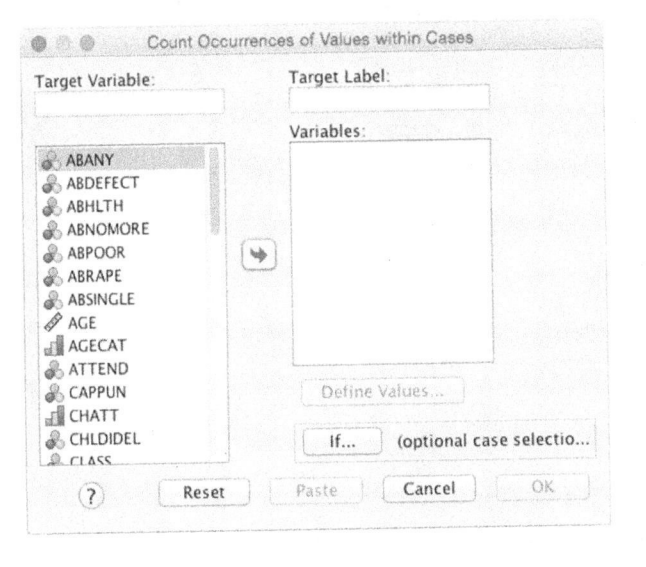

In the upper left-hand corner of the box, you will see a field labeled "Target Variable:" where you can type the name of your new variable (ABORT). To the right, you will see another field labeled "Target Label:" where you can type a descriptive label for your new variable, such as "Simple Abortion Index."

Once you have typed the variable name and label, transfer both ABDEFECT and ABSINGLE from the variable list to the "Variables:" field. Remember, you can do this by highlighting the variable name and then clicking on the right-pointing arrow. Alternatively, you can transfer both variables at the same time by using the **Ctrl** key (**APPLE** key for Macintosh users) on your keyboard. Whichever method you choose, your screen should look like this once you are done.

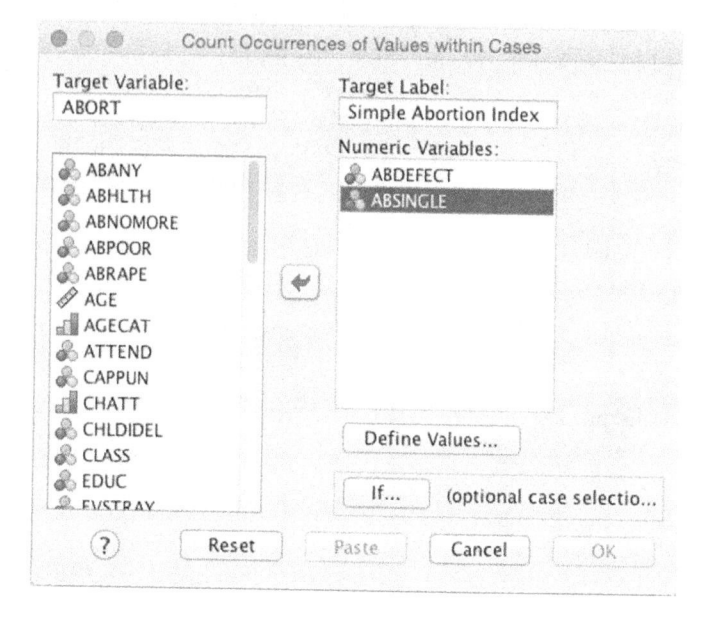

So far, all we have done is tell SPSS Statistics the variables for which specified values will be counted. We have not, however, told SPSS Statistics which value(s) to count. To do that, we need to click the **Define Values** button to open the Count Values within Cases: Values to Count dialog box. Use this dialog box to tell SPSS Statistics which value(s) of ABDEFECT and ABSINGLE to count. For this index, we want SPSS Statistics to count the value of 2, or the number of respondents who said they do not support a woman's right to have an abortion in either case (if there is a chance of a birth defect or if the woman is single). To do this, type **2** in the "Value:" field on the left, and then click the **Add** button. You should now see the value of 2 displayed in the large "Values to Count:" field.

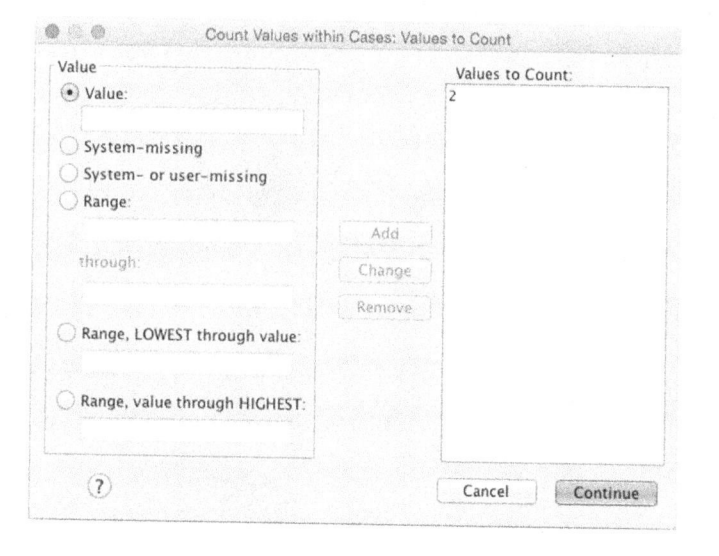

Now click **Continue** to return to the Count Occurrences dialog box.

We are almost ready to set SPSS Statistics on its task. Before we do that, however, we have to deal with missing values. Remember, before we started, we made sure the values of 0 (IAP), 8 (DK), and 9 (NA) for ABDEFECT and ABSINGLE were defined as "missing." Since we do not want SPSS Statistics to count respondents with missing codes, we have to tell it to count only respondents who answered 1 ("Yes") or 2 ("No") on both questions.

In order to remove the people with missing value codes from consideration, click the **If** button next to the parenthetical text "optional case selection condition." This opens the Count Occurrences: If Cases dialog box.

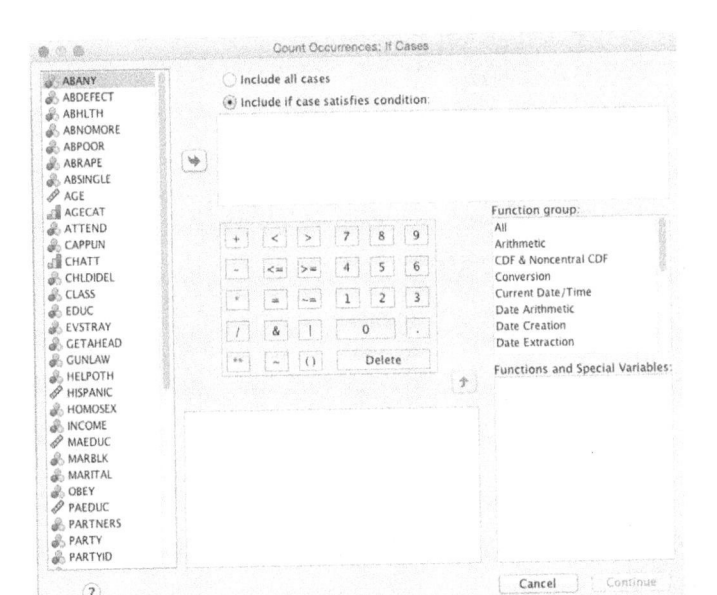

Begin by clicking the round button next to the "Include if case satisfies condition:" field. Now you can either type or paste the following expression in that field: NMISS (abdefect, absingle) = 0. You can do this by clicking in the field and then using your keypad to type the expression. Alternatively, you can paste the expression by following these directions:

- In the "Function group:" list, select "Missing Values."

- Scroll through the "Functions and Special Variables:" list on the bottom right-hand side of the dialog box until you locate the "NMISS (variable[,. . .])" function. This function[6] is used to count the number of variables with missing value codes. Once you have located "NMISS (variable[,. . .])," highlight it, and click on the arrow to the left of the list to move it to the empty field.

- The blinking question mark (?) shows that SPSS Statistics is waiting for you to specify the names of the variables. To do this, simply highlight **ABDEFECT** in the variable list on the left, and then transfer it with the right-pointing arrow. You will notice that ABDEFECT has replaced the blinking question mark.

- Type a **comma** (,), and then follow the same process to transfer the variable ABSINGLE.

- Now, you can use the calculator in the middle of the dialog box to finish the expression by clicking **= 0.**

The expression, as shown below, tells SPSS Statistics to count only when the values 1 or 2 are present for both variables. If respondents answered 0, 8, or 9 for either variable, the index ABORT will be set to "missing."

---

6. SPSS Statistics contains an extensive library of functions for data manipulation and statistical computations that cannot be accomplished with procedures found on the Data and Transform drop-down menus. Detailed information about functions may be found by clicking **Help → Index** and looking under "functions."

Now click **Continue** and then **OK** in the Count Occurrences dialog box to set SPSS Statistics going on its assigned task.

You should now be back in the Data View portion of the Data Editor. Scroll to the far right side, and you will see your new ABORT variable in the last column. You may notice that many respondents (Case Nos. 1, 2, and 4, for instance) have a dot (.) as opposed to a value for ABORT. That is okay; it is just the way SPSS Statistics tells you that this person has a missing value (0, 8, or 9) on either ABDEFECT or ABSINGLE and therefore did not receive a score on our new index.

# DEMONSTRATION 8.4: DEFINING ABORT

You may also notice that, unlike the scores for most other variables on our data file, the scores for ABORT include decimal places. If this is true, it is because the default number of decimals for your copy of SPSS Statistics has been set to 2. You can tell the program to discard the unused decimal places when you define ABORT.

To do so, simply click on the **Variable View** tab. Once you are in the Variable View window, scroll down until you see ABORT in the last row. Now, define your new index, similar to the way we defined new, recoded variables in the previous chapter. In this case, do the following:

- Set the decimals at 0.

- Set the width at 1.

- You should already have a variable label, but you can change it if you want.

- Set the level of measurement to ordinal.

- Add values and labels as shown below (see figure at the top of the next page):

  ○ 0 = "Yes/Approve" (in both cases)

  ○ 1 = "Conditional Support" ("Yes" in one case, "No" in one case)

  ○ 2 = "No/Disapprove" (in both cases)

# DEMONSTRATION 8.5: CHECKING NEW INDEX—COMPARING SCORES ON OLD AND NEW VARIABLES

After you have defined your new variable, go back to the Data View portion of the Data Editor, and locate ABORT in the far right-hand column. You will see that the decimal places are gone, and each respondent has one of three scores: 0, 1, or 2.

Now we want to check our new index, or verify that we created it correctly. One simple way to determine whether we constructed our index properly is to compare a few respondents' scores on the original variables (ABDEFECT and ABSINGLE) with their scores on our index (ABORT). For instance, determine how Respondents 1, 2, 3, and 13 answered for ABDEFECT and ABSINGLE and their index scores. We have done it ourselves, as shown below.

| | ABDEFECT | ABSINGLE | Expected Index Score | Actual ABORT Score |
|---|---|---|---|---|
| Respondent 1 | 1 | 1 | 0 | 0 |
| Respondent 2 | 0 | 0 | Missing | Missing |
| Respondent 3 | 2 | 2 | 2 | 2 |
| Respondent 13 | 2 | 1 | 1 | 1 |

Now, without looking at your data file, determine what score each respondent should have gotten on your new ABORT index. If we constructed the index correctly, their expected score should match their actual score on ABORT. As you can see above, Respondent 13 responded "No" (2) on ABDEFECT and "Yes" (1) on ABSINGLE, so he or she should get a score of 1 on our new index, ABORT. Similarly, since Respondent 2 has a 0 for both ABDEFECT and ABSINGLE, she or he should be scored as "Missing" on our newly created index.

Now, go ahead and determine the expected ABORT scores for Respondents 1 and 3, as well. Once you have done that, compare the expected index scores with the actual ABORT scores. If you constructed the index properly, the expected and actual scores should match. If not, you will need to go back to the index creation process and see where a mistake was made.

# DEMONSTRATION 8.6: RUNNING FREQUENCIES FOR ABORT

An even better way to see whether we really accomplished what we set out to do is to run frequencies for the variable ABORT.

Once you do that, you should see the following table:

## ABORT Simple Abortion Index

| | | Frequency | Percent | Valid Percent | Cumulative Percent |
|---|---|---|---|---|---|
| Valid | 0 Yes/Approve | 408 | 27.2 | 43.7 | 43.7 |
| | 1 Conditional Support | 300 | 20.0 | 32.1 | 75.8 |
| | 2 No/Disapprove | 226 | 15.1 | 24.2 | 100.0 |
| | Total | 934 | 62.3 | 100.0 | |
| Missing | System | 566 | 37.7 | | |
| Total | | 1500 | 100.0 | | |

---

**SPSS Statistics Command 8.3: Creating a Simple Index Using Count**

*Creating Index*

Click **Transform → Count**

Type new variable name in "Target Variable:" field → Type new variable label in "Target Label:" field → Transfer variables for which specified values will be counted to "Variables:" field

Click **Define Values** → Insert value(s) to be counted

Click **Add → Continue**

> → Click **If** → **Include if case satisfies condition:** → Type or paste expression (e.g., "NMISS [abdefect, absingle] = 0")
>
> Click **Continue** → **OK**
>
> *Defining New Variable*
>
> Access **Variable View tab** → Scroll to new variable in last row
>
> Set type, width, values, measure
>
> *Checking New Variable*
>
> Compare expected and actual index scores
>
> Run frequencies for new variable

As the table shows, 408 people, or 44% of GSS respondents (valid percent), scored 0 on the index, meaning that they approved of abortion in both instances. Conversely, 226 people, or 24% of respondents, scored 2, which means that they disapproved of abortion in both cases. In the middle category, we found 32% (300 respondents) who approved in one case but not the other. It should also be noted that a considerable number of people (566) were excluded on the basis of missing data; that, however, does not impact the valid percentages.

Congratulations! You've just created a composite index. We realize you may still be wondering why that's such good news. After all, it wasn't your idea to create the thing in the first place!

## ABINDEX: Index Based on Six Abortion Variables

While our first index was created from only two of the abortion items, we can easily create a more thorough index using more items. In addition to providing us with a wider range of scores, having more items will increase our confidence in the index. As with quizzes, we'd have more confidence in a six-item quiz than in a two-item quiz. For our new index, we will use all of the abortion items *except* ABANY, supporting a woman's unrestricted choice.

For this index, we will ask SPSS Statistics to count the number of times respondents approve (1 = "Yes") of abortion. Unlike the previous index, the more supportive respondents are of abortion, the higher the scores will be. Respondents who disapprove of abortion will have lower scores. The ABINDEX scores will range from 0 (disapprove of abortion in all instances) to 6 (approve of abortion in all cases), with some respondents falling in between depending on their support or disapproval in various circumstances.

Usually, before beginning, we would ask you to make sure the appropriate values (0, 8, and 9) for each variable are defined as "missing." Since we used these variables in the previous demonstrations, they should be ready to use in the next one—although no one would be hurt if you double-checked.

# DEMONSTRATION 8.7: ABINDEX

Since we are following the same basic procedures we used previously, the steps should be somewhat familiar to you. As a guide, we've outlined the process in brief below.

- Click **Transform** → **Count Values within Cases.**
- Click **Reset** to remove all previous settings.
- Type new variable name (ABINDEX) in "Target Variable:" field.
- Type a label for new variable (descriptive variable label of your choice) in "Target Label:" field (e.g., "Six-Item Abortion Index").

- Transfer six abortion variables (ABDEFECT, ABHLTH, ABNOMORE, ABPOOR, ABRAPE, ABSINGLE) to "Numeric Variables:" field[7] → Click **Define Values** → Click button next to **Value:** option.

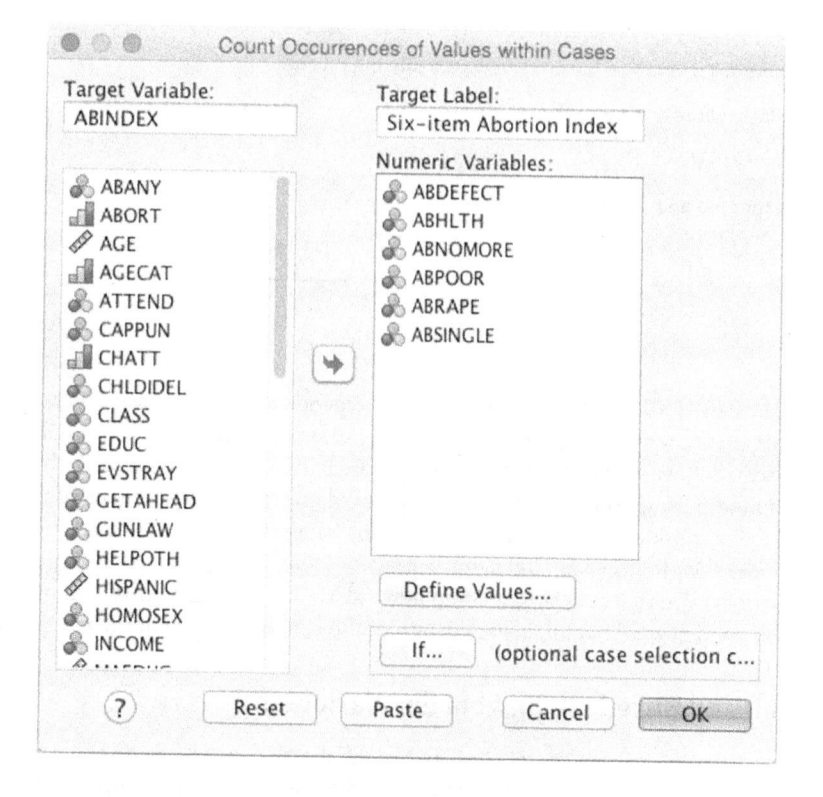

- Type **1** → Click **Add** → Click **Continue** *(because we are counting the "Yes" responses).*

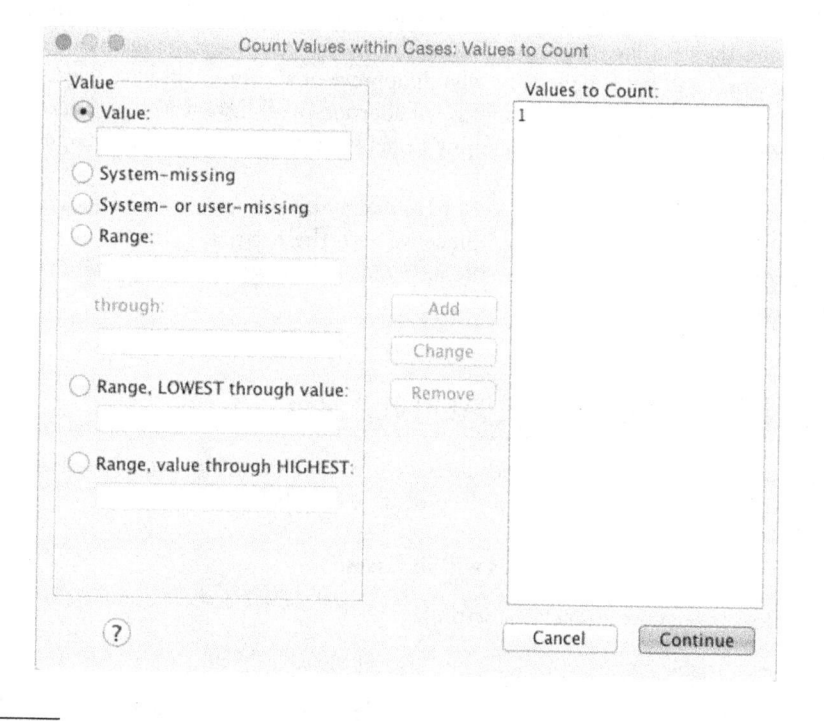

---

7. If the previous index, ABORT, is in the variable list, be careful you do NOT transfer it to the "Numeric Variables:" field as well.

- Click **If**.
- Click button next to "Include if case satisfies condition:" option.

- Type or paste expression "NMISS (ABDEFECT, ABHLTH, ABNOMORE, ABPOOR, ABRAPE, ABSINGLE) = 0."

- Click **Continue → OK**.

Now, all we have to do is tidy up our new variable, ABINDEX, by accessing the Variable View tab and setting the decimals, width, values (0 = No Support; 6 = High Support), and level of measurement (ordinal).

Once you have done that, you may want to return to the Data View portion of the Data Editor and check your new index by comparing the expected and actual ABINDEX scores for a few respondents/cases chosen at random.

# DEMONSTRATION 8.8: RUNNING FREQUENCIES

Better yet, let's go ahead and run a frequency distribution for ABINDEX. Here's what you should find.

## ABINDEX Six-Item Abortion Index

|         |               | Frequency | Percent | Valid Percent | Cumulative Percent |
|---------|---------------|-----------|---------|---------------|--------------------|
| Valid   | 0 No Support  | 84        | 5.6     | 9.6           | 9.6                |
|         | 1             | 68        | 4.5     | 7.7           | 17.3               |
|         | 2             | 79        | 5.3     | 9.0           | 26.3               |
|         | 3             | 176       | 11.7    | 20.0          | 46.3               |
|         | 4             | 62        | 4.1     | 7.1           | 53.4               |
|         | 5             | 62        | 4.1     | 7.1           | 60.4               |
|         | 6 High Support| 348       | 23.2    | 39.6          | 100.0              |
|         | Total         | 879       | 58.6    | 100.0         |                    |
| Missing | System        | 621       | 41.4    |               |                    |
| Total   |               | 1500      | 100.0   |               |                    |

## WRITING BOX 8.1   DESCRIPTION OF ABINDEX

Respondents' attitudes toward abortion have been summarized in the form of an index, ABINDEX. Scores on the index, which range from 0 to 6, are based on responses to six items asked in the questionnaire, each of which indicates some degree of support for a woman's right to choose an abortion (or opposition to it). The six items were presented as different circumstances in which one might approve or disapprove of abortion as a choice:

Strong chance of serious defect (ABDEFECT)

Woman's health seriously endangered (ABHLTH)

Married—wants no more children (ABNOMORE)

Low income—can't afford more children (ABPOOR)

Pregnant as a result of rape (ABRAPE)

Not married (ABSINGLE)

*Note:* GSS variable names for items are presented in parentheses.

Respondents were given 1 point for each circumstance they felt justified a woman's choice to have an abortion. Thus, respondents who scored 6 on the index (42% of the sample) felt that each of the circumstances was sufficient justification. Those who scored 0 on the index (a little more than 9% of the sample) were unconditionally opposed to abortion in any or all of these circumstances. A person who scored 3 on the index felt that three of the circumstances warranted abortion, but the other three did not (46% of GSS respondents).

That is enough for now. However, before ending this session, make sure you save both of your new variables (ABORT and ABINDEX) in a file with an appropriate name, such as "DEMOPLUS .SAV," so we can find and use them later.

It is important to reiterate that anyone using the Student Version of SPSS Statistics has to be sensitive to the fact that the Student Version is limited to 50 variables. Consequently, you may need to follow the instructions in Chapter 5, "Demonstration 5.10," regarding saving your data. For those of you using any of the other versions of SPSS Statistics, this is not an issue.

## CONCLUSION

In this chapter, we've seen that it is often possible to measure social scientific concepts in a number of different ways. Sometimes, the data set contains a single item that does the job nicely. Measuring gender by asking people for their gender is a good example. In other cases, the mental images that constitute our concepts (e.g., religiosity, political orientation, or prejudice) are varied and ambiguous. Typically, no single item in a data set provides a complete representation of what we have in mind.

Often, we can resolve this problem by combining two or more indicators of the concept into a composite index. As we've seen, SPSS Statistics offers the tools necessary for such data transformations. If you continue your studies in social research, you will discover that there are many more sophisticated techniques for creating composite measures. However, the simple indexing techniques you have learned in this chapter will serve you well in the analyses that lie ahead.

## Main Points

- Concepts can be measured in a number of different ways.

- In some cases, a single item is enough to measure a concept.

- In the case of a controversial and emotionally charged issue such as abortion, where opinion is varied and intricate, no one item is capable of capturing the complexity of opinion.

- In such cases, composite measures made up of multiple indicators of a single concept can be very useful.

- The advantages of using composite measures include measuring the concept of interest more accurately, encompassing multiple dimensions of the concept, and being sensitive to more variation between the extremes of a variable.

- An index is a form of composite measure.

- The Count Values within Cases command allows us to create a new summary variable or index based on the scores of existing variables.

- We created one fairly simple index (ABORT) and one more complicated index (ABINDEX) with Count Values within Cases. Both indices were designed to measure overall feelings about abortion.

- After you create a new variable, it is important to check your work by running frequencies.

- When saving new, recoded variables, those working with the student version of SPSS Statistics must be aware of the limitation to 50 variables; those working with a full version of SPSS Statistics are *not* limited in terms of the number of variables they can save.

## Key Terms

Count command 127

Index 128

## SPSS Statistics Commands Introduced in This Chapter

8.1.  Identifying Variables—File Info

8.2.  Running Frequencies for Several Variables (Not Clustered)

8.3.  Creating a Simple Index Using Count

## Review Questions

1. What is a composite measure?

2. What is an index?

3. Why do researchers create indices? What are the advantages of using an index?

4. In this chapter, we created indices using which command: Analyze, Compute, Count, or Recode?

5. What dialog box do we use to specify which value(s) of certain variables are to be counted?

6. After creating an index, why do you access the Variable View tab?

7. Can indices be based on the scores of more than two variables?

*(Continued)*

[Continued]

8.  Can the procedure used to create indices in this chapter be used if the variables are not coded the same way?

9.  What is one disadvantage of using Count Values within Cases to create an index?

10. In this chapter, we created two indices that helped summarize American attitudes toward abortion.

Setting this issue aside for a moment, what other complicated issues or ambiguous concepts are you personally interested in investigating further? Identify three issues or concepts, at least one of which could be investigated using your DEMO.SAV data file.

## SPSS Statistics Lab Exercise 8.1

NAME: _____

CLASS: _____

INSTRUCTOR: _____

DATE: _____

In this exercise, you will be given an opportunity to create three indices. In order to complete the exercises, you should access the EXERPLUS.SAV file we asked you to create at the end of SPSS Statistics Lab Exercise 7.1. If you did not save the recoded variables, don't worry; when we use them in later exercises, you can simply go back and recode them following the commands in SPSS Statistics Lab Exercise 7.1. At the end of this exercise, we will ask you to save the indices you create on your EXERPLUS.SAV file; so if you are working in a lab setting, make sure you have a USB jump/ flash/thumb drive handy or access to a network drive or cloud (or some other way to safely store your files).

### INDEX 1: POLIN

The first index is based on two variables contained in your EXERPLUS.SAV (or EXER.SAV) data file, POLABUSE and POLATTAK. Simply follow the steps below and supply the information requested.

1. What does the variable POLABUSE measure?

2. What does the variable POLATTAK measure?

3. List the values and labels for POLABUSE and POLATTAK.

| **Value** | **Label** |
|---|---|
| _____ | _____ |
| _____ | _____ |
| _____ | _____ |
| _____ | _____ |

Now define 0, 8, and 9 as "missing" for the variables POLABUSE and POLATTAK. Our new variable/index will be named POLIN (for POLice INdex). POLIN scores are as follows:

0—"Approve/Yes" in both cases

1—"Conditional Approval/Yes" in one case but not the other

2—"Disapprove/No" in both cases

4. The _____ (higher/lower) the index score, the *more the respondent agrees* that there are situations in which he or she would approve of a police officer striking an adult male citizen.

5. The _____ (higher/lower) the index score, the *less the respondent agrees* that there are situations in which he or she would approve of a police officer striking an adult male citizen.

Now, compute new variable/index POLIN. (Hint: Click **Transform → Count**.) Then, define your new variable. (Hint: Access the **Variable View** tab, and then set decimals, width, values/labels, and measure.)

6. Access the **Data View** tab. Use the information in the matrix to complete the first two columns indicating the values for the variables POLABUSE and POLATTAK (Respondents 1–3, 6–8).

*(Continued)*

(Continued)

After completing the first two columns, use the information to fill in the expected index score for each case.

Now, compare the expected index score with the actual POLIN score for each case. Based on this "test," use the space below to indicate whether your index appears to have been completed properly or whether you need to go back and reconstruct the index.

| | Value on POLABUSE | Value on POLATTAK | Expected Index Score | Actual POLIN Score |
|---|---|---|---|---|
| Respondent 1 | | | | |
| Respondent 2 | | | | |
| Respondent 3 | | | | |
| Respondent 4 | | | | |
| Respondent 5 | | | | |
| Respondent 6 | | | | |
| Respondent 7 | | | | |
| Respondent 8 | | | | |

Run frequencies for POLIN, and attach your output to this sheet.

7. Of those who answered,

_____% received a score of 0 on the index.

_____% received a score of 1 on the index.

_____% received a score of 2 on the index.

## INDEX 2: POLFORCE

Now, it is time to compute an index on your own. Create a more complex index (POLFORCE) based on the following four variables: POLABUSE, POLATTAK, POLESCAP, and POLMURDR. Be sure to define 0, 8, and 9 as "missing" for each variable before you begin.

8. After you construct and define your index, run frequencies, and attach your output to this sheet. Then, describe your findings below. What does this index tell us about Americans' attitudes toward the use of force by police officers?

## INDEX 3: CONSTRUCTING AN INDEX OF YOUR CHOICE

Choose variables from the EXER.SAV (or, of course, EXERPLUS.SAV) file, and create an index of your choice. When you are finished, answer the following questions:

9. What variables did you choose, and why?

10. After you construct and define your index, run frequencies, and attach your output to this sheet. Then, describe your findings below. After you are done, be sure to save the indices you created in this lab exercise in your EXERPLUS.SAV file so we can use them in later analyses.

# SUGGESTIONS FOR FURTHER ANALYSIS

In the preceding chapters, we've given you a number of research possibilities to begin exploring based on the variables contained in your DEMOPLUS.SAV (and DEMO.SAV) file. The topics we have focused on so far include religion, politics, and abortion. In the event that you've exhausted those possibilities and want to look beyond them, here are some additional topics for you to consider.

## DESIRED FAMILY SIZE

One of the major social problems facing the world today is that of overpopulation. A brief summary of population growth on the planet illustrates the trend.

| Year | Population | Doubling Time |
|------|-----------|---------------|
| 0 | 0.25 billion | — |
| 1650 | 0.50 billion | 1,650 years |
| 1850 | 1.00 billion | 200 years |
| 1930 | 2.00 billion | 80 years |
| 1975 | 4.00 billion | 45 years |
| 1994 | 5.64 billion | 39 years |
| 1998 | 5.93 billion | 49 years |
| 2002 | 6.27 billion | 54 years |
| 2006 | 6.53 billion | 60 years |
| 2010 | 6.86 billion | 62 years |
| 2014 | 7.25 billion | 73 years |
| 2017 | 7.43 billion | 63 years |

These data show several things. For example, the world's population has increased more than 20-fold since the beginning of the Christian era. More important, until recently, the rate of growth has been increasing steadily. This is most easily seen in the rightmost column, showing what demographers call the **doubling time**. It took 1,650 years for the world's population to increase from a quarter of a billion people to half a billion. The time required for the population to double dramatically shortened until 1994. By 2006, the doubling time had increased to about 60 years. In 2017, the doubling time sits at 63 years. Even with this modest increase in doubling time, however, today's children can expect to be senior citizens in a world with more than 15 billion people.

Although during most of human existence, extremely high death rates were matched by equally high birth rates, during the past few generations, death rates have plummeted around the world because of improved public health measures, medical discoveries, and improved food production. This has resulted in the astounding increase in population.

The current pace of population growth simply cannot go on forever. Although scientists may disagree on the number of people the planet can support, there is simply no question that there is a limit. At some point, population growth must be slowed even more and stopped—perhaps even reversed.

There are two ways to end population growth: Either death rates can be returned to their former high levels, or birth rates can be reduced. Because most of us would choose the latter solution, demographers have been very interested in variables that measure desired family size.

# DEMONSTRATION 9.1: RESPONDENTS' IDEAL FAMILY SIZE (CHLDIDEL)

Your data set contains a variable, CHLDIDEL, that presents responses to the question, "What do you think is the ideal number of children for a family to have?" If every family had only two children, then births and deaths would eventually roughly balance each other out, producing a condition of population stabilization, or zero population growth (excluding the effect of migration). What percentage of the population do you suppose chose that as the ideal? Some favored larger families, and others said they thought only one child was the ideal.

Why don't you find out what the most common response was by running a frequency distribution, as shown below, as well as the appropriate measures of central tendency?[1]

## CHLDIDEL Ideal Number of Children

|  | | Frequency | Percent | Valid Percent | Cumulative Percent |
|---|---|---|---|---|---|
| Valid | 0 | 7 | .5 | .7 | .7 |
| | 1 | 16 | 1.1 | 1.6 | 2.3 |
| | 2 | 449 | 29.9 | 45.4 | 47.8 |
| | 3 | 246 | 16.4 | 24.9 | 72.7 |
| | 4 | 108 | 7.2 | 10.9 | 83.6 |
| | 5 | 17 | 1.1 | 1.7 | 85.3 |
| | 6 | 4 | .3 | .4 | 85.7 |
| | 7 SEVEN+ | 7 | .5 | .7 | 86.4 |
| | 8 AS MANY AS WANT | 134 | 8.9 | 13.6 | 100.0 |
| | Total | 988 | 65.9 | 100.0 | |
| Missing | −1 IAP | 512 | 34.1 | | |
| Total | | 1500 | 100.0 | | |

Later in this book, when we focus on bivariate analysis, you may want to explore the causes of people's attitudes about ideal family size. For instance, it may be interesting to consider whether the number of siblings that respondents have (SIBS) impacts their conception of ideal family size (CHLDIDEL).

---

1. Define the values −1 and 9 as "missing" for CHLDIDEL, if that has not already been done in your file.

# WRITING BOX 9.1

Almost half the respondents (48%) say two children would be ideal, while about a fourth (26%) say three. Eleven percent offer an ambiguous answer, saying that "as many as you want" is the ideal number. About 3% of the sample say they want fewer than two children, and the rest want four or more. The two-child family has become the norm in the United States. The mode is two children. The median is 3, and the mean is 3.35. (It should be noted that the actual mean may be higher since category 7 was truncated, meaning that "7" represented those people who chose seven *or more* children.) As recently as 2012, the median was 2 and the mean was 3.2, which would seem to indicate at least an intended growth in average family sizes going forward.

## CHILD-REARING

What do you think are the most important qualities for children to develop as they grow up? Respondents to the General Social Survey (GSS) were asked that question also.

To frame the question more specifically, they were presented with several of the answers people commonly give and were asked how important each was. The interviewer read the following list (which we've annotated with the GSS variable names). If you had to choose, which thing on this list would you pick as the most important for a child to learn to prepare him or her for life?

| OBEY | To obey |
| POPULAR | To be well liked or popular |
| THNKSELF | To think for himself or herself |
| WORKHARD | To work hard |
| HELPOTH | To help others when they need help |

Once the respondents indicated which of these they felt was most important, they were asked the following:

Which comes next in importance?

Which comes third?

Which comes fourth?

This set of responses allowed the researchers to code the final responses as "Least important."

## DEMONSTRATION 9.2: IMPORTANT QUALITIES FOR CHILDREN

As with earlier topics, take a moment to notice how you feel about such matters. Then, see if you can anticipate what public opinion is about these qualities of children.

It will be useful, by the way, to observe your reasoning process as you attempt to anticipate public opinion. What observations, clues, or cues prompt you to think that OBEY is the most important, or POPULAR, or whichever one you picked as the one most people would choose?

After making a prediction, you can see how people actually responded to the questions. You can use either of the univariate techniques reviewed in earlier chapters (frequencies or graphs) to examine how respondents to the 2016 GSS answered these questions. In this case, let's go ahead and run appropriate graphs and charts for these variables.[2] Once you've done that, you should review your

---

2. Define the values 0, 8, and 9 as "missing" for the variables OBEY, POPULAR, THNKSELF, WORKHARD, and HELPOTH.

earlier reasoning, either to confirm your predictions or to figure out where you went wrong. What can you infer from the differences among your opinions, your predictions, and the actual results?

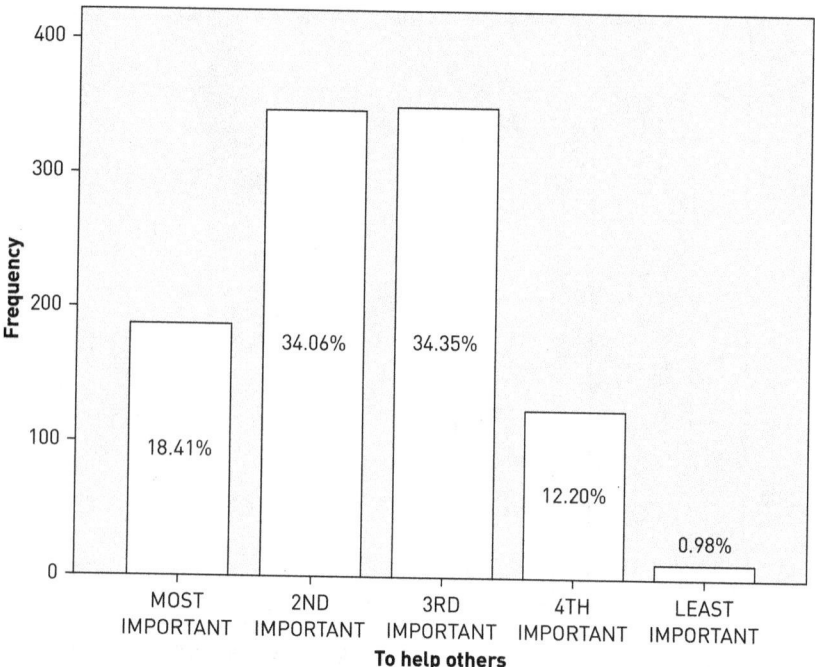

## ATTITUDES ABOUT SEXUAL BEHAVIOR

As with most other things, Americans differ in their feelings about sexual behavior. We thought you might be interested in this area of public opinion, so we've included three GSS variables dealing with two different kinds of sexual behavior. HOMOSEX asks about homosexual sex relations, while PREMARSX focuses on premarital sex. Both variables measure respondents' attitudes toward the behavior of others. Either might be taken as an indication of overall beliefs, but it is important always to remember exactly what variables represent.

One question the use of these variables raises is whether self-reports of behavior can be considered generally reliable. A second question you may want to think about is whether this method of data collection (surveys) should be used primarily to measure opinions and attitudes rather than behavior.

We realize that you may very well have strong opinions about premarital sex and homosexuality. Your job as a social science researcher, however, is to find out what Americans as a whole think and do. Which do you think people tolerate more: premarital sex or homosexuality? Give it some thought, and then check it out using one of the techniques we covered earlier.

It's not too early to begin asking yourself what would cause people to be more tolerant or less so with respect to these behaviors. When we turn to bivariate analysis later on, you'll have a chance to test some of your expectations.

# DEMONSTRATION 9.3: INDEX OF SEXUAL PERMISSIVENESS

Here's an idea that could take you deeper into this general topic. See if you can use the **Transform Count Values within Cases** command to create a composite measure of sexual permissiveness, combining the two items so the higher the index score, the more likely respondents will be sexually permissive.

Go ahead and construct an index called SEXPERM. As always, you will need to make sure of the nonresponses for HOMOSEX and PREMARSX. In this instance, there are four codes that should be defined as "missing" (0, 5, 8, and 9). As a result, you cannot use the "Discrete missing values" option discussed earlier (SPSS Statistics Command 5.4) because it allows you to list only three missing values. In cases where you want to designate four or more values as "missing," use the "Range plus one discrete missing value" option as described in SPSS Statistics Command 9.1.

- Access **Variable View tab**.
- Open Missing Variables dialog box by double-clicking on right side of cell that corresponds to appropriate variable and column labeled "Missing."
- Select **Range plus one discrete missing value** option.
- Type 5 in space next to "Low," 9 in space next to "High," and 0 in box next to "Discrete value" option. This tells SPSS Statistics to designate any value from 5 to 9 and 0 as "missing" for this variable.
- Click **OK**.

---

### SPSS Statistics Command 9.1: Setting Values and Labels as "Missing" Using "Range Plus One" Option

Access **Variable View tab**

Double-click on right side of cell that corresponds to appropriate variable and column "Missing"

Click on circle next to "Range plus one optional discrete missing value"

Insert appropriate low, high, and discrete values

Click **OK**

---

Don't forget to repeat this process for both HOMOSEX and PREMARSX. Once you are done, you will be ready to begin constructing your index by selecting **Transform → Count Values within Cases**.

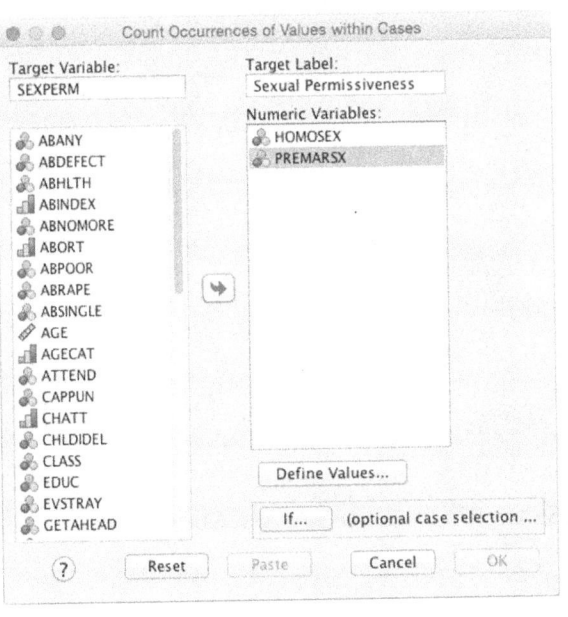

Since Response Code 4, "Not Wrong," indicates permissiveness, you will need to tell Count to count the instances of 4 for both variables.

Use the NMISS function to ensure that only those cases that have responses for both questions are used to construct the index.

After you have created SEXPERM, be sure to add value labels.

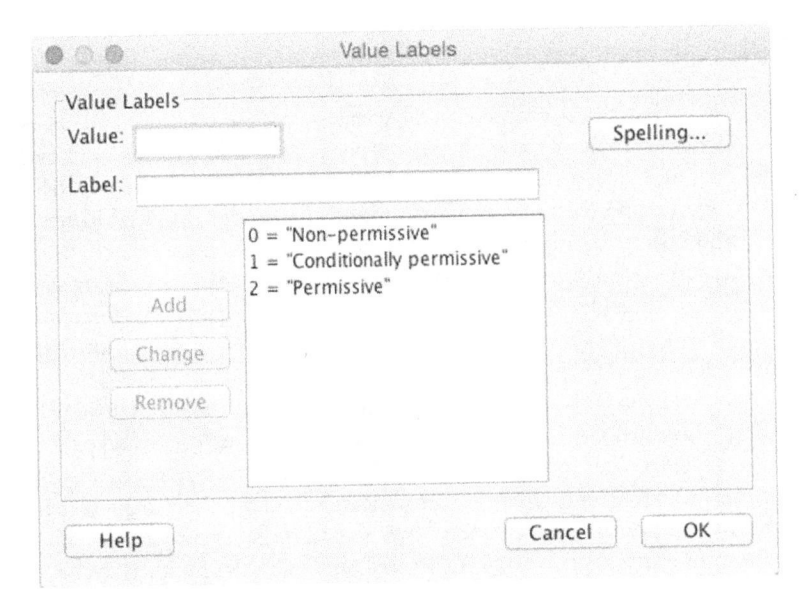

Then, run frequencies to check your index. What conclusions would you draw about the sexual attitudes and behavior of Americans? Are they generally permissive or not? You can check your findings against ours shown below.

## SEXPERM Sexual Permissiveness

|  |  | Frequency | Percent | Valid Percent | Cumulative Percent |
|---|---|---|---|---|---|
| Valid | 0 Non-permissive | 143 | 9.5 | 32.0 | 32.0 |
|  | 1 Conditionally permissive | 106 | 7.1 | 23.7 | 55.7 |
|  | 2 Permissive | 198 | 13.2 | 44.3 | 100.0 |
|  | Total | 447 | 29.8 | 100.0 |  |
| Missing | System | 1053 | 70.2 |  |  |
| Total |  | 1500 | 100.0 |  |  |

# WRITING BOX 9.3   DESCRIPTION OF SEXPERM INDEX

SEXPERM is an index of sexual permissiveness, based on two indicators. HOMOSEX asks respondents whether "sexual relations between two adults of the same sex is always wrong, almost always wrong, wrong only sometimes, or not wrong at all." Those who chose the last response received a score of 1 on the index. The other item in the index, PREMARSX, asked a similar question about a man and a woman having "sex relations before marriage" and was scored the same as HOMOSEX. Thus, respondents who approved of both homosexuality and premarital sex received a score of 2 on the index; those who disapproved (even a little) of both were scored 0. Those who approved of only one (usually premarital sex) and disapproved of the other (even a little) were scored 1. The sexual permissiveness index thus has a range of 0 to 2. A considerable proportion of respondents (32%) had a score of 0, meaning a little less than one-third of GSS respondents disapproved of both premarital sex and homosexuality. A quarter (24%) scored 1, indicating that they were permissive toward one of the two behaviors. Another 44% had a score of 2, indicating that they approved of both premarital sex and homosexuality.

# PREJUDICE

Prejudice is a topic that has concerned social scientists for a long time, and the persistence of the problem keeps it a topic of interest and research. Your data file includes two items from the GSS that deal with aspects of anti-Black prejudice: MARBLK and RACDIF4. Both items deal with different components of prejudice and racial attitudes. MARBLK measures whether respondents (who may be of any race) would favor or oppose a close relative marrying a Black person, whereas RACDIF4 deals with the causes of differences in socioeconomic status. You may want to look at Appendix A for the exact wording of these questions. Remember, it's always important to know exactly how survey questions were asked in order to understand what the responses really mean.

These items present you with an interesting picture of racial attitudes and prejudice in the United States. Where, for instance, do you think the majority of adult Americans stand on the issue of interracial marriage when it comes to a close relative? Do you think most respondents would support or oppose interracial marriage under these circumstances? You may be able to guess that opposition to interracial marriage, in general, has decreased over the years. Before you look at this variable, however, take a moment to try to guess what the level of public support for interracial marriage is when it comes to a close family member. Then, use one of the techniques introduced in earlier chapters to see how well you've been able to anticipate opinion on this issue.

Next, try to estimate overall opinion on the other variable, RACDIF4. It may be somewhat more difficult for you to estimate opinion on this issue, but after you have come up with an estimate, check to see whether you were correct by running frequencies.

You may want to consider creating a composite measure of prejudice called PREJIND from these two variables: MARBLK and RACDIF4. Remember, as in the last demonstration, you need to do a few things before you start constructing your index, beginning with defining the appropriate values for each variable as "missing" and then recoding as noted subsequently.

Designate the values 0, 8, and 9 as "missing" for both MARBLK and RACDIF4. Notice that the values and labels for these variables differ. Consequently, to create an index using Count, you should recode MARBLK to create RACMAR as follows.

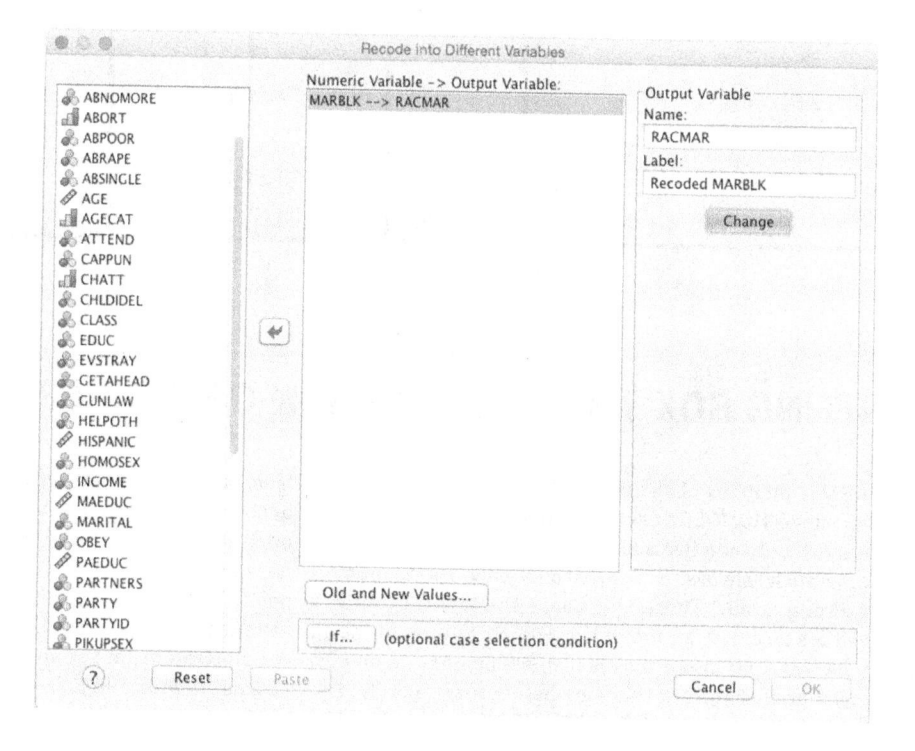

Pay particular attention to the new values and labels before proceeding:

| MARBLK | | RACMAR |
|---|:---:|---|
| Old Values/Labels | | New Values/Labels |
| 1 Strongly favor | → | 2 No/Not oppose marriage |
| 2 Favor | | |
| 4 Oppose | → | 1 Yes/Oppose marriage |
| 5 Strongly oppose | → | |

*Note:* When a different variable is created, old values that are not assigned new values for recoding are set to "missing" in the new variable unless the "Copy old value(s)" option is selected.

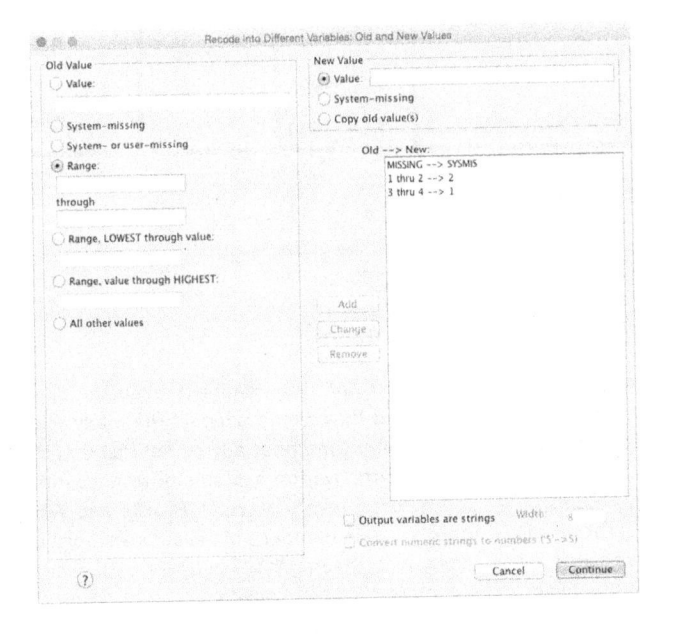

Now use the **Transform Count Values within Cases** command to create a composite measure of prejudice. Combine the two items (your new, recoded variable RACMAR and RACDIF4) so that the higher the index score, the less likely respondents were prejudiced.

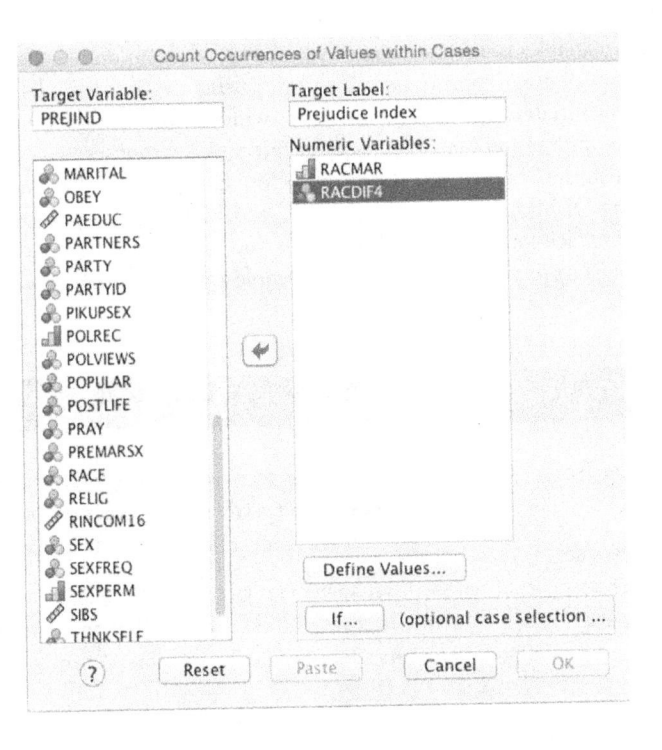

Afterward, be sure to define your new variable, and then run frequencies.

## PREJIND Prejudice Index

| | | Frequency | Percent | Valid Percent | Cumulative Percent |
|---|---|---|---|---|---|
| Valid | 0 Prejudiced | 160 | 10.7 | 26.8 | 26.8 |
| | 1 Conditionally prejudiced | 308 | 20.5 | 51.6 | 78.4 |
| | 2 Not prejudiced | 129 | 8.6 | 21.6 | 100.0 |
| | Total | 597 | 39.8 | 100.0 | |
| Missing | System | 903 | 60.2 | | |
| Total | | 1500 | 100.0 | | |

## WRITING BOX 9.4

PREJIND is an index intended to measure respondents' levels of prejudice. Respondents could get between 0 and 2 points on the index, with lower scores representing higher degrees of prejudice.

Twenty-seven percent of the respondents had PREJIND scores of 0, indicating that they both opposed interracial marriage for a close family member and answered affirmatively to RACDIF4. Nearly four-fifths responded positively to at least one item, while the remainder of the sample (22%) said they would support the interracial marriage of a close family member and do not feel that the lack of willpower or motivation explains differences in jobs, income, and housing levels between Blacks and Whites. Interestingly, smaller numbers of persons anchor both ends of the index, with the majority (just over half) occupying the middle, more moderate position.

## CONCLUSION

There are several other variables in the data set. As you may recall from our discussion in the previous chapters, you can get an overview of the whole thing by using the command **Utilities Variables**. Once you see the list of variables on the left side of the window, you can click any of the variable names to get short descriptions and the codes used for categorical responses.

By the time you finish this chapter, you should be feeling fairly comfortable with SPSS Statistics and the GSS (including DEMO, DEMOPLUS, EXER, and EXERPLUS) data sets. Now you can build on your developing facility. In Part III of this book, you are going to try your hand at bivariate analysis, which lets you start to search for the reasons people are the way they are.

## Main Points

- DEMO.SAV contains a variety of variables that open a number of research possibilities.

- In addition to religion, politics, and abortion, the data set contains variables that deal with issues such as desired family size, child-rearing, attitudes toward sexual behavior, and prejudice.

- Overpopulation is an issue of grave concern that can be dealt with in two primary ways, by increasing the death rate or decreasing the birth rate.

- Because most people prefer a solution that decreases birth rates rather than increases death rates, public opinion regarding ideal family size is an issue of great interest to many researchers.

- If you are interested in child development, public attitudes regarding child-rearing may be of particular interest to you.

- Attitudes toward sexual behavior can be combined to create an interesting measure of sexual permissiveness.

- It is important to note that the variables dealing with sexual behavior, HOMOSEX and PREMARSX, measure

attitudes toward the behavior of others, not the respondents' own behavior.

- Two variables deal with different aspects of prejudice, specifically anti-Black prejudice.

- You can use several of the techniques reviewed in earlier chapters to examine these and other topics in more depth.

- Some of the key techniques we have covered so far include frequencies, measures of central tendency and dispersion, recoding, graphs and charts, and index construction.

## Key Term

Doubling time  143

## SPSS Statistics Command Introduced in This Chapter

9.1.  Setting Values and Labels as "Missing" Using "Range Plus One" Option

## Review Questions

1. What topics besides religion, politics, and abortion are represented by the variables contained in your DEMO.SAV file?

2. List the variables on your DEMO.SAV file that pertain to ideal family size.

3. List two SPSS Statistics techniques reviewed previously that you could use to determine how respondents to the 2016 General Social Survey feel about family size.

4. List the variables on your DEMO.SAV file that pertain to child-rearing.

5. List two SPSS Statistics techniques reviewed earlier that you could use to determine which qualities respondents value in children.

6. List the variables on your DEMO.SAV file that pertain to attitudes about sexual behavior.

7. Do the variable(s) listed in response to Question 6 measure attitudes or behavior?

8. Why might some researchers argue that a measure of self-reported behavior is potentially unreliable?

9. List the variables on your DEMO.SAV file that pertain to prejudice.

10. List two SPSS Statistics techniques reviewed previously that you could use to examine either the topic of sexual attitudes/behavior or prejudice in more depth.

11. Of the four new topics introduced in this chapter, which would you be most interested in examining further, and why?

# SPSS Statistics Lab Exercise 9.1

NAME: _____

CLASS: _____

INSTRUCTOR: _____

DATE: _____

Your EXERPLUS.SAV data file contains a number of additional topics and research possibilities for you to consider, including attitudes about gender roles, law enforcement, the environment, mass media use, national government spending priorities, teen sex, and affirmative action.

In this exercise, you will be asked to choose and examine one of these topics in more depth. Our goal is to allow you to use and apply several of the SPSS Statistics techniques introduced in earlier chapters. In addition, we want you to gain more practice not only with using SPSS Statistics but also with interpreting your findings and writing up research results. Throughout the past few chapters, we have periodically supplied you with Writing Boxes, which illustrate how a social scientist might communicate findings in writing. Remember, the ability to interpret and communicate your findings in writing is crucial. While this skill is as difficult to teach as it is to master, our experience has been that the more you read research reports in the media, scholarly journals, and the like, and the more you practice creating your own research reports, the better your chances of success.

Reminder: All of the techniques we ask you to use in this exercise were discussed in Chapters 5 through 8. If you have any trouble recalling a particular command, please consult the appropriate chapter. There is a list of SPSS Statistics Commands at the end of each chapter and on this book's companion website (https://study.sagepub.com/babbie10e).

1.  From the list provided above, choose a topic or issue you are interested in investigating further.

2.  Use the Utilities Variables command to identify the variables in your EXERPLUS.SAV file that pertain to this issue or topic. Then, list the abbreviated variable name, variable label, and values for each item in the space provided below.

| Abbreviated Variable Name | Variable Label/Description | Values |
|---|---|---|

3.  Using the Internet, the library, or another research tool, investigate the issue or topic you have chosen. Then, write a few short paragraphs in the space below (similar to those in the Writing Boxes in this chapter) that accomplish the following:

    •  Provide a general overview or introduction to this issue or topic.

    •  State why the issue or topic is of interest to you (as well as others).

    •  Highlight at least one of the central questions and controversies that make this issue or topic ripe for social research and further investigation.

*(Continued)*

(Continued)

4. In the space provided below, indicate which of the values for each variable identified in Question 2 should be defined as "missing." Once you have done that, use SPSS Statistics to define these values as "missing."

5. Run frequencies for each variable listed in response to Question 2. Then, summarize your findings in a paragraph or two in the space provided below. Be sure to print your frequencies and attach them to this sheet.

6. Run the appropriate graphs or charts for each variable listed in response to Question 2. Then, summarize your findings in a few short paragraphs in the space below. Be sure to include a title on each of your charts, print them out, and attach them to this sheet.

7. Choose two of the following techniques:

   • Running measures of central tendency and dispersion

   • Recoding

   • Index construction

   Then, use the techniques you chose to investigate the issue or topic you are considering in more depth. After examining the issue or topic, summarize your findings below. In addition, print out and attach your output to this sheet.

# BIVARIATE ANALYSIS

This set of chapters adds another dimension to your analyses. By moving from the analysis of one variable (univariate analysis) to the analysis of two variables (bivariate analysis), we open the possibility of exploring cause and effect.

Thus, in Chapter 10, we'll begin to examine what factors cause some people to be more religious than others. In this analysis, we'll be guided by an earlier analysis, which put forward a "deprivation theory" of church involvement.

In Chapters 11 and 12, our newly learned bivariate techniques will help us explore two important political and social issues. We will begin by trying to discover the roots of political orientation: Why are some people more liberal than others? Why do some people belong to the Democratic Party while others belong to the Republican Party, and still others declare themselves Independents? What are some consequences of political orientation? What differences does political orientation make in terms of other attitudes and orientations?

Chapter 12 takes us deeper inside the hotly controversial issue of abortion. You probably already have a few ideas about why some people are supportive of a woman's right to choose an abortion and others are opposed. Now, you are going to have an opportunity to test your expectations and learn something about the roots of different points of view in this national debate.

In these chapters (10–12), we limit our analyses to percentage tables, a basic format for investigations in social research. However, there are many other methods for measuring the extent to which variables are related to one another. We'll examine some of these in Chapters 13 and 14, where we focus on some common measures of association such as lambda, gamma, Pearson's $r$, and linear regression. You'll learn the logic that underlies these measures, as well as how they help us assess the strength (and in some cases, the direction) of association between variables.

Chapter 15 adds another set of techniques for your use in assessing the associations you discover among variables. Whenever samples have been chosen from a larger population, as is the case with the General Social Survey data, there is always some danger that the associations we discover among variables in our sample are merely results of sampling error and do not represent a genuine pattern in the larger population. Chapter 15 demonstrates several techniques social researchers use to guard against being misled in that fashion.

Finally, as we did in Part II, we'll conclude our examination of bivariate analysis in Chapter 16 with some suggestions for other avenues of inquiry.

# EXAMINING THE SOURCES OF RELIGIOSITY

U p to this point, we have largely limited our discussion to **univariate analysis**, the analysis of one variable. Now, however, we are going to turn our attention to **bivariate analysis**, the analysis of two variables at a time. This will allow us to shift our focus from description (mainly the province of univariate analysis) to the more exciting world of explanation.

It may be useful for you to think about the differences between univariate and bivariate analyses in terms of the number of variables under analysis, the major question to be answered, and the primary goal of the research, as laid out in Table 10.1.

| TABLE 10.1 ■ Distinctions Between Univariate and Bivariate Analysis | | |
| --- | --- | --- |
| | **Univariate Analysis** | **Bivariate Analysis** |
| Number of variables | 1 | 2 |
| Major question | What? | Why? |
| Primary goal | Description | Explanation |

Consequently, whereas in the previous section we looked at the extent of people's religiosity, we now turn our attention to trying to explain "why": *Why* are some people more religious than others? What *causes* some people to be more religious than others? How can we *explain* the fact that some people are more religious than others?

## THE DEPRIVATION THEORY OF RELIGIOSITY

The reading titled "A Theory of Involvement" by Charles Y. Glock, Benjamin R. Ringer, and Earl R. Babbie,[1] which you can find on the study website that accompanies this text (https://study.sagepub .com/babbie10e), presents one explanation for differing degrees of religiosity, the social deprivation theory of religiosity. Simply put, the authors say that people who are denied gratification within secular society will be more likely to turn to church as an alternative source of gratification.

In their analysis, they looked for variables that distinguished those who were getting more gratification in secular society from those who were getting less. For example, they reasoned that the United States is still a male-dominated society, meaning that women are denied the level of gratification enjoyed by men. Women often earn less for the same work, are denied equal access to prestigious

---

1. Glock, C. Y., Ringer, B. B., & Babbie, E. R. (1967). A theory of involvement. In *To comfort and to challenge: A dilemma of the contemporary church* (Chapter 5). Berkeley: University of California Press.

occupations, are underrepresented in politics, and so on. According to the deprivation theory, therefore, women should be more religious than are men.

The data analyses done by Glock et al. (1967), based on a sample of Episcopalian church members, confirmed their hypothesis. The question we might now ask is whether the same is true of the general U.S. population. Our data allow us to test that hypothesis.

# TESTING OUR HYPOTHESIS: CORRELATING RELIGIOSITY AND GENDER

You may recall that at the end of Chapter 7, we asked you to save your recoded variables in a file named DEMOPLUS.SAV. Since we want to use some of our recoded variables in this chapter, go ahead and open the DEMOPLUS.SAV file. If you did not save your recoded variables, don't worry. You can easily recode the necessary variables (ATTEND → CHATT; AGE → AGECAT) by following the recoding commands in Chapter 7.

As we noted earlier, this analysis requires us to advance our analytic procedures to bivariate analysis involving two variables: a cause and an effect. If you think back to our discussion of theory and hypotheses in Chapter 1, you may recall that in this case, religiosity would be the effect, or dependent variable, and gender the cause, or independent variable. This means that gender causes—to some extent—degree of religiosity. Based on this notion, we might construct a hypothesis that states:

> You are more likely to be religious (dependent variable) if you are a woman (category of independent variable—gender) than if you are a man (category of independent variable—gender).

It is often easy to confuse the categories of the variable with the variable itself. Keep in mind that in this case, "woman" and "man" are categories of the independent variable "gender."

To test this hypothesis, we need measures of both the independent and dependent variables. The independent variable (gender) is easy: The variable SEX handles that nicely. But what about our dependent variable (religiosity)? As you'll recall from our earlier discussion, several measures are available to us. For the time being, let's use church attendance as our measure, even though we've noted that it is not a perfect indicator of religiosity in its most general meaning.

You will remember that when we looked at ATTEND in Chapter 7, it had nine categories. If we were to crosstabulate ATTEND and SEX without recoding ATTEND, we would expect a table with 18 (9 × 2) cells. To make our table more manageable, we are going to use the recoded CHATT as our measure of church attendance.

Once we have identified the independent variable (SEX) and dependent variable (CHATT), we are going to ask SPSS Statistics to construct a crosstab or **crosstabulation**.[2] A crosstab is a table or matrix that shows the distribution of one variable for each category of a second variable. Crosstabs are powerful tools because they allow us to determine whether the two variables under consideration are associated. In this case, for instance, is gender (SEX) related to or associated with church attendance (CHATT)?

# DEMONSTRATION 10.1: RUNNING CROSSTABS TO TEST OUR HYPOTHESIS

To access the crosstabs dialog box, click **Analyze Descriptive Statistics Crosstabs.**

Once you work your way through these menu selections, you should reach a window that looks like the one on the next page.

---

2. Some texts and statistical packages refer to crosstabulations as *bivariate distributions*, *contingency tables*, or *two-way frequency distributions*, but SPSS Statistics just refers to them as crosstabs.

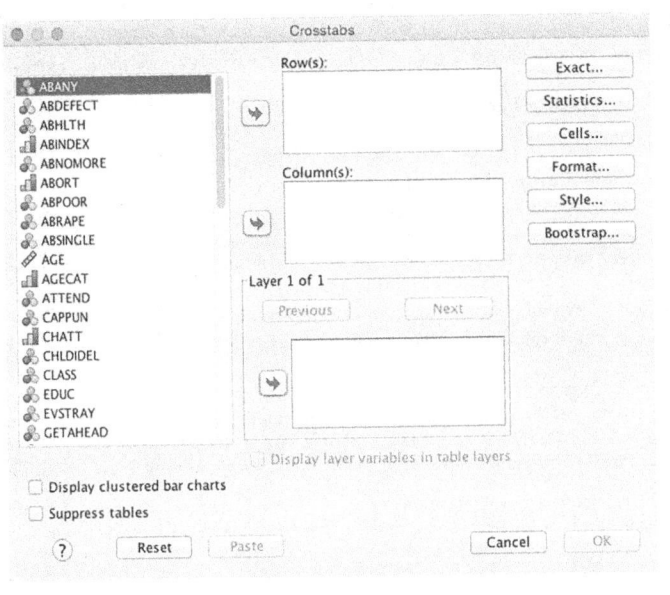

Because the logic of a crosstab will be clearer when we have an example to look at, just follow these steps on faith, and we'll justify your faith in a moment.

When running crosstabs, it is customary to specify the dependent variable as the row variable and the independent variable as the column variable. We will follow this convention by specifying CHATT (dependent variable) as the row variable and SEX (independent variable) as the column variable. (See Table 10.2 for help in determining independent and dependent variables.)

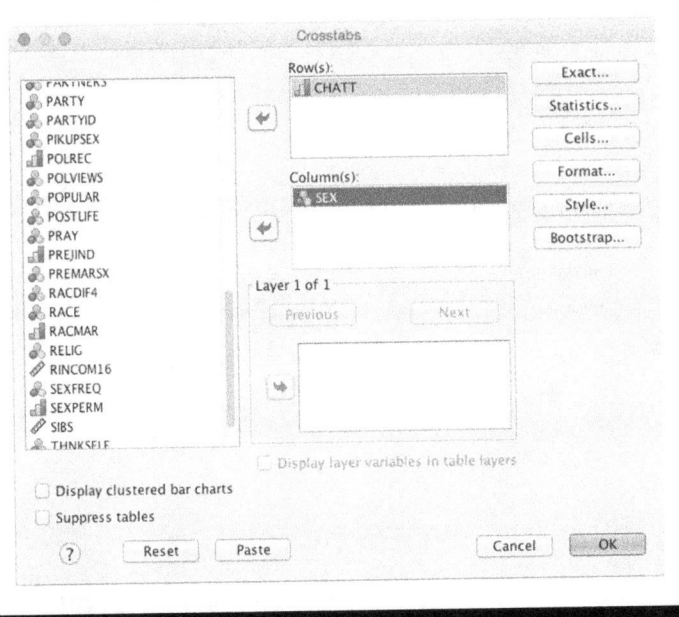

| TABLE 10.2 ■ Tips for Identifying Independent and Dependent Variables[a] |
| --- |
| When running crosstabs on SPSS Statistics, it is important that you first determine which variable is the independent and which is the dependent. Then, specify the independent as the column variable and the dependent as the row variable. Identifying independent and dependent variables can sometimes be tricky. If you are having difficulty differentiating between the independent and dependent variables, try using one of the following strategies:[b] |
| 1. Restate the hypothesis as an "If _____ (independent variable), then_____ (dependent variable)" statement. |
| *Example:* If you are female (independent variable—gender), then you are more likely to be religious (dependent variable—religiosity). |

*(Continued)*

**TABLE 10.2 ■ (Continued)**

2. The independent variable "influences" the dependent variable.

*Example:* Ask yourself if religiosity can "influence" gender. Once you have reasoned that the answer is "no," switch it around. Can gender "influence" religiosity? Since in this case, the answer is "maybe," you know that gender is the independent variable, and religiosity is the dependent variable.

3. The independent variable is the one that comes first in time (i.e., "before" the dependent variable).

*Example:* Ask yourself which came first, gender or religiosity? Since gender is determined before religiosity, you know that gender is the independent variable.

a. For further discussion, see Russell K. Schutt, *Investigating the Social World: The Process and Practice of Research*, 3rd edition (Thousand Oaks, CA: Pine Forge Press, 2001), pp. 39–41; Chava Frankfort-Nachmias & Anna Leon-Guerrero, *Social Statistics for a Diverse Society*, 2nd edition (Thousand Oaks, CA: Pine Forge Press, 2000), pp. 6–8.

b. If it isn't clear which variable is the independent or dependent, it may be that you are dealing with an ambiguous relationship or a case in which either variable could be treated as the independent. We examine this possibility in the next chapter.

Now we want to tell SPSS Statistics to compute column percentages. To do this, simply choose **Cells** at the right of the Crosstabs window. The "Crosstabs: Cell Display" dialog box will appear. Select **Column** in the "Percentages" area; then, click **Continue**.

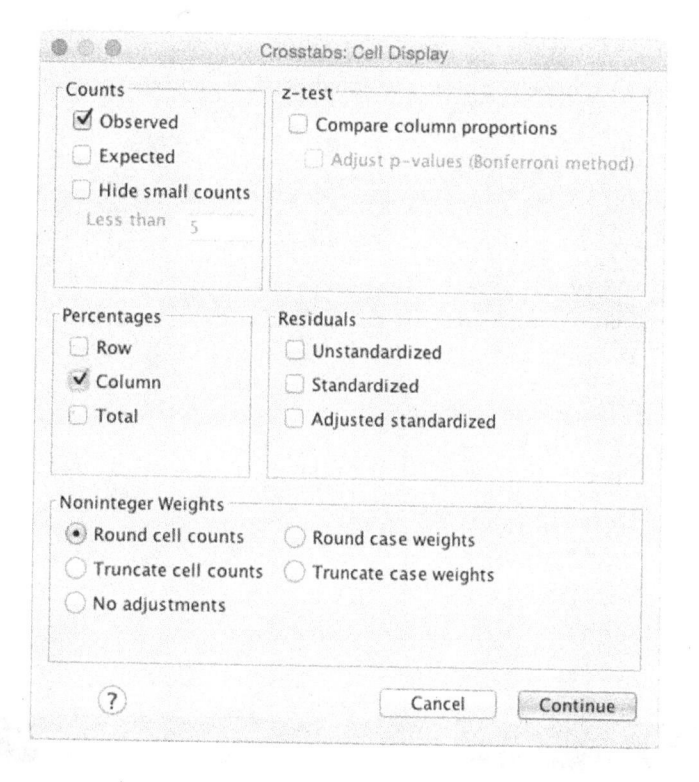

Now hit the **OK** button to execute this command, and in a moment, you should get the result shown at the top of the next page.

## Examining Your Output

Take a moment to examine the crosstab you created. You should notice that as requested, the categories of the independent variable (Male, Female—SEX) are displayed across the top in the columns. The categories of the dependent variable (About weekly, About monthly, Seldom, Never—CHATT) are displayed down the left side of the table in the rows. Now, look at the numbers in each of the squares, or *cells*. You can see that there are two sets of numbers in each cell: the *frequency* (or count) and *column percentage*.

## CHATT Recoded Church Attendance * SEX
## Respondent's Sex Crosstabulation

| | | | SEX Respondent's Sex | | Total |
|---|---|---|---|---|---|
| | | | 1 MALE | 2 FEMALE | |
| CHATT Recoded Church Attendance | 1 About weekly | Count | 177 | 250 | 427 |
| | | % within SEX Respondent's sex | 26.2% | 30.7% | 28.7% |
| | 2 About monthly | Count | 90 | 150 | 240 |
| | | % within SEX Respondent's sex | 13.3% | 18.4% | 16.1% |
| | 3 Seldom | Count | 207 | 247 | 454 |
| | | % within SEX Respondent's sex | 30.7% | 30.3% | 30.5% |
| | 4 Never | Count | 201 | 167 | 368 |
| | | % within SEX Respondent's sex | 29.8% | 20.5% | 24.7% |
| Total | | Count | 675 | 814 | 1489 |
| | | % within SEX Respondent's sex | 100.0% | 100.0% | 100.0% |

If you look in the first cell in the first row of results, you see there are 177 males who attend church about weekly. Below the frequency or count, you find the column percentage. In this instance, we know that 26.2% of male respondents reported attending church about weekly. The column percentage is calculated by dividing the cell frequency (177) by the column total (675) and then multiplying by 100.

In contrast, 250 or 30.7% of female respondents reported attending church about weekly. Once again, the column percentage (30.7) was calculated by dividing the cell frequency (250) by the column total (814) and then multiplying by 100. Luckily, you do not have to go through the process of calculating the column percentages by hand because you have SPSS Statistics to do the work for you.

If we want, we can also note that 39.5% of the men attend church either about weekly or about monthly (26.2% + 13.3%; "About weekly" + "About monthly"). Note also that 49.1% of the women attend either about weekly or about monthly (30.7% + 18.4%; "About weekly" + "About monthly").

In addition to the cell frequencies and column percentages, the table also contains *row totals* and *column totals* (sometimes called *marginals*). These are the frequencies for each variable. In this case, the column totals or marginals tell us that 675 of the respondents to this particular survey question are male, and 814 are female, while the row totals, or marginals, tell us that 427 respondents attend church about weekly, 240 about monthly, 454 seldom, and 368 never.

The column and row totals are followed by the column and row marginal percentages. The column marginal percentages are 100% for each column; the row marginal percentages tell us what percentage of all respondents attend church about weekly (28.7%), about monthly (16.1%), seldom (30.5%), and never (24.7%).

---

### SPSS Statistics Command 10.1: Running Crosstabs—Specifying the Dependent and Independent Variables

Click **Analyze** → **Descriptive Statistics** → **Crosstabs**

Highlight dependent variable → Click arrow pointing to "Row(s):" box

Highlight independent variable → Click arrow pointing to "Column(s):" box

Click **Cells** → Select **Column** in the "Percentages" box

Click **Continue** → **OK**

The *Total* on the bottom right tells us that a total of 1,489 of our 1,500 GSS random subsample respondents gave valid responses to both the SEX and CHATT (recoded ATTEND) questions. This number is often referred to as *N* in statistical analyses.

### Interpreting Crosstabs

The demonstration asked you to run crosstabs to test a hypothesis with two variables, one that is ordinal (CHATT—dependent variable) and one that is nominal (SEX—independent variable). SEX has two categories, while CHATT has four. The larger the number of categories, the more tricky it becomes to read or interpret a table. Therefore, to start, we'll keep things simple by focusing on a table with two nominal variables with just two categories each. Then, we will look at a few crosstabs with variables that have more than two categories.

### Interpreting Crosstabs: Association, Strength, and Direction

As we noted earlier, we run crosstabs to determine whether there is an *association* between two variables. In addition, crosstabs may tell us other important things about the relationship between the two variables—namely, the *strength of association* and, in some cases, the direction of association. We should stress that you can determine the direction of association *only* when both the variables in your table are greater than nominal—that is, capable of "greater than, less than" relationships. If your table contains one or more nominal variables, it is *not* possible to determine the direction.

Once you have created your crosstab, ask yourself the following questions:

1.  Is there an *association* between the two variables?

    If the answer to Question 1 is yes (or maybe) . . .

2.  What is the *strength of association* between the two variables?

    If both variables are ordinal . . .

3.  What is the direction of association?

# DEMONSTRATION 10.2: INTERPRETING A CROSSTAB WITH LIMITED CATEGORIES

Since we have been focusing on the relationship between religiosity and gender, let's run a crosstab with an indicator of religiosity (POSTLIFE) and gender (SEX). POSTLIFE measures respondents' belief in life after death and is measured at the nominal level. In accordance with the deprivation theory, we may hypothesize that women are more likely than men to believe in life after death. Consequently, POSTLIFE is the dependent variable, and SEX is once again the independent variable.

Before running crosstabs, make sure to define the values 0, 8, and 9 as "missing" for the variable POSTLIFE. Now go ahead and request crosstabs, specifying POSTLIFE (dependent variable) as the row variable, SEX (independent variable) as the column variable, and cells to be percentaged by column. If you are working through this chapter all in one session, remember to click **Reset** or move CHATT back to the variable list before proceeding.

### First Question: Is There an Association?

As we noted earlier, the first question you want to ask is whether there is an association between the variables. In examining a crosstab to determine whether an *association* exists between two variables, what we are really trying to determine is whether knowing the value of one variable helps us predict the value of the other variable. In other words, if gender is associated with belief in the

## POSTLIFE Belief in Life After Death * SEX
## Respondent's Sex Crosstabulation

| | | | SEX Respondent's Sex | | Total |
|---|---|---|---|---|---|
| | | | 1 MALE | 2 FEMALE | |
| POSTLIFE Belief in life after death | 1 YES | Count | 458 | 632 | 1090 |
| | | % within SEX Respondent's sex | 75.5% | 85.4% | 80.9% |
| | 2 NO | Count | 149 | 108 | 257 |
| | | % within SEX Respondent's sex | 24.5% | 14.6% | 19.1% |
| Total | | Count | 607 | 740 | 1347 |
| | | % within SEX Respondent's sex | 100.0% | 100.0% | 100.0% |

afterlife, knowing the independent variable (SEX) should help us predict the value of the dependent variable (POSTLIFE). If gender and belief in the afterlife are *not* related or associated, knowing the value of SEX will *not* help us predict the value of POSTLIFE.

To determine whether SEX and POSTLIFE are associated, we read across the rows of the dependent variable to see if there are differences in the column percentages.[3] Let's go ahead and do that for the table we just created. By reading across the first row, we see that women (85.4%) are more likely than men (75.5%) to believe in life after death.

You can also examine the second category of the dependent variable, or the second row (those who do not believe in life after death). Here, we see that a slightly higher percentage of men (24.5%) are likely to report that they do not believe in life after death than are women (14.6%).

The crosstab suggests that women are a little more likely to believe in the afterlife than are men, but knowing respondents' gender does not help conclusively with predicting whether or not people believe in life after death. Perhaps this is worth examining further?

## Second Question: How Strong Is the Association?

If there seems to be an association between the variables, the next logical question is, How strong is the association? In Chapter 13, we provide you with statistical techniques that provide measures of strength for associations. For now, we'll provide a crude method of assessing the strength of associations, which is to examine the size of the differences in the percentages. One general rule to keep in mind is that the larger the percentage differences across the categories, the stronger the association between the variables. Conversely, the smaller the percentage differences across categories, the weaker the association.

Some researchers use a rough ***10-percentage-point rule***. That is, if the percentage point difference is 10 or more, the relationship between the variables is probably worth examining further. Of course, the larger the percentage point difference, the stronger the association. Keep in mind that this "rule of thumb" is just a rough indicator. Whereas some researchers may see a 6- or 8-percentage-point difference as indicating a potentially noteworthy relationship, others may not. (Percentage point "rules" also tend to fluctuate depending on how many columns and/or rows make up the table. For example, a greater number of columns often means that a smaller percentage point difference can be noteworthy.)

In the case of our crosstab between POSTLIFE and SEX, we have just short of a 10-percentage-point difference (85.4% – 75.5% = 9.9%). Based on the 10-percentage-point rule, the relationship would be judged to be weak, unless we rounded up to 10%. However, bear in mind that a number

---

3. One useful rule to keep in mind is that when a table is presented with column percentages—that is, calculated as a percentage of the column totals (as it is in this case and will be for the remainder of the text)—the table should be read across the columns. Conversely, when a table shows row percentages, calculated as a percentage of the row totals, it should be read down the rows.

of researchers may still feel that an 8-percentage-point (or greater) difference warrants some further investigation. In this case, it would seem prudent to investigate further.

Finally, because POSTLIFE and SEX are nominal variables, we cannot ask the third question regarding the direction of association. That question applies only when *both* the variables in your table are measured at the ordinal level or higher.

# DEMONSTRATION 10.3: CORRELATING ANOTHER MEASURE OF RELIGIOSITY AND GENDER

Your file contains a third measure of religiosity we can use to continue our examination: PRAY. As the name implies, this variable measures how often respondents pray: several times a day, once a day, several times a week, and so on.

Take a moment to examine the response categories for the variable PRAY. Remember, you can do this in a number of ways (accessing the **Variable View** tab and then clicking on **Values**, or using the **Utilities** → **Variables** commands).

Based on your examination, it should be clear that PRAY is measured at the ordinal level. It should also be apparent that before running crosstabs, you need to define the values 0, 8, and 9 for this variable as "missing." Once you have done that, go ahead and run crosstabs, specifying PRAY as the row variable and SEX as the column variable, with cells percentaged by column. Once again, if you are doing this in the same session as your previous work, you should click **Reset** or move POSTLIFE back to the variable list before you begin.

## PRAY How Often Does R Pray * SEX Respondent's Sex Crosstabulation

| | | | SEX Respondent's Sex | | Total |
| | | | 1 MALE | 2 FEMALE | |
|---|---|---|---|---|---|
| PRAY How often does R pray | 1 SEVERAL TIMES A DAY | Count | 167 | 274 | 441 |
| | | % within SEX Respondent's sex | 24.8% | 34.0% | 29.8% |
| | 2 ONCE A DAY | Count | 157 | 286 | 443 |
| | | % within SEX Respondent's sex | 23.3% | 35.4% | 29.9% |
| | 3 SEVERAL TIMES A WEEK | Count | 65 | 83 | 148 |
| | | % within SEX Respondent's sex | 9.7% | 10.3% | 10.0% |
| | 4 ONCE A WEEK | Count | 51 | 49 | 100 |
| | | % within SEX Respondent's sex | 7.6% | 6.1% | 6.8% |
| | 5 LT ONCE A WEEK | Count | 84 | 49 | 133 |
| | | % within SEX Respondent's sex | 12.5% | 6.1% | 9.0% |
| | 6 NEVER | Count | 149 | 66 | 215 |
| | | % within SEX Respondent's sex | 22.1% | 8.2% | 14.5% |
| Total | | Count | 673 | 807 | 1480 |
| | | % within SEX Respondent's sex | 100.0% | 100.0% | 100.0% |

Now, take a moment to examine your table. Remember, because one of your variables (SEX) is measured at the nominal level, it is not possible to determine the direction of association between the variables. It is possible, however, to draw some tentative conclusions regarding whether there is a relationship between the variables and, if so, the strength of the association.

Once you have examined your table, compare your answer to the description in Writing Box 10.1. Keep in mind that because crosstabs give us only a rough indication of the strength of association, your interpretation may be somewhat different from the one below.

## WRITING BOX 10.1

As we see in the table, women pray more often than men. For example, 69% of the women in the sample say they pray at least once a day, compared with 48% of the men. Or, looking at the other end of the table, we see that men are more likely (42%) to say they pray once a week or less, including never, than are women (30%).

## DRAWING CONCLUSIONS CAREFULLY: REASSESSING OUR ORIGINAL HYPOTHESIS

Now that we have had a chance to examine three crosstabs involving gender and religiosity, it is important to go back to our original hypothesis. Would you say that we have found support for the thesis put forth by Glock and his coauthors? Remember, we began with a hypothesis based on the deprivation theory, which suggests that people who are deprived of gratification in secular society are more likely to turn to religion as an alternative source of gratification.

Based on our analysis, does the evidence support an assumption of the thesis—that women are still deprived of gratification in American society in comparison with men? Why, or why not? It is important to note that even when we find relationships between variables—such as religiosity and gender—that are worth investigating further, we still have not *proven* our theory. For instance, while there seems to be a fairly strong association between PRAY and SEX, this association is probably best looked at as *evidence of*, not *proof of*, a causal relationship. Because two variables can be associated without there necessarily being a causal relationship, we need to proceed with care when interpreting our findings.

## DEMONSTRATION 10.4: INTERPRETING A CROSSTAB WITH ORDINAL VARIABLES—RELIGIOSITY AND AGE

Now that you've had a chance to practice interpreting crosstabs with variables measured at the nominal level, we will consider a case in which both variables are measured at the ordinal level. As we noted earlier, the greater the number of categories, the more difficult it is to interpret your output.

In addition to focusing on gender, Glock et al. argued that the United States is a youth-oriented society, with gratification being denied to elderly people. Whereas some traditional societies tend to revere their elders, this is not the case in the United States. The deprivation thesis, then, would predict that older respondents are more religious than younger ones. The researchers confirmed this expectation in their data from Episcopalian church members.

Let's check out the relationship between age and religiosity in our GSS data. To make the table manageable, we'll use the recoded AGECAT variable created earlier in Chapter 7.[4] So request a crosstab using[5]

---

4. If you did not save the recoded variable AGECAT, simply go back to Chapter 7 and follow the Recode command to create AGECAT before moving ahead with the demonstrations in this chapter.

5. If you are doing this in the same session as your previous work in this chapter, remember to click **Reset** before specifying your row and column variables for this demonstration.

- CHATT (our dependent variable) as a row variable,
- AGECAT (our independent variable) as a column variable, and
- cells to be percentaged by column.

The resulting table should look like this:

## CHATT Recoded Church Attendance * AGECAT Recoded Age Crosstabulation

| | | | AGECAT Recoded Age | | | | |
| | | | 1 Under 21 | 2 21–39 years old | 3 40–64 years old | 4 65 and older | Total |
|---|---|---|---|---|---|---|---|
| CHATT Recoded Church Attendance | 1 About weekly | Count | 10 | 99 | 188 | 128 | 425 |
| | | % within AGECAT Recoded Age | 30.3% | 20.8% | 28.7% | 39.9% | 28.6% |
| | 2 About monthly | Count | 6 | 96 | 97 | 40 | 239 |
| | | % within AGECAT Recoded Age | 18.2% | 20.2% | 14.8% | 12.5% | 16.1% |
| | 3 Seldom | Count | 9 | 156 | 214 | 73 | 452 |
| | | % within AGECAT Recoded Age | 27.3% | 32.8% | 32.7% | 22.7% | 30.5% |
| | 4 Never | Count | 8 | 124 | 156 | 80 | 368 |
| | | % within AGECAT Recoded Age | 24.2% | 26.1% | 23.8% | 24.9% | 24.8% |
| Total | | Count | 33 | 475 | 655 | 321 | 1484 |
| | | % within AGECAT Recoded Age | 100.0% | 100.0% | 100.0% | 100.0% | 100.0% |

## Interpreting Crosstabs With Ordinal Variables

Because our table contains two ordinal variables, our method of interpretation varies slightly from when we were looking at a table with at least one nominal variable.

Consider the hypothetical example in Table 10.3 of a crosstab with two ordinal variables (Variables A and B). Notice that we have identified the highest percentage in each row of our hypothetical table. Because the highest percentages occur in the three cells that form a diagonal from the upper left to the lower right, this is an indication of a *positive association* between Variables A and B.

| TABLE 10.3    ■    Hypothetical Example of a Positive Association | | | |
|---|---|---|---|
| Variable B (Dependent) | Variable A (Independent) | | |
| | Low | Medium | High |
| Low | 25% | 25% | 50% |
| Medium | 25% | 50% | 25% |
| High | 50% | 25% | 25% |
| Total | 100% | 100% | 100% |

Positive associations are ones in which increases in one variable are related to increases in the other variable. You may be able to think of some variables that you suspect are positively related. One common example is level of education and income. You could hypothesize that the more education you have, the more money you are likely to earn. If this is truly the case, these variables are positively related or associated. In terms of religiosity, you may hypothesize that church attendance and the amount you pray are positively related—meaning that the more you attend church, the more likely you are to pray.

Now consider another example (Table 10.4) depicting a negative relationship between two hypothetical variables. Once again, you will notice that we have indicated the highest percentage in each row. However, in this case, the higher percentages occur in the three cells that form a diagonal line from the bottom left to the upper right side of the table. This indicates a **negative association** between the variables—an increase in one variable is associated with a decrease in the other variable.

**TABLE 10.4  ■  Hypothetical Example of a Negative Association**

| Variable B (Dependent) | Variable A (Independent) | | |
|---|---|---|---|
| | Low | Medium | High |
| Low | 50% | 25% | 25% |
| Medium | 25% | 50% | 25% |
| High | 25% | 25% | 50% |
| Total | 100% | 100% | 100% |

Can you think of two variables that you suspect may be negatively related? How about levels of education and prejudice? Students' alcohol consumption and GPA? If the variables are negatively associated, you will find that as education increases, the level of prejudice decreases. Similarly, as alcohol consumption increases, GPA decreases.

## Examining Your Output

Of course, as we move from hypothetical tables to tables with "real social data," we seldom, if ever, find such clear positive or negative relationships.

Look back at your crosstab of AGECAT and CHATT. If you take a moment to identify the highest percentage in each row, you will quickly notice that it does not form a diagonal line depicting a positive or negative association, such as the hypothetical examples we just looked at. Instead, as is typical when you are dealing with real-life data, the relationship is a little more "messy." Nevertheless, with some slight variations, we can see that older respondents are more likely to report that they attend church than are younger respondents. This would tend to support the deprivation thesis in terms of age, at least to some extent. You should be aware that variations such as those seen here become more common as the number of groups being compared increases.

Once again, while the table gives us an indication of association and strength, other statistics—such as the measures of association we discuss in Chapter 13—are much better indicators of the strength and direction of association.

# DEMONSTRATION 10.5: CORRELATING OTHER MEASURES OF RELIGIOSITY AND AGE

We can request more than one table in our Crosstabs window. You will notice that the commands for this procedure are the same as those listed in SPSS Statistics Command 10.1, except that in this case, we are going to click on two dependent variables and place them both in the "Row(s):" field.

Once you open your Crosstabs window, highlight **POSTLIFE** and move it to the "Row(s):" field. Then, do the same with **PRAY**, placing it in the "Row(s):" field directly below **POSTLIFE**. Now, go ahead and move **AGECAT** to the "Column(s):" field, request that your cells be percentaged by column, and click **OK**.[6]

Now, take a moment to examine your tables. As you do this, keep in mind that one table has an ordinal and a nominal variable, while the other contains two ordinal variables.

## POSTLIFE Belief in Life After Death * AGECAT Recoded Age Crosstabulation

| | | | AGECAT Recoded Age | | | | |
|---|---|---|---|---|---|---|---|
| | | | 1 Under 21 | 2 21–39 years old | 3 40–64 years old | 4 65 and older | Total |
| POSTLIFE Belief in life after death | 1 YES | Count | 26 | 343 | 490 | 226 | 1085 |
| | | % within AGECAT Recoded Age | 96.3% | 80.5% | 81.7% | 78.2% | 80.8% |
| | 2 NO | Count | 1 | 83 | 110 | 63 | 257 |
| | | % within AGECAT Recoded Age | 3.7% | 19.5% | 18.3% | 21.8% | 19.2% |
| Total | | Count | 27 | 426 | 600 | 289 | 1342 |
| | | % within AGECAT Recoded Age | 100.0% | 100.0% | 100.0% | 100.0% | 100.0% |

## PRAY How Often Does R Pray * AGECAT Recoded Age Crosstabulation

| | | | AGECAT Recoded Age | | | | |
|---|---|---|---|---|---|---|---|
| | | | 1 Under 21 | 2 21–39 years old | 3 40–64 years old | 4 65 and older | Total |
| PRAY How often does R pray | 1 SEVERAL TIMES A DAY | Count | 7 | 109 | 213 | 109 | 438 |
| | | % within AGECAT Recoded Age | 21.9% | 23.1% | 32.6% | 34.1% | 29.7% |
| | 2 ONCE A DAY | Count | 6 | 129 | 204 | 103 | 442 |
| | | % within AGECAT Recoded Age | 18.8% | 27.4% | 31.2% | 32.2% | 29.9% |
| | 3 SEVERAL TIMES A WEEK | Count | 7 | 53 | 64 | 24 | 148 |
| | | % within AGECAT Recoded Age | 21.9% | 11.3% | 9.8% | 7.5% | 10.0% |
| | 4 ONCE A WEEK | Count | 0 | 32 | 43 | 25 | 100 |
| | | % within AGECAT Recoded Age | 0.0% | 6.8% | 6.6% | 7.8% | 6.8% |
| | 5 LT ONCE A WEEK | Count | 6 | 48 | 53 | 26 | 133 |
| | | % within AGECAT Recoded Age | 18.8% | 10.2% | 8.1% | 8.1% | 9.0% |
| | 6 NEVER | Count | 6 | 100 | 76 | 33 | 215 |
| | | % within AGECAT Recoded Age | 18.8% | 21.2% | 11.6% | 10.3% | 14.6% |
| Total | | Count | 32 | 471 | 653 | 320 | 1476 |
| | | % within AGECAT Recoded Age | 100.0% | 100.0% | 100.0% | 100.0% | 100.0% |

---

6. Don't forget to click **Reset** or move CHATT back to the variable list before proceeding with this demonstration.

While examining the tables, you may want to consider the following questions and others you may think of: Do age and belief in the afterlife appear to have an association? How about age and prayer? Are older people more likely to believe in the afterlife than are younger people? Do younger people report praying less often or more often than do elderly people, or are they about the same? Based on your interpretation, what conclusions might you draw in regard to our original hypothesis about the relationship between age and religiosity? Is there support for the notion that the older you are, the more religious you are likely to be? Why, or why not? Once you have taken a few minutes to examine these tables, compare your interpretation to that in Writing Box 10.2.

## WRITING BOX 10.2

Age appears to have some impact on belief in life after death. About four fifths of respondents hold this belief in each of the age groups, except for those under 21, where 96% hold this belief.

The relationship between age and prayer seems to guide us in a particular direction. If we look only at praying several times a day, we find that as age increases, so does the likelihood of frequent prayer. Why might this be true? Do people become more concerned about their relationship with a higher power as they age? Or is age a marker for the time when people of that age were born and the state of religiosity in general at that time? Or is there another explanation?

If we combine the first two response categories—representing prayer at least once a day—then we find that 41% of the youngest group say that they pray at least once a day. This increases to 51% among the 21-to-39 group, rises further to 64% among the 40-to-64 group, and reaches a high of 66% in the oldest group.

## Epsilon

Before concluding our initial examination of crosstabs, we want to mention one simple statistic you may find useful. *Epsilon* (ε) is a statistic often used to summarize percentage differences such as those in the tables above. Epsilon is calculated by identifying the largest and smallest percentages in a given row and then subtracting the smallest from the largest.

For example, look back at the first crosstab we ran in this chapter (Demonstration 10.1) comparing gender and church attendance. In comparing men and women in terms of "about weekly" church attendance, the percentage difference (epsilon) is 4.5 points (30.7 – 26.2). This simple statistic is useful because it gives us a tool for comparing sex differences on other measures of religiosity.

When discussing epsilon, it is important to note that technically, tables that have more than two columns have several epsilons, one for each pair of cells being compared. In these cases, researchers will often use epsilon to refer to the largest difference between cell percentages in a given row. As mentioned earlier in the chapter, it is also important to consider the number of columns that make up the table. A crosstabulation with more columns is more likely to exhibit a smaller epsilon than is one with fewer columns. Consider that two columns would have 50% each if the responses split evenly between them. A table with five columns would have 20% in each cell if the responses were divided evenly. Thus, an epsilon of 5 for the former may not seem impressive but would be noteworthy in the latter case.

Returning to our crosstab of church attendance and sex, these data seem to show that women are somewhat more likely than men to attend church frequently. This would seem to support the deprivation theory of religiosity to a limited extent. Take a moment to determine epsilon for the other tables we created in this chapter and see the results suggest similar support for the hypothesis.

This completes our initial foray into the world of bivariate analysis. We hope you've gotten a good sense of the potential for detective work in social research.

# CONCLUSION

In this chapter, we made a critical logical advance in the analysis of social scientific data. Up to now, we have focused our attention on description. With this examination of religiosity, we've crossed over into explanation. We've moved from asking *what* to asking *why*.

Much of the excitement in social research revolves around discovering why people think and act as they do. You've now had an initial exposure to the logic and computer techniques that make such inquiries possible.

Let's apply your new capabilities to other subject matter. In the next chapters, we're going to examine the sources of different political orientations and why people feel as they do about abortion.

## Main Points

- In this chapter, we shifted our focus from univariate analysis to bivariate analysis.

- Univariate analysis is the analysis of one variable at a time.

- Bivariate analysis is the analysis of two variables at a time.

- Univariate and bivariate analysis differ in terms of the number of variables analyzed, major questions asked, and primary research goals.

- We began our bivariate analysis by considering why some people are more religious than others.

- In this analysis, we were guided by the social deprivation theory of religiosity.

- We used this theory to develop a hypothesis stating that women are more likely to be religious than are men.

- This hypothesis contains two variables: gender (independent variable/cause) and religiosity (dependent variable/effect).

- It is important not to confuse the categories of a variable with the variable itself.

- We tested this hypothesis by running crosstabs with column percentages.

- When running crosstabs, it is customary to specify the dependent variable as the row variable and the independent variable as the column variable.

- Throughout the chapter, we ran several crosstabs correlating religiosity (as measured by CHATT, PRAY, and POSTLIFE) with gender (as measured by SEX) and then age (as measured by AGECAT).

- You can run crosstabs with both nominal and ordinal variables

- As a general rule, the more categories in your variables, the more difficult it becomes to interpret your crosstab table.

- When interpreting crosstabs, we are generally looking to see whether an association exists between two variables.

- We look for an association by reading across categories of the dependent variable.

- A difference of 10 or more percentage points is sometimes taken as an indication that an association between variables is worth investigating further. This is just a general rule of thumb, however, and additional factors that bear on this decision, such as the number of columns, are discussed in this chapter.

- In addition to allowing us to look for an association between the variables, crosstabs give us a rough indication of the strength and, in some cases, the direction of association.

- Bear in mind, however, that the measures of association we focus on in Chapter 13 give us a much better basis for drawing conclusions about the nature, strength, and direction of association between variables.

- An association between variables is best looked at as evidence of, not proof of, a causal relationship.

- Epsilon is a simple statistic used to summarize percentage differences.

## Key Terms

10-percentage-point rule 167
Association 166
Bivariate analysis 161
Cells 164
Column percentage 164
Column totals 165

Crosstabulation 162
Epsilon (ε) 173
Frequency 164
Marginals 165
Negative association 171
Positive association 170

Row totals 165
Strength of association 166
Total (N) 166
Univariate analysis 161

## SPSS Statistics Command Introduced in This Chapter

10.1. Running Crosstabs—Specifying the Dependent and Independent Variables

## Review Questions

1. What is univariate analysis?

2. What is bivariate analysis?

3. What are the major differences between univariate and bivariate analysis in terms of the number of variables analyzed, major questions asked, and primary goals of the research?

4. In a hypothesis, the variable that is said to "cause" (to some extent) variation in another variable is referred to as what type of variable?

5. What three general questions might you ask yourself when examining a crosstab with two ordinal variables?

*Identify the independent and dependent variables in the following hypotheses (Questions 6 and 7):*

6. Those employed by companies with more than 20 employees are more likely to have some form of managed-choice health care than are those employed by companies with fewer employees.

7. In the United States, women are more likely to vote Democratic than men are.

8. What are the categories of the independent variable in the hypothesis in Question 7?

9. When running crosstabs, is it customary to specify the dependent variable as the row or column variable?

10. If you were running crosstabs to test the relationship between the variables in the hypothesis in Question 6, which variable would you specify as the row variable, and which would you specify as the column variable?

11. If you produce a crosstab for the variables SEX and PARTYID (with the following categories: Democrat, Republican, Independent, and other), is it possible to determine the direction of association between these two variables? Why, or why not?

12. A researcher produces a crosstab for the variables AGECAT and level of happiness (with the following categories: low, medium, and high) and finds a negative relationship between these two variables. Does this mean that the older you are, the happier you are likely to be or the older you are, the less happy you are likely to be?

13. A researcher produces a crosstab for the variables class (with the following categories: lower, working, middle, and upper) and level of contentment (with the following categories: low, medium, and high) and finds that members of the upper class are more likely to be content than are members of the middle, working, and lower classes. Based on this hypothetical example, how would you describe the direction of association between these variables?

14. What is epsilon?

15. How is epsilon calculated?

16. Can there be more than one epsilon in a table that has more than two columns?

17. If you run crosstabs and find a strong relationship between the independent and dependent variables in your hypothesis, are you better off looking at this association as evidence of or proof of a causal relationship?

# SPSS Statistics Lab Exercise 10.1

NAME: _____

CLASS: _____

INSTRUCTOR: _____

DATE: _____

*To complete the following exercises, you should load the data file EXERPLUS.SAV.*

A number of studies have addressed the relationship between race and attitudes toward sex roles. In a 1992 study, Jill Grigsby* argued that Whites are more likely than Blacks to believe that a woman's working has a detrimental impact on her children.

We are going to test this hypothesis using the variables RACE (as a measure of race) and FECHLD (as a measure of opinions regarding the impact of women working outside the home on their children). Follow the steps listed below, and supply the information requested in the spaces provided (Questions 1–10).

1. Restate the hypothesis linking RACE and FECHLD.

2. Identify the independent and dependent variables in the hypothesis.

3. When running crosstabs, which variable should you specify as the row variable?

4. When running crosstabs, which variable should you specify as the column variable?

5. What is the level of measurement for RACE?

6. What is the level of measurement for FECHLD?

7. Now run crosstabs with column percentages to test the hypothesis. (Do not forget to define 0, 8, and 9 as missing values for FECHLD before you begin.) When you have produced your table, present your results by filling in the following information:

   a. List the categories of the independent variable in the spaces provided on Line A.

   b. In the spaces provided on Line B, list the percentage of respondents who "strongly agree" and "agree" with the statement that a woman's working does not hurt children (i.e., sum of those who "strongly agree" + "agree" on FECHLD).

---

*Grigsby, J. S. (1992). Women change places. *American Demographics*, 14(11), 48.

(Continued)

(Continued)

FECHLD by RACE

Line A _____

_____

_____

Line B _____

_____

_____

8. Are the results consistent with your hypothesis as stated in response to Question 1? Explain.

9. Compare Blacks and Whites in terms of agreement ("strongly agree" + "agree") with the statement that a woman's working does not hurt children, and give the percentage difference (epsilon) below.

10. Do your findings show evidence of a causal relationship between RACE and FECHLD? Explain.

Continue to research the causes of differing attitudes toward sex roles by selecting one independent and one dependent variable from the following lists:

Independent variables: SEX, RACE, CLASS (select one)

Dependent variables: FEFAM, FEHIRE, FEPRESCH (select one)

As before, run crosstabs with column percentages to test your hypothesis, and then fill in the information requested in the spaces provided (Questions 11–18).

11. State and explain your hypothesis involving the independent variable and dependent variable you chose from the lists above.

12. Identify the independent and dependent variables in your hypothesis.

13. When running crosstabs, which variable should you specify as the column variable, and which should you specify as the row variable?

14. Identify the level of measurement for each of the variables in your hypothesis.

15. Now run crosstabs with column percentages to test your hypothesis. Remember to define the appropriate values as "missing" for both of your variables. Then complete the exercise below:

    a. List the abbreviated variable names of your independent and dependent variables on Line A.

    b. List the categories of the independent variable in the spaces provided on Line B. (Use only as many blank spaces as necessary.)

    c. List the percentage of respondents who "strongly agree" and "agree" for either FEFAM, FEHIRE, or FEPRESCH on Line C (i.e., sum of those who "strongly agree" + "agree" for the variable you have chosen); use only as many blank spaces as necessary.

LINE A _____ by _____

              **[Dependent Variable]**              **[Independent Variable]**

LINE B _____   _____

      _____   _____

      _____   _____

LINE C _____   _____

      _____   _____

      _____   _____

16. Are these results consistent with your hypothesis as stated in response to Question 11? Explain.

17. Compute epsilon.

18. Do your findings show evidence of a causal relationship between your independent and dependent variables? Explain.

*Continue to research the causes of differing attitudes toward sex roles by selecting one independent and one dependent variable from the following lists:*

Independent variables: AGE, EDUC (select one)

Dependent variables: FEFAM, FEHIRE, FEPRESCH (select one)

*This time, however, recode the independent variable before proceeding. Then, run crosstabs with column percentages to test your hypothesis, and fill in the information requested in the spaces provided (Questions 19–23).*

19. State and explain your hypothesis involving the recoded independent variable and dependent variable you chose from the lists above.

(Continued)

20. Identify the independent and dependent variables in your hypothesis.


21. When running crosstabs, which variable should you specify as the column variable, and which should you specify as the row variable?


22. Identify the level of measurement for each of the variables in your hypothesis.


23. Now run crosstabs with column percentages to test your hypothesis. (Remember to define the appropriate values as "missing" before proceeding.) Then, print and attach a copy of your table to this sheet. Analyze and then write a short description of your findings below (similar to those in Writing Box 10.1). In particular, you may want to consider whether the results are consistent with your hypothesis and whether there appears to be an association between the variables. If so, how strong is the association? If applicable, what is the direction of association? Based on your examination, is this association worth investigating further? Why, or why not? Include relevant percentages.


24. Access the SPSS Statistics Help feature Tutorial, and review the section titled "Crosstabulation Tables."

    *Hint:* Click **Help → Tutorial → Crosstabulation Tables**

# POLITICAL ORIENTATIONS AS CAUSE AND EFFECT

In looking for the sources of religiosity, we worked with a coherent theory (the deprivation theory). As we noted earlier, this process is called *deductive research*, and it is usually the preferred approach to data analysis. Sometimes, however, it's appropriate to take a less structured route, beginning with data and then proceeding to theory. As you may recall, this process is known as *inductive research*. As we turn our attention to politics in this chapter, we're going to be more inductive than deductive so you can become familiar with this approach as well.

In Chapter 6, we examined two 2016 General Social Survey (GSS) variables: POLVIEWS and PARTYID. In the analyses to follow, we'll look at the relationship between these variables. You can do that now that you understand the crosstabs command. Next, we'll explore some of the variables that cause differences in political philosophies and party identification, such as age, religion, gender, race, education, class, and marital status. Finally, we'll look at POLVIEWS and PARTYID as independent variables to determine what impact they have on other variables.

## THE RELATIONSHIP BETWEEN POLVIEWS AND PARTYID

Let's begin with the recoded forms of our two key political variables, POLVIEWS and PARTYID. You may recall that when we recoded these items in Chapter 7, we named them POLREC and PARTY. We then recommended that you save these variables on a file named DEMOPLUS.SAV. Go ahead and open your DEMOPLUS.SAV file now. If you did not save the recoded variables, don't worry. Simply follow the recoding commands listed in Chapter 7 before continuing.

As we indicated earlier, the consensus is that Democrats are more liberal than Republicans, and Republicans are more conservative than Democrats, although everyone recognizes the existence of liberal Republicans and conservative Democrats. The GSS data allow us to see what the relationship between these two variables actually is. Because neither variable is logically prior to the other, we could treat either as the independent variable. For our present purposes, it is probably useful to explore both possibilities: (1) Political philosophy causes party identification (political philosophy as the independent variable), and (2) party identification causes political philosophy (party identification as the independent variable).

## DEMONSTRATION 11.1: POLREC BY PARTY

To begin, then, let's see if Democrats are more liberal or more conservative than Republicans. Before beginning your examination, make sure you define the value 4 ("Other") for the variable PARTY as "missing." Now, go ahead and run crosstabs, specifying

- POLREC as the row variable,
- PARTY as the column variable, and
- cells to be percentaged by column.

## POLREC Recoded POLVIEWS * PARTY Political Party Crosstabulation

| | | | PARTY Political Party | | | | |
| --- | --- | --- | --- | --- | --- | --- | --- |
| | | | 1 Democrat | 2 Independent | 3 Republican | 4 Other | Total |
| POLREC Recoded POLVIEWS | 1 Liberal | Count | 234 | 151 | 21 | 5 | 411 |
| | | % within PARTY Political Party | 49.3% | 26.3% | 6.1% | 16.1% | 28.8% |
| | 2 Moderate | Count | 165 | 264 | 71 | 14 | 514 |
| | | % within PARTY Political Party | 34.7% | 45.9% | 20.6% | 45.2% | 36.1% |
| | 3 Conservative | Count | 76 | 160 | 252 | 12 | 500 |
| | | % within PARTY Political Party | 16.0% | 27.8% | 73.3% | 38.7% | 35.1% |
| Total | | Count | 475 | 575 | 344 | 31 | 1425 |
| | | % within PARTY Political Party | 100.0% | 100.0% | 100.0% | 100.0% | 100.0% |

The data in this table confirm the general expectation. Of the Democrats in the GSS sample, 49% describe themselves as liberals, in contrast to 6% of the Republicans. The Independents fall between the two parties, with 26% saying they are liberals. The relationship can also be seen by reading across the bottom row of percentages: 16% of the Democrats, versus 73% of the Republicans, call themselves conservatives.

# DEMONSTRATION 11.2: PARTY BY POLREC

We can also turn the table around logically and ask whether liberals or conservatives are more likely to identify with the Democratic Party (or which are more likely to say they are Republicans). You can get this table by simply reversing the location of the two variable names in the earlier command: Run the crosstabs procedure again; only this time, make PARTY the row variable and POLREC the column variable. The results are shown at the top of the next page.

Again, the relationship between the two variables is evident. Liberals are more likely (56%) to say they are Democrats than are moderates (57%) or conservatives (only 15%). Could you also state the relationship between POLREC and PARTY in terms of the likelihood that people of various political orientations will support the Republican Party? Absolutely. Either way of stating the relationship is appropriate.

In summary, then, an affinity exists between liberalism and Democrats and between conservatism and Republicans. At the same time, it is not a perfect relationship, and you can find plenty of liberal Republicans and conservative Democrats in the tables.

Now, let's switch gears and see if we can begin to explain why people are liberals or conservatives, Democrats or Republicans. In the previous chapter, when we began our discussion of bivariate analyses, we examined why some people are more religious than others. Now, in this chapter, we are going to ask similar questions about political orientation and party identification: Why are

## PARTY Political Party *
## POLREC Recoded POLVIEWS Crosstabulation

| | | | POLREC Recoded POLVIEWS | | | |
| --- | --- | --- | --- | --- | --- | --- |
| | | | 1 Liberal | 2 Moderate | 3 Conservative | Total |
| PARTY Political Party | 1 Democrat | Count | 234 | 165 | 76 | 475 |
| | | % within POLREC Recoded POLVIEWS | 56.9% | 32.1% | 15.2% | 33.3% |
| | 2 Independent | Count | 151 | 264 | 160 | 575 |
| | | % within POLREC Recoded POLVIEWS | 36.7% | 51.4% | 32.0% | 40.4% |
| | 3 Republican | Count | 21 | 71 | 252 | 344 |
| | | % within POLREC Recoded POLVIEWS | 5.1% | 13.8% | 50.4% | 24.1% |
| | 4 Other | Count | 5 | 14 | 12 | 31 |
| | | % within POLREC Recoded POLVIEWS | 1.2% | 2.7% | 2.4% | 2.2% |
| Total | | Count | 411 | 514 | 500 | 1425 |
| | | % within POLREC Recoded POLVIEWS | 100.0% | 100.0% | 100.0% | 100.0% |

some people more liberal (or conservative) than others? Why do some people identify themselves as Democrats, while others identify themselves as Republicans, Independents, or "other"? What causes people to be liberals or conservatives, Democrats or Republicans?

## Age and Politics

Often, the search for causal variables involves the examination of **demographic** (or background) **variables**, such as age, religion, sex, race, education, class, and marital status. Such variables often have a powerful impact on attitudes and behaviors. Let's begin with age.

A common belief is that younger people are more liberal than are older people—that people get more conservative as they get older. As you can imagine, liberals tend to see this as a trend toward stodginess, whereas conservatives tend to explain it as a matter of increased wisdom. Regardless of the explanation you might prefer, let's see if it's even true that older people are more conservative than are younger people.

# DEMONSTRATION 11.3: POLREC BY AGECAT

To find out, run crosstabs. In this case, age (as measured by AGECAT) would be the independent variable, and political views (as measured by POLREC) would be the dependent variable.[1] Consequently, you should specify POLREC as the row variable and AGECAT as the column variable. See the next page for what you should get.

---

1. If you did not save the recoded variable AGECAT, go back to Chapter 7 and follow the recoding commands before continuing.

## POLREC Recoded POLVIEWS *
## AGECAT Recoded Age Crosstabulation

|  |  |  | AGECAT Recoded Age | | | | |
|---|---|---|---|---|---|---|---|
|  |  |  | 1 Under 21 | 2 21–39 years old | 3 40–64 years old | 4 65 and older | Total |
| POLREC Recoded POLVIEWS | 1 Liberal | Count | 10 | 147 | 175 | 83 | 415 |
|  |  | % within AGECAT Recoded Age | 33.3% | 32.4% | 27.7% | 26.2% | 29.0% |
|  | 2 Moderate | Count | 10 | 178 | 227 | 101 | 516 |
|  |  | % within AGECAT Recoded Age | 33.3% | 39.2% | 35.9% | 31.9% | 36.0% |
|  | 3 Conservative | Count | 10 | 129 | 230 | 133 | 502 |
|  |  | % within AGECAT Recoded Age | 33.3% | 28.4% | 36.4% | 42.0% | 35.0% |
| Total |  | Count | 30 | 454 | 632 | 317 | 1433 |
|  |  | % within AGECAT Recoded Age | 100.0% | 100.0% | 100.0% | 100.0% | 100.0% |

How would you interpret the table above? Do older age groups appear to be more conservative than younger age groups? Are older age groups more liberal than younger age groups, or would you interpret the table in another way? One thing you probably notice is that the relationship between age and ideology is not as strong as you may have thought initially, though there is certainly a relationship—what is it?

# DEMONSTRATION 11.4: PARTY BY AGECAT

What would you expect to find in terms of political party identification (as measured by PARTY)? Do you expect to find growing strength for Republicans as people grow older? Are young people more likely to identify themselves as Democrats? Here's an opportunity to test these ideas. Why don't you try it yourself and see what you get? Then compare your table with the one on the next page.

### Interpreting Your Table: The Relationship Between Age and Party Identification

How would you interpret this table? What's the relationship between age and party identification? See if you can interpret this table yourself before moving on.

As you can see, in the relationship between AGECAT and PARTY, younger people are much less likely to call themselves Democrats than are older people. When we examine the third row, we discover that young people are just as likely to call themselves Republicans as are older people. (It is important to note that the sample size for the "Under 21" column is very small, increasing the probability of sampling error for this group.)

As such, the middle row, those identifying themselves as Independents, is perhaps most interesting of all. This identification appears to be more common among the young than among

**PARTY Political Party \***
**AGECAT Recoded Age Crosstabutation**

| | | | AGECAT Recoded Age | | | | |
|---|---|---|---|---|---|---|---|
| | | | 1 Under 21 | 2 21–39 years old | 3 40–64 years old | 4 65 and older | Total |
| PARTY Political Party | 1 Democrat | Count | 5 | 145 | 223 | 113 | 486 |
| | | % within AGECAT Recoded Age | 15.2% | 30.9% | 34.3% | 35.4% | 33.0% |
| | 2 Independent | Count | 15 | 222 | 267 | 100 | 604 |
| | | % within AGECAT Recoded Age | 45.5% | 47.2% | 41.0% | 31.3% | 41.0% |
| | 3 Republican | Count | 11 | 91 | 144 | 103 | 349 |
| | | % within AGECAT Recoded Age | 33.3% | 19.4% | 22.1% | 32.3% | 23.7% |
| | 4 Other | Count | 2 | 12 | 17 | 3 | 34 |
| | | % within AGECAT Recoded Age | 6.1% | 2.6% | 2.6% | 0.9% | 2.3% |
| Total | | Count | 33 | 470 | 651 | 319 | 1473 |
| | | % within AGECAT Recoded Age | 100.0% | 100.0% | 100.0% | 100.0% | 100.0% |

the old. Thus, older people are more likely than younger ones to identify with a political party; younger people are more likely to describe themselves as independent. The clearest relationship in this table is that the likelihood of identifying with some political party increases dramatically with age.

Realize that the observed pattern is amenable to more than one explanation. It could be that people become more likely to identify with the major parties as they grow older. On the other hand, the relationship might reflect a trend phenomenon: a disenchantment with the major parties in recent years, primarily among young people. To test these competing explanations, you would need to analyze **longitudinal data**, those representing the state of affairs at different points in time. Because the GSS has been conducting surveys since 1972, we have such data extending back more than a quarter century, making such further analysis possible.

## Religion and Politics

In the United States, the relationship between religion and politics is somewhat complex, especially with regard to Roman Catholics. Let's begin with political philosophies. We will ask SPSS Statistics to run crosstabs for RELIG with POLREC.

# DEMONSTRATION 11.5: POLREC BY RELIG

Before we run crosstabs, however, we need to make our measure of religious affiliation (RELIG) more manageable. You may recall from our earlier discussion that RELIG contains 16 categories.

Because we are primarily interested in the four largest categories (Protestant, Catholic, Jewish, and agnostic/atheist) as opposed to the smaller categories labeled "Other" (Mormon, Buddhist, and Moslem), we want to instruct SPSS to define the latter as "missing."

You can review the labels and values for this item by accessing the Variable View tab and then double-clicking in the rectangle that corresponds with RELIG and Values (or by looking at the codebook in Appendix A). Do that now, and you will see that we want to define the values 0, 5 to 13, 98, and 99 as "missing." Now, go ahead and define these values as "missing" by using the "Range plus one discrete missing value" option. In this case, we want to list the range of values as 5 through 99 and the discrete value as 0.

Now you are ready to run your crosstabs for RELIG (independent/column variable) and POLREC (dependent/row variable).

### POLREC Recoded POLVIEWS * RELIG R's Religious Preference Crosstabulation

| | | | RELIG R's Religious Preference | | | | |
| --- | --- | --- | --- | --- | --- | --- | --- |
| | | | 1 PROTESTANT | 2 CATHOLIC | 3 JEWISH | 4 NONE | Total |
| POLREC Recoded POLVIEWS | 1 Liberal | Count | 145 | 94 | 16 | 124 | 379 |
| | | % within RELIG R's religious preference | 20.6% | 27.8% | 64.0% | 43.5% | 28.1% |
| | 2 Moderate | Count | 249 | 137 | 7 | 90 | 483 |
| | | % within RELIG R's religious preference | 35.4% | 40.5% | 28.0% | 31.6% | 35.8% |
| | 3 Conservative | Count | 309 | 107 | 2 | 71 | 489 |
| | | % within RELIG R's religious preference | 44.0% | 31.7% | 8.0% | 24.9% | 36.2% |
| Total | | Count | 703 | 338 | 25 | 285 | 1351 |
| | | % within RELIG R's religious preference | 100.0% | 100.0% | 100.0% | 100.0% | 100.0% |

We did not define "None" as "missing" because, as you can see, it is a meaningful category. Notice that agnostics and atheists ("None," 44%) have a higher likelihood of identifying themselves as politically liberal than Protestants or Catholics, as do Jews (64%). Jews are also the least likely to identify as conservative (8%). Among members of the other three categories, Agnostics and Atheists ("None") are the least conservative (25%), followed by Catholics (32%) and then Protestants (44%).

If you were to make a gross generalization about the relationship between religious affiliation and political philosophy, you might place Protestants and Catholics on the right end of the political spectrum and Jews and "Nones" (Agnostics and Atheists) on the left, with the caveat that Protestants tend to be more conservative than Catholics.

## DEMONSTRATION 11.6: PARTY BY RELIG

Political party identification, however, is a somewhat different matter. Like Jews, Roman Catholics have been an ethnic minority throughout much of U.S. history, and the Democratic Party, in the past century at least, has focused more on minority rights than has the Republican Party. That could explain a relationship between religion and political party in which Catholics and Jews tend to identify as Democrats. Why don't you run that table now? Make PARTY the row variable and RELIG the column variable.

## PARTY Political Party * RELIG R's Religious Preference Crosstabulation

| | | | RELIG R's Religious Preference | | | | |
| | | | 1 PROTESTANT | 2 CATHOLIC | 3 JEWISH | 4 NONE | Total |
|---|---|---|---|---|---|---|---|
| PARTY Political Party | 1 Democrat | Count | 208 | 127 | 16 | 97 | 448 |
| | | % within RELIG R's religious preference | 28.7% | 36.9% | 64.0% | 32.8% | 32.3% |
| | 2 Independent | Count | 270 | 137 | 6 | 153 | 566 |
| | | % within RELIG R's religious preference | 37.3% | 39.8% | 24.0% | 51.7% | 40.7% |
| | 3 Republican | Count | 232 | 75 | 3 | 34 | 344 |
| | | % within RELIG R's religious preference | 32.0% | 21.8% | 12.0% | 11.5% | 24.8% |
| | 4 Other | Count | 14 | 5 | 0 | 12 | 31 |
| | | % within RELIG R's religious preference | 1.9% | 1.5% | 0.0% | 4.1% | 2.2% |
| Total | | Count | 724 | 344 | 25 | 296 | 1389 |
| | | % within RELIG R's religious preference | 100.0% | 100.0% | 100.0% | 100.0% | 100.0% |

As we see in the table, Jews are the most likely to identify themselves with the Democratic Party, with 64% reporting such affiliation. Catholics have the next highest likelihood of identifying themselves as Democrats at 37%, followed by Agnostics/Atheists ("Nones") at 33%. Protestants, on the other hand, are far more likely (32%) than members of any other of these groups to report an affiliation with the Republican Party.

If you are interested in these two variables, you might want to explore the relationship between politics and the other religious variables we've examined: POSTLIFE and PRAY. On the other hand, you could look for other consequences of RELIG. What else do you suppose might be affected by differences of religious affiliation?

## Gender and Politics

Gender is a demographic variable associated with a great many attitudes and behaviors. Take a minute to think about the reasons women might be more liberal or more conservative than men.

# DEMONSTRATION 11.7: PARTY AND POLREC BY SEX

Once you've developed expectations regarding the relationship between gender and political views, use SPSS Statistics to examine the actual association between these variables. Begin by running crosstabs for SEX and POLREC.

## POLREC Recoded POLVIEWS *
## SEX Respondent's Sex Crosstabulation

| | | | SEX Respondent's Sex | | Total |
|---|---|---|---|---|---|
| | | | 1 MALE | 2 FEMALE | |
| POLREC Recoded POLVIEWS | 1 Liberal | Count | 187 | 229 | 416 |
| | | % within SEX Respondent's sex | 28.6% | 29.2% | 28.9% |
| | 2 Moderate | Count | 217 | 302 | 519 |
| | | % within SEX Respondent's sex | 33.2% | 38.5% | 36.1% |
| | 3 Conservative | Count | 249 | 254 | 503 |
| | | % within SEX Respondent's sex | 38.1% | 32.4% | 35.0% |
| Total | | Count | 653 | 785 | 1438 |
| | | % within SEX Respondent's sex | 100.0% | 100.0% | 100.0% |

According to the table, a larger percentage of men (38%, vs. 32% of women) identify themselves as conservative. Furthermore, a slightly larger percentage of women (30%) identify themselves as liberal compared with men (29%). With epsilon equal to 6, the relationship between gender and political ideology may warrant further investigation, but the relationship appears not to be particularly strong.

You can also run crosstabs for SEX and PARTY. Here are the results.

## PARTY Political Party *
## SEX Respondent's Sex Crosstabulation

| | | | SEX Respondent's Sex | | Total |
|---|---|---|---|---|---|
| | | | 1 MALE | 2 FEMALE | |
| PARTY Political Party | 1 Democrat | Count | 188 | 298 | 486 |
| | | % within SEX Respondent's sex | 28.0% | 37.0% | 32.9% |
| | 2 Independent | Count | 292 | 315 | 607 |
| | | % within SEX Respondent's sex | 43.5% | 39.1% | 41.1% |
| | 3 Republican | Count | 172 | 179 | 351 |
| | | % within SEX Respondent's sex | 25.6% | 22.2% | 23.7% |
| | 4 Other | Count | 20 | 14 | 34 |
| | | % within SEX Respondent's sex | 3.0% | 1.7% | 2.3% |
| Total | | Count | 672 | 806 | 1478 |
| | | % within SEX Respondent's sex | 100.0% | 100.0% | 100.0% |

The association between party identification and gender is indeed noteworthy. Women are more likely to identify with the Democratic Party (37%) than are men (28%), with an epsilon of 9. Among other things, this may reflect the fact that the Democratic Party has been more explicit in its support for women's issues in recent years than has the Republican Party.

## Race and Politics

Given our brief discussion previously about politics and religious minority groups, such as Jews and Roman Catholics, what relationship do you expect to find between politics and race? The variable available to you for analysis (RACE) codes only "White," "Black," and "other," so it's not possible to examine this relationship in great depth, but you should be able to make some educated guesses about how Caucasians and African Americans might differ politically.

# DEMONSTRATION 11.8: POLREC BY RACE

After you've thought about the likely relationship between race and politics, why don't you run the tables and test your ability to predict such matters? Begin by exploring the association, if any, of race with political orientation.

### POLREC Recoded POLVIEWS *
### RACE Race of Respondent Crosstabulation

| | | | RACE Race of Respondent | | | |
| | | | 1 WHITE | 2 BLACK | 3 OTHER | Total |
|---|---|---|---|---|---|---|
| POLREC Recoded POLVIEWS | 1 Liberal | Count | 294 | 71 | 51 | 416 |
| | | % within RACE Race of respondent | 27.4% | 30.3% | 38.6% | 28.9% |
| | 2 Moderate | Count | 371 | 99 | 49 | 519 |
| | | % within RACE Race of respondent | 34.6% | 42.3% | 37.1% | 36.1% |
| | 3 Conservative | Count | 407 | 64 | 32 | 503 |
| | | % within RACE Race of respondent | 38.0% | 27.4% | 24.2% | 35.0% |
| Total | | Count | 1072 | 234 | 132 | 1438 |
| | | % within RACE Race of respondent | 100.0% | 100.0% | 100.0% | 100.0% |

The table shows that Whites are notably more likely to be conservative (38%) than are Blacks (27%). There is a smaller but still noteworthy difference when it comes to liberalism: Blacks are more likely than Whites (30% and 27%, respectively) to identify themselves as liberal.

# DEMONSTRATION 11.9: PARTY BY RACE

While the correlation between political views and race may not have been as pronounced as you expected, the relationship between race and political party identification is very strong, reflecting the Democratic Party's orientation toward minority groups. Blacks are far more likely to identify as Democrats (59%) than are Whites (26%). While a similar percentage of Whites claim the Republican label as the Democratic one (29%), just 2% of Blacks identify as Republicans, illustrating stark differences in political party affiliation between Blacks and Whites.

## PARTY Political Party *
## RACE Race of Respondent Crosstabulation

| | | | RACE Race of Respondent | | | |
|---|---|---|---|---|---|---|
| | | | 1 WHITE | 2 BLACK | 3 OTHER | Total |
| PARTY Political Party | 1 Democrat | Count | 284 | 143 | 59 | 486 |
| | | % within RACE Race of respondent | 26.0% | 59.1% | 41.5% | 32.9% |
| | 2 Independent | Count | 473 | 77 | 57 | 607 |
| | | % within RACE Race of respondent | 43.2% | 31.8% | 40.1% | 41.1% |
| | 3 Republican | Count | 312 | 18 | 21 | 351 |
| | | % within RACE Race of respondent | 28.5% | 7.4% | 14.8% | 23.7% |
| | 4 Other | Count | 25 | 4 | 5 | 34 |
| | | % within RACE Race of respondent | 2.3% | 1.7% | 3.5% | 2.3% |
| Total | | Count | 1094 | 242 | 142 | 1478 |
| | | % within RACE Race of respondent | 100% | 100% | 100% | 100% |

### Education and Politics

Education, a common component of social class, is likely to be of interest to you, especially if you are currently a college student. From your own experience, what would you expect to be the relationship between education and political philosophy?

# DEMONSTRATION 11.10:
# RECODING EDUC → EDCAT

Before we test the relationship between these variables, we need to recode our measure of education (EDUC) to make it more manageable. We will create a new variable called EDCAT and save it on our DEMOPLUS.SAV file.

Before you begin recoding, make sure to define the values 97, 98, and 99 for EDUC as "missing." Then, follow the instructions on the following pages.

| EDUC | | EDCAT | |
|---|---|---|---|
| Old Values | | New Values | Labels |
| Lowest to 11 | → | 1 | Less than high school |
| 12 | → | 2 | High school graduate |
| 13 to 15 | → | 3 | Some college |
| 16 | → | 4 | College graduate |
| 17 to 20 | → | 5 | Graduate studies (beyond college) |

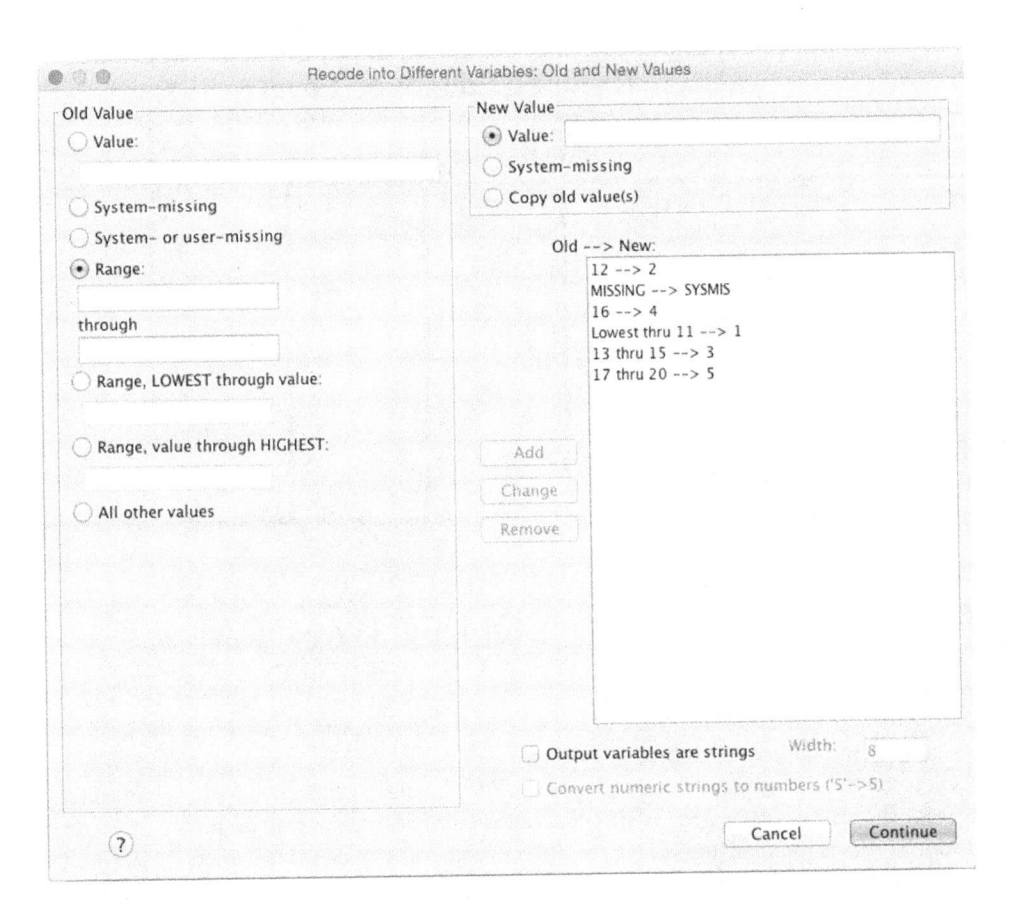

Don't forget to go back and add the labels for EDCAT in the Variable View.

After you have successfully recoded and labeled EDCAT, check your results by running frequencies on the new variable. Your table should look like the one below.

## EDCAT Recoded Education Level

| | | Frequency | Percent | Valid Percent | Cumulative Percent |
|---|---|---|---|---|---|
| Valid | 1 Less than high school | 180 | 12.0 | 12.1 | 12.1 |
| | 2 High school graduate | 427 | 28.5 | 28.6 | 40.7 |
| | 3 Some college | 401 | 26.7 | 26.9 | 67.5 |
| | 4 College graduate | 266 | 17.7 | 17.8 | 85.3 |
| | 5 Graduate studies (beyond college) | 219 | 14.6 | 14.7 | 100.0 |
| | Total | 1493 | 99.5 | 100.0 | |
| Missing | System | 7 | .5 | | |
| Total | | 1500 | 100.0 | | |

# DEMONSTRATION 11.11: POLREC BY EDCAT

Now we are ready to run crosstabs for EDCAT (independent/column variable) and POLREC (dependent/row variable) so you can find out whether your expectations regarding the relationship between these variables are accurate.

As you can see in the table on the next page, while liberalism generally increases with education (except for the least educated group), this does not mean that conservatism declines with increasing education. Perhaps the most important row on the table is the middle one, which shows that those with less than a college degree tend to be more moderate than those with bachelor's and advanced degrees.

## POLREC Recoded POLVIEWS * EDCAT Recoded Education Level Crosstabulation

| | | | EDCAT Recoded Education Level | | | | | |
| --- | --- | --- | --- | --- | --- | --- | --- | --- |
| | | | 1 Less than high school | 2 High school graduate | 3 Some college | 4 College graduate | 5 Graduate studies (beyond college) | Total |
| POLREC Recoded POLVIEWS | 1 Liberal | Count | 37 | 83 | 108 | 92 | 95 | 415 |
| | | % within EDCAT Recoded Education Level | 22.4% | 20.6% | 27.7% | 35.1% | 43.8% | 28.9% |
| | 2 Moderate | Count | 67 | 178 | 154 | 64 | 56 | 519 |
| | | % within EDCAT Recoded Education Level | 40.6% | 44.3% | 39.5% | 24.4% | 25.8% | 36.1% |
| | 3 Conservative | Count | 61 | 141 | 128 | 106 | 66 | 502 |
| | | % within EDCAT Recoded Education Level | 37.0% | 35.1% | 32.8% | 40.5% | 30.4% | 35.0% |
| Total | | Count | 165 | 402 | 390 | 262 | 217 | 1436 |
| | | % within EDCAT Recoded Education Level | 100.0% | 100.0% | 100.0% | 100.0% | 100.0% | 100.0% |

# DEMONSTRATION 11.12: PARTY BY EDCAT

But how about political party? You decide how to structure your crosstabs SPSS Statistics command to obtain the table shown on the next page.

The relationship here is consistent with the findings in the previous table in that the less educated tend to be independents. Those with a 4-year college degree are generally split (with some differences) between the categories. Those who have attended graduate school, however, tend to be Democrats or Independents. One thing is for certain: The trend does not monotonically move toward Democrat or Republican as years of education increase. This may have to do with other interdependent factors, such as the major one chooses in college or family income. Another issue we have neglected to discuss in detail is that our EDCAT variable is an estimate of degree level. Perhaps actual degree earned produces a different picture. All three of those variables (major, income, and degree), by the way, are in the full GSS2016.SAV data file, available free of charge on our student study website (https://study.sagepub.com/babbie10e)—so the adventure of finding out awaits you!

## PARTY Political Party * EDCAT Recoded
## Education Level Crosstabulation

| | | | EDCAT Recoded Education Level | | | | | |
|---|---|---|---|---|---|---|---|---|
| | | | 1 Less than high school | 2 High school graduate | 3 Some college | 4 College graduate | 5 Graduate studies (beyond college) | Total |
| PARTY Political Party | 1 Democrat | Count | 57 | 128 | 124 | 85 | 89 | 483 |
| | | % within EDCAT Recoded Education Level | 32.0% | 30.5% | 31.2% | 32.4% | 40.8% | 32.7% |
| | 2 Independent | Count | 92 | 177 | 162 | 92 | 84 | 607 |
| | | % within EDCAT Recoded Education Level | 51.7% | 42.2% | 40.7% | 35.1% | 38.5% | 41.2% |
| | 3 Republican | Count | 26 | 108 | 102 | 74 | 41 | 351 |
| | | % within EDCAT Recoded Education Level | 14.6% | 25.8% | 25.6% | 28.2% | 18.8% | 23.8% |
| | 4 Other | Count | 3 | 6 | 10 | 11 | 4 | 34 |
| | | % within EDCAT Recoded Education Level | 1.7% | 1.4% | 2.5% | 4.2% | 1.8% | 2.3% |
| Total | | Count | 178 | 419 | 398 | 262 | 218 | 1475 |
| | | % within EDCAT Recoded Education Level | 100.0% | 100.0% | 100.0% | 100.0% | 100.0% | 100.0% |

# SOME SURPRISES: CLASS, MARITAL STATUS, AND POLITICS

Sometimes, the inductive method of analysis produces some surprises. As an example, you might take a look at the relationship between our political variables and the demographic variables CLASS and MARITAL.[2]

## Social Class

You might expect that social class is related to political philosophy and party identification because the Democratic Party has traditionally been strong among the working class, whereas the well-to-do have seemed more comfortable as Republicans. If you are so inclined, why don't you check whether this relationship still holds true? You can use the variable CLASS, which is a measure of subjective social class, asking respondents how they view themselves in this regard.

After you have done that, try to interpret your tables in much the same way we did with the tables before. What do your tables show? Is there a relationship between subjective social class and political philosophy or party identification? Are the results consistent with your expectations, or are they surprising in some way?

---

2. Define 0 and 5 to 9 as "missing" for CLASS and 9 as "missing" for MARITAL.

**Marital Status**

In addition, you may also want to take a look at the relationship between marital status and political orientation. If even the suggestion of a relationship between marital status and political orientation sounds far-fetched to you, the results of this analysis may be surprising.

Once you've run the tables, try to interpret them and think of any good reasons for the observed differences. Here's a clue: Try to think of other variables that might account for the patterns you've observed. Later, when we engage in multivariate analysis, you'll have a chance to check out some of your explanations.

# THE IMPACT OF PARTY AND POLITICAL PHILOSOPHY

Let's shift gears now and consider politics as an independent variable. What impact do you suppose political philosophy and/or political party might have on people's attitudes toward some of the political issues we looked at earlier? Ask yourself where liberals and conservatives would stand on the following issues: GUNLAW, or registration of firearms, and CAPPUN, or capital punishment. Then, run the tables to find out if your hunches are correct. Remember, when POLREC is the independent variable, you need to alter its location in the crosstabs command, making it the column variable.

After you've examined the relationship between political philosophies and these more specific political issues, consider the impact of political party as well. In forming your expectations here, you might want to review recent platforms of the two major parties or the speeches of candidates from the two parties. Then, see if the political party identification of the American public aligns with the views of the parties on these issues.

# SAVING RECODED VARIABLE: EDCAT

Before concluding your SPSS Statistics session, be sure to save the data set, including the newly recoded variable EDCAT, under the name DEMOPLUS.SAV so we can use it later on.

# CONCLUSION

We hope this chapter has given you a good look at how exciting the detective work called social science research can be. We're willing to bet that some of the results you've uncovered in this chapter pretty much squared with your understanding of American politics, whereas other findings came as a surprise.

The skills you are learning in this book, along with your access to SPSS Statistics and the GSS data, make it possible for you to conduct your own investigations into the nature of American politics and other issues that may interest you. In the chapter that follows, we're going to return to our examination of attitudes toward abortion. This time, we want to learn what causes differences in attitudes on this controversial topic.

## Main Points

- While in the previous chapter we began with a theory of religiosity, in this chapter, we took a more inductive approach, using the data to see what associations might emerge.

- We examined the causes (and effects) of political orientation by focusing primarily on the recoded forms of our two main political variables: POLVIEWS and PARTYID.

*(Continued)*

(Continued)

- We examined what causes some people to be liberals or conservatives, Democrats or Republicans.

- In searching for causal variables, we focused primarily on demographic items such as age, religion, gender, race, education, class, and marital status.

- The bulk of the chapter was devoted to explaining what causes people to hold various political views

or to identify with one political party or another. In these analyses, we identified POLREC and PARTY as dependent variables.

- It is also possible to look at political views and party identification as independent variables to see how they might determine people's attitudes on political issues such as gun control and capital punishment.

## Key Terms

Demographic variables  183

Longitudinal data  185

## SPSS Statistics Commands Introduced in This Chapter

No new commands were introduced in this chapter.

## Review Questions

1. What is the difference between deductive and inductive data analysis?

2. Which approach did we use in Chapter 10 to examine religiosity?

3. Which approach did we use to examine political orientations in this chapter (Chapter 11)?

4. What did we find when we crosstabulated POLREC and PARTY?

5. Do our findings suggest that all conservatives are Republican and all liberals are Democrats?

6. Name three demographic variables in your DEMO. SAV data file.

7. Is the variable CAPPUN a demographic variable? How about INCOME?

8. Of the three religious categories we examined, which is the most liberal? Which is the most conservative?

9. Summarize the relationship between gender and our political variables.

10. There is a strong relationship between race and party identification. Describe that relationship. Can we conclude from this that there is an equally strong relationship between race and political views?

11. Describe the relationship between education levels and party identification.

12. Summarize the relationship between marital status and political orientation. How can we explain these results?

13. Does either political philosophy or party identification determine attitudes about issues such as gun control or capital punishment?

# SPSS Statistics Lab Exercise 11.1

NAME: _____

CLASS: _____

INSTRUCTOR: _____

DATE: _____

*To complete the following exercises, you need to load the EXERPLUS.SAV data file.*

1. What causes some people to feel that the national government is spending too little on improving and protecting Americans' health? We will use the variables NATHEAL and HEALTH to begin to address this question.

   - Define the values 0, 8, and 9 as "missing" for both NATHEAL and HEALTH.

   - Run crosstabs with NATHEAL as your dependent variable, HEALTH as your independent variable, and cells to be percentaged by column.

   - Print your output.

   - On Line A below, write the names of the categories of HEALTH using as many spaces as necessary. On Line B, fill in the spaces noting the percentage who answered "Too little" on NATHEAL for each category of HEALTH.

NATHEAL by HEALTH

Line A _____     _____

_____     _____

_____     _____

Line B _____     _____

_____     _____

_____     _____

Do the column percentages in the summary table above suggest that there is a relationship between the variables? If so, what is that relationship?

2. Choose one demographic variable from your EXERPLUS.SAV data file, and state your expectations regarding the relationship between that variable (as the independent variable) and NATHEAL (as the dependent variable). (Depending on which variable you chose, you may need to recode it to make it more manageable.)

   a. Was it necessary for you to recode the demographic variable you chose as your independent variable? If so, explain how you recoded the variable by listing the name of the variable you recoded, the name of the new (recoded) variable, the old value labels, and the new value labels.

   **GSS Variable**                                                    **Recoded Variable**

   b. Run crosstabs with NATHEAL as your dependent variable and the variable you chose as the independent variable, and print your table.

*(Continued)*

(Continued)

  c. Then, on Line A below, write the name of your independent variable. On Line B, write the names of the categories of your independent variable using as many spaces as necessary. On Line C, fill in the spaces, noting the percentage who answered "Too little" on NATHEAL for each category of the independent variable.

Line A NATHEAL by _____

Line B _____          _____

  _____          _____

  _____          _____

Line C_____          _____

  _____          _____

  _____          _____

  d. Do the column percentages in the summary table you created above suggest that there is a relationship between the variables? _____

  e. Summarize and explain your findings below. You may want to note, for instance, whether the findings match your expectations and whether you were surprised by the findings.

3. Choose one of the following variables as your dependent variable: NATEDUC, NATRACE, or NATFARE. Note the name of the variable you chose and what it measures below.

  _____

  a. Now, choose a second variable from your data set as your independent variable. Note the name of the variable and what it measures below. If it is necessary to recode your variable, note how you did that below.

  _____

  **GSS Variable**                                             **Recoded Variable**

  b. What are your expectations regarding the relationship between your independent and dependent variables?

  c. Run crosstabs, and print your table. Then, summarize and explain your findings below. You may want to note, for instance, whether there is a relationship between your independent and dependent variables. Do the findings match your expectations? Were you at all surprised by the results? If so, why? If not, why not?

In this chapter, we examined the relationship between PARTY and POLREC in two ways: (1) PARTY as the "cause," or independent variable, and (2) POLREC as the "cause," or independent variable. In the following exercise, we are going to consider the relationship between two variables on your EXERPLUS.SAV file having to do with opinions about sex education in the public schools and whether marijuana should be legal (SEXEDUC and GRASS), both of which can be technically examined as the "cause" and as the "effect." In other words, both variables can be considered either the independent or dependent variable.

4. How might the variables SEXEDUC and GRASS be related to each other?

   a. Define the values 0 and 3 through 9 as "missing" for SEXEDUC.

   b. Construct a hypothesis in which SEXEDUC is the independent variable and GRASS is the dependent variable.

   c. Using your recoded variables, test your hypothesis by running crosstabs. Print and attach your output to this sheet. Then, in the space provided below, analyze your findings. You may want to consider questions such as these: How does the dependent variable change with changes in the independent variable? How strong is the relationship between the variables?

5. Now, construct a hypothesis in which GRASS is the independent variable and SEXEDUC is the dependent variable.

   a. Use your recoded variables, and test the hypothesis by running crosstabs. Print and attach your output to this sheet. Then, in the space provided below, analyze your findings. You may want to consider questions such as these: How does the dependent variable change with changes in the independent variable? How strong is the relationship between the variables?

6. Now, choose two other variables on your EXERPLUS.SAV file that can be treated as the "cause" and as the "effect."

   • Once you have identified the variables, make sure you define the appropriate values for each variable as "missing"; recode if necessary.

   • Then, run crosstabs to examine the relationship between the variables. Remember, you should run crosstabs twice, examining each variable as the "cause" (or independent variable).

   • Once you have run crosstabs, print your output, and attach it to this sheet. Then, write a short description of your findings below. Your primary goal is to identify and describe the general pattern (and any exceptions to that pattern) in the tables. In addition, you may want to ask yourself: What is the nature of association between the variables in each table? How does the dependent variable change with changes in the independent variable? How strong is the association between the variables? What general pattern(s) is/are evident in each table? Are there any exceptions to this pattern that are worth noting? Is one variable "better" viewed as the "cause" or independent variable?

# WHAT CAUSES DIFFERENT ATTITUDES TOWARD ABORTION?

One of the most controversial issues of recent years has concerned whether a woman has the right to have an abortion. Partisans on both sides of this issue are often extremely vocal and demonstrative.

In this chapter, we're going to use your new analytic skills to begin exploring the causes of different points of view on abortion. Whereas in the previous two chapters, we focused on running and interpreting crosstabs, in this chapter, we want to use our output to create summary tables that help us understand relationships between variables. Specifically, why are some people permissive toward abortion and others not? As we pursue this question, we can profit from an excellent review of the research on abortion attitudes: Cook, Jelen, and Wilcox's *Between Two Absolutes: Public Opinion and the Politics of Abortion*.[1] Chapter 2 from that book is available on the *Adventures in Social Research* student study website (https://study.sagepub.com/babbie10e) to serve as a background for the analyses we'll undertake in this chapter. You may also find it suggestive of additional directions for analysis, if you would like to pursue this topic beyond the first steps we take here.

## DEMONSTRATION 12.1: GENDER AND ABORTION

Go ahead and open your DEMOPLUS.SAV file so we can use some of the variables we created earlier.

As you think about possible causes of different attitudes toward abortion, the first one that probably comes to mind is gender, given that abortion affects women more directly than it does men. In a quote that has become a popular pro-choice bumper sticker, Florence Kennedy put it this way several years ago: "If men could get pregnant, abortion would be a sacrament." There is reason to believe, therefore, that women would be more supportive of abortion than would men. Let's see.

On the next page is a table that summarizes attitudes toward abortion by gender. It is not SPSS Statistics output, but we've created it from several SPSS Statistics tables. Your task is to figure out how to produce the SPSS Statistics tables that would allow you to create this table.[2]

---

1. Cook, A. E., Jelen, T., & Wilcox, C. (1992). *Between two absolutes: Public opinion and the politics of abortion*. Boulder, CO: Westview Press.

2. If you are having trouble figuring out how to access the information used to create this table, don't worry. The commands are as follows: Run crosstabs for the seven abortion variables (row variables) and SEX (column variable), cells to be percentaged by column. You should get seven crosstabs that can be used to create this table (i.e., the percentage of men and women who responded "Yes" to each item). Make sure you are clear as to how this table was created before moving ahead because we will ask you to set up similar tables later in the chapter.

| Percentage Approving of Abortion Under the Following Conditions | | Men | Women |
|---|---|---|---|
| ABHLTH | Woman's health endangered | 89 | 88 |
| ABRAPE | Resulted from rape | 78 | 77 |
| ABDEFECT | Serious defect likely | 77 | 73 |
| ABNOMORE | Family wants no more | 52 | 45 |
| ABANY | For any reason | 48 | 46 |
| ABPOOR | Can't afford more children | 46 | 44 |
| ABSINGLE | Woman is unmarried | 46 | 43 |

Contrary to what we expected, women are not more supportive of abortion than are men. Actually, men are as supportive or more so. On variables where there are differences between men and women, the epsilons range between 1 and 7 percentage points. This enlightening perspective runs counter to contemporary media portrayal of men being more conservative or restrictive than women when it comes to the issue of abortion. Why do you suppose there may be a discrepancy between what we've just uncovered and that discourse?

We used the individual items concerning abortion for this analysis because it was possible that men and women would differ on some items but not on others and/or differ by varying amounts. For instance, we might have expected women to be more supportive on the item concerning the woman's health, but this was not the case.

As an alternative strategy for examining the sources of attitudes toward abortion, let's make use of the index ABORT that we created in Chapter 8 by combining responses to ABDEFECT and ABSINGLE. Based on the summary table shown previously, we would expect men to exhibit slightly more support for abortion than would women. And our modified expectations are more accurate, as you'll discover when you create the following table.

## ABORT Simple Abortion Index * SEX
## Respondent's Sex Crosstabulation

| | | | SEX Respondent's Sex | | Total |
|---|---|---|---|---|---|
| | | | 1 MALE | 2 FEMALE | |
| ABORT Simple Abortion Index | 0 Yes/Approve | Count | 198 | 210 | 408 |
| | | % within SEX Respondent's sex | 45.2% | 42.3% | 43.7% |
| | 1 Conditional Support | Count | 142 | 158 | 300 |
| | | % within SEX Respondent's sex | 32.4% | 31.9% | 32.1% |
| | 2 No/Disapprove | Count | 98 | 128 | 226 |
| | | % within SEX Respondent's sex | 22.4% | 25.8% | 24.2% |
| Total | | Count | 438 | 496 | 934 |
| | | % within SEX Respondent's sex | 100.0% | 100.0% | 100.0% |

Recall that a score of 0 on the index represents those who supported a woman's right to have an abortion in both circumstances: if there was a chance of a birth defect and if she was single. Overall, 44% of the sample took that position. This table indicates an almost three percentage point difference between men and women, with men slightly more likely (45.2%) to score 0 on the index than women (42.3%).

So far, then, we have learned that while men are slightly more likely to be supportive of abortion, gender is certainly not the sole explanation (if any noteworthy explanation at all) for differences in attitudes toward abortion. Let's see whether age has an impact.

# DEMONSTRATION 12.2: AGE AND ABORTION

As Cook and her colleagues (1992) pointed out, abortion is somewhat more relevant to young people because they are more likely to experience unwanted pregnancies than are older people. What would that lead you to expect about a relationship between age and support for abortion? Think about that, and then use SPSS Statistics to run the tables that answer the question for you.

Recall that we recoded AGE into AGECAT and saved the variable on our DEMOPLUS.SAV file. We'll want to use AGECAT for our examination of the relationship between age and abortion attitudes. Now you can request the SPSS Statistics tables that relate age to abortion attitudes.

Here's a summary of the tables you should have created.

| Percentage Approving of Abortion Under the Following Conditions | | Under 21 | 21 to 39 | 40 to 64 | Over 64 |
|---|---|---|---|---|---|
| ABHLTH | Woman's health endangered | 80 | 91 | 88 | 87 |
| ABRAPE | Resulted from rape | 70 | 82 | 77 | 73 |
| ABDEFECT | Serious defect likely | 70 | 75 | 74 | 77 |
| ABANY | For any reason | 50 | 48 | 48 | 42 |
| ABPOOR | Can't afford more children | 40 | 51 | 45 | 39 |
| ABNOMORE | Family wants no more | 30 | 49 | 51 | 42 |
| ABSINGLE | Woman is unmarried | 30 | 44 | 47 | 39 |

Take a minute to look over the data presented in this summary table. How do the analytic results square with your expectations? These data suggest that age is not a clear predictor of attitude toward abortion. Those 21 and under tend to be less likely than any of the other groups to support abortion than those in the middle groups, ranging from 21 all the way up to 64. The data suggest that this youngest group is more conservative on this issue that the others. Can you think of reasons why we may have stumbled across this result?

Those aged 21 to 39 are more likely than those in other age groups to support abortion in instances where a woman's health is endangered, the pregnancy resulted from rape, or the mother can't afford more children. For most of these conditions, support neither increases monotonically nor decreases monotonically.

As an aside, these data change each time the General Social Survey (GSS) is administered. Remember that we use the 2016 GSS for the analyses in this book. One change that is particularly noteworthy is the overall support from any age or gender. ABSINGLE, whether the mother is unmarried, garners less support overall than any other circumstance. This has not been the case in the past. What might explain this dynamic phenomenon? Could it have something to do with increased acceptance of single-parent families?

Now let's run crosstabs using our ABORT index and AGECAT to see what we find. This table indicates that the relationship between age and abortion as measured by our ABORT index continues to be murky. Whereas 30% of those 21 and under approve of abortion in both cases, this percentage is higher in all of the other age categories (44%, 46%, 39%), though without monotonically increasing or decreasing. Likewise, the percentage who disapprove of abortion in both cases changes from 30% (21 and under) to 23% (21–39) to 25% (40–64) to 24% (65 and older.) Again, there isn't a clear continuous pattern. What is clear is that those 21 and under seem to have a somewhat lower likelihood of approval in both instances included in our index.

## ABORT Simple Abortion Index * AGECAT Recoded Age Crosstabulation

| | | | AGECAT Recoded Age | | | | |
| --- | --- | --- | --- | --- | --- | --- | --- |
| | | | 1 Under 21 | 2 21–39 years old | 3 40–64 years old | 4 65 and older | Total |
| ABORT Simple Abortion Index | 0 Yes/ Approve | Count | 3 | 129 | 191 | 83 | 406 |
| | | % within AGECAT Recoded Age | 30.0% | 44.0% | 46.0% | 39.0% | 43.6% |
| | 1 Conditional Support | Count | 4 | 96 | 119 | 80 | 299 |
| | | % within AGECAT Recoded Age | 40.0% | 32.8% | 28.7% | 37.6% | 32.1% |
| | 2 No/ Disapprove | Count | 3 | 68 | 105 | 50 | 226 |
| | | % within AGECAT Recoded Age | 30.0% | 23.2% | 25.3% | 23.5% | 24.3% |
| Total | | Count | 10 | 293 | 415 | 213 | 931 |
| | | % within AGECAT Recoded Age | 100.0% | 100.0% | 100.0% | 100.0% | 100.0% |

# DEMONSTRATION 12.3: RELIGION AND ABORTION

If we began this analysis by asking you what variable you thought might account for attitudes toward abortion, there is a good chance you would have guessed religion, given the unconditional and public opposition of the Roman Catholic Church. Your growing facility with SPSS Statistics and the 2016 GSS data make it possible for you to test that expectation.

Let's start with the possible impact of religious affiliation. Here's a summary of what you should discover if you run the several abortion items by RELIG. (Remember to define the values 0 and 5 to 99 as "missing" for the variable RELIG before running crosstabs and creating your summary table.)

| Percentage Approving of Abortion Under the Following Conditions | | Protestant | Catholic | Jewish | None |
| --- | --- | --- | --- | --- | --- |
| ABHLTH | Woman's health endangered | 86 | 85 | 100 | 94 |
| ABRAPE | Resulted from rape | 73 | 73 | 95 | 91 |
| ABDEFECT | Serious defect likely | 69 | 71 | 100 | 89 |
| ABNOMORE | Family wants no more | 38 | 43 | 90 | 73 |
| ABANY | For any reason | 36 | 41 | 72 | 70 |
| ABSINGLE | Woman is unmarried | 34 | 37 | 79 | 69 |
| ABPOOR | Can't afford more children | 36 | 36 | 72 | 74 |

There are several observations you might make about these data. To begin with, the expectation that Catholics would be the most opposed to abortion is not confirmed. In fact, Protestants are just as likely, if not slightly more likely, to disapprove of abortion under all of these seven conditions. Based on our summary table, we can conclude that upward of 69% of both Protestants and Catholics are likely to approve of abortion in cases of health, rape, and birth defect, while between only 34% and 43% are likely to support it in the other cases.

You might also note that the level of support for abortion among American Catholics is greatly at variance with the Roman Catholic Church's official position. Under the traumatic conditions summarized at the top of the table, 71% to 85% of Catholics say they would approve of abortion. Even under the less traumatic conditions, 36% to 43% of Catholics would support a woman's right to an abortion.

In contrast, Jews and those with no religious affiliation are consistently more supportive of a woman's right to an abortion. It is interesting to note that 95% to 100% of the Jewish respondents said they would support abortion in two of the three most traumatic cases. In the other cases, Jewish respondents' approval ranges from 72% to 90%.

To examine this relationship further, you could also use the index ABORT to see if this pattern is reflected in scores on a composite measure. Your table should look like the one below.

## ABORT Simple Abortion Index * RELIG R's Religious Preference Crosstabulation

| | | | RELIG R's Religious Preference | | | | Total |
|---|---|---|---|---|---|---|---|
| | | | 1 PROTESTANT | 2 CATHOLIC | 3 JEWISH | 4 NONE | |
| ABORT Simple Abortion Index | 0 Yes/Approve | Count | 152 | 78 | 15 | 129 | 374 |
| | | % within RELIG R's religious preference | 33.9% | 35.9% | 78.9% | 68.3% | 42.8% |
| | 1 Conditional Support | Count | 164 | 77 | 4 | 39 | 284 |
| | | % within RELIG R's religious preference | 36.5% | 35.5% | 21.1% | 20.6% | 32.5% |
| | 2 No/ Disapprove | Count | 133 | 62 | 0 | 21 | 216 |
| | | % within RELIG R's religious preference | 29.6% | 28.6% | 0.0% | 11.1% | 24.7% |
| Total | | Count | 449 | 217 | 19 | 189 | 874 |
| | | % within RELIG R's religious preference | 100.0% | 100.0% | 100.0% | 100.0% | 100.0% |

In our earlier examinations of religion, we've sometimes gone beyond affiliation to examine the measure of religiosity, or religiousness. How do you suppose church attendance would relate to abortion attitudes? To find out, let's use CHATT, the recoded variable created earlier.

Run the appropriate tables. Here's a summary of what you should have learned.

| Percentage Approving of Abortion Under the Following Conditions | | Weekly | Monthly | Seldom | Never |
|---|---|---|---|---|---|
| ABHLTH | Woman's health endangered | 79 | 85 | 95 | 94 |
| ABRAPE | Resulted from rape | 57 | 73 | 88 | 90 |
| ABDEFECT | Serious defect likely | 55 | 74 | 85 | 89 |
| ABANY | For any reason | 25 | 42 | 58 | 63 |
| ABNOMORE | Family wants no more | 24 | 45 | 58 | 66 |
| ABPOOR | Can't afford more children | 25 | 42 | 53 | 62 |
| ABSINGLE | Woman is unmarried | 20 | 38 | 55 | 63 |

What does this table tell you about religion and abortion attitudes? The overall relationship is pretty clear: Increased church attendance is related to decreased support for abortion in every circumstance. There is a substantial difference, however, between those who attend church about weekly and those who attend less often. Those who attend one to three times per month are considerably more likely to support unconditional abortion than are those who attend church weekly. Even in the case of the traumatic conditions at the top of the table, only those who attend church weekly stand out overwhelmingly in their comparatively low level of support (when a woman's health is endangered, the margin is smallest).

The fact that the "seldom" and "never" groups do not differ that much in these calculations is a result of what we call a **ceiling effect**. Whenever the overall percentage of people agreeing with something approaches 100%, considerable variation among subgroups is not possible. In the extreme case, if everyone agreed on something, there would be no way for men and women to differ, for example, because 100% of both would have to agree. Similarly, there could be no differences among age groups, religions, and so on. When the overall percentage approaches zero, a similar situation occurs that we call a **floor effect**.

Now, check the relationship between CHATT and the abortion index, ABORT, and then compare your results with ours below.

## ABORT Simple Abortion Index * CHATT Recoded Church Attendance Crosstabulation

|  |  |  | CHATT Recoded Church Attendance | | | | |
|---|---|---|---|---|---|---|---|
|  |  |  | 1 About weekly | 2 About monthly | 3 Seldom | 4 Never | Total |
| ABORT Simple Abortion Index | 0 Yes/Approve | Count | 52 | 55 | 157 | 144 | 408 |
|  |  | % within CHATT Recoded Church Attendance | 19.3% | 37.4% | 54.5% | 64% | 43.9% |
|  | 1 Conditional Support | Count | 98 | 56 | 88 | 57 | 299 |
|  |  | % within CHATT Recoded Church Attendance | 36.3% | 38.1% | 30.6% | 25% | 32.2% |
|  | 2 No/ Disapprove | Count | 120 | 36 | 43 | 24 | 223 |
|  |  | % within CHATT Recoded Church Attendance | 44.4% | 24.5% | 14.9% | 11% | 24.0% |
| Total |  | Count | 270 | 147 | 288 | 225 | 930 |
|  |  | % within CHATT Recoded Church Attendance | 100.0% | 100.0% | 100.0% | 100.0% | 100.0% |

Are these results consistent with those in the summary table we created? Do you find evidence of a ceiling effect in this table as well? The GSS data we've provided for your use permit you to explore this general topic even further, if you wish. Why don't you check out the effect of POSTLIFE and PRAY on abortion attitudes (try ABANY: "for any reason")? Before running the tables, however, take some time to reflect on what might logically be expected. How might beliefs about an afterlife affect support for or opposition to abortion? You may be surprised by what you learn. Then again, maybe you won't be surprised!

# WRITING BOX 12.1

It might seem ironic that those who believe in a life after death are less likely to support abortion than are those who do not—and vice versa—but that's what the data indicate. Of those who believe in an afterlife, only 41% give unconditional support to a woman's right to have an abortion, contrasted with 64% of those who disbelieve in an afterlife.

Religiosity, as measured by prayer, also affects attitudes toward abortion. Among those who pray several times a day, only 28% give unconditional support for abortion, as do about 46% of those who pray once a day. The real difference shows up among those who pray only once a week: 57% of respondents who pray once a week (68% for those who report praying less than once a week but more than never) and 75% of those who never pray support a woman's right to an abortion unconditionally.

# DEMONSTRATION 12.4: POLITICS AND ABORTION

A strong and consistent relationship exists between political philosophy and abortion attitudes. What do you suppose that relationship is? Who would you expect to be the more supportive of abortion: liberals or conservatives? To carry out this investigation, you'll probably want to use the recoded variable POLREC.

Now you can examine the relationship between political philosophy and abortion attitudes to see if your hunch is correct. Here's a summary of what you should discover.

| Percentage Approving of Abortion Under the Following Conditions | | Liberal | Moderate | Conservative |
|---|---|---|---|---|
| ABHLTH | Woman's health endangered | 96 | 90 | 81 |
| ABRAPE | Resulted from rape | 90 | 82 | 63 |
| ABDEFECT | Serious defect likely | 87 | 78 | 64 |
| ABNOMORE | Family wants no more | 70 | 50 | 32 |
| ABANY | For any reason | 68 | 49 | 30 |
| ABPOOR | Can't afford more children | 67 | 43 | 32 |
| ABSINGLE | Woman is unmarried | 66 | 43 | 29 |

How would you describe these results? Before reading ahead, try your hand at writing a sentence or two to report on the impact of political philosophy on abortion attitudes.

One way to summarize the relationship between political philosophy and abortion attitudes is to say the following: Liberals are strongly and consistently more supportive of a woman's right to an abortion than are conservatives, with moderates falling in between. (As an aside, between 2012 and 2016, the GSS results show that the existing gap in support for a woman's right to abortion between liberals and conservatives has grown by at least a few percentage points in every circumstance.)

To pursue this relationship further, you may want to use the ABORT index (see figure at the top of the next page).

Are these results consistent with those in the summary table above? Does the interpretation of the relationship between political philosophy and abortion attitudes as being strong and consistent hold up? Another direction you might want to take in investigating the relationship between politics and abortion attitudes concerns political party identification. As you no doubt realize, the Democratic Party has been generally more supportive of a woman's right to have an abortion than has the Republican Party. This difference was dramatically portrayed by the positions of the U.S. presidential and vice presidential candidates during the 2000 and 2004 elections. Economic recession and war took some of the spotlight away from the abortion issue during the 2008 and 2012 presidential

## ABORT Simple Abortion Index * POLREC
## Recoded POLVIEWS Crosstabulation

| | | | POLREC Recoded POLVIEWS | | | |
| --- | --- | --- | --- | --- | --- | --- |
| | | | 1 Liberal | 2 Moderate | 3 Conservative | Total |
| ABORT Simple Abortion Index | 0 Yes/Approve | Count | 173 | 141 | 87 | 401 |
| | | % within POLREC Recoded POLVIEWS | 65.8% | 43.1% | 28.3% | 44.7% |
| | 1 Conditional Support | Count | 57 | 116 | 111 | 284 |
| | | % within POLREC Recoded POLVIEWS | 21.7% | 35.5% | 36.2% | 31.7% |
| | 2 No/Disapprove | Count | 33 | 70 | 109 | 212 |
| | | % within POLREC Recoded POLVIEWS | 12.5% | 21.4% | 35.5% | 23.6% |
| Total | | Count | 263 | 327 | 307 | 897 |
| | | % within POLREC Recoded POLVIEWS | 100.0% | 100.0% | 100.0% | 100.0% |

elections. While not as dramatic as in 2000 and 2004, the issue had greater visibility in 2016 than in the two prior presidential election cycles.

How do you suppose the official differences separating the parties show up in the attitudes of the rank and file? Among the general public, who do you suppose are the most supportive of abortion: Democrats or Republicans? See if you can find out for yourself by creating a summary table similar to those above and then running crosstabs with PARTY (our measure of party identification) and ABANY ("for any reason"). Once you have done that, see if the findings are consistent with your expectations.

# WRITING BOX 12.2

The relationship between political party identification and support for abortion is what you may have anticipated, based on official party platforms and the pronouncements of party spokespersons. Of the Democrats, 58% give unconditional support to a woman's right to an abortion. Among Republicans, only 32% do so. Not surprisingly, independents fall almost directly in the middle, with 47% giving unconditional support for abortion.

# DEMONSTRATION 12.5:
# SEXUAL ATTITUDES AND ABORTION

Recalling that abortion attitudes are related to differences in political philosophy, it might occur to you that other philosophical differences might be relevant as well. In Chapter 6, we discussed three items in the GSS data set that deal with the permissiveness or restrictiveness of sexual attitudes.[3] The GSS data set also contains a variable related to personal sexual behavior. Here are the four variables:

PREMARSX—attitudes toward premarital sex

HOMOSEX—attitudes toward homosexual relationships

XMOVIE—attendance at an X-rated movie during the year

PIKUPSEX—respondent had sex with a casual date within the past year

Here's the relationship between attitudes toward premarital sex (PREMARSX) and toward abortion. Notice how permissiveness on one is related to permissiveness on the other.

## ABORT Simple Abortion Index * PREMARSX
## Sex Before Marriage Crosstabulation

| | | | PREMARSX Sex Before Marriage | | | | |
| --- | --- | --- | --- | --- | --- | --- | --- |
| | | | 1 ALWAYS WRONG | 2 ALMST ALWAYS WRG | 3 SOMETIMES WRONG | 4 NOT WRONG AT ALL | Total |
| ABORT Simple Abortion Index | 0 Yes/ Approve | Count | 7 | 5 | 14 | 150 | 176 |
| | | % within PREMARSX Sex before marriage | 7.4% | 22.7% | 26.4% | 54.9% | 39.7% |
| | 1 Conditional Support | Count | 39 | 9 | 24 | 86 | 158 |
| | | % within PREMARSX Sex before marriage | 41.1% | 40.9% | 45.3% | 31.5% | 35.7% |
| | 2 No/ Disapprove | Count | 49 | 8 | 15 | 37 | 109 |
| | | % within PREMARSX Sex before marriage | 51.6% | 36.4% | 28.3% | 13.6% | 24.6% |
| Total | | Count | 95 | 22 | 53 | 273 | 443 |
| | | % within PREMARSX Sex before marriage | 100.0% | 100.0% | 100.0% | 100.0% | 100.0% |

Now, why don't you check to see if the same pattern holds for the other sexual permissiveness items (see tables on pages 210 and 211)?

As you probably expected, abortion attitudes are related to attitudes toward premarital sex, to homosexuality, to attendance at an X-rated movie, and to whether the respondent had sex with a casual date in the past year. In other words, those who are sexually permissive tend to be permissive in the area of abortion as well.

---

3. Use the "Range plus one optional discrete missing value" option to define the values 0, 5, 8, and 9 as "missing" for the variables PREMARSX and HOMOSEX. In addition, remember to define the values 0, 8, and 9 as "missing" for the variables XMOVIE and PIKUPSEX.

## ABORT Simple Abortion Index * HOMOSEX
## Homosexual Sex Relations Crosstabulation

| | | | HOMOSEX Homosexual Sex Relations | | | | |
|---|---|---|---|---|---|---|---|
| | | | 1 ALWAYS WRONG | 2 ALMST ALWAYS WRG | 3 SOMETIMES WRONG | 4 NOT WRONG AT ALL | Total |
| ABORT Simple Abortion Index | 0 Yes/ Approve | Count | 66 | 5 | 29 | 298 | 398 |
| | | % within HOMOSEX Homosexual sex relations | 19.2% | 16.7% | 50.0% | 62.6% | 43.9% |
| | 1 Conditional Support | Count | 122 | 20 | 25 | 121 | 288 |
| | | % within HOMOSEX Homosexual sex relations | 35.6% | 66.7% | 43.1% | 25.4% | 31.8% |
| | 2 No/ Disapprove | Count | 155 | 5 | 4 | 57 | 221 |
| | | % within HOMOSEX Homosexual sex relations | 45.2% | 16.7% | 6.9% | 12.0% | 24.4% |
| Total | | Count | 343 | 30 | 58 | 476 | 907 |
| | | % within HOMOSEX Homosexual sex relations | 100.0% | 100.0% | 100.0% | 100.0% | 100.0% |

## ABORT Simple Abortion Index * XMOVIE Seen
## X-Rated Movie in Last Year Crosstabulation

| | | | XMOVIE Seen X-Rated Movie in Last Year | | |
|---|---|---|---|---|---|
| | | | 1 YES | 2 NO | Total |
| ABORT Simple Abortion Index | 0 Yes/Approve | Count | 89 | 139 | 228 |
| | | % within XMOVIE Seen X-rated movie in last year | 60.5% | 41.5% | 47.3% |
| | 1 Conditional Support | Count | 38 | 101 | 139 |
| | | % within XMOVIE Seen X-rated movie in last year | 25.9% | 30.1% | 28.8% |
| | 2 No/Disapprove | Count | 20 | 95 | 115 |
| | | % within XMOVIE Seen X-rated movie in last year | 13.6% | 28.4% | 23.9% |
| Total | | Count | 147 | 335 | 482 |
| | | % within XMOVIE Seen X-rated movie in last year | 100.0% | 100.0% | 100.0% |

## ABORT Simple Abortion Index * PIKUPSEX R Had Sex With Casual Date Last Year Crosstabulation

| | | | PIKUPSEX R Had Sex With Casual Date Last Year | | Total |
| --- | --- | --- | --- | --- | --- |
| | | | 1 HAD SEX WITH PICKUP | 2 NOT SELECTED | |
| ABORT Simple Abortion Index | 0 Yes/Approve | Count | 28 | 24 | 52 |
| | | % within PIKUPSEX R had sex with casual date last year | 66.7% | 57.1% | 61.9% |
| | 1 Conditional Support | Count | 6 | 9 | 15 |
| | | % within PIKUPSEX R had sex with casual date last year | 14.3% | 21.4% | 17.9% |
| | 2 No/Disapprove | Count | 8 | 9 | 17 |
| | | % within PIKUPSEX R had sex with casual date last year | 19.0% | 21.4% | 20.2% |
| Total | | Count | 42 | 42 | 84 |
| | | % within PIKUPSEX R had sex with casual date last year | 100.0% | 100.0% | 100.0% |

# OTHER FACTORS YOU CAN EXPLORE ON YOUR OWN

A number of other factors can affect attitudes toward abortion. We'll suggest a few more demographic variables here for you to check out, and you may want to review the excerpt from Cook et al. on the website (https://study.sagepub.com/babbie10e) for further ideas.

You might suspect that education is related to abortion attitudes. If so, which direction do you suppose that relationship goes? Why do you suppose that is? Race is another standard demographic variable that might be related to abortion attitudes. You should examine the relationship between attitudes toward abortion in particular circumstances and race carefully because race may have slightly different effects on different items.

Finally, you might want to explore the relationship between abortion attitudes and some family variables. How do you suppose abortion attitudes relate to respondents' views of the ideal number of children to have? The family variable that may surprise you in its relationship to abortion attitudes is MARITAL. You may recall that in Chapter 11, we also uncovered a surprising effect of marital status on political philosophy. Check this one out, and we'll take a more in-depth look once we begin our multivariate analyses.

# CONCLUSION

In this chapter, you've had an opportunity to search for explanations of the vast differences in people's feelings about abortion. We've found that religion and politics, for example, are powerful influences. We've also just seen that permissiveness and restrictiveness regarding abortion are strongly related to permissiveness and restrictiveness on issues of sexual behavior. Gender, on the other hand, does not seem to be strongly related to attitudes toward abortion, nor does age have a monotonic relationship.

Thus far, we've limited the search for explanations to bivariate analyses. In the analyses to come, we'll dig even deeper into the reasons for differences of opinion. Ultimately, you should gain a well-rounded understanding of the logic of social scientific research, as well as mastering some of the fundamental techniques for acting on that logic through SPSS Statistics.

## Main Points

- This chapter focused on the causes of differing attitudes toward abortion.

- Cook, Jelen, and Wilcox's book *Between Two Absolutes: Public Opinion and the Politics of Abortion* was used as a starting point for our analysis.

- Throughout the chapter, we examined the relationship between attitudes toward abortion and several potential independent or causal variables.

- In addition to examining SPSS Statistics output (primarily crosstabs), we also created our own

summary tables based on several SPSS Statistics tables. These summary tables made it easy to examine the relationship between attitudes toward abortion and several independent variables.

- Gender and age tend not to be related to attitudes toward abortion, whereas religion, politics, and sexual attitudes are.

- You may also want to try looking for relationships between attitudes toward abortion and other demographic variables, such as race, education, and ideal family size.

## Key Terms

Ceiling effect  206

Floor effect  206

## SPSS Statistics Commands Introduced in This Chapter

No new commands were introduced in this chapter.

## Review Questions

1. One way we explored the relationship between attitudes toward abortion and several potential independent variables was by constructing a summary table based on SPSS Statistics output. How were these tables constructed?

2. What are the commands used to instruct SPSS Statistics to construct a table looking at the relationship between our abortion index ABORT and gender?

3. Do our findings support the contention that women are more likely to support abortion than are men?

4. Why did we use the recoded variable AGECAT as opposed to the variable AGE to examine the relationship between age and attitudes toward abortion?

5. Summarize the relationship between abortion attitudes and religious affiliation.

6. Do the majority of American Catholics differ from the Roman Catholic Church on abortion in particular circumstances? If so, what circumstances?

7. What is the ceiling effect?

8. What is the floor effect?

9. We found that liberals are more likely than conservatives to support abortion. Does this mean that Democrats are more likely to support abortion than are Republicans?

10. Are those favoring small families more or less likely to support abortion?

11. Is there any difference between those who are separated and those who are divorced in terms of their unconditional support for abortion?

12. Is there a relationship between attitudes toward sexual behavior and attitudes toward abortion?

## SPSS Statistics Lab Exercise 12.1

NAME: _____

CLASS: _____

INSTRUCTOR: _____

DATE: _____

*To complete the following exercises, you need to retrieve the data file EXERPLUS.SAV.*

We are going to begin by looking at what causes people to be permissive (or restrictive) in the area of teen sex. We will focus primarily on the three variables from your data file that deal with this issue: PILLOK, SEXEDUC, and TEENSEX.

1. What does each of the following variables measure?

   a. PILLOK

   b. SEXEDUC

   c. TEENSEX

2. List the values and labels of each of the following variables in the spaces provided below. Check to make sure all "missing" and "don't know" codes have been designated as missing values for each variable:

   - PILLOK (missing values: 0, 8, 9)

   - SEXEDUC (missing values: 0, 3, 8, 9)

   - TEENSEX (missing values: 0, 5, 8, 9)

*Hint:* If needed, use "Range plus one optional discrete missing value" to designate missing values for SEXEDUC and TEENSEX.

   a. PILLOK

   | Value | Label |
   |-------|-------|
   | _____ | _____ |
   | _____ | _____ |
   | _____ | _____ |
   | _____ | _____ |

   b. SEXEDUC

   | Value | Label |
   |-------|-------|
   | _____ | _____ |
   | _____ | _____ |
   | _____ | _____ |

*(Continued)*

(Continued)

    c. TEENSEX

| Value | Label |
|-------|-------|
| _____ | _____ |
| _____ | _____ |
| _____ | _____ |
| _____ | _____ |

3. Recode the variables PILLOK and TEENSEX as indicated below.

    a. PILLOK—recode to create PILLREC

        1 to 2 → 1 Permissive

        3 to 4 → 2 Restrictive

    b. TEENSEX—recode to create TEENREC

        3 to 4 → 1 Permissive

        1 to 2 → 2 Restrictive

4. Relabel SEXEDUC in the following manner:

    1—Permissive (favor)

    2—Restrictive (oppose)

*Hint:* Access **Variable View** tab → Click cell corresponding with SEXEDUC and column labeled "Values" → Remove label (1—Favor; 2—Oppose) and add labels listed above.

5. Use SEX and our three measures of permissiveness on teen sex (PILLREC, TEENREC, and SEXEDUC) to instruct SPSS Statistics to run tables that can be used to fill in the summary table below.

| Percentage Permissive Toward Issues Concerning Teen Sexual Behavior | Men | Women |
|---|---|---|
| PILLREC | | |
| SEXEDUC | | |
| TEENREC | | |

6. What do the column percentages in this table tell you about the strength of the relationship between gender and permissiveness toward teen sex? If there is a relationship, specify how the dependent variable changes with changes in the independent variable.

7. Now, we will move away from demographic variables. Try using FEFAM (which, as you may recall, is one of our measures of attitudes toward family and sex roles) and our three measures of permissiveness on teen sex (PILLREC, TEENREC, and SEXEDUC) to instruct SPSS Statistics to run tables that can be used to fill in the summary table below. (Don't forget to define 0, 8, and 9 as "missing" for FEFAM.)

| Percentage Permissive Toward Issues Concerning Teen Sexual Behavior | FEFAM: Better for Man to Work, Woman to Tend Home | | | |
|---|---|---|---|---|
| | Strongly Agree | Agree | Disagree | Strongly Disagree |
| PILLREC | | | | |
| SEXEDUC | | | | |
| TEENREC | | | | |

8. What do the column percentages in this table tell you about the strength of the relationship between attitudes toward family/sex roles and permissiveness toward teen sex? If there is a relationship, specify how the dependent variable changes with changes in the independent variable.

9. Use FEPRESCH and our three measures of permissiveness on teen sex (PILLREC, TEENREC, and SEXEDUC) to instruct SPSS Statistics to run tables that can be used to fill in the following summary table. (Don't forget to define 0, 8, and 9 as "missing" for FEPRESCH.)

| Percentage Permissive Toward Issues Concerning Teen Sexual Behavior | FEPRESCH: Preschool Kids Suffer if Mother Works | | | |
|---|---|---|---|---|
| | Strongly Agree | Agree | Disagree | Strongly Disagree |
| PILLREC | | | | |
| SEXEDUC | | | | |
| TEENREC | | | | |

10. What do the column percentages in this table tell you about the strength of the relationship between attitudes toward family/sex roles and permissiveness on teen sex? If there is a relationship, specify how the dependent variable changes with changes in the independent variable.

11. Now, choose another variable from EXERPLUS.SAV that you think may be related to permissiveness toward teen sex. Write the name of the variable, and explain why you chose it (i.e., how it might be related to permissiveness toward teen sex).

12. List the values and labels of the item you chose and indicate whether it is necessary to recode/relabel. If so, explain how you did that below. Remember, you may also need to define values as "missing" for your variable.

*(Continued)*

(Continued)

13. Examine the relationship between the variable you chose and our three measures of permissiveness toward teen sex (PILLREC, SEXEDUC, and TEENREC). Then, fill in the following summary table with the results of your analysis. If you need more space, use a separate sheet of paper. (Don't forget, depending on which variable you choose, you may have to designate "DK" as "missing.")

**Percentage Permissive Toward Teen Sex**

LABELS OF VARIABLE CHOSEN    _____

_____

_____

_____

PILLREC    _____

_____

_____

_____

_____

SEXEDUC    _____

_____

_____

_____

_____

TEENREC    _____

_____

_____

_____

14. What do the column percentages in this table tell you about the strength of the relationship between _____ [variable you chose] and permissiveness toward teen sex? If there is a relationship, specify how the dependent variable changes with changes in the independent variable.

15. In previous SPSS Statistics lab exercises, we examined several variables on your data file that ask respondents under which circumstances, if any, they would support a police officer striking an adult male (POLABUSE, POLATTAK, POLESCAP, and POLMURDR). The GSS data set also contains another variable related to this issue: POLHITOK, whether the respondent would ever approve of a police officer striking a citizen. In Lab Exercise 8.1, we created an index, named POLIN, based on two of these items, POLABUSE and POLATTAK. In the following exercises, we want you to explore these variables further, specifically by asking why some people are more supportive than others of the use of violence by police officers.

a. To begin, choose two of the demographic variables from your file that you think may be associated with attitudes toward the use of force by police officers. List the abbreviated variable names, and explain why you think these variables may be related to attitudes toward the use of force.

b. Is it necessary to recode either of the demographic variables to make them more amenable to examination? If so, recode the variable(s), and show how you did that in the space below. If necessary, define appropriate values for each variable as "missing."

c. Use SPSS Statistics to explore the association between these demographic variables and the five variables related to violence on the part of law enforcement officers (POLABUSE, POLATTAK, POLESCAP, POLHITOK, and POLMURDR).

d. On a separate sheet, create two summary tables similar to those we focused on in the demonstrations in this chapter, one table for each independent demographic variable. Your tables should be formatted as follows:

"Percentage Approving of Police Officer Striking a Citizen Under the Following Conditions"

Demographic/Independent Variable 1 _____

|  | Categories/Labels of Demographic/Independent Variable | | | | |
|---|---|---|---|---|---|
|  | Value/Label | Value/Label | Value/Label | Value/Label | Value/Label |
| POLABUSE |  |  |  |  |  |
| POLATTAK |  |  |  |  |  |
| POLESCAP |  |  |  |  |  |
| POLHITOK |  |  |  |  |  |
| POLMURDR |  |  |  |  |  |

e. After creating your summary tables, write a few sentences showing what each table tells us about the relationship between the independent/demographic variables you are working with and POLABUSE, POLATTAK, POLESCAP, POLHITOK, and POLMURDR.

(Continued)

f. Now, examine the relationship between the two demographic variables you chose and POLIN. If you did not save POLIN on your EXERPLUS.SAV file, simply follow the instructions in SPSS Statistics Lab Exercise 8.1 to create the index before moving ahead. Once you have run your crosstabs, print and attach your output to this sheet. Then, summarize your findings in a few sentences. What do your findings tell us about the relationship between the variables? Are the variables associated? If so, how strongly? Be sure to cite percentages.

*Reminder: Before ending this session, be sure to save your new recoded variables on your EXERPLUS.SAV file.*

# MEASURES OF ASSOCIATION FOR NOMINAL AND ORDINAL VARIABLES

In the preceding analyses, we depended on percentage tables as our format for examining the relationships among variables. While crosstabs are a useful way to examine the relationship between two variables, it is often difficult to get a clear sense of how strong the association between the variables is. While a relationship appears to exist between POLREC and PARTY, for example, it can be difficult to say how strong the association is. In this chapter, we are going to explore some measures that allow us to determine more precisely the strength of a relationship. In contrast to the way percentage tables lay out the details, these techniques, called ***measures of association***, by and large summarize relationships (strength and, in some cases, direction).

Another way you might think of measures of association is in contrast to the statistics (measures of central tendency and dispersion) we introduced in Chapter 5. Both are considered ***descriptive statistics***, but measures of central tendency and dispersion summarize the distribution of categories of a single variable, whereas measures of association summarize the strength of association between two variables. Additionally, when two variables are at either the ordinal or interval/ratio level of measure, measures of association indicate the direction of association. These capabilities enable us to use measures of association to answer two important questions:

1. How strong is the association or relationship between two variables?

2. For ordinal and interval/ratio variables, what is the direction of association between two variables?

We begin our discussion with a thought experiment designed to introduce you to the logic of statistical association. We will then focus on two of the most commonly used measures of association for nominal variables, each of which is appropriate for variables at different levels of measurement: lambda ($\lambda$) and gamma ($\gamma$). In Chapter 14, we will cover measures of association for interval and ratio variables: Pearson's $r$, the coefficient of determination ($r^2$), and linear regression. In each case, we will begin by introducing the logic of the measure and then show you how it can be calculated using SPSS Statistics. Finally, at the end of Chapter 14, we will briefly discuss measures appropriate for mixed types of variables.

## THE LOGIC OF STATISTICAL ASSOCIATION: PROPORTIONATE REDUCTION OF ERROR

To introduce the logic of statistical association, we would like you to take a minute for a "thought experiment." Imagine that there is a group of 100 people in a lecture hall and you are standing in the hallway outside the room. The people will come out of the room one at a time, and your task will be to guess the gender of each before he or she comes into view. Take a moment to consider your best strategy for making these guesses.

If you know nothing about the people in the room, there really is no useful strategy for guessing—no way to make educated guesses. But now suppose you know that 60 of the people in the room are women. This would make educated guesses possible: You should guess "woman" every time. By doing this, you would be right 60 times and wrong 40 times.

Now, suppose that every time a person prepares to emerge from the room, his or her first name is announced. This would probably improve your guessing substantially. You'd guess "woman" for every Nancy or Joanne and "man" for every Joseph or Wendell. Even so, you probably wouldn't be totally accurate, given the ambiguity of names such as Pat, Chris, Taylor, and Leslie.

It is useful to notice that we could actually calculate how much knowing first names improved your guessing. Let's say you would have made 40 errors out of 100 guesses without knowing names and only 10 errors when you knew the names. You would have made 30 fewer mistakes. Out of an original 40 mistakes, that's a 75% improvement. Statisticians refer to this as a ***proportionate reduction of error (PRE)***. The measures of association we are going to focus on are largely based on this logic.

# LAMBDA (λ): A MEASURE APPROPRIATE FOR NOMINAL VARIABLES

***Lambda*** (λ) is a measure of association appropriate for use with two nominal variables, and it operates on the PRE logic. Essentially, this means that the two variables are related to each other to the extent that knowing a person's attribute on one will help you guess his or her attribute on the other (i.e., the extent to which one variable is "associated" with, affects, or has an impact on another variable).

## An Indication of Strength of Association

The value of lambda, which can vary between 0.00 and 1.00, indicates the strength of association or relationship between two nominal variables. The closer the value of lambda is to 1.00, the stronger the relationship between the variables. Conversely, the closer the value of lambda is to 0.00, the weaker the relationship between the variables.

You'll remember that nominal variables are just sets of categories with no greater-than or less-than relationships between them. Based on that, you have probably already correctly surmised that lambda provides *no* indication of the direction of association. In the absence of an order between categories, there can be no direction of relationship. For example, even if there were a strong relationship between eye color and hair color, it would make no sense to say it was positive or negative.

Table 13.1 summarizes the way that lambda is used.

| TABLE 13.1   ■   A Summary of Lambda (λ) | |
| --- | --- |
| **Measure of Association** | **Lambda** |
| Type of variables | Nominal × Nominal |
| Values (strength) | 0.00 to +1.00 |
| | 0 = no association |
| | 1.00 = perfect association |
| Direction | Not applicable |

## Example 1: The Logic of Lambda (λ)

Here's a very simple example of lambda.[1] Suppose we have data on the employment status of 1,000 people. Half are employed; half are unemployed. If we were to begin presenting you with person after person, asking you to guess whether each was employed or not, you'd get about half

---

1. Throughout this chapter, we review how measures of association are computed in an effort to provide the rationale for matching the measure to the level of data. Instructors and students who would rather focus on interpretation are encouraged to skip these sections and proceed directly to the demonstrations.

wrong and half right by guessing blindly. So the logic of lambda begins with the assumption that you'd make 500 errors in this case. Let's call these your "uneducated errors." Now, take a look at the table below, which gives you additional information: the ages of the subjects.

| | Young | Old | Total |
|---|---|---|---|
| Employed | 0 | 500 | 500 |
| Unemployed | 500 | 0 | 500 |
| Total | 500 | 500 | 1,000 |

Now, suppose we were to repeat the guessing exercise. This time, however, you would know whether each person is young or old. What would be your strategy for guessing employment status? Clearly, you should make an educated guess of "unemployed" for every young person and "employed" for every old person. Do that, and you'll make no errors. You will have reduced your errors by 500, in comparison with the first attempt. Given that you will have eliminated all of your former errors, we could also say that you have reduced your errors by 100%.

Here's the simple equation for lambda that allows you to calculate the reduction of errors:

$$\frac{(Uneducated\ errors) - (Educated\ errors)}{(Uneducated\ errors)} = \frac{500 - 0}{500} = 1.00$$

Notice that the calculation results in 1.00, which we treat as 100% in the context of lambda. So in this hypothetical exercise, age is a perfect predictor of employment status: 100% of the variation in employment status can be accounted for by the variation in age.

## Example 2: The Logic of Lambda (λ)

To be sure the logic of lambda is clear, let's consider another hypothetical example, similar to the previous example.

| | Young | Old | Total |
|---|---|---|---|
| Employed | 250 | 250 | 500 |
| Unemployed | 250 | 250 | 500 |
| Total | 500 | 500 | 1,000 |

In this new example, we still have half young and half old, and we also have half employed and half unemployed. Notice the difference in the relationship between the two variables, however. Just by inspection, you should be able to see that they are independent of each other. In this case, age has no impact on employment status.

The lack of a relationship between age and employment status here is reflected in the "educated" guesses you would make about employment status if you knew a person's age. That information wouldn't help you at all, and you would get half of the young people wrong and half of the old people wrong. By making uneducated guesses, you would make 500 errors, and knowing these peoples' ages, you would still make 500 errors.

Lambda reflects this new situation:

$$\frac{(Uneducated\ errors) - (Educated\ errors)}{(Uneducated\ errors)} = \frac{500 - 500}{500} = 0.00$$

Knowing age would have reduced your errors by 0%. Moreover, none (0%) of the variation in employment status can be accounted for by the variation in age.

# DEMONSTRATION 13.1: INSTRUCTING SPSS STATISTICS TO CALCULATE LAMBDA (λ)

The real relationships between variables are seldom this simple, of course, so let's look at a real example using SPSS Statistics and the General Social Survey (GSS) data. You'll be pleased to discover that you won't have to calculate the errors or the proportion of reduction because SPSS Statistics does these calculations for you.

Go ahead and open your DEMOPLUS.SAV file. Then, set up a crosstabs request using ABANY as the row variable and RELIG as the column variable.[2]

For the time being, we will not request percentages. To double-check that this option is *not* selected, you can click on **Cells** and turn off percentages by "Column."[3] Then return to the Crosstabs window by clicking **Continue**. Before executing the crosstabs command, however, click the **Statistics** button. Here's what you should see:

---

2. Define the values 0, 8, and 9 as "missing" for the variable ABANY. Define the values 0 and 5 to 99 as "missing" for the variable RELIG.
3. Usually, percentages are requested in order to see how the column percentages change or move. We omitted them here only to make the table somewhat easier to read.

You will notice that SPSS Statistics gives you a variety of options, including some of the measures of association we are going to introduce in this chapter (as well as some we will not introduce but which you may want to explore on your own). You can see that lambda is listed in the box on the left-hand side under "Nominal" because, as we know, lambda is a measure of association used for two nominal variables.

Click **Lambda**, and a check mark will appear in the small box to the left. Once you have done that, you can leave the Statistics window by clicking **Continue** and then execute the crosstabs command by selecting **OK**. Here's the result that should show up in your Output window:

## ABANY Abortion if Woman Wants for Any Reason * RELIG R's Religious Preference Crosstabulation

| | | RELIG R's Religious Preference | | | | |
| --- | --- | --- | --- | --- | --- | --- |
| | | 1 PROTESTANT | 2 CATHOLIC | 3 JEWISH | 4 NONE | Total |
| ABANY Abortion if woman wants for any reason | 1 YES | 166 | 89 | 13 | 134 | 402 |
| | 2 NO | 291 | 127 | 5 | 58 | 481 |
| Total | | 457 | 216 | 18 | 192 | 883 |

We've omitted the request for percentages in this table because it will be useful to see the actual number of cases in each cell of the table; however, keep in mind that in most cases, you want to request percentages to see how the column percentages change or move from one category of the independent variable to the next. At the far right of the table, notice that 402 people supported the idea of a woman being able to get an abortion just because she wants one, while 481 were opposed. If we were to make uneducated guesses about people's opinions on this issue, we'd do best always to guess "opposed." But by doing that, we would make 402 errors.

If we knew each person's religion, however, we would improve our record somewhat. Here's what would happen.

| Religion | Guess | Errors |
| --- | --- | --- |
| Protestant | No | 166 |
| Catholic | No | 89 |
| Jewish | Yes | 5 |
| None | Yes | 58 |
| Total | | 318 |

Compare this table with your output to ensure that you understand how we created it. To calculate lambda, then,

$$\lambda = \frac{(Uneducated\ errors) - (Educated\ errors)}{(Uneducated\ errors)} = \frac{402 - 318}{402} = .209$$

This indicates, therefore, that we have improved our guessing of abortion attitudes by 20% as a result of knowing religious affiliation. How SPSS Statistics reports the result is shown below. SPSS Statistics reports more information than we need right now, so let's focus our attention on the second row of numbers. Because we have been testing whether we could predict abortion attitudes (ABANY) by knowing religion, that makes ABANY the dependent variable. As you can see, the value of lambda in that instance is 0.209, the value we got by calculating it for ourselves.

## Directional Measures

| | | | Value | Asymptotic Standard Error[a] | Approximate T[b] | Approximate Significance |
|---|---|---|---|---|---|---|
| Nominal by Nominal | Lambda | Symmetric | .101 | .016 | 5.910 | .000 |
| | | ABANY Abortion if woman wants for any reason Dependent | .209 | .032 | 5.910 | 000 |
| | | RELIG R's religious preference Dependent | .000 | .000 | .[c] | .[c] |
| | Goodman and Kruskal tau | ABANY Abortion if woman wants for any reason Dependent | .077 | .017 | | .000[d] |
| | | RELIG R's religious preference Dependent | .034 | .008 | | .000[d] |

a. Not assuming the null hypothesis.

b. Using the asymptotic standard error assuming the null hypothesis.

c. Cannot be computed because the asymptotic standard error equals 0.

d. Based on chi-square approximation

Knowing a person's religious affiliation, then, allows us to predict his or her attitude on abortion 21% more accurately. The implicit assumption in this analysis is that religious affiliation is associated with or to some extent "causes" attitudes toward abortion. We use the value of lambda as an indication of how strong the causal link is.

However, it is important that you bear in mind that *association alone does not prove causation.* When we observe a statistical relationship between two variables, that relationship strengthens the probability that one causes the other, but it is not sufficient proof. To be satisfied that a causal relationship exists, social scientists also want the link to make sense logically. (In this case, the role of churches and clergy in the abortion debate offers that reasoning.) And finally, we want to be sure that the observed relationship is not an artifact produced by the effects of a third variable. A relationship between two variables is said to be an artifact of a third variable if the relationship results from that third variable acting on both variables being analyzed. This last possibility will be examined later when we focus on multivariate analysis.

For curiosity's sake, notice the third row, which treats RELIG as the dependent variable. This deals with the possibility that we might be able to guess people's religions by knowing where they stand on abortion. Take a moment to look at these values in the crosstabulation above.

If we were to make uneducated guesses about people's religions, we'd always guess Protestant because Protestants are, by far, the largest group. Knowing attitudes toward abortion wouldn't help matters, either. We'd still guess Protestant, even among those who were in favor of abortion rights. If RELIG were the dependent variable, then, knowing ABANY would improve our guessing by 0%, which is the calculation presented by SPSS Statistics.

# INTERPRETING LAMBDA AND OTHER MEASURES

After all this discussion of lambda, you may still be wondering what a value of .209, for instance, actually means in terms of the strength of the relationship between these two variables. Does it signify a strong, relatively strong, moderate, or weak association? Is it something worth noting, or does it indicate such a weak relationship that it is not even worth paying attention to? Unfortunately, there are no easy answers to these questions. Because we are going to say more about what is called *statistical significance* in the next chapter, we do want to give you some (albeit general) basis for interpreting these values.

We can say for certain that not only for lambda but also for all of the PRE measures of association we are considering in this chapter, a value of 1.00 (both positive and negative in the case of gamma and Pearson's *r*) indicates a perfect association or the strongest possible relationship between two variables. Conversely, with the exception noted previously, a value of 0.00 indicates no relationship between the variables. We can also say that the closer the value is to 1.00 (both positive and negative in the case of gamma and Pearson's *r*), the stronger the relationship. And the closer the value is to 0.00, the weaker the relationship.

Determining whether or not a relationship is noteworthy depends on what other researchers have found. If other researchers had not discovered any variables that related to abortion attitudes, then our lambda of .209 would be important. As you will see later, there are variables that have much stronger relationships to abortion than does religion—so strong that they make our .209 quite unremarkable. In short, all relationships must be interpreted in the context of other findings in the same general area of inquiry.

That said, in order to give you a sense of one way you can approach these statistics, we include some general guidelines in Table 13.2 for interpreting the strength of association between variables. As the title of the table clearly indicates, these are merely loose guidelines with arbitrary cutoff points that must be understood within the context of our prior discussion regarding the absence of any absolute "rules" of interpretation.

| TABLE 13.2 ■ Some General Guidelines for Interpreting Strength of Association (Lambda [λ], Gamma [γ], etc.) | |
| --- | --- |
| **Strength of Association** | **Value of Measures of Association (Lambda [λ], Gamma [γ], etc.)** |
| None | 0.00 |
| Weak/uninteresting association | ±.01 to .09 |
| Moderate/worth noting | ±.10 to .29 |
| Evidence of strong association/extremely interesting | ±.30 to .99 |
| Perfect/strongest possible association | ±1.00 |

*Note:* This table is adapted from a more in-depth discussion in J. F. Healey et al. (1999), *Exploring social issues: Using SPSS for Windows 95* (Belmont, CA: Wadsworth). In the text, the authors noted that whereas "this scale may strike you as too low . . . remember that, in the social sciences, we deal with *probabilistic* causal relationships . . . [so] expecting measures of association to approach 1 is unreasonable. Given the complexity of the social world the (admittedly arbitrary) guideline presented is serviceable in most instances" (p. 84). In comparison to similar guides to interpretation, the scale presented here is fairly low. C. Frankfort-Nachmias and A. Leon-Guerrero (2000), *Social statistics for a diverse society,* 2nd ed. (Thousand Oaks, CA: Pine Forge Press), for instance, included a table that gives the following guide to interpretation: .00 (no relationship); ±.20 (weak relationship); ±.40 (moderate relationship); ±.60 (strong relationship); ±.80 (very strong relationship); ±1.00 (perfect relationship). They went on to note that "these are only rough guidelines" (p. 259).

You will note that Table 13.2 lists the possible values as positive or negative. While the value of lambda is, as we noted, always a positive value between 0.00 and 1.00, the values of the other measures we will discuss later in this chapter (see discussions of gamma and Pearson's *r* next) run from –1.00 to +1.00 and, thus, include both positive and negative values.

## Caveat: Interpreting Lambdas of 0.00

Now that we have told you quite firmly that lambdas of 0.00 always indicate that there is no association between the variables, we need to revise our statement slightly. Lambdas of 0.00 must be treated with great caution. When one of the totals for the dependent variable is much larger than the rest, lambda can take on the value zero even when an inspection of the percentages indicates a strong relationship. Moreover, lambda is typically not useful when crosstabulating two *dichotomous variables.*

To be safe, lambda should be used only when the marginal totals are relatively equal in magnitude and when at least one of the variables is not a dichotomy (i.e., when at least one of the variables has at least three categories). If those requirements are not met, a chi-square-based measure of association, such as Cramer's *V*, should be used.

Based on these general guidelines, what might you say about the strength of the relationship between ABANY and RELIG? Take a moment to develop your answer and then compare your response to Writing Box 13.1.[4]

# WRITING BOX 13.1

The relationship between ABANY and RELIG can be summarized by a value of .209 on lambda. This means that if we wanted to predict how someone felt about abortion, we would make about 21% fewer errors if we knew that person's religious affiliation than we would make without knowing that.

Now, why don't you choose two nominal variables and then experiment with instructing SPSS Statistics to calculate lambda? If you need help recalling how to run lambda on SPSS Statistics, refer to SPSS Statistics Command 13.1 below.

---

### SPSS Statistics Command 13.1:
### Running Crosstabs With Lambda (λ)

Click **Analyze** → **Descriptive Statistics** → **Crosstabs**

Specify dependent variable as the "Row(s):" variable

Specify independent variable as the "Column(s):" variable

Click **Cells**

Make sure "Column" under "Percentages" is not selected [there should not be a check mark next to "Column"][5]

→ Click **Continue**

→ Click **Statistics** → **Lambda**

→ Click **Continue** → **OK**

---

# GAMMA (γ): A MEASURE APPROPRIATE FOR ORDINAL VARIABLES

Whereas lambda is used to examine the association between two nominal variables, *gamma* (γ) is a measure of association based on the logic of proportionate reduction of error appropriate for two ordinal variables (or one ordinal variable and one nominal dichotomous variable).

## An Indication of Strength and Direction (With a Caveat) of Association

Unlike lambda, gamma not only indicates the strength of association but also indicates the direction of association between two ordinal variables. With each variable having a greater-than/less-than

---

4. A more complete discussion may be found in Hubert M. Blalock's *Social Statistics* (London, UK: McGraw-Hill, 1960), pp. 310–311.

5. Usually, percentages are requested in order to see how the column percentages change or move. We purposefully omitted the percentages in Demonstration 13.1 in order to make the table easier to read.

relationship between its categories, we can observe whether or not high values of one variable are associated with high values of the other (a positive association) or if high values of one variable are associated with low values of the other (a negative association). The values of gamma range from –1.00 to +1.00.

In terms of the strength of association, the closer gamma is to –1.00 or +1.00, the stronger the relationship between the two variables, whereas the closer to 0.00, the weaker the association between the variables.

In terms of the **direction of association**, a negative sign indicates a negative association; as one variable increases, the other decreases. (The items change in opposite directions.) Conversely, a positive sign indicates a positive association; both items change in the same direction. (They both either increase or decrease.)

A negative association between social class and prejudice, for instance, indicates that the variables change in opposite directions: As one increases, the other decreases. Conversely, a positive association between social class and prejudice indicates that the variables change in the same direction: They both either increase or decrease (see Table 13.3).

We want to underscore the fact that you can determine the direction of association between two variables only if they are both measured on scales that express greater-than/less-than relationships between their points. Furthermore, if an ordinal variable's values have been arbitrarily assigned in such a way that high numbers or values indicate an absence of what is being measured and low numbers or values indicate a presence of the phenomenon, the sign (– or +) of the relationship will be reversed.

| TABLE 13.3 ■ Direction of Association: Using Class and Prejudice as an Example | |
|---|---|
| Negative Association | Value of Gamma Is Negative (–) |
| | As social class increases, prejudice decreases. |
| | ↑Social class, ↓Prejudice |
| | OR |
| | As social class decreases, prejudice increases. |
| | ↓Social class, ↑Prejudice |
| Positive Association | Value of Gamma Is Positive (+) |
| | As social class increases, so, too, does prejudice. |
| | ↑Social class, ↑Prejudice |
| | OR |
| | As social class decreases, so, too, does prejudice. |
| | ↓Social class, ↓Prejudice |

For an example of what we mean by *arbitrary* values, think back to when we reduced the number of ordinal categories on the variable ATTEND to create CHATT. In that case, we chose the value of 1 to represent "About weekly," 2 to represent "About monthly," and so on. These are arbitrary values in the sense that we could just as easily have arranged the categories in the opposite direction so that 1 represented "Never," 2 represented "Seldom," 3 represented "About monthly," and 4 represented "About weekly." With reversed codes, you need to keep in mind that a negative value for gamma in this case would not correctly indicate a direction of association; it would merely be a result of the way we had arbitrarily arranged the categories of an item.

Table 13.4 summarizes the way that gamma is used.

| TABLE 13.4 ■ A Summary of Gamma (γ) | |
|---|---|
| **Measure of Association** | **Gamma** |
| *Type of variables* | Ordinal × Ordinal |
| *Values (strength)* | −1.00 to +1.00 |
| | 0 = no association |
| | −1.00 = perfect (negative) association |
| | +1.00 = perfect (positive) association |
| *Direction* | + indicates positive association (variables change or move in same direction, i.e., both ↓↓ OR both ↑↑) |
| | − indicates negative association (variables change or move in opposite directions, i.e., as one goes ↑, other goes ↓ OR as one goes ↓, other goes ↑) |
| | Caveat: Have the values been arbitrarily assigned? If so, the + or − signs may be reversed. |

## Example 1: The Logic of Gamma (γ)

We judge two variables to be related to each other to the extent that knowing what a person is like in terms of one variable helps us guess what he or she is like in the other. Whereas the application of this logic in the case of lambda lets us make predictions for individuals (e.g., if a person is Protestant, we guess he or she is also Republican), in the case of gamma, the logic is applied to pairs of people.

To see the logic of gamma, let's consider the following nine people, placed in a matrix that indicates their social class standing and their level of prejudice: two ordinal variables.

| Prejudice | Lower Class | Middle Class | Upper Class |
|---|---|---|---|
| Low | Jim | Tim | Kim |
| Medium | Mary | Harry | Carrie |
| High | Nan | Jan | Fran |

Our purpose in this analysis is to determine which of the following best describes the relationship between social class and prejudice:

1. The higher your social class, the more prejudiced you are.

2. The higher your social class, the less prejudiced you are.

3. Your social class has no effect on your level of prejudice.

To begin our analysis, we should note that the only pairs who are appropriate to our question are those who differ in both social class and prejudice. Jim and Harry are an example; they differ in both social class and level of prejudice. Here are the 18 pairs that qualify for analysis:

| | | |
|---|---|---|
| Jim-Harry | Kim-Mary | Harry-Nan |
| Jim-Carrie | Kim-Harry | Harry-Fran |
| Jim-Jan | Kim-Nan | |
| Jim-Fran | Kim-Jan | |
| Tim-Mary | Mary-Jan | Carrie-Nan |

| Tim-Nan | Mary-Fran | Carrie-Jan |
|---------|-----------|------------|
| Tim-Carrie | | |
| Tim-Fran | | |

Take a minute to assure yourself that no other pair of people satisfies the criterion that they differ in both social class and prejudice.

If you study the table, you should be able to identify pairs of people who would support Conclusions 1 and 2; we'll come back to Conclusion 3 a little later.

Suppose now that you have been given the list of pairs, but you've never seen the original table. Your task is to guess which member of each pair is the more prejudiced. Given that you will simply be guessing blindly, chances are that you'll get about half right and half wrong: nine correct answers and nine errors. Gamma helps us determine whether knowing how two people differ on social class would reduce the number of errors we'd make in guessing how they differ on prejudice.

Let's consider Jim-Harry for a moment. If they were the only two people you could study, and if you had to reach a conclusion about the relationship between social class and prejudice, what would you conclude? Notice that Harry is higher in social class than Jim (middle class vs. lower class), and Harry is also higher in prejudice (medium vs. low). If you were to generalize from this single pair of observations, there is only one conclusion you could reach: "The higher your social class, the more prejudiced you are." As we noted earlier, this is referred to as a positive association: the higher on one variable, the higher on the other. In the more specific language of gamma, we'll refer to this as a *same pair*: The direction of the difference between Jim and Harry on one variable is the same as the direction of their difference on the other. Harry is higher than Jim on both.

Suppose you had to base your conclusion on the Jim-Jan pair. What would you conclude? Look at the table, and you'll see that Jan, like Harry, is higher than Jim on both social class and prejudice. This pair would also lead you to conclude that the higher your social class, the more prejudiced you are. Jim-Jan, then, is another same pair in the language of gamma.

Suppose, on the other hand, we observed only Tim and Mary. They would lead us to a very different conclusion. Mary is lower than Tim on social class, but she is higher on prejudice. If this were the only pair you could observe, you'd have to conclude that the higher your social class, the lower your prejudice. In the language of gamma, Tim-Mary is an *opposite pair*: The direction of their difference on one variable is the opposite of their difference on the other.

Now, we hope you've been feeling uncomfortable about the idea of generalizing from only one pair of observations, although that's what many people often do in everyday life. In social research, however, we would never do that.

Moving a little bit in the direction of normal social research, let's assume that you have observed all nine of the individuals in the table. What conclusion would you draw about the association between social class and prejudice? Gamma helps you answer this question.

Let's see how well each of the alternative conclusions might assist you in guessing people's prejudice based on knowing about their social class. If you operated on the basis of the conclusion that prejudice increases with social class, for example, and I told you Fran is of a higher social class than Harry, you would correctly guess that Fran is more prejudiced. If, on the other hand, I told you that Harry is higher in social class than Nan, you would incorrectly guess that Harry is more prejudiced.

Take a minute to go through the list of pairs above and make notations of which ones are same pairs and which are opposite pairs. Once you've done that, count the numbers of same and opposite pairs.

You should get nine of each type of pair. This means if you assume that prejudice increases with social class, you will get the nine opposite pairs wrong; if you assume prejudice decreases with social class, you will get the nine same pairs wrong. In other words, neither strategy for guessing levels of prejudice based on knowing social class will do you any good in this case. In either case, we make as many errors as we would have made if we didn't know the social class differences in the pairs. Gamma gives us a method for calculating that result.

The formula for gamma is as follows:

$$\gamma = \frac{Same - Opposite}{Same + Opposite}$$

To calculate gamma, you must first count the number of same pairs and the number of opposite pairs. Once you've done that, the math is pretty simple.

Now, you can complete the formula as follows:

$$\gamma = \frac{9-9}{9+9} = \frac{0}{18} = 0$$

In gamma, this result is interpreted as 0%, meaning that knowing how two people differ on social class would improve your guesses as to how they differ on prejudice by 0—or not at all.

Consider the following modified table, however. Suppose for the moment that there are only three people to be studied:

| Prejudice | Lower Class | Middle Class | Upper Class |
|---|---|---|---|
| Low | Jim | | |
| Medium | | Harry | |
| High | | | Fran |

Just by inspection, you can see how perfectly these three people fit the pattern of a positive association between social class and prejudice. Each of the three pairs—Jim-Harry, Harry-Fran, and Jim-Fran—is a same pair. There are no opposite pairs. If we were to give you each of these pairs, telling you who is higher in social class, the assumption of a positive association between the two variables would let you guess who is higher in social class with perfect accuracy.

Let's see how this situation would look in terms of gamma.

$$\gamma = \frac{same - opposite}{same + opposite} = \frac{3-0}{3+0} \; 1.00 \; or \; 100\%$$

In this case, we would say that gamma equals 1.00, meaning you have reduced the number of errors by 100%. To understand this meaning of gamma, we need to go back to the idea of guessing differences in prejudice without knowing social class.

Recall that if you were guessing blindly, you'd be right about half of the time and wrong about half of the time. In this hypothetical case, you'd be wrong 1.5 times out of 3. (That would be your average if you repeated the exercise hundreds of times.) As we've seen, however, knowing social class in this instance lets us reduce the number of errors by 1.5—down to zero. It is in this sense that we say we have reduced our errors by 100%.

Now, let's consider a slightly different table.

| Prejudice | Lower Class | Middle Class | Upper Class |
|---|---|---|---|
| Low | | | Nan |
| Medium | | Harry | |
| High | Kim | | |

Notice that in this case, we could also have a perfect record, if we use the assumption of a negative association between social class and prejudice: the higher your social class, the lower your prejudice. The negative association shows up in gamma as follows:

$$\gamma = \frac{same - opposite}{same + opposite} = \frac{0-3}{0+3} = -1.00 \text{ or } 100\%$$

Once again, the gamma indicates that we have reduced our errors by 100%. The minus sign in this result simply signals that the relationship is negative.

## Example 2: The Logic of Gamma (γ)

We are finally ready for a more realistic example. Just as you would not want to base a generalization on as few cases as we've been considering so far, neither would it make sense to calculate gamma in such situations. Notice how gamma helps you assess the relationship between two variables when the results are not as obvious to those inexperienced in statistics.

| Prejudice | Lower Class | Middle Class | Upper Class |
|---|---|---|---|
| Low | 200 | 400 | 700 |
| Medium | 500 | 900 | 400 |
| High | 800 | 300 | 100 |

In this table, the names of individuals have been replaced with the number of people having a particular social class and level of prejudice. There are 200 lower-class people in the table, for example, who are low on prejudice. On the other hand, there are 100 upper-class people who are high on prejudice.

Perhaps you can get a sense of the relationship in this table by simple observation. The largest cells are those lying along the diagonal running from lower left to upper right. This would suggest a negative association between the two variables (direction of association). Gamma lets us determine with more confidence whether that's the case and gives us a yardstick for measuring how strong the relationship is (strength of association).

In the simpler examples, every pair of cells represented one pair because there was only one person in each cell. Now, it's a little more complex. Imagine for a moment just one of the people in the upper left cell (lower class, low prejudice). If we matched that person up with the 900 people in the center cell (middle class, medium prejudice), we'd have 900 pairs. The same would result from matching each of the people in the first cell with all of those in the second. We can calculate the total number of pairs produced by the two cells by simple multiplication: 200 × 900 gives us 180,000 pairs. Notice, by the way, that these are same pairs.

As a further simplification, notice that there are 900 + 400 + 300 + 100 people who will match with the upper left cell to form same pairs. That makes a total of 1,700 × 200 = 340,000. Here's an overview of all of the same pairs in the table:

$$200 \times (900 + 300 + 400 + 100) = 340,000$$
$$500 \times (300 + 100) = 200,000$$
$$400 \times (400 + 100) = 200,000$$
$$900 \times 100 = 90,000$$
$$\text{Total same pairs} = 830,000$$

Following the same procedure, here are all of the opposite pairs:

$$700 \times (500 + 800 + 900 + 300) = 1,750,000$$
$$400 \times (800 + 300) = 440,000$$

$$400 \times (500 + 800) = 520,000$$

$$900 \times 800 = 720,000$$

Total opposite pairs = 3,430,000

Even though this procedure produces quite a few more pairs than we've been dealing with, the formula for gamma still works the same way:

$$\gamma = \frac{Same - Opposite}{Same + Opposite} = \frac{830,000 - 3,430,000}{830,000 + 3,430,000} = \frac{-2,600,000}{4,260,000} = -.61$$

The minus sign in this result confirms that the relationship between the two variables is a negative one (direction). The numerical result indicates that knowing the social class ranking in each pair reduces our errors in predicting their ranking in terms of prejudice by 61% (strength).

Suppose, for the moment, that you had tried to blindly predict differences in prejudice for each of the 4,260,000 pairs. You would have been wrong about 2,130,000 times. By assuming that the person with higher social class is less prejudiced, you would have made only 830,000 errors, and 2,130,000 – 830,000 = 1,300,000 fewer errors. Dividing the 1,300,000 improvement by the 2,130,000 baseline gives us .61, indicating that you have reduced your errors by 61%.

# DEMONSTRATION 13.2: INSTRUCTING SPSS STATISTICS TO CALCULATE GAMMA (γ)—EXAMPLE 1

Now, here's the good news. Although it's important for you to understand the logic of gamma, it is no longer necessary for you to do the calculations by hand. Whenever you run crosstabs in SPSS Statistics, you can request that gamma be calculated by making that request when you set up the table.

Go to crosstabs. Make EDCAT the column variable and CLASS the row variable.[6] Then, click on **Statistics**.

---

6. We walked through the steps of recoding EDUC to create the new variable EDCAT in Chapter 11. If you did not save EDCAT on your DEMOPLUS.SAV file, simply refer back to the recode commands in that chapter before continuing with this demonstration. For the variable CLASS, the values 0, 5, 8, and 9 should be defined as "missing."

Notice that "Gamma" is appropriately listed as a choice under "Ordinal" data. Click it. If "Lambda" still has a check mark next to it, turn it off before selecting **Continue** to return to the main window. Once you have returned to the Crosstabs window, you can instruct SPSS Statistics to run the procedure by selecting **OK**. You should get the following crosstab table, as well as the table reporting on gamma (titled "Symmetric Measures" on the next page).

## CLASS Subjective Class Identification * EDCAT Recoded Education Level Crosstabulation

| | | EDCAT Recoded Education Level | | | | | |
|---|---|---|---|---|---|---|---|
| | | 1 Less than high school | 2 High school graduate | 3 Some college | 4 College graduate | 5 Graduate studies (beyond college) | Total |
| CLASS Subjective class identification | 1 LOWER CLASS | 39 | 58 | 35 | 8 | 8 | 148 |
| | 2 WORKING CLASS | 96 | 238 | 218 | 82 | 52 | 686 |
| | 3 MIDDLE CLASS | 38 | 123 | 141 | 159 | 143 | 604 |
| | 4 UPPER CLASS | 5 | 4 | 5 | 16 | 14 | 44 |
| Total | | 178 | 423 | 399 | 265 | 217 | 1482 |

Notice that gamma is reported as .439. This means that knowing a person's level of education would improve our estimate of his or her class by 44%. Based on our "general guidelines" for interpreting measures of association (Table 13.2), you can see that this value of gamma is fairly high and is therefore evidence of a strong, extremely interesting association between these two variables.

Remember that in addition to indicating the strength of the association between two variables, which in this case is fairly high, gamma also tells us the direction of association. In this instance, the positive sign indicates a positive association between the variables. That is, as level of education rises, so does class.

### Symmetric Measures

| | | Value | Asymptotic Standard Error[a] | Approximate T[b] | Approximate Significance |
|---|---|---|---|---|---|
| Ordinal by Ordinal | Gamma | .439 | .028 | 14.630 | .000 |
| N of Valid Cases | | 1482 | | | |

a. Not assuming the null hypothesis.

b. Using the asymptotic standard error assuming the null hypothesis.

## WRITING BOX 13.2

Education is a powerful predictor of social class, as these data illustrate. The gamma value of +.439 indicates that our ability to predict accurately which of two people has the higher social class is improved by more than 44% if we know their respective educational levels.

## DEMONSTRATION 13.3: RUNNING GAMMA (γ)— EXAMPLE 2 (REVERSE SCORING CASE)

Now that you are fairly comfortable requesting gamma, let's look at an example in which the arbitrary arrangement of the categories means that you cannot rely on the positive or negative sign as an indication of the direction of association between the variables.

For this example, let's look at the association between CHATT and AGECAT. Go ahead and run crosstabs; then, make CHATT the row variable and AGECAT the column variable. Once you have done that, click on **Statistics** and request "Gamma."

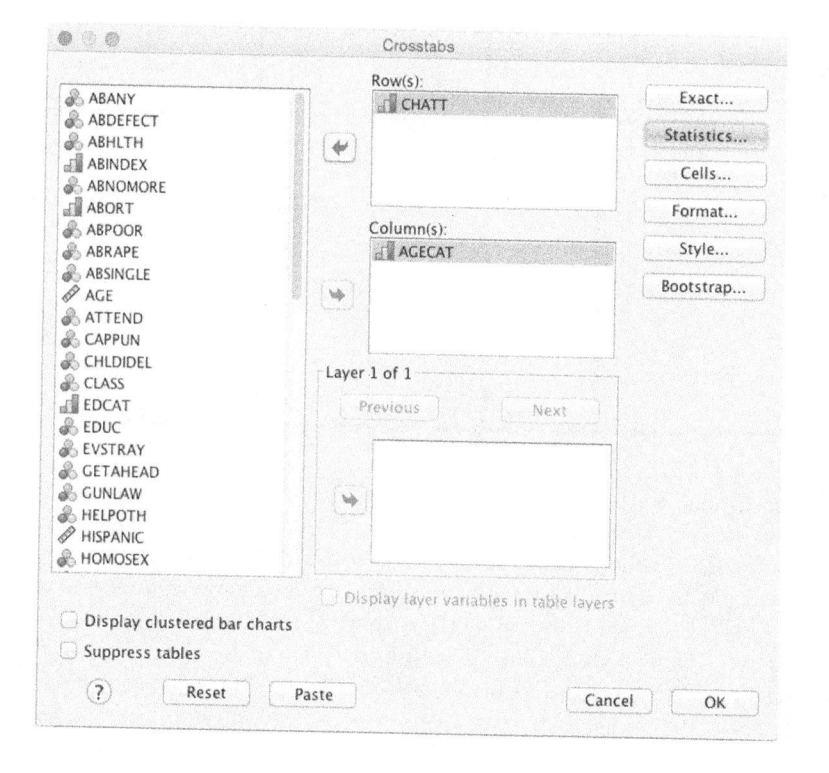

Crosstabs: Statistics

☐ Chi-square                    ☐ Correlations

Nominal
☐ Contingency coefficient

Ordinal
☑ Gamma

☐ Phi and Cramer's V            ☐ Somers' d

☐ Lambda                        ☐ Kendall's tau-b

☐ Uncertainty coefficient       ☐ Kendall's tau-c

Nominal by Interval             ☐ Kappa
☐ Eta                           ☐ Risk

                                ☐ McNemar

☐ Cochran's and Mantel–Haenszel statistics
Test common odds ratio equals: 1

(?)            Cancel        Continue

Your output should look like the tables below.

## CHATT Recoded Church Attendance * AGECAT Recoded Age Crosstabulation

| | | AGECAT Recoded Age | | | | |
|---|---|---|---|---|---|---|
| | | 1 Under 21 | 2 21–39 years old | 3 40–64 years old | 4 65 and older | Total |
| CHATT Recoded Church Attendance | 1 About weekly | 10 | 99 | 188 | 128 | 425 |
| | 2 About monthly | 6 | 96 | 97 | 40 | 239 |
| | 3 Seldom | 9 | 156 | 214 | 73 | 452 |
| | 4 Never | 8 | 124 | 156 | 80 | 368 |
| Total | | 33 | 475 | 655 | 321 | 1484 |

## Symmetric Measures

| | | Value | Asymptotic Standard Error[a] | Approximate T[b] | Approximate Significance |
|---|---|---|---|---|---|
| Ordinal by Ordinal | Gamma | −.106 | .033 | −3.240 | .001 |
| N of Valid Cases | | 1484 | | | |

a. Not assuming the null hypothesis.

b. Using the asymptotic standard error assuming the null hypothesis.

Notice that gamma is reported as −.106. This means that knowing a person's age would improve our estimate of his or her church attendance by 11%.

Although you might think that the negative sign means there is a negative relationship between age and church attendance, we know now that this is not the case. In this example, the minus sign results from our choosing to arrange attendance categories arbitrarily, from the most frequent at the top to the least frequent at the bottom. If we had arranged the categories in the opposite direction, the gamma would have been positive.

Whenever you ask SPSS to calculate gamma, it is important that you note how the variable categories are arranged. If coding is not consistent—that is, if low codes don't indicate low amounts of what is being measured and vice versa—gamma's signs will be reversed. You can also determine the direction of the association by inspecting the table. Looking at the first row in the table above, it is fairly clear that church attendance tends to increase as age increases; hence, the relationship between the two variables is a positive one.

Now, take a moment to compare the two tables we just created: CLASS-EDCAT and CHATT-AGECAT. You can see that in the first case, the values of CLASS run down the left-hand side from lowest (top) to highest (bottom), whereas the values of EDCAT run across the top from the lowest education level (left side) to the highest (far right side). Because the categories are arranged in this way, you can be sure that the sign (positive in this case) is meaningful.

**EXAMPLE 1: CLASS × EDCAT**

| | EDCAT | | | | |
|---|---|---|---|---|---|
| | Less Than High School | High School | Some College | College Graduate | Graduate Students+ |
| CLASS | LOWEST education level → HIGHEST education level | | | | |
| Lower | LOWEST | | | | |
| Working | Class | | | | |
| Middle | ↓ | | | | |
| Upper | HIGHEST | | | | |
| | Class | | | | |

However, if you examine the second example (CHATT-AGECAT), you can see a major difference. In this case, CHATT is arranged down the left side from the most frequent attendance (top) to the least frequent attendance (bottom), whereas AGECAT is arrayed across the top from the youngest (left side) to the oldest (right side).

As a result, in this case the sign is reversed. If we rearranged the categories for CHATT, we would get the opposite sign. However, instead of recoding the variable, it is easier just to make sure you are careful when reading the table and pay attention to cases such as this in which the sign is reversed.

**EXAMPLE 2: CHATT × AGECAT**

| | AGECAT | | | |
|---|---|---|---|---|
| | Under 21 | 21 to 39 | 40 to 64 | 65 and older |
| CHATT | YOUNGEST age category → OLDEST age category | | | |
| About weekly | Attend | | | |
| About monthly | MOST often | | | |
| Seldom | ↓ | | | |
| Never | Attend LEAST often | | | |

To gain some more experience with gamma, why don't you select two ordinal variables that interest you and examine their relationships with each other by using gamma? Remember to pay attention to cases such as the one we just reviewed in which the scoring is reversed.

---

**SPSS Statistics Command 13.2:**
**Running Crosstabs With Gamma (γ)**

Click **Analyze** → **Descriptive Statistics** → **Crosstabs**

Specify dependent variable as the "Row(s):" variable

Specify independent variable as the "Column(s):" variable

Click **Cells**

Make sure "Column" under "Percentages" is not selected [there should not be a check mark next to "Column"][7]

Click **Continue**

Click **Statistics** → **Gamma**

Click **Continue** → **OK**

---

# ADDITIONAL MEASURES OF ASSOCIATION

The measures of association we have focused on are each appropriate for variables at a particular level of measurement. For instance, lambda is used to examine the association between two nominal variables, whereas gamma is used to explore the relationship between two ordinal variables; later, in Chapter 14, we will explore Pearson's $r$, the coefficient of determination ($r^2$), and regression, which are appropriate for two interval/ratio items. Table 13.5 lists the measures we have reviewed in this chapter, along with their appropriate level of measurement.

| TABLE 13.5 ■ Measures of Association Reviewed in This Chapter | |
|---|---|
| **Level of Measurement** | **Measure of Association (Range of Values) of Each Variable** |
| Nominal | Lambda [0 to +1] |
| Ordinal (& Dichotomous Nominal) | Gamma [–1 to +1] |

Keep in mind, however, that the measures we reviewed are just a few of the most popular measures available for nominal and ordinal variables. In Table 13.6, we list some other measures applicable for variables at particular levels of measurement. You can access all of these (and other measures) using SPSS Statistics. However, we want to stress that you should use these measures with caution because, like the others we reviewed in the chapter, each has its own peculiar benefits and limitations. For instance, unlike gamma (γ), which is a symmetrical measure of association, Somers's $d$ is an asymmetrical measure of association. So with Somers's $d$, if you switched the positions (columns vs. rows) of the variables, the value would be different. With gamma (γ), the value would remain the same.

---

7. Usually, percentages are requested in order to see how the column percentages change or move. We purposefully omitted the percentages in Demonstrations 13.2 and 13.3 in order to make the tables easier to read.

| TABLE 13.6   ■   Additional Measures of Association | |
|---|---|
| **Level of Measurement** | |
| **Nominal** | Goodman and Kruskal's tau |
| | Phi |
| | Cramer's *V* |
| **Ordinal** | Somers's *d* |
| | Kendall's tau-*b* |
| | Kendall's tau-*c* |

# ANALYZING THE ASSOCIATION BETWEEN VARIABLES AT DIFFERENT LEVELS OF MEASUREMENT

In some cases, you may discover that you want to analyze the association between variables at different levels of measurement: for instance, nominal by ordinal, nominal by interval/ratio, and so on. While there are specialized bivariate measures of association for use when two variables have different levels of measurement, the safest course of action for the novice is to use a measure of association that meets the assumptions for the variable with the lowest level of measurement.

This often means that one variable will have to be recoded to reduce its level of measurement. For instance, when we examined the relationship between church attendance (ordinal) and age (interval/ratio), we recoded people's ages into ordinal categories to carry out the analysis in a meaningful way.

While it would not be appropriate to use Pearson's $r$ or $r^2$ (measures of association for interval/ratio variables) to correlate our CHATT and AGE, it is perfectly legitimate to use gamma to correlate CHATT with AGECAT.

While it is beyond the scope of this chapter to review all of the statistical measures appropriate for each particular situation, those of you who are interested in pursuing the relationship between mixed variables may want to consult a basic statistics or research methods text for a discussion of appropriate measures.[8]

# CONCLUSION

In this chapter, we've seen a number of statistical techniques that can be used to summarize the degree of relationship or association between two variables. We've seen that the appropriate technique depends on the level of measurement represented by the variables involved. Lambda ($\lambda$) is appropriate for nominal variables, while gamma ($\gamma$) is appropriate for ordinal and dichotomous nominal variables.

We realize that you may have had trouble knowing how to respond to the results of these calculations. How do you decide, for example, whether a gamma of .25 is high or low? Should you get excited about it or yawn and continue looking? The following chapter on statistical significance offers one basis for making such decisions.

---

8. Among the many basic statistics texts you may want to consult are the following: Freeman, L. C. (1968). *Elementary applied statistics: For students in behavioral science*. New York, NY: J. Wiley & Sons; Siegel, S., & Castellan, N. J. (1989). *Nonparametric statistics for the behavioral sciences* (2nd ed.). New York, NY: McGraw-Hill; Frankfort-Nachmias, C., & Leon-Guerrero, A. (2015). *Social statistics for a diverse society* (7th ed.). Thousand Oaks, CA: Sage. P. L. Alreck and R. B. Settle's (1985) *The Survey Research Handbook* (Homewood, IL: R. D. Irwin), pp. 287–362, contains a table titled "Statistical Measures of Association" (Table 10-5, p. 303), which, depending on the type of independent and dependent variables you are working with (i.e., categorical or continuous), specifies appropriate measures of association. The table is accompanied by a discussion of statistical analysis and interpretation.

## Main Points

- In this chapter, we looked at new ways to examine the relationships among variables.

- Measures of association summarize the strength (and in some cases, the direction) of association between two variables in contrast to the way percentage tables lay out the details.

- This chapter focuses on only two of the many measures available: lambda ($\lambda$) and gamma ($\gamma$).

- The measures are largely based on the logic of proportionate reduction of error.

- Lambda ($\lambda$) is appropriate for two nominal variables; its values range from 0 to 1.

- Lambda ($\lambda$) is an asymmetrical measure of association.

- Gamma ($\gamma$) is appropriate for two ordinal variables (as well as dichotomous nominal variables); its values range from –1 to +1.

- Gamma ($\gamma$) is a symmetrical measure of association.

- The closer the value is to positive or negative 1, the stronger the relationship between the items (with +1 or –1 indicating a perfect association). The closer the value is to 0, the weaker the relationship between the items (with 0 indicating no association between the items).

- There are no absolute rules for interpreting strength of association.

- Pearson's $r$, $r^2$, and linear regression analysis are appropriate for analyzing relationships between interval and ratio variables (see Chapter 14).

- There are a variety of appropriate statistics for examining the relationship between mixed types of variables.

## Key Terms

Descriptive statistics  219
Dichotomous variables  225
Direction of association  227
Gamma ($\gamma$)  226

Lambda ($\lambda$)  220
Measures of association  219
Opposite pair  229

Proportionate reduction
  of error (PRE)  220
Same pair  229

## SPSS Statistics Commands Introduced in This Chapter

13.1.  Running Crosstabs With Lambda ($\lambda$)

13.2.  Running Crosstabs With Gamma ($\gamma$)

## Review Questions

1. If two variables are strongly associated, does that mean they are necessarily causally related?

2. What does PRE stand for? Explain what that means.

3. List two measures of association.

4. Measures of association give us an indication of the _____ of association and (if the variables are ordinal or higher) the_____ of association between two variables.

5. Lambda ($\lambda$) is appropriate for variables at which level of measurement?

6. Gamma ($\gamma$) is appropriate for variables at which level of measurement?

7. Pearson's $r$ and the coefficient of determination ($r^2$) are appropriate for variables at which level of measurement?

8. List the range of values for each of the following measures:

   Lambda

   Gamma

*(Continued)*

(Continued)

9. The closer to _____ or _____ (value), the stronger the relationship between the variables.

10. The closer to _____ (value), the weaker the relationship between the variables.

11. A value of _____ or _____ indicates a perfect (or the strongest) relationship between the variables.

12. What does a positive association between two variables indicate? What does a negative association between two variables indicate?

13. Does a negative value for gamma necessarily indicate that the variables are negatively associated? Explain.

14. Name one measure of association you might use to examine the strength of association between the variable CHATT (ordinal) and SEX (nominal), without recoding these two variables.

# SPSS Statistics Lab Exercise 13.1

NAME: _____

CLASS: _____

INSTRUCTOR: _____

DATE: _____

*To complete these exercises, load your EXERPLUS.SAV data file.*

Run crosstabs with column percentages for the variables RACE (independent) and POLHITOK (dependent). Then, request the appropriate measure of association, and answer Questions 1 through 7. Be sure to define the values 0, 8, and 9 as "missing" for POLHITOK.

1. What is the level of measurement for the variable RACE?

2. What is the level of measurement for the variable POLHITOK?

3. What measure of association is appropriate to examine the relationship between these variables?

4. Record the percentage of respondents who said "Yes" to POLHITOK for each category of the variable RACE.

|  | Race | | |
|---|---|---|---|
|  | White | Black | Other |
| Yes |  |  |  |

5. Do the column percentages change or move, signifying a relationship between RACE and POLHITOK? Explain.

6. The strength/value of _____ (measure of association) is _____ (value/strength of measure of association).

7. Would you characterize the relationship between these two variables as weak, moderate, or strong? Explain.

Choose two nominal variables from your data set. Run crosstabs with column percentages for the variables. Then, request the appropriate measure of association, and answer Questions 8 through 12. Reminder: Be sure to define the appropriate values as "missing" for each of your variables.

8. List the two variables you chose, designating one as the independent variable and one as the dependent variable. Then, state briefly why you chose them and what you expect to find in terms of the relationship between these variables (i.e., construct a hypothesis relating your variables).

*(Continued)*

(Continued)

9. What measure of association is appropriate to examine the relationship between these variables?

10. Do the column percentages change or move across categories of the variables, signifying a relationship between these variables? Explain.

11. The strength/value of _____ (measure of association) is _____ (value/strength of measure of association).

12. Would you characterize the relationship between these two variables as weak, moderate, or strong? Explain.

Run Crosstabs with column percentages for the variables RACWORK (independent) and DISCAFF (dependent). Then, request the appropriate measure of association, and answer Questions 13 through 20. Before proceeding with your analysis, remember to define the values 0, 6, 8, and 9 as "missing" for RACWORK. In addition, be sure to define 0, 8, and 9 as "missing" for DISCAFF.

13. What is the level of measurement for the variable RACWORK?

14. What is the level of measurement for the variable DISCAFF?

15. What measure of association is appropriate to examine the relationship between these variables?

16. Record the percentage of respondents who said "Very likely" and "Somewhat likely" to DISCAFF for each category of the variable RACWORK.

|  | RACWORK | | | | |
|---|---|---|---|---|---|
|  | All White | Mostly White | Half White— Half Black | Mostly Black | All Black |
| Very likely |  |  |  |  |  |
| Somewhat likely |  |  |  |  |  |

17. Do the column percentages change or move across categories of the variables, signifying a relationship between RACWORK and DISCAFF? Explain.

18. The strength/value of _____ (measure of association) is
    _____ (value/strength of measure of association).

19. Would you characterize the relationship between these two variables as weak, moderate, or strong? Explain.

20. What is the direction of association between these variables?

Choose two ordinal variables from your data set. Run crosstabs with column percentages for the variables. Then, request the appropriate measure of association, and answer Questions 21 through 26. Reminder: Be sure to label appropriate values for each variable as "missing."

21. List the two variables you chose, designating one as the independent variable and one as the dependent variable. Then, state briefly why you chose them and what you expect to find in terms of the relationship between these variables (i.e., construct a hypothesis relating your variables).

22. What measure of association is appropriate to examine the relationship between these variables?

23. Do the column percentages change or move across categories of the variables, signifying a relationship between these variables? Explain.

24. The strength/value of _____ (measure of association) is
    _____ (value/strength of measure of association).

25. Would you characterize the relationship between these two variables as weak, moderate, or strong? Explain.

26. What is the direction of association between these variables?

# CORRELATION AND REGRESSION ANALYSIS

In the previous chapter, we carefully examined the nature and logic of statistical association through proportionate reduction of error (PRE). The discussion in Chapter 13 was limited to measures of association for nominal and ordinal variables. Lambda ($\lambda$) and gamma ($\gamma$) were both introduced and explored. Of course, we understand that other measures of association can be utilized for nominal and ordinal variables, as presented in Table 13.6.

We begin our discussion in this chapter with Pearson's $r$, often referred to as a correlation coefficient. After enumerating the details of this statistic, we explore the logic of correlation. We will then focus on linear regression analysis, which includes a discussion of $r^2$, the coefficient of determination. You'll see that $r^2$ is, in fact, a PRE statistic, just like lambda and gamma. Lastly, we will revisit measures appropriate for mixed types of variables.

## PEARSON'S $r$: A MEASURE APPROPRIATE FOR INTERVAL/RATIO VARIABLES

Finally, we are going to work with **Pearson's r**, also known as a *product-moment correlation coefficient* and sometimes simply referred to as a *correlation coefficient*. Pearson's $r$ is a measure of association that reflects the PRE logic and is appropriate to continuous, interval/ratio (I/R) variables such as age, education, and income.

### An Indication of Strength and Direction of Association

Like gamma, the value of Pearson's $r$ ranges from –1.00 to +1.00, indicating both the strength and direction of the relationship between two I/R variables. Once again, –1.00 indicates a perfect negative association, +1.00 indicates a perfect positive association, and 0.00 indicates no association. Table 14.1 summarizes the way Pearson's $r$ is used.

### Example 1: The Logic of Pearson's $r$

Although this measure also reflects the PRE logic, its meaning in that regard is not quite as straightforward as for the discrete variables analyzed by lambda and gamma. Although it made sense to talk about "guessing" someone's gender or employment status and being either right or wrong, there is little chance that we would ever guess someone's annual income in exact dollars or his or her exact age in days. Our best strategy would be to guess the mean income, and we'd be wrong almost every time. Pearson's $r$ lets us determine whether knowing one variable would help us come closer in our guesses of the other variable, and it calculates how much closer we would come.

| TABLE 14.1 ■ Summary of Pearson's *r* | |
|---|---|
| **Measure of association** | **Pearson's *r*** |
| *Type of variables* | I/R × I/R |
| *Values (strength)* | –1.00 to +1.00 |
| | 0 = no association |
| | –1.00 = perfect (negative) association |
| | +1.00 = perfect (positive) association |
| *Direction* | + indicates positive association (variables change or move in same direction, i.e., both ↓↓ *OR* both ↑↑) |
| | – indicates negative association (variables change or move in opposite directions, i.e., as one goes ↑, other goes ↓, *OR* as one goes ↓, other goes ↑) |

To understand *r*, let's take a simple example of eight young people and see whether there is a correlation between their heights (in inches) and their weights (in pounds). To begin, then, let's meet the eight subjects.

| | Height | Weight |
|---|---|---|
| Eddy | 68 | 144 |
| Mary | 58 | 111 |
| Marge | 67 | 137 |
| Terry | 66 | 153 |
| Albert | 61 | 165 |
| Larry | 74 | 166 |
| Heather | 67 | 92 |
| Ruth | 61 | 128 |

Take a minute to study the heights and weights. Begin with Eddy and Mary, at the top of the list. Eddy is both taller and heavier than Mary. If we were forced to reach a conclusion about the association between height and weight based on only these two observations, we would conclude that there is a positive correlation: The taller you are, the heavier you are. We might even go a step further and note that every additional inch of height corresponds to about 3 pounds of weight.

On the other hand, if you needed to base a conclusion on observations of Eddy and Terry, see what that conclusion would be. Terry is 2 inches shorter but 9 pounds heavier than Eddy. Our observations of Eddy and Terry would lead us to just the opposite conclusion: The taller you are, the lighter you are.

Sometimes, it's useful to look at a **scattergram**, which graphs the cases at hand in terms of the two variables.[1] The diagram that follows presents the eight cases in this fashion. Notice that a general pattern of increasing height seems to be associated with increasing weight, although a couple of cases don't fit that pattern.

---

1. We are going to review how you can instruct SPSS Statistics to produce a scattergram (also called a scatterplot) toward the end of this chapter.

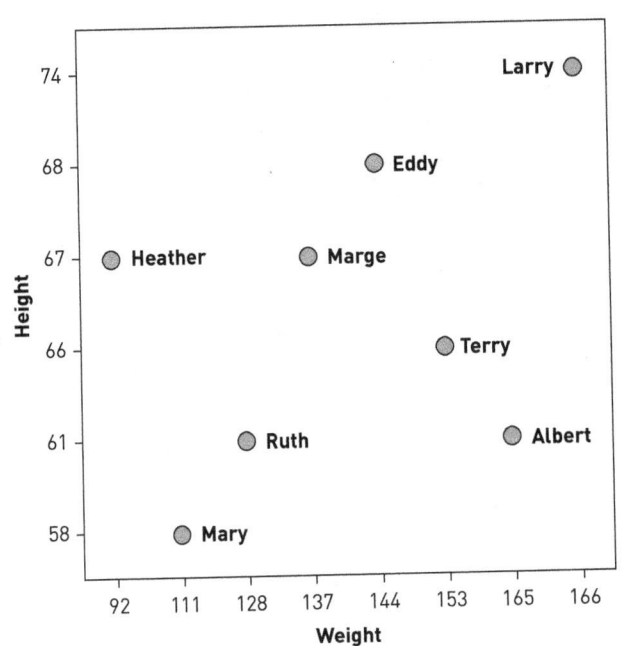

Pearson's *r* allows for the fact that the relationship between height and weight may not be completely consistent; nevertheless, it lets us discover any prevailing tendency in that regard. In the gamma logic presented previously, we might consider a strategy of guessing who is heavier or lighter on the basis of who is taller or shorter, assuming either a positive (taller means heavier) or negative (taller means lighter) relationship between the two variables. With *r*, however, we'll take account of *how much* taller or heavier.

To calculate *r*, we need to know the mean value of each variable. As you recall, this is calculated by adding all of the values on a variable and dividing by the number of cases. If you do these calculations in the case of height, you'll discover that the eight people, laid end to end, would stretch to 522 inches, for a mean height of 65.25 inches. Do the same calculation for their weights, and you'll discover that the eight people weigh a total of 1,096 pounds, for a mean of 137 pounds.

From now on, we are going to focus less on the actual heights and weights of our eight people and deal more with the extent to which they differ from the means. The table below shows how much each person differs from the means for height and weight. Notice that plus and minus signs have been used to indicate whether a person is above or below the mean. (If you want to check your calculations in this situation, you should add all of the deviations from height and notice that they total zero; the same is true for deviations from mean weight.)

| | Height | Weight | H-dev | W-dev |
|---|---|---|---|---|
| Eddy | 68 | 144 | +2.75 | +7 |
| Mary | 58 | 111 | −7.25 | −26 |
| Marge | 67 | 137 | +1.75 | 0 |
| Terry | 66 | 153 | +0.75 | +16 |
| Albert | 61 | 165 | −4.25 | +28 |
| Larry | 74 | 166 | +8.75 | +29 |
| Heather | 67 | 92 | +1.75 | −45 |
| Ruth | 61 | 128 | −4.25 | −9 |
| Means | 65.25 | 137 | | |

As our next step, we want to determine the extent to which heights and weights vary from their means overall. Although we have shown the plus and minus signs above, it is important to note that both +2.00 and –2.00 represent deviations of 2 inches from the mean height. For reasons that will become apparent shortly, we are going to capture both positive and negative variations by squaring each of the deviations from the means. The squares of both +2.00 and –2.00 are the same: 4.00. The table below shows the squared deviations for each person on each variable. We've also totaled the squared deviations and calculated their means.

|        | Height | Weight | H-dev | W-dev | Sq H-dev | Sq W-dev |
|--------|--------|--------|-------|-------|----------|----------|
| Eddy   | 68     | 144    | +2.75 | +7    | 7.5625   | 49       |
| Mary   | 58     | 111    | –7.25 | –26   | 52.5625  | 676      |
| Marge  | 67     | 137    | +1.75 | 0     | 3.0625   | 0        |
| Terry  | 66     | 153    | +0.75 | +16   | 0.5625   | 256      |
| Albert | 61     | 165    | –4.25 | +28   | 18.0625  | 784      |
| Larry  | 74     | 166    | +8.75 | +29   | 76.5625  | 841      |
| Heather| 67     | 92     | +1.75 | –45   | 3.0625   | 2,025    |
| Ruth   | 61     | 128    | –4.25 | –9    | 18.0625  | 81       |
| Mean   | 65.25  | 137    |       |       | Totals   | 4,712    |
|        |        |        |       |       | 179.5000 |          |

Now, we're going to present a couple of steps that would require more complicated explanations than we want to subject you to in this book, so if you can simply hear what we say without asking why, that's sufficient at this point. (But if you are interested in learning the logic of the intervening steps, that's great. You should check out discussions of variance and standard deviations in statistics textbooks.) Dividing the sum of the squared deviations by 1 less than the number of cases ($N - 1$) yields a quantity that statisticians call the variance. With a large number of cases, this quantity is close to the mean of the sum of squared deviations.

The variances in this case are 25.643 for height and 673.143 for weight. The square root of the variance is called the standard deviation. (Perhaps you are already familiar with these concepts, or perhaps you have heard the terms but didn't know what they mean.) Thus, the standard deviation for height is 5.063891; for weight, it is 25.94499.

Now we are ready to put all of these calculations to work for us. We are going to express all of the individual deviations from mean height and mean weight in units equal to the standard deviations. For example, Eddy was +2.75 inches taller than the average. Eddy's new deviation from the mean height becomes +0.54 (+2.75 ÷ 5.064). His deviation from the mean weight becomes +0.27 (+7 ÷ 25.945).

Our purpose in these somewhat complex calculations is to standardize deviations from the means of the two variables because the values on those variables are of very different scales. From the data, we knew that Eddy was 1.75 inches taller and 7 pounds heavier than the mean; we didn't have a way of knowing whether his height deviation was greater or less than his weight deviation. By dividing each deviation by the standard deviation for that variable, we can now see that Eddy's deviation on height is actually greater than his deviation in terms of weight. These new measures of deviation are called **z scores**. The table below presents each person's z score for both height and weight.

|       | Height | Weight | z height | z weight | z cross |
|-------|--------|--------|----------|----------|---------|
| Eddy  | 68     | 144    | 0.54     | 0.27     | 0.15    |
| Mary  | 58     | 111    | –1.43    | –1.00    | 1.43    |
| Marge | 67     | 137    | 0.35     | 0.00     | 0.00    |

| | Height | Weight | z height | z weight | z cross |
|---|---|---|---|---|---|
| Terry | 66 | 153 | 0.15 | 0.62 | 0.09 |
| Albert | 61 | 165 | −0.84 | 1.08 | −0.91 |
| Larry | 74 | 166 | 1.73 | 1.12 | 1.93 |
| Heather | 67 | 92 | 0.35 | −1.73 | −0.60 |
| Ruth | 61 | 128 | −0.84 | −0.35 | 0.29 |
| Total | | | | | 2.38 |

You'll notice that there is a final column of the table labeled "z cross." This is the result of multiplying each person's z score on height by the z score on weight. You'll notice that we've begun rounding the numbers to two decimal places. That level of precision is sufficient for our present purposes.

Thanks to your perseverance, we are finally ready to calculate Pearson's $r$ product-moment correlation. By now, it's pretty simple.

$r$ = sum of (z scores for height × z scores for weight) divided by $N - 1$

In our example, this amounts to

$$r = 2.38 \div 8 - 1 = .34$$

There is no easy, commonsense way to represent the meaning of $r$. Technically, it has to do with the extent to which variations in one variable can explain variations in the other. In fact, if you square $r$, you get the coefficient of determination, .12 in this case. This number can be interpreted as follows: 12% of the variation in one variable can be accounted for by the variation in the other. Recall that the variation in a variable reflects the extent to which individual cases deviate (or vary) from the mean value.

Reverting to the logic of PRE, this means that knowing a person's height reduces by 12% the extent of our errors in guessing how far he or she is from the mean weight.

In large part, $r$'s value comes with use. When you calculate correlations among several pairs of variables, the resulting $r$'s will tell which pairs are more highly associated with each other than is true of other pairs.

# INTERPRETING PEARSON'S $r$ AND THE COEFFICIENT OF DETERMINATION ($r^2$)

We can say for certain that for the measures of association we are considering in this chapter, a value of 1.00 (both positive and negative in the case of Pearson's $r$) indicates a perfect association or the strongest possible relationship between two variables. Conversely, a value of 0.00 indicates no relationship between the variables.

We can also say that the closer the value is to 1.00 (both positive and negative in the case of Pearson's $r$), the stronger the relationship. And the closer the value is to 0.00, the weaker the relationship.

That said, in order to give you a sense of one way you can approach these statistics, we include in Table 14.2 some general guidelines for interpreting the strength of association between variables. As the title of the table clearly indicates, these are merely loose guidelines with arbitrary cutoff points that must be understood within the context of our discussion before regarding the absence of any absolute "rules" of interpretation. Ultimately, determining whether or not a relationship is noteworthy depends on what association values other researchers have found.

| TABLE 14.2   ■   Some General Guidelines for Interpreting Strength of Association (Pearson's *r*, Coefficient of Determination) | |
| --- | --- |
| **Strength of Association** | **Value of Measures of Association (Pearson's *r*, Coefficient of Determination)** |
| None | 0.00 |
| Weak/uninteresting association | ±.01 to .09 |
| Moderate/worth noting | ±.10 to .29 |
| Evidence of strong association/extremely interesting | ±.30 to .99 |
| Perfect/strongest possible association | ±1.00 |

*Note:* This table has been adapted from a more in-depth discussion in Healey et al. (1999).

# INSTRUCTING SPSS STATISTICS TO CALCULATE PEARSON'S *r*

Here's the really good news. Your reward for pressing through all of the prior calculations in order to gain some understanding of what *r* represents is that you may never have to do it again. SPSS Statistics will do it for you.

Let's consider the possible relationship between two of the continuous variables in the data set: AGE and RINCOM16. If you think about it, you should expect that people tend to earn more money as they grow older, so let's check the correlation between age and respondents' incomes. (Note: RINCOM16 is the respondent's personal income as of 2016; INCOME is total family income as of 2016.) You might be reluctant to calculate the deviations, squared deviations, and so on for the 1,500 respondents in your data set (if not, you need a hobby), but computers thrive on such tasks.

# DEMONSTRATION 14.1: RECODING RINCOM16 → RECINC

Before we tell SPSS Statistics to take on the task of computing correlations for us, we need to do a little housekeeping. First, request a frequency distribution for RINCOM16 in SPSS Statistics.

There are two problems with using RINCOM16 the way it is currently coded. First, we need to be sure codes 0 (IAP), 26 (REFUSED), 98 (DK), and 99 (NA) are not included in our analysis. They may be eliminated by recoding them "system-missing," if they are not already coded as such. This may have already been done in the data file you are using, but it is certainly important to take a moment to check. Second, the code categories are not equal in width. For example, code category 8 includes respondents whose incomes were between $8,000 and $9,999, whereas code category 9 includes incomes between $10,000 and $12,499. The categories form an ordinal scale that is not appropriate for use with Pearson's *r*.

We can use Recode to improve on the coding scheme used for recording incomes.[2] If we assume that incomes are spread evenly across categories, then we can simply substitute the midpoints of the interval widths for the codes used in RINCOM16. That way, we can approximate an I/R scale and rid ourselves of the problems created by the interval widths not being equal. Note that code

---

2. The authors greatly appreciate the suggestion of this analysis by Professor Gilbert Klajman, Montclair State University.

# RINCOM16 Respondent's Income

| | | Freq. | % | Valid % | Cumulative Percent |
|---|---|---|---|---|---|
| Valid | 1 UNDER $1 000 | 11 | .7 | 1.3 | 1.3 |
| | 2 $1 000 TO 2 999 | 28 | 1.9 | 3.3 | 4.5 |
| | 3 $3 000 TO 3 999 | 18 | 1.2 | 2.1 | 6.6 |
| | 4 $4 000 TO 4 999 | 13 | .9 | 1.5 | 8.1 |
| | 5 $5 000 TO 5 999 | 18 | 1.2 | 2.1 | 10.2 |
| | 6 $6 000 TO 6 999 | 18 | 1.2 | 2.1 | 12.3 |
| | 7 $7 000 TO 7 999 | 9 | .6 | 1.0 | 13.4 |
| | 8 $8 000 TO 9 999 | 20 | 1.3 | 2.3 | 15.7 |
| | 9 $10000 TO 12499 | 24 | 1.6 | 2.8 | 18.5 |
| | 10 $12500 TO 14999 | 15 | 1.0 | 1.7 | 20.2 |
| | 11 $15000 TO 17499 | 26 | 1.7 | 3.0 | 23.3 |
| | 12 $17500 TO 19999 | 23 | 1.5 | 2.7 | 25.9 |
| | 13 $20000 TO 22499 | 41 | 2.7 | 4.8 | 30.7 |
| | 14 $22500 TO 24999 | 43 | 2.9 | 5.0 | 35.7 |
| | 15 $25000 TO 29999 | 52 | 3.5 | 6.0 | 41.7 |
| | 16 $30000 TO 34999 | 68 | 4.5 | 7.9 | 49.7 |
| | 17 $35000 TO 39999 | 58 | 3.9 | 6.7 | 56.4 |
| | 18 $40000 TO 49999 | 82 | 5.5 | 9.5 | 65.9 |
| | 19 $50000 TO 59999 | 72 | 4.8 | 8.4 | 74.3 |
| | 20 $60000 TO 74999 | 75 | 5.0 | 8.7 | 83.0 |
| | 21 $75000 TO $89999 | 46 | 3.1 | 5.3 | 88.4 |
| | 22 $90000 TO $109999 | 35 | 2.3 | 4.1 | 92.4 |
| | 23 $110000 TO $129999 | 17 | 1.1 | 2.0 | 94.4 |
| | 24 $130000 TO $149999 | 12 | .8 | 1.4 | 95.8 |
| | 25 $150000 TO $169999 | 6 | .4 | .7 | 96.5 |
| | 26 $170000 OR OVER | 30 | 2.0 | 3.5 | 100.0 |
| | Total | 860 | 57.3 | 100 | |
| Missing | 0 IAP | 589 | 39.3 | | |
| | 27 REFUSED | 42 | 2.8 | | |
| | 98 DK | 9 | .6 | | |
| | Total | 640 | 42.7 | | |
| Total | | 1500 | 100 | | |

25, $150,000 or more, has no upper limit; we just took an educated guess that the midpoint would be about $160,000. Even though we don't have each respondent's actual income, this recoding approach will enable us to use Pearson's $r$ to search for relationships between income and other variables. As SPSS Statistics commands, the recoding looks like this:

## TRANSFORM → RECODE → INTO DIFFERENT VARIABLES

| Old Variable RINCOM16 | | New Variable RECINC |
|---|---|---|
| Values | | Values |
| 1 | → | 500 |
| 2 | → | 2,000 |
| 3 | → | 3,500 |
| 4 | → | 4,500 |
| 5 | → | 5,500 |
| 6 | → | 6,500 |
| 7 | → | 7,500 |
| 8 | → | 9,000 |
| 9 | → | 11,250 |
| 10 | → | 13,750 |
| 11 | → | 16,250 |
| 12 | → | 18,750 |
| 13 | → | 21,250 |
| 14 | → | 23,750 |
| 15 | → | 27,500 |
| 16 | → | 32,500 |
| 17 | → | 37,500 |
| 18 | → | 45,000 |
| 19 | → | 55,000 |
| 20 | → | 67,500 |
| 21 | → | 82,500 |
| 22 | → | 100,000 |
| 23 | → | 120,000 |
| 24 | → | 140,000 |
| 25 | → | 160,000 |
| System or user missing | → | System-missing |

Once you have completed the recoding, access the **Variable View** tab and define your new variable RECINC (i.e., set the width, decimals, etc.). Also, don't forget to save your recoded variable on your DEMOPLUS.SAV file so we can use it later on.

Now, go ahead and run Frequencies for RECINC.

Here's what the recoded variable looks like:

## RECINC Recoded R's Income

| | | Frequency | Percent | Valid Percent | Cumulative Percent |
|---|---|---|---|---|---|
| Valid | 500 | 11 | .7 | 1.3 | 1.3 |
| | 2000 | 28 | 1.9 | 3.4 | 4.7 |
| | 3500 | 18 | 1.2 | 2.2 | 6.9 |
| | 4500 | 13 | .9 | 1.6 | 8.4 |
| | 5500 | 18 | 1.2 | 2.2 | 10.6 |
| | 6500 | 18 | 1.2 | 2.2 | 12.8 |
| | 7500 | 9 | .6 | 1.1 | 13.9 |
| | 9000 | 20 | 1.3 | 2.4 | 16.3 |
| | 11250 | 24 | 1.6 | 2.9 | 19.2 |
| | 13750 | 15 | 1.0 | 1.8 | 21.0 |
| | 16250 | 26 | 1.7 | 3.1 | 24.1 |
| | 18750 | 23 | 1.5 | 2.8 | 26.9 |
| | 21250 | 41 | 2.7 | 4.9 | 31.8 |
| | 23750 | 43 | 2.9 | 5.2 | 37.0 |
| | 27500 | 52 | 3.5 | 6.3 | 43.3 |
| | 32500 | 68 | 4.5 | 8.2 | 51.4 |
| | 37500 | 58 | 3.9 | 7.0 | 58.4 |
| | 45000 | 82 | 5.5 | 9.9 | 68.3 |
| | 55000 | 72 | 4.8 | 8.7 | 77.0 |
| | 67500 | 75 | 5.0 | 9.0 | 86.0 |
| | 82500 | 46 | 3.1 | 5.5 | 91.6 |
| | 100000 | 35 | 2.3 | 4.2 | 95.8 |
| | 120000 | 17 | 1.1 | 2.0 | 97.8 |
| | 140000 | 12 | .8 | 1.4 | 99.3 |
| | 160000 | 6 | .4 | .7 | 100.0 |
| | Total | 830 | 55.3 | 100.0 | |
| Missing | System | 670 | 44.7 | | |
| Total | | 1500 | 100.0 | | |

# DEMONSTRATION 14.2: USING SPSS STATISTICS TO COMPUTE PEARSON'S *r*

Now make sure codes 98 and 99 are defined as "missing" for AGE.

With the housekeeping out of the way, you need only move through this menu path to launch SPSS Statistics on the job of computing *r*. Unlike the measures of association for nominal and ordinal variables we have discussed, Pearson's *r* is *not* available in the Crosstabs window. This stands to reason because you typically would not want to create a crosstabulation of I/R variables; the table would be too large to be of any real use.

Instead, Pearson's *r* is appropriately available in the Bivariate Correlations dialog box. To access this window, simply follow these steps:

**Analyze → Correlate → Bivariate**

This will bring you to the following window:

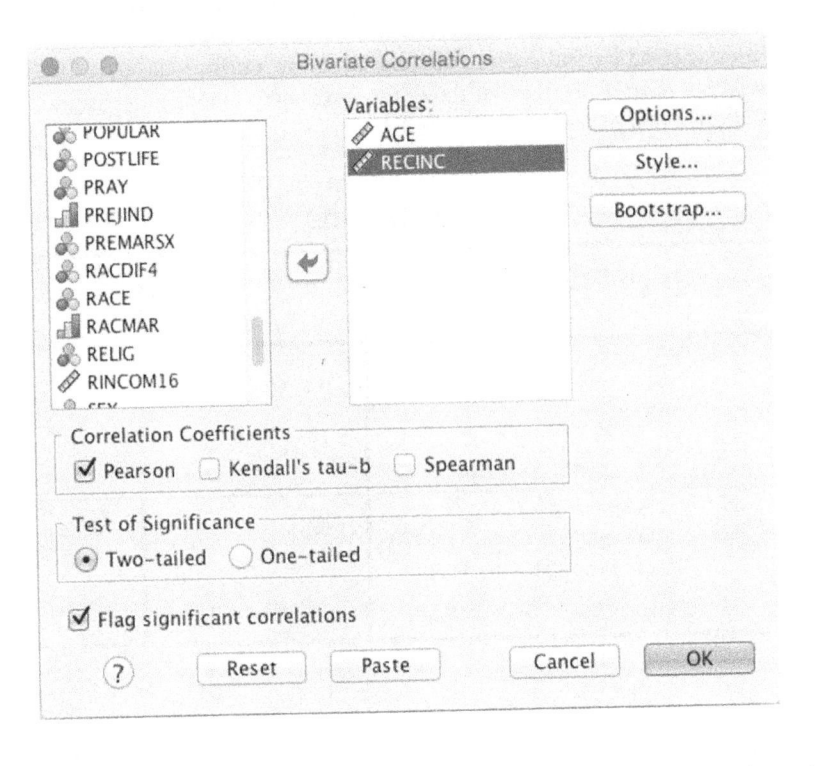

Transfer AGE and RECINC to the "Variables:" field. (Be sure to use AGE and not AGECAT because we want the unrecoded variable.) Below the "Variables:" list, you'll see that we can choose from among three forms of correlation coefficients. Our previous discussion has described Pearson's *r*, so click **Pearson** if it is not selected already.

Did you ever think about what we would do if we had an AGE for someone, but we did not know his or her RECINC? Because we would have only one score, we would have to throw that person out of our analysis. But suppose we had three variables, and we were missing a score on a case. Would we throw out just the pair that had a missing value, or would we throw out the whole case? SPSS Statistics lets us do it either way. Click on **Options**, and you will see that we can choose to exclude cases either pairwise or listwise. If we exclude pairwise, we discard a pair only when either score is missing, but with listwise exclusion, we discard the entire case if only one score is missing. We will use pairwise exclusion.

Given the time and money it takes to collect data, it's usually best to keep as much of it as we can. Unless there is a specific reason for using listwise exclusion, it is best to preserve as much of the data as possible by using pairwise exclusion.

Once you have selected **Exclude cases pairwise**, click on **Continue** and then **OK**. Your reward will be a *correlation matrix*, a table that shows the correlations among all variables (including, as we will see, the correlation of each item with itself).

## Correlations

| | | AGE Age of Respondent | RECINC Recoded R's Income |
|---|---|---|---|
| AGE Age of respondent | Pearson Correlation | 1 | .192** |
| | Sig. (2-tailed) | | .000 |
| | N | 1495 | 828 |
| RECINC Recoded R's Income | Pearson Correlation | .192** | 1 |
| | Sig. (2-tailed) | .000 | |
| | N | 828 | 830 |

**. Correlation is significant at the 0.01 level (2-tailed).

The Pearson's *r* product-moment correlation between AGE and RECINC is .192.[3] Notice that the correlation between AGE and itself is perfect (1), which makes sense if you think about it. You now know that the .192 is a measure of the extent to which deviations from the mean income can be accounted for by deviations from the mean of age. By squaring *r* (.192 × .192 = .037), we learn that about 3.7% of the variation in income can be accounted for by the variation in how old people are. Squaring *r* yields $r^2$, also known as the coefficient of determination. The *coefficient of determination* ($r^2$) is a PRE measure that can be interpreted in the same way as gamma or lambda. (We discussed these measures of association for nominal and ordinal variables in Chapter 13.)

We are going to ignore the references to "Significance" until later, in Chapter 15. For now, just know that this indicates the statistical significance of the association.

---

### SPSS Statistics Command 14.1: Producing a Correlation Matrix With Pearson's *r*

Click **Analyze** → **Correlate** → **Bivariate**

Highlight variable name → Click right-pointing arrow to transfer variable to "Variables:" field

Repeat previous step until all variables have been transferred

Click **Pearson** → **Options** → Exclude cases either pairwise OR listwise

Click **Continue** → **OK**

---

# DEMONSTRATION 14.3: REQUESTING SEVERAL CORRELATION COEFFICIENTS

What else do you suppose might account for differences in income? If you think about it, you might decide that education is a possibility. Presumably, the more education you get, the more money you'll make. Your understanding of *r* through SPSS Statistics will let you check it out.

---

3. See Table 14.2 for some general guidelines you can use to interpret the value of Pearson's *r*.

The Correlations command allows you to request several correlation coefficients at once. Go back to the Bivariate Correlations window, and add EDUC to the list of variables being analyzed.[4] Once again, exclude cases pairwise before executing the command.

Here's what you should get in your Output window. (Hint: If you didn't get this, go back and make sure you defined the value 99 as "missing" for the variable EDUC, and then, try it again.)

## Correlations

| | | AGE Age of Respondent | RECINC Recoded R's Income | EDUC Highest Year of School Completed |
|---|---|---|---|---|
| AGE Age of respondent | Pearson Correlation | 1 | .192** | −.002 |
| | Sig. (2-tailed) | | .000 | .944 |
| | N | 1495 | 828 | 1488 |
| RECINC Recoded R's Income | Pearson Correlation | .192** | 1 | .324** |
| | Sig. (2-tailed) | .000 | | .000 |
| | N | 828 | 830 | 830 |
| EDUC Highest year of school completed | Pearson Correlation | −.002 | .324** | 1 |
| | Sig. (2-tailed) | .944 | .000 | |
| | N | 1488 | 830 | 1493 |

**. Correlation is significant at the 0.01 level (2-tailed).

---

4. Make sure to define the values 97, 98, and 99 for EDUC as "missing" before continuing with this demonstration.

Take a moment to examine your new correlation matrix. It is slightly more complex than the previous example. The fact that each variable correlates perfectly with itself should offer assurance that we are doing something right.

The new matrix also tells us that there is a stronger correlation between EDUC and RECINC: .324. Squaring the $r$ ($.324^2 = .105$) yields the coefficient of determination ($r^2$) and tells us that 11% of the variance in income can be accounted for by how much education people have attained.

# WRITING BOX 14.1

Respondents' years of education are more strongly related to income than are their ages. While age is only moderately related to income ($r = .192$), highest year of school completed is more strongly related to income ($r = .324$). Interestingly, a weak inverse relation ($r = -.002$) exists between age and highest year of school, telling us that younger adults are more likely to obtain more years of schooling than are older people.

(Note that this is despite the fact that the youngest adults in the sample are temporally limited by their age to a ceiling of years of education that they could possibly have earned.) Perhaps this relation is an indicator of rising expectations for educational achievement in more recent years. At any rate, this, in part, accounts for the weaker relationship found between age and income than between education and income.

## A Note of Caution

We'll be using the Correlations command and related statistics as the book continues. In closing this discussion, we'd like you to recall that Pearson's $r$ is appropriate only for I/R (interval and ratio) variables. The same is true for $r^2$, the coefficient of determination, which is also for use only with I/R variables. Calculating these statistics would not be appropriate in the analysis of nominal variables such as RELIG and MARITAL, for example. But what do you suppose would happen if we asked SPSS Statistics to correlate $r$ for those two variables? Again, exclude cases pairwise before you execute the command.

### Correlations

|  |  | AGE Age of Respondent | MARITAL Marital Status |
|---|---|---|---|
| AGE Age of respondent | Pearson Correlation | 1 | -.389** |
|  | Sig. (2-tailed) |  | .000 |
|  | N | 1495 | 1494 |
| MARITAL Marital status | Pearson Correlation | -.389** | 1 |
|  | Sig. (2-tailed) | .000 |  |
|  | N | 1494 | 1499 |

**. Correlation is significant at the 0.01 level (2-tailed).

As you can see, SPSS Statistics does not recognize that we've asked it to do a stupid thing. It stupidly complies. It tells us that there is a somewhat significant (see next chapter) relationship between a person's marital status and the religion he or she belongs to, but the correlation calculated here has no real meaning.

SPSS Statistics has been able to do the requested calculation because it stores "Married" as 1 and "Widowed" as 2 and stores "Protestant" as 1, "Catholic" as 2, and so on, but these numbers have no numerical meaning in this instance. Catholics are not "twice" Protestants, and widowed people are not "twice" married people.

Here's a thought experiment we hope will guard against this mistake: (a) Write down the telephone numbers of your five best friends; (b) add them up and calculate the "mean" telephone number; (c) call that number and see if an "average" friend answers. Or go to a Chinese restaurant with a group of friends and have everyone in your party select one dish by its number on the menu. Add all of those numbers, and calculate the mean. When the waiter comes, get several orders of the "average" dish, and see if you have any friends left.

Pearson's *r* is designed for the analysis of relationships among continuous, I/R variables. We have just entrusted you with a powerful weapon for understanding. Use it wisely. Remember: Statistics don't mislead—those who calculate statistics stupidly mislead.

# REGRESSION ANALYSIS

The discussion of Pearson's *r* correlation coefficient opens the door for discussion of a related statistical technique that is also appropriate for I/R-level variables: ***regression***. When we looked at the scattergram of weight and height in the hypothetical example that introduced the discussion of correlation, you will recall that we tried to "see" a general pattern in the distribution of cases. Regression makes that attempt more concrete.

## Example 1: The Logic of Regression

To begin, let's imagine an extremely simple example that relates the number of hours spent studying for an examination and the grades that students got on the exam. Here are the data in a table:

| Student | Hours | Grade |
|---------|-------|-------|
| Fred | 0 | 0 |
| Mary | 2 | 25 |
| Sam | 4 | 50 |
| Edith | 6 | 75 |
| Earl | 8 | 100 |

First question: Can you guess which of us prepared this example? Second question: Can you see a pattern in the data presented? The pattern, pretty clearly, is this: The more you study, the better the grade you will get. Let's look at these data in the form of a graph. (This is something you can do by hand, using graph paper, but we used SPSS's scattergram.)

As you can see, the five people in this example fall along a straight line across the graph. This line is called the ***regression line***. As you may recall from plane geometry, it is possible to represent a straight line on a graph in the form of an equation. In this case, the equation would be as follows:

$$Grade = 12.5 \times Hours$$

To determine a person's grade using this equation, you need only multiply the number of hours he or she studied by 12.5. Multiply Earl's 8 hours of study by 12.5, and you get his grade of 100. Multiply Edith's 6 hours by 12.5, and you get 75. Multiply Fred's 0 hours by 12.5, and, well, you know Fred.

Whereas correlation considers the symmetrical association between two variables, regression adds the notion of causal direction. One of the variables is the dependent variable—grades, in this example—and the other is the independent variable or cause—hours of study. Thus, the equation we just created is designed to predict a person's grade based on how many hours he or she studied. If we were to tell you that someone not included in these data studied 5 hours for the exam, you could predict that that person got a 62.5 on the exam (5 × 12.5).

If all social science analyses produced results as clear as these, you probably wouldn't need SPSS Statistics or a book such as this one. In the example we just discussed, there is a perfect relationship between the two variables, without deviation or error. We call this a ***deterministic relationship***. In practice, however, the facts are usually more complex, and SPSS Statistics is up to the challenge.

Given a set of data with an imperfect relationship between two variables, SPSS Statistics can discover the line that comes closest to passing through all of the points on the graph. To understand the meaning of the notion of coming close, we need to recall the squared deviations found in our calculation of Pearson's *r*.

Suppose Sam had gotten 70 on the exam, for example. Here's what he would look like on the graph we just drew.

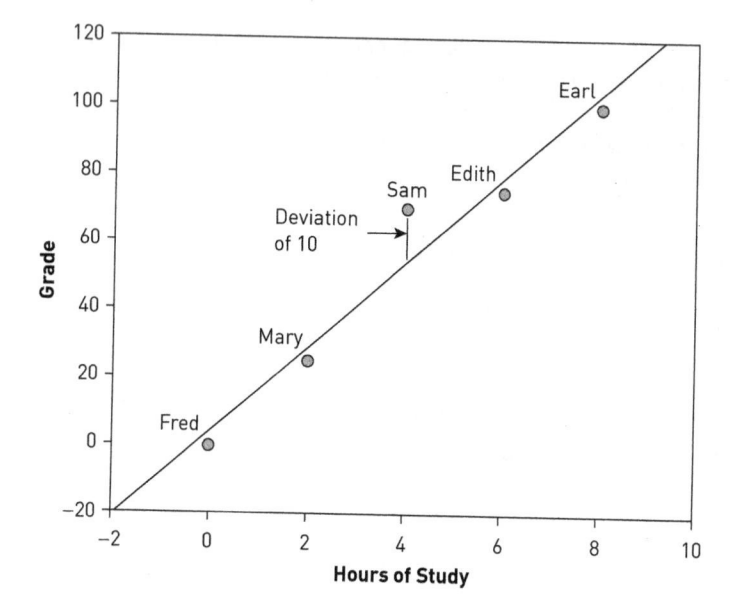

Notice that the improved Sam does not fall on the original regression line: His grade represents a deviation of 10 points. With a real set of data, most people fall to one side or the other of any line we might draw through the data. SPSS Statistics, however, is able to determine the line that would produce the smallest deviations overall—measured by squaring all of the individual deviations and adding them. This calculated regression line is sometimes called the ***least-squares regression line***.

To use this technique to real advantage, you need more instruction than is appropriate for this book. However, we want to introduce you to regression because it is a popular technique among many social scientists. Fortunately, requesting such an analysis from SPSS Statistics is fairly simple.

# DEMONSTRATION 14.4: REGRESSION

To experiment with the regression technique, let's make use of a new variable: SEI. This variable rates the socioeconomic prestige of respondents' occupations on a scale from a low of 0 to a high of 100 based on other studies that have asked a sample from the general population to rate different occupations.

Here's how we would ask SPSS Statistics to find the equation that best represents the influence of PAEDUC on EDUC. You should realize that there are a number of ways to request this information, but we'd suggest you do it as follows. (Just do it this way, and nobody gets hurt, okay?)

Under **Analyze**, select **Regression → Linear**. Then select **EDUC** as the "Dependent:" variable and **PAEDUC** as the "Independent(s):" variable.

Click Options, and select Exclude cases pairwise; then, hit Continue.

Click **OK**, and SPSS Statistics is off and running. Here's the output you should get in response to this instruction.

## Model Summary

| Model | R | R Square | Adjusted R Square | Std. Error of the Estimate |
|---|---|---|---|---|
| 1 | .417[a] | .174 | .173 | 2.580 |

a. Predictors: (Constant), PAEDUC Highest year school completed, father

## ANOVA[a]

| Model | | Sum of Squares | df | Mean Square | F | Sig. |
|---|---|---|---|---|---|---|
| 1 | Regression | 1552.574 | 1 | 1552.574 | 233.22 | .000[b] |
| | Residual | 7369.324 | 1107 | 6.657 | | |
| | Total | 8921.898 | 1108 | | | |

a. Dependent Variable: EDUC Highest year of school completed

b. Predictors: (Constant), PAEDUC Highest year school completed, father

## Coefficients[a]

| Model | | Unstandardized Coefficients | | Standardized Coefficients | t | Sig. |
|---|---|---|---|---|---|---|
| | | B | Std. Error | Beta | | |
| 1 | (Constant) | 10.326 | .242 | | 42.723 | .000 |
| | PAEDUC Highest year school completed, father | .295 | .019 | .417 | 15.272 | .000 |

a. Dependent Variable: EDUC Highest year of school completed

The key information we are looking for is contained in the final table, titled "Coefficients": the **intercept**, labeled "Constant" (10.326), and the **slope**, labeled "PAEDUC" (.295). These are the data we need to complete our regression equation. Use them to fill the equation as follows:

$$Y = a + bX$$

$$EDUC = 10.326 + (PAEDUC \times 0.295)$$

This means that we would predict the education level of a respondent whose father was a high school graduate (12 years of schooling) as follows:

$$EDUC = 10.326 + (12 \times 0.295) = 13.866 \text{ years of education}$$

On the other hand, we would predict the education level of a respondent whose father was a college graduate (16 years of schooling) as

$$\text{EDUC} = 10.326 + (16 \times 0.295) = 15.046 \text{ years of education}$$

Notice that along with the regression coefficient and constant, we are also provided other information, including both Pearson's $r$ (.417) and $r^2$ (.174), the coefficient of determination.

---

**SPSS Statistics Command 14.2: Regression**

Click **Analyze** → **Regression** → **Linear**

Highlight dependent variable and click right-pointing arrow to transfer it to "Dependent:" field

Highlight independent variable and click right-pointing arrow to transfer it to "Independent(s):" field

Click **OK**

---

# DEMONSTRATION 14.5: PRESENTING DATA GRAPHICALLY—PRODUCING A SCATTERPLOT WITH A REGRESSION LINE

Another way to explore the relationship between SEI and EDUC is to instruct SPSS to produce a scatterplot with a regression line. *Scatterplot* is a term SPSS Statistics uses to identify what we referred to earlier in our discussion of Pearson's $r$ as a scattergram. A scatterplot/scattergram is simply a graph with a horizontal ($x$) axis and a vertical ($y$) axis. As you saw earlier, each dot on the graph represents the point of intersection for each individual case. It is the "scatter" of dots taken as a whole that, along with the regression line, indicates the strength and direction of association between the variables.

Instructing SPSS Statistics to produce a scatterplot with a regression line allows us to see the distribution and array of cases while saving us the time-consuming task of creating the graph on our own (which, as you can imagine with 1,500 cases, would be quite daunting).

To produce a scatterplot, all you have to do is open the Scatterplot window by clicking **Graphs** → **Legacy Dialogs** and then choosing **Scatter/Dot** in the drop-down menu.

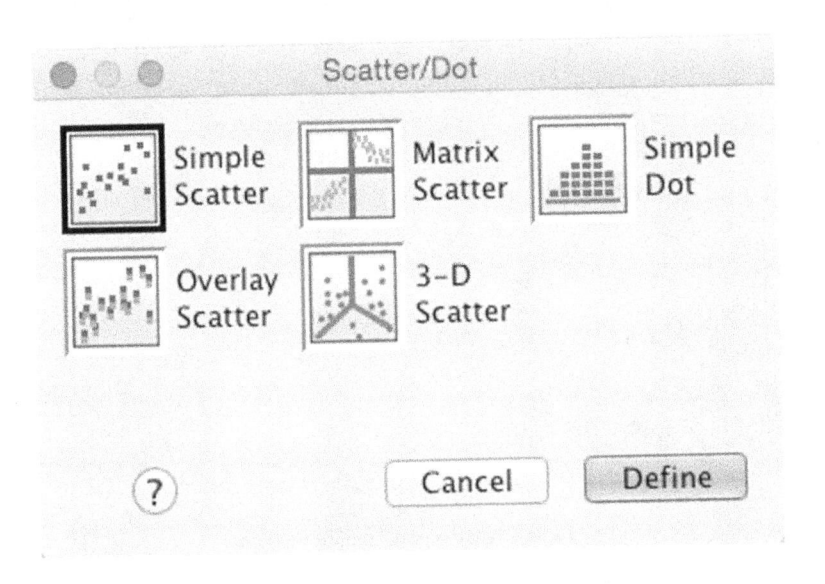

When you have opened the Scatter/Dot box, as shown above, select **Simple Scatter** if it is not already highlighted; then click **Define**. You should now be looking at the Simple Scatterplot dialog box, as shown below.

Following the example we used above, place **EDUC** (the dependent variable) along the *y*-axis. Then place **PAEDUC** (the independent variable) along the *x*-axis. When you are finished with this process, you can hit **OK**, and the following graph should appear on your screen.

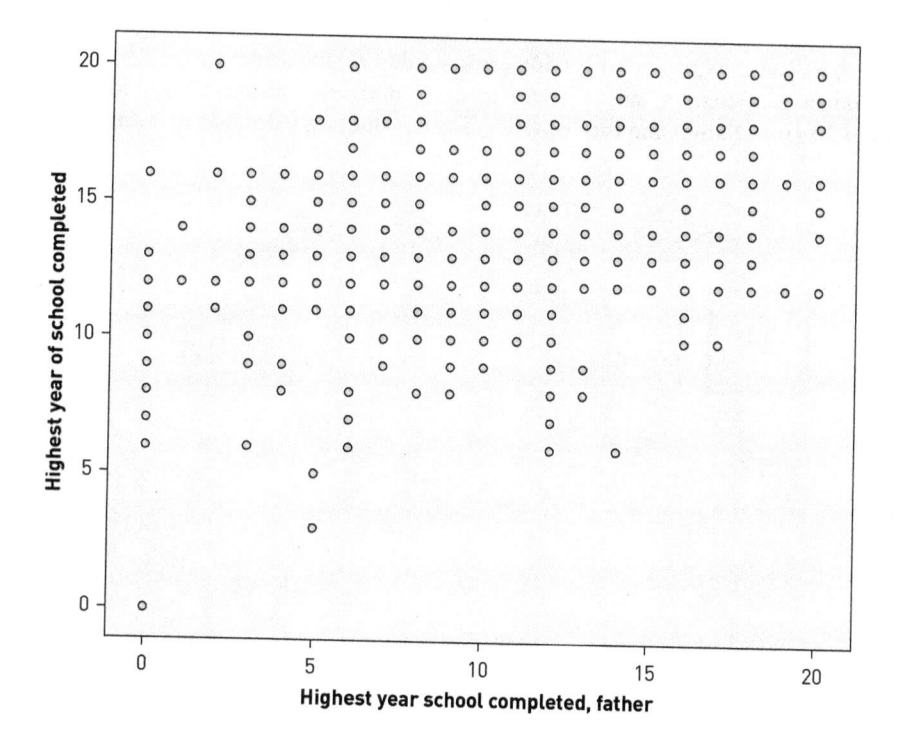

As requested, our independent variable, PAEDUC, is arrayed along the *x* (horizontal) axis, and our dependent variable, EDUC, is arrayed along the *y* (vertical) axis. You can also see the splatter of dots on the graph, each representing a particular case.

However, we are going to use the Chart Editor to add our regression line, which, as we saw earlier, is simply a single straight line that will run through our scatterplot and come as close as possible to touching all of the "dots," or data points. Double-click on the graph, and the SPSS Chart Editor will appear.

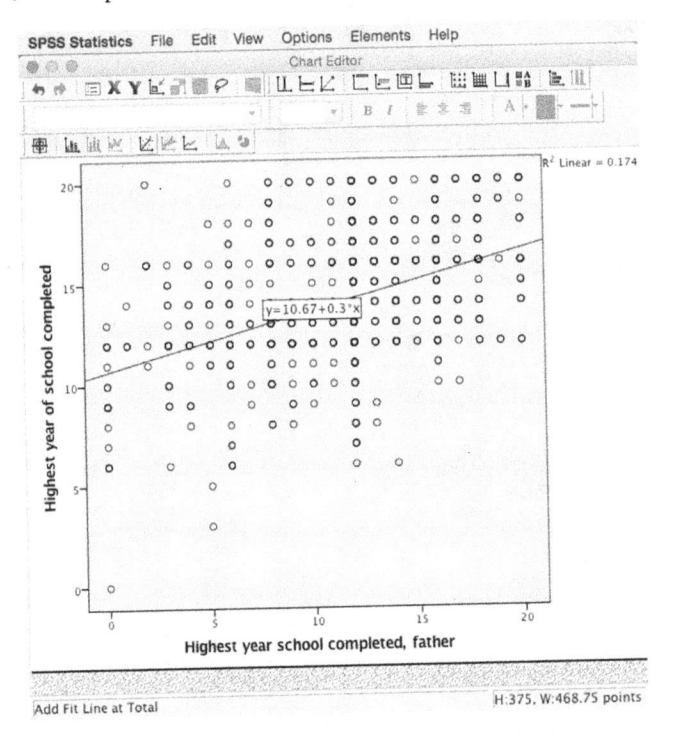

There is a button that allows you to quickly request the "fit line," which, in this case, refers to the line of best fit as measured by the sum of the least squares or ordinary least squares (OLS) regression line. As you can see below, it's the fifth button from the left on the lower toolbar.

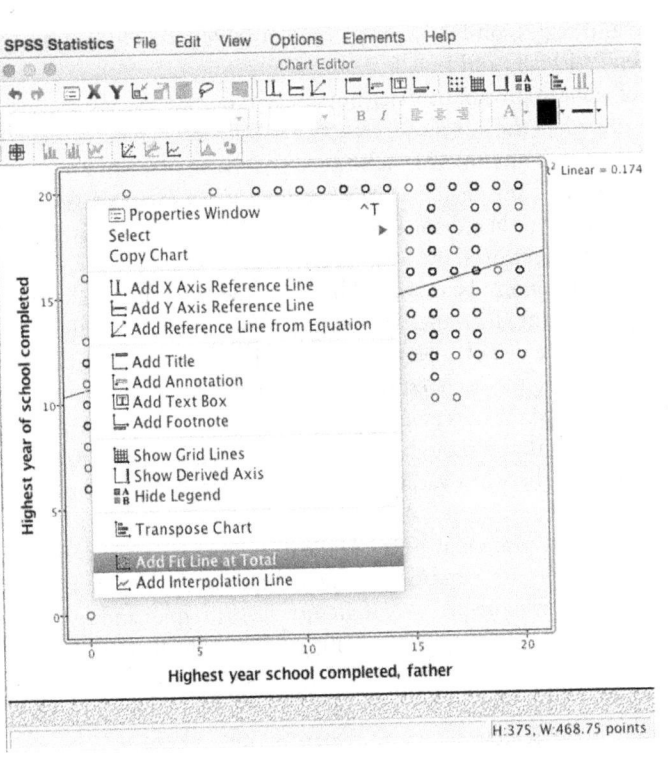

Here's another way to add the line representing the linear regression equation. With the Chart Editor active, right-click on the chart to show the Properties window.

Click on **Add Fit Line at Total** to insert the regression line. Then, close the Chart Editor. You'll find the result of that action below.

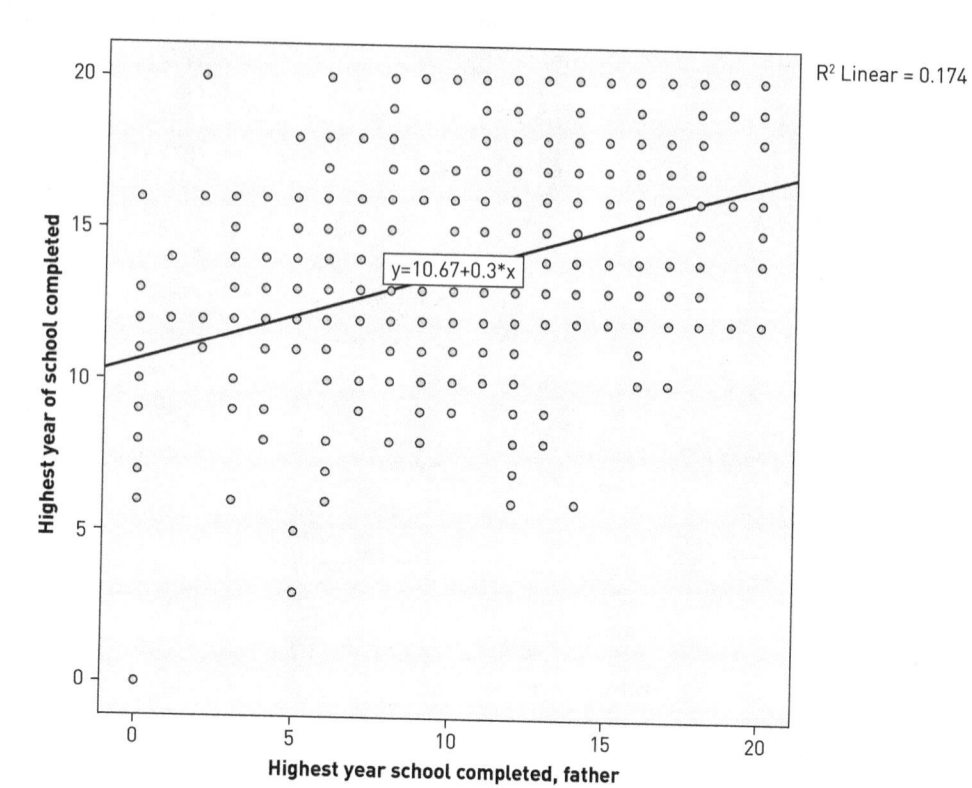

## An Indication of Direction and Strength of Association

The scatterplot and regression line serve as a visual indication of the direction and strength of association between PAEDUC and EDUC.

The direction of association can be determined based on the way the regression line sits on the scatterplot. Generally, when the line moves from the bottom left-hand side of the graph to the upper right-hand side of the graph (uphill), this indicates a positive association between the variables (they both either increase or decrease in the same direction), whereas a regression line that runs from the upper left to the lower right side of the scatterplot (downhill) indicates a negative association between the items (as one increases, the other decreases).

The strength of association can be estimated based on the extent to which the dots (cases) are scattered around the regression line. The closer the dots are to the regression line, the stronger the association between the variables. (In the case of a "perfect" or deterministic relationship, the dots will sit exactly on the regression line, indicating the strongest possible association between the variables.) Conversely, the farther spread out or scattered the dots are, the weaker the relationship between the items.

We want to emphasize that although this type of visual representation allows us to estimate the strength of association between variables, there is no agreement regarding what constitutes a "strong" versus a "moderate" or "weak" association.

Consequently, your best option may be to use the scatterplot with a regression line in conjunction with a measure such as Pearson's $r$ and/or $r^2$, which allows you to obtain a value summarizing the association between variables more precisely than just the scatterplot and regression line do. Keep in mind that because both options are appropriate for continuously distributed I/R variables, they can be used to examine the same types of items.

Now, try to see if you can describe the strength and direction of association between PAEDUC and EDUC as shown in the scatterplot with a regression line above.

What is the direction of association? Are the variables positively or negatively related (i.e., does the regression line run uphill or downhill)? What can you estimate in terms of the strength of association between PAEDUC and EDUC? Are the dots or cases clustered around the regression line, or are they spread out?

# WRITING BOX 14.2

The positive relationship between father's educational attainment and respondent's educational attainment can be seen by inspection of the scatterplot. While the many cases are widely dispersed, there is a discernible pattern concentrating on the lower left and upper right quadrants. Adding the regression line confirms that assessment.

---

### SPSS Statistics Command 14.3: Producing a Scatterplot With a Regression Line

Click **Graphs** → **Legacy Dialogs** → **Scatter/Dot** → **Simple Scatter** → **Define**

Highlight independent variable → Click right-pointing arrow to transfer to x-axis

Highlight dependent variable → Click right-pointing arrow to transfer to y-axis

Click **OK**

*To Add Regression Line*

Double-click on scatterplot to open SPSS Statistics Chart Editor → With Chart Editor active, right-click on chart to display Properties window

Click **Add Fit Line at Total** to insert regression line

Close Chart Editor

---

That's enough fun for now. We'll return to regression in the next chapter when we discuss multivariate analysis.

# MEASURES OF ASSOCIATION FOR INTERVAL AND RATIO VARIABLES

The measures of association we have focused on in this chapter are appropriate for variables measured at the interval and/or ratio level of measurement (I/R variables). Table 14.3 lists the measures we have reviewed, along with their appropriate level of measurement.

| TABLE 14.3 ■ Measures of Association Reviewed in This Chapter | |
|---|---|
| **Level of Measurement** | **Measure of Association (Range of Values) of Each Variable** |
| Interval/ratio | Pearson's $r$ [−1 to +1] |
| | $r^2$ [0 to 1] |
| | Linear regression |

Keep in mind, however, that there are situations where one might need to analyze variables that are not I/R along with those that are I/R. While one can certainly use statistical techniques that lie beyond the scope of this book (e.g., logistic regression for dichotomous dependent variables and I/R independent variables), there are some ways to incorporate different types of variables into linear regression analysis. We have to first make the variables "appropriate," as explained below.

## ANALYZING THE ASSOCIATION BETWEEN VARIABLES AT DIFFERENT LEVELS OF MEASUREMENT

In some cases, you may discover that you want to analyze the association between variables at different levels of measurement: for instance, nominal by ordinal, nominal by I/R, and so on. While there are specialized bivariate measures of association for use when two variables have different levels of measurement, the safest course of action for the novice is to use a measure of association that meets the assumptions for the variable with the lowest level of measurement.

This usually means that one variable will have to be recoded to reduce its level of measurement. For instance, when we examined the relationship between church attendance (ordinal) and age (I/R) in Chapter 13, we recoded people's ages into ordinal categories.

While it would not be appropriate to use Pearson's *r* to correlate our CHATT and AGE, it is perfectly legitimate to use gamma to correlate CHATT with AGECAT.

With linear regression, there is a technique that allows us to incorporate into the equation an independent variable that is not originally an I/R variable. This technique is known as "creating a set of *dummy* variables." There is a brief discussion of this technique in Chapter 7 of Wagner's *Using IBM SPSS Statistics for Research Methods and Social Science Statistics*.[5] Single dummy variables are addressed later on in *Adventures in Social Research* (the book you are reading right now!) in Chapter 17.

While it is beyond the scope of this chapter to review all of the statistical measures appropriate for every situation you might encounter, those of you who are interested in pursuing relationships between mixed variables may want to consult a basic statistics or research methods text for a discussion of appropriate measures.[6] Keep in mind that a variety of basic statistics texts are now easily accessible on the Internet. In addition, several websites help students identify appropriate statistical tests. Here is just one of the numerous sites available: HyperStat Online, http://davidmlane.com/hyperstat/index.html.

## CONCLUSION

In this chapter, we've seen a number of statistical techniques that can be used to summarize the degree of relationship or association between two variables. We've seen that the appropriate technique depends on the level of measurement represented by the variables involved. Lambda is appropriate for nominal, gamma for ordinal, and Pearson's *r* product-moment correlation and regression for I/R variables.

We realize that you may have had trouble knowing how to respond to the results of these calculations. How do you decide, for example, whether a Pearson's *r* of .25 is high or low? Should you get excited about it or yawn and continue looking? The following chapter on statistical significance offers one basis for making such decisions.

---

5. Wagner, W. E., III. (2016). *Using IBM SPSS Statistics for research methods and social science statistics* (6th ed.). Thousand Oaks, CA: Sage.

6. Among the many basic statistics texts you may want to consult are Freeman's *Elementary Applied Statistics* (1968), Siegel and Castellan's *Nonparametric Statistics for the Behavioral Sciences* (1989), and Frankfort-Nachmias and Leon-Guerrero's *Social Statistics for a Diverse Society* (2006). Alreck and Settle's *The Survey Research Handbook* (1985, pp. 287–362) contains a table titled "Statistical Measures of Association" (Table 10-5, p. 303), which, depending on the type of independent and dependent variables you are working with (i.e., categorical or continuous), specifies appropriate measures of association. The table is accompanied by a discussion of statistical analysis and interpretation.

# Main Points

- In this chapter, we looked at new ways to examine the relationships among interval/ratio (I/R) variables.

- Measures of association summarize the strength (and, in some cases, the direction) of association between two variables in contrast to the way percentage tables lay out the details.

- This chapter focuses on only some of the many measures available: Pearson's $r$, $r^2$ (the coefficient of determination), and regression.

- The coefficient of determination ($r^2$) is based on the logic of proportionate reduction of error (PRE).

- Pearson's $r$ is appropriate for two I/R items; its values range from –1 to +1.

- The coefficient of determination, $r^2$, is also appropriate for two I/R items; it is a PRE statistic whose values range from 0 to 1.

- The closer the Pearson's $r$ value is to positive or negative 1, the stronger the relationship between the items (with +1 or –1 indicating a perfect association). The closer the value is to 0, the weaker the relationship between the items (with 0 indicating no association between the items).

- There are no set rules for interpreting strength of association.

- Like Pearson's $r$, linear regression is also appropriate for I/R variables.

- Another way to explore the strength and direction of association between two I/R variables is to produce a scatterplot with a linear regression line.

- A variety of statistics are appropriate for examining the relationship between mixed types of variables.

# Key Terms

Coefficient of
    determination ($r^2$)  256
Correlation matrix  256
Deterministic relationship  260
Intercept  262

Least-squares regression
    line  260
Pearson's $r$  245
Regression  259
Regression line  259

Scattergram  246
Slope  262
$z$ scores  248

# SPSS Statistics Commands Introduced in This Chapter

14.1.  Producing a Correlation Matrix With Pearson's $r$

14.2.  Regression

14.3.  Producing a Scatterplot With a Regression Line

# Review Questions

1.  If two variables are strongly associated, does that necessarily mean they are causally related?

2.  What is PRE?

3.  List two measures of association for interval/ratio (I/R) variables.

4.  Measures of association give us an indication of the _____ of association and (if the variables are ordinal or higher)

the _____ of association between two variables.

5.  Pearson's $r$ and the coefficient of determination ($r^2$) are appropriate for variables at which level of measurement?

6.  List the range of values for each of the following measures:

- Pearson's $r$

- Coefficient of determination ($r^2$)

*(Continued)*

(Continued)

7. The closer Pearson's *r* is to _____ or _____ (value), the stronger the relationship between the variables.

8. The closer Pearson's *r* or *r²* is to _____ (value), the weaker the relationship between the variables.

9. A Pearson's *r* value of _____ or _____ indicates a perfect (or the strongest) relationship between the variables.

10. What does a positive association between two variables indicate? What does a negative association between two variables indicate?

11. Linear regression is appropriate for two variables at which level of measurement?

12. What type of graph did we review in this chapter that allows us to examine the strength and direction of association between two I/R variables?

# SPSS Statistics Lab Exercise 14.1

NAME: _____

CLASS: _____

INSTRUCTOR: _____

DATE: _____

*To complete these exercises, load your EXERPLUS.SAV data file.*

Produce a correlation matrix, exclude cases pairwise, and request Pearson's *r* for the variables MAEDUC (independent) and EDUC (dependent). Then, answer Questions 1 through 5.

1. What is the level of measurement for the variable MAEDUC?

   *Ratio*

2. What is the level of measurement for the variable EDUC?

   *Ratio*

3. Pearson's *r* for MAEDUC and EDUC is _____*.453*_____, while $r^2$ is ____*20.5%*____.

4. Would you characterize the relationship between these two variables as weak, moderate, or strong? Explain.  *writing box 14.1 moderate*

5. What proportion of the variation in EDUC can be explained by the variation in MAEDUC? (Hint: You've already calculated the PRE measure that will reveal this amount.) ____*20.5%*____

Produce a scatterplot with a regression line for the variables EDUC (independent) and TVHOURS (dependent). Then, answer Questions 6 through 11. Before proceeding with your analysis, be sure to define the values 97, 98, and 99 as "missing" for the variable EDUC. In addition, define the values –1, 98, and 99 as "missing" for the variable TVHOURS.

6. What is the level of measurement for the variable EDUC?

   *Ratio*

7. What is the level of measurement for the variable TVHOURS?

   *Scale (Ratio)*

8. What is the regression equation for EDUC and TVHOURS?

   $Y =$ _____ + _____ $\times X$    *5.54 - 0.18*

9. What is the direction of the relationship between the variables? ___*down hill*___ As years of education increases, does the number of hours of television watched increase or decrease?

   ___*decrease*___

10. The relationship of the "dots" or cases to the regression line suggests what about the strength of the relationship between these two variables?  *writing box 14.2*

*(Continued)*

(Continued)

11. Produce a correlation matrix with Pearson's *r*, excluding cases pairwise. Then, further describe the strength of the relationship between EDUC and TVHOURS by noting what the value of Pearson's *r* is and whether the relationship is weak, moderate, or strong.

12. Now, choose two variables from your data set that you think may be associated. After defining appropriate values for each variable as "missing," analyze the relationship between the variables by instructing SPSS to calculate the appropriate measure of association. If you want to recode either of your variables, feel free to do so. Remember, if you choose two variables at different levels of measurement, you can follow our suggestion toward the end of the chapter that you use a measurement that meets the assumptions for the variable with the lowest level of measurement. If you choose two interval/ratio variables, also produce a scatterplot with a regression line.

Once you have completed your analysis, print your output, and attach it to this sheet. Then, take a few moments to describe your findings in the space provided below. In particular, you may want to consider noting the following:

- What variables you chose and why
- The levels of measurement of each
- Whether you had to recode either item or designate any values as "missing"
- What measure of association you instructed SPSS to calculate
- The value of that measure
- What it indicates about the relationship between these variables (strength and direction)

If you are having any trouble producing an analysis of your findings in prose, you may want to reread the writing boxes throughout Chapters 13 and 14.

# TESTS OF SIGNIFICANCE

Thus far, in Chapters 10 through 14, we've looked at the relationships between pairs of variables. Throughout, you may have been frustrated over the ambiguity of what constitutes a "strong" or a "weak" relationship. As we noted in the last chapter, there is no absolute answer to this question. The strength and significance of a relationship between two variables depend on many things.

If you are trying to account for differences among people on some variable, such as prejudice, the explanatory power of one variable, such as education, needs to be contrasted with the explanatory power of other variables. Thus, you might be interested in knowing whether education, political affiliation, or region of upbringing has the greatest impact on a person's prejudice.

Sometimes, the importance of a relationship is based on practical policy implications. Thus, the impact of some variable in explaining (and potentially reducing) auto theft rates, for example, might be converted to cost to society in dollars. Other relationships might be expressed in terms of lives saved, students graduating from college, and so forth.

## STATISTICAL SIGNIFICANCE

In this chapter, we're going to introduce you to another standard for judging the relationships among variables—one commonly used by social scientists. Whereas in Chapters 13 and 14, we discussed measures of association that allow us to examine the strength (and in the case of ordinal and interval/ratio [I/R] variables, the direction) of association, in this chapter, we explore tests that will allow you to estimate *statistical significance*. Tests of statistical significance allow us to estimate the likelihood that a relationship between variables in a sample actually exists in the population as opposed to being an illusion due to chance or sampling error.

Whenever analyses are based on random samples selected from a population rather than on data collected from everyone in that population, there is always the possibility that what we learn from the samples may not truly reflect the whole population. Thus, we might discover in a sample that women are more religious than men, but that could be simply an artifact of our sample: We happened to pick too many religious women and/or too few religious men. Tests of significance allow us to estimate the likelihood that our finding, a relationship between gender and religiosity in this case, could have happened by chance. If the chances of our finding are very unlikely—say, only about 5 in 100—then we have the confidence needed to generalize our finding from the sample to the population from which it was drawn.

## SIGNIFICANCE TESTS: PART OF THE LARGER BODY OF INFERENTIAL STATISTICS

Significance tests are part of a larger body of statistics known as inferential statistics. *Inferential statistics* can probably best be understood in contrast to descriptive statistics, with which you are already familiar. Together, descriptive and inferential statistics constitute two of the main types of statistics that social researchers use. Up to this point (Chapters 5 through 14), our focus has been largely on descriptive statistics, which allows us to describe or summarize the main features of our data or the relationships between variables in our data set. In contrast, inferential statistics allows us to go a step further by making it possible to draw conclusions or make inferences that extend beyond the items in our particular data set to the larger population. In short, we can use inferential statistics to help us learn what our sample tells us about the population from which it was drawn. In the case of tests of significance, for instance, we can estimate whether an observed association between variables in our sample is generalizable to the larger population.

# STATISTICAL SIGNIFICANCE VERSUS MEASURES OF ASSOCIATION

Social scientists often test the statistical significance of relationships discovered among variables. Although these tests do not constitute a direct measure of the strength of a relationship, they tell us the likelihood that the observed relationship could have resulted from the vagaries of probability sampling, which, as first discussed in Chapter 3, we call *sampling error*. These tests relate to the strength of relationships in that the stronger an observed relationship is, the less likely it could be the result of sampling error. Correspondingly, it is more likely that the observed relationship represents something that exists in the population as a whole.

You will find that social scientists use measures of association and tests of significance in conjunction with each other because, together, they allow us to address three important questions about the relationships between variables:

1. *How strong is the relationship?* (Measures of association/descriptive statistics such as lambda [$\lambda$], gamma [$\gamma$], etc.; Chapter 13)

2. In the case of ordinal and I/R variables, *what is the direction of association?* (Measures of association/descriptive statistics such as gamma [$\gamma$], Pearson's $r$, the coefficient of determination [$r^2$], etc.; Chapters 13 and 14)

3. *Is the relationship statistically significant?* (Tests of significance/inferential statistics such as chi-square [$\chi^2$], $t$ test, etc.; Chapter 15)

In this chapter, we turn our attention to Question 3 and some of the measures that can be used to estimate statistical significance, primarily chi-square ($\chi^2$), $t$ tests, and ANOVA (analysis of variance).

# CHI-SQUARE ($\chi^2$)

To learn the logic of statistical significance, let's begin with **chi-square** ($\chi^2$), a measure based on the kinds of crosstabulations we've examined in previous chapters. Chi-square, one of the most widely used tests of significance, is most appropriate for nominal items, although it can be used with ordinal variables or a combination of nominal and ordinal variables. Chi-square estimates the probability that the association between variables is a result of random chance or sampling error by comparing the actual or observed distribution of responses with the distribution of responses we would expect if there were absolutely no association between two variables.

To help make this clearer, let's take some time now to look at the logic of statistical significance in general and chi-square in particular.

## The Logic of Statistical Significance: Chi-Square ($\chi^2$)

For a concrete example, let's return to one of the tables that examines the relationship between religion and abortion attitudes.

Let's reexamine the relationship between religious affiliation and unconditional support for abortion. Do a crosstabulation of ABANY (row variable) and RELIG (column variable), making sure to request column percentages.[1]

**Analyze → Descriptive Statistics → Crosstabs**

Click the **Cells** button at the top right.

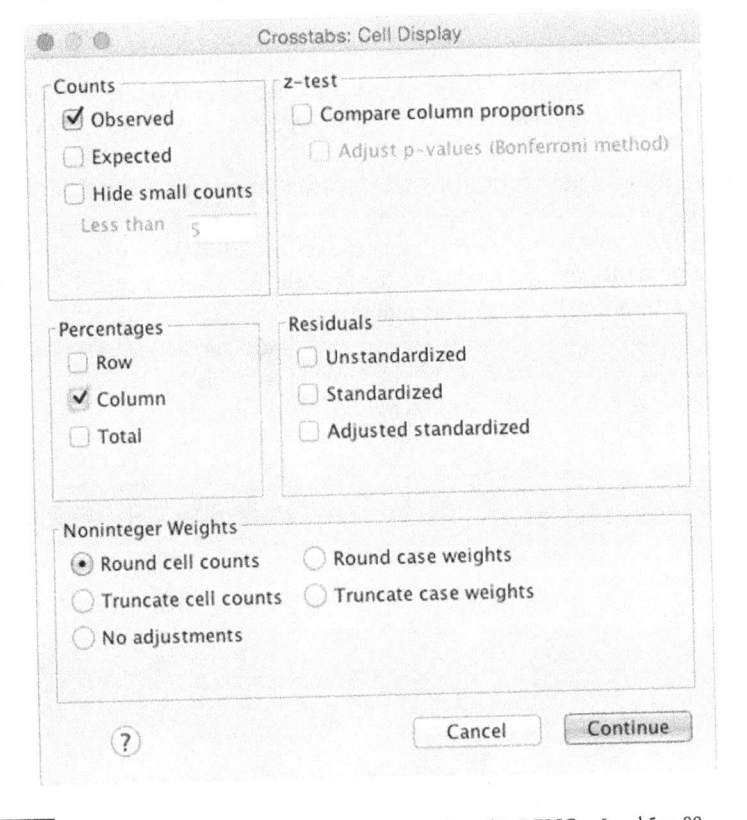

---

1. Define the following values as "missing" for each variable: ABANY—0, 8, and 9; RELIG—0 and 5 to 99.

Here is the output that will be produced:

## ABANY Abortion if Woman Wants for Any Reason * RELIG R's Religious Preference Crosstabulation

| | | | RELIG R's Religious Preference | | | | |
| --- | --- | --- | --- | --- | --- | --- | --- |
| | | | 1 PROTESTANT | 2 CATHOLIC | 3 JEWISH | 4 NONE | Total |
| ABANY Abortion if woman wants for any reason | 1 YES | Count | 166 | 89 | 13 | 134 | 402 |
| | | % within RELIG R's religious preference | 36.3% | 41.2% | 72.2% | 70% | 45.5% |
| | 2 NO | Count | 291 | 127 | 5 | 58 | 481 |
| | | % within RELIG R's religious preference | 63.7% | 58.8% | 27.8% | 30% | 54.5% |
| Total | | Count | 457 | 216 | 18 | 192 | 883 |
| | | % within RELIG R's religious preference | 100.0% | 100.0% | 100.0% | 100.0% | 100.0% |

The question this table (which contains the actual or observed frequencies) is designed to answer is whether a person's religious affiliation affects his or her attitude toward abortion. You'll recall that we concluded that it does: Catholics and Protestants are the most opposed to abortion, and Jews and those with no religion are the most supportive. The question we now confront is whether the observed differences point to some genuine pattern in the U.S. population at large or whether they result from a quirk of sampling.

To assess the **_observed relationship_** as shown in the table above, we are going to begin by asking what we would expect to find if there were no relationship between religious affiliation and abortion attitudes. An important part of the answer lies in the rightmost column in the preceding table. It indicates that 45% of the whole sample supported a woman's unconditional right to an abortion (Yes), and 55% did not (No). (Note that in this instance, we are rounding 45.5 to 45 and 55.4 to 55 so that the total IS equal to 100%.

If there were no relationship between religious affiliation and abortion attitudes, we should expect to find 45% of the Protestants approving (Yes), 45% of the Catholics approving, 45% of the Jews approving, and so forth. But we recall that the earlier results did not match this perfect model of no relationship, so the question is whether the disparity between the model and our observations would fall within the normal degree of sampling error.

To measure the extent of the disparity between the model and what's been observed, we need to calculate the number of cases we'd expect in each cell of the table if there were no relationship. The table below shows how to calculate the **_expected cell frequencies_**.

| ABANY | Protestant | Catholic | Jewish | None |
| --- | --- | --- | --- | --- |
| Yes | 457 | 216 | 18 | 192 |
| | × 0.45 | × 0.45 | × 0.45 | × 0.45 |
| No | 457 | 216 | 18 | 192 |
| | × 0.55 | × 0.55 | × 0.55 | × 0.55 |

Make sure you understand how we constructed this table before moving ahead.

Consequently, if there were no relationship between religious affiliation and abortion attitudes, we would expect 45% of the 443 Protestants (443 × 0.45 = 199) to approve and 55% of the 443 Protestants (443 × 0.55 = 244) to disapprove.

If you continue this series of calculations, you should arrive at the following set of expected cell frequencies.

| ABANY | Protestant | Catholic | Jewish | None |
|---|---|---|---|---|
| Yes | 206 | 97 | 8 | 86 |
| No | 251 | 119 | 10 | 106 |

The next step in calculating chi-square is to calculate the difference between expected and observed values in each cell of the table. For example, if religion had no effect on abortion, we would have expected to find 199 Protestants approving; in fact, we observed only 164. Thus, the discrepancy in that cell is –35. The discrepancy for Catholics approving is –14 (observed – expected = 86 – 100). The table below shows the discrepancies for each cell.

| ABANY | Protestant | Catholic | Jewish | None |
|---|---|---|---|---|
| Yes | –40 | –8 | 5 | 48 |
| No | 40 | 8 | –5 | –48 |

Finally, for each cell, we square the discrepancy and divide it by the expected cell frequency. For the Protestants approving of abortion, then, the squared discrepancy is 1,225 (–35 × –35). Dividing that by the expected frequency of 199 yields 6.16. When we repeat this for each cell, we get the following results.

| ABANY | Protestant | Catholic | Jewish | None |
|---|---|---|---|---|
| Approve | 7.77 | 0.66 | 3.13 | 26.79 |
| Disapprove | 6.37 | 0.54 | 2.50 | 21.74 |

Chi-square is the sum of all of these latest cell figures: 69.5. We have calculated a summary measure of the discrepancy between what we would have expected to observe if religion did not affect abortion and what we actually observed. Now, the only remaining question is whether that resulting number should be regarded as large or small. Statisticians often speak of the ***goodness of fit*** in this context: How well do the observed data fit a model of two variables being unrelated to each other? The answer to this latest question takes the form of a probability: the probability that a chi-square this large could occur as a result of sampling error. A probability of .05 in this context would mean that a certain chi-square would happen 5 times in 100 samples. A probability of .001 would mean that it would happen only 1 time in 1,000 samples.

To evaluate our chi-square of 69.5, we need to look it up in a table of chi-square values, which you'll find in the back of most statistics textbooks or by searching the Internet. Such tables have several columns marked by different probabilities (e.g., .30, .20, .10, .05, .01, .001, etc.). The tables also have several rows representing different ***degrees of freedom*** (**df**).

If you think about it, you'll probably see that the larger and more complex a crosstabulation is, the greater the likelihood that there will be discrepancies from the perfect model of expected frequencies. We take account of this with one final calculation.

Degrees of freedom are calculated from the data table as (rows – 1) × (columns – 1). In our table, there are four columns and two rows, giving us (3 × 1) degrees of freedom. Thus, we would look across the third row in the table of chi-square values, which would look, in part, like this:

| df | .05 | .01 | .001 |
|---|---|---|---|
| 3 | 7.815 | 11.341 | 16.268 |

These numbers tell us that a chi-square as high as 7.815 from a table such as ours would occur only 5 times in 100 samples if there were no relationship between religious affiliation and abortion attitudes among the whole U.S. population. A chi-square as high as 11.341 would happen only once in 100 samples, and a chi-square as high as 16.268 would happen only once in 1,000 samples.

Thus, we conclude that our chi-square of 69.5 could result from sampling error less than once in 1,000 samples. This is often abbreviated as $p < .001$: The probability is less than 1 in 1,000.

They have no magical meaning, but the .05 and .001 levels of significance are often used by social scientists as a convention for concluding that an observed relationship reflects a similar relationship in the population rather than arising from sampling error. Most social scientists agree that relationships with significance values of .05 or less are so unlikely to have occurred by chance that they can be called significant. The lower the probability, the more statistically significant the relationship is. Accordingly, if a relationship is significant at the .001 level, we can be more confident of our conclusion than if it were significant at the higher .05 level.

Going back to our example, then, because the value of chi-square is 69.5—which is greater than the value printed in the reference table for the appropriate *df* at the probability of .05 (and greater than the values at .01 and .001, for that matter)—the relationship between our variables (ABANY and RELIG) can be considered statistically significant.

There you have it: far more than you ever thought you'd want to know about chi-square. By sticking it out and coming to grasp the logical meaning of this statistical calculation, you've earned a reward.

# DEMONSTRATION 15.1: INSTRUCTING SPSS STATISTICS TO CALCULATE CHI-SQUARE

Rather than going through all of the preceding calculations, we could have simply modified our crosstabs request slightly (and after seeing how easy it is to instruct SPSS Statistics to run chi-square, you will probably wish we had just done this much earlier). Begin by clicking **Statistics** at the upper right of the Crosstabs window.

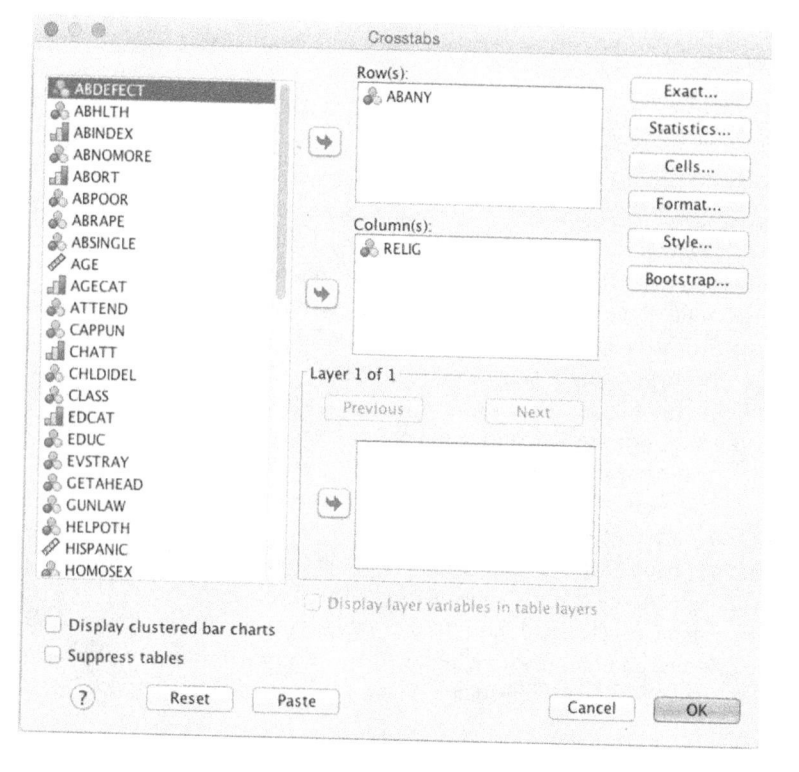

Note that in the lower left of the Crosstabs window, you can select "Suppress tables," as in the above image, so that the crosstabulation table is not presented (since we already produced that earlier in the chapter). In this case, we are interested only in learning what SPSS comes up with for the value of chi-square.

When the Statistics window pops up, select **Chi-Square** in the upper left corner. Then, click **Continue** and **OK** to run the crosstabs request.

## Chi-Square Tests

| | Value | df | Asymptotic Significance (2-sided) |
|---|---|---|---|
| Pearson Chi-Square | 67.991[a] | 3 | .000 |
| Likelihood Ratio | 68.878 | 3 | .000 |
| Linear-by-Linear Association | 63.722 | 1 | .000 |
| N of Valid Cases | 883 | | |

a. 0 cells (0.0%) have expected count less than 5. The minimum expected count is 8.19.

### Reading Your Output

We are interested primarily in the first row of figures in this report. Notice that the 67.991 value of chi-square is slightly different from our hand calculation. This is because of our rounding in our cell calculations, and it shouldn't worry you one bit.

Notice that we're told that there are 3 degrees of freedom, just as we determined earlier.

Finally, SPSS Statistics has calculated the probability of getting a chi-square this high with 3 degrees of freedom and has run out of space after three zeros to the right of the decimal point.

Thus, the probability is far less than .001, as we determined earlier by checking a table of chi-square values.

The reference to a minimum expected frequency of 8.19 is worth noting. Because the calculation of chi-square involves divisions by expected cell frequencies, it can be greatly inflated if any of them are very small. By convention, adjustments to chi-square should be made if more than 20% of the expected cell frequencies are below 5. You should check a comprehensive statistics text if you want to know more about this.

---

**SPSS Statistics Command 15.1:**
**Producing Crosstabs With Chi-Square**

Click **Analyze** → **Descriptive Statistics** → **Crosstabs**

Highlight dependent variable → Click arrow to transfer to "Row(s):" field

Highlight independent variable → Click arrow to transfer to "Column(s):" field

Click **Cells** → **Click Column in Percentages box**

Click **Continue** → **Statistics** → **Chi-Square**

Click **Continue** → **OK**

---

### Practice Running Chi-Square

While it is fresh in your mind, why don't you have SPSS Statistics calculate some more chi-squares for you? You may recall that gender had little impact on abortion attitudes as indicated by ABANY. Why don't you see what the chi-square is? Once you have done so, compare your interpretation of your findings with that in Writing Box 15.1.

## WRITING BOX 15.1

With a chi-square of just 0.251, we find, once again, that gender has little impact on attitudes toward abortion. With a probability of .617, the observed relationship is not statistically significant.

To experiment more with chi-square, you might rerun some of the other tables relating various demographic variables to abortion attitudes. Notice how chi-square offers a basis for comparing the relative importance of different variables that may determine attitudes on this controversial topic.

## SIGNIFICANCE AND ASSOCIATION

It bears repeating here that tests of significance are different from measures of association, although they are related to each other. The stronger an association is between two variables, the more likely that association will be judged statistically significant—that is, not a simple product of sampling error. Other factors also affect statistical significance, however. As we've already mentioned, the number of degrees of freedom in a table is relevant. So is the size of the sample: The larger the sample, the more likely an association will be judged significant.

Researchers often distinguish between statistical significance (examined in this section) and **substantive significance**. The latter refers to the importance of an association, and it can't be determined by empirical analysis alone. As we suggested at the outset of this chapter, substantive significance depends on practical and theoretical factors. All this notwithstanding, social researchers often find statistical significance to be a useful device in gauging associations.

That said, you may still be wondering how you should interpret findings that show, for instance, that there is a strong but not statistically significant relationship between two variables. Or conversely, what you should say if you find that there is a fairly weak but nonetheless statistically significant relationship between two items. Table 15.1 is intended to help as you approach the sometimes daunting task of interpreting tests of significance and association. While there are no "rules" of interpretation, this table can be looked at as a general guide as you begin to bring together the concepts of association and significance.

| TABLE 15.1 ■ A Guide to Interpreting Tests of Association and Significance | | | |
|---|---|---|---|
| **Strength of Association** | **Statistical Significance** | **Interpretation** | **Comment** |
| Strong | Significant | Knowledge of the independent variable improves prediction of the dependent variable, and the relationship can be generalized from the sample to the population. | Look what I've discovered. |
| Strong | Nonsignificant | Although knowledge of the independent variable improves prediction of the dependent variable in the sample, the relationship cannot be generalized to the population. | Close, but no banana. |
| Weak | Significant | Knowledge of the independent variable is of little help in predicting the dependent variable, but that knowledge may be generalized to the population. | That's no big thing. |
| Weak | Nonsignificant | Knowing about the independent variable provides little help in the prediction of the dependent variable in the sample, and this knowledge cannot be generalized to the population. | Back to the drawing board. |

For instance, if your findings show that the association between two variables is strong and statistically significant, you can look across the first row of the table to get some guidance in interpreting these results. Again, however, this table is meant to serve only as a general guide to interpreting tests of association and significance. Consequently, you may (and probably should) find that you do not agree with the interpretation offered in every case.

Whereas chi-square operates on the logic of the contingency table, to which you've grown accustomed by using the crosstabs procedure, we're going to turn next to a test of significance based on means.

## *t* Tests

Who do you suppose lives longer, men or women? Whichever group lives longer should, as a result, have a higher average age at any given time. Regardless of whether you know the answer to this question for the U.S. population as a whole, let's see if our General Social Survey (GSS) data can shed some light on the issue.

We could find the average ages of men and women in our GSS sample with the simple command path:

**Analyze → Compare Means → Means**

Because age is the characteristic on which we want to compare men and women, **AGE** is the dependent variable, and **SEX** is the independent variable.[2] Transfer those variables to the appropriate fields in the window. Then, click **OK**.

---

2. Define the values 98 and 99 as "missing" for the variable AGE.

## Report

AGE Age of Respondent

| SEX Respondent's Sex | Mean | N | Std. Deviation |
|---|---|---|---|
| 1 MALE | 48.14 | 679 | 17.541 |
| 2 FEMALE | 50.01 | 816 | 17.388 |
| Total | 49.16 | 1495 | 17.476 |

As you can see, our sample reflects the general population in that women have a mean age of 50.01, compared with the mean age of 48.14 for men. The task facing us now parallels the one pursued in the discussion of chi-square. Does the observed difference, quite small as it is, reflect a pattern that exists in the whole population, or is it simply a result of a sampling procedure? Would another sample indicate that men are older than women or that there is no difference at all?

In the previous section, we ran crosstabs with chi-square to estimate the statistical significance of the observed association between gender and religiosity, two nominal variables. We will not rely on crosstabs and chi-square here because our dependent variable, AGE, is an I/R item that contains many categories. Consequently, the crosstabs procedure would produce a table too large and unwieldy to analyze easily. Instead, we will rely on one of the most commonly used inferential statistics—*t* tests. While there are three types of *t* tests available on SPSS Statistics, we are going to utilize the ***independent-samples* t *test* (*two-sample* t *test*)**.

Given that we've moved very deliberately through the logic and calculations of chi-square, we are going to avoid such details in the present discussion. The **t *test***, which is best suited for dependent variables at the I/R level of measurement, examines the distribution of values on one variable (AGE) between different groups (men and women—two categories of one variable, SEX), and it calculates the probability that the observed difference in means results from sampling error alone. As with chi-square, it is customary to use the value of .05 or less to identify a statistically significant association.

# DEMONSTRATION 15.2: INSTRUCTING SPSS STATISTICS TO RUN INDEPENDENT-SAMPLES *T* TEST

To request a *t* test from SPSS Statistics in order to examine the relationship between AGE and SEX, enter the following command path:

**Analyze → Compare Means → Independent-Samples T Test**

You will notice that the drop-down menu lists the three types of *t* tests available on SPSS Statistics: "One-Sample T Test," "Independent-Samples T Test," and "Paired-Samples T Test." As noted previously, we are interested in the "Independent-Samples T Test" option. After following the command path just noted, you should see the following screen.

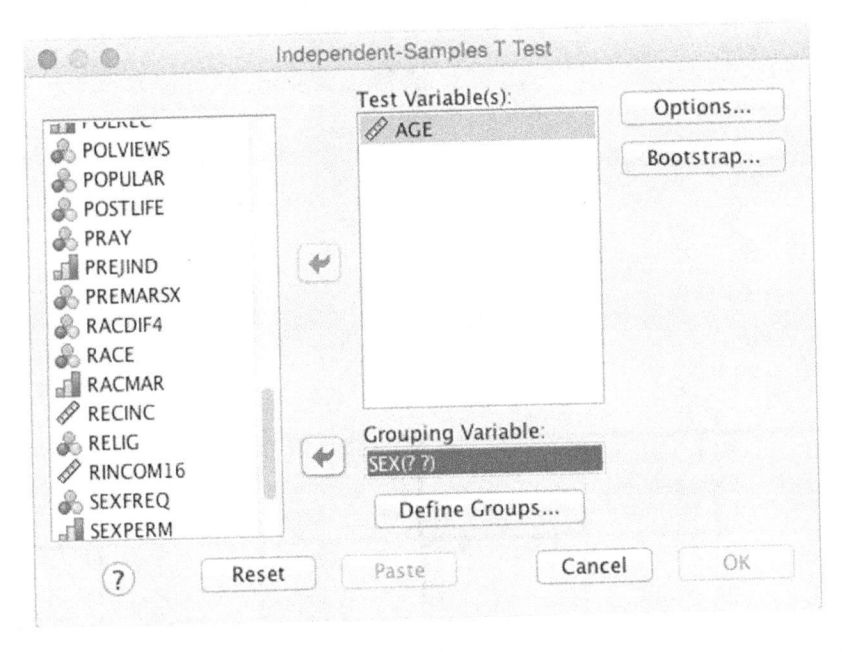

In this window, we want to enter **AGE** as the test variable and **SEX** as the grouping variable. This means that SPSS Statistics will group respondents by sex and then examine and compare the mean ages of the two gender groups.

Notice that when you enter the grouping variable, SPSS Statistics puts "SEX(??)" in that field. Although the comparison groups are obvious in the case of SEX, it might not be so obvious with other variables, so SPSS Statistics wants some guidance. Click **Define Groups**. . . .

Type **1** (male) into the "Group 1:" field and **2** (female) into the "Group 2:" field. Click **Continue**. Notice that the two question marks next to the grouping variable, SEX, are gone. In their place, you should see the new values to be used for comparison: 1 and 2.

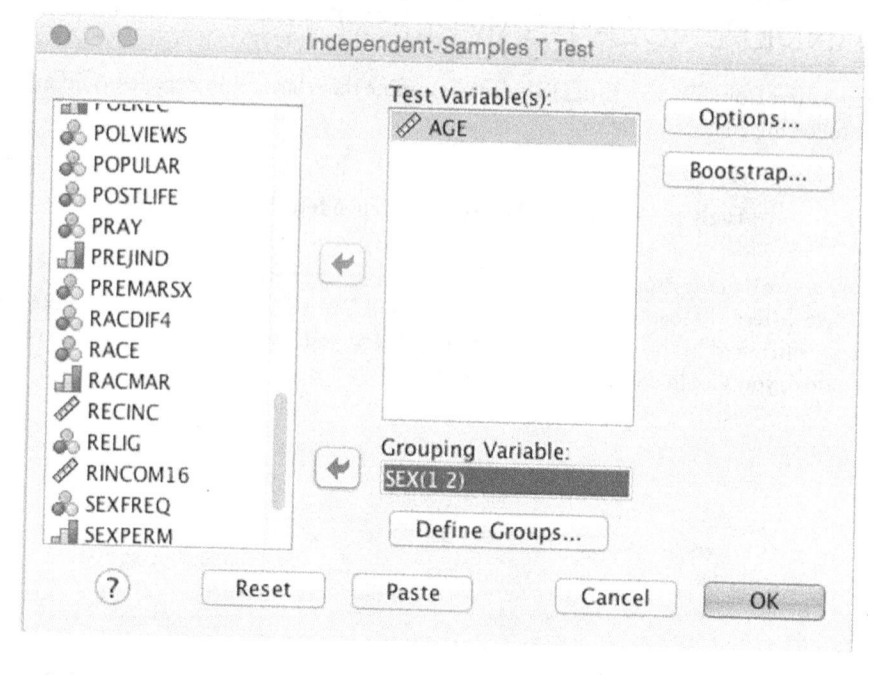

Now, click **OK**.

## Group Statistics

| | SEX Respondent's Sex | N | Mean | Std. Deviation | Std. Error Mean |
|---|---|---|---|---|---|
| AGE Age of respondent | 1 MALE | 679 | 48.14 | 17.541 | .673 |
| | 2 FEMALE | 816 | 50.01 | 17.388 | .609 |

## Independent Samples Test

| | | Levene's Test for Equality of Variances | | t-Test for Equality of Means | | | | | 95% Confidence Interval of the Difference | |
|---|---|---|---|---|---|---|---|---|---|---|
| | | F | Sig. | t | df | Sig. (2-tailed) | Mean Difference | Std. Error Difference | Lower | Upper |
| AGE Age of respondent | Equal variances assumed | .270 | .603 | −2.058 | 1493 | .040 | −1.866 | .907 | −3.645 | −.087 |
| | Equal variances not assumed | | | −2.056 | 1439.4 | .040 | −1.866 | .908 | −3.646 | −.086 |

## Reading Your Output

The program gives you much more information than you need for present purposes, so let's identify the key elements. Some of the information is a repeat of what we got earlier from the Means command: means, standard deviations, and standard errors for men and women. In the "Group Statistics" box under "Mean," for example, we see once again that the average age is 48.14 for men and 50.01 for women.

The results regarding significance that we are most interested in now are given in the box below, labeled "Independent Samples Test," under the heading "t-test for Equality of Means." If you look there under the subheading "Sig. (2-tailed)," in the top row labeled "Equal variances assumed," you will see the probability we are looking for: .040.

As you will anticipate, .040 in this context indicates a probability of just 40 in 1,000. The "2-tailed" notation requires just a little more explanation.

In our sample, the average age for women is 1.87 years higher than for men (50.01 − 48.14). SPSS Statistics has calculated that about 40 times in 1,000 samples, sampling error might produce a difference this great in either direction. That is, if the average age of men and the average age of women in the population were exactly the same and we were to select 1,000 samples like this one, we could expect 40 of those samples to show women at least 1.87 years older than men or women as much as 1.87 years younger than men.

When you don't have theoretical reasons to anticipate a particular relationship, it is appropriate for you to use the "2-tailed" probability in evaluating differences in means such as these. For our purposes, we'll stick with the 2-tailed test.

---

### SPSS Statistics Command 15.2: Running t Test (Independent-Samples t Test)

Click **Analyze → Compare Means → Independent-Samples T Test**

Highlight test variable in variable list → Click arrow pointing to the "Test Variable(s):" box

Highlight name of grouping variable in variable list → Click arrow pointing to the "Grouping Variable:" box

Click **Define Groups** → Define "Group 1" and "Group 2"

Click **Continue → OK**

---

# DEMONSTRATION 15.3: t TEST—EDUC BY SEX

Your GSS data set contains many variables that allow you to explore gender differences further. For example, say you were interested in the average difference in pay seen between men and women in the United States. It would be reasonable for better educated workers to earn more than poorly educated workers, so if the men in our sample have more education than the women, that might explain the difference in pay. Let's see.

Return to the T Test window and substitute EDUC for AGE as the test variable.[3] Leave "SEX(1 2)" as the grouping variable.

Run the new t test (see figures on the next page).

What conclusion do you draw from these results? Notice first that the men and women in our sample have identical mean numbers of years of education (men = 13.79; women = 13.85). The difference of 0.06 makes no practical distinction between men and women, and it is not statistically significant at a probability of .719.

---

3. Define the values 97, 98, and 99 as "missing" for the variable EDUC.

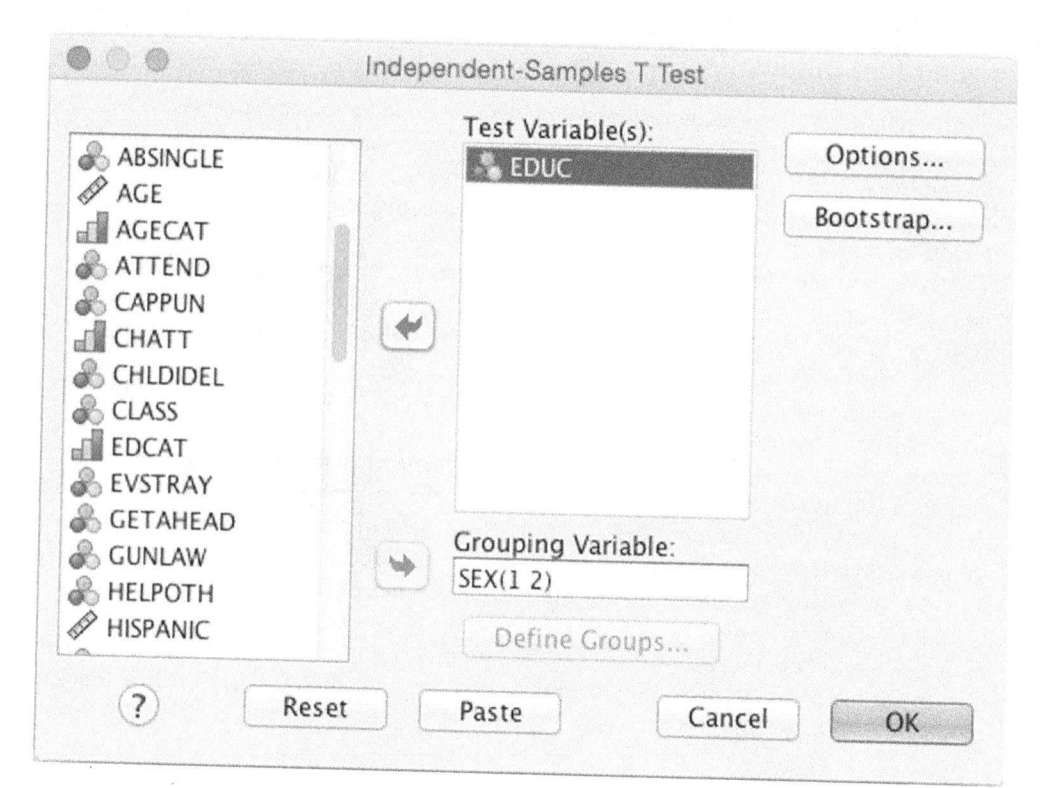

## Group Statistics

| | SEX Respondent's Sex | N | Mean | Std. Deviation | Std. Error Mean |
|---|---|---|---|---|---|
| EDUC Highest year of school completed | 1 MALE | 678 | 13.79 | 2.866 | .110 |
| | 2 FEMALE | 815 | 13.85 | 2.815 | .099 |

## Chi-Square Tests

| | Value | df | Asymptotic Significance (2-sided) |
|---|---|---|---|
| Pearson Chi-Square | 67.991a | 3 | .000 |
| Likelihood Ratio | 68.878 | 3 | .000 |
| Linear-by-Linear Association | 63.722 | 1 | .000 |
| N of Valid Cases | 883 | | |

a. 0 cells (0.0%) have expected count less than 5. The minimum expected count is 8.19.

With no distinguishable difference between men's and women's educational backgrounds in our sample, it is unlikely that education can be claimed to be a "legitimate reason" for women earning less than men. That's not to say that there aren't other legitimate reasons that may account for the difference in pay. For instance, it is often argued that women tend to concentrate in less prestigious jobs than do men: nurses rather than doctors, secretaries rather than executives, teachers rather than principals.

Leaving aside the reasons for such occupational differences, differences in jobs held might account for the differences in pay. Your GSS2016.SAV GSS data contain information about the respondents' occupational categories. You can determine whether the women in this sample have lower-status jobs, on average, than do the men.

# ANALYSIS OF VARIANCE

The *t* test is limited to the comparison of two groups at a time (e.g., male and female). If we wanted to compare the levels of education of different religious groups, we'd have to compare Protestants and Catholics, Protestants and Jews, Catholics and Jews, and so forth. And if some of the comparisons found significant differences and other comparisons did not, we'd be hard-pressed to reach an overall conclusion about the nature of the relationship between the two variables.

The *analysis of variance* (*ANOVA*) is a technique that resolves this shortcoming of the *t* test. It examines the means of subgroups in the sample and analyzes the variances as well. That is, it examines more than whether the actual values are clustered around the mean or spread out from it.

If we were to ask ANOVA to examine the relationship between RELIG and EDUC, it would determine the mean years of education for each of the different religious groups, noting how they differed from one another. Those "between-group" differences would be compared with the "within-group" differences (variance): how much Protestants differed among themselves, for example. ANOVA then reconciles both sets of comparisons to calculate the likelihood that the observed differences are merely the result of sampling error.

# DEMONSTRATION 15.4: INSTRUCTING SPSS STATISTICS TO RUN ANOVA

To get a clearer picture of ANOVA, ask SPSS Statistics to perform the analysis we've been discussing. You can probably figure out how to do that, but here's a hint.

**Analyze → General Linear Model → Univariate[4]**

Put **EDUC** into the "Dependent Variable:" field and **RELIG** into the "Fixed Factor(s):" field. Next, open the Univariate: Options dialog box by clicking on the **Options** button on the right (see figures on the next page).

To enable viewing the years of education for each of the religious groups, put a check mark by "Descriptive statistics." To request an equality of variance test, put a check mark next to "Homogeneity tests" by clicking the empty box next to it. Then, click **Continue** and **OK**.

## Reading Your Output

Page 288 shows the SPSS Statistics report on the analysis. Again, we've gotten more information than we need for our present purposes.

The first table of interest is labeled "Descriptive Statistics." It displays the means, standard deviations, and numbers of respondents in each religious category. Note that the Jewish respondents (mean = 16.00) have over 1 year more of education than do any of the other categories. The means for all other groups are close to each other, with those in the "None" (14.19) category being highest, Protestants next at 13.63, and Catholics having the lowest mean at 13.54.

---

4. If you have used earlier versions of SPSS Statistics, you may notice a difference here. The simple factorial ANOVA procedure has been replaced with the GLM univariate procedure (General Factorial). This allows the generation of ANOVA tables but does not require a defined range of factor variables.

## Descriptive Statistics

**Dependent Variable: EDUC Highest Year of School Completed**

| RELIG R's Religious Preference | Mean | Std. Deviation | N |
|---|---|---|---|
| 1 PROTESTANT | 13.63 | 2.696 | 729 |
| 2 CATHOLIC | 13.54 | 2.986 | 348 |
| 3 JEWISH | 16.00 | 2.614 | 25 |
| 4 NONE | 14.19 | 2.821 | 296 |
| Total | 13.77 | 2.820 | 1398 |

## Levene's Test of Equality of Error Variances[a]

**Dependent Variable: EDUC Highest Year of School Completed**

| F | df1 | df2 | Sig. |
|---|---|---|---|
| 1.417 | 3 | 1394 | .236 |

Tests the null hypothesis that the error variance of the dependent variable is equal across groups.

a. Design: Intercept + RELIG

## Tests of Between-Subjects Effects

**Dependent Variable: EDUC Highest Year of School Completed**

| Source | Type III Sum of Squares | df | Mean Square | F | Sig. |
|---|---|---|---|---|---|
| Corrected Model | 209.251[a] | 3 | 69.750 | 8.922 | .000 |
| Intercept | 69080.926 | 1 | 69080.926 | 8836.651 | .000 |
| RELIG | 209.251 | 3 | 69.750 | 8.922 | .000 |
| Error | 10897.659 | 1394 | 7.818 | | |
| Total | 276118.000 | 1398 | | | |
| Corrected Total | 11106.910 | 1397 | | | |

a. R Squared = .019 (Adjusted R Squared = .017)

The second table, "Levene's Test of Equality of Error Variances," shows whether or not the variances between the groups are the same. In our table, we are checking to see whether the variability in education is the same for each of the categories of religion. If they differed significantly in variability, then our test of differences in means could be distorted by differences in variability among the groups rather than differences between the means. The Levene statistic tests for equal amounts of variation within the groups.

If the amounts of variation are significantly different, ANOVA should not be used. We know the significance level of the Levene test by looking at the probability labeled "Sig." in the table. If the significance level is .05 or less, the variances are considered significantly different, and the ANOVA test should not be used. If the significance level is greater than .05, the variances are considered equal, and ANOVA can be used. In our example, the significance level is .236.

Once the variances are determined to be equal, we can proceed to the table titled "Tests of Between-Subjects Effects" and simply look at the row titled "Corrected Model." This refers to the amount of variance in EDUC that can be explained by variations in RELIG. Because our present purpose is to learn about tests of statistical significance, let's move across the row to the statistical significance of the explained variance. You can see that the significance level for the corrected model F statistic (8.922) is .000.[5] This means that if religion and education were unrelated to each other in the population, we might expect samples that would generate this amount of explained variance less than once in 1,000 samples.

Perhaps you will find it useful to think of ANOVA as something like a statistical broom. We began by noting a lot of variance in educational levels of our respondents; imagine people's educations spread all over the place. In an attempt to find explanatory patterns in that variance, we use ANOVA to sweep the respondents into subgroups based on religious affiliation. (Stay with us on this.) The questions are (a) whether variations in education are substantially less within each of the piles than we originally observed in the whole sample and (b) whether the mean years of education in each of the subgroups are quite different from one another.

So imagine a set of tidy piles that are quite distant from one another. ANOVA provides a statistical test of this imagery.

---

### SPSS Statistics Command 15.3: ANOVA (GLM Univariate)

Click **Analyze → General Linear Model → Univariate**

Highlight dependent variable → Click arrow pointing to "Dependent Variable:" field

Highlight factor variable → Click arrow pointing to "Fixed Factor(s):" field

Click **Options** → Check box next to "Homogeneity tests"

Click **Continue → OK**

---

It is also possible for ANOVA to consider two or more independent variables, but that goes beyond the scope of this book. We have introduced you to ANOVA because we feel it is useful, and we wanted to open up the possibility of your using this popular technique; however, you will need more specialized training in the performance of analysis of variance to use it effectively.

## WRITING BOX 15.2

Protestants and Catholics are relatively similar in years of education—13.6 and 13.5 years, respectively— while those who do not have a religious affiliation have a higher average education level at 14.2 years, and Jews average 16 years, significantly more than the other groups.

## A STATISTICAL TOOLBOX: A SUMMARY

As we near the end of our discussion of bivariate analysis, we think it may be useful as a review, and a summary of sorts, to provide you with a table listing descriptive and inferential statistics by their appropriate levels of measurement. You will note that those statistics we reviewed in depth are listed in boldface. In addition, we included a few references to some basic statistics we did not cover but you may find useful as you pursue your own research.

Please keep in mind that Table 15.2 is not exhaustive. It references only a few of the many statistics that social researchers find useful when working with items at various levels of measurement.

---

5. Make sure the following values for each variable are defined as "missing": AGE—0, 98, 99; EDUC—97, 98, 99.

**TABLE 15.2 ■ A Statistical Toolbox**

| Statistics for Measuring | Level of Measure | | |
|---|---|---|---|
| | Nominal | Ordinal | I/R |
| **Descriptive statistics** | | | |
| *Central tendency* | **Mode** | **Median** | **Mean** |
| *Dispersion* | | **Range** | **Variance** |
| | | **Interquartile range** | **Standard deviation** |
| *Association (PRE and non-PRE)* | **Lambda (λ)** | **Gamma (γ)** | $r^2$ |
| | Cramer's *V* | Somers's *d* | **Pearson's *r*** |
| | Phi | Kendall's tau-*b* | beta |
| | Contingency | | |
| | Coefficient | | |
| **Inferential statistics** | | | |
| Tests of significance | **Chi-Square (χ²)** | **Chi-Square (χ²)** | **Independent-samples *t* test** |
| | | | **ANOVA** |

# CONCLUSION

This chapter has taken on the difficult question of whether the observed relationship between two variables is important or not. It is natural that you would want to know whether and when you have discovered something worth writing home about.

No one wants to shout, "Look what I've discovered!" and have others say, "That's no big thing." Ultimately, there is no simple test of the substantive significance of a relationship between variables. If we found that women earn less than men, who could say if that difference amounts to a lot less or just a little bit less? In a more precise study, we could calculate exactly how much less in dollars, but we would still not be in a position to say absolutely whether that amount was a lot or a little. If women made a dollar a year less than men on the average, we'd all probably agree that this was not an important difference. If men earned 100 times as much as women, on the other hand, we'd probably all agree that this was a big difference. However, few of the differences we discover in social science research are that dramatic.

In this chapter, we've examined a very specific approach social scientists often take to address the issue of significance. As distinct from notions of *substantive* significance, we have examined *statistical* significance. In each of the measures we've examined—chi-square (χ²), *t* test, and analysis of variance—we've asked how likely it would be that sampling error could produce the observed relationship if there were actually no relationship in the population from which the sample was drawn.

This assumption of "no relationship" is sometimes referred to as the ***null hypothesis***. The tests of significance we've examined all deal with the probability that the null hypothesis is correct. If the probability is relatively high, then we conclude that there is no relationship between the two variables under study in the whole population. If the probability is small that the null hypothesis could be true, then we conclude that the observed relationship reflects a genuine pattern in the population.

## Main Points

- In this chapter, we introduced tests of statistical significance.

- As opposed to measures of association, which focus on the strength and direction of the relationship, tests of significance allow us to estimate whether the relationship can be considered statistically significant.

- *Statistical significance* generally refers to the likelihood that an observed relationship between variables in a sample could have occurred as a result of chance or sampling error.

- Tests of significance also allow you to determine whether or not an observed association between items in a sample is likely to exist in the population.

- In this chapter, we moved from focusing primarily on descriptive statistics to inferential statistics.

- Inferential statistics includes the three tests of significance we reviewed here: chi-square, *t* tests, and ANOVA.

- Chi-square is most appropriate for nominal variables, although it can be used with ordinal variables.

- Traditionally, a chi-square with a probability of .05 or less is considered significant.

- The *t* test is most appropriate if the dependent variable is at the interval/ratio level of measurement.

- ANOVA addresses the limitations of the *t* test in dealing with more than two categories of an independent variable.

- There is an important difference between substantive and statistical significance. For example, a difference may be statistically significant but not matter for real-world purposes.

## Key Terms

Analysis of variance (ANOVA)  287
Chi-square (χ²)  274
Degrees of freedom (*df*)  277
Expected cell frequencies  276
Goodness of fit  277

Independent-samples *t* test
  (two-sample *t* test)  282
Inferential statistics  273
Null hypothesis  291

Observed relationship  276
Statistical significance  273
Substantive significance  280
*t* test  282

## SPSS Statistics Commands Introduced in This Chapter

15.1.  Producing Crosstabs With Chi-Square

15.2.  Running *t* Test (Independent-Samples *t* Test)

15.3.  ANOVA (GLM Univariate)

## Review Questions

1.  What does the term *statistical significance* mean?

2.  If you are interested in estimating the strength of association between variables, would you rely on tests of significance or measures of association?

3.  If you are interested in determining whether or not an observed relationship between variables in your

    sample is likely to exist in the population, would you rely on tests of significance or measures of association?

4.  What are inferential statistics?

5.  How do inferential statistics differ from descriptive statistics?

6. Chi-square $(\chi^2)$ is considered appropriate for variables at what level of measurement?

7. Chi-square is based on a comparison of _____ frequencies and _____ frequencies.

8. If a chi-square has a probability level greater than .05, is it generally considered significant by traditional social science standards?

9. Would a chi-square with a probability of .01 be considered significant by traditional social science standards?

10. Would we have more confidence if an association were significant at the .05 or the .001 level?

11. The $t$ test is considered appropriate if your dependent variable is at what level of measurement?

12. Does the $t$ test allow us to determine whether the means, the variances, or both the means and variances of two groups are statistically different from each other?

13. How does ANOVA resolve the shortcomings of the $t$ test? Explain.

14. Does ANOVA examine the means, variances, or both the means and variances of subgroups in a sample?

15. In this chapter, we have focused primarily on statistical significance. How does this differ from substantive significance?

# SPSS Statistics Lab Exercise 15.1

NAME: _____

CLASS: _____

INSTRUCTOR: _____

DATE: _____

*To complete the following exercises, you need to load the EXERPLUS.SAV data file.*

1. Define the values 0, 8, and 9 as "missing" for AFFRMACT. Then, recode AFFRMACT as follows to create the new variable AFFREC. When you have done that, be sure to set the decimal places for AFFREC to 0 and add value labels.

| Old Values | | New Values | Labels |
|---|---|---|---|
| 1 to 2 | → | 1 | Support |
| 3 to 4 | → | 2 | Oppose |
| System- or user-missing | → | System-missing | |

Run crosstabs listing RACE and SEX as the independent variables and AFFREC as the dependent variable. Request column percentages and chi-square. Then, answer Questions 2 through 8.

2. Record the percentage of respondents who said they "Support" preferences (AFFREC) for each independent variable (RACE and SEX).

| | White | Black | Other | Chi-Square Asymp. Sig. |
|---|---|---|---|---|
| *Percentage* | | | | |
| *Support* | | | | |
| | Male | Female | | Chi-Square Asymp. Sig. |
| *Percentage* | | | | |
| *Support* | | | | |

3. (RACE) Do the percentages change or move between categories of the variable, signifying a relationship between RACE and AFFREC? Explain how you know.

4. (RACE) What is the significance of chi-square? Is it less than, equal to, or more than .05?

5. (RACE) Is the relationship between RACE and AFFREC statistically significant?

6. (SEX) Do the percentages change or move between categories of the variable, signifying a relationship between SEX and AFFREC? Explain how you know.

7. (SEX) What is the significance of chi-square? Is it less than, equal to, or more than .05?

*(Continued)*

(Continued)

8. (SEX) Is the relationship between SEX and AFFREC statistically significant?

9. Choose two variables from the data set (nominal and/or ordinal) that you think may be related. List the variables, and explain briefly how you think they are related.

10. Explore the relationship between the variables using crosstabs and chi-square. Print your output and describe your findings in a few sentences, focusing in particular on whether the relationship between the variables you chose is statistically significant.

Run a *t* test specifying AGE, PAEDUC, and EDUC as the test variables and RACE as the grouping variable. Keep in mind that you will have to ask SPSS Statistics to limit the comparison to Whites and Blacks, omitting the "Other" category. Once you have run the procedure, complete Questions 11 and 12.

11. Fill in the blanks with the appropriate information.

| | | RACE | |
| --- | --- | --- | --- |
| | | White | Black |
| AGE | Mean | 49.66, .025 | 46.74, .025 |
| | Sig. (2-tailed) | | |
| PAEDUC | Mean | 11.95, .012 | 10.69, .012 |
| | Sig. (2-tailed) | | |
| EDUC | Mean | 13.70, .016 | 13.19, .016 |
| | Sig. (2-tailed) | | |

| | What Is the Mean Difference? | Is the Mean Difference Significant? |
| --- | --- | --- |
| AGE | 2.914 | yes |
| PAEDUC | 1.262 | yes |
| EDUC | .513 | yes |

12. On the basis of these results, what conclusions, if any, can you draw about racial inequality in the United States? How much inequality is there? Is there inequality in education, life expectancy, or both? For example, do your data indicate that Whites have a higher average age, suggesting that they live longer? What, if anything, does this say about racial inequality today?

We want to find out whether there is a relationship between the amount of TV people watch and their social class, using the variables CLASS and TVHOURS from your EXERPLUS.SAV file. To start the process, make sure any codes that indicate missing information, such as DK, NA, and so on, have been defined as "missing" values.

Use the Univariate procedure (hint: **Analyze → General Linear Model → Univariate**) to produce an ANOVA with TVHOURS as the dependent variable and CLASS as the fixed factor. On the Options screen, mark both "Descriptive statistics" and "Homogeneity tests." Use the output to answer Questions 13–16.

13. From your results, what is the average number of hours per day spent watching TV by each of the social classes? How many respondents were in each class?

| Class | Mean Hours Watching TV | Number of Respondents |
|---|---|---|
| Lower class | 4.49 | 105 |
| Working class | 3.11 | 421 |
| Middle class | 2.87 | 428 |
| Upper class | 2.50 | 34 |

14. Find the F statistics and significance levels for both the Levene test and the independent variable.

| | F Value | Significance Level |
|---|---|---|
| Levene test | 5.721 | < .001 |
| Independent variable | 8.980 | < .001 |

15. Describe the relationship between hours spent watching TV and social class.

equal variances are not assumed

16. Using the information you gathered, explain why the relationship you described can or cannot be generalized from the EXER.SAV sample to the United States population. (Hint: The GSS is a random sample of noninstitutionalized adults in the United States, and the EXER.SAV is a randomly drawn subsample containing 1,500 of those 1,974 respondents.)

# SUGGESTIONS FOR FURTHER BIVARIATE ANALYSES

By now, you've amassed a powerful set of analytic tools. In a world where people make casual assertions about sociological topics, you're now in a position to determine the facts about how the U.S. population feels about a variety of topics. And with your new bivariate skills, you can begin to explain why people feel as they do.

Remember, in Chapters 10 through 15, we introduced you to a number of techniques that make this type of analysis possible, including crosstabs (Chapters 10–12); measures of association—lambda ($\lambda$), gamma ($\gamma$), Pearson's $r$, and regression—(Chapters 13–14); and tests of significance—chi-square ($\chi^2$), $t$ test, and ANOVA—(Chapter 15). Our goal in this chapter is to encourage you to use these techniques to explore some of the other variables contained on your data files.

To get you started, we are going to suggest some analyses you might undertake. In Chapter 9, we suggested some topics—drawn from the items on your DEMOPLUS.SAV file—that you might pursue with the techniques of univariate analysis. Let's start by returning to those topics.

## DEMONSTRATION 16.1: DESIRED FAMILY SIZE

Your DEMOPLUS.SAV file contains the variable CHLDIDEL, which asked respondents what they considered the ideal number of children for a family. A little more than half of the respondents said that two was best. Because that is also the number of children that would represent population

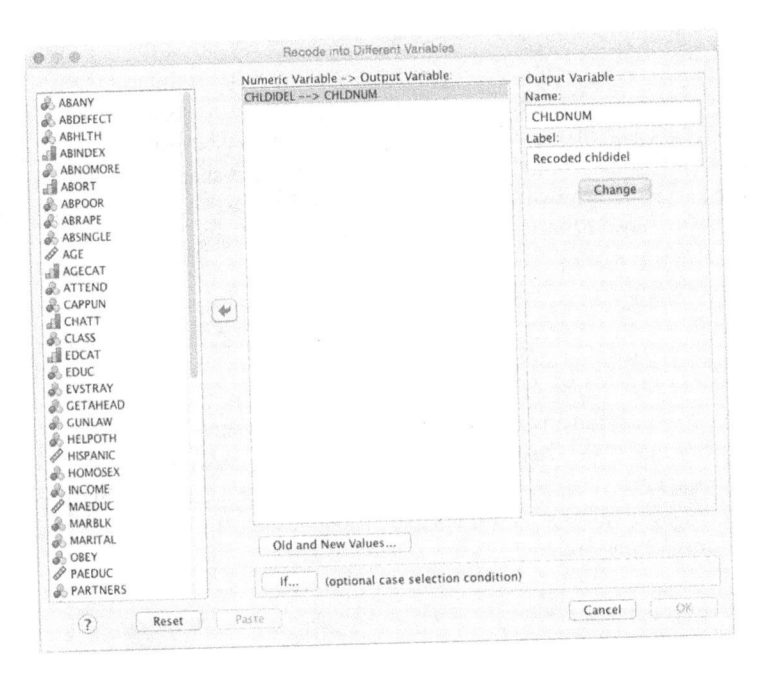

stabilization, you might want to begin by recoding this variable to create two response categories. If you are having difficulty with this, here is a hint to point you in the right direction: Select **Transform → Recode → Into Different Variables** (see figure on the previous page).

Then, recode CHLDIDEL to create a new variable, CHLDNUM, with the following values and labels:[1]

| Old Values | New Values | Labels |
|---|---|---|
| 0 to 2 | 1 | 0 to 2 |
| 3 to 8 | 2 | 3 or more |

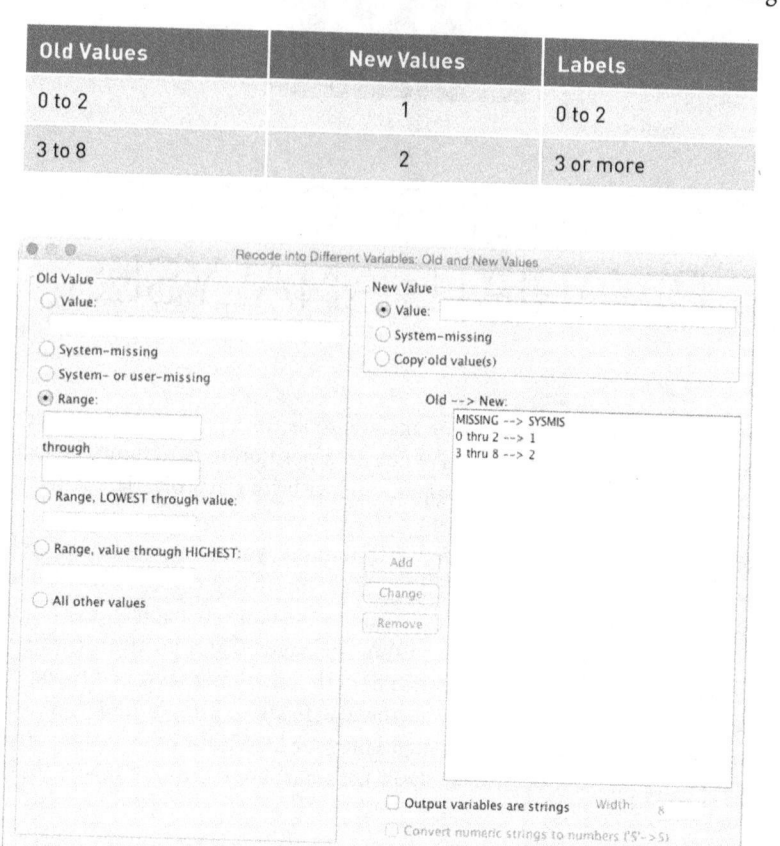

Once you've recoded CHLDIDEL into the more manageable variable CHLDNUM, you can use some of the bivariate techniques you learned to examine the causes of differences.

As a start, you might want to see if the amount of education a person has is related to opinions about ideal family size. The better-educated members of the population are, for instance, generally more concerned about environmental issues. Now, you can explore if they are also more committed to small families. How about age? Support for small families is a fairly recent development in the United States, against a historical backdrop of large farm families. Does this mean that young people would be more supportive of small families than would older people? You find out!

Religion and race are good candidates for factors that might shape opinions about ideal family size because the nature of family life is often central to subcultural patterns. We saw that Catholics and Protestants were resistant to abortion. How do they feel about limiting family size in general? You can know the answer in a matter of minutes.

Several family variables may very well relate to attitudes toward ideal family size. Marital status and whether respondents have ever been divorced might be relevant. Can you see why that would be worth exploring? What would you hypothesize? The data set contains SIBS (the number of brothers and sisters the respondent has), which may be relevant. You might want to see if the experience of having brothers and sisters has any impact on opinions about what's best in family size.

We found that gender was basically unrelated to abortion attitudes. How about ideal family size? Do you think men and women differ in their images of the perfect family? If you think so, in which direction do you think that difference goes? Take a moment to see if they are at all related to opinions about ideal family size.

---

1. Before proceeding, define the following values as "missing" for CHLDIDEL: −1 and 9.

Once you have explored one or more of these possibilities, take a moment to describe your findings in a few sentences or paragraphs.

Finally, what about the variables we examined in relation to abortion attitudes? Is there a relationship between ideal family size (CHLDNUM) and attitudes toward abortion (ABINDEX)? We created ABINDEX in Chapter 8, so it should be saved on your DEMOPLUS.SAV file. If not, simply go back to the chapter and re-create it before proceeding.

Take a moment to consider which measure of association and test of statistical significance are appropriate in this case. If you have trouble making this determination, refer to the discussions in Chapters 13, 14, and 15.

Now that you have done the hard work, you are ready to determine whether there is a relationship between family size and attitudes toward abortion. After you have completed your analysis and written a short description of your findings, compare it with Writing Box 16.1, an example of how a social scientist examining this relationship might describe his or her findings in prose.

## WRITING BOX 16.1

The relationship between the number of children people want to have and support for abortion is indeed statistically significant by the chi-square measurement; the level of significance is .000. Gamma (–.365) provides evidence of a moderate association worth noting. Respondents who strongly approve of abortion are less likely to want more than two children. Likewise, those who strongly disapprove of abortion are more likely to say that their ideal number of children is three or more.

## CHILD-REARING

In Chapter 9, we took an initial look at different opinions about what was important in the development of children. The key variables were as follows:

| OBEY | To obey |
|------|---------|
| POPULAR | To be well liked or popular |
| THNKSELF | To think for himself or herself |
| WORKHARD | To work hard |
| HELPOTH | To help others when they need help |

If you examined these variables, then you discovered some real differences in how people want their children to turn out. Now let's see what causes those differences because opinions on this topic can reflect some more general attitudes and worldviews.

Once again, such demographic variables as sex, age, race, and religion might make a difference. OBEY, for example, reflects a certain authoritarian leaning. Perhaps it is related to political variables, such as PARTYID and POLVIEWS; perhaps it is not. There's only one way to find out!

HELPOTH measures an altruistic dimension. That's something that religions often encourage. Maybe there's a relation between this variable and some of the religion variables.

Also consider the variable THNKSELF, which values children learning to think for themselves. What do you expect will influence this? Education perhaps? How about age and sex? Do you think older respondents would be relatively cool with children thinking for themselves? Would men or women be more supportive? Don't rule out religious and political variables. Some of these results are likely to confirm your expectations; some are not.

When it comes to the value of children thinking for themselves, you may find that some of the other attitudinal variables in the General Social Survey (GSS) data set are worth looking at. Consider those who have told us that they are permissive on premarital sex and homosexuality. Do you think they would be more or less likely to value children learning to think for themselves?

You might want to pursue any number of directions in looking for the causes of different attitudes toward the qualities most valued in children.

# ATTITUDES ABOUT SEXUAL BEHAVIOR

You may want to focus on the three sexual variables. What do you suppose would cause differences of opinion regarding premarital sexual relations and homosexuality? What do you suppose determines who goes to X-rated movies? You have the ability and the tools to find out for yourself.

Near the end of the movie *Casablanca*, the police chief instructs his officers to "round up the usual suspects." You might do well to round up the usual demographic variables as a way of beginning your examination of sexual attitudes: age, gender, race, religion, education, social class, and marital status, for example.

Before examining each of these relationships, take some time to think about any links you might logically expect. Will men or women be more permissive toward homosexuality? Will married, single, or divorced people be more supportive of premarital sex? How do you expect that young and old people will differ in their X-rated movie-viewing habits? As you investigate these attitudes, be careful about assuming that the three items are just different dimensions of the same orientation. The kinds of people who are permissive about premarital sex are not necessarily the same ones who are permissive about homosexuality, for example.

# DEMONSTRATION 16.2: INVESTIGATING SEXUAL PERMISSIVENESS FURTHER

Another possibility is to use the index of sexual permissiveness (SEXPERM) we created in Chapter 9 to explore why some people are more permissive than others when it comes to attitudes toward sex.

Writing Box 16.2 contains an example of how a social scientist examining this issue might convey his or her findings in prose. In this case, we examined the possibility that two basic demographic variables may be related to sexual permissiveness: AGE (as represented by the recoded variable AGECAT) and SEX. After making sure to define appropriate values for each variable as "missing," determine which measure of association and test of statistical significance are appropriate to examine the relationship between SEXPERM, AGECAT, and SEX. After exploring the relationship between these variables, take some time to describe your findings. Then, compare your analysis with the short description in Writing Box 16.2.

## WRITING BOX 16.2

The relationship between gender (SEX) and sexual permissiveness (SEXPERM) is neither strong ($\lambda = .017$) nor significant ($p = .437$) when measured by lambda (using the symmetric computation). A nonsignificant chi-square ($p = .298$) bolsters the finding that there is no statistically significant gender difference with regard to sexual permissiveness. Respondents' ages, however, are related to permissiveness. Not only does chi-square ($p = .000$) indicate a statistically significant relationship, but so does gamma ($\gamma = -.27$; $p = .000$), showing a moderate negative relationship worth noting between age and sexual permissiveness.

## Prejudice

Several items in your DEMOPLUS.SAV file address different aspects of racial prejudice about African Americans. RACMAR measures respondents' attitudes toward the legality of interracial marriage, whereas RACDIF1, RACDIF2, RACDIF3, and RACDIF4 measure attitudes about Black–White differences.

Certainly, RACE is the most obvious variable to examine, and you probably won't be surprised at what you find. Don't stop there, however. There are other variables that provide even more dramatic relationships. Education, politics, and social class offer fruitful avenues for understanding the roots of attitudes on these variables. You may be surprised by the impact of religious variables.

As a different approach, you might be interested in whether the belief that homosexuality is morally wrong reflects prejudice against gays and lesbians. In exploring this hypothesis, it's worth checking whether responses to that item are related to prejudice against Blacks.

## ADDITIONAL RESOURCES

The National Opinion Research Center (NORC) maintains a website that has not only a codebook for the GSS but also a fairly extensive bibliography. This is a particularly useful resource if you want to identify studies, reports, books, and articles that use the GSS variables with which you are working.

You can access the site at http://gss.norc.org/Get-Documentation. From that site, you have several options. You may, for instance, search the reference section directly by clicking "Bibliography" toward the right-hand side of the page. This, however, may not be directly useful unless you know exactly for what you are looking. The bibliography does have a search function that allows you to search titles for keywords. This can be a useful approach to narrowing the extensive bibliography.

Another alternative may be to start by searching by either subject or mnemonic (an index of abbreviated variable names) under the "Search GSS Variables" menu on the GSS data explorer page: https://gssdataexplorer.norc.org. For example, if you are interested in pursuing the subject of child-rearing further, simply click **Filter by Module/Subject;** then select your topic (**Children**). After clicking "search," you will be provided with a list of subjects and mnemonics relevant to "Children." If, for instance, you want to find more variables that might be relevant to the variable you have selected, you will see a list of links on the right side of the variable page.

If you wish to browse variable names directly, once you access the site, click Search GSS Variables. Here, you will be provided the entire list of GSS variables ever used since 1972. The Search function is what allows you to narrow down your search. From here, you might have uncovered additional keywords to take back to your bibliography search.

## CONCLUSION

The preceding suggestions should be enough to keep you busy, but you shouldn't feel limited by them. The most fruitful guides to your analyses should be your own personal interests. Keep in mind that the DEMO.SAV (or DEMOPLUS.SAV) file contains a number of additional variables covering issues such as the environment, mass media use, national government spending priorities, gender roles, law enforcement, teen sex, and the Internet. Think about which topics from the DEMO.SAV file interest or concern you. Now, you have a chance to learn something about them on your own. You don't have to settle for polemical statements about "the way things are." You now have the tools you need to find out for yourself.

In examining these bivariate relationships, you may want to begin with crosstabs because that technique gives you the most detailed view of the data. At the same time, you should use this exercise as an opportunity to experiment with the other bivariate techniques we've examined. Try chi-squares where appropriate, for example. As you find interesting relationships between variables, you may want to test these relationships' statistical significance to get another view of what they mean.

What you've learned so far may be sufficient to satisfy most of your day-to-day curiosity. You can learn what public opinion really is on a given topic, and you can determine what kinds of people hold differing views on that topic. In the remaining chapters of this book, however, we are going to show you an approach to understanding that goes much deeper. As we introduce you to multivariate analysis, you're going to have an opportunity to sample a more complex mode of understanding than most people are even aware of.

## Main Points

- Now that you are capable of describing both what Americans think about a variety of issues and why they think that way, we suggest some additional bivariate analyses for you to pursue on your own.

- We focus on four topics drawn from the items in your DEMOPLUS.SAV file as examples of the types of investigations you may want to pursue: desired family size, child-rearing, attitudes about sexual behavior, and prejudice.

- Don't be limited by these suggestions, however. Pursue topics and issues that interest or concern you. After all, this is your adventure!

- Keep in mind that your DEMO.SAV file contains 46 General Social Survey items covering a number of important and controversial issues and topics in American life; your EXER.SAV file contains a different selection of 46 variables, as well. The full version of the GSS, also available to you, contains 799 variables.

- When pursuing relations between two variables, you should begin with crosstabs and then experiment with the other techniques we reviewed in this section, including measures of association and tests of statistical significance.

## Key Terms

No new terms were introduced in this chapter.

## SPSS Statistics Commands Introduced in This Chapter

No new commands were introduced in this chapter.

## Review Questions

1. Use the National Opinion Research Center website (http://www.norc.org/GSS+Website) discussed in the "Additional Resources" section at the end of this chapter to identify an article or study that pertains to each of the following topics. Then, list the names, authors, and publication dates of the articles.

   a. Desired family size

   b. Child-rearing

   c. Attitudes toward sexual behavior

   d. Prejudice

2. Write a summary of one of the articles you found in response to Question 1. Include the following in your summary: the variables examined, statistics used, and author's findings.

3. Discuss how you might apply the techniques and procedures we covered in Part III (Chapters 10–15) on bivariate analysis (e.g., crosstabs, measures of association, and tests of statistical significance) to examine each of the following topics.

   a. Desired family size

   b. Child-rearing

   c. Attitudes toward sexual behavior

   d. Prejudice

# SPSS Statistics Lab Exercise 16.1

NAME: _____

CLASS: _____

INSTRUCTOR: _____

DATE: _____

In Lab Exercise 9.1, we asked you to use univariate techniques to examine one of the topics from your EXERPLUS. SAV file in more depth: attitudes about gender roles, law enforcement, the environment, mass media use, national government spending priorities, teen sex, affirmative action, and so on.

In this lab exercise, you will be given an opportunity to expand your analysis of this issue by applying some of the bivariate techniques discussed in Chapters 10 through 15.

1. List the general topic or issue you examined in Lab Exercise 9.1.

2. List the variables in your EXERPLUS.SAV file that pertain to this topic or issue.

3. In Lab Exercise 9.1, did you either recode or create an index based on any of the variables you were working with? If so, list the abbreviated variable name(s) below.

4. Choose one of the variables listed in response to Question 2 or 3 that you are interested in examining further. List it in the space below.

   *Dependent variable:* _____

5. List the names of two other items (independent variables) from the EXERPLUS.SAV file that you think may be causally related to or associated with your dependent variable.

   *Independent Variable 1:* _____

   *Independent Variable 2:* _____

6. Write two hypotheses linking your dependent variable (Question 4) and independent variables (Question 5).

   *Hypothesis 1:* _____

   *List the dependent variable in Hypothesis 1:* _____

   *List the independent variable in Hypothesis 1:* _____

(Continued)

(Continued)

*Hypothesis 2:* _____

*List the dependent variable in Hypothesis 2:* _____

*List the independent variable in Hypothesis 2:* _____

7. From the list of bivariate techniques below, circle the procedures appropriate for examining the relationship in Hypothesis 1 (Question 6) further. Circle at least one technique in each "group": (a) Chapters 10–12; (b) Chapters 13–14; (c) Chapter 15.

   a. Chapters 10 through 12: Crosstabs

      Crosstabs

   b. Chapters 13 and 14: Measures of association

      Lambda

      Gamma

      Correlation matrix with Pearson's $r$

      Coefficient of determination ($r^2$)

      Regression

      Scatterplot with a regression line

   c. Chapter 15: Tests of significance

      Chi-square

      $t$ test

      ANOVA

8. From the list of bivariate techniques reviewed in Chapters 10 through 15, circle the procedures appropriate for examining the relationship in Hypothesis 2 (Question 6) further. Circle at least one technique in each "group": (a) Chapters 10–12; (b) Chapter 13–14; (c) Chapter 15.

   a. Chapters 10 through 12: Crosstabs

      Crosstabs

   b. Chapter 13 and 14: Measures of association

      Lambda

      Gamma

      Correlation matrix with Pearson's $r$

      Coefficient of determination ($r^2$)

      Regression

      Scatterplot with a regression line

   c. Chapter 15: Tests of significance

      Chi-square

      $t$ test

      ANOVA

9. Now, use the techniques you identified as appropriate in response to Question 7 to examine the relationship between the variables in Hypothesis 1. After you have completed your analysis, do the following:

   - Print and attach a copy of your output to this sheet.

   - Summarize your findings in prose below.

10. Now, use the techniques you identified as appropriate in response to Question 8 to examine the relationship between the variables in Hypothesis 2. After you have completed your analysis, do the following:

    - Print and attach a copy of your output to this sheet.

    - Summarize your findings in prose below.

11. Choose a variable from your EXERPLUS.SAV file._____

12. Access the National Opinion Research Center website (http://www.norc.org/GSS+Website) discussed in the "Additional Resources" section at the end of this chapter. Locate an article, study, or report that references this variable. Remember to first look up the variable; then, find the link to research at the bottom of that page, under "Notes." Read the article, and write a critique that includes the following:

    - Article title

    - Author

    - Main point(s) of article

    - How the author uses/refers to the variable

    - What you learned from the article (as it pertains to the variable)

    - How you might explore this variable further in future research

# MULTIVARIATE ANALYSIS

Now that you've mastered the logic and techniques of bivariate analysis, we are going to take you one step further: to the examination of three or more variables at a time, known as multivariate analysis.

In Chapter 17, we'll delve more deeply into religious orientation to gain a more comprehensive understanding of this variable. In Chapter 18, we will pick up some loose threads of our bivariate analysis of political orientation and party identification and pursue them further with our new analytic capability.

In Chapter 19, we will set as our purpose the prediction of attitudes toward abortion. We'll progress, step by step, through a number of variables previously found to have an impact on abortion attitudes, and we'll accumulate them in a composite measure that will operate as a powerful predictor of opinions.

Finally, Chapter 20 launches us into uncharted areas of social research, which you should now be empowered to chart for yourself.

# MULTIPLE CAUSATION

## Examining Religiosity in Greater Depth

In Part III, we focused primarily on the relationship between two variables: an independent variable and a dependent variable. If we continued to limit ourselves solely to the examination of two variables at a time, our understanding of the social world would remain incomplete, not to mention dissatisfying.

Bivariate analysis alone cannot help us understand the social world because in the "real world," two or more factors often have an impact on, influence, or cause variation in a single dependent variable. Consequently, to understand the complexities of the social world, we need to introduce a more sophisticated form of statistical analysis that allows us to examine the impact of more than one independent variable on a single dependent variable.

Social scientists refer to this type of analysis as **multivariate analysis**, the *simultaneous* analysis of three or more variables. The next step after bivariate analysis, multivariate analysis moves us beyond the limitations of univariate and bivariate analysis, allowing us to develop a more complete understanding of the complexities of the social world.

We are going to introduce multivariate analysis by looking at the simplest of outcomes, multiple causation.

## MULTIPLE CAUSATION

In Chapter 10, we discussed several variables, including gender and age, that might affect the levels of respondents' religiosity. It is often the case with social phenomena that people's attitudes and behaviors are affected by more than one factor. The task of the social scientist, then, is to discover all of those factors that influence the dependent variable under question and discover how those factors work together to produce a result. If both age and gender affect religiosity independently, perhaps a combination of the two would predict it even better.

## DEMONSTRATION 17.1: THE IMPACT OF AGE AND SEX ON RELIGIOSITY

To begin our multivariate analysis, let's see how well we can predict religiosity if we consider AGE and SEX simultaneously. Does religiosity increase with age among both men and women separately? Moreover, do the two variables have a cumulative effect on religiosity? That is, are older women the most religious and younger men the least?

To begin our exploration of this topic, let's open our DEMOPLUS.SAV file and access the crosstabs dialog box. In this case, we want to use CHATT as the dependent/row variable and AGECAT (recoded AGE) as the independent/column variable.

Now, select **SEX** in the list of variables. Notice that the arrows activated would let you transfer SEX to the row or column fields—but don't do that! Instead, transfer it to the third field, near the bottom of the window.

We have now told SPSS Statistics to examine the relationship between AGECAT and CHATT while controlling for SEX. The result of this simple act is that now we will get two crosstabs, one showing the relationship between AGECAT and CHATT for men and another showing the association between AGECAT and CHATT for women.

Now, to run crosstabs, make sure that cells are percentaged by column, and then, execute the command (i.e., click **Cells → Percentages: Column → Continue → OK**).

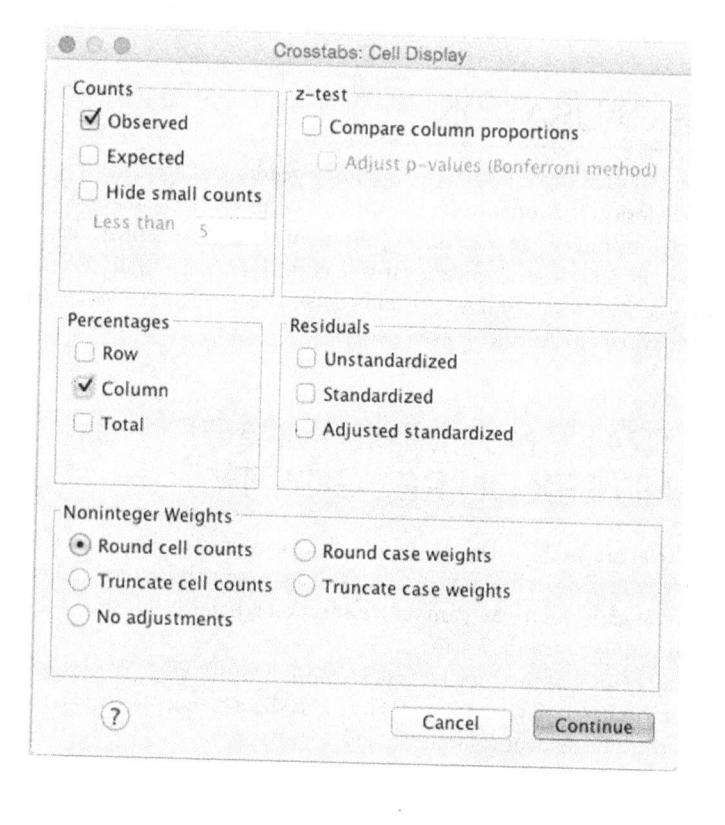

As we noted, this command produces more than one table. We have asked SPSS Statistics to examine the impact of AGECAT on CHATT separately for men and women. Thus, we are rewarded with the following three-variable crosstabulation.

## CHATT Recoded Church Attendance * AGECAT Recoded Age * SEX Respondent's Sex Crosstabulation

| | | | | AGECAT Recoded Age | | | | |
|---|---|---|---|---|---|---|---|---|
| | | | | 1 Under 21 | 2 21–39 years old | 3 40–64 years old | 4 65 and older | Total |
| SEX Respondent's Sex | | | | | | | | |
| 1 MALE | CHATT Recoded Church Attendance | 1 About weekly | Count | 6 | 41 | 86 | 43 | 176 |
| | | | % within AGECAT Recoded Age | 33.3% | 18.5% | 29.2% | 31.2% | 26.2% |
| | | 2 About monthly | Count | 4 | 32 | 38 | 16 | 90 |
| | | | % within AGECAT Recoded Age | 22.2% | 14.4% | 12.9% | 11.6% | 13.4% |
| | | 3 Seldom | Count | 5 | 84 | 84 | 33 | 206 |
| | | | % within AGECAT Recoded Age | 27.8% | 37.8% | 28.5% | 23.9% | 30.6% |
| | | 4 Never | Count | 3 | 65 | 87 | 46 | 201 |
| | | | % within AGECAT Recoded Age | 16.7% | 29.3% | 29.5% | 33.3% | 29.9% |
| | Total | | Count | 18 | 222 | 295 | 138 | 673 |
| | | | % within AGECAT Recoded Age | 100.0% | 100.0% | 100.0% | 100.0% | 100.0% |
| 2 FEMALE | CHATT Recoded Church Attendance | 1 About weekly | Count | 4 | 58 | 102 | 85 | 249 |
| | | | % within AGECAT Recoded Age | 26.7% | 22.9% | 28.3% | 46.4% | 30.7% |
| | | 2 About monthly | Count | 2 | 64 | 59 | 24 | 149 |
| | | | % within AGECAT Recoded Age | 13.3% | 25.3% | 16.4% | 13.1% | 18.4% |
| | | 3 Seldom | Count | 4 | 72 | 130 | 40 | 246 |
| | | | % within AGECAT Recoded Age | 26.7% | 28.5% | 36.1% | 21.9% | 30.3% |
| | | 4 Never | Count | 5 | 59 | 69 | 34 | 167 |
| | | | % within AGECAT Recoded Age | 33.3% | 23.3% | 19.2% | 18.6% | 20.6% |
| | Total | | Count | 15 | 253 | 360 | 183 | 811 |
| | | | % within AGECAT Recoded Age | 100.0% | 100.0% | 100.0% | 100.0% | 100.0% |

*(Continued)*

(Continued)

| | | | | AGECAT Recoded Age | | | | |
|---|---|---|---|---|---|---|---|---|
| SEX Respondent's Sex | | | | 1 Under 21 | 2 21–39 years old | 3 40–64 years old | 4 65 and older | Total |
| Total | CHATT Recoded Church Attendance | 1 About weekly | Count | 10 | 99 | 188 | 128 | 425 |
| | | | % within AGECAT Recoded Age | 30.3% | 20.8% | 28.7% | 39.9% | 28.6% |
| | | 2 About monthly | Count | 6 | 96 | 97 | 40 | 239 |
| | | | % within AGECAT Recoded Age | 18.2% | 20.2% | 14.8% | 12.5% | 16.1% |
| | | 3 Seldom | Count | 9 | 156 | 214 | 73 | 452 |
| | | | % within AGECAT Recoded Age | 27.3% | 32.8% | 32.7% | 22.7% | 30.5% |
| | | 4 Never | Count | 8 | 124 | 156 | 80 | 368 |
| | | | % within AGECAT Recoded Age | 24.2% | 26.1% | 23.8% | 24.9% | 24.8% |
| | Total | | Count | 33 | 475 | 655 | 321 | 1484 |
| | | | % within AGECAT Recoded Age | 100.0% | 100.0% | 100.0% | 100.0% | 100.0% |

Notice that the table is divided into three parts: male, female, and total. The "Total" part of the table contains the same information that would have been provided had we not selected SEX as a "layer." For our purposes, we can create a summary table, as follows, that is easier to read, allowing us to consider more easily differences across age, with a specific focus on gender.

| Percentage Who Attend Worship Services About Weekly | | | | |
|---|---|---|---|---|
| | Under 21 | 21 to 39 | 40 to 64 | 65 and Older |
| Men | — | 19% | 29% | 31% |
| Women | — | 23% | 28% | 46% |

A dash (—) in this table indicates that there are too few cases for meaningful percentages. We required at least 10 cases, a common standard.

There are two primary observations to be made regarding this table. First, women are more likely to attend worship services than are men within each age group. Second, the previously observed relationship between AGECAT and CHATT remains present for both men and women. In other words, the introduction of a third or control variable (SEX) did not alter or diminish the strength of the relationship between AGECAT and CHATT. So age and church attendance do appear to be related both among women and among men.

The SPSS Statistics procedure we just ran is sometimes referred to as controlling for a third variable, and it is often used to elaborate on bivariate relationships. **Elaboration** is a technique that helps us examine the relationship between two variables (an independent and dependent) while controlling for a third variable.

In this example, for instance, we specified CHATT as our dependent variable, AGECAT as our independent variable, and SEX as our **control variable** (or third variable). This allowed us to examine the relationship between church attendance and age while controlling for sex. Consequently, our output was in two tables: one showing the relationship between CHATT and AGECAT for men and the other showing the relationship between CHATT and AGECAT for women.[1]

---

### SPSS Statistics Command 17.1: Running Crosstabs With a Control or Third Variable

**Analyze → Descriptive Statistics → Crosstabs**

Highlight dependent variable → Click arrow pointing to "Row(s):" field

Highlight independent variable → Click arrow pointing to "Column(s):" field

Highlight control/third variable → Click arrow pointing toward bottom field ("Layer 1 of 1")

Click **Cells** → "Column" box under "Percentages"

Click **Continue → OK**

---

# DEMONSTRATION 17.2: FAMILY STATUS AND RELIGIOSITY

If you read the excerpt by Glock et al. (1967) on the *Adventures in Social Research* student study website (https://study.sagepub.com/babbie10e), you will recall that according to social deprivation theory, "family status" is also related to religiosity. Those who had "complete families" (spouse and children) were the least religious among the 1,952 Episcopal Church members, suggesting that those lacking families were turning to the church for gratification.

Using crosstabs, set CHATT as the row variable and MARITAL as the column variable.[2] See pages 316–317 for what you should get.

These data do not confirm the earlier finding. Those who are currently married or who are legally separated but not divorced, for instance, are more likely than divorced and never-married people to attend church about weekly. Those who were married and are now widowed have the highest rates of weekly church attendance. It does not appear that those without conventional family status (i.e., those divorced or never married) are turning to the church for an alternative source of gratification.

Perhaps the explanation for this lies in historical changes. In the years separating these two studies, there have been many changes with regard to family life in the United States. Divorced people, single-parent families, unmarried couples living together—these and other variations on the traditional family have become more acceptable and certainly more common. It would make sense, therefore, that people who lacked regular family status in 2016 did not feel as deprived as such people may have in the early 1950s.

# DEMONSTRATION 17.3: FAMILY STATUS AND RELIGIOSITY, CONTROLLING FOR AGE

Before setting this issue aside, however, we should take a minute to consider whether the table we've just seen is concealing anything. In particular, can you think of any other variable that is related to both attendance at worship services and marital status? If so, that variable might be clouding the relations between marital status and religiosity.

---

1. While a complete discussion of the elaboration model is beyond the scope of this text, this technique is explored in detail in most texts on social statistics and research methods. See, for instance, Chapter 15 of Earl Babbie's *The Practice of Social Research*, 13th edition (Belmont, CA: Wadsworth Cengage Learning, 2013).

2. Define the value 9 as "missing" for the variable MARITAL.

## CHATT Recoded Church Attendance * MARITAL Marital Status * SEX Respondent's Sex Crosstabulation

| SEX Respondent's Sex | | | | MARITAL Marital Status | | | | | Total |
|---|---|---|---|---|---|---|---|---|---|
| | | | | 1 MARRIED | 2 WIDOWED | 3 DIVORCED | 4 SEPARATED | 5 NEVER MARRIED | |
| 1 MALE | CHATT Recoded Church Attendance | 1 About weekly | Count | 97 | 13 | 25 | 6 | 36 | 177 |
| | | | % within MARITAL Marital status | 34.0% | 37.1% | 20.0% | 27.3% | 17.4% | 26.3% |
| | | 2 About monthly | Count | 41 | 3 | 14 | 3 | 29 | 90 |
| | | | % within MARITAL Marital status | 14.4% | 8.6% | 11.2% | 13.6% | 14.0% | 13.4% |
| | | 3 Seldom | Count | 84 | 6 | 37 | 4 | 76 | 207 |
| | | | % within MARITAL Marital status | 29.5% | 17.1% | 29.6% | 18.2% | 36.7% | 30.7% |
| | | 4 Never | Count | 63 | 13 | 49 | 9 | 66 | 200 |
| | | | % within MARITAL Marital status | 22.1% | 37.1% | 39.2% | 40.9% | 31.9% | 29.7% |
| | Total | | Count | 285 | 35 | 125 | 22 | 207 | 674 |
| | | | % within MARITAL Marital status | 100.0% | 100.0% | 100.0% | 100.0% | 100.0% | 100.0% |
| 2 FEMALE | CHATT Recoded Church Attendance | 1 About weekly | Count | 126 | 43 | 38 | 12 | 31 | 250 |
| | | | % within MARITAL Marital status | 35.5% | 43.0% | 28.6% | 26.1% | 17.2% | 30.7% |
| | | 2 About monthly | Count | 66 | 10 | 25 | 11 | 38 | 150 |
| | | | % within MARITAL Marital status | 18.6% | 10.0% | 18.8% | 23.9% | 21.1% | 18.4% |
| | | 3 Seldom | Count | 104 | 27 | 42 | 13 | 61 | 247 |
| | | | % within MARITAL Marital status | 29.3% | 27.0% | 31.6% | 28.3% | 33.9% | 30.3% |
| | | 4 Never | Count | 59 | 20 | 28 | 10 | 50 | 167 |
| | | | % within MARITAL Marital status | 16.6% | 20.0% | 21.1% | 21.7% | 27.8% | 20.5% |
| | Total | | Count | 355 | 100 | 133 | 46 | 180 | 814 |
| | | | % within MARITAL Marital status | 100.0% | 100.0% | 100.0% | 100.0% | 100.0% | 100.0% |

| SEX Respondent's Sex | | | | MARITAL Marital Status | | | | | |
|---|---|---|---|---|---|---|---|---|---|
| | | | | 1 MARRIED | 2 WIDOWED | 3 DIVORCED | 4 SEPARATED | 5 NEVER MARRIED | Total |
| Total | CHATT Recoded Church Attendance | 1 About weekly | Count | 223 | 56 | 63 | 18 | 67 | 427 |
| | | | % within MARITAL Marital status | 34.8% | 41.5% | 24.4% | 26.5% | 17.3% | 28.7% |
| | | 2 About monthly | Count | 107 | 13 | 39 | 14 | 67 | 240 |
| | | | % within MARITAL Marital status | 16.7% | 9.6% | 15.1% | 20.6% | 17.3% | 16.1% |
| | | 3 Seldom | Count | 188 | 33 | 79 | 17 | 137 | 454 |
| | | | % within MARITAL Marital status | 29.4% | 24.4% | 30.6% | 25.0% | 35.4% | 30.5% |
| | | 4 Never | Count | 122 | 33 | 77 | 19 | 116 | 367 |
| | | | % within MARITAL Marital status | 19.1% | 24.4% | 29.8% | 27.9% | 30.0% | 24.7% |
| | Total | | Count | 640 | 135 | 258 | 68 | 387 | 1488 |
| | | | % within MARITAL Marital status | 100.0% | 100.0% | 100.0% | 100.0% | 100.0% | 100.0% |

The variable we are thinking of is age. We've already seen that age is related to church attendance. It is also probably related to marital status in that young people (lower in church attendance) are the most likely to be "never married." And older people (higher in church attendance) are the most likely to be widowed. It is possible, therefore, that the widowed are higher in church attendance because they're mostly older, and those never married are lower in church attendance only because they're young. This kind of reasoning lies near the heart of multivariate analysis, and the techniques you've mastered allow you to test this possibility (see figure at the top of the next page).

Return to the Crosstabs window and add AGECAT as the control or third variable. Once you've reviewed the resulting tables, see if you can construct the following summary table.

| | Percentage Who Attend Church About Weekly | | | | |
|---|---|---|---|---|---|
| | Married | Widowed | Divorced | Separated | Never Married |
| Under 21 | — | — | — | — | 31% |
| 21 to 39 | 29% | — | 41% | 17% | 13% |
| 40 to 64 | 34% | 24% | 22% | 30% | 23% |
| 65 and older | 45% | 47% | 21% | — | — |

Again, remember that dashes in this table indicate that there are too few cases for meaningful percentages.

Once again, these findings do not seem to confirm the theory that those lacking families turn to the church for gratification, whereas those with families are the least religious. The widowed, separated, and married appear to be among the most religious in each category. The lack of data for so many cells in our table is unfortunate in that those additional figures might have helped complete the puzzle.

You can also observe in this table that the effect of age on church attendance is maintained regardless of marital status—with one exception. Older respondents are more likely to attend religious services than are younger ones, except among those who have never married, where there is a small decline. Social scientists often use the term ***replication*** for the analytic outcome we've just observed. Having discovered that church attendance increases with age overall, we've now found that this relationship holds true regardless of marital status, except perhaps with those who are never married, revealing a *conditional relationship*. That's an important discovery in terms of the generalizability of what we have learned about the causes of religiosity.

# DEMONSTRATION 17.4: SOCIAL CLASS AND RELIGIOSITY

Glock and his colleagues (1967) also found that religiosity increased as social class decreased; that is, those in the lower class were more religious than those in the upper class. This fit nicely into the deprivation thesis, that those deprived of status in the secular society would turn to the church as an alternative source of gratification. The researchers indicated, however, that this finding might be limited to the Episcopalian Church members under study. They suggested that the relationship might not be replicated in the general public. You have the opportunity to check it out.

Let's begin with our measure of subjective social class. Run crosstabs with column percentages, requesting CHATT as the row variable and CLASS as the column variable.[3] See the next page for what you should get.

---

3. Define the values 0 and 5 to 9 as "missing" for the variable CLASS.

## CHATT Recoded Church Attendance * CLASS Subjective Class Identification Crosstabulation

| | | | CLASS Subjective Class Identification | | | | |
|---|---|---|---|---|---|---|---|
| | | | 1 LOWER CLASS | 2 WORKING CLASS | 3 MIDDLE CLASS | 4 UPPER CLASS | Total |
| CHATT Recoded Church Attendance | 1 About weekly | Count | 40 | 180 | 185 | 20 | 425 |
| | | % within CLASS Subjective class identification | 27.2% | 26.4% | 30.5% | 45.5% | 28.7% |
| | 2 About monthly | Count | 17 | 120 | 95 | 5 | 237 |
| | | % within CLASS Subjective class identification | 11.6% | 17.6% | 15.7% | 11.4% | 16.0% |
| | 3 Seldom | Count | 37 | 202 | 201 | 11 | 451 |
| | | % within CLASS Subjective class identification | 25.2% | 29.6% | 33.2% | 25.0% | 30.5% |
| | 4 Never | Count | 53 | 180 | 125 | 8 | 366 |
| | | % within CLASS Subjective class identification | 36.1% | 26.4% | 20.6% | 18.2% | 24.7% |
| Total | | Count | 147 | 682 | 606 | 44 | 1479 |
| | | % within CLASS Subjective class identification | 100.0% | 100.0% | 100.0% | 100.0% | 100.0% |

These data do not definitively confirm the earlier findings. In fact, the findings seem to run contrary to our expectations. Examine the first row, for instance, and you see that those in the middle class are more likely to attend church on about a weekly basis than are those in the lower and working classes. To be sure of this conclusion, you might want to rerun the table, controlling for sex, age, and income.

At the same time, you can test the generalizability of the previously observed effects of sex and age on church attendance. Do they hold up among members of different social classes? Once you have examined this possibility, compare your findings with those in Writing Box 17.1 below.

## WRITING BOX 17.1

The finding that women attend church more regularly than men is replicated in each of the social class groups, with the exception of those in the upper class. Once again, both men (29%) and women (32%) in the middle class appear somewhat more likely to attend religious services about weekly than those in the lower and working classes.

By the same token, the relationship between age and church attendance is also replicated among the several social class groups, with some minor variations. That is, older respondents attend church more often than younger ones, regardless of their social class.

## OTHER VARIABLES TO EXPLORE

Notice that our analyses so far in this chapter have used CHATT as the dependent variable: the measure of religiosity. Recall our earlier comments on the shortcomings of single-item measures of variables. Perhaps our analyses have been misleading by seeking to explain church attendance.

Perhaps different conclusions might be drawn if we studied beliefs in an afterlife or frequency of prayer. Why don't you test some of the earlier conclusions by using other measures of religiosity? If you are really ambitious—and why wouldn't you be?—you can create a composite index of religiosity and look for causes.

Similarly, we have limited our preceding investigations in this chapter to the variables examined by Glock and his colleagues (1967). Now that you have gotten the idea about how to create and interpret multivariate tables, you should broaden your exploration of variables that might be related to religiosity. What are some other demographic variables that might affect religiosity? Or you might want to explore the multivariate relationships between religiosity and some of the attitudinal variables we've been exploring: political philosophies, sexual attitudes, and so forth. In each instance, you should examine the bivariate relationships first and then move on to the multivariate analyses.

# CHI-SQUARE AND MEASURES OF ASSOCIATION

Thus far, we've introduced the logic of multivariate analysis through the use of crosstabs and controlling for a third variable. You've already learned some other techniques that can be used in your examination of several variables simultaneously.

## Chi-Square ($\chi^2$)

First, we should remind you that you may want to use a chi-square test of statistical significance when you use crosstabs. It's not required, but you may find it useful as an independent assessment of the relationships you discover.

## Measures of Association

Second, you may also want to experiment using an appropriate measure of association, such as lambda or gamma, to test the strength and, in certain cases, the direction of association.

## Multiple Regression

You may recall our fairly brief discussion of regression at the end of Chapter 14. At that point, we discussed a form of regression known as simple linear regression, or just **linear regression**, which involves one independent variable and one dependent variable. Regression can also be a powerful technique for exploring multivariate relationships.

When you are conducting multivariate analysis involving one dependent variable and more than one independent variable, the technique is referred to as **multiple regression**. In both cases, regression is appropriate for two or more interval/ratio (I/R) or continuous variables. The linear regression methods addressed in this book are based on **ordinary least-squares (OLS) regression**, meaning that this regression method minimizes the squared deviations between the observed data and the regression line.

To use either linear or multiple regression effectively, you need much more instruction than we propose to offer in this book. Still, we want to give you a brief overview of multiple regression, in much the same way as we did when we introduced linear regression earlier.

In our previous use of regression (linear regression, Chapter 14), we examined the impact of PAEDUC (father's educational attainment) on EDUC, respondents' educational attainment. Now, we'll open the possibility that other variables in the data set might also affect educational attainment.

## Dummy Variables

In addition to PAEDUC, we are going to consider two other independent variables: SEX and RACE. These variables were chosen because many argue that in today's workforce, men are still treated differently than women, and Whites are still treated differently than African Americans.

You will notice, however, that both SEX and RACE are nominal variables, not I/R variables. Since we told you that regression is appropriate for I/R continuous variables, you may begin to wonder how we can propose to use two nominal variables in a regression equation. That's a very good question.

The answer lies in the fact that researchers sometimes treat such items as *dummy variables* to make them appropriate for a regression analysis. In regard to the variable SEX, for example, one can transform gender into a measure of "maleness," with male respondents being 100% male and female respondents being 0% male.

## Recoding SEX to Create a Dummy Variable: MALE

Let's recode SEX as described previously into the new variable MALE. So take the following steps:

**Transform → Recode → Into Different Variables**

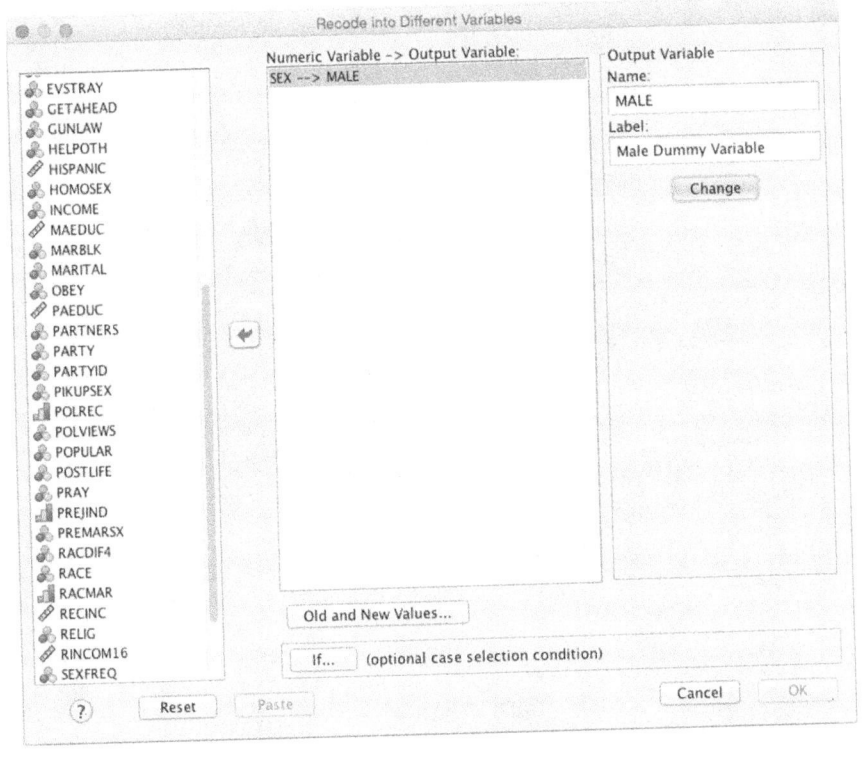

Select **SEX** as the numeric variable. Let's call the new variable **MALE**. Using the Old and New Values window, make these assignments (see figure at the top of the next page).

Execute the Recode command by clicking **Continue** and then **OK**.

Before moving on to the variable RACE, make sure you set the decimal places for MALE to 0. You may also want to give a brief description of MALE and define your values and labels (e.g., "male" and "not male"). It might be a good idea to check the Data View window and verify that your coding is accurate: Cases with a 1 for SEX should also have a 1 for MALE, while cases with a 2 for SEX should have a 0 for MALE.

## Recoding RACE to Create a Dummy Variable: WHITE

We will use the same basic procedure to recode RACE as we used to recode SEX. Open the Recode dialog box by selecting **Transform → Recode → Into Different Variables**.

Designate **RACE** as the numeric variable, and name the new variable **WHITE**. Then, use the Old and New Values window to accomplish your recode.

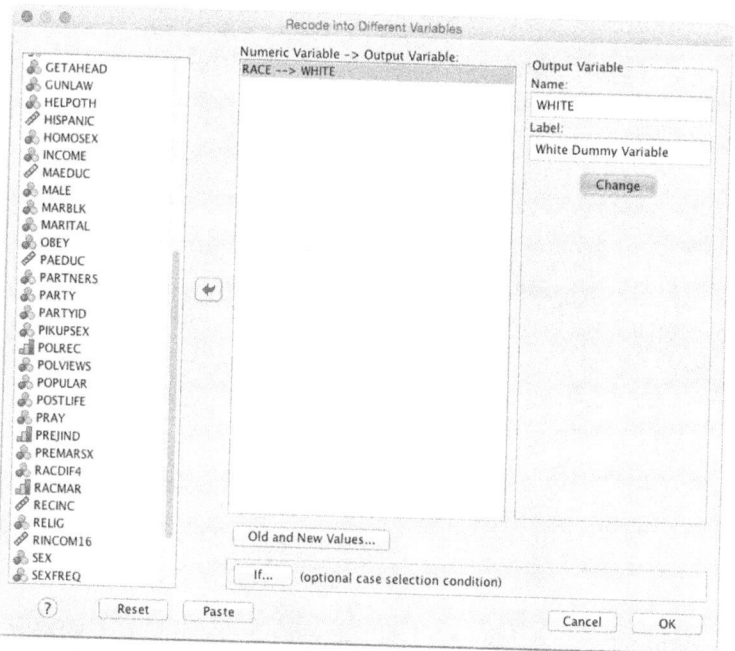

You will notice that unlike the variable SEX, RACE contains three values: 1 ("White"), 2 ("Black"), and 3 ("other"). Consequently, in this case, we are going to recode RACE as follows:

| Old Variable RACE | | New Variable WHITE |
|:---:|:---:|:---:|
| **Values** | | **Values** |
| 1 | → | 1 |
| 2 to 3 | → | 0 |

With this coding scheme, the dummy code 1 designates 100% majority group status; 0 designates 0% majority group status. Once you have set the new values, click **Continue** and **OK** to execute the command.

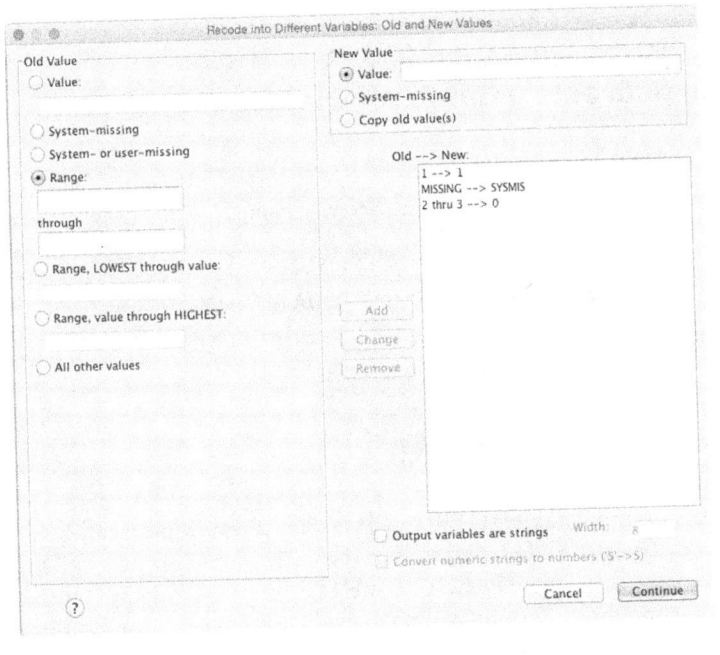

Before we ask SPSS Statistics to run our regression analysis, make sure you set the decimal places for your new variable (WHITE) to 0. In addition, you may want to provide a brief description of the variable and define the values and labels (e.g., "white" and "not white"). Again, it wouldn't hurt to take a look in the Data View window to verify that your coding is accurate: Cases with a 1 for RACE should also have a 1 for WHITE, and cases with a 2 or 3 for RACE should have a 0 for WHITE.

---

### SPSS Statistics Command 17.2:
### Recoding to Create a Dummy Variable

**Transform → Recode → Into Different Variables**

Highlight name of variable recoding → Click arrow pointing toward "Numeric Variable" field

Type name of new variable in field under "Output Variable" labeled "Name:"

Click **Change → Old and New Values → Recode Old/Add New Values**

Click **Continue → OK**

---

## MULTIPLE REGRESSION

Now that we have created our dummy variables, we are ready to request the multiple regression analysis.

**Analyze → Regression → Linear** takes us to the window we want. Select **EDUC**, and make it the dependent variable. Then, place **PAEDUC**, **WHITE**, and **MALE** in the "Independent(s):" field. In the "Method:" drop-down menu, the "Enter" method is probably displayed by default. If not, select it by clicking on the down arrow.

Run this command by clicking **OK**, and you will receive a mass of output. Without going into all the details, we are simply going to show you how it establishes the equation we asked for. We'll take the output a piece at a time. For our purposes, we'd like you to skip through the output on your screen until you find the following tables:

### Model Summary

| Model | | R | R Square | Adjusted R Square | Std. Error of the Estimate |
|---|---|---|---|---|---|
| 1 | | .423a | .179 | .176 | 2.588 |

a. Predictors: (Constant), MALE Male Dummy Variable; PAEDUC Highest year school completed, father; WHITE White Dummy Variable

## ANOVA[a]

| Model | | Sum of Squares | df | Mean Square | F | Sig. |
|---|---|---|---|---|---|---|
| 1 | Regression | 1609.132 | 3 | 536.377 | 80.079 | .000[b] |
| | Residual | 7401.437 | 1105 | 6.698 | | |
| | Total | 9010.570 | 1108 | | | |

a. Dependent Variable: EDUC Highest year of school completed

b. Predictors: (Constant), MALE Male Dummy Variable; PAEDUC Highest year school completed, father; WHITE White Dummy Variable

## Coefficients[a]

| Model | | Unstandardized Coefficients | | Standardized Coefficients | t | Sig. |
|---|---|---|---|---|---|---|
| | | B | Std. Error | Beta | | |
| 1 | (Constant) | 10.532 | .280 | | 37.575 | .000 |
| | PAEDUC Highest year school completed, father | .293 | .019 | .413 | 15.050 | .000 |
| | WHITE White Dummy Variable | .371 | .190 | .054 | 1.951 | .051 |
| | MALE Male Dummy Variable | −.248 | .156 | −.043 | −1.588 | .113 |

a. Dependent Variable: EDUC Highest year of school completed

We have given SPSS Statistics three variables that we felt might help predict occupational prestige. To create our equation, we take two numbers from the "Unstandardized Coefficients" column: the constant (10.532) and the β (beta) value (called the slope) for PAEDUC (0.293), WHITE (0.371), and MALE (−0.248). Locate those in your output. We use these numbers to create the following equation for EDUC, based on the standard regression model for the predicted value of Y:

$$\hat{Y} = a + bX_1 + bX_2 + bX_3$$

$$\text{EDUC} = 10.532 + (\text{PAEDUC} \times 0.293)^* + (\text{WHITE} \times 0.371) + (\text{MALE} \times -0.248)$$

$$= 10.532 + (\text{PAEDUC} \times 0.293)^* + (\text{WHITE} \times 0.371) - (\text{MALE} \times 0.248)$$

We'll explain the asterisk in the above equation shortly. In the meantime, how would you predict years of education of a White male whose father had 12 years of education? Here is a hint to get you started:

$$\text{EDUC} = 10.532 + (12 \times 0.293) - (\underline{\quad} \times \underline{\quad}) - (\underline{\quad} \times \underline{\quad}) = \underline{\quad}$$

The column titled "Standardized Coefficients" gives you a guide to the *relative impact* of the different variables. Take a minute to consider some independent variable that has no impact on the dependent variable. What slope would it be given? If you think about it, the only proper weight would be zero. That would mean that a person's value on that variable would never make any difference in predicting the dependent variable. By the same token, the larger the slope for any given variable, the larger its part in determining the resulting prediction.

It is possible that a variable that is supposed to be a better predictor, such as PAEDUC, could have a smaller slope than an item such as MALE, which is not supposed to be as good a predictor of EDUC. How can this happen? The solution to this puzzle lies in the different scales used in the different variables. MALE goes only as high as 1 ("male"), whereas PAEDUC obviously goes much higher to accommodate differences in the levels of education of respondents. Slopes must be standardized before they can be compared. Standardized slopes are what the slopes would be if each of the variables used the same scale.

SPSS Statistics prints standardized slopes under the column "Standardized Coefficients." The data presented indicate that PAEDUC (0.413) has the greatest impact on EDUC, followed distantly by WHITE (0.054) and MALE (-0.043). Interpreted, this means that father's education has the greatest impact on one's own educational level, followed by "maleness" and then "racial majorityness."

Significance levels of the coefficients also add information about the likelihood of their impact on the dependent variable. Look at the column labeled "Sig." Here, this value can be interpreted as we have discussed earlier in this book. As a rule of thumb, anything at .05 or less is considered significant; such values are usually denoted with an asterisk in a report. The only independent variable in this equation that turned out to be statistically significant (.000) was PAEDUC, father's educational attainment. This explains the appearance of the mysterious asterisk in the equation!

Other variables exist within your DEMO.SAV file that you could add to the mix of independent variables for a regression analysis. One such variable that might prove particularly interesting is MAEDUC, mother's educational attainment. How does the impact of mother's educational attainment compare with that of PAEDUC, father's educational attainment? Go back to the linear regression dialog box and begin that adventure!

---

### SPSS Statistics Command 17.3: Multiple Regression

**Analyze → Regression → Linear**

Highlight name of dependent variable → Click arrow pointing toward "Dependent:" field

Highlight name of first independent variable → Click arrow pointing to "Independent(s):" field

Repeat last step as many times as necessary until all independent variables are listed in the "Independent(s):" field

Click down arrow next to box labeled "Method"

Click **Enter → OK**

---

## CONCLUSION

In this chapter, we have given you an initial peek into the logic and techniques of multivariate analysis. As you've seen, the difference between bivariate and multivariate analysis is much more than a matter of degree. Multivariate analysis does more than bring in additional variables: It represents a new logic for understanding social scientific relationships.

In this introduction to multivariate analysis, we've looked at how it lets us explore the nature of multiple causation, specifically how two or more independent variables may affect a dependent variable. In addition, we've used multivariate techniques to test the generalizability of relationships.

In the latter regard, we have begun using multivariate techniques for the purpose of considering hidden relationships among variables, as when we asked whether the widowed attended church frequently not because of their marital status but because they were mostly older people. We'll pursue this kind of detective work further in the chapters to come.

## Main Points

- This chapter introduced a new, more sophisticated form of statistical analysis: multivariate analysis.

- Multivariate analysis is the simultaneous analysis of three or more variables.

- The crosstabs procedure can be used to analyze the relationship between an independent variable and a dependent variable while controlling for a third variable.

- We examined multiple causes of religiosity in more depth by focusing on items such as AGECAT, SEX, MARITAL, and CLASS.

- Other analytic techniques that may aid in the examination of several items at once include chi-square, measures of association, and regression.

- We introduced simple linear regression (ordinary least-squares method) in Chapter 14.

- In this chapter, we introduced another regression procedure: multiple regression.

- Nominal and ordinal items can be recoded to create dummy variables that are suitable for regression analysis or other analyses in which interval/ratio variables are a prerequisite.

## Key Terms

Control variable 314
Dummy variables 321
Elaboration 314

Linear regression 320
Multiple regression 320
Multivariate analysis 311

Ordinary least-squares (OLS) regression 320
Replication 318

## SPSS Statistics Commands Introduced in This Chapter

17.1. Running Crosstabs With a Control or Third Variable

17.2. Recoding to Create a Dummy Variable

17.3. Multiple Regression

## Review Questions

1. Describe the major differences among univariate, bivariate, and multivariate analysis.

2. If a researcher uncovers a relationship between class (independent variable) and prejudice (dependent variable), what technique introduced in this chapter might he or she use to examine the relationship further?

3. Describe the relationship between social class and church attendance. Do the findings support the "social deprivation" theory? Why, or why not?

4. To what does *replication* refer?

5. Name at least two other techniques you learned (before reading Chapter 16) that you could use in your multivariate examinations.

6. Simple linear regression involves the analysis of _____ [number] independent and _____ [number] dependent variables.

7. Multiple regression involves the analysis of _____ [number] independent and _____ [number] dependent variables.

8. Regression is appropriate for variables at what level(s) of measurement?

9. What is a dummy variable?

10. Why did we recode SEX to create MALE for our multiple regression example? Why didn't we just use SEX as our measure of gender?

*(Continued)*

(Continued)

11. What is a better predictor of EDUC—PAEDUC or MALE? PAEDUC or WHITE? PAEDUC or MAEDUC?

12. As you read your multiple regression output, which of the following gives you a sense of the relative impact of the independent variable: unstandardized coefficients, standardized coefficients, $t$, or sig.?

# SPSS Statistics Lab Exercise 17.1

NAME: _____

CLASS: _____

INSTRUCTOR: _____

DATE: _____

*To complete the following exercises, you need to load the data file EXERPLUS.SAV.*

1. Examine the simultaneous impact of class and race on support for national spending on crime. The variable NATCRIME reflects the percentage of respondents who felt that the national government is spending too little fighting crime. Before proceeding, designate the values indicated below as "missing" for each item. Then, run crosstabs with column percentages and request chi-square. Use your output to complete the summary table, and answer Questions 2–4:

   Dependent variable—NATCRIME (define 0, 8, 9 as "missing")

   Independent variable 1—CLASS (define 5–9, 0 as "missing")

   Independent variable 2—RACE (define 0, 3 as "missing")

| | NATCRIME | | | | |
|---|---|---|---|---|---|
| | **Lower** | **Working** | **Middle** | **Upper** | **Sig. (chi-square)** |
| *White* | | | | | |
| *Black* | | | | | |

2. (Whites) The percentage who feel that the national government is spending too little fighting crime _____ [increases, decreases, neither increases nor decreases] as class increases. The value of chi-square indicates that there _____ [is/is not] a statistically significant relationship.

3. (Blacks) The percentage who feel that the national government is spending too little fighting crime _____ [increases, decreases, neither increases nor decreases] as class increases. The value of chi-square indicates that there _____[is/is not] a statistically significant relationship.

4. Summarize the major findings from the table. Explain the primary observations that can be made regarding your findings and the table above. You may want to note, for instance, the relationship between race and support for government spending on crime, as well as the relationship between class and support for government spending on crime. Also, note whether the two variables have a cumulative effect on support for national spending on crime. That is, are lower-class Blacks more likely to feel that the government is spending too little fighting crime than are upper-class Whites?

5. Examine the simultaneous impact of class and gender on support for national spending on welfare. The variable NATFARE represents the percentage of respondents who felt that the national government is spending too little on welfare. Before proceeding, designate the values indicated below as "missing" for each item. Then, run crosstabs, and request chi-square. Use your output to complete the summary table, and answer Question 6:

   Dependent variable—NATFARE (define 0, 8, and 9 as "missing")

   Independent variable 1—CLASS

   Independent variable 2—SEX

*(Continued)*

(Continued)

| | NATFARE | | | | |
|---|---|---|---|---|---|
| | Lower | Working | Middle | Upper | Sig. (chi-square) |
| Male | | | | | |
| Female | | | | | |

6. Summarize the major findings from the table. Explain the primary observations that can be made regarding the results of the analysis. You may want to note, for instance, the relationship between gender and support for government spending on welfare, as well as the relationship between class and support for government spending on welfare. Also, note whether the two variables have a cumulative effect on support for national spending on welfare. That is, are lower-class women more likely to feel that the government is spending too little on welfare than are upper-class men? In addition, be sure to discuss whether the findings are statistically significant.

Examine the simultaneous impact of two independent variables of your choice on support for the national government's spending on education (NATEDUC). Run crosstabs, request chi-square, and then answer the following questions and complete the summary table (use as many rows as necessary). Don't forget to define DK as "missing" for NATEDUC and the other variables you choose.

In addition, if you need to recode one or both of your independent variables, indicate how you did that in your response to Question 7.

7. List the two independent variables you chose. Describe how you recoded variables, if applicable.

8. Justify your choice of the two independent variables, and explain how you expect them to be related to NATEDUC.

9. NATEDUC: Percentage who feel that government is spending too little on education

| | NATEDUC | | | |
|---|---|---|---|---|
| | Too little | About right | Too much | Chi-square |
| | | | | |
| | | | | |

| | NATEDUC | | | |
|---|---|---|---|---|
| | Too little | About right | Too much | Chi-square |
| | | | | |
| | | | | |

10. Summarize your findings in detail below. Be sure to explain the primary observations that can be made regarding the table and discuss whether the findings are statistically significant.

11. Choose one dependent and two independent variables, and write the names of the variables you chose below.

Dependent variable _____

Independent variable 1 _____

Independent variable 2 _____

12. Write two hypotheses explaining the relationship between each independent variable and the dependent variable.

Hypothesis 1: _____

_____

Hypothesis 2: _____

_____

Examine the simultaneous impact of the two independent variables on the dependent variable. Run crosstabs with chi-square and an appropriate measure of association. Then, create a summary table below detailing the relationship (Question 14). Remember to define DKs as "missing." Also, if necessary, recode your variables, and indicate how you did that in the space below Question 15.

13. Measure of association _____

14. Summary table

(Continued)

(Continued)

15. Summarize your findings in detail below. Be sure to explain the primary observations that can be made regarding the table. Discuss the strength and, if possible, the direction of association. Also, indicate whether the findings are statistically significant and whether they support your hypotheses.

If necessary, recode RACE to create the dummy variable WHITE, similar to the way we did it in the chapter. Then, designate the following values as "missing":

EDUC (define 97–99 as missing)

AGE (define 98–99 as missing)

TVHOURS (define –1, 98–99 as missing)

Now, open the Linear Regression window, and designate TVHOURS as the dependent variable and EDUC, WHITE, and AGE as the independent variables.

16. What is the constant for the regression equation? _____

17. What are β (beta) values for the slopes of each variable?

    EDUC _____; WHITE _____; AGE _____

18. Fill in the blanks to create a prediction equation for TVHOURS.

    TVHOURS = _____ + (EDUC × _____) + (WHITE × _____) + (AGE × _____)

19. How many hours per day would you predict that a 25-year-old White high school graduate would watch TV?

20. How many hours per day would you predict that a 48-year-old non-White college graduate would watch TV?

21. Which of the three independent variables is most strongly related to TVHOURS? Explain the logic of your choice.

22. Of the three independent variables in the regression equation, which are (is) statistically significant? How do you know?

23. What PRE measure is given in the linear regression output? _____ What is its value in this case? _____ Interpret the meaning of that value for the relationship between these variables.

# DISSECTING THE
# POLITICAL FACTOR

In Chapter 11, we began exploring some of the causes of political philosophies and party identification. Now you are equipped to dig more deeply. Let's start with the relationship between political philosophy and party identification. As you'll recall, our earlier analysis showed a definite relationship, although it was not altogether consistent. Perhaps we can clarify it.

## POLITICAL PHILOSOPHY AND PARTY IDENTIFICATION

On the whole, Democrats in our sample were more liberal than independents or Republicans. Also, Republicans were the most conservative, although there wasn't as large a distinction between Democrats and independents as you might have expected. Here's the basic table from Chapter 11 examining the relationship between political philosophy (POLREC) and party identification (PARTY).[1]

### POLREC Recoded POLVIEWS *
### PARTY Political Party Crosstabulation

| | | | PARTY Political Party | | | | |
| --- | --- | --- | --- | --- | --- | --- | --- |
| | | | 1 Democrat | 2 Independent | 3 Republican | 4 Other | Total |
| POLREC Recoded POLVIEWS | 1 Liberal | Count | 234 | 151 | 21 | 5 | 411 |
| | | % within PARTY Political Party | 49.3% | 26.3% | 6.1% | 16.1% | 28.8% |
| | 2 Moderate | Count | 165 | 264 | 71 | 14 | 514 |
| | | % within PARTY Political Party | 34.7% | 45.9% | 20.6% | 45.2% | 36.1% |
| | 3 Conservative | Count | 76 | 160 | 252 | 12 | 500 |
| | | % within PARTY Political Party | 16.0% | 27.8% | 73.3% | 38.7% | 35.1% |
| Total | | Count | 475 | 575 | 344 | 31 | 1425 |
| | | % within PARTY Political Party | 100.0% | 100.0% | 100.0% | 100.0% | 100.0% |

---

1. In Chapter 7, we recoded the variables POLVIEWS and PARTYID to create POLREC and PARTY, respectively.

For purposes of this analysis, let's focus on the percentages of those who identified themselves as conservative. In the table above, the percentage difference separating the Democrats and Republicans calling themselves conservative amounts to 57 points. You'll recall from Chapter 10, perhaps, that percentage differences are sometimes designated by the Greek letter *epsilon* (ε).

# DEMONSTRATION 18.1: CONTROLLING FOR EDUCATION

If you were to undertake a study of the political party platforms and/or the speeches of political leaders from the two major parties, you would conclude that Democrats are, in fact, somewhat more liberal than Republicans and that Republicans are, in fact, somewhat more conservative than Democrats. If the relationship between political philosophy and party identification is not as clear as we might like, then perhaps some of the respondents simply don't know how the two parties are generally regarded.

Who do you suppose would be the least likely to know the philosophical leanings of the two parties? Perhaps those with the least education would be unaware of them. If that were the case, then we should expect a clearer relationship between political philosophy and party identification among the more educated respondents than among the less educated.

Why don't you open your DEMOPLUS.SAV file and run the SPSS Statistics command that lets you create the following three-variable summary table?[2]

|  | Percentage Saying They Are Conservative | | | | |
|---|---|---|---|---|---|
|  | Less Than High School | High School Graduate | Some College | College Graduate | Graduate Studies |
| Democrat | 34% | 17% | 12% | 16% | 9% |
| Independent | 27% | 32% | 24% | 29% | 28% |
| Republican | 76% | 63% | 73% | 82% | 83% |
| Democrat–Republican Epsilon (ε) | 42 | 46 | 61 | 66 | 74 |

The clearest relationship between party and political philosophy appears among those with the highest levels of education (some college, college graduates, and postcollege education). Among those with relatively high levels of education, the epsilon between Democrats and Republicans is 61 among those with some college, 66 among college graduates, and 74 for those who have pursued graduate studies. However, Democrats and Republicans are separated by an epsilon of 46 percentage points among those who graduated high school and an epsilon of 42 percentage points among those with less than a high school education.

Independents at all but one education level (less than high school) say they are more conservative than Democrats but much less so than Republicans. So it seems like additional education leads to greater political polarization? Consider the category with the greatest epsilon: graduate studies. Perhaps the type of graduate degree one pursues has more to do with this than simply the pursuit of graduate studies itself? Or perhaps there is yet another explanation?

When we look at the relationship between two variables, such as political philosophy and party identification, among subgroups determined by some other variable, such as education, we often say that we are ***controlling for a third variable***.

Social scientists use the expression "controlling for" in the sense of creating controlled conditions: only college graduates, only those with some college, and so on. We also speak of "holding education

---

2. To construct this summary table, run crosstabs with column percentages, specifying EDCAT as the column (independent) variable, POLREC as the row (dependent) variable, and PARTY as the control variable.

constant" in the sense that education is no longer a variable (it is a ***constant***) when we look at only one educational group at a time.

Why don't you experiment with this logic, testing the generalizability of the relationship between political philosophy and party identification among other subgroups formed by holding other variables constant?

# DEMONSTRATION 18.2: THE MYSTERY OF POLITICS AND MARITAL STATUS

In Chapter 11, we encouraged you to explore the relationship between marital status and politics. If you took us up on the invitation, you should have found an interesting relationship between marital status and political philosophy.

## Recoding MARITAL

Because relatively few respondents were "Separated," we should combine them with some other group. It would seem to make sense to combine the separated with the divorced, reasoning that separation is often experienced as an interim step toward divorce.

Let's recode MARITAL into a new variable, MARITAL2, with **Transform → Recode → Into Different Variables**.

Once in the Recode window, you should enter **MARITAL** as the "Input Variable" and **MARITAL2** as the "Output Variable." Click on **Change** to move MARITAL2 to the recode list. Then, in the Old and New Values window, recode as follows:

| Old Variable MARITAL | | New Variable MARITAL2 | |
|---|---|---|---|
| Values | | Values | Labels |
| 1 | → | 1 | Married |
| 2 | → | 2 | Widowed |
| 3 to 4 | → | 3 | Divorced/Separated |
| 5 | → | 4 | Never Married |

Don't forget to use **Add** to record the instructions. Then, you can **Continue** and **OK** your way to the recoded variable.

Before we move on, make sure you set the decimal places for your new variable to 0 and define the values and labels for MARITAL2 to prevent confusion among the categories in the following analyses.

## POLREC by MARITAL2

Now, create a crosstab with POLREC as the column variable and MARITAL2 as the row variable. Ask SPSS Statistics for column percentages and chi-square. The top two figures on page 336 show what you should get.

The chi-square test of statistical significance shows that this relationship is statistically significant. So why are married and widowed respondents more conservative than others? Similarly, why is it that those who have never been married are most likely to be liberal? Your multivariate skills will allow you to explore this matter in more depth than was possible before.

## POLREC by MARITAL2 by AGECAT

Perhaps age is the key. Perhaps those who have never been married tend to be more liberal because they also tend to be younger. At the bottom of the next page is a summary table created from the results of the crosstab of POLREC by MARITAL2 by AGECAT. See if you can duplicate this yourself.

## POLREC Recoded POLVIEWS * MARITAL2 Recoded Marital Crosstabulation

| | | | MARITAL2 Recoded Marital | | | | |
| | | | 1 Married | 2 Widowed | 3 Divorced/ separated | 4 Never married | Total |
|---|---|---|---|---|---|---|---|
| POLREC Recoded POLVIEWS | 1 Liberal | Count | 179 | 29 | 79 | 129 | 416 |
| | | % within MARITAL2 Recoded Marital | 28.6% | 21.6% | 25.6% | 34.8% | 28.9% |
| | 2 Moderate | Count | 196 | 52 | 127 | 144 | 519 |
| | | % within MARITAL2 Recoded Marital | 31.4% | 38.8% | 41.2% | 38.8% | 36.1% |
| | 3 Conservative | Count | 250 | 53 | 102 | 98 | 503 |
| | | % within MARITAL2 Recoded Marital | 40.0% | 39.6% | 33.1% | 26.4% | 35.0% |
| Total | | Count | 625 | 134 | 308 | 371 | 1438 |
| | | % within MARITAL2 Recoded Marital | 100.0% | 100.0% | 100.0% | 100.0% | 100.0% |

## Chi-Square Tests

| | Value | df | Asymptotic Significance (2-sided) |
|---|---|---|---|
| Pearson Chi-Square | 28.558[a] | 6 | .000 |
| Likelihood Ratio | 29.128 | 6 | .000 |
| Linear-by-Linear Association | 12.641 | 1 | .000 |
| N of Valid Cases | 1438 | | |

a. 0 cells (0.0%) have expected count less than 5. The minimum expected count is 38.76.

| | Percentage Who Say They Are Conservative | | | |
| | Married | Widowed | Divorced/ Separated | Never Married |
|---|---|---|---|---|
| Under 21 | — | — | — | 33% |
| 21 to 39 | 34% | — | 29% | 24% |
| 40 to 64 | 41% | — | 33% | 30% |
| 65 and older | 46% | 43% | 37% | — |

While there are a number of cells with too few cases to include in the analysis, this table does help clarify matters somewhat. The married are somewhat more conservative than those who are divorced/separated or never married. The difference seems to be lesser at older ages.

## POLREC by MARITAL2 by SEX

How about sex? Perhaps it can shed some light on this relationship. Why don't you run the tables that would result in this summary?

| | Percentage Who Say They Are Conservative | | | |
|---|---|---|---|---|
| | Married | Widowed | Divorced/Separated | Never Married |
| Men | 47% | 44% | 39% | 24% |
| Women | 34% | 38% | 28% | 29% |

As before, the married remain relatively conservative, and the divorced and never married remain less conservative. This holds true for men and women. Men are more likely to be conservative in all categories except "never married," where women are more likely to be conservative.

## POLREC by MARITAL2 by EDCAT

To pursue this further, you might want to consider education. Here's the summary table you should generate if you follow this avenue.

| | Percentage Who Say They Are Conservative | | | |
|---|---|---|---|---|
| | Married | Widowed | Divorced/Separated | Never Married |
| Less than high school | 41% | 35% | 36% | 35% |
| High school graduate | 39% | 49% | 29% | 29% |
| Some college | 38% | 42% | 38% | 20% |
| College graduate | 45% | 44% | 40% | 31% |
| Graduate studies + | 38% | — | 25% | — |

Here, we seem to have dug a dry well. Education does not seem to clarify the relationship we first observed between marital status and political philosophy. This is the point in an analysis where you sometimes wonder if you should ever have considered this line of inquiry.

## POLREC by MARITAL2 by RACE

See what happens when we introduce race as a control. It, too, provides no additional insight for our analysis.

| | Percentage Who Say They Are Conservative | | | |
|---|---|---|---|---|
| | Married | Widowed | Divorced/Separated | Never Married |
| White | 43 | 45 | 34 | 28 |
| Black | 30 | — | 35 | 21 |
| Other | 26 | — | — | 28 |

## POLREC as Independent Variable

When we consistently fail to find a clear answer to a question—Why do people of different marital statuses differ in their political philosophies?—it is sometimes useful to reconsider the question itself. Thus far, we have been asking why marital status would affect political philosophy. Perhaps we have the question reversed.

What if political philosophy affects marital status? Is that a possibility? Perhaps those who are politically conservative are also socially conservative. Maybe it would be especially important for them to form and keep traditional families. During the past few presidential elections, the political conservatives made "traditional family values" a centerpiece of their campaigns. Let's see what the table would look like if we percentaged it in the opposite direction. (Hint: Place POLREC as the column variable and MARITAL2 as the row variable this time.)

## MARITAL2 Recoded Marital * POLREC Recoded POLVIEWS Crosstabulation

| | | | POLREC Recoded POLVIEWS | | | |
|---|---|---|---|---|---|---|
| | | | 1 Liberal | 2 Moderate | 3 Conservative | Total |
| MARITAL2 Recoded Marital | 1 Married | Count | 179 | 196 | 250 | 625 |
| | | % within POLREC Recoded POLVIEWS | 43.0% | 37.8% | 49.7% | 43.5% |
| | 2 Widowed | Count | 29 | 52 | 53 | 134 |
| | | % within POLREC Recoded POLVIEWS | 7.0% | 10.0% | 10.5% | 9.3% |
| | 3 Divorced/ separated | Count | 79 | 127 | 102 | 308 |
| | | % within POLREC Recoded POLVIEWS | 19.0% | 24.5% | 20.3% | 21.4% |
| | 4 Never married | Count | 129 | 144 | 98 | 371 |
| | | % within POLREC Recoded POLVIEWS | 31.0% | 27.7% | 19.5% | 25.8% |
| Total | | Count | 416 | 519 | 503 | 1438 |
| | | % within POLREC Recoded POLVIEWS | 100% | 100.0% | 100.0% | 100.0% |

Notice that, again, the chi-square value is statistically significant and, in fact, identical to when we ran this analysis with the variables in the reverse order.

Look at the first row in the crosstab table. The percentage married increases steadily with increasing conservatism across the table. Singlehood, on the other hand, decreases just as steadily. Perhaps marital status is more profitably seen as a dependent variable in this context—affected to some extent by worldviews such as those reflected in political philosophy.

## Chi-Square Tests

| | Value | df | Asymptotic Significance (2-sided) |
|---|---|---|---|
| Pearson Chi-Square | 28.558[a] | 6 | .000 |
| Likelihood Ratio | 29.128 | 6 | .000 |
| Linear-by-Linear Association | 12.641 | 1 | .000 |
| N of Valid Cases | 1438 | | |

a. 0 cells (0.0%) have expected count less than 5. The minimum expected count is 38.76.

Sometimes, the direction of a relationship—which is the dependent and which is the independent variable—is clear. If we discover that voting behavior is related to gender, for instance, we can be sure that gender can affect voting, but how you vote can't change your gender. In other situations, such as the present one, the direction of a relationship is somewhat ambiguous. Ultimately, this decision must be based on theoretical reasoning. There is no way that the analysis of data can determine which variable is dependent and which is independent.

If you wanted to pursue the present relationship, you might treat marital status as a dependent variable, subjecting its relationship with political philosophies to a multivariate analysis. Try, for instance, rerunning the crosstab, using AGECAT as a control variable. After you examine your output, compare your findings with those in Writing Box 18.1.

## WRITING BOX 18.1

Age has confirmed the original relationship between political orientations and marital status. Among those in each of the age categories, conservatives are consistently more likely to be married than liberals. It is also worth remembering that the youngest respondents (those 21 and under) are most likely never to have been married.

Now, why don't you continue your analysis using SEX, EDCAT, and RACE as control variables? When you are done, create your own summary as we did in the writing box.

## POLITICAL ISSUES

In Chapter 11, we began looking for the causes of opinions on two political issues: GUNLAW (registration of firearms) and CAPPUN (capital punishment). Now that you have the ability to undertake a multivariate analysis, you can delve more deeply into the causes of public opinion. Let's think a little about capital punishment for a moment. Here are some variables that might logically affect how people feel about the death penalty.

POLREC and PARTY are obvious candidates. Liberals are generally more opposed to capital punishment than are conservatives. Similarly, Republicans have tended to support it more than have Democrats. You might check to see how these two variables work together on death penalty attitudes.

Given that capital punishment involves the taking of a human life, you might expect some religious effects. How do the various religious affiliations relate to support for or opposition to capital punishment? What about belief in an afterlife? Do those who believe in life after death find it easier to support the taking of a life? How do religious and political factors interact in this arena? Those opposed to capital punishment base their opposition on the view that it is wrong to take a human life. The same argument is made by those who oppose abortion. Logically, you would expect those opposed to abortion also to oppose capital punishment. Why don't you check it out? You may be surprised by what you find.

Another approach to understanding opinions about capital punishment might focus on which groups in society are most likely to be victims of it. Men are more likely to be executed than are women. Blacks are often executed disproportionately in comparison with their numbers in the population.

# CONCLUSION

These few suggestions should launch you on an extended exploration of the nature of political orientations. Whereas people often speak casually about political matters, you are now in a position to check out the facts and begin to understand why people feel as they do about political issues. Multivariate analysis techniques let you uncover some of the complexities that can make human behavior difficult to understand.

## Main Points

- You can use your multivariate analysis skills to delve into the nature of political orientation.

- We began by exploring the relationship between political philosophy and party identification while controlling for education.

- You can test the generalizability of the relationship between two items by controlling for a third variable or holding a third variable constant.

- The direction of the relationship between variables (which is the dependent and which is the independent) is not always clear.

- In exploring the relationship between political philosophy and marital status, we took turns examining both as the independent variable.

- We discovered that marital status is perhaps better seen as the dependent variable in this context.

- You can use your multivariate analysis skills to discover why people hold the opinions they do on volatile political issues such as gun control and capital punishment.

## Key Terms

Constant 335

Controlling for a third variable 334

## SPSS Statistics Commands Introduced in This Chapter

No new commands were introduced in this chapter.

## Review Questions

1. What does it mean to "control" for a third variable?

2. Is this the same as or different from "holding a variable constant"?

3. If we wanted to instruct SPSS Statistics to create crosstabs examining the relationship between POLREC and PARTY while controlling for SEX, where in the Crosstabs window would we transfer SEX (i.e., to which field: "Row[s]," "Column[s]," or the third box near the bottom of the window)?

4. In examining the relationship between political philosophy and party identification, what other variables (besides sex and education) might you want to control for? Name at least two.

5. When conducting a multivariate analysis, how do we ultimately know which variable is the dependent one and which is the independent one?

6. If we were performing a multivariate analysis and found a relationship between RACE and voting behavior, could RACE be the dependent variable? Why, or why not?

7. Name three variables from your data set that you think may logically affect or have an impact on how people feel about gun control (GUNLAW), and explain why.

# SPSS Statistics Lab Exercise 18.1

NAME: _____

CLASS: _____

INSTRUCTOR: _____

DATE: _____

*To complete the following exercises, you need to load the data file EXERPLUS.SAV.*

Designate 0 and 6 to 9 as "missing" for RACWORK. Then, recode the variable to create RACWORK2:

| RACWORK | | RACWORK2 | |
|---|---|---|---|
| Old Values | | New Values | Labels |
| 1 to 2 | → | 1 | Mostly White |
| 3 | → | 2 | Half White, Half Black |
| 4 to 5 | → | 3 | Mostly Black |

Now, use crosstabs to examine the relationship between RACWORK2 (recoded RACWORK) and AFFREC (recoded AFFRMACT). *(We recoded AFFRMACT to create AFFREC in SPSS Statistics Lab Exercise 15.1. If you did not save AFFREC to your EXERPLUS.SAV file, refer to the recoding instructions in Chapter 15 before proceeding.)* Designate RACWORK2 as the column variable and AFFREC as the row variable, and request column percentages and chi-square. Then, use your output to answer the questions below.

1. The table shows that those who work mostly with Whites are _____ [more likely/ less likely/not any more or less likely] than those who work mostly with Blacks to support affirmative action.

2. The significance of chi-square is _____ [less than/more than] .05, so the relationship between AFFREC and RACWORK2 _____ [is/is not] statistically significant.

3. List three variables from the data file EXERPLUS.SAV that you want to use to examine why those who work with mostly Whites are less supportive of affirmative action than are those who work with mostly Blacks.

   Variable 1: _____

   Variable 2: _____

   Variable 3: _____

4. Justify your choice of Variable 1 above (i.e., give theoretical reasons for choosing this variable).



5. Justify your choice of Variable 2 above (i.e., give theoretical reasons for choosing this variable).

*(Continued)*

(Continued)

6. Justify your choice of Variable 3 above (i.e., give theoretical reasons for choosing this variable).

7. Examine the relationship between AFFREC and RACWORK2 while controlling for Variable 1 above. Run crosstabs with chi-square. If you had to recode Variable 1, make sure you explain how you did that. Then, create a summary table based on the results of your crosstab, and show it below. (If you need help creating a summary table, see the tables in the chapter for guidance.)

8. Summarize below the major findings from your table. Explain what, in your view, are the primary observations that can be made regarding the table. Be sure to note, for instance, whether the findings support your expectations. Use chi-square as a criterion for judging whether the differences in your table are significant. (If your findings are statistically significant, you may want to go back and measure the strength of the relationship and then discuss how you did that and what you found.)

9. Examine the relationship between AFFREC and RACWORK2 while controlling for Variable 2 above. Run crosstabs with chi-square. If you had to recode Variable 2, make sure you explain how you did that. Then, create a summary table based on the results of your crosstab, and show it below.

10. Summarize the major findings from your table. Explain what, in your view, are the primary observations that can be made regarding the table. Be sure to note, for instance, whether the findings support your expectations. Use chi-square as a criterion for judging whether the differences in your table are significant. (If your findings are statistically significant, you may want to go back and measure the strength of the relationship and then discuss how you did that and what you found.)

11. Examine the relationship between AFFREC and RACWORK2 while controlling for Variable 3 above. Run crosstabs with chi-square. If you had to recode Variable 3, make sure you explain how you did that. Then, create a summary table based on the results of your crosstab, and show it below.

12. Summarize the major findings from your table below. Explain what, in your view, are the primary observations that can be made regarding the table. Be sure to note, for instance, whether the findings support your expectations. Use chi-square as a criterion for judging whether the differences in your table are significant. (If your findings are statistically significant, you may want to go back and measure the strength of the relationship and then discuss how you did that and what you found.)

# A POWERFUL PREDICTION OF ATTITUDES TOWARD ABORTION

In previous analyses, we've seen how complex attitudes about abortion are. As we return to our analysis of this controversial topic, you have additional tools for digging deeper. Let's begin with the religious factor. Then, we'll turn to politics and other variables.

## RELIGION AND ABORTION

In Chapter 12, we found that both religious affiliation and measures of religiosity were related to abortion attitudes. The clearest relationships were observed in terms of the unconditional right to abortion because only a small minority are opposed to abortion in all circumstances.

Protestants and Catholics are generally less supportive of abortion than are Jews and "nones." And on measures of religiosity, opposition to abortion increases with increasing religiosity. The most religious are the most opposed to a woman's right to choose an abortion.

With your multivariate skills, you can examine this issue more deeply. Consider the possibility, for example, that one of these relationships is an artifact of the other. A variable is an artifact of another if it is a direct structural result of the other variable. In this case, it may be that a person's religion directly and necessarily causes that person to hold particular beliefs about abortion.

## DEMONSTRATION 19.1: RELIGIOUS AFFILIATION AND CHURCH ATTENDANCE

To explore the possibility that one of the relationships we found in Chapter 12 is merely an artifact of another association, you can begin by opening your DEMOPLUS.SAV file and examining the relationship between religious affiliation (RELIG) and church attendance (CHATT).[1]

Remember to request cells be percentaged by column (see figures on p. 348).

The chart at the top of p. 349 shows what SPSS Statistics will produce for you.

As you can see, there is a relationship between these two variables. Protestants and Catholics are the most likely to attend worship services weekly. Not surprisingly, about 94% of those with no religious affiliation attend religious services seldom or never.

---

1. For RELIG, the values 0 and 5 to 99 should be defined as "missing."

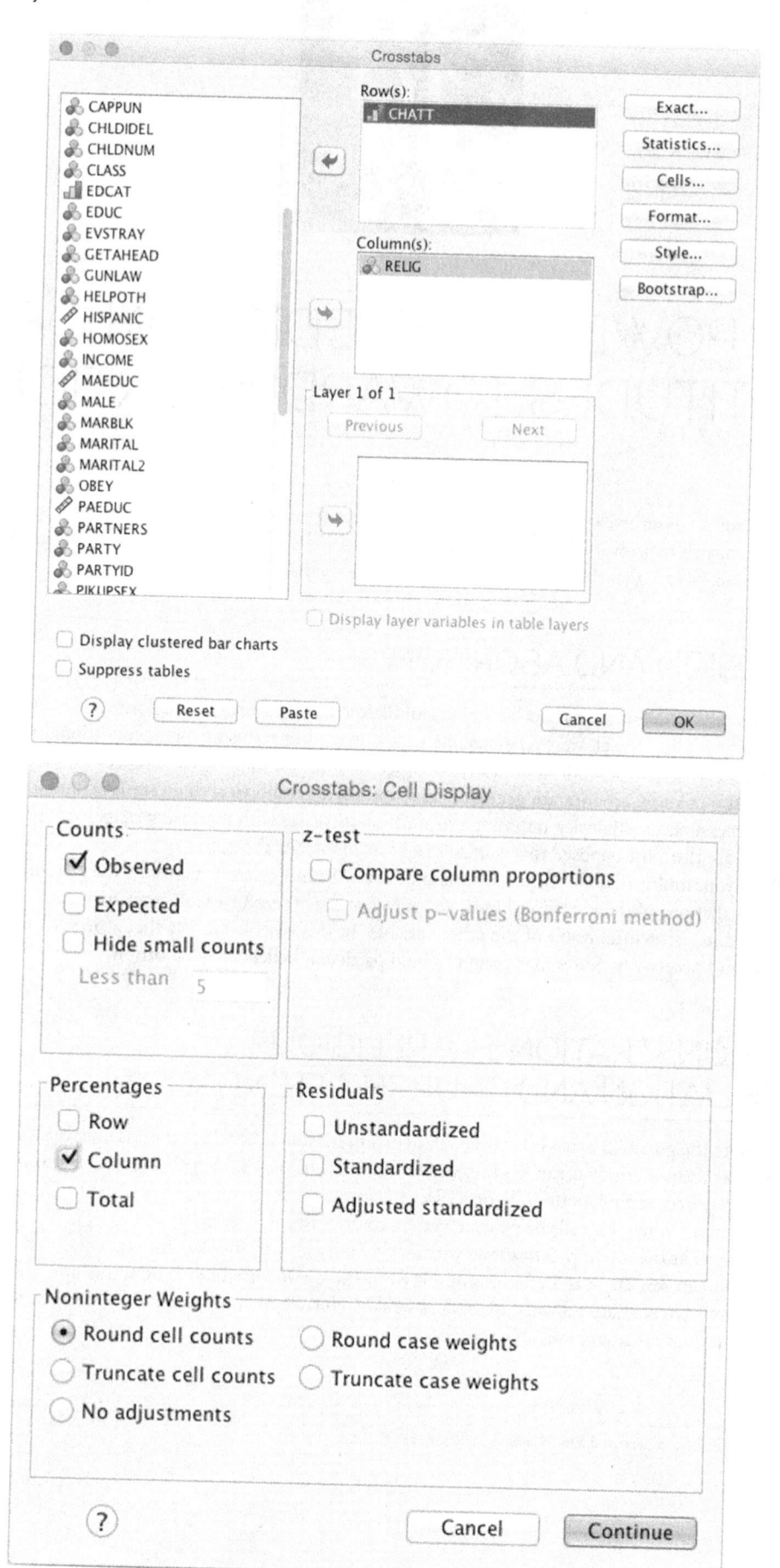

## CHATT Recoded Church Attendance * RELIG R's
## Religious Preference Crosstabulation

| | | | RELIG R's Religious Preference | | | | |
|---|---|---|---|---|---|---|---|
| | | | 1 PROTESTANT | 2 CATHOLIC | 3 JEWISH | 4 NONE | Total |
| CHATT Recoded Church Attendance | 1 About weekly | Count | 288 | 109 | 2 | 8 | 407 |
| | | % within RELIG R's religious preference | 39.5% | 31.4% | 8.3% | 2.7% | 29.1% |
| | 2 About monthly | Count | 139 | 68 | 4 | 12 | 223 |
| | | % within RELIG R's religious preference | 19.0% | 19.6% | 16.7% | 4.0% | 16.0% |
| | 3 Seldom | Count | 203 | 124 | 8 | 88 | 423 |
| | | % within RELIG R's religious preference | 27.8% | 35.7% | 33.3% | 30% | 30.3% |
| | 4 Never | Count | 100 | 46 | 10 | 189 | 345 |
| | | % within RELIG R's religious preference | 13.7% | 13.3% | 41.7% | 64% | 24.7% |
| Total | | Count | 730 | 347 | 24 | 297 | 1398 |
| | | % within RELIG R's religious preference | 100.0% | 100.0% | 100.0% | 100.0% | 100.0% |

If we combine the two most frequent categories, we see that more than half of the whole sample attend church at least monthly. There are big differences, however, among the four religious groups.

| | Percentage Who Attend at Least Monthly |
|---|---|
| Protestants | 59% |
| Catholics | 51% |
| Jews | 25% |
| None | 7% |

# DEMONSTRATION 19.2: RELIGIOUS AFFILIATION, CHURCH ATTENDANCE, AND ABORTION

Because religious affiliation and church attendance are related to each other and each is related to abortion attitudes, there are two possibilities for us to explore. For example, perhaps church attendance seems to affect abortion attitudes only because Protestants and Catholics (relatively opposed to abortion) attend more often. Or conversely, perhaps Protestants and Catholics seem more opposed to abortion simply because they attend church more often, and church attendance drives abortion attitudes.

We can test for these possibilities by running a multivariate table, taking account of all three variables.

## Recoding RELIG and ATTEND Into Different Variables

To simplify our analysis, let's recode RELIG into two categories—"Christians" and "None," those respondents expressing no religious preference. While it would be interesting to compare Christians with those with other religious preferences, Christians (Protestants plus Catholics) and those responding "None" have sufficient numbers of cases for meaningful analysis. We will then recode ATTEND into two categories as well. We will recode the variables into the creatively named new variables RELIG2 and ATTEND2. So let's use **Transform → Recode → Into Different Variables**.

Make the recodes listed below, beginning with **RELIG** and then moving to **ATTEND**. Once you have recoded the items, access the **Variable View** tab, and label your recoded variables. If you need to verify the process for recoding into different variables, consult SPSS Statistics Command 19.1.[2]

| Recode RELIG | | | |
|---|---|---|---|
| Old Values | | New Values | Labels |
| 1 to 2 | → | 1 | Christian |
| 3 | → | System-missing | — |
| 4 | → | 2 | None |
| Recode ATTEND | | | |
| Old Values | | New Values | Labels |
| 4 to 8 | → | 1 | Often |
| 0 to 3 | → | 2 | Seldom |

---

## SPSS Statistics Command 19.1: Recoding Into Different Variables

**Transform → Recode → Into Different Variables**

→ Highlight variable name → Click right-pointing arrow to move variable to "Numeric Variable → Output Variable:" field

→ Click **Old and New Values** → Define Old and New Values in the Recode Into Different Variables: Old and New dialog box

→ Click **Add** to change Old → New Values

→ Click **Continue → OK**

Click **Variable View** tab → Click right side of area that corresponds to recoded variable name and labels → Add new labels

---

2. Previously, we declared all cases except those coded Protestant, Catholic, Jew, and None as missing. Now, we are going to collapse Protestants and Catholics into a category named "Christian." Jewish respondents are being declared missing because they are too few for meaningful analysis. The code for "None" (4) is being changed to 2 simply to keep the code categories contiguous.

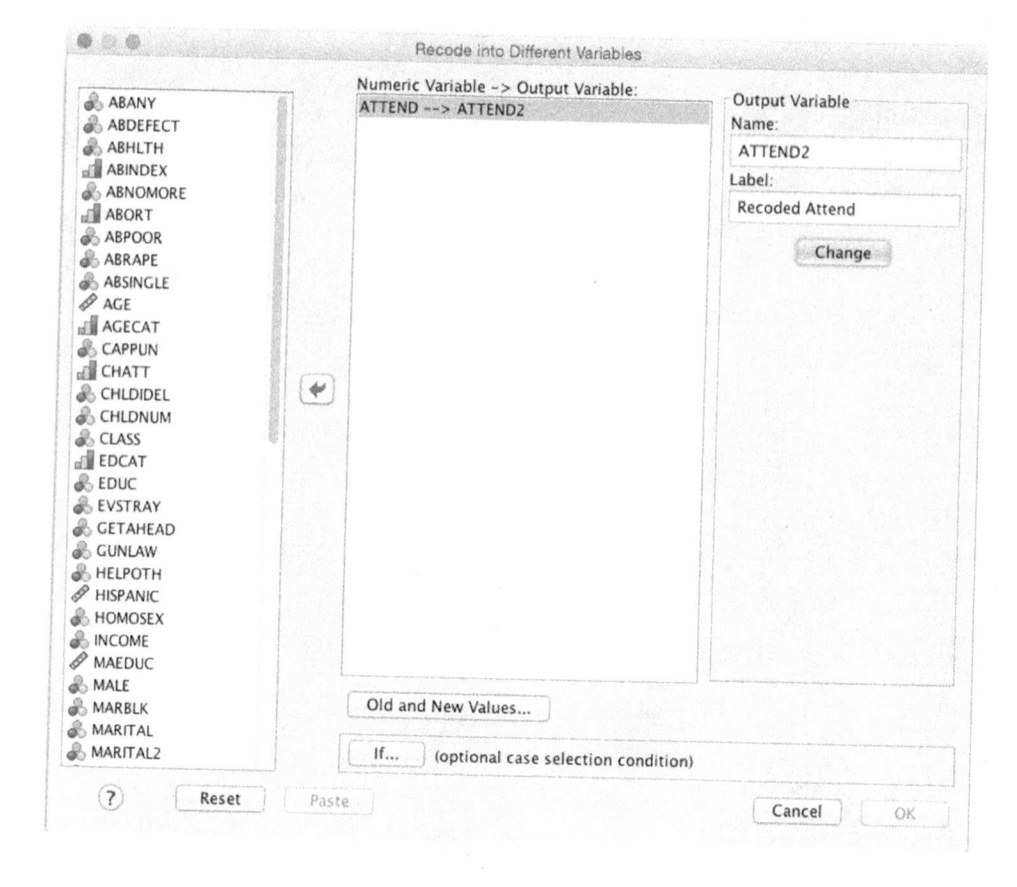

## Crosstab Recoded Variables

Now, run a crosstab with column percentages. Designate ATTEND2 as the row variable and RELIG2 as the column variable.

### ATTEND2 Recoded Attend * RELIG2 Recoded RELIG Crosstabulation

| | | | RELIG2 Recoded RELIG | | |
| --- | --- | --- | --- | --- | --- |
| | | | 1 Christian | 2 None | Total |
| ATTEND2 Recoded Attend | 1 Often | Count | 604 | 20 | 624 |
| | | % within RELIG2 Recoded RELIG | 56.1% | 6.7% | 45.4% |
| | 2 Seldom | Count | 473 | 277 | 750 |
| | | % within RELIG2 Recoded RELIG | 43.9% | 93.3% | 54.6% |
| Total | | Count | 1077 | 297 | 1374 |
| | | % within RELIG2 Recoded RELIG | 100.0% | 100.0% | 100.0% |

As you can see, the relationship between religious affiliation and church attendance is still obvious after categories are collapsed on both variables.

Now, let's review the relationships between each variable and abortion, again using the recoded variables.

## Relationship Between ABORT and Recoded Items

Notice that the relationship between affiliation and abortion is now represented by an epsilon of 34 percentage points. The relationship between church attendance and abortion has an epsilon of 33 percentage points. At this point, these findings seem to suggest that each independent variable may itself influence abortion attitudes.

### ABORT Simple Abortion Index * RELIG2 Recoded RELIG Crosstabulation

| | | | RELIG2 Recoded RELIG | | |
| --- | --- | --- | --- | --- | --- |
| | | | 1 Christian | 2 None | Total |
| ABORT Simple Abortion Index | 0 Yes/Approve | Count | 230 | 129 | 359 |
| | | % within RELIG2 Recoded RELIG | 34.5% | 68.3% | 42.0% |
| | 1 Conditional Support | Count | 241 | 39 | 280 |
| | | % within RELIG2 Recoded RELIG | 36.2% | 20.6% | 32.7% |
| | 2 No/Disapprove | Count | 195 | 21 | 216 |
| | | % within RELIG2 Recoded RELIG | 29.3% | 11.1% | 25.3% |
| Total | | Count | 666 | 189 | 855 |
| | | % within RELIG2 Recoded RELIG | 100.0% | 100.0% | 100.0% |

## ABORT Simple Abortion Index * ATTEND2 Recoded ATTEND Crosstabulation

| | | | ATTEND2 Recoded ATTEND | | Total |
|---|---|---|---|---|---|
| | | | 1 Often | 2 Seldom | |
| ABORT Simple Abortion Index | 0 Yes/Approve | Count | 107 | 301 | 408 |
| | | % within ATTEND2 Recoded ATTEND | 25.7% | 58.7% | 43.9% |
| | 1 Conditional Support | Count | 154 | 145 | 299 |
| | | % within ATTEND2 Recoded ATTEND | 36.9% | 28.3% | 32.2% |
| | 2 No/Disapprove | Count | 156 | 67 | 223 |
| | | % within ATTEND2 Recoded ATTEND | 37.4% | 13.1% | 24.0% |
| Total | | Count | 417 | 513 | 930 |
| | | % within ATTEND2 Recoded ATTEND | 100.0% | 100.0% | 100.0% |

# POLITICS (POLREC, PARTY) AND ABORTION (ABORT)

As we saw in Chapter 12, political philosophies and party identification have a strong impact on attitudes toward abortion. You might want to refresh your memory by rerunning those tables. (You now know how. Wow!)

## ABORT Simple Abortion Index * POLREC Recoded POLVIEWS Crosstabulation

| | | | POLREC Recoded POLVIEWS | | | Total |
|---|---|---|---|---|---|---|
| | | | 1 Liberal | 2 Moderate | 3 Conservative | |
| ABORT Simple Abortion Index | 0 Yes/ Approve | Count | 173 | 141 | 87 | 401 |
| | | % within POLREC Recoded POLVIEWS | 65.8% | 43.1% | 28.3% | 44.7% |
| | 1 Conditional Support | Count | 57 | 116 | 111 | 284 |
| | | % within POLREC Recoded POLVIEWS | 21.7% | 35.5% | 36.2% | 31.7% |
| | 2 No/ Disapprove | Count | 33 | 70 | 109 | 212 |
| | | % within POLREC Recoded POLVIEWS | 12.5% | 21.4% | 35.5% | 23.6% |
| Total | | Count | 263 | 327 | 307 | 897 |
| | | % within POLREC Recoded POLVIEWS | 100.0% | 100.0% | 100.0% | 100.0% |

The impact of political philosophy on unconditional support for a woman's right to choose abortion results in an epsilon of 38 percentage points. As we saw earlier, however, political party identification—despite official party differences on the issue of abortion—has a smaller effect, showing a 23-percentage-point difference between Democrats and Republicans.

## ABORT Simple Abortion Index * PARTY Political Party Crosstabulation

| | | | PARTY Political Party | | | | Total |
|---|---|---|---|---|---|---|---|
| | | | 1 Democrat | 2 Independent | 3 Republican | 4 Other | |
| ABORT Simple Abortion Index | 0 Yes/ Approve | Count | 161 | 165 | 68 | 9 | 403 |
| | | % within PARTY Political Party | 52.4% | 45.0% | 29.4% | 47.4% | 43.6% |
| | 1 Conditional Support | Count | 89 | 113 | 91 | 6 | 299 |
| | | % within PARTY Political Party | 29.0% | 30.8% | 39.4% | 31.6% | 32.4% |
| | 2 No/ Disapprove | Count | 57 | 89 | 72 | 4 | 222 |
| | | % within PARTY Political Party | 18.6% | 24.3% | 31.2% | 21.1% | 24.0% |
| Total | | Count | 307 | 367 | 231 | 19 | 924 |
| | | % within PARTY Political Party | 100.0% | 100.0% | 100.0% | 100.0% | 100.0% |

# DEMONSTRATION 19.3: THE INTERACTION OF RELIGION AND POLITICS ON ABORTION ATTITUDES

In a multivariate analysis, we might next want to explore the possible interaction of religion and politics on abortion attitudes. For example, in Chapter 12, we found that Protestants and Catholics were somewhat more conservative than "nones." Perhaps their political orientations account for the differences that the religious groups have on the issue of abortion.

With your multivariate skills, testing this new possibility is a simple matter. Take a minute to figure out the SPSS Statistics command that would provide for such a test. Then, enter it, and review the results. (Hint: Run crosstabs with column percentages, POLREC as the column variable, ABORT as the row variable, and RELIG2 as the control/third variable.) Here's a summary table of the results you should find if you are working with the latest recode for RELIG2. Be sure you can replicate this on your own.

| | Percentage Who Support Right to Abortion (Simple Abortion Index) | | |
|---|---|---|---|
| | Liberal | Moderate | Conservative |
| Christian | 53% | 34% | 25% |
| None | 82% | 72% | 47% |
| Epsilon ($\varepsilon$) | 29 | 38 | 22 |

This table demonstrates the independent impact of religion and politics on abortion attitudes. In addition, what would you say it tells us about the religious effect observed earlier? Does it occur among all of the political groups? What, if anything, do the epsilons for each political group tell us about the religious effect?

Overall, you can see that the joint impact of politics and religion is represented by an epsilon of 57 percentage points (82–25), a rather powerful degree of prediction for opinions on this controversial issue.

# DEMONSTRATION 19.4: CONSTRUCTING AN INDEX OF IDEOLOGICAL TRADITIONALISM

To support our continued analysis, let's create an index to combine the religious and political factors. For the time being, we'll call it our "index of ideological traditionalism." You may recall from our earlier discussion that there are several ways to construct indices. In Chapter 8, we introduced you to a method using the Count command. In this chapter, we are going to introduce you to another method that uses the **Compute Variable command**.

As you are now aware, a number of steps are involved in creating an index. However, all the work is worth it because, in the end, we will have a composite measure that captures religious and political predisposition to support abortion. In other words, we will have built an index based on our two religious items (ATTEND2 and RELIG2) and one political item (POLREC) that allows us to predict attitudes toward abortion.

In this case, our index will range from 0 (traditional) to 4 (nontraditional). Before we begin constructing our new index of ideological traditionalism, which we will call IND, it may be useful to give you a brief overview of the seven steps.

*Step 1:*      Create new index, IND.

*Steps 2 to 5:*   Assign points on the index based on responses to the three component variables: POLREC, RELIG2, and ATTEND2. As noted, our index scores will run from 0 ("Opposed to abortion") to 4 ("Supportive of abortion"). We will assign points as follows:

*Step 2:*      If Liberal (1) on POLREC, get two points on IND.

*Step 3:*      If Moderate (2) on POLREC, get one point on IND.

*Step 4:*      If None (2) on RELIG2, get one point on IND.

*Step 5:*      If Seldom (2) on ATTEND2, get one point on IND.

*Step 6:*      Use COMPUTE to handle missing data.

*Step 7:*      Access **Variable View** tab and define IND (e.g., decimals, labels, etc.).

Now that you have reviewed the steps involved in creating IND, let's go through each of the steps one at a time.

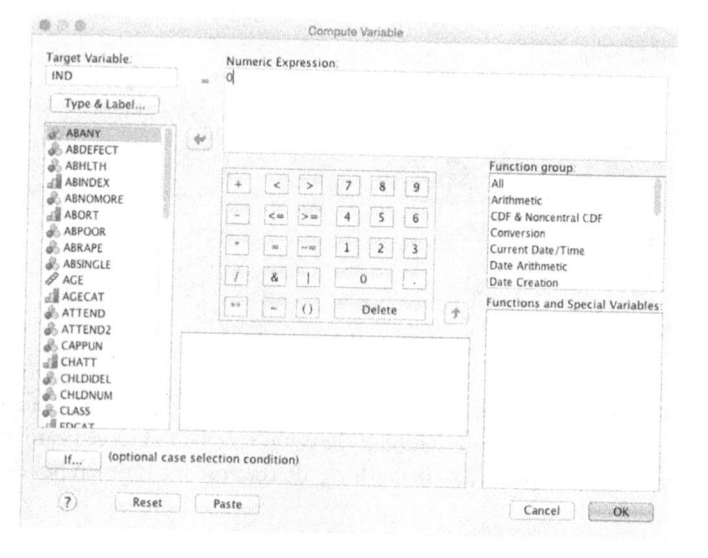

## Step 1: Create IND

To begin, select **Transform → Compute Variable**.

In the Compute Variable box, create a new "Target Variable:" called **IND** (for index). We'll start by giving everyone a 0, so type 0 or use the calculator pad to move 0 into the "Numeric Expression:" box. Your expression should now read "IND = 0," as shown in the figure at the bottom of the previous page.

Run this instruction by selecting **OK**.

## Step 2: Assign Points—If Liberal (1) on POLREC, Get Two Points on IND

Now, we are ready to begin assigning points on our index. Open the Compute Variable box once again by selecting **Transform → Compute Variable**.

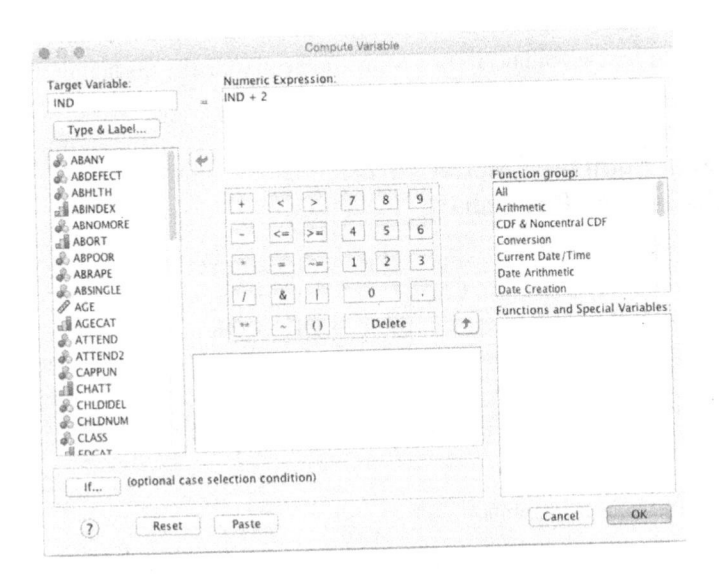

Let's begin by giving people two points if they have a 1 on POLREC (Liberal). To do this, change the "Numeric Expression" to **IND + 2**.

Now, click **If** at the bottom of the window, and in the Compute Variable: If Cases box, select the "Include if case satisfies condition:" option. Then, type or click **POLREC = 1** into the rectangular space, as shown below.

Run this instruction by selecting **Continue**, **OK**, and then **OK** again to change the existing variable IND. SPSS Statistics may ask whether you indeed wish to change the existing IND variable, as shown below. Click **OK**.

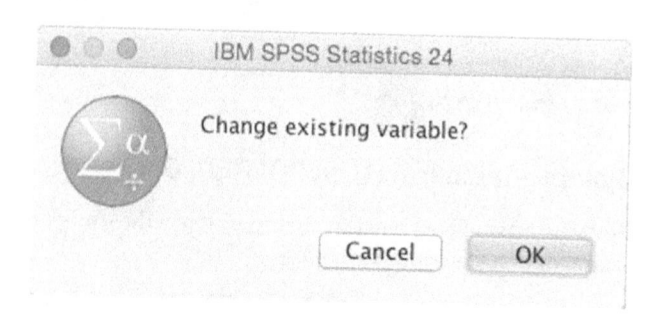

At this point, we have given liberals two points, and everyone else (including those with missing data) has zero points.

### Step 3: Assign Points—If Moderate (2) on POLREC, Get One Point on IND

Now, let's give the moderates one point on the index. Return to the Compute Variable window, and make the following two changes: Change the "Numeric Expression" to **IND + 1**. Change the "If" statement to **POLREC = 2**. Select **Continue → OK → OK** to run this instruction.

Thus far, we have established an index as follows:

- Liberals have two points.

- Moderates have one point.

- Conservatives have zero points.

- Those who are none of the above have zero points on the index.

You may want to look at IND in the Data window or run Frequencies anytime during this process to see how the index is shaping up.

### Step 4: Assign Points—If None (2) on RELIG2, Get One Point on IND

Now, we are ready to add to the index. Go back to the Compute Variable window, and enter the following specifications:

- Leave the "Numeric Expression" as **IND + 1**.

- Change the "If" statement to **RELIG2 = 2**.

Run this instruction by clicking **Continue → OK → OK**. Now, we've added one point for each respondent who indicated no religious preference.

### Step 5: Assign Points—If Seldom (2) on ATTEND2, Get One Point on IND

Finally, return to the Compute Variable window, and enter these specifications:

- Leave the "Numeric Expression" as **IND + 1**.

- Change the "If" statement to **ATTEND2 = 2**.

Run this expression, and review the logic of what we have done.

We've now created an index that presumably captures religious and political predispositions to support a woman's right to an abortion. Scores on the index run from 0 ("Opposed to abortion") to 4 ("Supportive of abortion").

## Step 6: Handle Missing Data

There is one glitch in this index that we need to correct before moving on: those respondents for whom we have missing data. We don't know about the religious behavior or political orientations of those respondents for whom data were missing for ATTEND2, POLREC, or RELIG2. Since we can't provide an index score for respondents we don't know about, we must eliminate them from our analysis.

We can do this easily by using the NMISS function in the Compute procedure to set any cases to $SYSMIS (system-missing) if they have missing information.

To do this, select **Transform → Compute Variable**, and then, follow these instructions:

- With IND in the "Target Variable:" box, type **$SYSMIS** in the "Numeric Expression:" field, as shown below.

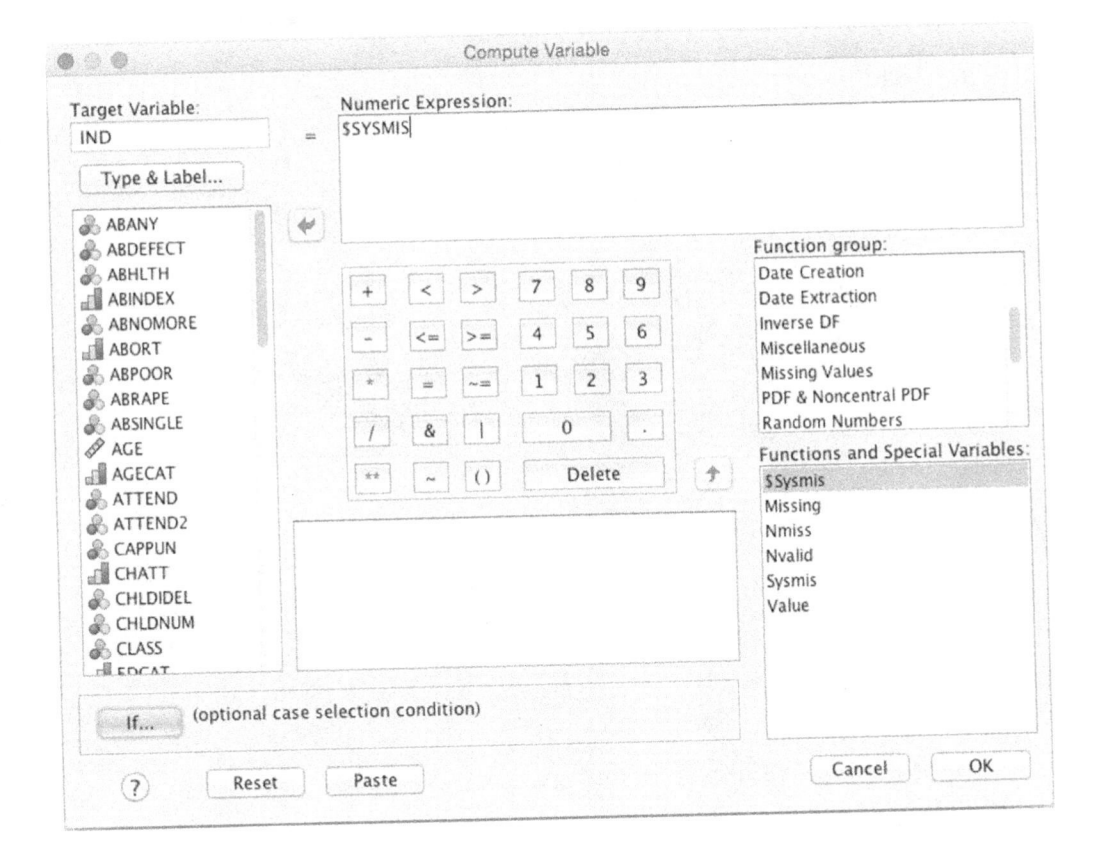

- Now click **If**.

- Click the button next to "Include if case satisfies condition."

- Type the following expression in the rectangular box: **NMISS(relig2, attend2, polrec) > 0**.

- Click **Continue → OK → OK**.

## Step 7: Define IND

All that remains (thankfully!) is to define our new index. You can do that by accessing the **Variable View** tab and setting the decimals, width, and values (remember, for this index, 0 = traditional and 4 = nontraditional).

| | Name | Type | Width | Decimals | Label | Values | Missing | Columns | Align | Measure | |
|---|---|---|---|---|---|---|---|---|---|---|---|
| 26 | PARTNERS | Numeric | 2 | 0 | How many sex partner's R had i... | (-1, IAP)... | -1, 98, 99 | 8 | Right | Nominal | |
| 27 | PARTYID | Numeric | 1 | 0 | Political party affiliation | (0, STRONG ... | 8, 9 | 8 | Right | Nominal | |
| 28 | PIKUPSEX | Numeric | 1 | 0 | R had sex with casual date last ... | (0, IAP)... | 0, 8, 9 | 8 | Right | Nominal | |
| 29 | POLVIEWS | Numeric | 1 | 0 | Think of self as liberal or conser... | (0, IAP)... | 0, 8, 9 | 8 | Right | Nominal | |
| 30 | POPULAR | Numeric | 1 | 0 | To be well liked or popular | (0, IAP)... | 0, 8, 9 | 8 | Right | Nominal | |
| 31 | POSTLIFE | Numeric | 1 | 0 | Belief in life after death | (0, IAP)... | 0, 8, 9 | 8 | Right | Nominal | |
| 32 | PRAY | Numeric | 1 | 0 | How often Does R pray | (0, IAP)... | 0, 8, 9 | 8 | Right | Nominal | |
| 33 | PREMARSX | Numeric | 1 | 0 | Sex before marriage | (0, IAP)... | 0, 8, 9 | 8 | Right | Nominal | |
| 34 | RACDIF4 | Numeric | 1 | 0 | Differences due to lack of will | (0, IAP)... | 0, 8, 9 | 8 | Right | Nominal | |
| 35 | RACE | Numeric | 1 | 0 | Race of respondent | (0, IAP)... | 0 | 8 | Right | Nominal | |
| 36 | RELIG | Numeric | 2 | 0 | R's religious preference | (0, IAP)... | 5 - 99, 0 | 8 | Right | Scale | |
| 37 | RINCOM16 | Numeric | 8 | 0 | Respondents income | (0, IAP)... | 27 - 99, 0 | 8 | Right | Nominal | |
| 38 | SEX | Numeric | 1 | 0 | Respondents sex | (1, MALE)... | 0 | 8 | Right | Nominal | |
| 39 | SEXFREQ | Numeric | 2 | 0 | Frequency of sex during last year | (-1, IAP)... | -1, 8, 9 | 8 | Right | Scale | |
| 40 | SIBS | Numeric | 2 | 0 | Number of brothers and sisters | (-1, IAP)... | -1, 98, 99 | 8 | Right | Nominal | |
| 41 | THNKSELF | Numeric | 1 | 0 | To think for ones self | (0, IAP)... | 0, 8, 9 | 8 | Right | Nominal | |
| 42 | WORKHARD | Numeric | 1 | 0 | To work hard | (0, IAP)... | 0, 8, 9 | 8 | Right | Nominal | |
| 43 | XMOVIE | Numeric | 1 | 0 | Seen x-rated movie in last year | (0, IAP)... | 0, 8, 9 | 8 | Right | Nominal | |
| 44 | CHATT | Numeric | 1 | 0 | Recoded Church Attendance | (1, About w... | None | 10 | Right | Ordinal | |
| 45 | AGECAT | Numeric | 1 | 0 | Recoded Age | (1, Under 2... | None | 10 | Right | Ordinal | |
| 46 | POLREC | Numeric | 1 | 0 | Recoded Polviews | (1, Liberall... | None | 10 | Right | Nominal | |
| 47 | PARTY | Numeric | 1 | 0 | Political Party | (1, Democra... | None | 10 | Right | Ordinal | |
| 48 | ABORT | Numeric | 1 | 0 | Simple Abortion Index | (0, Yes/App... | None | 10 | Right | Ordinal | |
| 49 | ABINDEX | Numeric | 1 | 0 | Six-item Abortion Index | (0, No Supp... | None | 10 | Right | Ordinal | |
| 50 | SEXPERM | Numeric | 1 | 0 | Sexual Permissiveness | (0, Non-per... | None | 10 | Right | Ordinal | |
| 51 | RACMAR | Numeric | 1 | 0 | Recoded MARBLK | (1, Yes/Opp... | None | 10 | Right | Ordinal | |
| 52 | PREJIND | Numeric | 1 | 0 | Prejudice Index | (0, Prejudic... | None | 10 | Right | Ordinal | |
| 53 | EDCAT | Numeric | 1 | 0 | Recoded Education Level | (1, Less tha... | None | 10 | Right | Scale | |
| 54 | RECINC | Numeric | 8 | 0 | Recoded R's Income | None | None | 10 | Right | Nominal | |
| 55 | CHLDNUM | Numeric | 1 | 0 | Recoded chldidel | (1, 0 to 2)... | None | 10 | Right | Nominal | |
| 56 | MALE | Numeric | 1 | 0 | Male Dummy Variable | None | None | 10 | Right | Nominal | |
| 57 | WHITE | Numeric | 1 | 0 | White Dummy Variable | None | None | 10 | Right | Nominal | |
| 58 | MARITAL2 | Numeric | 1 | 0 | Recoded Marital | (1, Married)... | None | 10 | Right | Nominal | |
| 59 | RELIG2 | Numeric | 1 | 0 | Recoded Relig | (1, Christia... | None | 10 | Right | Nominal | |
| 60 | ATTEND2 | Numeric | 1 | 0 | Recoded Attend | (1, Often)... | None | 10 | Right | Nominal | |
| 61 | IND | Numeric | 1 | 0 | Ideological Traditionalism Index | (0, Traditio... | None | 10 | Right | Nominal | |
| 62 | | | | | | | | | | | |

Data View    **Variable View**

IBM SPSS Statistics Processor is ready        Unicode:ON

---

## SPSS Statistics Command 19.2:
## Creating an Index Using Compute Variable

*Step 1: Create New Index*

Click **Transform → Compute Variable**

Type name of new index in "Target Variable:" field → Type/paste 0 in "Numeric Expression:" field

Click **OK**

*Step 2: Add Points to Index*

Click **Transform → Compute Variable**

Keep new index name in "Target Variable:" field → Begin assigning points by adding appropriate points to new variable (e.g., IND = #)

Click **If → Include if case satisfies condition** → Type/paste condition under which points should be added to new index (e.g., if respondent was liberal: POLREC = 1)

Click **Continue → OK → OK**

Repeat this step as many times as necessary until you have completed adding points to index.

*(Continued)*

(Continued)

*Step 3: Handle Missing Data*

Click **Transform → Compute Variable**

Keep new index name in "Target Variable:" field → Type **$SYSMIS** in "Numeric Expression:" field

Click **If → Include if case satisfies condition** → Type "**NMISS** (variable names that compose index) **→ 0**"

Click **Continue → OK → OK**

*Step 4: Define New Index*

Click **Variable View** tab → Set decimals, width, labels, etc.

## Run Frequencies to Check IND

Having created such an index, it is always good practice to check the frequencies. Run Frequencies on IND, and you should get this:

### IND Ideological Traditionalism Index

| | | Frequency | Percent | Valid Percent | Cumulative Percent |
|---|---|---|---|---|---|
| Valid | 0 Traditional | 265 | 17.7 | 20.0 | 20.0 |
| | 1 | 348 | 23.2 | 26.3 | 46.3 |
| | 2 | 389 | 25.9 | 29.4 | 75.7 |
| | 3 | 204 | 13.6 | 15.4 | 91.1 |
| | 4 Nontraditional | 118 | 7.9 | 8.9 | 100.0 |
| | Total | 1324 | 88.3 | 100.0 | |
| Missing | System | 176 | 11.7 | | |
| Total | | 1500 | 100.0 | | |

## Does IND Predict Attitudes Toward Abortion?

After all that work, let's finally see how well our index predicts abortion attitudes. To do this, run the table at the top of the next page.

As you can see, the index provides a very strong prediction of support for the unconditional right to an abortion, monotonically increasing from 16% to 82% for an epsilon of 66 percentage points. Let's see if we can improve on our ability to predict.

# SEXUAL ATTITUDES AND ABORTION

Earlier, we discovered that attitudes about various forms of sexual behavior were also related to abortion attitudes. As you'll recall, people were asked whether they felt that premarital sex and

## ABORT Simple Abortion Index * IND Ideological Traditionalism Index Crosstabulation

| | | | IND Ideological Traditionalism Index | | | | | |
|---|---|---|---|---|---|---|---|---|
| | | | 0 Traditional | 1 | 2 | 3 | 4 Non traditional | Total |
| ABORT Simple Abortion Index | 0 Yes/ Approve | Count | 26 | 71 | 102 | 88 | 65 | 352 |
| | | % within IND Ideological Traditionalism Index | 16.4% | 31.1% | 43.6% | 71.5% | 82.3% | 42.8% |
| | 1 Conditional Support | Count | 53 | 95 | 83 | 27 | 8 | 266 |
| | | % within IND Ideological Traditionalism Index | 33.3% | 41.7% | 35.5% | 22.0% | 10.1% | 32.3% |
| | 2 No/ Disapprove | Count | 80 | 62 | 49 | 8 | 6 | 205 |
| | | % within IND Ideological Traditionalism Index | 50.3% | 27.2% | 20.9% | 6.5% | 7.6% | 24.9% |
| Total | | Count | 159 | 228 | 234 | 123 | 79 | 823 |
| | | % within IND Ideological Traditionalism Index | 100.0% | 100.0% | 100.0% | 100.0% | 100.0% | 100.0% |

homosexuality were "always wrong," "almost always wrong," "sometimes wrong," or "not wrong at all." In addition, respondents were asked whether they had attended an X-rated movie during the past year.

Each of these items was related to abortion attitudes, with those most permissive in sexual matters also being more permissive about abortion.

# DEMONSTRATION 19.5: RECODE PREMARSX AND HOMOSEX

Because we want to explore this phenomenon, why don't you recode HOMOSEX and PREMARSX into *dichotomies* (only two values) of "Always or almost always wrong" versus "Only sometimes or never wrong"? That will make it easier to conduct the following analysis.

Just as when we recoded ATTEND and RELIG, we want to recode HOMOSEX and PREMARSX "into different variables":[3] HOMOSEX2 and PREMRSX2. To review the steps involved in recoding into the same variable, see SPSS Statistics Command 19.1. In addition, the following hints may be useful to get you started.

Keep in mind that because both HOMOSEX and PREMARSX have the same values and labels, you can create the dichotomies for these two sexual attitude variables with a single command; then, use one more command to create new value labels.

---

3. For HOMOSEX and PREMARSX, the values 0 and 5 to 9 should be defined as "missing."

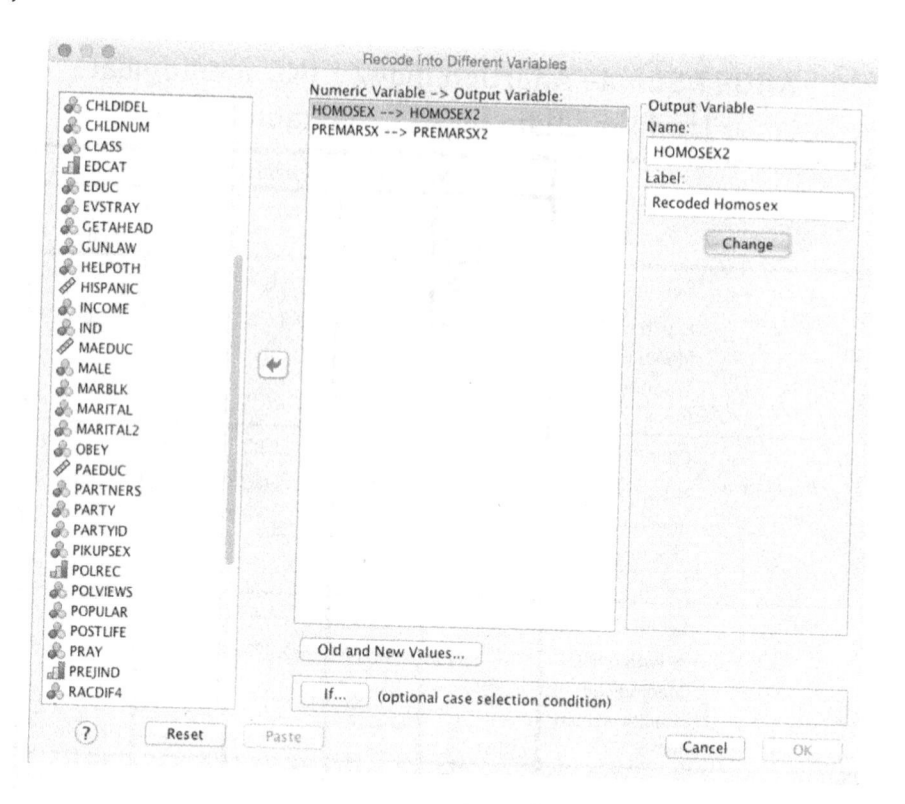

Transform → Recode → Into Different Variables

| Old Values for Both HOMOSEX and PREMARSX | | New Values | Labels |
|---|---|---|---|
| 1 to 2 | → | 1 | Wrong |
| 3 to 4 | → | 2 | Okay |

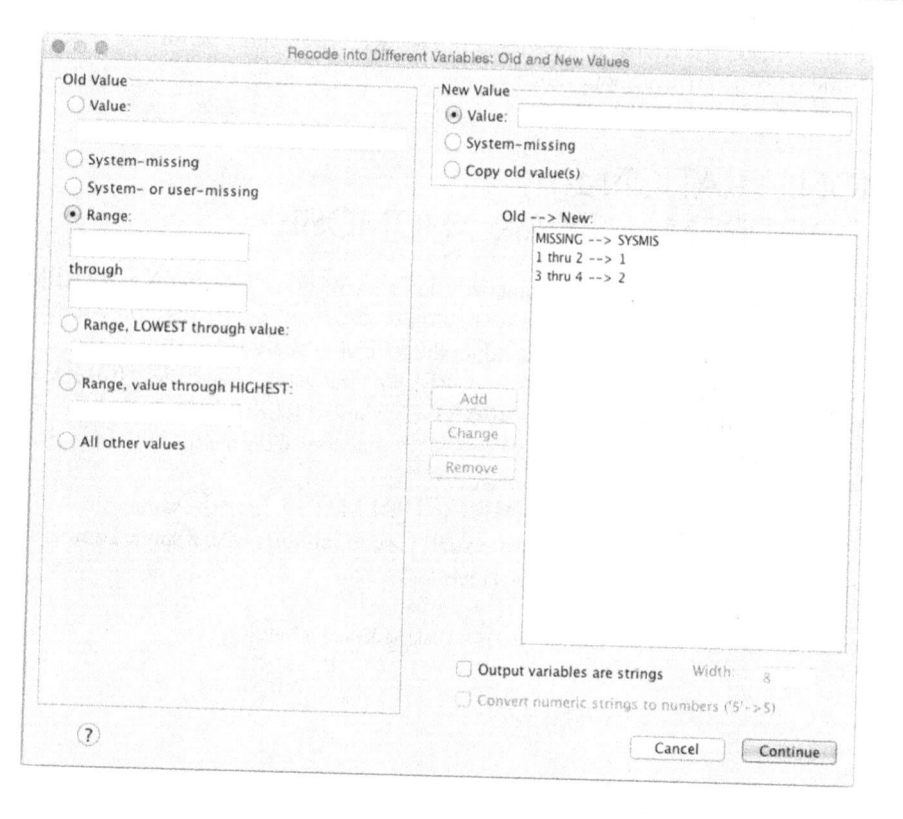

# WRITING BOX 19.1

We see by inspection that the index of ideological traditionalism strongly predicts whether people have attended an X-rated movie, progressing steadily from 13% of those scored 0 (traditional) on the index to 38% among those scored 4 (nontraditional) and 41% of those scoring a 3 on the index. The nontraditional respondents are far more likely to have seen an X-rated movie. Also, over a third of traditional respondents (37%) had casual sex on a date (is that traditional behavior?), while less than half of nontraditional respondents (44%) engaged in casual sex on a date (though 57% of those scoring a 3 on the index had engaged in sex on a date; clearly, there seems to be a difference here, as well). There also seems to be a noteworthy difference among traditional respondents, nontraditional respondents, and those in between on the question of which married respondents had ever strayed from their spouses. Of those on the traditional end of the scale, just 7% have strayed, while 14% reported straying at the nontraditional end. (The values in between are all higher than at either end of the index, ranging here from 14% to 17%).

## DEMONSTRATION 19.6: THE RELATIONSHIP BETWEEN SEXUAL PERMISSIVENESS AND IND

Now, let's see whether the sexual behavior attitudes are related to our "political–religious" index that predicts abortion attitudes so powerfully. Why don't you run each of those tables now? Here's a summary of what you should find.

| Percentage Who Are Permissive About . . . | Index of Ideological Traditionalism | | | | |
|---|---|---|---|---|---|
| | 0 Traditional | 1 | 2 | 3 | 4 Nontraditional |
| Premarital sex | 42% | 69% | 81% | 93% | 99% |
| Homosexuality | 20% | 48% | 67% | 81% | 95% |

Even though there is a great difference in the overall level of permissiveness on these issues, we can see that the political–religious index is clearly related to each one. People are generally more permissive toward premarital sex than homosexuality at all levels of ideological traditionalism. The gap is large among those who are classified as traditional (or close to traditional) and smallest among those identified as nontraditional (4 on the scale).

Why don't you also go ahead and check whether the index predicts whether people have taken in an X-rated movie during the past year (XMOVIE), whether people have had casual sex on a date (PIKUPSEX), or whether married individuals have ever cheated on their spouses (EVSTRAY)? Once you have completed your analysis, compare your findings with those in Writing Box 19.1.

If you want to continue your analysis, you might consider determining whether the previously observed relationship between attitudes about sexual behavior and attitudes about abortion are a product of religious and political factors. You might also consider expanding the index to include other items on sexual attitudes.

These suggestions are just a few of the many avenues you could take if you are interested in pursuing this line of inquiry further. Clearly, we have gone a long way toward accounting for people's opinions on the issue of abortion. At the same time, we've moved quickly to give you a broad view. If attitudes toward abortion interest you, you could go in any number of directions to follow up with a more focused and deliberate analysis.

## CONCLUSION

You've had an opportunity now to see how social scientists might set out to understand people's attitudes toward abortion. We know that this is a topic about which you hear a great deal in the popular media, and it may be an issue that concerns you and about which you have strong opinions. The previous analyses should give you some insight into the sources of opinions on this topic.

We hope this chapter has also expanded your understanding of the possibilities for multivariate analysis. Whereas bivariate analysis allows for some simple explanations of human thoughts and behaviors, multivariate analysis permits more sophisticated investigations and discoveries.

## Main Points

- You can use your multivariate analysis skills to delve more deeply into the sources of opinion on controversial issues such as abortion.

- The primary goal in this chapter is to try to predict attitudes toward abortion.

- To that end, we went through a number of items that earlier were found to have an impact on abortion attitudes: religious affiliation, measures of religiosity, political philosophy, and sexual attitudes.

- We constructed a composite measure or index, called IND, to predict support for a woman's right to have an abortion.

- IND was made up of the following component variables: ATTEND2, POLREC, and RELIG2.

- After working through the demonstrations in this chapter, you should have a better understanding of how a social scientist might begin to account for opinion on an issue such as abortion.

- With the univariate, bivariate, and multivariate analysis skills you have learned, you should now be able to design a more careful and deliberate study dealing with this or another issue or topic that interests and excites you.

## Key Terms

Compute Variable command   356

Dichotomies   363

## SPSS Statistics Commands Introduced in This Chapter

19.1.   Recoding Into Different Variables

19.2.   Creating an Index Using Compute Variable

## Review Questions

*Answer Questions 1 through 5 T (true) or F (false).*

1. In the 2016 General Social Survey (GSS), frequency of attendance at religious services was related to abortion attitudes, but religious affiliation was not.

2. According to the 2016 GSS, opposition to abortion tends to decrease with decreasing measures of religiosity.

3. According to the 2016 GSS, religious affiliation and church attendance are related to each other, but neither is related to abortion attitudes.

4. In the 2016 GSS, political philosophy was related to abortion attitudes, but party identification was not.

5. In the 2016 GSS, those who were somewhat permissive about premarital and homosexual sex also tended to oppose abortion.

6. List the commands for instructing SPSS Statistics to recode an original variable (into different variables).

7. If you save your data set after recoding an original variable, what should you remember to do?

8. List two findings from our multivariate analysis of the relationship among abortion, religious affiliation, and church attendance.

9. Name the three items we used to construct our index of ideological traditionalism, IND.

10. Scores on IND ranged from _____ to _____.

11. Does a score of 4 on IND indicate support for or opposition to abortion?

12. How well did IND predict abortion attitudes?

13. How might you expand the index IND to include one (or more) of the variables dealing with sexual attitudes?

# SPSS Statistics Lab Exercise 19.1

NAME: _____

CLASS: _____

INSTRUCTOR: _____

DATE: _____

*To complete the following exercises, you need to load the data file EXERPLUS.SAV.*

In this exercise, we are going to create a simple index combining attitudes toward teen sex (PILLOK, SEXEDUC, and TEENSEX). The goal is to construct an index/composite measure called IND2 that can be used to predict attitudes toward sex and family roles (FEPRESCH and FECHLD). To create IND2, simply follow the steps listed below. After we set up the index initially, you will be given a chance to expand it and explore its capabilities on your own.

1.  Define the following values for each item listed below as "missing":

    PILLOK—0, 8, 9

    SEXEDUC—0, 3 to 9 (Hint: Use "Range plus one discrete missing value.")

    TEENSEX—0, 5 to 9 (Hint: Use "Range plus one discrete missing value.")

    FEPRESCH—0, 8, 9

    FECHLD—0, 8, 9

2.  Recode PILLOK, TEENSEX, FEPRESCH, and FECHLD into dichotomies as shown below. Use **Transform →
    Recode → Into Different Variables** to recode the original variables. As noted earlier, if you save your data
    set after this exercise, be sure to use "Save As" and give the data set a new name so you are able to get
    back to the original, unrecoded data.

| PILLOK | | | |
|---|---|---|---|
| **Old Values** | | **New Values** | **Labels** |
| 1 to 2 | → | 1 | Okay/Agree |
| 3 to 4 | → | 2 | Wrong/Disagree |

| TEENSEX | | | |
|---|---|---|---|
| **Old Values** | | **New Values** | **Labels** |
| 1 to 2 | → | 2 | Wrong |
| 3 to 4 | → | 1 | Okay |

| FEPRESCH | | | |
|---|---|---|---|
| **Old Values** | | **New Values** | **Labels** |
| 1 to 2 | → | 1 | Agree |
| 3 to 4 | → | 2 | Disagree |

*(Continued)*

(Continued)

| FECHLD | | | |
|---|---|---|---|
| **Old Values** | | **New Values** | **Labels** |
| 1 to 2 | → | 1 | Agree |
| 3 to 4 | → | 2 | Disagree |

3. Create a simple index called IND1 built on the items PILLOK, SEXEDUC, and TEENSEX (which we just recoded). There are a number of ways to create IND1. Feel free to design your own method or follow the general steps below. You may want to refer to our discussion in the chapter (and SPSS Statistics Command 19.1) if you need to refresh your memory.

   Step 1:   Create IND2.

   Step 2:   Assign points for IND2 based on scores for three component items (PILLOK, SEXEDUC, TEENSEX) as follows:

   - If Wrong/Disagree (2) on PILLOK, give one point on IND2.
   - If Oppose (2) on SEXEDUC, give one point on IND2.
   - If Wrong (2) on TEENSEX, give one point on IND2.

   Our goal is to create an index (IND2) with scores ranging from 0 (least traditional attitudes toward sex and family roles—or, if you like, least conservative/most liberal views) to 3 (most traditional attitudes toward sex and family roles—most conservative/least liberal views).

   Step 3:   Missing data.

   Step 4:   Define IND2.

   When you are done, you will have created an index (IND2) that captures predispositions to hold traditional attitudes toward sex and family roles. Again, scores on the index range from 0 (least traditional) to 3 (most traditional).

4. Run Frequencies for IND2, and use your output to fill in the blanks below.

   **IND2**                                                                 **Valid Percentage**

   0 Least traditional                           _____

   1                                             _____

   2                                             _____

   3 Most traditional                           _____

5. See how well IND2 predicts attitudes toward sex and family roles. Run crosstabs with column percentages and chi-square, specifying FEPRESCH and FECHLD as row variables and IND2 as the column variable. Then, use your output to fill in the blanks below:

| | | IND2 | | | |
|---|---|---|---|---|---|
| | | **0 Least Traditional** | **1** | **2** | **3 Most Traditional** |
| FEPRESCH | Agree | | | | |
| FECHLD | Agree | | | | |

6. Does the index (IND2) provide a strong prediction of support for attitudes toward sex and family roles as measured by FEPRESCH and FECHLD? Discuss the findings of your analysis in detail below. (Keep in mind that FEPRESCH and FECHLD ask different questions.)

7. You are now on your own! Expand IND2 to include one or more items of your choosing from your data file EXERPLUS.SAV. (Keep in mind that you may need to recode your item[s] before adding them to IND2.) When you have expanded the index, run Frequencies, and then, see how well your new expanded index predicts attitudes toward sex and family roles. Print both your frequencies and table[s], and discuss your findings in detail below.

8. Continue your analysis by checking whether your new, expanded index predicts FEFAM and FEHIRE. Print your table[s], and discuss your findings in detail below. (Keep in mind that you may need to recode FEFAM and FEHIRE.)

# SUGGESTIONS FOR FURTHER MULTIVARIATE ANALYSES

In each of the previous analytic chapters, we have tried to leave a large number of "loose ends" for you to pursue on your own. If you are using this book in connection with a college class, you may want to follow up on some of those leads in the form of a term paper or a class project.

This chapter will build on some of those suggestions and offer some additional possibilities for your analyses. We begin with some suggestions for exploring ideal family size. We will then move to discuss other possible issues to investigate, such as child-rearing, the Protestant ethic, and prejudice. Do not limit yourself to these ideas! Even within the fairly limited data sets that accompany this book, there are many analytic possibilities we do not consider in these pages.

## IDEAL FAMILY SIZE AND ABORTION

Before leaving the topic of abortion altogether, we'd like to suggest another explanatory variable you might consider: ideal family size. We've seen previously that those who favor small families are more supportive of abortion than are those who favor large families. Now you are able to pursue this matter further using the data on your DEMOPLUS.SAV file. Here's the basic relationship with which you might start. Notice that we're using the recoded variable CHLDNUM that we created in Chapter 16 and the Simple Abortion index we created in Chapter 8.

### ABORT Simple Abortion Index * CHLDNUM Recoded CHLDIDEL Crosstabulation

| | | | CHLDNUM Recoded CHLDIDEL | | Total |
|---|---|---|---|---|---|
| | | | 10 to 2 | 23 or more | |
| ABORT Simple Abortion Index | 0 Yes/Approve | Count | 108 | 72 | 180 |
| | | % within CHLDNUM Recoded CHLDIDEL | 49.5% | 31.0% | 40.0% |
| | 1 Conditional Support | Count | 77 | 83 | 160 |
| | | % within CHLDNUM Recoded CHLDIDEL | 35.3% | 35.8% | 35.6% |
| | 2 No/ Disapprove | Count | 33 | 77 | 110 |
| | | % within CHLDNUM Recoded CHLDIDEL | 15.1% | 33.2% | 24.4% |
| Total | | Count | 218 | 232 | 450 |
| | | % within CHLDNUM Recoded CHLDIDEL | 100.0% | 100.0% | 100.0% |

## Symmetric Measures

| | | Value | Asymptotic Standard Error[a] | Approximate T[b] | Approximate Significance |
|---|---|---|---|---|---|
| Ordinal by Ordinal | Gamma | .371 | .069 | 5.068 | .000 |
| N of Valid Cases | | 450 | | | |

a. Not assuming the null hypothesis.

b. Using the asymptotic standard error assuming the null hypothesis.

Why don't you see whether the index of ideological traditionalism (IND) is related to the ideal family sizes that people reported? Then, compare your findings with Writing Box 20.1.

# WRITING BOX 20.1

There is an overall relationship between scores on the abortion opinion index and family size preferences: Those who scored high on the index were more likely to prefer small families. The gamma calculation ($\gamma = .371$, statistically significant at $p < .000$) indicates that this is a relationship worth further exploration.

What happens, however, when you control for other variables? Does this relationship stand up? Among those supporting abortion, does the index of traditional values have an impact?

To take a more focused approach, you might review two articles that appear on the *Adventures in Social Research* student study website (https://study.sagepub.com/babbie10e): Renzi's "Ideal Family Size as an Intervening Variable Between Religion and Attitudes Towards Abortion" (1975) and D'Antonio and Stack's "Religion, Ideal Family Size, and Abortion: Extending Renzi's Hypothesis" (1980).[1] While somewhat dated, these articles can be used as a starting point and in conjunction with more recent studies in this area. Remember, you can access an extensive bibliography using the National Opinion Research Center site we recommended earlier in this book (http://gss.norc.org/get-documentation/bibliography).

Once you have accessed and read some of these articles, see if you can replicate portions of the published analyses. Perhaps you can identify additional variables that should be taken into account.

# CHILD-REARING

In Chapter 16, we began to look into some of the factors that might affect people's views of the qualities most important to develop in children. As a reminder, the qualities were as follows:

- OBEY—to obey

- POPULAR—to be well liked or popular

- THNKSELF—to think for himself or herself

- WORKHARD—to work hard

- HELPOTH—to help others when they need help

---

1. Renzi, M. (1975). Ideal family size as an intervening variable between religion and attitudes towards abortion. *Journal for the Scientific Study of Religion, 14*, 23–27; D'Antonio, W. V., & Stack, S. (1980). Religion, ideal family size, and abortion: Extending Renzi's hypothesis. *Journal for the Scientific Study of Religion, 19*, 397–408.

We suggested that you start your analysis with some basic demographic variables, such as age, sex, and race. We encouraged you to consider relationships you might logically expect, such as more educated respondents placing a higher value on children thinking for themselves.

Now you are able to explore all of the possibilities in greater depth. To stay with the example of education and independence of thought in children, you could see whether certain variables shed more light on that relationship. You might check POLVIEWS, for example. Before you do, ask yourself what you expect to find. You might also check the effect of gender while you're at it.

Earlier, we suggested that you look at the impact of the sexual attitude items. Those who are permissive regarding violations of the established norms for sexual conduct often feel that they are thinking for themselves in that regard. How do such people feel about encouraging independence of thought in young people? With your multivariate skills, you can examine that matter with some sophistication.

Perhaps you will find it useful to combine some of the "quality" items into an index. On the face of it, OBEY and THNKSELF appear to reflect valuing opposite traits. Are they negatively related to each other? Would they fit into an index of "conformity–independence" perhaps? If that seems a fruitful index to create, to which other variables might it relate?

## THE PROTESTANT ETHIC

Perhaps one of the most famous books in the social sciences is Max Weber's *The Protestant Ethic and the Spirit of Capitalism* (1905/1958).[2] In it, Weber traced the religious (Calvinist) roots of the ethic of hard work and thrift, which he concluded forged the beginnings of capitalism. This ethic is something you might like to explore.

A central notion of the Protestant ethic as described by Weber is the belief that individuals are responsible for their own economic well-being, which they should achieve through hard work. People's wealth is taken as a sign of how hardworking and diligent they are. In its most extreme form, the Protestant ethic sees poverty as the result of slothfulness and laziness and wealth as the product of persistence and effort.

The GETAHEAD item in your General Social Survey (GSS) data set provides a measure of at least one dimension of the Protestant ethic that you might like to explore. To measure the degree to which people took responsibility for their own economic well-being, respondents were read this statement: "Some people say that people get ahead by their own hard work; others say that lucky breaks or help from other people are more important." Following the statement, they were asked, "Which do you think is most important?" Why don't you begin by examining how GETAHEAD is related to other variables? It seems logical, for example, that GETAHEAD would be related to WORKHARD.

Are people who are in disadvantaged groups or who have low incomes more apt to believe that their fates are governed by luck rather than hard work? Or does a belief that luck is the basis for success provide a rationalization for people who have little power to control the events that affect their lives? Because these variables are not the ratio measures that Pearson's *r* assumes, you can't take the results literally, but perhaps they can give you a first glimpse. Do not use this technique as a substitution for other, statistically appropriate examinations.

If you follow these suggestions, you'll need to be prepared for some surprises—even disappointments—so it may take some hard work (not inappropriate) for you to create a measure of commitment to the Protestant ethic that you like. Then, you can begin the multivariate search for the causes of this point of view. Be sure to check out the attitudes of actual Protestants, but don't expect to find a straightforward answer.

## CAPITAL PUNISHMENT, GENDER, AND RACE

In your analysis of the Protestant ethic, you may have looked at racial items such as MARBLK or NATRACE. If not, you may want to do so now. Logically, the belief that people get ahead by hard work alone would seem to rule out the limits imposed by prejudice and discrimination. You can explore the relationships among some of the work ethic and prejudice items to see if this is the case.

---

2. Weber, M. (1958). *The Protestant ethic and the spirit of capitalism* (T. Parsons, Trans.). New York, NY: Scribner. (Originally published 1905 as *Die protestantische Ethik und der Geist des Kapitalismus*)

The variables on our DEMOPLUS.SAV file allow us to explore other aspects of race and racial prejudice. You probably recall that the file contains the variable CAPPUN, which measures support of and opposition to the death penalty; by utilizing some of the bivariate and multivariate skills we have acquired, we can explore this issue and its relationship to other variables, such as gender and race, in more depth.

According to Amnesty International, about 60% of the countries in the world have now abolished the death penalty. In the 20 years from 1994 to 2013, the number of countries that actually carried out executions fell from 37 to 22. In 2013, the vast majority of executions took place in China; 80% of executions outside China took place in Iran, Iraq, and Saudi Arabia.[3]

In the United States today (2017), the death penalty is still practiced in 31 states and provided for under U.S. federal civilian and military law. In all, 20 prisoners were put to death in the United States during 2016, reflecting a steady decrease since executions peaked at 98 in 1998. However, as of July 2014, more than 2,800 inmates in the United States were on death row awaiting execution.[4] Often, executions are delayed by inmates' appeals or court challenges to death penalty laws. This can be explained in part not only by the nature of the U.S. judicial system but also by the fact that capital punishment remains enormously controversial. While attitudes toward the death penalty in the United States have fluctuated over time, currently about two thirds of the population favor capital punishment and about one third would like to see it abolished.[5]

Our data let us explore some of the factors influencing attitudes toward the death penalty in the United States.

# DEMONSTRATION 20.1: CAPPUN BY SEX

Some argue that gender influences attitudes toward the death penalty—specifically, that women are taught to be more nurturing and, especially when life without parole is an alternative to execution, are more likely to favor abolition of the death penalty. With the help of SPSS Statistics, we can quickly test this theory.

Before running crosstabs, be sure to designate the appropriate values as "missing" for CAPPUN and SEX. Then, run crosstabs with percentages. Your results should match the table below.

## CAPPUN Favor or Oppose Death Penalty for Murder * SEX Respondent's Sex Crosstabulation

| | | | SEX Respondent's Sex | | |
| --- | --- | --- | --- | --- | --- |
| | | | 1 MALE | 2 FEMALE | Total |
| CAPPUN Favor or oppose death penalty for murder | 1 FAVOR | Count | 427 | 428 | 855 |
| | | % within SEX Respondent's sex | 65.6% | 57.1% | 61.0% |
| | 2 OPPOSE | Count | 224 | 322 | 546 |
| | | % within SEX Respondent's sex | 34.4% | 42.9% | 39.0% |
| Total | | Count | 651 | 750 | 1401 |
| | | % within SEX Respondent's sex | 100.0% | 100.0% | 100.0% |

3. Amnesty International. (2014). *Death sentences and executions 2013*. London, UK: Author. Retrieved from http://issuu.com/amnestypublishing/docs/death_sentences_and_executions_2013

4. Death Penalty Information Center. (2017). *Death row inmates by state*. Retrieved October 10, 2017, from http://www.deatpenaltyinfo.org/death-row-inmates-state-and-size-death-row-year

5. For additional facts and figures surrounding this issue, you may want to check out Amnesty International's webpage at http://www.amnesty.org/en/death-penalty. Alternatively, you may want to access the Bureau of Justice Statistics' "Capital Punishment Statistics" page at http://bjs.ojp.usdoj.gov/index.cfm?ty=tp&tid=18. The information at http://www.deathpenaltyinfo.org is also illuminating. Remember, you can also find a host of other information on this topic by using your favorite search engine or visiting your library.

The table shows a relationship between these variables: Women are more likely than men to oppose the death penalty by more than 8 percentage points. That's a notable difference but not one to get too excited about. Perhaps other variables in our data set, such as RACE, will allow us to explore attitudes toward the death penalty further.

# DEMONSTRATION 20.2: CAPPUN BY SEX, CONTROLLING FOR RACE

In our country, because of long-standing patterns of economic, residential, and educational discrimination, Blacks have had very different community experiences with violence and the criminal justice system. Although they are a minority, Blacks make up the majority of our prison population. Violence is commonly experienced in impoverished Black urban neighborhoods.

As we discussed in earlier chapters, the introduction of a control variable will sometimes reveal more about the nature of a simple two-variable relationship, such as between CAPPUN and SEX. Relationships can become stronger when a control variable is applied, while under different circumstances, a relationship can become weaker or disappear. Sometimes the addition of a control variable has no effect at all.

Why don't you see what happens to the relationship between CAPPUN and SEX when we control for RACE? As usual, before you run your table, be sure to designate the appropriate values as "missing" for RACE.

As the table on the next page shows, for Whites, we get a very similar point spread (although opposition for White respondents was a little lower than for the total population) between males and females to that in the earlier table. As you can see, 36% of the women and 31% of the men oppose the death penalty.

## CAPPUN Favor or Oppose Death Penalty for Murder• SEX Respondent's Sex * RACE Race of Respondent Crosstabulation

| RACE Race of respondent | | | | SEX Respondent's Sex | | Total |
|---|---|---|---|---|---|---|
| | | | | 1 MALE | 2 FEMALE | |
| 1 WHITE | CAPPUN Favor or oppose death penalty for murder | 1 FAVOR | Count | 344 | 351 | 695 |
| | | | % within SEX Respondent's sex | 69.4% | 64.1% | 66.6% |
| | | 2 OPPOSE | Count | 152 | 197 | 349 |
| | | | % within SEX Respondent's sex | 30.6% | 35.9% | 33.4% |
| Total | | | Count | 496 | 548 | 1044 |
| | | | % within SEX Respondent's sex | 100.0% | 100.0% | 100.0% |
| 2 BLACK | CAPPUN Favor or oppose death penalty for murder | 1 FAVOR | Count | 52 | 38 | 90 |
| | | | % within SEX Respondent's sex | 54.2% | 29.2% | 39.8% |
| | | 2 OPPOSE | Count | 44 | 92 | 136 |
| | | | % within SEX Respondent's sex | 45.8% | 70.8% | 60.2% |
| Total | | | Count | 96 | 130 | 226 |
| | | | % within SEX Respondent's sex | 100.0% | 100.0% | 100.0% |
| 3 OTHER | CAPPUN Favor or oppose death penalty for murder | 1 FAVOR | Count | 31 | 39 | 70 |
| | | | % within SEX Respondent's sex | 52.5% | 54.2% | 53.4% |
| | | 2 OPPOSE | Count | 28 | 33 | 61 |
| | | | % within SEX Respondent's sex | 47.5% | 45.8% | 46.6% |
| Total | | | Count | 59 | 72 | 131 |
| | | | % within SEX Respondent's sex | 100.0% | 100.0% | 100.0% |
| Total | CAPPUN Favor or oppose death penalty for murder | 1 FAVOR | Count | 427 | 428 | 855 |
| | | | % within SEX Respondent's sex | 65.6% | 57.1% | 61.0% |
| | | 2 OPPOSE | Count | 224 | 322 | 546 |
| | | | % within SEX Respondent's sex | 34.4% | 42.9% | 39.0% |
| Total | | | Count | 651 | 750 | 1401 |
| | | | % within SEX Respondent's sex | 100.0% | 100.0% | 100.0% |

When we look at Blacks, we see that men are actually also less likely (46%) than women (71%) to oppose the death penalty for murder. Moreover, the opposition is much higher among Blacks than Whites for both men and women. The total percentage differences between Whites and Blacks opposing the death penalty is noteworthy. Of the Blacks, 60% oppose while only 33% of the Whites oppose—a 27-point spread.

In the "Other" racial category, men are more likely to oppose using the death penalty for murder than are women. This illustrates a *conditional relationship* dependent on race since the relationship between SEX and CAPPUN is dependent upon the category of RACE.

The introduction of RACE as a control variable raises important questions about why men and women of different racial groups are so different in their attitudes toward the death penalty. In the background lies an even bigger question of why such large differences exist between Blacks' and Whites' attitudes. These are the types of questions social researchers explore in more detail using bivariate and multivariate skills—those we discussed in the past several chapters. We leave the exciting possibilities for additional exploration in your able, bivariate and multivariate hands.

# CONCLUSION

The National Rifle Association and other proponents of extensive gun distribution (see GUNLAW) are fond of saying, "Guns don't kill people; people kill people." Of course, without high-powered guns, it would be a lot more difficult. This opens the door to considerable research that can be done using the GSS about politics, public opinion, and guns. Well, in a more pacific spirit, we'd like to suggest that SPSS Statistics doesn't analyze data; analysts analyze data. While you can't perform the many analyses quickly or at all without a high-powered tool like SPSS, the good news is that you are now a bona fide, certifiable data analyst with knowledge about how to use SPSS Statistics. SPSS is a tool that, in the hands of an educated analyst, can benefit society.

We've taken you through bivariate and multivariate analysis to demonstrate the importance of ascertaining the sometimes hidden meanings lying behind the responses people give to survey questions. That's a big part of the *adventure* of social research. (We wanted to call this book *Earl, Billy, and Jeanne's Excellent Adventure*, but you know publishers.) We've given you about all the guidance and assistance we planned when we started this adventure. Remember, in Chapter 1, we said you'll just add yourself to the mix. Well, it's show time! You're on your own now, although you should have a support network behind you. If you read this book in connection with a college course, you have your instructor.

The final section of this book expands the horizons of social research even further. It suggests a number of ways you might reach out beyond the GSS data set we have provided for your introductory experience with the adventure of social research.

## Main Points

- This chapter offers suggestions for further multivariate analyses.

- If you are using this book in connection with a college course, these suggestions may be useful in helping you design a term paper or class project.

- Even within the limited data sets that accompany this text, there are numerous analytic possibilities we have not explored or considered.

- The suggestions offered here are built on the questions and issues addressed in your data files DEMOPLUS.SAV and EXERPLUS.SAV (and GSS2016.SAV).

- The suggestions cover issues such as abortion, child-rearing, the Protestant ethic, and capital punishment.

- These suggestions are just a small portion of the analytic possibilities stemming from the data contained in your data files.

## Key Term

Conditional relationship 377

## SPSS Statistics Commands Introduced in This Chapter

No new commands were introduced in this chapter.

## Review Questions

1. Use the National Opinion Research Council website discussed earlier ("Additional Resources") to access at least one article or study that pertains to each of the following topics (http://gss.norc.org/get-documentation). Read the articles, and see if you can identify a variable related to each of the following topics that was *not* discussed in this chapter. List the variable, and explain its relationship to the topic.

   a.  Abortion

   b.  Child-rearing

   c.  Protestant ethic

   d.  Capital punishment

2. Which of the studies that you accessed in response to Question 1 would you be interested in attempting to replicate, and why?

3. Discuss how you might apply the techniques and procedures we covered in Chapters 17 through 19 on multivariate analysis to examine the following topics/issues:

   a.  Abortion

   b.  Child-rearing

   c.  Protestant ethic

   d.  Capital punishment

# SPSS Statistics Lab Exercise 20.1

NAME: _____

CLASS: _____

INSTRUCTOR: _____

DATE: _____

In Lab Exercise 16.1, we asked you to use bivariate techniques to examine one of the topics from the EXERPLUS.SAV file: attitudes about gender roles, law enforcement, the environment, mass media use, national government spending priorities, teen sex, affirmative action, and so on.

In this exercise, you will be given an opportunity to expand your analysis of the issue you chose by applying some of the multivariate techniques discussed in Chapters 17 through 19.

1. List the general topic or issue you examined in Lab Exercise 16.1.



2. List the variables (including any recoded variables or indexes) in your EXERPLUS.SAV file that pertain to this issue.




3. In Lab Exercise 16.1, you developed two hypotheses. List Hypotheses 1 and 2 below, identifying the dependent and independent variables in each.

    a. Hypothesis 1:

      • Independent variable: _____

      • Dependent variable: _____

    b. Hypothesis 2:

      • Independent variable: _____

      • Dependent variable: _____

4. Describe the strength and significance of the relationship between the variables in Hypothesis 1. In particular, you should note whether the relationship is worth exploring further.




5. Describe the strength and significance of the relationship between the variables in Hypothesis 2. In particular, you should note whether the relationship is worth exploring further.




6. Based on your responses to Questions 4 and 5, choose one hypothesis you would like to explore further (list abbreviated variable names). If neither hypothesis is worth exploring further, develop a new

*(Continued)*

(Continued)

hypothesis, and run through the exercises in SPSS Statistics Lab Exercise 16.1 again before continuing with this exercise. Once you have identified a hypothesis worth exploring further, fill in the blanks below.

- Independent variable: _____

- Dependent variable: _____

7. List a variable from your EXERPLUS.SAV file that you think may be related to the independent and dependent variables listed in response to Question 6. Explain your reasoning.

- Third variable A: _____

8. List another variable from your EXERPLUS.SAV file that you think may be related to the independent and dependent variables listed in response to Question 6. Explain your reasoning.

- Third variable B: _____

9. From the list of techniques reviewed in previous chapters, circle the procedures appropriate to examine the relationship among your independent variable, dependent variable, and third variable A (Question 7). (Hint: You should circle at least one technique in each group.)

   a. Group 1:

   - Running crosstabs with a control variable

   b. Group 2:

   - Recoding to create a dummy variable

   - Multiple regression

   - Recoding into different variables

   - Creating an index using Compute

   c. Group 3:

   - Measure of association (lambda, gamma, correlation matrix with Pearson's $r$, $r^2$, regression, scatterplot with regression line)

   - Tests of significance (chi-square, $t$ test, ANOVA)

10. From the list of techniques reviewed in previous chapters, circle the procedures appropriate to examine the relationship among your independent variable, dependent variable, and third variable B (Question 8). (Hint: You should circle at least one technique in each group.)

   a. Group 1:

   - Running crosstabs with a control variable

   b. Group 2:

   - Recoding to create a dummy variable

   - Multiple regression

- Recoding into different variables
- Creating an index using Compute

c. Group 3:

- Measure of association (lambda, gamma, correlation matrix with Pearson's $r$, $r^2$, regression, scatterplot with regression line)
- Tests of significance (chi-square, $t$ test, ANOVA)

11. Use the techniques you identified as appropriate in response to Question 9 to examine the relationship among your independent variable, dependent variable, and third variable A. Once you have conducted your analysis, do the following:

- Print and attach your output to this sheet.
- Summarize your findings in prose.

12. Use the techniques you identified as appropriate in response to Question 10 to examine the relationship between your independent variable, dependent variable, and third variable B. Once you have conducted your analysis, do the following:

- Print and attach your output to this sheet.
- Summarize your findings in prose.

# THE ADVENTURE CONTINUES

In the concluding chapters, we want to explore several ideas that may support your continued investigations into the nature of human beings and the societies they create.

It struck us that you might be interested in conducting your own survey—perhaps as a class project. Consequently, in Chapter 21, we begin by taking a step back to look at the process of social research and the research proposal. We then focus specifically on survey research. In particular, we delve into designing and administering a survey, defining and entering data in SPSS Statistics, and writing a research report. In Chapter 22, we suggest other avenues for pursuing your social investigations. Among other things, we talk about the unabridged General Social Survey (GSS), other data sources you might explore, and other computer programs you might find useful.

We hope that by the time you finish these chapters, you will have fully realized the two purposes that lie behind our writing this book: to help you learn (1) the logic of social research and (2) how to pursue that logic through the use of SPSS Statistics. In addition, we hope you will have experienced some of the excitement and challenges that make social research such a marvelous adventure.

# DESIGNING AND EXECUTING YOUR OWN SURVEY

The General Social Survey (GSS) data sets provided with this book are of special interest to researchers because they offer a window into American public opinion. We thought you might be interested in learning about the thoughts and actions of people across the country.

At the same time, it occurred to us that many of you may be interested in conducting your own survey to investigate topics, issues, and populations not addressed by the GSS or other data sets. Conducting your own survey is a good idea because data analysis in a classroom setting is sometimes more meaningful if the data are more personal. Perhaps you would like to analyze the opinions and behaviors of your own class (if it's a large one), the opinions of students elsewhere in your school, or even the attitudes of members of your community.

If you are interested in conducting a survey, this chapter and some of the material contained on the *Adventures in Social Research* student study website (https://study.sagepub.com/babbie10e) are designed to help you get started developing and administering the survey, defining and entering the data in SPSS Statistics, and writing a research report. (You already know how to analyze the data!) This is our answer (albeit brief) to those students and readers who ask, "How can I do this myself?" While we cannot hope to provide you with an in-depth understanding of the intricacies of survey research in such a short time, we do give you a brief overview of the steps involved in designing and implementing your own survey. When possible, we will also point you toward a few other resources that you may find useful as you launch your own original study.

## THE SOCIAL RESEARCH PROCESS AND PROPOSAL

Before we focus on designing and executing your own survey, we want to take a step back and place survey research and data analysis, which have been the central focus of this book, in the context of the social research process as a whole.

Our primary focus in this book has been a secondary analysis of a portion of a nationwide survey, the 2016 GSS. As you are aware, survey research is just one of many methods of data collection used by social researchers. Other methods include—but are not limited to—experimentation, participant observation, focus groups, intensive interviews, and content analysis.

Not only has our focus been limited to just one method of data collection, but it has also been limited to one step (albeit crucial) in the social research process—data analysis. We have focused on the use of one of the most popular computer software programs, SPSS Statistics, to analyze survey data. As we discuss in the next chapter, there are other software packages you might want to consider using as well.

Because our focus has been on the statistical analysis of survey data using SPSS Statistics, our discussions of the practice and process of social research have been necessarily limited to data analysis. Before conducting your own study, you may find it helpful to review the entire social research process. You can get some tips on writing a research proposal (which is often the first step in the research process) and, most importantly, find out how to locate texts that will give you more detailed descriptions of parts of the research process not covered here.

The *Adventures in Social Research* student study website (https://study.sagepub.com/babbie10e) includes an excerpt from Russell K. Schutt's comprehensive research methods text, *Investigating the Social World* (2012).[1] The excerpt focuses on the major steps involved in designing a research project and gives some guidelines for writing a research proposal. As Bachman and Schutt (2008) noted, the research proposal is a crucial step in the social research process because it goes "a long way toward shaping the final research report and will make it easier to progress at later research stages."[2] Schutt's text is just one of many research methods texts that you may find useful.

Others include Earl Babbie's *The Practice of Social Research* (2013), Kenneth Bailey's *Methods of Social Research* (1994), Thomas Sullivan's *Methods of Social Research* (2001), Chava Frankfort-Nachmias and David Nachmias's *Research Methods in the Social Sciences* (2015), Bridget Somekh and Cathy Lewin's *Research Methods in the Social Sciences* (2005), Alan Bryman's *Social Research Methods* (2012), and W. Lawrence Neuman's *Social Research Methods: Qualitative and Quantitative Approaches* (2010).[3] While this list is by no means exhaustive, it should be useful in beginning your search for a text that will provide you with a comprehensive overview of social research.

# DESIGNING AND EXECUTING YOUR OWN SURVEY

Like all methods of data collection, survey research has its own peculiar advantages and disadvantages, benefits and liabilities. Nevertheless, a carefully constructed and executed survey can yield results that are considered valid, reliable, and generalizable. The 2016 GSS is a good example of a carefully designed and implemented survey, yielding data from which findings can be generalized to all English-speaking, noninstitutionalized American adults 18 years of age and older.

To design and conduct a survey that meets scientific standards, you need to pay particular attention to the steps required for survey research: research design, sampling, questionnaire construction, data collection, data processing, data analysis, and report writing.

To help you design and implement your own survey, we have included an excerpt from a guide called "SPSS Survey Tips" by the company that makes SPSS Statistics on the *Adventures in Social Research* website (https://study.sagepub.com/babbie10e). This guide discusses some of the key considerations in planning, developing, and executing a survey. You should think of these as useful tips rather than hard-and-fast rules. Keep in mind it is unlikely that all social scientists or pollsters would agree with every recommendation. Moreover, in the "real world," the process of developing and implementing a survey is seldom as neat as the sequential ordering of the tips may suggest.

Despite these caveats, we think that you will find "SPSS Survey Tips" a useful and concise overview of the steps involved in developing and implementing your own survey. In addition, you may also want to consult one of the many texts devoted to the principles and techniques of survey research. In particular, we draw your attention to Pamela Alreck and Robert Settle's *Survey Research Handbook* (2004), Earl Babbie's *Survey Research Methods* (1990), Floyd J. Fowler Jr.'s *Survey Research Methods* (2014), and Peter Nardi's *Doing Survey Research* (2014).[4]

---

1. Schutt, R. K. (2012). *Investigating the social world: The process and practice of research* (7th ed.). Thousand Oaks, CA: Sage.

2. Bachman, R., & Schutt, R. K. (2008). *Fundamentals of research in criminology and criminal justice.* Thousand Oaks, CA: Sage, p. 306.

3. Babbie, E. (2013). *The practice of social research* (13th ed.). Belmont, CA: Wadsworth Cengage Learning; Bailey, K. (1994). *Methods of social research* (4th ed.). New York, NY: The Free Press; Sullivan, T. J. (2001). *Methods of social research.* Fort Worth, TX: Harcourt College Publishers; Frankfort-Nachmias, C., & Leon-Guerrero, A. (2015). *Social statistics for a diverse society* (7th ed.). Thousand Oaks, CA: Sage; Somekh, B., & Lewin, C. (2005). *Research methods in the social sciences.* Thousand Oaks, CA: Sage; Bryman, A. (2012). *Social research methods* (4th ed.). Oxford, UK: Oxford University Press; Neuman, W. L. (2010). *Social research methods: Qualitative and quantitative approaches* (7th ed.). Boston, MA: Pearson.

4. Alreck, P. L., & Settle, R. B. (2004). *Survey research handbook* (3rd ed.). New York, NY: McGraw-Hill Irwin; Babbie, E. R. (1990). *Survey research methods* (2nd ed.). Belmont, CA: Wadsworth Cengage Learning; Fowler, F. J., Jr. (2014). *Survey research methods* (5th ed.). Thousand Oaks, CA: Sage; Nardi, P. M. (2014). *Doing survey research: A guide to quantitative methods* (3rd ed.). Boulder, CO: Paradigm.

## Sample Questionnaire

To help you collect your own data, we have included in Appendix B of this book a sample questionnaire. This survey asks some of the same questions found in the subset of GSS items included in your DEMO.SAV and EXER.SAV files. We've also provided the tools you may need to make modifications you think would serve the interest of local relevance. If you wish, you can make copies of the questionnaire and use it to collect your own data.[5] If you are more ambitious, you might choose to design a totally different questionnaire that deals with whatever variables interest you. There is no need for you to be limited to the GSS variables we've analyzed in this book or suggested in the sample questionnaire. You have learned a technology that is much more broadly usable than that. To get ideas about the kinds of things sociologists and other social scientists study, you might go to the library and surf the research categories in *Sociological Abstracts*.

Whatever survey you choose to conduct, the following section tells you how to get your data into a form that SPSS Statistics will accept for analysis.

# GETTING READY FOR DATA ANALYSIS USING SPSS STATISTICS

Once you have designed and administered your questionnaire (or collected your data), you are ready to begin analyzing your data. Getting data ready for analysis with SPSS Statistics is really a three-step process:

*Step 1:* Define your data

*Step 2:* Edit and code your data

*Step 3:* Enter your raw data

# STEP 1: DEFINE YOUR DATA

The first step, often called **data definition**, involves giving each item from your questionnaire a variable name, setting the data type, describing the variable, indicating values and labels, designating missing values, setting the item's level of measurement, and designating a place to store this information.

This process can begin even before you have completed collecting the data, if you are certain that the questionnaire itself is not going to be altered or revised.

# DEMONSTRATION 21.1: EXAMPLE 1—DEFINING ID

To walk you through this process, we are going to use the sample questionnaire provided in Appendix B of this book. You may want to take a moment to review the questionnaire before we begin defining the first variable, ID.

Go ahead and launch SPSS Statistics. If you get the "What would you like to do now?" dialog box, simply click **Cancel**. Now you should be looking at the Data Editor. Since we will define our data in the Variable View screen, make sure to click on the tab with that name if it is not already displayed.

As you know from previous chapters, Variable View contains descriptions of the variables contained in a data file. In Variable View, each row describes a variable, while the variable attributes (name, type, width, decimals, etc.) are contained in the columns. Unlike your earlier experience

---

5. We have also included an empty data file, LOCAL.SAV, on the *Adventures in Social Research* website. As we will discuss later in the chapter, this file is already defined and can be used to enter data from a sample population.

with Variable View, now you are creating a variable definition rather than simply modifying one that has been supplied by someone else.

We will define the first variable ID (the case identification number) from our sample questionnaire. Since each row in Variable View represents a variable, looking at our sample questionnaire, you can see that the variables we'll be putting in the numbered rows start with ID, then move to CHLDIDEL, OBEY, POPULAR, and so on until we come to the last variable, SEX. For each variable, we will start by typing its name in the first column and then work our way across the columns from left to right ("Name" to "Measure").

## Variable Names

To begin, double-click on the first cell in the upper left corner (the one that corresponds with Row No. 1 and the "Name" column). Now, type the abbreviated variable name, ID.[6]

Now, go ahead and hit **Enter**. Once you do that, you will notice that the cell that corresponds with Row No. 1 and the second column ("Type") becomes the active cell. Moreover, SPSS Statistics automatically gives you the default variable attributes for ID.

## Type

There are several types of data, including "comma," "dot," "scientific notation," and others. To get a sense of the various types of data, double-click on the small gray box with the three dots (ellipses) in the right side of the Row No. 1 "Type" cell.

---

6. If you are designing your own survey and planning to use SPSS Statistics to analyze the data, there are several "rules" to keep in mind when constructing abbreviated variable names. Among the most important rules are these: Each name must begin with a letter (letters, digits, periods, or the symbols @, #, _, or $ can follow), variable names should generally not exceed eight characters in length, variable names cannot end with a period, and each variable name on a file must be unique.

SPSS Statistics has probably chosen "Numeric" by default. If not, click the **Numeric** button, and select **OK**. If the "Numeric" type has already been selected, simply click **Cancel** or the **X** (Close button) to exit. All of the data we have used in this book and that you will collect with the sample questionnaire are numeric.

## Decimal

For a moment, skip over the "Width" column, and click on the right side of the cell corresponding with Row No. 1 and the "Decimal" column. When you do, you will notice that a set of up and down arrows appears, allowing you to either increase or decrease the decimal places. Since our variable, ID, does not require any decimal places, click the down arrow until it reaches 0.

## Width

Now, go ahead and click on the right side of the cell corresponding with Row No. 1 and the "Width" column. Once again, you will see up and down arrows allowing you to specify the width or the number of characters for the column. While this column is not crucial for our purposes, you can go ahead and decrease the width to 3 or more if you wish.

## Label

Now go ahead and double-click in the cell corresponding with Row No. 1 and the "Label" column. This cell allows you to insert the variable label or a brief description of your variable. Variable labels can be up to 255 characters long if necessary.

In this case, once you have double-clicked on the cell, go ahead and insert a variable label for ID, such as "Respondent's Identification Number." When you do that, you will see that the width of the column expands somewhat.

Once you are done, simply select **Enter**, or use your cursor to click on the next cell, "Values."

## Values

Once again, double-click on the gray box with the ellipses on the right side of the cell to open the Value Labels box. The Value Labels box allows you to assign values and labels for your variable.

For instance, if we were defining the variable SEX, we would want to enter the values 1 and 2 for "male" and "female," respectively. The numeral 1 would be placed in the "Value:" box and "male" in the "Value Label:" box. Then, you would click **Add**. The numeral 2 would then be placed in the "Value:" box and "female" in the "Value Label:" box. Then, again, you would click **Add** and then **OK**.

In the case of ID, however, we do not need to assign values and labels because each respondent has a unique identification number. When we go through the next variable, CHLDIDEL, you will have an opportunity to practice filling in the values and labels.

Click on the **Cancel** or **X** button to close the Value Labels box.

## Missing

There are no missing values for ID, so we do not have to open the Missing Values dialog box in this case. However, if we wanted to define missing values (as we will in the case of CHLDIDEL), all we would have to do is double-click on the gray box with ellipses in the right side of the cell.

Then, in the Missing Values box, we would define the missing values as we have done previously by choosing, in the case of ID, "No missing values" (the default setting in SPSS Statistics). For another variable, we might choose "Discrete missing values," "Range of missing values," or "Range plus one discrete missing value."

If you opened the Missing Values box, you can click **Cancel** or **X** to exit.

## Columns and Align

The next two columns ("Columns" and "Align") allow us to define the width of the columns in the Data Editor and specify the alignment of data values. By default, SPSS Statistics sets the column width to 8 and aligns data on the right. If you wish to change either of these settings, you can double-click on the right-hand side of the cell and use the arrows. Since we don't need to change either the column width or alignment, we can skip to the last column, "Measure."

## Measure

The last step in the process of defining your variable is to indicate the level of measurement. When you click on the right side of the cell that corresponds with Row No. 1 and the "Measure" column, you will see a down arrow. By clicking on the down arrow, you can specify the level of measurement as "Scale" (interval/ratio), "Ordinal," or "Nominal."

In the case of ID, the level of measurement is nominal, with each case having its own category. Remember that an ID number of 20 is not twice as "ID" as an ID number of 10, and no ID number is "more" ID than any other.

After you change the level of measurement to "Nominal," you are done defining the first variable. If you like, click on the **Data View** tab at the bottom left side of the screen. You will now see that ID is magically placed in the first column at the top left-hand corner of your Data Editor.

To return to the Variable View screen, either double-click on the variable name (ID) at the top of the column, or click the **Variable View** tab.

## DEMONSTRATION 21.2: EXAMPLE 2—DEFINING CHLDIDEL

Now that you have successfully defined the first variable from our sample questionnaire, why don't we go ahead and practice by defining the second item, CHLDIDEL, together as well. This time, we will list the commands in an easy-to-read format. You should already be in the Variable View screen. We will place CHLDIDEL in Row No. 2. Each of the following commands refers to variable attributes in Row No. 2.

- Double-click on the cell corresponding with Row No. 2 and the "Name" column.
- Type CHLDIDEL.
- Click **Enter.**

- By default, SPSS Statistics will set the "Type" to numeric, so there is no need to change that setting.

- Click on the right side of the cell corresponding with Row No. 2 and the "Decimal" column.

- Use the down arrow to set the decimal to 0.

- Click on the right side of the cell corresponding with Row No. 2 and the "Width" column.

- Use the down arrow to change the width to 2.

- Double-click the cell corresponding with Row No. 2 and the "Label" column.

- Type a descriptive variable label, such as "Respondent's ideal number of children."

- Click **Enter**, or use cursor to move to next column, "Values."

- Double-click in the gray box to open Value Labels dialog box.

- Type –1 in the "Value:" box, type IAP (inapplicable) in the "Value Labels:" box, and click **Add**.

You will notice that "–1 = IAP" is now specified in the box below. If you wanted to change or revise the statement for any reason, you would simply highlight "–1 = IAP." Once you did that, you would notice that you would be able to select **Remove** to delete the statement.

- Now go ahead and enter the other values and labels for CHLDIDEL: seven plus DK and NA.

Keep in mind that the sample questionnaire contains questions taken from your DEMO.SAV and EXER.SAV files. Consequently, you can refer to those files or the codebook (Appendix A) to verify the values and labels for the variables in the sample questionnaire (Appendix B).

- Click **Enter**, or use your cursor to move to the next column.

- Click in the gray box on the right side of the "Missing" column to open the Missing Values dialog box.

- Select **Discrete missing values** and type the values –1 and 9.

- Click **OK**.

- By default, SPSS Statistics has probably already selected "Scale" as the level of measurement. If not, use the down arrow to set the level of measurement to "Scale."

- Click on the **Data View** tab, and you will see CHLDIDEL in the second column in your Data Editor window.

You have now successfully defined the first two items in our sample questionnaire, ID and CHLDIDEL. As you can probably see, while it is not a difficult process, defining all of the variables from a questionnaire, even one as small as our sample questionnaire, can be fairly time-consuming.

---

## SPSS Statistics Command 21.1: Defining a Variable

Make sure the Variable View screen is the active window

Double-click cell corresponding with appropriate row and "Name" column → Type abbreviated variable name → **Enter**

Move through cells corresponding with that row and each applicable column from left ("Name") to right ("Measure") → Click or double-click on right side of a cell to access either arrows or appropriate dialog box (for our purposes, the most important columns are "Name," "Decimals," "Labels," "Values Missing," and "Measure")

Once done, click **Data View** tab

Your new variable will be situated in a column at the top of the screen

## Copying Variables With Shared Attributes: Abortion Variables

One way to cut down on the time-consuming process of defining variables is to copy and paste variables that share similar attributes or characteristics.

The seven abortion variables in our sample questionnaire, for instance, all use the numeric code 1 to represent "Yes," 2 to represent "No," 0 to represent "IAP," 8 to represent "DK," and 9 to represent "NA." Moreover, in each case, 0, 8, and 9 are defined as missing values. In cases such as these, it is not necessary to define each variable individually; instead, you can simply copy a variable. We will use the abortion variables to illustrate how this works.

# DEMONSTRATION 21.3: COPYING A VARIABLE

Now that you are comfortable defining variables with SPSS Statistics, go ahead and define ABDEFECT, the first abortion variable in our sample questionnaire. Place ABDEFECT in Row No. 3 directly below CHLDIDEL.[7] If you need to review the steps for defining a variable, refer to SPSS Statistics Command 21.1.

Once you have defined ABDEFECT, you can easily define the other six abortion variables (ABNOMORE, ABHLTH, ABPOOR, ABRAPE, ABSINGLE, and ABANY) by copying and pasting. To do this, click on the row number (3) to the left of the cell containing ABDEFECT. When you do that, you will notice that the row is highlighted.

Now choose **Edit → Copy** from the drop-down menu.[8]

---

7. We are placing ABDEFECT in Row No. 3 for illustrative purposes only. If you were actually to set up this data file, Row No. 3 would be occupied by OBEY, Row No. 4 by POPULAR, Row No. 5 by THNKSELF, and so on. The proper order is displayed on the LOCAL.SAV file on the *Adventures in Social Research* website.

8. Alternatively, you can right-click with your mouse and choose **Copy** (or CTRL + click on a Macintosh computer with a one-button mouse).

Then, go ahead and select the row (most likely Row No. 4) where you would like to place the next variable (ABNOMORE). Now, all you have to do is select **Edit → Paste Variables**.[9] By selecting "Paste Variables" instead of the simple Paste command, you'll get the following box, which allows you to add all of the like variables at one time without having to repeat the same pasting over and over.

Select the number of variables you would like to create with the same specifications as ABDEFECT, and then click **OK.** Voilà!

_____
9. You can also right-click with your mouse and select **Paste**, though we recommend you use the Paste Variables command.

The only thing you need to do after that is to insert a correct variable name and label for each.

---

### SPSS Statistics Command 21.2: Copying a Variable

In Variable View, click left side of row to be copied

Click **Edit → Copy** OR right-click with mouse → **Copy** OR (for Macintosh one-button mouse users) **CTRL + click → Copy**

Click on left side of row you're copying to

Click **Edit → Paste Variables**

Select the number of variables to produce from the specifications of the copied variable

Click **OK**

---

## DEMONSTRATION 21.4: SAVING YOUR NEW FILE

Before you end this (or any other) data definition session, remember to save the new file with a name that will remind you of its contents.

To save a new data file, make the Data Editor the active window. Then, from the menu, choose **File → Save As** to open the Save Data As dialog box. Now, click on the down arrow to the right of the "Save in:" field to choose the appropriate drive.

Then, in the "File name:" field, type a descriptive file name, and click **Save.**

---

## SPSS Statistics Command 21.3: Saving a New Data File

With Data Editor active, click **File → Save As**

Use down arrow to right of "Save in:" field to select appropriate drive

Type file name in "File name:" field

Click **Save**

---

### LOCAL.SAV

Now that you have mastered the commands for defining a variable and saving your new data file, we are going to let you in on a little secret. To save you the time and trouble of having to define all of the variables in the sample questionnaire, we have included a file named LOCAL.SAV on the *Adventures in Social Research* website. It contains the data definitions for this particular questionnaire.

In short, because we know you are getting toward the end of the book and are probably anxious to begin your own adventure, we wanted to save you the time and work of having to define all the variables included in the sample questionnaire. So we did it for you (think of it as a gift of sorts)! For now, however, just keep the existence of LOCAL.SAV in the back of your mind. We'll show you how to use it after we discuss the next step (Step 2) in the process of getting your data ready for analysis with SPSS Statistics—editing and coding your data.

## STEP 2: EDIT AND CODE YOUR DATA

The second step in the process of getting your data ready for analysis with SPSS Statistics is editing and **coding** your data. People do not always follow instructions when filling out a questionnaire. Verbal or written responses have to be transformed into a numeric code for processing with SPSS Statistics. For ease of entry, questionnaires should be edited for proper completion and coding before you attempt to key or enter them into an SPSS Statistics file.

To the extent that we could, we designed the sample questionnaire to be self-coding. By having a number next to each response for the **closed-ended questions**, the interviewer assigns a code as the respondent answers the question. In some cases, we have had to use **open-ended questions**, either because there would be too many responses to print on the questionnaire or because we couldn't anticipate all of the possible responses.

Essentially, four steps are involved in editing and coding your data: making sure each questionnaire has a unique ID number, coding open-ended questions, making sure the codes are easy to read, and editing each questionnaire.

### Unique ID Number

Each questionnaire should have a unique number in the "ID" field. We do this not because we want to identify individuals but because errors are frequently made in the coding process and then show up later.

For instance, we coded SEX as 1 for "male" and 2 for "female," but in our analysis, we might find a respondent with SEX coded 7. What we would need to do is find the record with the erroneous code 7. To do this, we would look up the ID number, go back to the original questionnaire, find out what code SEX should have been, and fix it.

### Coding Open-Ended Questions

Next in the editing process, we have to code the open-ended questions. All of the people coding questions should be following the same written instructions for coding. For instance, at the end of Appendix B of this book, we include a list of occupations and their socioeconomic statuses for coding SEI, the socioeconomic index.

Other coding schemes might not be as elaborate. For instance, in a medical study, patients might be asked about the illnesses that brought them to the hospital. Coding might be as simple as classifying the illnesses as acute or chronic.

### Ensuring That Codes Are Easy to Read

Finally, the codes need to be written so they are easy to read. We have designed our questionnaire to be *edge-coded*. If you look in the right margin, you will see that we put a space for each variable's code. We included these numbers because some statistics software requires that variables be placed in specific columns across each record. Happily, that is not a requirement of SPSS Statistics for Windows or Macintosh. We'll just use the numbered blanks as a convenient place to write our codes.

### Editing Questionnaires

Whether you are going to edit the sample questionnaire we have been using as an example throughout this section or another questionnaire you designed on your own, you should get a copy of the codes used to define the file with which you are working (e.g., a copy of the work you did in Step 1 when you defined your data). For this example, we will access the codes used to define our LOCAL.SAV file.

## DEMONSTRATION 21.5: ACCESSING FILE INFORMATION FOR CODING AND EDITING

When you open the LOCAL.SAV data file that is available on the *Adventures in Social Research* website, you will notice that the data cells are empty. Don't panic; they are supposed to be empty. This is the empty but defined data file LOCAL.SAV we mentioned earlier.

To display the codes for your use in coding your data in SPSS Statistics, you can either check the Variable View portion of the Data Editor or click **Utilities → Variables**.

Here is an example of the coding information you will find for the variable MARITAL, responses to Question 4 on the questionnaire: "Are you married, widowed, divorced, or separated, or have you never been married?"

For people who are married, code 1 is used. For people who are widowed, 2 is used; divorced, 3; and so on. Notice that code 9, "No answer," has an "NA" next to it. This means that 9 has been designated a missing code. All missing codes are thrown out of the analysis. If respondents fail to answer a question or if they give two responses for one question, they should be assigned the missing-value code for that variable.

Now that you have the information, you can go through each questionnaire, one question at a time, to make sure the coding is correct, that there is only one code per question, and so on.

---

**SPSS Statistics Command 21.4:**
**Accessing File Information for Coding and Editing**

Utilities → **Variables**

From list on the left, select variable for which you want coding information

---

# STEP 3: ENTER YOUR RAW DATA

Once you have edited and coded each of your questionnaires, you can move to the final step in the process: entering your raw data. Once again, we are going to use our sample questionnaire as an example.

Because the LOCAL.SAV file is on the *Adventures in Social Research* website, in order to enter data on it, you need to save the file to a local disk or drive (or a network drive, if you are connected to such). Go ahead and do that now. Once you are done, you can open the file, and we will run through the process of entering data.

After opening your file, you should be looking at a data matrix in the Data View portion of the Data Editor that is empty except for the variable names across the top and record numbers down the left side. This is where we will enter our raw data. You will notice that the order of the variables across the record is the same as the order of the variables on the questionnaire. We placed them in that order to make data entry easier and less error-prone.

# DEMONSTRATION 21.6: MOVING THROUGH DATA VIEW

You can easily move from cell to cell in the data matrix. Pressing just the **Tab** key moves the active cell to the right, and pressing the **Shift** and **Tab** keys together moves the active cell to the left. You can tell the active cell by its thick black border.

Pressing the **Enter** key moves the active cell down to the next row (to the next record or respondent). The directional arrows on your keyboard will also move the active cell, one cell at a time. The mouse can be used to make a cell active just by pointing and clicking. Long-distance moves can be made by pressing **CTRL + Home** (*OR* **APPLE + Home** for Macintosh computers) to move to the leftmost cell on the first case or **CTRL + End** (*OR* **APPLE + Home** for Macintosh computers) to move to the rightmost cell on the last case.

---

**SPSS Statistics Command 21.5:**
**Some Tips for Moving Through Data View**

**Tab**: Moves active cell to right

**Shift + Tab**: Moves active cell to left

**Enter**: Moves active cell down to next row

**Directional arrows**: Move active cell, one cell at a time

**CTRL + Home** on Windows computers *OR* **APPLE + Home** on Macintosh computers: Moves active cell to leftmost cell, first case

**CTRL + End** on Windows computers *OR* **APPLE + End** on Macintosh computers: Moves active cell to rightmost cell, last case

---

# DEMONSTRATION 21.7: ENTERING DATA

To enter data, simply select the appropriate cell in the Data Editor, making it the active cell. When you do that, you will notice that the record number and the variable name appear in the rectangle at the top left-hand corner of the Data Editor, directly below the toolbar. You can now enter the appropriate value.

When you enter your data, you will notice that they first appear in the **Cell Editor** at the top of the Data Editor window, just below the toolbar. Simply press **Enter** or **Tab** or move to another cell to record your data.

---

### SPSS Statistics Command 21.6: Entering Numeric Data[10]

In Data View, click appropriate cell → Type value

Click **Enter** OR move to another cell to record data

---

# DEMONSTRATION 21.8: REVISING OR DELETING DATA

Data may be changed at any time just by moving to the appropriate cell, keying in new values, and pressing **Enter** or moving to another cell.

If a particular case turns into a disaster, you can get rid of the entire case by clicking on the record number at the extreme left of a record and pressing the **Delete** key.

---

### SPSS Statistics Command 21.7: Deleting an Entire Case

Click record number at far left side → **Delete**

---

# DEMONSTRATION 21.9: SAVING YOUR DATA FILE

After you are done entering data, or if you want to stop entering data and continue at a later time, make sure you save your data. By clicking **File** and **Save**, you will save your data under the name used at the beginning of the session (for instance, LOCAL.SAV or whatever other name you used when you saved the LOCAL.SAV file on your local or network drive).

If you wish to save it under another name, click on **File** and **Save As**. Be sure to note to which drive or other device you save.

# WRITING A RESEARCH REPORT

After you design and execute your survey and enter and analyze the data, finally it is time to report your results. To help you through this crucial aspect of the research process, we have included an excerpt on the *Adventures in Social Research* website (https://study.sagepub.com/babbie10e) that, among other things, presents guidelines for reporting analyses you may find useful.

---

10. We specify "Numeric" because the data we work with in the text are numeric. More importantly, to enter anything other than numeric data in SPSS Statistics, you must first specify the variable type. Consequently, the commands for entering nonnumeric data are somewhat different from those discussed here.

In addition, many research methods texts (including some of those we referenced earlier, such as Schutt, Alreck and Settle, Babbie, and others) devote sections to writing research reports.

You may also want to reference one of the many books devoted to writing, particularly those designed with social scientists in mind, such as Howard Becker's *Writing for Social Scientists* (2007) or Lee Cuba's *A Short Guide to Writing About Social Science* (2001).[11]

# CONCLUSION

Although a fair amount of work is involved in developing your own survey, entering and analyzing your own data, and then reporting your results, there can also be a special excitement about coming to an understanding of the opinions and behaviors of a group of people with whom you are directly familiar. The benefits of conducting your own study are even more evident if your survey focuses on topics and issues that are meaningful, relevant, or otherwise important to you or to those in your community.

In fact, the main advantage of designing and executing your own original or primary research is that you can focus specifically on those issues, topics, populations, and variables that interest you. Since you are in charge of the design, implementation, analysis, and reporting of your study, you do not have to depend on the work of other social scientists who may have approached the issue, topic, or problem differently. The downside, of course, is the fact that conducting your own study often requires a tremendous investment of time and resources.

Nevertheless, we think you will find that even though both primary and secondary research have advantages and disadvantages, the rewards and excitement that come from both types make the time, energy, and commitment involved worth it.

---

11. Becker, H. S. (2007). *Writing for social scientists: How to start and finish your thesis, book, or article* (2nd ed.). Chicago, IL: University of Chicago Press; Cuba, L. J. (2001). *A short guide to writing about social science* (4th ed.). New York, NY: Longman.

## Main Points

- This chapter is designed to help you construct and administer your own survey, enter the data in SPSS Statistics, and write a research report.

- The *Adventures in Social Research* website (https://study.sagepub.com/babbie10e) includes an excerpt designed to give you a sense of the steps involved in the social research process and some hints on writing a research proposal (often the first step in the research process).

- Various considerations are involved in constructing and implementing a survey that is reliable, valid, and generalizable.

- "SPSS Survey Tips," also at the book's companion website, gives you an overview of how to design and execute your own survey.

- Appendix B of this book contains a sample questionnaire with questions drawn from the 2016 General Social Survey.

- There are three main steps involved in getting ready for data analysis using SPSS Statistics:

  o Step 1: Define your data

  o Step 2: Edit and code your data

  o Step 3: Enter your raw data

- The LOCAL.SAV file includes the data definition for the sample questionnaire.

- An excerpt on the *Adventures in Social Research* website (https://study.sagepub.com/babbie10e) discusses one of the most important and difficult aspects of the social research process: writing a research report.

## Key Terms

| | | |
| --- | --- | --- |
| Cell Editor 400 | Coding 397 | Edge-coded 398 |
| Closed-ended questions 397 | Data definition 387 | Open-ended questions 397 |

## SPSS Statistics Commands Introduced in This Chapter

21.1.  Defining a Variable

21.2.  Copying a Variable

21.3.  Saving a New Data File

21.4.  Accessing File Information for Coding and Editing

21.5.  Some Tips for Moving Through Data View

21.6.  Entering Numeric Data

21.7.  Deleting an Entire Case

## Review Questions

1.  Name two methods social scientists use to collect data (besides survey research).

2.  Name three decisions involved in designing a social research project.

3.  Why is it important to write a research proposal?

4.  Briefly describe at least four of the tips included in "SPSS Survey Tips."

5.  List the three primary steps involved in getting ready for data analysis using SPSS Statistics.

6.  To what does *data definition* refer?

7.  Name two guidelines or rules for choosing a variable name that SPSS Statistics will accept.

8.  What is a shortcut that can be used to define variables that share similar attributes?

9.  What does the LOCAL.SAV file on the *Adventures in Social Research* website contain?

10.  List two things you need to do when editing and coding your data.

11.  List two ways you can move through the data matrix.

12.  When you key in data, where does it appear before it is recorded (i.e., before you press **Enter** or move to another cell)?

13.  Name two considerations involved in writing a research report.

14.  Name two guidelines for reporting analyses.

# SPSS Statistics Lab Exercise 21.1

NAME: _____

CLASS: _____

INSTRUCTOR: _____

DATE: _____

*Our goal in this exercise is to allow you to practice defining, editing, coding, and entering data that you collect from a small number of respondents.*

1. Make 15 copies of the sample questionnaire available in Appendix B and also on the *Adventures in Social Research* website (https://study.sagepub.com/babbie10e). (As an alternative, make 15 copies of a questionnaire you designed on your own.) Then, administer the questionnaire to 15 respondents. (Since this is practice only, they can be friends, family, colleagues, etc.)

2. After collecting the data, go through the three steps involved in getting data ready for analysis using SPSS Statistics:

   a. Define your data.

   b. Edit and code your data.

   c. Enter your raw data.

3. After you have entered your data, choose five variables, run Frequencies, and attach your output to this sheet.

4. Access the SPSS Statistics Tutorial (**Help → Tutorial**). Then, work through the portion labeled "Using the Data Editor."

# FURTHER OPPORTUNITIES
# FOR SOCIAL RESEARCH

Well, we've come to the end of our introduction to SPSS Statistics. In this final chapter, we want to suggest ways in which you can expand beyond the scope of this book. In particular, we are going to focus briefly on the unabridged General Social Survey (GSS), other data sets, and other computer programs you may find useful as you continue your social research adventure.

## THE UNABRIDGED GSS

The GSS subsamples that accompany this book, DEMO.SAV and EXER.SAV, each include a random subsample of 1,500 cases from the 2016 General Social Survey (GSS). The DEMO.SAV file contains 43 variables, and the EXER.SAV file contains 46 variables. Of course, the data available through the GSS are vastly more extensive. In 2016, researchers asked 2,867 respondents hundreds of questions. The cumulative data file that merges all of the General Social Surveys conducted between 1972 (when the first GSS was conducted) and 2016 contains more than 56,000 cases and 5,400 variables of interest to researchers around the country and, indeed, around the world.

As we noted earlier, the National Opinion Research Center (NORC) at the University of Chicago maintains an Internet site called GSS Data Explorer. You can access the GSS Data Explorer at https://gssdataexplorer.norc.org. The GSS Data Explorer site houses an interactive cumulative index to the GSS, indexing variables by subject as well as abbreviated variable name. In addition, it contains a search engine that locates abstracts of research reports produced from GSS data, an electronic edition of the complete GSS codebook, an extensive GSS bibliography, and a data extraction system that permits downloading GSS data in a format that can be used with any version of SPSS Statistics.

Now that you are familiar with how to use GSS data with SPSS Statistics, you may be able to locate other GSS data sets through your school. You can get additional information about accessing GSS data from the Roper Center for Public Opinion Research at http://www.ropercenter.cornell .edu. (Search data sets for GSS.)

An important reference book for your use with the data is the *GSS 1972–2016 Cumulative Codebook* (2017), edited by Tom W. Smith, Michael Dalvern, Jeremy Freese, and Michael Hout. Available both in book and computer form, the *Cumulative Codebook* may be purchased from the Roper Center. Or if you wish, use the electronic version mentioned above, available at the *Adventures in Social Research* website (https://study.sagepub.com/babbie10e).

The 2017 edition of the *Cumulative Codebook* contains information on all aspects of the GSS from 1972 to 2016, including exact questions, response codes, frequency counts, and so on. The table of contents for the latest edition, which is shown below, will give you an overview of the type of information included in this valuable resource.

Table of Contents

Introduction

Changes in Design

Abbreviations and Data Identification Numbers

Index to Data Set

Codes for the 1972 to 2016 Surveys (Includes variable names, exact question text, response categories and codes, and unweighted marginal frequencies for questions in selected years)

General Social Survey Topical Modules

International Social Survey Program (ISSP) Modules

Additional GSS Variables

Appendices

Page 407 shows a sample of some of the information available to you in the main body of the *Cumulative Codebook* (2017). This selection shows how coding has been accomplished for two of the abortion items, ABDEFECT and ABNOMORE, included in your DEMO.SAV file.

223. Please tell me whether or not you think it should be possible for a pregnant woman to obtain a legal abortion if . . . READ EACH STATEMENT, AND CIRCLE ONE CODE FOR EACH.

In addition to allowing you to work with many more variables than we've included in the present file, the larger GSS data set permits you to conduct longitudinal research—to analyze changes in opinions and behaviors over the years.

The initial experience of the GSS data set in connection with this book has put you in touch with a powerful research resource that we hope you'll be able to use more extensively in the future.

# OTHER DATA SETS

As if the full GSS weren't enough, thousands of other data sets are appropriate for analysis with SPSS Statistics.

To begin, there is a global network of data archives, or data libraries, which operate somewhat like book libraries. Instead of lending books, these archives lend or sell sets of data that have been collected previously. NORC, which administers the GSS, is one such archive. Other major archives include the Roper Center for Public Opinion Research at Cornell University and the Inter-university Consortium for Political and Social Research (ICPSR) at the University of Michigan.

A great deal of the data housed in data archives today is accessible via the Internet. We have already given you the Web addresses for NORC and the Roper Center. Other academic research centers, some of which include similar archives or links to archives, are these:

- Survey Research Center, at Princeton University (https://psrc.princeton.edu)

- ICPSR, at the University of Michigan (http://www.icpsr.umich.edu/icpsrweb/ICPSR)

- Survey Research Center, at the University of Michigan (http://www.src.isr.umich.edu)

- Marist College Institute for Public Opinion, at Marist College (http://maristpoll.marist .edu)

The data sets available for secondary analysis at these and other archives include, for example, studies conducted by university faculty researchers that may have been financed by federal research grants. Thus, the results of studies that may have cost hundreds of thousands of dollars to conduct can be yours for the nominal cost of copying and shipping the data.

The Roper Center, for instance, is a repository not only for all data on American public opinion but also for data collected in other countries as well. For instance, the center maintains a Latin American Data Bank that acquires, processes, and archives public opinion surveys conducted by

Please tell me whether or not you think it should be possible for a pregnant woman to obtain a legal abortion if ...

READ EACH STATEMENT, AND CIRCLE ONE CODE FOR EACH.

A. If there is a strong chance of serious defect in the baby?

[VAR: ABDEFECT]

| RESPONSE | PUNCH | YEAR | | | | | | | | | | | | | | | ALL |
|---|---|---|---|---|---|---|---|---|---|---|---|---|---|---|---|---|---|
| | | 1972-82 | 1982B | 1983-87 | 1987B | 1988-91 | 1993-98 | 2000 | 2002 | 2004 | 2006 | 2008 | 2010 | 2012 | 2014 | 2016 | |
| Yes | 1 | 10980 | 236 | 4625 | 236 | 3056 | 5354 | 1397 | 703 | 624 | 1425 | 952 | 921 | 919 | 1231 | 1353 | 34012 |
| No | 2 | 2195 | 92 | 1210 | 94 | 707 | 1255 | 377 | 193 | 232 | 495 | 321 | 304 | 313 | 402 | 447 | 8637 |
| Don't know | 8 | 419 | 25 | 187 | 21 | 141 | 250 | 83 | 24 | 33 | 68 | 61 | 32 | 52 | 54 | 58 | 1508 |
| No answer | 9 | 32 | 1 | 50 | 2 | 16 | 17 | 4 | 4 | 9 | 15 | 18 | 24 | 24 | 27 | 32 | 275 |
| Not applicable | 0 | 0 | 0 | 1470 | 0 | 1987 | 3458 | 956 | 1841 | 1914 | 2507 | 671 | 763 | 666 | 824 | 977 | 18034 |

B. If she is married and does not want any more children?

[VAR: ABNOMORE]

| RESPONSE | PUNCH | YEAR | | | | | | | | | | | | | | | ALL |
|---|---|---|---|---|---|---|---|---|---|---|---|---|---|---|---|---|---|
| | | 1972-82 | 1982B | 1983-87 | 1987B | 1988-91 | 1993-98 | 2000 | 2002 | 2004 | 2006 | 2008 | 2010 | 2012 | 2014 | 2016 | |
| Yes | 1 | 5920 | 111 | 2387 | 125 | 1640 | 3021 | 720 | 400 | 360 | 818 | 579 | 587 | 577 | 780 | 859 | 18884 |
| No | 2 | 7133 | 216 | 3452 | 206 | 2129 | 3539 | 1050 | 493 | 502 | 1107 | 716 | 636 | 669 | 862 | 964 | 23674 |
| Don't know | 8 | 542 | 26 | 181 | 20 | 132 | 293 | 85 | 29 | 30 | 65 | 40 | 36 | 44 | 50 | 43 | 1616 |
| No answer | 9 | 31 | 1 | 52 | 2 | 19 | 23 | 6 | 2 | 6 | 13 | 17 | 22 | 18 | 22 | 24 | 258 |
| Not applicable | 0 | 0 | 0 | 1470 | 0 | 1987 | 3458 | 956 | 1841 | 1914 | 2507 | 671 | 763 | 666 | 824 | 977 | 18034 |

the survey research community in Latin America. Other archives maintain similar data banks for opinion collected by researchers around the world. To begin, you may want to access the Roper Center site given above for a list of some of the many international links (see the menu on the main page, under "Polling Data").

You probably also realize that, like many governments, the U.S. government conducts a great many surveys that produce data suitable for analysis with SPSS Statistics. The U.S. Census is a chief example, and it is possible for researchers to obtain and analyze data collected in the decennial censuses. You can visit the U.S. Census Bureau online at http://www.census.gov.

Other examples include the following:

- Bureau of Justice Statistics (https://www.bjs.gov)

- Bureau of Labor Statistics (http://www.bls.gov/data)

For access to almost the full range of statistics produced by more than 100 U.S. federal agencies, you may want to log on to FedStats: One Stop Shopping for Federal Statistics (http://fedstats.sites .usa.gov).

It is worth recalling that when Émile Durkheim set about his major analysis of suicide in Europe, he was forced to work with printed government reports of suicide rates in various countries and regions. Moreover, his analysis needed to be done by hand. With the advent of computers for mass data storage and analytic programs such as SPSS Statistics, the possibilities for secondary analysis have been revolutionized. You live in an enviable time!

This is, of course, just the tip of the iceberg. These limited recommendations don't even begin to scratch the surface of the numerous sites available to help you locate and access statistical data on the Internet. While you should make use of the Web to locate and, in some cases, access data, however, please bear in mind that you also have to be cautious when conducting online searches. Anyone can post information online, so the accuracy of the data or other information you locate may not necessarily be conducive to sound social research. Also bear in mind that different search engines are likely to identify different sites, even when provided with the same search terms.

# OTHER COMPUTER PROGRAMS

We have organized this book around the use of SPSS Statistics because this program is so widely used by social scientists. Quite frankly, we spent a fair amount of time considering other programs as the focus for the book, but we ultimately decided that using SPSS Statistics would be most useful to the greatest number of students. And by the way, the popularity of SPSS Statistics is due largely to its excellence as a tool for social research.

At the same time, we want you to know that there are several other excellent analytic programs. We'll mention some of these here in case you have access to them. You should realize that the commands and procedures used in other programs will differ from those of SPSS Statistics, but the logic of data analysis that we've presented in this book applies across the various programs.

The program package that is probably the next most commonly used by social scientists is SAS (Statistical Analysis System), mentioned in Chapter 1. Like SPSS Statistics, it is an omnibus package of techniques that goes far beyond those we've introduced in this book. Interestingly, SAS functions within a broader set of programs for accounting, management, and other activities. You can learn more about SAS by accessing the SAS home page at http://www.sas.com.

**SYSTAT** is another widely used package of programs designed for social science research. Like SAS and SPSS Statistics, SYSTAT is an omnibus package with graphing, statistical, and other analytical capabilities much more advanced than those we have discussed here. SYSTAT was developed by Dr. Leland Wilkinson while he was a professor at the University of Illinois at Chicago. For a complete overview of this software, its general features, and system requirements, see the SYSTAT home page at http://systatsoftware.com.

A few other programs you may find useful for social science data analysis include Minitab (http://www.minitab.com), P-STAT (http://www.pstat.com), and STATA (http://www.stata.com).

# CONCLUSION

We hope that you've had some fun as you've worked through this book and that you've learned some important research techniques and some facts about the American public. We hope you have discovered that social research, as well as being very important—especially considering the range of social problems we confront today—is a fascinating enterprise.

Like the investigative detective, the social researcher must possess large amounts of curiosity and ingenuity. Sit beside a social researcher at work, and you'll hear him or her muttering things such as, "Wait a minute. If that's the case, then I'd expect to find . . ."; "Hey! That probably explains why . . ." "OMG! That means. . . ." Maybe you've caught yourself practicing these social scientific incantations. If so, congratulations and welcome. If not, you have a delightful adventure waiting for you just around the corner. We'll see you there.

## Main Points

- The unabridged 2016 General Social Survey (GSS) contains 2,867 cases and 960 variables.

- The DEMO.SAV file is made up of a random subsample of 1,500 cases and 43 of the variables from the 2016 GSS.

- The EXER.SAV file includes a random subsample of 1,500 cases and a different selection of 46 variables from the 2016 GSS.

- Since the first GSS in 1972, more than 56,000 respondents have been asked more than 5,400 different questions.

- There are many ways to access the unabridged GSS.

- The *Cumulative Codebook* is a valuable resource for researchers using the GSS.

- The GSS is just one of many data sets available to social researchers.

- Data sets of interest to social scientists (of which there are many) are often housed in one of the data archives and, in some cases, can be accessed via the Internet.

- The federal government is an important source of statistical data of interest to social scientists.

- We focused this text on SPSS Statistics because it is so widely used by social researchers. It is easy for beginners to learn and has many capabilities and much power for the advanced user; however, it is not the only statistical package available.

- In addition to SPSS Statistics, other excellent software programs often used by social researchers include (but are not limited to) SAS, SYSTAT, and STATA.

## Key Term

SYSTAT 408

## SPSS Statistics Commands Introduced in This Chapter

No new commands were introduced in this chapter.

## Review Questions

1. How many variables are contained on your DEMO.SAV file and your EXER.SAV file?

2. How many cases are contained on your DEMO.SAV file and your EXER.SAV file?

3. How many variables are contained in the entire 2016 General Social Survey (GSS)?

4. How many respondents took part in the GSS in 2016?

5. What is the GSS Data Explorer, and what type of information does it contain?

6. How can you access the GSS data?

7. What type of information does the *Cumulative Codebook* (2017) contain?

8. What are data archives?

9. Name two data archives.

10. Name two specific data sets relevant to your particular discipline.

11. Besides SPSS Statistics, what statistical package is most commonly used by social scientists?

# APPENDIX A: THE CODEBOOK

This codebook contains information for each of the variables in your DEMO.SAV and EXER .SAV files.

## SUBSAMPLE 1: DEMO.SAV

As noted in Chapter 3, DEMO.SAV is used in the demonstrations in the body of the chapters. This subsample contains 1,500 cases and 43 variables drawn from the 2016 General Social Survey (GSS).

**ABANY**

| | | Value | Count | Percent |
|---|---|---|---|---|
| Standard Attributes | Position | 1 | | |
| | Label | Abortion if woman wants for any reason | | |
| | Type | Numeric | | |
| | Format | F1 | | |
| | Measurement | Nominal | | |
| | Role | Input | | |
| Valid Values | 1 | YES | 441 | 29.4% |
| | 2 | NO | 502 | 33.5% |
| Missing Values | 0 | IAP | 516 | 34.4% |
| | 8 | DK | 25 | 1.7% |
| | 9 | NA | 16 | 1.1% |

**ABDEFECT**

| | | Value | Count | Percent |
|---|---|---|---|---|
| Standard Attributes | Position | 2 | | |
| | Label | Strong chance of serious defect | | |
| | Type | Numeric | | |
| | Format | F1 | | |
| | Measurement | Nominal | | |
| | Role | Input | | |
| Valid Values | 1 | YES | 710 | 47.3% |
| | 2 | NO | 236 | 15.7% |
| Missing Values | 0 | IAP | 516 | 34.4% |
| | 8 | DK | 23 | 1.5% |
| | 9 | NA | 15 | 1.0% |

## ABHLTH

| Standard Attributes | | Value | Count | Percent |
|---|---|---|---|---|
| | Position | 3 | | |
| | Label | Woman's health seriously endangered | | |
| | Type | Numeric | | |
| | Format | F1 | | |
| | Measurement | Nominal | | |
| | Role | Input | | |
| Valid Values | 1 | YES | 834 | 55.6% |
| | 2 | NO | 110 | 7.3% |
| Missing Values | 0 | IAP | 516 | 34.4% |
| | 8 | DK | 27 | 1.8% |
| | 9 | NA | 13 | 0.9% |

## ABNOMORE

| Standard Attributes | | Value | Count | Percent |
|---|---|---|---|---|
| | Position | 4 | | |
| | Label | Married—wants no more children | | |
| | Type | Numeric | | |
| | Format | F1 | | |
| | Measurement | Nominal | | |
| | Role | Input | | |
| Valid Values | 1 | YES | 459 | 30.6% |
| | 2 | NO | 493 | 32.9% |
| Missing Values | 0 | IAP | 516 | 34.4% |
| | 8 | DK | 21 | 1.4% |
| | 9 | NA | 11 | 0.7% |

## ABPOOR

| Standard Attributes | | Value | Count | Percent |
|---|---|---|---|---|
| | Position | 5 | | |
| | Label | Low income—can't afford more children | | |
| | Type | Numeric | | |
| | Format | F1 | | |
| | Measurement | Nominal | | |
| | Role | Input | | |
| Valid Values | 1 | YES | 428 | 28.5% |
| | 2 | NO | 521 | 34.7% |
| Missing Values | 0 | IAP | 516 | 34.4% |
| | 8 | DK | 24 | 1.6% |
| | 9 | NA | 11 | 0.7% |

## ABRAPE

| | | Value | Count | Percent |
|---|---|---|---|---|
| Standard Attributes | Position | 6 | | |
| | Label | Pregnant as result of rape | | |
| | Type | Numeric | | |
| | Format | F1 | | |
| | Measurement | Nominal | | |
| | Role | Input | | |
| Valid Values | 1 | YES | 737 | 49.1% |
| | 2 | NO | 215 | 14.3% |
| Missing Values | 0 | IAP | 516 | 34.4% |
| | 8 | DK | 17 | 1.1% |
| | 9 | NA | 15 | 1.0% |

## ABSINGLE

| | | Value | Count | Percent |
|---|---|---|---|---|
| Standard Attributes | Position | 7 | | |
| | Label | Not married | | |
| | Type | Numeric | | |
| | Format | F1 | | |
| | Measurement | Nominal | | |
| | Role | Input | | |
| Valid Values | 1 | YES | 421 | 28.1% |
| | 2 | NO | 538 | 35.9% |
| Missing Values | 0 | IAP | 516 | 34.4% |
| | 8 | DK | 11 | 0.7% |
| | 9 | NA | 14 | 0.9% |

## AGE

| | | Value | Count | Percent |
|---|---|---|---|---|
| Standard Attributes | Position | 8 | | |
| | Label | Age of respondent | | |
| | Type | Numeric | | |
| | Format | F2 | | |
| | Measurement | Scale | | |
| | Role | Input | | |
| N | Valid | 1495 | | |
| | Missing | 5 | | |

*(Continued)*

(Continued)

|  |  | Value | Count | Percent |
|---|---|---|---|---|
| Central Tendency and Dispersion | Mean | 49.16 |  |  |
|  | Standard Deviation | 17.476 |  |  |
|  | Percentile 25 | 34.00 |  |  |
|  | Percentile 50 | 50.00 |  |  |
|  | Percentile 75 | 62.00 |  |  |
| Labeled Values | 89 | 89 OR OLDER | 7 | 0.5% |
|  | 98 | DK | 0 | 0.0% |
|  | 99 | NA | 5 | 0.3% |

## ATTEND

|  |  | Value | Count | Percent |
|---|---|---|---|---|
| Standard Attributes | Position | 9 |  |  |
|  | Label | How often R attends religious services |  |  |
|  | Type | Numeric |  |  |
|  | Format | F1 |  |  |
|  | Measurement | Nominal |  |  |
|  | Role | Input |  |  |
| Valid Values | 0 | NEVER | 368 | 24.5% |
|  | 1 | LT ONCE A YEAR | 79 | 5.3% |
|  | 2 | ONCE A YEAR | 217 | 14.5% |
|  | 3 | SEVRL TIMES A YR | 158 | 10.5% |
|  | 4 | ONCE A MONTH | 105 | 7.0% |
|  | 5 | 2–3X A MONTH | 135 | 9.0% |
|  | 6 | NRLY EVERY WEEK | 78 | 5.2% |
|  | 7 | EVERY WEEK | 252 | 16.8% |
|  | 8 | MORE THN ONCE WK | 97 | 6.5% |
| Missing Values | 9 | DK, NA | 11 | 0.7% |

## CAPPUN

|  |  | Value | Count | Percent |
|---|---|---|---|---|
| Standard Attributes | Position | 10 |  |  |
|  | Label | Favor or oppose death penalty for murder |  |  |
|  | Type | Numeric |  |  |
|  | Format | F1 |  |  |
|  | Measurement | Nominal |  |  |
|  | Role | Input |  |  |
| Valid Values | 1 | FAVOR | 855 | 57.0% |
|  | 2 | OPPOSE | 546 | 36.4% |

|  | | Value | Count | Percent |
|---|---|---|---|---|
| Missing Values | 0 | IAP | 0 | 0.0% |
|  | 8 | DK | 79 | 5.3% |
|  | 9 | NA | 20 | 1.3% |

## CHLDIDEL

|  | | Value | Count | Percent |
|---|---|---|---|---|
| Standard Attributes | Position | 11 | | |
|  | Label | Ideal number of children | | |
|  | Type | Numeric | | |
|  | Format | F1 | | |
|  | Measurement | Nominal | | |
|  | Role | Input | | |
| Valid Values | 0 | | 7 | 0.5% |
|  | 1 | | 16 | 1.1% |
|  | 2 | | 449 | 29.9% |
|  | 3 | | 246 | 16.4% |
|  | 4 | | 108 | 7.2% |
|  | 5 | | 17 | 1.1% |
|  | 6 | | 4 | 0.3% |
|  | 7 | SEVEN+ | 7 | 0.5% |
|  | 8 | AS MANY AS WANT | 134 | 8.9% |
| Missing Values | −1 | IAP | 512 | 34.1% |
|  | 9 | DK, NA | 0 | 0.0% |

## CLASS

|  | | Value | Count | Percent |
|---|---|---|---|---|
| Standard Attributes | Position | 12 | | |
|  | Label | Subjective class identification | | |
|  | Type | Numeric | | |
|  | Format | F1 | | |
|  | Measurement | Nominal | | |
|  | Role | Input | | |
| Valid Values | 1 | LOWER CLASS | 148 | 9.9% |
|  | 2 | WORKING CLASS | 687 | 45.8% |
|  | 3 | MIDDLE CLASS | 608 | 40.5% |
|  | 4 | UPPER CLASS | 44 | 2.9% |
|  | 5 | NO CLASS | 0 | 0.0% |
| Missing Values | 0 | IAP | 0 | 0.0% |
|  | 8 | DK | 9 | 0.6% |
|  | 9 | NA | 4 | 0.3% |

## EDUC

| Standard Attributes | | Value | Count | Percent |
|---|---|---|---|---|
| Standard Attributes | Position | 13 | | |
| | Label | Highest year of school completed | | |
| | Type | Numeric | | |
| | Format | F2 | | |
| | Measurement | Nominal | | |
| | Role | Input | | |
| Valid Values | 0 | | 1 | 0.1% |
| | 3 | | 2 | 0.1% |
| | 4 | | 1 | 0.1% |
| | 5 | | 1 | 0.1% |
| | 6 | | 12 | 0.8% |
| | 7 | | 10 | 0.7% |
| | 8 | | 23 | 1.5% |
| | 9 | | 28 | 1.9% |
| | 10 | | 41 | 2.7% |
| | 11 | | 61 | 4.1% |
| | 12 | | 427 | 28.5% |
| | 13 | | 131 | 8.7% |
| | 14 | | 193 | 12.9% |
| | 15 | | 77 | 5.1% |
| | 16 | | 266 | 17.7% |
| | 17 | | 61 | 4.1% |
| | 18 | | 74 | 4.9% |
| | 19 | | 26 | 1.7% |
| | 20 | | 58 | 3.9% |
| Missing Values | 97 | IAP | 0 | 0.0% |
| | 98 | DK | 1 | 0.1% |
| | 99 | NA | 6 | 0.4% |

## EVSTRAY

| Standard Attributes | | Value | Count | Percent |
|---|---|---|---|---|
| Standard Attributes | Position | 14 | | |
| | Label | Have sex other than spouse while married | | |
| | Type | Numeric | | |
| | Format | F1 | | |
| | Measurement | Nominal | | |
| | Role | Input | | |

| | | Value | Count | Percent |
|---|---|---|---|---|
| Valid Values | 1 | YES | 122 | 8.1% |
| | 2 | NO | 537 | 35.8% |
| | 3 | NEVER MARRIED | 257 | 17.1% |
| Missing Values | 0 | IAP | 567 | 37.8% |
| | 8 | DK | 0 | 0.0% |
| | 9 | NA | 17 | 1.1% |

## GETAHEAD

| | | Value | Count | Percent |
|---|---|---|---|---|
| Standard Attributes | Position | 15 | | |
| | Label | Opinion of how people get ahead | | |
| | Type | Numeric | | |
| | Format | F1 | | |
| | Measurement | Nominal | | |
| | Role | Input | | |
| Valid Values | 1 | HARD WORK | 670 | 44.7% |
| | 2 | BOTH EQUALLY | 174 | 11.6% |
| | 3 | LUCK OR HELP | 129 | 8.6% |
| | 4 | OTHER | 0 | 0.0% |
| Missing Values | 0 | IAP | 519 | 34.6% |
| | 8 | DK | 5 | 0.3% |
| | 9 | NA | 3 | 0.2% |

## GUNLAW

| | | Value | Count | Percent |
|---|---|---|---|---|
| Standard Attributes | Position | 16 | | |
| | Label | Favor or oppose gun permits | | |
| | Type | Numeric | | |
| | Format | F1 | | |
| | Measurement | Nominal | | |
| | Role | Input | | |
| Valid Values | 1 | FAVOR | 682 | 45.5% |
| | 2 | OPPOSE | 284 | 18.9% |
| Missing Values | 0 | IAP | 516 | 34.4% |
| | 8 | DK | 15 | 1.0% |
| | 9 | NA | 3 | 0.2% |

## HELPOTH

| Standard Attributes | | | Value | Count | Percent |
|---|---|---|---|---|---|
| Standard Attributes | Position | | 17 | | |
| | Label | To help others | | | |
| | Type | Numeric | | | |
| | Format | F1 | | | |
| | Measurement | Nominal | | | |
| | Role | Input | | | |
| Valid Values | 1 | MOST IMPORTANT | | 187 | 12.5% |
| | 2 | 2ND IMPORTANT | | 346 | 23.1% |
| | 3 | 3RD IMPORTANT | | 349 | 23.3% |
| | 4 | 4TH IMPORTANT | | 124 | 8.3% |
| | 5 | LEAST IMPORTANT | | 10 | 0.7% |
| Missing Values | 0 | IAP | | 473 | 31.5% |
| | 8 | DK | | 0 | 0.0% |
| | 9 | NA | | 11 | 0.7% |

## HISPANIC

| Standard Attributes | | | Value | Count | Percent |
|---|---|---|---|---|---|
| Standard Attributes | Position | | 18 | | |
| | Label | Hispanic specified | | | |
| | Type | Numeric | | | |
| | Format | F2 | | | |
| | Measurement | Scale | | | |
| | Role | Input | | | |
| N | Valid | | 1499 | | |
| | Missing | | 1 | | |
| Central Tendency and Dispersion | Mean | | 1.87 | | |
| | Standard Deviation | | 4.690 | | |
| | Percentile 25 | | 1.00 | | |
| | Percentile 50 | | 1.00 | | |
| | Percentile 75 | | 1.00 | | |
| Labeled Values | 0 | IAP | | 0 | 0.0% |
| | 1 | NOT HISPANIC | | 1312 | 87.5% |
| | 2 | MEXICAN, MEXICAN AMERICAN, CHICANO/A | | 99 | 6.6% |
| | 3 | PUERTO RICAN | | 22 | 1.5% |
| | 4 | CUBAN | | 10 | 0.7% |
| | 5 | SALVADORIAN | | 7 | 0.5% |
| | 6 | GUATEMALAN | | 5 | 0.3% |

| | Value | Count | Percent |
|---|---|---|---|
| 7 | PANAMANIAN | 2 | 0.1% |
| 8 | NICARAGUAN | 1 | 0.1% |
| 9 | COSTA RICAN | 0 | 0.0% |
| 10 | CENTRAL AMERICAN | 3 | 0.2% |
| 11 | HONDURAN | 4 | 0.3% |
| 15 | DOMINICAN | 6 | 0.4% |
| 16 | WEST INDIAN | 0 | 0.0% |
| 20 | PERUVIAN | 1 | 0.1% |
| 21 | EQUADORIAN | 0 | 0.0% |
| 22 | COLOMBIAN | 1 | 0.1% |
| 23 | VENEZUELAN | 1 | 0.1% |
| 24 | Argentinian | 2 | 0.1% |
| 25 | Chilean | 0 | 0.0% |
| 30 | SPANISH | 14 | 0.9% |
| 31 | BASQUE | 0 | 0.0% |
| 35 | FILIPINO/A | 1 | 0.1% |
| 40 | LATIN AMERICAN | 0 | 0.0% |
| 41 | SOUTH AMERICAN | 1 | 0.1% |
| 42 | American | 1 | 0.1% |
| 45 | LATIN | 0 | 0.0% |
| 46 | LATINO/A | 2 | 0.1% |
| 47 | HISPANIC | 2 | 0.1% |
| 50 | OTHER, NOT SPECIFIED | 2 | 0.1% |
| 98 | DK | 0 | 0.0% |
| 99 | NA | 1 | 0.1% |

## HOMOSEX

| | | Value | Count | Percent |
|---|---|---|---|---|
| Standard Attributes | Position | 19 | | |
| | Label | Homosexual sex relations | | |
| | Type | Numeric | | |
| | Format | F1 | | |
| | Measurement | Nominal | | |
| | Role | Input | | |
| Valid Values | 1 | ALWAYS WRONG | 364 | 24.3% |
| | 2 | ALMST ALWAYS WRG | 31 | 2.1% |
| | 3 | SOMETIMES WRONG | 60 | 4.0% |

(Continued)

(Continued)

| | | Value | Count | Percent |
|---|---|---|---|---|
| Missing Values | 4 | NOT WRONG AT ALL | 491 | 32.7% |
| | 5 | OTHER | 0 | 0.0% |
| | 0 | IAP | 516 | 34.4% |
| | 8 | DK | 21 | 1.4% |
| | 9 | NA | 17 | 1.1% |

## INCOME

| | | Value | Count | Percent |
|---|---|---|---|---|
| Standard Attributes | Position | 20 | | |
| | Label | Total family income | | |
| | Type | Numeric | | |
| | Format | F2 | | |
| | Measurement | Nominal | | |
| | Role | Input | | |
| Valid Values | 1 | LT $1000 | 32 | 2.1% |
| | 2 | $1000 TO 2999 | 22 | 1.5% |
| | 3 | $3000 TO 3999 | 9 | 0.6% |
| | 4 | $4000 TO 4999 | 3 | 0.2% |
| | 5 | $5000 TO 5999 | 9 | 0.6% |
| | 6 | $6000 TO 6999 | 8 | 0.5% |
| | 7 | $7000 TO 7999 | 6 | 0.4% |
| | 8 | $8000 TO 9999 | 24 | 1.6% |
| | 9 | $10000 – 14999 | 85 | 5.7% |
| | 10 | $15000 – 19999 | 52 | 3.5% |
| | 11 | $20000 – 24999 | 108 | 7.2% |
| | 12 | $25000 OR MORE | 919 | 61.3% |
| Missing Values | 0 | IAP | 0 | 0.0% |
| | 13 | REFUSED | 156 | 10.4% |
| | 98 | DK | 67 | 4.5% |
| | 99 | NA | 0 | 0.0% |

## MAEDUC

| | | Value | Count | Percent |
|---|---|---|---|---|
| Standard Attributes | Position | 21 | | |
| | Label | Highest year school completed, mother | | |
| | Type | Numeric | | |
| | Format | F2 | | |
| | Measurement | Scale | | |
| | Role | Input | | |

|  |  | Value | Count | Percent |
|---|---|---|---|---|
| N | Valid | 1355 |  |  |
|  | Missing | 145 |  |  |
| Central Tendency and Dispersion | Mean | 11.99 |  |  |
|  | Standard Deviation | 3.648 |  |  |
|  | Percentile 25 | 11.00 |  |  |
|  | Percentile 50 | 12.00 |  |  |
|  | Percentile 75 | 14.00 |  |  |
| Labeled Values | 97 | IAP | 56 | 3.7% |
|  | 98 | DK | 86 | 5.7% |
|  | 99 | NA | 3 | 0.2% |

## MARBLK

|  |  | Value | Count | Percent |
|---|---|---|---|---|
| Standard Attributes | Position | 22 |  |  |
|  | Label | Close relative marry Black |  |  |
|  | Type | Numeric |  |  |
|  | Format | F1 |  |  |
|  | Measurement | Nominal |  |  |
|  | Role | Input |  |  |
| Valid Values | 1 | STRONGLY FAVOR | 223 | 14.9% |
|  | 2 | FAVOR | 131 | 8.7% |
|  | 3 | NEITHER FAVOR NOR OPPOSE | 513 | 34.2% |
|  | 4 | OPPOSE | 77 | 5.1% |
|  | 5 | STRONGLY OPPOSE | 42 | 2.8% |
| Missing Values | 0 | IAP | 511 | 34.1% |
|  | 8 | DONT KNOW | 2 | 0.1% |
|  | 9 | NA | 1 | 0.1% |

## MARITAL

|  |  | Value | Count | Percent |
|---|---|---|---|---|
| Standard Attributes | Position | 23 |  |  |
|  | Label | Marital status |  |  |
|  | Type | Numeric |  |  |
|  | Format | F1 |  |  |
|  | Measurement | Nominal |  |  |
|  | Role | Input |  |  |

*(Continued)*

(Continued)

| | | Value | Count | Percent |
|---|---|---|---|---|
| Valid Values | 1 | MARRIED | 644 | 42.9% |
| | 2 | WIDOWED | 136 | 9.1% |
| | 3 | DIVORCED | 259 | 17.3% |
| | 4 | SEPARATED | 68 | 4.5% |
| | 5 | NEVER MARRIED | 392 | 26.1% |
| Missing Values | 9 | NA | 1 | 0.1% |

## OBEY

| | | Value | Count | Percent |
|---|---|---|---|---|
| Standard Attributes | Position | 24 | | |
| | Label | To obey | | |
| | Type | Numeric | | |
| | Format | F1 | | |
| | Measurement | Nominal | | |
| | Role | Input | | |
| Valid Values | 1 | MOST IMPORTANT | 122 | 8.1% |
| | 2 | 2ND IMPORTANT | 114 | 7.6% |
| | 3 | 3RD IMPORTANT | 172 | 11.5% |
| | 4 | 4TH IMPORTANT | 435 | 29.0% |
| | 5 | LEAST IMPORTANT | 173 | 11.5% |
| Missing Values | 0 | IAP | 473 | 31.5% |
| | 8 | DK | 0 | 0.0% |
| | 9 | NA | 11 | 0.7% |

## PAEDUC

| | | Value | Count | Percent |
|---|---|---|---|---|
| Standard Attributes | Position | 25 | | |
| | Label | Highest year school completed, father | | |
| | Type | Numeric | | |
| | Format | F2 | | |
| | Measurement | Scale | | |
| | Role | Input | | |
| N | Valid | 1110 | | |
| | Missing | 390 | | |
| Central Tendency and Dispersion | Mean | 11.86 | | |
| | Standard Deviation | 4.015 | | |
| | Percentile 25 | 10.00 | | |

|  |  | Value | Count | Percent |
|---|---|---|---|---|
|  | Percentile 50 | 12.00 |  |  |
|  | Percentile 75 | 14.00 |  |  |
| Labeled Values | 97 | IAP | 274 | 18.3% |
|  | 98 | DK | 113 | 7.5% |
|  | 99 | NA | 3 | 0.2% |

## PARTNERS

|  |  | Value | Count | Percent |
|---|---|---|---|---|
| Standard Attributes | Position | 26 |  |  |
|  | Label | How many sex partner's R had in last year |  |  |
|  | Type | Numeric |  |  |
|  | Format | F2 |  |  |
|  | Measurement | Nominal |  |  |
|  | Role | Input |  |  |
| Valid Values | 0 | NO PARTNERS | 206 | 13.7% |
|  | 1 | 1 PARTNER | 582 | 38.8% |
|  | 2 | 2 PARTNERS | 67 | 4.5% |
|  | 3 | 3 PARTNERS | 23 | 1.5% |
|  | 4 | 4 PARTNERS | 17 | 1.1% |
|  | 5 | 5–10 PARTNERS | 22 | 1.5% |
|  | 6 | 11–20 PARTNERS | 9 | 0.6% |
|  | 7 | 21–100 PARTNERS | 1 | 0.1% |
|  | 8 | MORE THAN 100 PARTNERS | 0 | 0.0% |
|  | 9 | 1 OR MORE, # unknown | 5 | 0.3% |
|  | 95 | SEVERAL | 0 | 0.0% |
| Missing Values | –1 | IAP | 567 | 37.8% |
|  | 98 | DK | 0 | 0.0% |
|  | 99 | NA | 1 | 0.1% |

## PARTYID

|  |  | Value | Count | Percent |
|---|---|---|---|---|
| Standard Attributes | Position | 27 |  |  |
|  | Label | Political party affiliation |  |  |
|  | Type | Numeric |  |  |
|  | Format | F1 |  |  |
|  | Measurement | Nominal |  |  |
|  | Role | Input |  |  |

*(Continued)*

(Continued)

| | | Value | Count | Percent |
|---|---|---|---|---|
| Valid Values | 0 | STRONG DEMOCRAT | 239 | 15.9% |
| | 1 | NOT STR DEMOCRAT | 247 | 16.5% |
| | 2 | IND,NEAR DEM | 210 | 14.0% |
| | 3 | INDEPENDENT | 250 | 16.7% |
| | 4 | IND,NEAR REP | 147 | 9.8% |
| | 5 | NOT STR REPUBLICAN | 199 | 13.3% |
| | 6 | STRONG REPUBLICAN | 152 | 10.1% |
| | 7 | OTHER PARTY | 34 | 2.3% |
| Missing Values | 8 | DK | 0 | 0.0% |
| | 9 | NA | 22 | 1.5% |

## PIKUPSEX

| | | Value | Count | Percent |
|---|---|---|---|---|
| Standard Attributes | Position | 28 | | |
| | Label | R had sex with casual date last year | | |
| | Type | Numeric | | |
| | Format | F1 | | |
| | Measurement | Nominal | | |
| | Role | Input | | |
| Valid Values | 1 | HAD SEX WITH PICK-UP | 79 | 5.3% |
| | 2 | NOT SELECTED | 93 | 6.2% |
| Missing Values | 0 | IAP | 1321 | 88.1% |
| | 8 | DK | 0 | 0.0% |
| | 9 | NA | 7 | 0.5% |

## POLVIEWS

| | | Value | Count | Percent |
|---|---|---|---|---|
| Standard Attributes | Position | 29 | | |
| | Label | Think of self as liberal or conservative | | |
| | Type | Numeric | | |
| | Format | F1 | | |
| | Measurement | Nominal | | |
| | Role | Input | | |

|  |  | Value | Count | Percent |
|---|---|---|---|---|
| Valid Values | 1 | EXTREMELY LIBERAL | 72 | 4.8% |
|  | 2 | LIBERAL | 188 | 12.5% |
|  | 3 | SLIGHTLY LIBERAL | 156 | 10.4% |
|  | 4 | MODERATE | 519 | 34.6% |
|  | 5 | SLGHTLY CONSERVATIVE | 210 | 14.0% |
|  | 6 | CONSERVATIVE | 227 | 15.1% |
|  | 7 | EXTRMLY CONSERVATIVE | 66 | 4.4% |
| Missing Values | 0 | IAP | 0 | 0.0% |
|  | 8 | DK | 43 | 2.9% |
|  | 9 | NA | 19 | 1.3% |

## POPULAR

|  |  | Value | Count | Percent |
|---|---|---|---|---|
| Standard Attributes | Position | 30 |  |  |
|  | Label | To be well liked or popular |  |  |
|  | Type | Numeric |  |  |
|  | Format | F1 |  |  |
|  | Measurement | Nominal |  |  |
|  | Role | Input |  |  |
| Valid Values | 1 | MOST IMPORTANT | 4 | 0.3% |
|  | 2 | 2ND IMPORTANT | 12 | 0.8% |
|  | 3 | 3RD IMPORTANT | 25 | 1.7% |
|  | 4 | 4TH IMPORTANT | 201 | 13.4% |
|  | 5 | LEAST IMPORTANT | 774 | 51.6% |
| Missing Values | 0 | IAP | 473 | 31.5% |
|  | 8 | DK | 0 | 0.0% |
|  | 9 | NA | 11 | 0.7% |

## POSTLIFE

|  |  | Value | Count | Percent |
|---|---|---|---|---|
| Standard Attributes | Position | 31 |  |  |
|  | Label | Belief in life after death |  |  |
|  | Type | Numeric |  |  |
|  | Format | F1 |  |  |
|  | Measurement | Nominal |  |  |
|  | Role | Input |  |  |

*(Continued)*

(Continued)

| | | Value | Count | Percent |
|---|---|---|---|---|
| Valid Values | 1 | YES | 1090 | 72.7% |
| | 2 | NO | 257 | 17.1% |
| Missing Values | 0 | IAP | 0 | 0.0% |
| | 8 | DK | 148 | 9.9% |
| | 9 | NA | 5 | 0.3% |

## PRAY

| | | Value | Count | Percent |
|---|---|---|---|---|
| Standard Attributes | Position | 32 | | |
| | Label | How often does R pray | | |
| | Type | Numeric | | |
| | Format | F1 | | |
| | Measurement | Nominal | | |
| | Role | Input | | |
| Valid Values | 1 | SEVERAL TIMES A DAY | 441 | 29.4% |
| | 2 | ONCE A DAY | 443 | 29.5% |
| | 3 | SEVERAL TIMES A WEEK | 148 | 9.9% |
| | 4 | ONCE A WEEK | 100 | 6.7% |
| | 5 | LT ONCE A WEEK | 133 | 8.9% |
| | 6 | NEVER | 215 | 14.3% |
| Missing Values | 0 | IAP | 0 | 0.0% |
| | 8 | DK | 4 | 0.3% |
| | 9 | NA | 16 | 1.1% |

## PREMARSX

| | | Value | Count | Percent |
|---|---|---|---|---|
| Standard Attributes | Position | 33 | | |
| | Label | Sex before marriage | | |
| | Type | Numeric | | |
| | Format | F1 | | |
| | Measurement | Nominal | | |
| | Role | Input | | |
| Valid Values | 1 | ALWAYS WRONG | 200 | 13.3% |
| | 2 | ALMST ALWAYS WRG | 54 | 3.6% |
| | 3 | SOMETIMES WRONG | 137 | 9.1% |
| | 4 | NOT WRONG AT ALL | 578 | 38.5% |
| | 5 | OTHER | 0 | 0.0% |
| Missing Values | 0 | IAP | 511 | 34.1% |
| | 8 | DK | 15 | 1.0% |
| | 9 | NA | 5 | 0.3% |

## RACDIF4

| | | Value | Count | Percent |
|---|---|---|---|---|
| Standard Attributes | Position | 34 | | |
| | Label | Differences due to lack of will | | |
| | Type | Numeric | | |
| | Format | F1 | | |
| | Measurement | Nominal | | |
| | Role | Input | | |
| Valid Values | 1 | YES | 398 | 26.5% |
| | 2 | NO | 560 | 37.3% |
| Missing Values | 0 | IAP | 511 | 34.1% |
| | 8 | DK | 28 | 1.9% |
| | 9 | NA | 3 | 0.2% |

## RACE

| | | Value | Count | Percent |
|---|---|---|---|---|
| Standard Attributes | Position | 35 | | |
| | Label | Race of respondent | | |
| | Type | Numeric | | |
| | Format | F1 | | |
| | Measurement | Nominal | | |
| | Role | Input | | |
| Valid Values | 1 | WHITE | 1105 | 73.7% |
| | 2 | BLACK | 250 | 16.7% |
| | 3 | OTHER | 145 | 9.7% |
| Missing Values | 0 | IAP | 0 | 0.0% |

## RELIG

| | | Value | Count | Percent |
|---|---|---|---|---|
| Standard Attributes | Position | 36 | | |
| | Label | R's religious preference | | |
| | Type | Numeric | | |
| | Format | F2 | | |
| | Measurement | Nominal | | |
| | Role | Input | | |
| Valid Values | 1 | PROTESTANT | 731 | 48.7% |
| | 2 | CATHOLIC | 348 | 23.2% |
| | 3 | JEWISH | 25 | 1.7% |
| | 4 | NONE | 297 | 19.8% |

(Continued)

(Continued)

| | Value | | Value | Count | Percent |
|---|---|---|---|---|---|
| | 5 | OTHER | | 23 | 1.5% |
| | 6 | BUDDHISM | | 13 | 0.9% |
| | 7 | HINDUISM | | 7 | 0.5% |
| | 8 | OTHER EASTERN | | 3 | 0.2% |
| | 9 | MOSLEM/ISLAM | | 11 | 0.7% |
| | 10 | ORTHODOX-CHRISTIAN | | 5 | 0.3% |
| | 11 | CHRISTIAN | | 24 | 1.6% |
| | 12 | NATIVE AMERICAN | | 1 | 0.1% |
| | 13 | INTER-NONDENOMINATIONAL | | 4 | 0.3% |
| Missing Values | 0 | IAP | | 0 | 0.0% |
| | 98 | DK | | 1 | 0.1% |
| | 99 | NA | | 7 | 0.5% |

## RINCOM16

| | | Value | Count | Percent |
|---|---|---|---|---|
| Standard Attributes | Position | 37 | | |
| | Label | Respondent's income | | |
| | Type | Numeric | | |
| | Format | F8 | | |
| | Measurement | Scale | | |
| | Role | Input | | |
| N | Valid | 860 | | |
| | Missing | 640 | | |
| Central Tendency and Dispersion | Mean | 15.35 | | |
| | Standard Deviation | 6.061 | | |
| | Percentile 25 | 12.00 | | |
| | Percentile 50 | 17.00 | | |
| | Percentile 75 | 20.00 | | |
| Labeled Values | 0 | IAP | 589 | 39.3% |
| | 1 | UNDER $1000 | 11 | 0.7% |
| | 2 | $1000 TO 2999 | 28 | 1.9% |
| | 3 | $3000 TO 3999 | 18 | 1.2% |
| | 4 | $4000 TO 4999 | 13 | 0.9% |
| | 5 | $5000 TO 5999 | 18 | 1.2% |
| | 6 | $6000 TO 6999 | 18 | 1.2% |
| | 7 | $7000 TO 7999 | 9 | 0.6% |
| | 8 | $8000 TO 9999 | 20 | 1.3% |
| | 9 | $10000 TO 12499 | 24 | 1.6% |
| | 10 | $12500 TO 14999 | 15 | 1.0% |

| | Value | Count | Percent |
|---|---|---|---|
| 11 | $15000 TO 17499 | 26 | 1.7% |
| 12 | $17500 TO 19999 | 23 | 1.5% |
| 13 | $20000 TO 22499 | 41 | 2.7% |
| 14 | $22500 TO 24999 | 43 | 2.9% |
| 15 | $25000 TO 29999 | 52 | 3.5% |
| 16 | $30000 TO 34999 | 68 | 4.5% |
| 17 | $35000 TO 39999 | 58 | 3.9% |
| 18 | $40000 TO 49999 | 82 | 5.5% |
| 19 | $50000 TO 59999 | 72 | 4.8% |
| 20 | $60000 TO 74999 | 75 | 5.0% |
| 21 | $75000 TO $89999 | 46 | 3.1% |
| 22 | $90000 TO $109999 | 35 | 2.3% |
| 23 | $110000 TO $129999 | 17 | 1.1% |
| 24 | $130000 TO $149999 | 12 | 0.8% |
| 25 | $150000 TO $169999 | 6 | 0.4% |
| 26 | $170000 OR OVER | 30 | 2.0% |
| 27 | REFUSED | 42 | 2.8% |
| 98 | DK | 9 | 0.6% |
| 99 | NA | 0 | 0.0% |

## SEX

| | | Value | Count | Percent |
|---|---|---|---|---|
| Standard Attributes | Position | 38 | | |
| | Label | Respondent's sex | | |
| | Type | Numeric | | |
| | Format | F1 | | |
| | Measurement | Nominal | | |
| | Role | Input | | |
| Valid Values | 1 | MALE | 681 | 45.4% |
| | 2 | FEMALE | 819 | 54.6% |

## SEXFREQ

| | | Value | Count | Percent |
|---|---|---|---|---|
| Standard Attributes | Position | 39 | | |
| | Label | Frequency of sex during last year | | |
| | Type | Numeric | | |
| | Format | F1 | | |
| | Measurement | Nominal | | |
| | Role | Input | | |

*(Continued)*

(Continued)

| Valid Values | | | Value | Count | Percent |
|---|---|---|---|---|---|
| Valid Values | 0 | | NOT AT ALL | 225 | 15.0% |
| | 1 | | ONCE OR TWICE | 85 | 5.7% |
| | 2 | | ONCE A MONTH | 113 | 7.5% |
| | 3 | | 2–3 TIMES A MONTH | 159 | 10.6% |
| | 4 | | WEEKLY | 131 | 8.7% |
| | 5 | | 2–3 PER WEEK | 144 | 9.6% |
| | 6 | | 4+ PER WEEK | 48 | 3.2% |
| Missing Values | –1 | | IAP | 567 | 37.8% |
| | 8 | | DK | 2 | 0.1% |
| | 9 | | NA | 26 | 1.7% |

## SIBS

| | | Value | Count | Percent |
|---|---|---|---|---|
| Standard Attributes | Position | 40 | | |
| | Label | Number of brothers and sisters | | |
| | Type | Numeric | | |
| | Format | F2 | | |
| | Measurement | Scale | | |
| | Role | Input | | |
| N | Valid | 1497 | | |
| | Missing | 3 | | |
| Central Tendency and Dispersion | Mean | 3.75 | | |
| | Standard Deviation | 3.282 | | |
| | Percentile 25 | 2.00 | | |
| | Percentile 50 | 3.00 | | |
| | Percentile 75 | 5.00 | | |
| Labeled Values | –1 | IAP | 0 | 0.0% |
| | 98 | DK | 1 | 0.1% |
| | 99 | NA | 2 | 0.1% |

## THNKSELF

| | | Value | Count | Percent |
|---|---|---|---|---|
| Standard Attributes | Position | 41 | | |
| | Label | To think for oneself | | |
| | Type | Numeric | | |
| | Format | F1 | | |
| | Measurement | Nominal | | |
| | Role | Input | | |

|  |  | Value | Count | Percent |
|---|---|---|---|---|
| Valid Values | 1 | MOST IMPORTANT | 439 | 29.3% |
|  | 2 | 2ND IMPORTANT | 167 | 11.1% |
|  | 3 | 3RD IMPORTANT | 189 | 12.6% |
|  | 4 | 4TH IMPORTANT | 174 | 11.6% |
|  | 5 | LEAST IMPORTANT | 47 | 3.1% |
| Missing Values | 0 | IAP | 473 | 31.5% |
|  | 8 | DK | 0 | 0.0% |
|  | 9 | NA | 11 | 0.7% |

## WORKHARD

|  |  | Value | Count | Percent |
|---|---|---|---|---|
| Standard Attributes | Position | 42 |  |  |
|  | Label | To work hard |  |  |
|  | Type | Numeric |  |  |
|  | Format | F1 |  |  |
|  | Measurement | Nominal |  |  |
|  | Role | Input |  |  |
| Valid Values | 1 | MOST IMPORTANT | 264 | 17.6% |
|  | 2 | 2ND IMPORTANT | 377 | 25.1% |
|  | 3 | 3RD IMPORTANT | 281 | 18.7% |
|  | 4 | 4TH IMPORTANT | 82 | 5.5% |
|  | 5 | LEAST IMPORTANT | 12 | 0.8% |
| Missing Values | 0 | IAP | 473 | 31.5% |
|  | 8 | DK | 0 | 0.0% |
|  | 9 | NA | 11 | 0.7% |

## XMOVIE

|  |  | Value | Count | Percent |
|---|---|---|---|---|
| Standard Attributes | Position | 43 |  |  |
|  | Label | Seen X-rated movie in last year |  |  |
|  | Type | Numeric |  |  |
|  | Format | F1 |  |  |
|  | Measurement | Nominal |  |  |
|  | Role | Input |  |  |
| Valid Values | 1 | YES | 278 | 18.5% |
|  | 2 | NO | 745 | 49.7% |
| Missing Values | 0 | IAP | 473 | 31.5% |
|  | 8 | DK | 0 | 0.0% |
|  | 9 | NA | 4 | 0.3% |

## SUBSAMPLE 2: EXER.SAV

EXER.SAV is used primarily in the exercises at the end of the chapters. This subsample contains 1,500 cases and 46 variables drawn from the 2016 General Social Survey (GSS).

### AFFRMACT

| Standard Attributes | | Value | Count | Percent |
|---|---|---|---|---|
| Standard Attributes | Position | 1 | | |
| | Label | Favor preference in hiring Blacks | | |
| | Type | Numeric | | |
| | Format | F1 | | |
| | Measurement | Nominal | | |
| | Role | Input | | |
| Valid Values | 1 | STRONGLY SUPPORT PREF | 143 | 9.5% |
| | 2 | SUPPORT PREF | 66 | 4.4% |
| | 3 | OPPOSE PREF | 300 | 20.0% |
| | 4 | STRONGLY OPPOSE PREF | 424 | 28.3% |
| Missing Values | 0 | IAP | 511 | 34.1% |
| | 8 | DK | 41 | 2.7% |
| | 9 | NA | 15 | 1.0% |

### AGE

| Standard Attributes | | Value | Count | Percent |
|---|---|---|---|---|
| Standard Attributes | Position | 2 | | |
| | Label | Age of respondent | | |
| | Type | Numeric | | |
| | Format | F2 | | |
| | Measurement | Scale | | |
| | Role | Input | | |
| N | Valid | 1495 | | |
| | Missing | 5 | | |
| Central Tendency and Dispersion | Mean | 49.16 | | |
| | Standard Deviation | 17.476 | | |
| | Percentile 25 | 34.00 | | |
| | Percentile 50 | 50.00 | | |
| | Percentile 75 | 62.00 | | |
| Labeled Values | 89 | 89 OR OLDER | 7 | 0.5% |
| | 98 | DK | 0 | 0.0% |
| | 99 | NA | 5 | 0.3% |

## CLASS

| Standard Attributes | | Value | Count | Percent |
|---|---|---|---|---|
| Standard Attributes | Position | 3 | | |
| | Label | Subjective class identification | | |
| | Type | Numeric | | |
| | Format | F1 | | |
| | Measurement | Nominal | | |
| | Role | Input | | |
| Valid Values | 1 | LOWER CLASS | 148 | 9.9% |
| | 2 | WORKING CLASS | 687 | 45.8% |
| | 3 | MIDDLE CLASS | 608 | 40.5% |
| | 4 | UPPER CLASS | 44 | 2.9% |
| | 5 | NO CLASS | 0 | 0.0% |
| Missing Values | 0 | IAP | 0 | 0.0% |
| | 8 | DK | 9 | 0.6% |
| | 9 | NA | 4 | 0.3% |

## COLATH

| Standard Attributes | | Value | Count | Percent |
|---|---|---|---|---|
| Standard Attributes | Position | 4 | | |
| | Label | Allow antireligionist to teach | | |
| | Type | Numeric | | |
| | Format | F1 | | |
| | Measurement | Nominal | | |
| | Role | Input | | |
| Valid Values | 4 | ALLOWED | 648 | 43.2% |
| | 5 | NOT ALLOWED | 310 | 20.7% |
| Missing Values | 0 | IAP | 516 | 34.4% |
| | 8 | DK | 21 | 1.4% |
| | 9 | NA | 5 | 0.3% |

## COLCOM

| Standard Attributes | | Value | Count | Percent |
|---|---|---|---|---|
| Standard Attributes | Position | 5 | | |
| | Label | Should communist teacher be fired | | |
| | Type | Numeric | | |
| | Format | F1 | | |
| | Measurement | Nominal | | |
| | Role | Input | | |

*(Continued)*

(Continued)

| | | Value | Count | Percent |
|---|---|---|---|---|
| Valid Values | 4 | FIRED | 294 | 19.6% |
| | 5 | NOT FIRED | 639 | 42.6% |
| Missing Values | 0 | IAP | 516 | 34.4% |
| | 8 | DK | 43 | 2.9% |
| | 9 | NA | 8 | 0.5% |

## COLHOMO

| | | Value | Count | Percent |
|---|---|---|---|---|
| Standard Attributes | Position | 6 | | |
| | Label | Allow homosexual to teach | | |
| | Type | Numeric | | |
| | Format | F1 | | |
| | Measurement | Nominal | | |
| | Role | Input | | |
| Valid Values | 4 | ALLOWED | 868 | 57.9% |
| | 5 | NOT ALLOWED | 97 | 6.5% |
| Missing Values | 0 | IAP | 516 | 34.4% |
| | 8 | DK | 15 | 1.0% |
| | 9 | NA | 4 | 0.3% |

## COLRAC

| | | Value | Count | Percent |
|---|---|---|---|---|
| Standard Attributes | Position | 7 | | |
| | Label | Allow racist to teach | | |
| | Type | Numeric | | |
| | Format | F1 | | |
| | Measurement | Nominal | | |
| | Role | Input | | |
| Valid Values | 4 | ALLOWED | 430 | 28.7% |
| | 5 | NOT ALLOWED | 532 | 35.5% |
| Missing Values | 0 | IAP | 516 | 34.4% |
| | 8 | DK | 18 | 1.2% |
| | 9 | NA | 4 | 0.3% |

## CONPRESS

| | | Value | Count | Percent |
|---|---|---|---|---|
| Standard Attributes | Position | 8 | | |
| | Label | Confidence in press | | |

| | | Value | Count | Percent |
|---|---|---|---|---|
| | Type | Numeric | | |
| | Format | F1 | | |
| | Measurement | Nominal | | |
| | Role | Input | | |
| Valid Values | 1 | A GREAT DEAL | 79 | 5.3% |
| | 2 | ONLY SOME | 407 | 27.1% |
| | 3 | HARDLY ANY | 529 | 35.3% |
| Missing Values | 0 | IAP | 473 | 31.5% |
| | 8 | DK | 10 | 0.7% |
| | 9 | NA | 2 | 0.1% |

### CONTV

| | | Value | Count | Percent |
|---|---|---|---|---|
| Standard Attributes | Position | 9 | | |
| | Label | Confidence in television | | |
| | Type | Numeric | | |
| | Format | F1 | | |
| | Measurement | Nominal | | |
| | Role | Input | | |
| Valid Values | 1 | A GREAT DEAL | 95 | 6.3% |
| | 2 | ONLY SOME | 487 | 32.5% |
| | 3 | HARDLY ANY | 435 | 29.0% |
| Missing Values | 0 | IAP | 473 | 31.5% |
| | 8 | DK | 7 | 0.5% |
| | 9 | NA | 3 | 0.2% |

### DISCAFF

| | | Value | Count | Percent |
|---|---|---|---|---|
| Standard Attributes | Position | 10 | | |
| | Label | Whites hurt by aff. action | | |
| | Type | Numeric | | |
| | Format | F1 | | |
| | Measurement | Nominal | | |
| | Role | Input | | |
| Valid Values | 1 | VERY LIKELY | 120 | 8.0% |
| | 2 | SOMEWHAT LIKELY | 410 | 27.3% |
| | 3 | NOT VERY LIKELY | 417 | 27.8% |

*(Continued)*

(Continued)

| | | Value | Count | Percent |
|---|---|---|---|---|
| Missing Values | 0 | IAP | 517 | 34.5% |
| | 8 | DONT KNOW | 27 | 1.8% |
| | 9 | NA | 9 | 0.6% |

## EDUC

| | | Value | Count | Percent |
|---|---|---|---|---|
| Standard Attributes | Position | 11 | | |
| | Label | Highest year of school completed | | |
| | Type | Numeric | | |
| | Format | F2 | | |
| | Measurement | Nominal | | |
| | Role | Input | | |
| Valid Values | 0 | | 1 | 0.1% |
| | 3 | | 2 | 0.1% |
| | 4 | | 1 | 0.1% |
| | 5 | | 1 | 0.1% |
| | 6 | | 12 | 0.8% |
| | 7 | | 10 | 0.7% |
| | 8 | | 23 | 1.5% |
| | 9 | | 28 | 1.9% |
| | 10 | | 41 | 2.7% |
| | 11 | | 61 | 4.1% |
| | 12 | | 427 | 28.5% |
| | 13 | | 131 | 8.7% |
| | 14 | | 193 | 12.9% |
| | 15 | | 77 | 5.1% |
| | 16 | | 266 | 17.7% |
| | 17 | | 61 | 4.1% |
| | 18 | | 74 | 4.9% |
| | 19 | | 26 | 1.7% |
| | 20 | | 58 | 3.9% |
| Missing Values | 97 | IAP | 0 | 0.0% |
| | 98 | DK | 1 | 0.1% |
| | 99 | NA | 6 | 0.4% |

## EVSTRAY

| | | Value | Count | Percent |
|---|---|---|---|---|
| Standard Attributes | Position | 12 | | |
| | Label | Have sex other than spouse while married | | |
| | Type | Numeric | | |
| | Format | F1 | | |
| | Measurement | Nominal | | |
| | Role | Input | | |
| Valid Values | 1 | YES | 122 | 8.1% |
| | 2 | NO | 537 | 35.8% |
| | 3 | NEVER MARRIED | 257 | 17.1% |
| Missing Values | 0 | IAP | 567 | 37.8% |
| | 8 | DK | 0 | 0.0% |
| | 9 | NA | 17 | 1.1% |

## FECHLD

| | | Value | Count | Percent |
|---|---|---|---|---|
| Standard Attributes | Position | 13 | | |
| | Label | Mother working doesn't hurt children | | |
| | Type | Numeric | | |
| | Format | F1 | | |
| | Measurement | Nominal | | |
| | Role | Input | | |
| Valid Values | 1 | STRONGLY AGREE | 357 | 23.8% |
| | 2 | AGREE | 408 | 27.2% |
| | 3 | DISAGREE | 183 | 12.2% |
| | 4 | STRONGLY DISAGREE | 36 | 2.4% |
| Missing Values | 0 | IAP | 511 | 34.1% |
| | 8 | DK | 5 | 0.3% |
| | 9 | NA | 0 | 0.0% |

## FEFAM

| | | Value | Count | Percent |
|---|---|---|---|---|
| Standard Attributes | Position | 14 | | |
| | Label | Better for man to work, woman tend home | | |

*(Continued)*

(Continued)

| | | Value | Count | Percent |
|---|---|---|---|---|
| | Type | Numeric | | |
| | Format | F1 | | |
| | Measurement | Nominal | | |
| | Role | Input | | |
| Valid Values | 1 | STRONGLY AGREE | 50 | 3.3% |
| | 2 | AGREE | 202 | 13.5% |
| | 3 | DISAGREE | 465 | 31.0% |
| | 4 | STRONGLY DISAGREE | 264 | 17.6% |
| Missing Values | 0 | IAP | 511 | 34.1% |
| | 8 | DK | 8 | 0.5% |
| | 9 | NA | 0 | 0.0% |

## FEHIRE

| | | Value | Count | Percent |
|---|---|---|---|---|
| Standard Attributes | Position | 15 | | |
| | Label | Should hire and promote women | | |
| | Type | Numeric | | |
| | Format | F1 | | |
| | Measurement | Nominal | | |
| | Role | Input | | |
| Valid Values | 1 | STRONGLY AGREE | 120 | 8.0% |
| | 2 | AGREE | 256 | 17.1% |
| | 3 | NEITHER AGREE NOR DISAGREE | 48 | 3.2% |
| | 4 | DISAGREE | 67 | 4.5% |
| | 5 | STRONGLY DISAGREE | 14 | 0.9% |
| Missing Values | 0 | IAP | 995 | 66.3% |
| | 8 | DONT KNOW | 0 | 0.0% |
| | 9 | NA | 0 | 0.0% |

## FEPRESCH

| | | Value | Count | Percent |
|---|---|---|---|---|
| Standard Attributes | Position | 16 | | |
| | Label | Preschool kids suffer if mother works | | |
| | Type | Numeric | | |
| | Format | F1 | | |

| | | Value | Count | Percent |
|---|---|---|---|---|
| | Measurement | Nominal | | |
| | Role | Input | | |
| Valid Values | 1 | STRONGLY AGREE | 32 | 2.1% |
| | 2 | AGREE | 218 | 14.5% |
| | 3 | DISAGREE | 539 | 35.9% |
| | 4 | STRONGLY DISAGREE | 194 | 12.9% |
| Missing Values | 0 | IAP | 511 | 34.1% |
| | 8 | DK | 6 | 0.4% |
| | 9 | NA | 0 | 0.0% |

## GRASS

| | | Value | Count | Percent |
|---|---|---|---|---|
| Standard Attributes | Position | 17 | | |
| | Label | Should marijuana be made legal | | |
| | Type | Numeric | | |
| | Format | F1 | | |
| | Measurement | Nominal | | |
| | Role | Input | | |
| Valid Values | 1 | LEGAL | 589 | 39.3% |
| | 2 | NOT LEGAL | 375 | 25.0% |
| Missing Values | 0 | IAP | 473 | 31.5% |
| | 8 | DK | 61 | 4.1% |
| | 9 | NA | 2 | 0.1% |

## HEALTH

| | | Value | Count | Percent |
|---|---|---|---|---|
| Standard Attributes | Position | 18 | | |
| | Label | Condition of health | | |
| | Type | Numeric | | |
| | Format | F1 | | |
| | Measurement | Nominal | | |
| | Role | Input | | |
| Valid Values | 1 | EXCELLENT | 230 | 15.3% |
| | 2 | GOOD | 482 | 32.1% |
| | 3 | FAIR | 205 | 13.7% |
| | 4 | POOR | 62 | 4.1% |
| Missing Values | 0 | IAP | 518 | 34.5% |
| | 8 | DK | 0 | 0.0% |
| | 9 | NA | 3 | 0.2% |

## HISPANIC

| Standard Attributes | | Value | Count | Percent |
|---|---|---|---|---|
| Standard Attributes | Position | 19 | | |
| | Label | Hispanic specified | | |
| | Type | Numeric | | |
| | Format | F2 | | |
| | Measurement | Scale | | |
| | Role | Input | | |
| N | Valid | 1499 | | |
| | Missing | 1 | | |
| Central Tendency and Dispersion | Mean | 1.87 | | |
| | Standard Deviation | 4.690 | | |
| | Percentile 25 | 1.00 | | |
| | Percentile 50 | 1.00 | | |
| | Percentile 75 | 1.00 | | |
| Labeled Values | 0 | IAP | 0 | 0.0% |
| | 1 | NOT HISPANIC | 1312 | 87.5% |
| | 2 | MEXICAN, MEXICAN AMERICAN, CHICANO/A | 99 | 6.6% |
| | 3 | PUERTO RICAN | 22 | 1.5% |
| | 4 | CUBAN | 10 | 0.7% |
| | 5 | SALVADORIAN | 7 | 0.5% |
| | 6 | GUATEMALAN | 5 | 0.3% |
| | 7 | PANAMANIAN | 2 | 0.1% |
| | 8 | NICARAGUAN | 1 | 0.1% |
| | 9 | COSTA RICAN | 0 | 0.0% |
| | 10 | CENTRAL AMERICAN | 3 | 0.2% |
| | 11 | HONDURAN | 4 | 0.3% |
| | 15 | DOMINICAN | 6 | 0.4% |
| | 16 | WEST INDIAN | 0 | 0.0% |
| | 20 | PERUVIAN | 1 | 0.1% |
| | 21 | EQUADORIAN | 0 | 0.0% |
| | 22 | COLOMBIAN | 1 | 0.1% |
| | 23 | VENEZUELAN | 1 | 0.1% |
| | 24 | Argentinian | 2 | 0.1% |
| | 25 | Chilean | 0 | 0.0% |
| | 30 | SPANISH | 14 | 0.9% |
| | 31 | BASQUE | 0 | 0.0% |
| | 35 | FILIPINO/A | 1 | 0.1% |
| | 40 | LATIN AMERICAN | 0 | 0.0% |
| | 41 | SOUTH AMERICAN | 1 | 0.1% |
| | 42 | American | 1 | 0.1% |
| | 45 | LATIN | 0 | 0.0% |
| | 46 | LATINO/A | 2 | 0.1% |
| | 47 | HISPANIC | 2 | 0.1% |
| | 50 | OTHER, NOT SPECIFIED | 2 | 0.1% |
| | 98 | DK | 0 | 0.0% |
| | 99 | NA | 1 | 0.1% |

## INCOME

| | | Value | Count | Percent |
|---|---|---|---|---|
| Standard Attributes | Position | 20 | | |
| | Label | Total family income | | |
| | Type | Numeric | | |
| | Format | F2 | | |
| | Measurement | Nominal | | |
| | Role | Input | | |
| Valid Values | 1 | LT $1000 | 32 | 2.1% |
| | 2 | $1000 TO 2999 | 22 | 1.5% |
| | 3 | $3000 TO 3999 | 9 | 0.6% |
| | 4 | $4000 TO 4999 | 3 | 0.2% |
| | 5 | $5000 TO 5999 | 9 | 0.6% |
| | 6 | $6000 TO 6999 | 8 | 0.5% |
| | 7 | $7000 TO 7999 | 6 | 0.4% |
| | 8 | $8000 TO 9999 | 24 | 1.6% |
| | 9 | $10000 – 14999 | 85 | 5.7% |
| | 10 | $15000 – 19999 | 52 | 3.5% |
| | 11 | $20000 – 24999 | 108 | 7.2% |
| | 12 | $25000 OR MORE | 919 | 61.3% |
| Missing Values | 0 | IAP | 0 | 0.0% |
| | 13 | REFUSED | 156 | 10.4% |
| | 98 | DK | 67 | 4.5% |
| | 99 | NA | 0 | 0.0% |

## MAEDUC

| | | Value | Count | Percent |
|---|---|---|---|---|
| Standard Attributes | Position | 21 | | |
| | Label | Highest year school completed, mother | | |
| | Type | Numeric | | |
| | Format | F2 | | |
| | Measurement | Scale | | |
| | Role | Input | | |
| N | Valid | 1355 | | |
| | Missing | 145 | | |
| Central Tendency and Dispersion | Mean | 11.99 | | |
| | Standard Deviation | 3.648 | | |
| | Percentile 25 | 11.00 | | |
| | Percentile 50 | 12.00 | | |
| | Percentile 75 | 14.00 | | |

(Continued)

(Continued)

| Labeled Values | | Value | Count | Percent |
|---|---|---|---|---|
| | 97 | IAP | 56 | 3.7% |
| | 98 | DK | 86 | 5.7% |
| | 99 | NA | 3 | 0.2% |

## MARITAL

| | | Value | Count | Percent |
|---|---|---|---|---|
| Standard Attributes | Position | 22 | | |
| | Label | Marital status | | |
| | Type | Numeric | | |
| | Format | F1 | | |
| | Measurement | Nominal | | |
| | Role | Input | | |
| Valid Values | 1 | MARRIED | 644 | 42.9% |
| | 2 | WIDOWED | 136 | 9.1% |
| | 3 | DIVORCED | 259 | 17.3% |
| | 4 | SEPARATED | 68 | 4.5% |
| | 5 | NEVER MARRIED | 392 | 26.1% |
| Missing Values | 9 | NA | 1 | 0.1% |

## NATCRIME

| | | Value | Count | Percent |
|---|---|---|---|---|
| Standard Attributes | Position | 23 | | |
| | Label | Halting rising crime rate | | |
| | Type | Numeric | | |
| | Format | F1 | | |
| | Measurement | Nominal | | |
| | Role | Input | | |
| Valid Values | 1 | TOO LITTLE | 491 | 32.7% |
| | 2 | ABOUT RIGHT | 184 | 12.3% |
| | 3 | TOO MUCH | 46 | 3.1% |
| Missing Values | 0 | IAP | 756 | 50.4% |
| | 8 | DK | 20 | 1.3% |
| | 9 | NA | 3 | 0.2% |

## NATDRUG

| | | Value | Count | Percent |
|---|---|---|---|---|
| Standard Attributes | Position | 24 | | |
| | Label | Dealing with drug addiction | | |
| | Type | Numeric | | |

|  |  | Value | Count | Percent |
|---|---|---|---|---|
| Standard Attributes | Position | 24 |  |  |
|  | Format | F1 |  |  |
|  | Measurement | Nominal |  |  |
|  | Role | Input |  |  |
| Valid Values | 1 | TOO LITTLE | 459 | 30.6% |
|  | 2 | ABOUT RIGHT | 204 | 13.6% |
|  | 3 | TOO MUCH | 63 | 4.2% |
| Missing Values | 0 | IAP | 756 | 50.4% |
|  | 8 | DK | 16 | 1.1% |
|  | 9 | NA | 2 | 0.1% |

## NATEDUC

|  |  | Value | Count | Percent |
|---|---|---|---|---|
| Standard Attributes | Position | 25 |  |  |
|  | Label | Improving nations education system |  |  |
|  | Type | Numeric |  |  |
|  | Format | F1 |  |  |
|  | Measurement | Nominal |  |  |
|  | Role | Input |  |  |
| Valid Values | 1 | TOO LITTLE | 525 | 35.0% |
|  | 2 | ABOUT RIGHT | 163 | 10.9% |
|  | 3 | TOO MUCH | 48 | 3.2% |
| Missing Values | 0 | IAP | 756 | 50.4% |
|  | 8 | DK | 7 | 0.5% |
|  | 9 | NA | 1 | 0.1% |

## NATFARE

|  |  | Value | Count | Percent |
|---|---|---|---|---|
| Standard Attributes | Position | 26 |  |  |
|  | Label | Welfare |  |  |
|  | Type | Numeric |  |  |
|  | Format | F1 |  |  |
|  | Measurement | Nominal |  |  |
|  | Role | Input |  |  |
| Valid Values | 1 | TOO LITTLE | 151 | 10.1% |
|  | 2 | ABOUT RIGHT | 241 | 16.1% |
|  | 3 | TOO MUCH | 323 | 21.5% |
| Missing Values | 0 | IAP | 756 | 50.4% |
|  | 8 | DK | 26 | 1.7% |
|  | 9 | NA | 3 | 0.2% |

## NATHEAL

| | | Value | Count | Percent |
|---|---|---|---|---|
| Standard Attributes | Position | 27 | | |
| | Label | Improving & protecting nation's health | | |
| | Type | Numeric | | |
| | Format | F1 | | |
| | Measurement | Nominal | | |
| | Role | Input | | |
| Valid Values | 1 | TOO LITTLE | 470 | 31.3% |
| | 2 | ABOUT RIGHT | 189 | 12.6% |
| | 3 | TOO MUCH | 72 | 4.8% |
| Missing Values | 0 | IAP | 756 | 50.4% |
| | 8 | DK | 10 | 0.7% |
| | 9 | NA | 3 | 0.2% |

## NATRACE

| | | Value | Count | Percent |
|---|---|---|---|---|
| Standard Attributes | Position | 28 | | |
| | Label | Improving the conditions of Blacks | | |
| | Type | Numeric | | |
| | Format | F1 | | |
| | Measurement | Nominal | | |
| | Role | Input | | |
| Valid Values | 1 | TOO LITTLE | 344 | 22.9% |
| | 2 | ABOUT RIGHT | 254 | 16.9% |
| | 3 | TOO MUCH | 80 | 5.3% |
| Missing Values | 0 | IAP | 756 | 50.4% |
| | 8 | DK | 56 | 3.7% |
| | 9 | NA | 10 | 0.7% |

## NEWS

| | | Value | Count | Percent |
|---|---|---|---|---|
| Standard Attributes | Position | 29 | | |
| | Label | How often does R read newspaper | | |
| | Type | Numeric | | |
| | Format | F1 | | |
| | Measurement | Nominal | | |
| | Role | Input | | |

| | | Value | Count | Percent |
|---|---|---|---|---|
| Valid Values | 1 | EVERY DAY | 222 | 14.8% |
| | 2 | FEW TIMES A WEEK | 136 | 9.1% |
| | 3 | ONCE A WEEK | 109 | 7.3% |
| | 4 | LESS THAN ONCE WK | 164 | 10.9% |
| | 5 | NEVER | 356 | 23.7% |
| Missing Values | 0 | IAP | 512 | 34.1% |
| | 8 | DK | 0 | 0.0% |
| | 9 | NA | 1 | 0.1% |

## PAEDUC

| | | Value | Count | Percent |
|---|---|---|---|---|
| Standard Attributes | Position | 30 | | |
| | Label | Highest year school completed, father | | |
| | Type | Numeric | | |
| | Format | F2 | | |
| | Measurement | Scale | | |
| | Role | Input | | |
| N | Valid | 1110 | | |
| | Missing | 390 | | |
| Central Tendency and Dispersion | Mean | 11.86 | | |
| | Standard Deviation | 4.015 | | |
| | Percentile 25 | 10.00 | | |
| | Percentile 50 | 12.00 | | |
| | Percentile 75 | 14.00 | | |
| Labeled Values | 97 | IAP | 274 | 18.3% |
| | 98 | DK | 113 | 7.5% |
| | 99 | NA | 3 | 0.2% |

## PARTNERS

| | | Value | Count | Percent |
|---|---|---|---|---|
| Standard Attributes | Position | 31 | | |
| | Label | How many sex partners R had in last year | | |
| | Type | Numeric | | |
| | Format | F2 | | |
| | Measurement | Nominal | | |
| | Role | Input | | |

*(Continued)*

(Continued)

| | Value | | Count | Percent |
|---|---|---|---|---|
| Valid Values | 0 | NO PARTNERS | 206 | 13.7% |
| | 1 | 1 PARTNER | 582 | 38.8% |
| | 2 | 2 PARTNERS | 67 | 4.5% |
| | 3 | 3 PARTNERS | 23 | 1.5% |
| | 4 | 4 PARTNERS | 17 | 1.1% |
| | 5 | 5-10 PARTNERS | 22 | 1.5% |
| | 6 | 11-20 PARTNERS | 9 | 0.6% |
| | 7 | 21-100 PARTNERS | 1 | 0.1% |
| | 8 | MORE THAN 100 PARTNERS | 0 | 0.0% |
| | 9 | 1 OR MORE, # unknown | 5 | 0.3% |
| | 95 | SEVERAL | 0 | 0.0% |
| Missing Values | -1 | IAP | 567 | 37.8% |
| | 98 | DK | 0 | 0.0% |
| | 99 | NA | 1 | 0.1% |

## PILLOK

| | | Value | Count | Percent |
|---|---|---|---|---|
| Standard Attributes | Position | 32 | | |
| | Label | Birth control to teenagers 14-16 | | |
| | Type | Numeric | | |
| | Format | F1 | | |
| | Measurement | Nominal | | |
| | Role | Input | | |
| Valid Values | 1 | STRONGLY AGREE | 264 | 17.6% |
| | 2 | AGREE | 327 | 21.8% |
| | 3 | DISAGREE | 224 | 14.9% |
| | 4 | STRONGLY DISAGREE | 143 | 9.5% |
| Missing Values | 0 | IAP | 511 | 34.1% |
| | 8 | DK | 23 | 1.5% |
| | 9 | NA | 8 | 0.5% |

## POLABUSE

| | | Value | Count | Percent |
|---|---|---|---|---|
| Standard Attributes | Position | 33 | | |
| | Label | Citizen said vulgar or obscene things | | |
| | Type | Numeric | | |
| | Format | F1 | | |
| | Measurement | Nominal | | |
| | Role | Input | | |

| | | Value | Count | Percent |
|---|---|---|---|---|
| Valid Values | 1 | YES | 95 | 6.3% |
| | 2 | NO | 911 | 60.7% |
| Missing Values | 0 | IAP | 473 | 31.5% |
| | 8 | DK | 19 | 1.3% |
| | 9 | NA | 2 | 0.1% |

## POLATTAK

| | | Value | Count | Percent |
|---|---|---|---|---|
| Standard Attributes | Position | 34 | | |
| | Label | Citizen attacking policeman with fists | | |
| | Type | Numeric | | |
| | Format | F1 | | |
| | Measurement | Nominal | | |
| | Role | Input | | |
| Valid Values | 1 | YES | 865 | 57.7% |
| | 2 | NO | 145 | 9.7% |
| Missing Values | 0 | IAP | 473 | 31.5% |
| | 8 | DK | 13 | 0.9% |
| | 9 | NA | 4 | 0.3% |

## POLESCAP

| | | Value | Count | Percent |
|---|---|---|---|---|
| Standard Attributes | Position | 35 | | |
| | Label | Citizen attempting to escape custody | | |
| | Type | Numeric | | |
| | Format | F1 | | |
| | Measurement | Nominal | | |
| | Role | Input | | |
| Valid Values | 1 | YES | 670 | 44.7% |
| | 2 | NO | 314 | 20.9% |
| Missing Values | 0 | IAP | 473 | 31.5% |
| | 8 | DK | 40 | 2.7% |
| | 9 | NA | 3 | 0.2% |

## POLHITOK

| | | Value | Count | Percent |
|---|---|---|---|---|
| Standard Attributes | Position | 36 | | |
| | Label | Ever approve of police striking citizen | | |
| | Type | Numeric | | |

*(Continued)*

(Continued)

| | | Value | Count | Percent |
|---|---|---|---|---|
| | Format | F1 | | |
| | Measurement | Nominal | | |
| | Role | Input | | |
| Valid Values | 1 | YES | 689 | 45.9% |
| | 2 | NO | 298 | 19.9% |
| Missing Values | 0 | IAP | 473 | 31.5% |
| | 8 | DK | 37 | 2.5% |
| | 9 | NA | 3 | 0.2% |

## POLMURDR

| | | Value | Count | Percent |
|---|---|---|---|---|
| Standard Attributes | Position | 37 | | |
| | Label | Citizen questioned as murder suspect | | |
| | Type | Numeric | | |
| | Format | F1 | | |
| | Measurement | Nominal | | |
| | Role | Input | | |
| Valid Values | 1 | YES | 155 | 10.3% |
| | 2 | NO | 843 | 56.2% |
| Missing Values | 0 | IAP | 473 | 31.5% |
| | 8 | DK | 25 | 1.7% |
| | 9 | NA | 4 | 0.3% |

## PORNLAW

| | | Value | Count | Percent |
|---|---|---|---|---|
| Standard Attributes | Position | 38 | | |
| | Label | Feelings about pornography laws | | |
| | Type | Numeric | | |
| | Format | F1 | | |
| | Measurement | Nominal | | |
| | Role | Input | | |
| Valid Values | 1 | ILLEGAL TO ALL | 335 | 22.3% |
| | 2 | ILLEGAL UNDER 18 | 637 | 42.5% |
| | 3 | LEGAL | 43 | 2.9% |
| Missing Values | 0 | IAP | 473 | 31.5% |
| | 8 | DK | 7 | 0.5% |
| | 9 | NA | 5 | 0.3% |

## RACE

| | | Value | Count | Percent |
|---|---|---|---|---|
| Standard Attributes | Position | 39 | | |
| | Label | Race of respondent | | |
| | Type | Numeric | | |
| | Format | F1 | | |
| | Measurement | Nominal | | |
| | Role | Input | | |
| Valid Values | 1 | WHITE | 1105 | 73.7% |
| | 2 | BLACK | 250 | 16.7% |
| | 3 | OTHER | 145 | 9.7% |
| Missing Values | 0 | IAP | 0 | 0.0% |

## RACWORK

| | | Value | Count | Percent |
|---|---|---|---|---|
| Standard Attributes | Position | 40 | | |
| | Label | Racial makeup of workplace | | |
| | Type | Numeric | | |
| | Format | F1 | | |
| | Measurement | Nominal | | |
| | Role | Input | | |
| Valid Values | 1 | ALL WHITE | 106 | 7.1% |
| | 2 | MOSTLY WHITE | 256 | 17.1% |
| | 3 | HALF WHITE-BLACK | 174 | 11.6% |
| | 4 | MOSTLY BLACK | 24 | 1.6% |
| | 5 | ALL BLACK | 7 | 0.5% |
| | 6 | WORKS ALONE | 0 | 0.0% |
| Missing Values | 0 | IAP | 908 | 60.5% |
| | 8 | DON'T KNOW | 14 | 0.9% |
| | 9 | NA | 11 | 0.7% |

## RINCOM16

| | | Value | Count | Percent |
|---|---|---|---|---|
| Standard Attributes | Position | 41 | | |
| | Label | Respondent's income | | |
| | Type | Numeric | | |
| | Format | F8 | | |
| | Measurement | Scale | | |
| | Role | Input | | |

*(Continued)*

(Continued)

| N | | Value | Count | Percent |
|---|---|---|---|---|
| | Valid | 860 | | |
| | Missing | 640 | | |
| Central Tendency and Dispersion | Mean | 15.35 | | |
| | Standard Deviation | 6.061 | | |
| | Percentile 25 | 12.00 | | |
| | Percentile 50 | 17.00 | | |
| | Percentile 75 | 20.00 | | |
| Labeled Values | 0 | IAP | 589 | 39.3% |
| | 1 | UNDER $1000 | 11 | 0.7% |
| | 2 | $1000 TO 2999 | 28 | 1.9% |
| | 3 | $3000 TO 3999 | 18 | 1.2% |
| | 4 | $4000 TO 4999 | 13 | 0.9% |
| | 5 | $5000 TO 5999 | 18 | 1.2% |
| | 6 | $6000 TO 6999 | 18 | 1.2% |
| | 7 | $7000 TO 7999 | 9 | 0.6% |
| | 8 | $8000 TO 9999 | 20 | 1.3% |
| | 9 | $10000 TO 12499 | 24 | 1.6% |
| | 10 | $12500 TO 14999 | 15 | 1.0% |
| | 11 | $15000 TO 17499 | 26 | 1.7% |
| | 12 | $17500 TO 19999 | 23 | 1.5% |
| | 13 | $20000 TO 22499 | 41 | 2.7% |
| | 14 | $22500 TO 24999 | 43 | 2.9% |
| | 15 | $25000 TO 29999 | 52 | 3.5% |
| | 16 | $30000 TO 34999 | 68 | 4.5% |
| | 17 | $35000 TO 39999 | 58 | 3.9% |
| | 18 | $40000 TO 49999 | 82 | 5.5% |
| | 19 | $50000 TO 59999 | 72 | 4.8% |
| | 20 | $60000 TO 74999 | 75 | 5.0% |
| | 21 | $75000 TO $89999 | 46 | 3.1% |
| | 22 | $90000 TO $109999 | 35 | 2.3% |
| | 23 | $110000 TO $129999 | 17 | 1.1% |
| | 24 | $130000 TO $149999 | 12 | 0.8% |
| | 25 | $150000 TO $169999 | 6 | 0.4% |
| | 26 | $170000 OR OVER | 30 | 2.0% |
| | 27 | REFUSED | 42 | 2.8% |
| | 98 | DK | 9 | 0.6% |
| | 99 | NA | 0 | 0.0% |

## SEX

| | | Value | Count | Percent |
|---|---|---|---|---|
| Standard Attributes | Position | 42 | | |
| | Label | Respondent's sex | | |
| | Type | Numeric | | |
| | Format | F1 | | |
| | Measurement | Nominal | | |
| | Role | Input | | |
| Valid Values | 1 | MALE | 681 | 45.4% |
| | 2 | FEMALE | 819 | 54.6% |

## SEXEDUC

| | | Value | Count | Percent |
|---|---|---|---|---|
| Standard Attributes | Position | 43 | | |
| | Label | Sex education in public schools | | |
| | Type | Numeric | | |
| | Format | F1 | | |
| | Measurement | Nominal | | |
| | Role | Input | | |
| Valid Values | 1 | FAVOR | 909 | 60.6% |
| | 2 | OPPOSE | 72 | 4.8% |
| | 3 | DEPENDS | 0 | 0.0% |
| Missing Values | 0 | IAP | 512 | 34.1% |
| | 8 | DK | 7 | 0.5% |
| | 9 | NA | 0 | 0.0% |

## SEXFREQ

| | | Value | Count | Percent |
|---|---|---|---|---|
| Standard Attributes | Position | 44 | | |
| | Label | Frequency of sex during last year | | |
| | Type | Numeric | | |
| | Format | F1 | | |
| | Measurement | Nominal | | |
| | Role | Input | | |

*(Continued)*

(Continued)

|  |  | Value | Count | Percent |
|---|---|---|---|---|
| Valid Values | 0 | NOT AT ALL | 225 | 15.0% |
|  | 1 | ONCE OR TWICE | 85 | 5.7% |
|  | 2 | ONCE A MONTH | 113 | 7.5% |
|  | 3 | 2–3 TIMES A MONTH | 159 | 10.6% |
|  | 4 | WEEKLY | 131 | 8.7% |
|  | 5 | 2–3 PER WEEK | 144 | 9.6% |
|  | 6 | 4+ PER WEEK | 48 | 3.2% |
| Missing Values | –1 | IAP | 567 | 37.8% |
|  | 8 | DK | 2 | 0.1% |
|  | 9 | NA | 26 | 1.7% |

## TEENSEX

|  |  | Value | Count | Percent |
|---|---|---|---|---|
| Standard Attributes | Position | 45 |  |  |
|  | Label | Sex before marriage: teens 14–16 |  |  |
|  | Type | Numeric |  |  |
|  | Format | F1 |  |  |
|  | Measurement | Nominal |  |  |
|  | Role | Input |  |  |
| Valid Values | 1 | ALWAYS WRONG | 598 | 39.9% |
|  | 2 | ALMST ALWAYS WRG | 160 | 10.7% |
|  | 3 | SOMETIMES WRONG | 117 | 7.8% |
|  | 4 | NOT WRONG AT ALL | 103 | 6.9% |
|  | 5 | OTHER | 0 | 0.0% |
| Missing Values | 0 | IAP | 511 | 34.1% |
|  | 8 | DK | 9 | 0.6% |
|  | 9 | NA | 2 | 0.1% |

## TVHOURS

|  |  | Value | Count | Percent |
|---|---|---|---|---|
| Standard Attributes | Position | 46 |  |  |
|  | Label | Hours per day watching TV |  |  |
|  | Type | Numeric |  |  |
|  | Format | F2 |  |  |
|  | Measurement | Scale |  |  |
|  | Role | Input |  |  |
| N | Valid | 986 |  |  |
|  | Missing | 514 |  |  |
| Central Tendency and Dispersion | Mean | 2.98 |  |  |
|  | Standard Deviation | 2.783 |  |  |
|  | Percentile 25 | 1.00 |  |  |
|  | Percentile 50 | 2.00 |  |  |
|  | Percentile 75 | 4.00 |  |  |
| Labeled Values | –1 | IAP | 512 | 34.1% |
|  | 98 | DK | 2 | 0.1% |
|  | 99 | NA | 0 | 0.0% |

# APPENDIX B: QUESTIONNAIRE FOR CLASS SURVEY

Questionnaire for Class Survey

ID _____  _____  _____ (CODE LEADING ZEROS)     1  2  3

CHLDIDEL   1. What do you think is the ideal number of children for a family to have?     4  5

_____  _____ (CODE LEADING ZERO IF < 10)

2. If you had to choose, which thing on this list would you say is the most important for a child to learn to prepare him or her for life? (CODE 1)

[INTERVIEWER: READ CHOICES BELOW]     6

OBEY       _____ A. to obey     7

POPULAR    _____ B. to be well liked or popular     8

THNKSELF   _____ C. to think for himself or herself     9

WORKHARD   _____ D. to work hard     10

HELPOTH    _____ E. to help others

a. Which comes next in importance? (Code 2)
b. Which comes third? (Code 3)
c. Which comes fourth? (Code 4)
d. Which comes fifth? (Code 5) (no response: Code 9)

SIBS       3. How many brothers and sisters did you have? Please count those born     11  12
           alive, but no longer living, as well as those alive now. Also include
           stepbrothers and stepsisters and children adopted by your parents.

_____  _____ (CODE NUMBER WITH LEADING ZERO)

MARITAL    4. Are you married, widowed, divorced, or separated, or have you never been married?     13
           _____ 1. married
           _____ 2. widowed
           _____ 3. divorced
           _____ 4. separated
           _____ 5. never married
           _____ 9. no answer

[INTERVIEWER: ASK QUESTION 5 ONLY IF MARRIED OR WIDOWED]     14

DIVORCE    5. Have you ever been divorced or legally separated?
           _____ 1. yes
           _____ 2. no
           _____ 3. no answer or not applicable

PARTYID    6. Generally speaking, do you usually think of yourself as a Republican,     15
           Democrat, independent, or something else?
           _____ 0. strong Democrat
           _____ 1. not very strong Democrat
           _____ 2. independent, close to Democrat
           _____ 3. independent, neither, or no response
           _____ 4. independent, close to Republican

_____ 5. not very strong Republican

_____ 6. strong Republican

_____ 7. other party, refused to say

_____ 9. no answer

POLVIEWS

7. We hear a lot of talk these days about liberals and conservatives. I'm going to read you a set of seven categories of political views that people might hold, arranged from extremely liberal to extremely conservative. Which best describes you, or haven't you thought much about this?

16

_____ 1. extremely liberal

_____ 2. liberal

_____ 3. slightly liberal

_____ 4. moderate, middle-of-the-road

_____ 5. slightly conservative

_____ 6. conservative

_____ 7. extremely conservative

_____ 9. no answer or not applicable

CAPPUN

8. Do you favor or oppose the death penalty for murder?

17

_____ 1. favor

_____ 2. oppose

_____ 9. don't know, no answer

GUNLAW

9. Would you favor or oppose a law that would require a person to obtain a police permit before he or she could buy a gun?

18

_____ 1. favor

_____ 2. oppose

_____ 9. don't know, no answer

GETAHEAD

10. Some people say that people get ahead by their own hard work; others say that lucky breaks or help from other people is more important. Which do you think is most important?

19

_____ 1. hard work most important

_____ 2. hard work, luck equally important

_____ 3. luck most important

_____ 9. other, don't know, no answer

RACDIF4

11. On the average, African Americans have worse jobs, incomes, and housing than White people. Do you think this is because African Americans just don't have the motivation or will to pull themselves up out of poverty?

20

_____ 1. yes

_____ 2. no

RACMAR

12. Do you think there should be laws against marriages between (Negroes/Blacks/African Americans) and Whites?

21

_____ 1. yes

_____ 2. no

_____ 8. don't know

_____ 9. no answer, not applicable

RACPUSH

13. Some people have expressed the opinion that (Negroes/Blacks/African Americans) shouldn't push themselves in to where they're not wanted. Which of these responses comes closest to how you, yourself, feel?

22

_____ 1. agree strongly

_____ 2. agree slightly

_____ 3. disagree slightly

_____ 4. disagree strongly

_____ 8. no opinion

_____ 9. no answer, not applicable

ABDEFECT    14. Please tell me whether or not you think it should be possible for a pregnant woman to obtain a legal abortion if . . .

‾‾
23

A. If there is a strong chance of serious defect in the baby?

_____ 1. yes

_____ 2. no

_____ 3. don't know, no answer

‾‾
24

ABNOMORE    B. If she is married and does not want any more children?

_____ 1. yes

_____ 2. no

_____ 3. don't know, no answer

‾‾
25

ABHLTH    C. If the woman's own health is seriously endangered by the pregnancy?

_____ 1. yes

_____ 2. no

_____ 3. don't know, no answer

‾‾
26

ABPOOR    D. If the family has a very low income and cannot afford any more children?

_____ 1. yes

_____ 2. no

_____ 3. don't know, no answer

‾‾
27

ABRAPE    E. If she became pregnant as a result of rape?

_____ 1. yes

_____ 2. no

_____ 3. don't know, no answer

‾‾
28

ABSINGLE    F. If she is not married and does not want to marry the man?

_____ 1. yes

_____ 2. no

_____ 3. don't know, no answer

‾‾
29

ABANY    G. If the woman wants it for any reason?

_____ 1. yes

_____ 2. no

_____ 3. don't know, no answer

RELIG    15. What is your religious preference? Is it Protestant, Catholic, Jewish, some other religion, or no religion?

‾‾
30

_____ 1. Protestant

_____ 2. Catholic

_____ 3. Jewish

_____ 4. none

_____ 5. other

_____ 9. no answer, no response

‾‾
31

ATTEND    16. How often do you attend religious services?

_____ 0. never

_____ 1. less than once a year

_____ 2. about once or twice a year

_____ 3. several times a year

_____ 4. about once a month

_____ 5. 2 or 3 times a month

_____ 6. nearly every week

_____ 7. every week

_____ 8. several times a week

_____ 9. don't know, no answer

POSTLIFE    17. Do you believe there is a life after death?

_____ 1. yes      $\overline{32}$

_____ 2. no

_____ 9. undecided, no answer, not applicable

PRAY    18. About how often do you pray?

_____ 1. several times a day      $\overline{33}$

_____ 2. once a day

_____ 3. several times a week

_____ 4. once a week

_____ 5. less than once a week

_____ 6. never

_____ 9. don't know, no answer, not applicable

PREMARSX    19. There has been a lot of discussion about the way morals and attitudes about sex are changing in this country. If a man and woman have sexual relations before marriage, do you think it is always wrong, almost always wrong, wrong only sometimes, or not wrong at all?      $\overline{34}$

_____ 1. always wrong

_____ 2. almost always wrong

_____ 3. wrong only sometimes

_____ 4. not wrong at all

_____ 9. don't know, no answer

HOMOSEX    20. What about sexual relations between two adults of the same sex? Do you think it is always wrong, almost always wrong, wrong only sometimes, or not wrong at all?      $\overline{35}$

_____ 1. always wrong

_____ 2. almost always wrong

_____ 3. wrong only sometimes

_____ 4. ot wrong at all

_____ 9 don't know, no answer

XMOVIE    21. Have you seen an X-rated movie in the last year?      $\overline{36}$

_____ 1. yes

_____ 2. no

_____ 3. don't know, no answer

EDUC    22. What is the highest grade in elementary school or high school that      —   —
you finished and got credit for?      37   38

[INTERVIEWER: IF RESPONDENT COMPLETED 12 GRADES, ASK QUESTION 23.]

23. Did you complete one or more years of college for credit, not including schooling
such as business college or technical or vocational school?

_____ 1. yes

_____ 2. no

[INTERVIEWER: IF YES TO QUESTION 23, GO TO QUESTION 24; ELSE GO TO QUESTION 25.]

24. How many years did you complete?

CODING INSTRUCTION: ADD YEARS FROM QUESTION 22 TO YEARS FROM
QUESTION 24 AND CODE WITH LEADING ZERO IF NECESSARY IN
COLUMNS 37 AND 38. USE CODE 99 FOR NO RESPONSE.

SEI     25. What is your occupation?      —   —

_____ (write in)      39   40

[INTERVIEWER: IF RESPONDENT HAS NOT BEEN EMPLOYED FULL-TIME, RECORD
HIS OR HER FATHER'S OCCUPATION.]

CODING INSTRUCTION: LOOK UP OCCUPATION ON HODGE, SIEGEL, AND ROSSI
PRESTIGE SCALE AND RECORD SCORE IN COLUMNS 39 AND 40. USE CODE 99 FOR
NO RESPONSE.

CLASS    26. If you were asked to describe your social class with      —
one of the following four terms, which would you say      41
you belong in the lower class, the working class, the
middle class, or the upper class?

_____ 1. lower class

_____ 2. working class

_____ 3. middle class

_____ 4. upper class

_____ 9. don't know, no answer

     —   —
     42   43

AGE     27. In what year were you born?

CODING INSTRUCTION: SUBTRACT BIRTH YEAR FROM THIS YEAR TO GET AGE IN
YEARS. CODE IN COLUMNS 42 AND 43. CODE 99 FOR NO RESPONSE.

INCOME16    28. In which of these groups did your total family income, from all      —   —
sources, fall last year, before taxes? Just tell me to stop when I say      44   45
the category that describes your family.

_____ 1. under $1,000

_____ 2 $1,000 to $2,999

_____ 3 $3,000 to $3,999

_____ 4 $4,000 to $4,999

_____ 5 $5,000 to $5,999

_____ 6 $6,000 to $6,999

_____ 7 $7,000 to $7,999

_____ 8 $8,000 to $9,999

_____ 9 $10,000 to $12,499

_____ 10 $12,500 to $14,999

_____ 11 $15,000 to $17,499

_____ 12 $17,500 to $19,999

_____ 13 $20,000 to $22,499

_____ 14 $22,500 to $24,999

_____ 15 $25,000 to $29,999

_____ 16 $30,000 to $34,999

_____ 17 $35,000 to $39,999

_____ 18 $40,000 to $49,999

_____ 19 $50,000 to $59,999

_____ 20 $60,000 to $74,999

_____ 21 $75,000 to $89,999

_____ 22 $90,000 to $109,999

_____ 23 $110,000 or over

_____ 99 refused, don't know, not applicable

RACE        29. CODING INSTRUCTION: CODE WITHOUT ASKING ONLY IF THERE IS
                NO DOUBT IN YOUR MIND.

                                                                               46

_____ 1. White

_____ 2. Black

_____ 3. other

SEX         30. CODING INSTRUCTION: CODE RESPONDENT'S SEX.

                                                                               47

_____ 1. male

_____ 2. female

# OCCUPATIONAL TITLE AND SOCIOECONOMIC PRESTIGE SCORES

Below are occupational titles and socioeconomic index scores for use in coding the question 25, SEI, on the above questionnaire. To find a respondent's SEI score, look through the occupational titles until you find one that matches or is similar to the respondent's occupation. Write the number that appears to the right of the occupation in the space provided for it in the right margin of question 25 on the questionnaire.

The occupational prestige scores were developed by Robert W. Hodge, Paul S. Siegel, and Peter H. Rossi at the University of Chicago (and updated in 1989 by Robert W. Hodge, Judith Treas, and Keiko Nakao). You can learn more about how the prestige scores were obtained by reading Appendices F and G in *General Social Survey, 1972–2010: Cumulative Codebook* (Smith, Marsden, & Hout, 2011).[1]

| Occupational Title | SEI Score |
|---|---|
| *PROFESSIONAL, TECHNICAL, AND KINDRED WORKERS* | |
| Accountants | 57 |
| Architects | 71 |
| Computer specialists | |
| Computer programmers | 51 |
| Computer systems analysts | 51 |
| Computer specialists, n.e.c. | 51 |
| *Engineers* | |
| Aerospace engineers | 71 |
| Chemical engineers | 67 |
| Civil engineers | 68 |
| Electrical and electronic engineers | 69 |
| Industrial engineers | 54 |
| Mechanical engineers | 62 |
| Metallurgical and materials engineers | 56 |
| Mining engineers | 62 |
| Petroleum engineers | 67 |
| Sales engineers | 51 |
| Engineers, n.e.c. | 67 |
| Farm management advisers | 54 |
| Foresters and conservationists | 54 |
| Home management advisers | 54 |
| Lawyers and judges | |
| Judges | 76 |
| Lawyers | 76 |
| *Librarians, archivists, and curators* | |
| Librarians | 55 |

| Occupational Title | SEI Score |
|---|---|
| Archivists and curators | 66 |
| Mathematical specialists | |
| Actuaries | 55 |
| Mathematicians | 65 |
| Statisticians | 55 |
| *Life and physical scientists* | |
| Agricultural scientists | 56 |
| Atmospheric and space scientists | 68 |
| Biological scientists | 68 |
| Chemists | 69 |
| Geologists | 67 |
| Marine scientists | 68 |
| Physicists and astronomers | 74 |
| Life and physical scientists, n.e.c. | 68 |
| Operations and systems researchers and analysts | 51 |
| Personnel and labor relation workers | 56 |
| *Physicians, dentists, and related practitioners* | |
| Chiropractors | 60 |
| Dentists | 74 |
| Optometrists | 62 |
| Pharmacists | 61 |
| Physicians, including osteopaths | 82 |
| Podiatrists | 37 |
| Veterinarians | 60 |
| Health practitioners, n.e.c. | 51 |
| *Nurses, dietitians, and therapists* | |

1. Smith, T. W., Marsden, P. V., & Hout, M. (2011). *General Social Surveys, 1972–2010: Cumulative codebook.* Storrs, CT: Roper Center for Public Opinion Research, University of Connecticut; Ann Arbor, MI: Inter-university Consortium for Political and Social Research.

| Occupational Title | SEI Score |
|---|---|
| Dietitians | 52 |
| Registered nurses | 62 |
| Therapists | 37 |
| *Health technologists and technicians* | |
| Clinical laboratory technologists and technicians | 61 |
| Dental hygienists | 61 |
| Health record technologists and technicians | 61 |
| Radiologic technologists and technicians | 61 |
| Therapy assistants | 37 |
| Health technologists and technicians, n.e.c. | 47 |
| *Religious workers* | |
| Clergy | 69 |
| Religious workers, n.e.c. | 56 |
| Social scientists | |
| Economists | 57 |
| Political scientists | 66 |
| Psychologists | 71 |
| Sociologists | 66 |
| Urban and regional planners | 66 |
| Social scientists, n.e.c. | 66 |
| *Social and recreation workers* | |
| Social workers | 52 |
| Recreation workers | 49 |
| *Teachers, college and university* | |
| College agriculture teachers | 78 |
| College atmospheric, earth, marine, and space teachers | 78 |
| College biology teachers | 78 |
| College chemistry teachers | 78 |
| College physics teachers | 78 |
| College engineering teachers | 78 |
| College mathematics teachers | 78 |
| College health specialists teachers | 78 |
| College psychology teachers | 78 |
| College business and commerce teachers | 78 |
| College economics teachers | 78 |
| College history teachers | 78 |
| College sociology teachers | 78 |
| College social science teachers, n.e.c. | 78 |
| College art, drama, and music teachers | 78 |

| Occupational Title | SEI Score |
|---|---|
| College coaches and physical education teachers | 78 |
| College education teachers | 78 |
| College English teachers | 78 |
| College foreign language teachers | 78 |
| College home economics teachers | 78 |
| College law teachers | 78 |
| College theology teachers | 78 |
| College trade, industrial, and technical teachers | 78 |
| Miscellaneous teachers, college and university | 78 |
| Teachers, college and university, subject not specified | 78 |
| *Teachers, except college and university* | |
| Adult education teachers | 43 |
| Elementary school teachers | 60 |
| Pre-kindergarten and kindergarten teachers | 60 |
| Secondary school teachers | 63 |
| Teachers, except college and university, n.e.c. | 43 |
| *Engineering and science technicians* | |
| Agriculture and biological technicians, except health | 47 |
| Chemical technicians | 47 |
| Draftsmen | 56 |
| Electrical and electronic engineering | |
| Technicians | 47 |
| Industrial engineering technicians | 47 |
| Mechanical engineering technicians | 47 |
| Mathematical technicians | 47 |
| Surveyors | 53 |
| Engineering and science technicians, n.e.c. | 47 |
| *Technicians, except health, engineering, and science* | |
| Airplane pilots | 70 |
| Air traffic controllers | 43 |
| Embalmers | 52 |
| Flight engineers | 47 |
| Radio operators | 43 |
| Tool programmers, numerical control | 47 |

| Occupational Title | SEI Score |
|---|---|
| Technicians, n.e.c. | 47 |
| Vocational and educational counselors | 51 |
| *Writers, artists, and entertainers* | |
| Actors | 55 |
| Athletes and kindred workers | 51 |
| Authors | 60 |
| Dancers | 38 |
| Designers | 58 |
| Editors and reporters | 51 |
| Musicians and composers | 46 |
| Painters and sculptors | 56 |
| Photographers | 41 |
| Public relations men and publicity writers | 57 |
| Radio and television announcers | 51 |
| Writers, artists, and entertainers, n.e.c. | 51 |
| Research workers, not specified | 51 |
| Professional, technical, and kindred workers—allocated | 51 |
| *MANAGERS AND ADMINISTRATORS, EXCEPT FARM* | |
| Assessors, controllers, and treasurers, local public administration | 61 |
| Bank officers and financial managers | 72 |
| Buyers and shippers, farm products | 41 |
| Buyers, wholesale and retail trade | 50 |
| Credit men | 49 |
| Funeral directors | 52 |
| Health administrators | 61 |
| Construction inspectors, public administration | 41 |
| Inspectors, except construction, public administration | 41 |
| Managers and superintendents, building | 38 |
| Office managers, n.e.c. | 50 |
| Officers, pilots, and pursers; ship | 60 |
| Officials and administrators; public administration, n.e.c. | 61 |

| Occupational Title | SEI Score |
|---|---|
| Officials of lodges, societies, and unions | 58 |
| Postmasters and mail superintendents | 58 |
| Purchasing agents and buyers, n.e.c | 48 |
| Railroad conductors | 41 |
| Restaurant, cafeteria, and bar managers | 39 |
| Sales managers and department heads, retail | 50 |
| Sales managers, except retail trade | 50 |
| School administrators, college | 61 |
| School administrators, elementary and secondary | 60 |
| Managers and administrators, n.e.c. | 50 |
| Managers and administrators, except farm—allocated | 50 |
| *SALES WORKERS* | |
| Advertising agents and sales representatives | 42 |
| Auctioneers | 32 |
| Demonstrators | 28 |
| Hucksters and peddlers | 18 |
| Insurance agents, brokers, and underwriters | 47 |
| Newsboys | 15 |
| Real estate agents and brokers | 44 |
| Stocks and bonds sales representatives | 51 |
| Sales representatives and sales clerks, n.e.c. | 34 |
| Sales representatives, manufacturing industries | 49 |
| Sales representatives, wholesale trade | 40 |
| Sales clerks, retail trade | 29 |
| Sales representatives, retail trade | 29 |
| Sales representatives of services and construction | 34 |
| Sales workers—allocated | 34 |
| *CLERICAL AND KINDRED WORKERS* | |
| Bank tellers | 50 |
| Billings clerks | 45 |
| Bookkeepers | 48 |
| Cashiers | 31 |

| Occupational Title | SEI Score |
|---|---|
| Clerical assistants, social welfare | 36 |
| Clerical supervisors, n.e.c | 36 |
| Collectors, bill and account | 26 |
| Counter clerks, except food | 36 |
| Dispatchers and starters, vehicle | 34 |
| Enumerators and interviewers | 36 |
| Estimators and investigators, n.e.c. | 36 |
| Expediters and production controllers | 36 |
| File clerks | 30 |
| Insurance adjusters, examiners, and investigators | 48 |
| Library attendants and assistants | 41 |
| Mail carriers, post office | 42 |
| Mail handlers, except post office | 36 |
| Messengers and office runners | 19 |
| Meter readers, utilities | 36 |
| *Office machine operators* | |
| Bookkeeping and billing machine operators | 45 |
| Calculating machine operator | 45 |
| Computer and peripheral equipment operators | 45 |
| Duplicating machine operators | 45 |
| Keypunch operators | 45 |
| Tabulating machine operators | 45 |
| Office machine operators, n.e.c. | 45 |
| Payroll and timekeeping clerks | 41 |
| Postal clerks | 43 |
| Proofreaders | 36 |
| Real estate appraisers | 43 |
| Receptionists | 39 |
| Secretaries | |
| Secretaries, legal | 46 |
| Secretaries, medical | 46 |
| Secretaries, n.e.c. | 46 |
| Shipping and receiving clerks | 29 |
| Statistical clerks | 36 |
| Stenographers | 43 |
| Stock clerks and storekeepers | 23 |

| Occupational Title | SEI Score |
|---|---|
| Teacher aides, except school monitors | 36 |
| Telegraph messengers | 30 |
| Telegraph operators | 44 |
| Telephone operators | 40 |
| Ticket, station, and express agents | 35 |
| Typists | 41 |
| Weighers | 36 |
| Miscellaneous clerical workers | 36 |
| Not specified clerical workers | 36 |
| Clerical and kindred workers—allocated | 36 |
| *CRAFTSMEN AND KINDRED WORKERS* | |
| Automobile accessories installers | 47 |
| Bakers | 34 |
| Blacksmiths | 36 |
| Boilermakers | 31 |
| Bookbinders | 31 |
| Brickmasons and stonemasons | 36 |
| Brickmasons and stonemasons, apprentice | 36 |
| Bulldozer operators | 33 |
| Cabinetmakers | 39 |
| Carpenters | 40 |
| Carpenter apprentices | 40 |
| Carpet installers | 47 |
| Cement and concrete finishers | 32 |
| Compositors and typesetters | 38 |
| Printing trades apprentices, except pressmen | 40 |
| Cranemen, derrickmen, and hoistmen | 39 |
| Decorators and window dressers | 37 |
| Dental laboratory technicians | 47 |
| Electricians | 49 |
| Electrician apprentices | 41 |
| Electric power line technicians and cable technicians | 39 |
| Electrotypers and stereotypers | 38 |
| Engravers, except photoengravers | 41 |
| Excavating, grading and road machine operators, except bulldozer | 33 |
| Floor layers, except tile setters | 40 |

| Occupational Title | SEI Score |
|---|---|
| Foremen, n.e.c. | 45 |
| Forgers and hammerers | 36 |
| Furniture and wood finishers | 29 |
| Furriers | 35 |
| Glaziers | 26 |
| Heat treaters, annealers, and temperers | 36 |
| Inspectors, scalers, and graders: log and lumber | 31 |
| Inspectors, n.e.c. | 31 |
| Jewelers and watchmakers | 37 |
| Job and die setters, metal | 48 |
| Locomotive engineers | 51 |
| Locomotive firemen | 36 |
| Machinists | 48 |
| Machinist apprentices | 41 |
| Mechanics and repair technicians | |
| Air-conditioning, heating, and refrigeration | 37 |
| Aircraft | 48 |
| Automobile body repair mechanics | 37 |
| Automobile mechanics | 37 |
| Automobile mechanic apprentices | 37 |
| Data processing machine repairmen | 34 |
| Farm implements | 33 |
| Heavy equipment mechanics, including diesel | 33 |
| Household appliance and accessory installers and mechanics | 33 |
| Loom fixers | 30 |
| Office machines | 34 |
| Radio and television | 35 |
| Railroad and car shop | 37 |
| Mechanic, except auto, apprentices | 41 |
| Miscellaneous mechanics and repair technicians | 35 |
| Millers; grain, flour, and feed | 25 |
| Millwrights | 40 |
| Molders, metal | 39 |
| Molder, apprentices | 39 |
| Motion picture projectionists | 34 |
| Opticians, and lens grinders and polishers | 51 |

| Occupational Title | SEI Score |
|---|---|
| Painters, construction and maintenance | 30 |
| Painter apprentices | 30 |
| Paperhangers | 24 |
| Pattern and model makers, except paper | 39 |
| Photoengravers and lithographers | 40 |
| Piano and organ tuners and repair technicians | 32 |
| Plasterers | 33 |
| Plasterer apprentices | 33 |
| Plumber and pipe fitters | 41 |
| Plumber and pipe fitter apprentices | 41 |
| Power station operators | 39 |
| Pressmen and plate printers, printing | 40 |
| Pressmen apprentices | 40 |
| Rollers and finishers, metal | 36 |
| Roofers and slaters | 31 |
| Sheetmetal workers and tinsmiths | 37 |
| Sheetmetal apprentices | 37 |
| Shipfitters | 36 |
| Shoe repairers | 33 |
| Sign painters and letterers | 30 |
| Stationary engineers | 35 |
| Stone cutters and stone carvers | 33 |
| Structural metal craftsmen | 36 |
| Tailors | 41 |
| Telephone installers and repair technicians | 39 |
| Telephone line technicians and splicers | 39 |
| Tile setters | 36 |
| Tool and die makers | 42 |
| Tool and die maker apprentices | 41 |
| Upholsterers | 30 |
| Specified craft apprentices, n.e.c. | 41 |
| Not specified apprentices | 41 |
| Craftsmen and kindred workers, n.e.c. | 47 |
| Former members of the Armed Forces | 47 |
| Craftsmen and kindred workers—allocate | 47 |

| Occupational Title | SEI Score |
|---|---|
| Current members of the Armed Forces | 47 |
| *OPERATIVES, EXCEPT TRANSPORT* | |
| Asbestos and insulation workers | 28 |
| Assemblers | 27 |
| Blasters and powdermen | 32 |
| Bottling and canning operatives | 23 |
| Chainmen, rod men, and axmen; surveying | 39 |
| Checkers, examiners, and inspectors; manufacturing | 36 |
| Clothing ironers and pressers | 18 |
| Cutting operatives, n.e.c. | 26 |
| Dressmakers and textile workers, except factory | 32 |
| Drillers, earth | 27 |
| Dry wall installers and lathers | 27 |
| Dyers | 25 |
| Filers, polishers, sanders, and buffers | 19 |
| Furnacemen, smeltermen, and pourers | 33 |
| Garage workers and gas station attendants | 22 |
| Graders and sorters, manufacturing | 33 |
| Produce graders and packers, except factory and farm | 19 |
| Heaters, metal | 33 |
| Laundry and dry cleaning operatives, n.e.c. | 18 |
| Meat cutters and butchers, except manufacturing | 32 |
| Meat cutters and butchers, manufacturing | 28 |
| Meat wrappers, retail trade | 19 |
| Metal platers | 29 |
| Milliners | 33 |
| Mine operatives, n.e.c. | 26 |
| Mixing operatives | 29 |
| Oilers and greasers, except auto | 24 |
| Packers and wrappers, n.e.c | 19 |
| Painters, manufactured articles | 29 |
| Photographic process workers | 36 |
| Precision machine operatives | |
| Drill press operatives | 29 |

| Occupational Title | SEI Score |
|---|---|
| Grinding machine operatives | 29 |
| Lathe and milling machine operatives | 29 |
| Precision machine operatives, n.e.c | 29 |
| Punch and stamping press operatives | 29 |
| Riveters and fasteners | 29 |
| Sailors and deckhands | 34 |
| Sawyers | 28 |
| Sewers and stitchers | 25 |
| Shoemaking machine operatives | 32 |
| Solderers | 29 |
| Stationary firemen | 33 |
| *Textile operatives* | |
| Carding, lapping, and combing operatives | 29 |
| Knitters, loopers, and toppers | 29 |
| Spinners, twisters, and winders | 25 |
| Weavers | 25 |
| Textile operatives, n.e.c. | 29 |
| Welders and flame-cutters | 40 |
| Winding operatives, n.e.c. | 29 |
| Machine operatives, miscellaneous specified | 32 |
| Machine operatives, not specified | 32 |
| Miscellaneous operatives | 32 |
| Not specified operatives | 32 |
| Operatives, except transport—allocated | 32 |
| *TRANSPORT EQUIPMENT OPERATIVES* | |
| Boat and canal operators | 37 |
| Bus drivers | 32 |
| Conductors and drivers, urban rail transit | 28 |
| Deliverypersons | 28 |
| Forklift and tow motor operatives | 29 |
| Motormen; mine, factory, logging camp, etc. | 27 |
| Parking attendants | 22 |
| Railroad brakemen | 35 |
| Railroad switchmen | 33 |
| Taxicab drivers and chauffeurs | 22 |
| Truck drivers | 32 |

| Occupational Title | SEI Score |
|---|---|
| Transport equipment operatives—allocated | 29 |
| *LABORERS, EXCEPT FARM* | |
| Animal caretakers, except farm | 29 |
| Carpenters' helpers | 23 |
| Construction laborers, except carpenters' helpers | 17 |
| Fishermen and oystermen | 30 |
| Freight and material handlers | 17 |
| Garbage collectors | 17 |
| Gardeners and groundkeepers, except farm | 23 |
| Longshoremen and stevedores | 24 |
| Lumbermen, raftsmen, and woodchoppers | 26 |
| Stockhandlers | 17 |
| Teamsters | 12 |
| Vehicle washers and equipment cleaners | 17 |
| Warehousemen, n.e.c. | 20 |
| Miscellaneous laborers | 17 |
| Not specified laborers | 17 |
| Laborers, except farm—allocated | 17 |
| *FARMERS AND FARM MANAGERS* | |
| Farmers (owners and tenants) | 41 |
| Farm managers | 44 |
| Farmers and farm managers—allocated | 41 |
| *FARMERS, LABORERS AND FARM FOREMEN* | |
| Farm forepersons | 35 |
| Farm laborers, wage workers | 18 |
| Farm laborers, unpaid family workers | 18 |
| Farm laborers, unpaid family workers | 18 |
| Farm service laborers, self-employed | 27 |
| Farm laborers, farm forepersons, and kindred workers—allocated | 19 |
| *SERVICE WORKERS, EXCEPT PRIVATE HOUSEHOLD* | |
| Cleaning service workers | |
| Chambermaids and maids, except private household | 14 |
| Cleaners | 12 |

| Occupational Title | SEI Score |
|---|---|
| Janitors and sextons | 16 |
| Food service workers | |
| Bartenders | 20 |
| Busboys | 22 |
| Cooks, except private household | 26 |
| Dishwashers | 22 |
| Food counters and fountain workers | 15 |
| Waiters | 20 |
| Food service workers, n.e.c, except private household | 22 |
| *Health service workers* | |
| Dental assistants | 48 |
| Health aides, except nursing | 48 |
| Health trainees | 36 |
| Midwives | 23 |
| Nursing aides, orderlies, and attendants | 36 |
| Practical nurses | 42 |
| *Personal service workers* | |
| Airline flight attendants | 36 |
| Attendants, recreation and amusement | 15 |
| Attendants, personal service, n.e.c. | 14 |
| Baggage porters and bellhops | 14 |
| Barbers | 38 |
| Boarding and lodging housekeepers | 22 |
| Bootblacks | 9 |
| Child care workers, except private households | 25 |
| Elevator operators | 21 |
| Hairdressers and cosmetologists | 33 |
| Personal service apprentices | 14 |
| Housekeepers, except private households | 36 |
| School monitors | 22 |
| Ushers, recreation and amusement | 15 |
| Welfare service aides | 14 |
| *Protective service workers* | |
| Crossing guards and bridge tenders | 24 |
| Firefighters, fire protection | 44 |

*Note:* n.e.c = not elsewhere classified.

# INDEX/GLOSSARY

**Abbreviated variable names** Shortened names used to uniquely identify variables in an SPSS data file. In older versions of SPSS, the variable name was limited to 8 characters. Even though variable names can be much longer (up to 64 characters in many modern languages and 32 characters in others), by convention, secondary data typically limit variable names to 8 characters, in part to maintain compatibility with older and other types of software and also because the variable label contains more information about the variable.

**Active cell** The cell in a database that will receive any user action taken, such as a mouse click. It is outlined on the screen with thick black lines.

**Active window** The window currently displayed on the screen

**Analysis of variance (ANOVA)** An analytical technique aimed at determining whether variables are related to one another. It is based on a comparison of the differences (income, for example) among three or more subgroups and the variance on the same variable within each of the subgroups. For example, how do the differences in average income among Whites, Blacks,

**Crosstabulation**   A matrix that shows the distribution of one variable for each category of a second variable; also referred to as a crosstab, bivariate distribution, contingency table, and two-way frequency distribution.

**Data definition**   The first step in getting data ready for analysis with SPSS Statistics. Among other things, it involves giving each item on a questionnaire a variable name, setting the data type, describing each variable, indicating values and labels for each variable, designating missing values, setting the level of measurement for each variable, and designating a place to store the information.

**Data Editor**   A spreadsheet or matrix designed to hold data for analysis that opens automatically when you begin an SPSS Statistics session. It can be used to create and edit data files.

**Data View**   This view in the SPSS Data Editor window provides a snapshot of the raw data itself. On Windows computers, Data View can be selected by the toggle in the lower left side of the Data Editor window. On Macintosh computers, Data View can be selected using the toggle switch in the lower middle of the Data Editor window.

**Deductive research**   A logical model in which the investigator begins with a theory and derives hypotheses to be tested by empirical observations. *Compare with* Inductive research.

**Degrees of freedom (df)**   In calculating the statistical significance of relationships, it is necessary to take account of the extent of possibilities for variation within a model: How many items of information must be specified before all of the rest are determined by those specified?

In the case of chi-square for a crosstabulation, this is calculated as the number of rows minus 1 times the number of columns minus 1. For example, in a 2 × 2 table, if we know the number of cases in one cell, all the rest can be determined; hence, there is 1 degree of freedom.

**Demographic variables**   Objective background variables, such as gender, age, occupation, and education, that tend to be related to many other variables, such as attitudes, behaviors, and life experiences.

**DEMO.SAV**   File on the student study site (https://study. sagepub.com/babbie10e) containing a randomly selected subsample of 1,500 cases and 43 variables drawn from the 2016 GSS. The items are arranged according to the following subject categories: demographics, abortion, family, religion, social-political opinions, and sexual attitudes and behavior.

**Dependent variable**   In a causal relationship, this is the effect. For example, to the extent that religious affiliation causes attitude toward abortion, the attitude is the dependent variable.

**Descriptive statistics**   Along with inferential statistics, one of the two main types of statistics used by social scientists. Statistics are widely used to describe and summarize.

**Deterministic relationship**   A (bivariate) relationship between two variables such that one variable can be perfectly predicted from the other variable with no errors

**Dialog box**   In SPSS Statistics, most menu selections open dialog boxes, such as the Frequencies dialog box or the Help Topics dialog box. These boxes are then used to select variables and other options for analysis.

researchers to note how public support for the president has changed throughout his or her administration. Contrast with cross-sectional data, which is collected at only one point in time.

**Marginals** Formed by the row totals and column totals of a bivariate table.
**Mean** A measure of central tendency; what most people associate with the term *average*. Sum the ages of some group of people, divide by the number of people in question, and the result is their mean age. Generally considered appropriate for the analysis of variables at the interval or ratio level of measurement.
**Measures of association** Statistics such as lambda, gamma, and Pearson's *r* that indicate the strength (and, in certain cases, the direction) of the relationship or association between two variables.
**Measures of central tendency** Central tendency is generally indicated through one of three statistics known collectively as measures of central tendency (mode, median, and mean). In order to choose an appropriate measure, the researcher must first consider the variable's level of measurement.

**Measures of dispersion** Statistics that describe how similar a group of observations is to one another. For interval and ratio variables, the standard deviation measures the spread of cases around the mean.
**Median** A measure of central tendency; the point in an ordered distribution at which half the cases are above and half are below. Generally considered appropriate for the analysis of variables at the ordinal level of measurement.
**Menu bar** One of the primary means to control and communicate with SPSS Statistics. Each window in SPSS Statistics has its own menu bar with selections appropriate for that window.
**Missing data** In conducting a survey, missing data or values can result from, for example, a respondent refusing to answer a question or from a particular question not applying to a certain respondent. In SPSS Statistics, missing data are excluded from most calculations.
**Mode** A measure of central tendency; an average indicating the most frequent answer, response, or attribute in a given distribution. Generally considered appropriate for the analysis of variables at the nominal level of measurement.
**Multiple indicators** One solution to the problems of reliability and validity lies in the creation of composite measures using multiple indicators of a single concept. For instance, to measure social class, an analyst may ask respondents questions about their income, education, occupational prestige, and so on. The answers (multiple indicators of a single concept) could then be used to create an overall measure of social class.
**Multiple regression** A regression model in which more than one independent variable is used to predict values of the dependent variable. Thus, we might create a regression equation that lets us predict incomes from knowing a person's age, education, and gender.
**Multivariate analysis** An analysis that involves more than two variables. *Compare with* Bivariate analysis and Univariate analysis.

CPSIA information can be obtained
at www.ICGtesting.com
Printed in the USA
JSHW041133150621
15756JS00005B/14